Book of

Weekend Breaks

Edited by Jonathan Cox

Edited and designed by
Time Out Guides Limited
Universal House
251 Tottenham Court Road
London W1P 0AB
Tel + 44 (0)20 7813 3000
Fax + 44 (0)20 7813 6001
guides@timeout.com
www.timeout.com

Editorial

Editor Jonathan Cox
Editorial Director Peter Fiennes
Deputy Editor Lesley McCave
Listings Editor Zoë Sanders
Listings Assistant Sharon Lougher
Proofreader Tamsin Shelton

Design

Art Director John Oakey
Art Editor Mandy Martin
Senior Designer Scott Moore
Designers Benjamin de Lotz, Lucy Grant
Scanning/Imaging Chris Quinn
Advertisement make-up Paul Mansfield
Picture Editor Kerri Miles
Deputy Picture Editor Olivia Duncan-Jones
Picture Admin Kit Burnet

Advertising

Group Advertisement Director Lesley Gill
Sales Director/Sponsorship Mark Phillips
Sales Manager Alison Gray
Sales Dominic Mensah, Rhidian Thomas, Laurent Ezekiel,
Edward Searle
Guides Production Controller Samantha Furniss
Copy Controller Philippa Sethi
Advertising Assistant Ingrid Sigerson

Administration

Publisher Tony Elliott
Managing Director Mike Hardwick
Financial Director Kevin Ellis
General Manager Nichola Coulthard
Marketing Director Gill Auld
Marketing Manager Christine Cort
Marketing Executives Mandy Martinez, Jo Tomlin,
Sandie Tozer, Jenny Noden
Accountants Catherine Bowen, Bridget Carter
Production Manager Mark Lamond

Chapters in this guide were researched and written by...

KENT North Kent Coast Derek Hammond; **Canterbury**
Andrew White; **Sandwich to Sandgate** Melanie Dakin;
North Kent Downs Angela Jameson; **Rye, Dungeness & Romney Marsh** Guy Dimond; **The Heart of Kent**
Simon Radcliffe; **The Kent Weald** Jonathan Cox.

SUSSEX & SURREY Battle & Hastings Will
Hodgkinson; **The Ashdown Forest** Beth Barling;
Lewes & around Lily Dunn; **Brighton** Frank Broughton;
South-west Sussex Rachael Philipps; **North Surrey Downs** Patrick Butler; **The Three Counties** Sarah Guy.

HAMPSHIRE & ISLE OF WIGHT Around Newbury
Will Hodgkinson; **Winchester & around** Nick Rider;
The New Forest NJ Stevenson; **Isle of Wight** Dorothy
Boswell; **Bournemouth & Poole** Melanie Dakin.

WILTSHIRE & BATH Salisbury & Stonehenge Derek
Hammond; **Bradford-on-Avon & around** Steve Rose;
Bath Derek Hammond; **Chippenham to Avebury**
Amanda White; **Malmesbury & around** Patrick Marmion.

THE COTSWOLDS Cirencester to Gloucester Jonathan
Cox; **Cheltenham to Stow** Rachael Philipps; **North
Cotswolds** Patrick Butler; **Stratford & Warwick** Zoë
Sanders; **Oxford** Stephen Patience; **South Oxfordshire**
Caroline Taverne; **Woodstock to Burford** Sarah Halliwell;
Chipping Norton to Banbury Bill Tuckey.

THE CHILTERNS TO YORK Windsor & around
Lesley McCave; **North Chilterns** Helen Barnard;
Hertfordshire Melanie Dakin; **Rutland** Derek Hammond;
Lincoln Frank Broughton; **York** Jonathan Cox.

EAST ANGLIA Cambridge Michael Ellis; **West Essex**
Steve Rose; **Lower Stour Valley** Nick Rider;
Upper Stour Valley Louise Gray; **Bury St Edmunds & around** John O'Connell; **The Suffolk Coast** Jonathan Cox.

Maps by JS Graphics, 17 Beadles Lane, Old Oxted, Surrey
RH8 9JG (01883 716387). Maps based on data supplied by
Lovell Johns Ltd.

Photography by Paul Avis, Jonathan Cox and the featured
establishments.

Published by the Penguin Group
Penguin Books Ltd, 27 Wrights Lane, London, W8 5TZ, England
Penguin Putnam Inc, 375 Hudson Street, New York, NY10014, USA
Penguin Books Australia Ltd, 487 Maroondah Hwy (PO Box 257), Ringwood, VIC3134, Australia
Penguin Books Canada Ltd, 10 Alcorn Avenue, Toronto, Ontario, Canada M4V 3B2
Penguin Books (NZ) Ltd, 182-190 Wairau Road, Auckland 10, New Zealand

Penguin Books Ltd, Registered Offices: Harmondsworth, Middlesex, England

First published 1999
10 9 8 7 6 5 4 3 2 1

Colour reprographics by Precise Litho, 34-35 Great Sutton Street, London EC1
Printed and bound by Southernprint (Web Offset) Ltd, Upton Industrial Estate, Poole, Dorset, BH16 5SN

Contents

Introduction

Considering the diminutive size of these islands, it's amazing how little most of us know about our own country. Now that holidays abroad are the norm rather than the exotic exception, it can seem that we have a far more intimate knowledge of the hill villages of the Vaucluse or the cafés of Rome than of the pubs of the Sussex Weald or the beaches of the Suffolk coast. Of course, there are patches of the UK we're familiar with, as we rush from home to favourite country boozer to relatives in town to friends by the sea, but what of all the other bits?

It's also true that most of us like to get away for the weekend (or at least dream of doing so) several times a year, and yet it's remarkable that so little has been published to help the weekend breaker make those difficult where-to-stay, what-to-see decisions. Those guides which are available tend to cover too wide an area (usually the whole country) and, thus, supply only sketchy information. In order to provide as full a coverage as possible, we've deliberately restricted the scope of this book to the south-east portion of England (although, with places such as Bath and York included, this is a very liberal definition).

The basic rationale behind choosing which areas to include and which to exclude is that they should be within two hours' rail or road travel from the capital. This is something of an elastic criterion, too. If you live in Epping, say, you'll be able to zip up to the Stour Valley in no time at all, whereas residents of Streatham will probably take a good hour just to get as far as Epping. The presence of York, Lincoln and Rutland in this book is testament to the speed on the rail links to these places.

The breaks featured here may radiate out from London, but this is by no means a book only for Londoners. We hope that a resident of Oxford will be just as interested in finding out more about the New Forest, and Kentish folk as keen to mug up on the attractions of Suffolk as anyone living within the M25.

For us, one of the most rewarding aspects of putting this guide together has been to learn just how much great stuff to see and do there is out there, and just how many first-rate restaurants and drinking holes are awaiting our custom. It's inspired us to want to get away and explore; we hope it'll do the same for you. Pompous old Samuel Johnson may have found everything he wanted of life in London – but he really should have got out more.

Jonathan Cox

Legend for Town Maps

▦	Place of interest	▦	Restricted road
▦	College or University	WC	Toilet with disabled access
▦	Station	WC	Toilet without disabled access
▦	Park	⊡	Car park
		✝	Church

How the book is arranged

For ease of use, we've split the guide into seven chapters, roughly corresponding to county boundaries. But, as the breaks we feature don't conveniently follow county lines, this has produced a number of anomalies. For instance, in the 'Hampshire & Isle of Wight' section, we're well aware that Newbury and Bournemouth aren't in either of these counties, but felt that such inconsistencies were preferable to unwieldy chapter names like 'Hampshire, West Berkshire, Dorset & the Isle of Wight'.

Accommodation rates & booking

'B&B' indicates that a full English breakfast is included in the room price; 'B&ContB' means that a continental breakfast is included. In other cases the price of breakfast is shown. Rates are per room unless succeeded by 'pp', in which case they are per person.

Booking accommodation in advance is always recommended; most of the places we feature in this book are very popular, and at least several weeks' (and often months') notice is required, particularly in peak season. Also, bear in mind that many establishments close for a couple of weeks during the year, so it is always risky to turn up without phoning first. If you care unable to find a room in any of the places we list, most tourist information centres should be able to help you find somewhere to rest your head.

Things to check when booking

We have attempted to find out most of the following accommodation information for you, but always double check if you don't want the risk of an unwelcome surprise.

Children & dogs – It's remarkable the number of places that treat kids and pets as one and the same. We have shown where there is an age restriction on children, and indicated the places that are happy to take dogs.

Maps & directions – The maps in this book are intended (with the exception of the town

plans) for general orientation and you will need a road atlas or other detailed map to find your way around. We have included instructions of how to find your way to the hotels, guesthouses and B&B establishments we list, unless their location needs no explanation.

Minimum stay – Some hotels and B&Bs insist on a minimum stay of two nights or more (usually over a Friday and Saturday).

No-smoking policies – Many places (hotels less so than B&Bs) have strict no-smoking policies in their bedrooms and/or throughout the building.

Wedding parties – Be warned that some of the larger hotels are often taken over by wedding parties at weekends.

Sponsor and advertisers

We would like to thank our sponsor MasterCard for their involvement in this book. We would also like to thank the advertisers. However, we stress that they have no control over editorial content. No establishment has been included because it has advertised, and no payment of any kind has influenced any review. The opinions given in this book are those of *Time Out* writers and entirely impartial.

Listings

All the listings information was fully checked and correct at the time of going to press, but owners and managers can change their arrangements at any time, and prices do rise. Therefore, it is always best to check opening times, admission fees and other details before you set off. While every effort and care has been made to ensure the accuracy of the information contained in this book, the publishers cannot accept responsibility for any errors it may contain.

Credit & debit cards

In the 'Where to stay' and 'Where to eat & drink' sections, the following abbreviations have been used – **AmEx**: American Express; **DC**: Diners Club; **MC**: MasterCard; **V**: Visa. **Debit** means that most major debit cards are accepted. **If no cards are shown, it means none are accepted**.

Let us know what you think

We hope you enjoy this book and welcome any comments or suggestions you might have. A reader's reply card is included at the back of the book and, in addition to the chance to **win a weekend in York** (*see page 3*), we'll be giving free copies of the next edition of the guide to the most helpful replies.

Special offers

We have exclusively negotiated the following offers for readers of the *Time Out Book of Weekend Breaks*. Most of these are for **three nights for the price of two**. These establishments are marked with `Offer` in the book.

Be aware that, in addition, many hotels and some B&Bs offer regular special weekend or package breaks. We have indicated those that do in our listings as 'Special breaks'; it is always wise to check when booking to see what deals are available.

East Sussex

Cleveland House
Winchelsea (01797 226256). *See page 34.*

Offer	from £120 for three nights (normal price from £180).
Exclusions	Christmas, New Year & Easter.
Valid	until 31 Mar 2000; 1 Oct 2000-31 Mar 2001; 1-28 Oct 2001

Griffin Inn
Fletching, nr Uckfield (01825 722890). *See page 60.*

Offer	from £170 (with bath) or £150 (with shower) for three nights (normal price from £255/£225)
Conditions	Maximum 8-room booking
Exclusions	Christmas & New Year
Valid	until 28 Oct 2001

Hampshire

Westover Hall
Milford-on-Sea (01590 643044). *See page 111.*

Offer	£30 off dinner, bed & breakfast rate per night for two people (normal price from £155 per night)
Conditions	minimum two nights
Exclusions	Saturdays
Valid	until 28 Oct 2001

Isle of Wight

Priory Bay Hotel
Seaview, Isle of Wight (01983 613146). *See page 116.*

Offer	£160-£472 for three nights (normal price from £240-£708)
Exclusions	Bank Holiday weekends; 1 July-31 Aug
Valid	until 28 Oct 2001

Seaview Hotel
Seaview, Isle of Wight (01983 612711). *See page 117.*

Offer	from £180 for three nights (normal price from £270) plus automatic upgrade to a superior room if available
Exclusions	Christmas & New Year; 1 Mar-31 Oct
Valid	until 28 Oct 2001

Kent

Bishopsdale Oast
Biddenden (01580 291027). *See page 39.*

Offer	from £42 (normal price from £60) per night plus a free bottle of house wine with the £19 4-course dinner.
Conditions	minimum two nights
Exclusions	Christmas & New Year; 1 May-31 Aug
Valid	until 28 Oct 2001

Chilston Park
Lenham, nr Maidstone (01622 859803). *See page 28.*

Offer	from £230 for three nights (normal price from £375)
Exclusions	Christmas, New Year & Valentine's Day
Valid	until 28 Oct 2001

Jarvis Marina Hotel
Ramsgate (01843 588276). *See page 10.*

Offer	from £65 per night (normally from £92)
Conditions	minimum two nights (including Sat)
Valid	until 28 Oct 2001

Kennel Holt Hotel
Cranbrook (01580 712032). *See page 40.*

Offer	from £270 for three nights (normal price from £405)
Exclusions	Friday, Saturday and Sunday nights; Bank Holiday weekends; 1 May-30 Sept
Valid	until 28 Oct 2001

Wiltshire

Chilvester Hill House
Calne (01249 813981/815785). *See page 147.*

Offer	from £160 for three nights (normal price from £240)
Conditions	must include Sat; three couples only: quote 'AA' on booking;
Exclusions	Bank Holiday weekends
Valid	until Easter 2000; 28 Oct 2000-Easter 2001

Manor House
Castle Combe (01249 782206). *See page 148.*

Offer	from £425 for three nights (normal package price from £510) including unlimited complimentary golf on the Sunday.
Exclusions	Bank Holiday weekends
Valid	until 28 Oct 2001

Rudloe Hall

Rudloe (01255 810555). *See page 148.*

Offer	from £192 for four nights (normal price from £256)
Conditions	must eat dinner at hotel one night
Valid	until 28 Oct 2001

Win a weekend in York

As well as the discounts on this page, you can also win a weekend for two in York. Simply fill in and return the reader's reply card in the back of this book. The winning name will be picked at random on 28 October 2001. The winner will receive two nights bed and breakfast for two people at the Bishop's Hotel in York (*see page 241*); first-class rail travel from London to York; two VIP passes for entry into to all of the city's major museums and attractions and a plane ride over the city. (The prize is subject to change to one of equal value.)

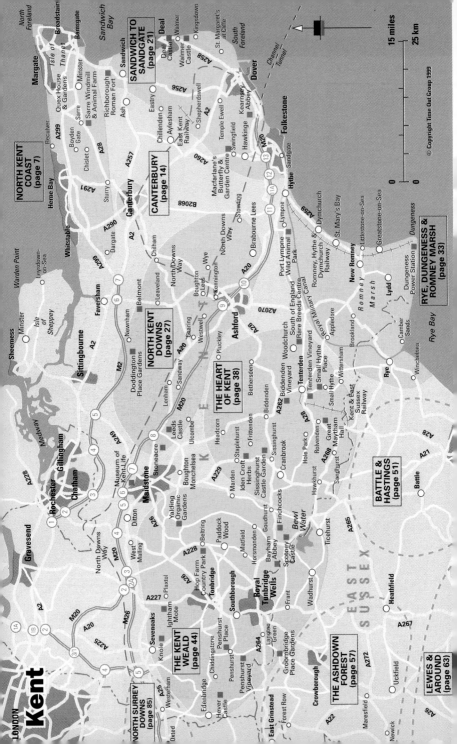

North Kent Coast

From classy Whitstable to the retro resorts of the Isle of Thanet.

Back in Roman times, a weekend bucket-and-spade break at Margate, Broadstairs or Ramsgate, all on the Isle of Thanet, would have involved an exciting ferry trip of at least a couple of hundred yards. The Wantsum Channel then stretched up to a mile across at its widest points – before the odd billion tons of silt washed on to the scene, reducing it to a six-foot drainage ditch that's easy to miss as you speed past in the car. The 26 miles or so of Thanet Coastal Path remain the area's prime attraction, fabulous for walking under white cliffs, arches and stacks to quiet coves… or crashing out behind a windbreak at one of the more popular sandy beaches.

Something fishy

Although **Whitstable** was always situated well on the mainland side of the channel, the arrival of the silt was great news for the town because along with it came its stock-in-trade of oysters, which was for years considered a poor man's source of gag-inducing nourishment. The ramshackle seafront is superb – Peter Cushing was a great fan, as a viewpoint plaque attests – cluttered with toy cottages, fishermen's huts and sailmakers. In the busy, modern harbour it's easy to get your feet splashed with the steamy water from cooking just-caught cockles, whelks and crab, which are on sale for a song. Cunningly built well below the level of high tides, Whitstable has somehow survived its inevitable historical flooding tragedies and offshore pollution, and retains an atmosphere of gentle bohemianism imported from London in its holiday heyday.

In an easterly direction along the north Kent coast is quiet **Herne Bay** and **Reculver**, site of a Roman fort that once guarded the northern entrance to the Wantsum, and a rebuilt seventh-century church on the same spot – you can see the Reculver Towers for miles around. A long stretch of desolate coast follows, leading into the

*Taking the plunge in **Whitstable** Harbour.*

rising slopes of Thanet's quiet seaside suburbia. Inland from all this coastline is some gorgeous, unspoiled countryside: attractions include the famous Wantsum Walk, St Augustine's Trail and some deeply fulfilling village pubs.

The land that time forgot

Margate's place in history is established as Britain's first ever seaside resort, while in the strictest terms of quality and choice it now seems more like the last. Back in the 1730s, Margate clocked up the first use of a beach deck-chair, the first ever donkey rides and seaside boarding houses. Benjamin Beale, a local man, revolutionised bathing with his patent modesty hood, which allowed naked therapeutic paddling from the back of a bathing machine. Throughout the Georgian and Victorian eras up until the 1960s, boatloads of cockneys used to pour down the Thames, offloading excitedly on Margate Pier (another famous first, sadly hit by storms in

---

By train from London

Trains run from **London Victoria** to **Ramsgate** about every half hour, and take **1 hr 50 mins**. Most of these stop at **Whitstable**, **Margate** and **Broadstairs** on the way.

Signs of **Whitstable** *times, including the* **Whitstable Oyster Fishery Company** *menu.*

1978 and just recently demolished). And still their descendants flock here for the trad summer holiday delights of the beach, the theatre and the seafront Strip. There's Grab City amusements, with its synthesised barrel-organ jingles; the white-knuckle thrills of Dreamland; the mixed aromas of seaweed from the harbour, hot doughnuts and pungent fish 'n' chips. Here, a pound in a slot will buy you an adults-only key-ring, a Lucky Lady charm or a pair of naughty undies – 'knickers for a knicker, pouches for a pound'. The Old Town and Market Place is the area with most atmosphere, albeit partly boarded-up or reduced to junk shops; handy for the Shell Grotto, too (*see page 10* **Shellhenge**). The modern town centre is busy but quite unremarkable. Nevertheless, if you're spending a weekend in the area, Margate is great value for a few hours' aimless mooching, chomping and setting off 10p cascade tilt alarms.

Across the headland from Margate, **Broadstairs** is the maiden aunt of Thanet resorts, haughtily disapproving of its noisy neighbours. 'Our English Watering Place' is how Charles Dickens described his favourite seaside town, and precious little has changed since – except for the steady theming of place-names to the likes of Dickens Walk, Dickens' Pantry, The Old Curiosity Shop, Bill Sykes' Market, the Barnaby Rudge pub, Dodger's and Quilp's restaurants, and so on. Every summer the town runs a week-long Dickens Festival (*see page 13*; Broadstairs' other main festival is August's Broadstairs Folk Week – phone 01843 604080 for information). For a weekend break to Thanet, Broadstairs represents the best bet for a base: there's more of a mix of accommodation; there's a decent selection of restaurants and pubs, and the sweep of dramatic coast really takes some beating. There's an inescapable retro ambience to the place, but that's no bad thing. Check out the tiny, pebble-dashed Windsor Cinema under the harbour's York Gate, and the proliferation of Formica 'milk bars', which disappeared from the rest of Britain 40 years ago; stop by at Morelli's (14 Victoria Parade) for a knickerbocker glory or a banana split; take a step back in time along the blooming clifftop prom, around the seven beautiful bays, and back to the bandstand in time for tea.

While **Ramsgate**, a couple of miles south of Broadstairs, offers many of the old-style seaside attractions – a long, sandy beach sheltered by towering cliffs, a clifftop model village and putting green – it doesn't rely excessively on the tourist dollar. OK, so the prime crowd-puller of Pegwell Bay, to the west, is a Viking longboat that has somehow survived the onslaught of small children since, ooh, 1949, but Ramsgate is primarily a working town, with a major continental ferry terminal and a teeming Royal Harbour. Climbing out of the harbour to the west, ramps scale the impressive brick-vaulted cliffs topped by the stately Victorian Yacht Club; to the east, Madeira Walk twists upward through a slalom of landscaped rock walls and waterfalls to the clifftop Wellington Terrace, which looks almost as impressive as Bath's Royal Crescent on the postcards, but is actually becoming rather tatty and dilapidated. As a visitor, there's little to see or do beyond the immediate vicinity of the seafront, shopping centre and harbour; but as is the case with the other Thanet towns, there's more than enough to happily fill a summer's day.

*Whitstable's excellent **Hotel Continental**.*

Where to stay

There's absolutely no problem finding an inexpensive, unremarkable family B&B or small hotel in any of the towns of Thanet and the north Kent coast. These selections highlight some of the more unusual options.

Crown Inn

Ramsgate Road, Sarre, CT11 0LF (01843 847808/fax 01843 847914). **Rates** (B&B) *single* £43.50; *double/twin* £56.90; *four-poster* £70; *family room* £66.75-£70. **Rooms** (all en suite) 7 double; 2 twin; 1 four-poster; 3 family. Special breaks. **Cards** AmEx, Debit, MC, V.

The very word 'quaint' could have been coined to describe the Crown halfway house on the Canterbury to Thanet road, a living antique with its four-poster luxury, snug restaurant and bar, and secret cherry brandy recipe (don't ask). Dating back to 1492 (when Sarre could still boast being one of the Cinque Ports; *see page 25* **That Cinque-ing feeling**), the inn has a lengthy celebrity guestlist including the ubiquitous Mr C Dickens, Douglas Fairbanks, Lloyd George, Mary Pickford… and the mob-capped ghost in Room 14. One room is specially adapted for disabled guests. Children and dogs are welcome.

Sarre is 7 miles NE of Canterbury on A28 towards Margate. Crown Inn is next to mini-roundabout on right.

Fishermen's Huts

On the seafront near the harbour, Whitstable (*see below* **Hotel Continental**). **Rates** (B&B) *two-person hut* £75-£85; *four-person hut* £100-£120. Special breaks. **Rooms** (all en suite) 2 two-person huts; 4 four-person huts. **Cards** AmEx, DC, Debit, MC, V.

Renovated from a state of total dilapidation six years ago, these original 1860s fishermen's net-sheds are now the perfect base for a summer break, full of air and atmosphere, opening direct on to the beach. The wooden huts are furnished comfortably in suitably minimalist fashion, with a sofabed, director's chairs and a plain table (laden with cups, a kettle, tea and coffee) in a bright yellow downstairs room, and a plain pine bed awaiting up a ladder-like flight of stairs. The huts were brought to life and run by Barry Green and family, who also own the Whitstable Oyster Fishery Company restaurant a few yards along the seafront. The larger huts are ideal for families.

On A290 into Whitstable; first left before harbour.

Hanson Hotel

41 Belvedere Road, Broadstairs, CT10 1PF (01843 868936). **Rates** (B&B) £19-£22pp. **Rooms** 2 single; 2 twin (1 en suite); 3 double (2 en suite); 2 family (en suite).

A small, friendly hotel nestling behind Virginia creeper in a Georgian mansion block once owned by Nelson's contemporary and 'hero of a hundred battles', Admiral Sutherland. Outrageously cosy basement bar, the pride of proprietors Jean and Trevor Webb. Children and dogs are welcome.

Follow High Street from Broadstairs station towards seafront; Belvedere Road is on right.

Shellhenge

No other tourist attraction in Britain can have been so consistently undersold and unappreciated as Margate's ancient 'Shell Grotto'. Since its discovery by workmen in 1835 – a handy child was the first drop-in visitor – the man-made chalk cavern, spectacularly studded with millions of shells, has been treated as little more than a side-show curiosity. Today's advertising rather lamely trumpets its credentials as 'the only underground Shell Temple in the world', adding in modest print, 'Believed to be 2,000 years old!', and citing plaudits from the likes of Prince Don Pedro Juan de Borbon, the Mayor of Yalta and, er, Judith Chalmers.

Access to the temple, from a tacky '70s shell shop, is down a flight of short stone steps, and along a rough-hewn chalk passage. At this point the passage splits left and right around a central rotunda, the walls embellished with intricate, expert shell mosaics in soot-blackened yellow, pink and blue: a three-pointed star; ram's horns and snakes; phallic icons; winged solar discs; a turtle deity, together with Bacchus and an eastern-style Ganesha. Walk further on, through a serpentine passage, to the larger altar room, encrusted with symbols of the sun, the moon and stars.

The mysteries of this awe-inspiring temple are manifold and, like all the greatest historical conundrums, apparently insoluble. Even the British Museum failed in its attempt to analyse and reproduce the fishy glue that has held the shells in place on porous chalk over centuries. As for the worshippers who carved this 150-foot temple from solid chalk and spent long years in its sacred decoration, there's simply no clue as to who they were or when they lived: Victorian oil-lamp deposits ruin any chance of accurate carbon dating. The discovery of turtle bones behind the main altar has recently led some experts around to the opinion held by HG Wells, that the temple is more likely nearer 3,000 years old. A truly major national site – Stonehenge was only completed around 1,500 BC – and not even subject to basic preservation guidelines.

Shell Grotto Grotto Hill, Northdown Road, Margate (01843 220008). **Open** *Easter-Oct* 10am-5pm Mon-Fri; 10am-4pm Sat, Sun. **Admission** £1.50; 75p under-11s.

Hotel Continental

29 Beach Walk, Whitstable, CT5 2BP (01227 280280/ fax 01227 280257/www.scoot.co.uk/hotel_continental). **Rates** (B&B) *single* £43; *double* £48-£84; *family room* from £72. **Rooms** (all en suite) 21 double; 2 family. **Cards** AmEx, DC, Debit, MC, V.

This sunny yellow art deco gem on Whitstable's eastern seafront is a complete and utter one-off. Once again, it's part of the local Whitstable Oyster Fishery Company empire, so rest assured the food at the Continental Restaurant (open to all) is wonderful. Whatever the weather, it's a pleasure to sit at the huge front window with your tipple and company of choice, and just gaze into the wide, open sky over the sea. Even better to wake up and see it from your window. It's worth splashing out a little extra for the rooms with sea views. Children welcome. All rooms no smoking.
On the Blean Road (A290); first left after harbour.

Jarvis Marina Hotel [Offer]

Harbour Parade, Ramsgate, CT11 8LZ (01843 588276/fax 01843 586866/www.jarvis.co.uk). **Rates** *single* £72; *double/twin* £82; *family* £82. Special breaks. **Rooms** (all en suite) 4 single; 47 double/twin; 7 family. **Cards** AmEx, DC, Debit, MC, V.

This large, ultra-modern brick affair enjoys a desirable position overlooking, as you can infer from the name, the marina. It may be the priciest hotel in the area, but you get what you pay for in terms of the range of amenities available, including an indoor heated pool, sauna, solarium and spa. Another bonus is the clean, smart rooms, which are all en suite and, for those who like to combine their weekends away with fixes of Sky Sport and CNN, come equipped with satellite TV. Hobson's Restaurant is open to non-guests, and the Club Bar enjoys great views over the busy harbour. Children and dogs welcome. No smoking rooms available.

Royal Albion Hotel

Albion Street, Broadstairs, CT10 1AN (01843 868071/ fax 01843 861509/enquiries@albion-bstairs.demon. co.uk/www.albion-bstairs.demon.co.uk).
Rates *single £57-£63; double £75-£83; family room* £73. Special breaks. **Rooms** (all en suite) 3 single; 14 double; 2 family. **Cards** AmEx, DC, Debit, MC, V.

The only AA stars in Thanet are found at this weighty stucco pile with unbeatable views over Viking Bay – as enjoyed by Dickens when he should have been finishing *Nicholas Nickleby*. Rooms are extremely comfortable, and the staff friendly. The sister establishment, the Marchesi Restaurant, a couple of doors down, is recommended for dinner. Children welcome. No smoking rooms available.
On corner of High Street opposite seafront in Broadstairs town centre.

Where to eat & drink

Tiptoeing precariously close to the incoming waves at Whitstable, the **Old Neptune** takes the idea of seaside pub to the absolute limit. The best pubs in Margate are around the Market Square area, also home to the **Wig & Pen Thai** and **Clementine's**, with its fine game and seafood specials. Getting into the Margate spirit, visit **Ye Olde Humbug** and **Honeycombe Shoppe** on Marine Drive Parade for a loose quarter of all those sweeties you haven't tasted since 1976.

In Broadstairs, the **Dolphin** on Albion Street features live music most nights; **Neptune's Hall** on Harbour Street, opposite, serves a super pint of Shepherd Neame. The **Charles Dickens** on the clifftop prom offers the best sea views. Foodies won't be let down at **Osteria Pizzeria Posillipo** (Albion Street; 01843 601133) or the **Mad Chef's Bistro** (Harbour Street; 01843 604609), despite the sad recent passing of the eponymous celeb crowd-pleaser.

In Ramsgate, the **Queen's Head** on Harbour Parade has a marvellous Victorian tile and sculpted brick façade, a cosy period bar and boules out back. **Harvey's Crab & Oyster House** (01843 591110) is a popular pub with harbour views from the first-floor restaurant. The best spot for a coffee and a snack, though, is undoubtedly the **Eagle** café, perched out on the end of the East Pier; the views are amazing.

Broadstairs Tandoori

41 Albion Street, Broadstairs (01843 865653).
Food served noon-2pm, 6-11pm, Mon-Sat; noon-2pm, 6-10.30pm, Sun. **Cards** AmEx, DC, Debit, MC, V.

Better-than-average pre-balti cuisine, deserving of a mention for its tag-line alone: 'the only Gurkha restaurant in Kent'. After a couple of days of seafood specialities, it's quite a relief to tuck into the BT's exemplary tandoori starters and seriously hardcore garlic nan. A slight question mark hangs over a dubious-sounding Nepalese speciality, tandrook khasi (£5.30), but, on our visit, any doubts were washed away by some Cobras (£3.20) and the khasi's pasanda-ish nut-egg-lamb combo (£5.30).

Summer frolics on **Margate** *Beach.*

Dove Inn

Plum Pudding Lane, Dargate (01227 751360).
Food served noon-2pm, 7-9pm, Tue-Sat; noon-2pm Sun. **Cards** Debit, MC, V.

Around three miles south-west of Whitstable off the A299, the Dove is that rare thing – a true gastropub (rather than a restaurant masquerading as a pub), serving great, imaginative (but not gimmicky) food at fair prices. A fine pint of Shepherd Neame is available at the bar, together with bar snacks, or you could have a full meal in one of the two rooms reserved for dining. Local produce is exploited to the full in dishes such as confit of duck salad with french beans and grain-mustard dressing (£5) and crown of mallard (£13); the local brown shrimps are another treat not to be missed. Booking is essential.

Gate Inn

Marshside, Chislet (01227 860498).
Food served 11am-2pm, 5-9pm, Mon-Fri; 11am-2.15pm, 6-9pm, Sat; noon-2.30pm, 7-9pm, Sun.

An idyllic country boozer secreted deep amid the marshes and high-banked lanes inland from nondescript Herne Bay. Bearded, loveably eccentric landlord Chris Smith makes his own Dragon's Breath mustard, presides over a celebrated and keenly priced specials board and keeps a mean pint of Shepherd Neame. In a textbook country pub garden, streams tinkle into a pond while geese, ducks and doves scrap for crumbs. Hostelry heaven.

Dickens' favourite holiday hotspot: **Broadstairs**.

Harbour Indian Cuisine

6-8 Westcliff Arcade, Ramsgate (01843 580290).
Food served noon-3pm, 6-10.45pm, Sun-Thur;
noon-3pm, 6-11.45pm, Fri, Sat. **Set meals** £20-£30
(minimum 2 people). **Cards** AmEx, DC, Debit, MC, V.

Large, smart Indian restaurant perched halfway up the
brick-vaulted cliffs on the town's western front. In summer, you can sit at tables outside on the steep pedestrian Westcliff Arcade and enjoy a gull's-eye view down
over the marina. There are few surprises on the menu
(main dishes £3-£5), but good fresh veg and spices and
generally classy old-school fare. Next door is the more
homey Thai option of Noknoi's Kitchen (01843 852750).

Pearson's

Horsebridge, Whitstable (01227 272005).
Food served noon-2.30pm, 6-10pm, Mon-Sat;
noon-10pm Sun. **Cards** Debit, MC, V.

Situated right on the seafront at Whitstable, the reputation of the fresh local seafood served up at Pearson's
Original Crab and Oyster House quite rightly extends
far beyond this fishy parish. Never mind the outward
appearance of a fairly unremarkable pub: get inside this
one-time smuggler's haunt and on the outside of a pint
and a Pearson's Paradise, a three-tier, two-person, 36-
quid mountain of lobster, crab, oysters, prawns, mussels, langoustines and clams. Most mains are £7-£13.

Tartar Frigate

Harbour Street, Broadstairs (01843 862013).
Food served noon-2pm, 7-9.30pm, Mon-Sat;
noon-4pm Sun. **Cards** AmEx, Debit, MC, V.

This highly rated Mediterranean-tinged fish restaurant
overlooks Viking Bay. The floral arches, cutesy dolls
and hundreds of Jeff Koons-ish ornaments may not be
to everybody's taste; the exemplary mozzarella skate
and pan-fried monkfish certainly should be. It's £13.50
for a choice of four courses Mon-Fri, but best pay a little extra and go à la carte (mains £11-£16).

Whitstable Oyster Fishery Company

Horsebridge, Whitstable (01227 276856).
Food served noon-1.45pm, 7-8.45pm, Tue-Fri;
noon-2.30pm, 6.30-9.45pm, Sat; noon-3.15pm,
6-8.30pm, Sun (phone to check). **Cards** AmEx, DC,
Debit, MC, V.

An excellent fish restaurant (and upstairs indie cinema!)
housed in the seafront warehouse that was once home
to the Royal Native Oyster Stores (Royal Fishers and
Dredgers incorporated 1793) – just across the street from
Pearson's. Minimal fuss, garnish and overelaboration,
and that goes for the clean red-and-white tablecloth look
of the restaurant as much as the food. The local cod
steaks with alioli are an absolute steal at £8.50. Other
mains can climb as high as £20.

What to see & do

Tourist information centres
6B High Street, **Broadstairs**, CT10 1LH
(01843 862242/www.tourism.thanet.gov.uk).
Open 9am-5pm Mon-Sat; 10am-4pm Sun.

22 High Street, **Margate**, CT9 1DS
(01843 220241/www.tourism.thanet.gov.uk).
Open 9am-5pm Mon-Sat; 10am-4pm Sun.

19-21 Harbour Street, **Ramsgate**, CT11 8HA
(01843 591086/www.tourism.thanet.gov.uk).
Open 9am-5pm Mon-Sat; 10am-4pm Sun.

7 Oxford Street, **Whitstable**, CT5 1DB
(01227 275482/canterburyvisitorinformation@
compuserve.com/www.canterbury.co.uk).
Open 9am-4pm Mon-Sat.

Bike hire
Ken's Bike Shop 26 Eaton Road, **Margate**
(01843 221422). Five minutes from the station.

Bleak House
Fort Road, Broadstairs (01843 862224).
Open *Feb-July, Sept-mid-Dec* 10am-6pm daily;
Aug 10am-9pm daily. **Admission** £3; £1.80 3s-11s;
£2.50 OAPs; £2 students.
This twin-purpose museum, devoted partially to
Dickens, and partially to smuggling and maritime mat-
ters, is housed in the novelist's favourite holiday home,
which dominates the harbour. The view across Viking
Bay from his authentically decked-out study is certain-
ly inspirational.

Clock House Maritime Museum
Pier Yard, Royal Harbour, Ramsgate (01843 587765).
Open *Apr-Sept* 10am-5pm daily; *Oct-Mar* 10am-
4.30pm daily. Last entry 30mins before closing.
Admission £1.50; 75p 5s-15s, OAPs; £4 family.
This local museum includes a weird section on the crick-
et team that plays matches out at sea on the deadly,
shifting Camber Sands.

Dickens' House Museum
Victoria Parade, Broadstairs (01843 862853).
Open *Apr-mid-Oct* 2-5pm daily.
Admission £1.50; 50p under-16s.
Another seafront Dickens haunt, this museum is stuffed
with plenty of letters and memorabilia, costume
exhibits and Victoriana. Broadstairs has hosted an
annual Dickens festival since 1937, commemorating the
author's association with the town. Running for a week
during June, it includes readings, talks, street events,
parades, costumed characters and a dramatic version
of a different Dickens book each year (phone 01843
601364 for details).

Dreamland Fun Park
Belgrave Road, Margate (01843 227011).
Open & **Admission** phone for details.
Cards Debit, MC, V.
The biggest seaside leisure complex in southern
England, featuring a rollercoaster from 1863, a new
Wild Mouse coaster, water rides, dodgems, waltzers
and other amusements.

Margate Caves
1 Northdown Road, Cliftonville (01843 220139).
Open *Easter-Oct* 10am-4pm daily (except July,
Aug & bank hols 10am-5pm). **Admission** £1.50;
75p 4s-11s.
1,000-year-old man-made chalk caverns, variously used
as a refuge from invaders, a secret church, a prison and
a smugglers' store.

Margate Museum
Market Square, Margate (01843 231213).
Open *Apr-Sept* 10am-5pm daily; *Oct-Mar* 9.30am-
4.30pm daily. Last entry 30mins before closing.
Admission £1; 50p 5s-15s, OAPs, students.
Housed in the old town hall-cum-police station, the
museum displays not-particularly-thrilling bits and
bobs on the history of Margate.

Quex House & Gardens/ Powell-Cotton Museum
Birchington (01843 842168).
Open & **Admission** phone for details.
A superb Regency house, furnished to view, set in 17
acres of gardens and woodland. The museum includes
oriental porcelain, African and Asian fine arts and 500
(once-) exotic animal dioramas courtesy of the great
Victorian explorer-naturalist-ethnographer Major PHG
Powell-Cotton.

Ramsgate Motor Museum
West Cliff Hall, Ramsgate (01843 581948).
Open *Easter-Sept* 10.30am-5.30pm daily.
Admission £2.50; 50p 6s-15s; £2 OAPs;
£1.50 students.
A subterranean clifftop museum packed with an extensive and astonishing array of vintage cars and motorcycles, all entertainingly presented in time-machine
dioramas. Everything from a 1900 Benz to the much-
derided Sinclair C5, including fantastic bubble-cars and
obscure scooters.

Sarre Windmill & Animal Farm
Canterbury Road, off A253, Sarre (01843 847573).
Open 10am-5pm daily. **Admission** £2; £1 4s-15s,
OAPs, students.
A rare fully-functioning Edwardian windmill, with
licensed tearooms selling home-made goodies from the
mill's own bakery.

Whitstable Museum & Gallery
Oxford Street, Whitstable (01227 276998).
Open 10.30am-1pm, 2-4pm, Mon, Tue, Thur-Sat.
Admission free.
Some impressive exhibitions from the local arty set, plus
all you need to know about Whitstable's Victorian
seafront rollerskating rink.

Whitstable Oyster & Fishery Exhibition
East Quay, Whitstable (01227 276856).
Open & **Admission** phone for details.
The oyster is your world here: taste it, learn about it,
and, if you're a child, get to fumble around with it.
Opening times are somewhat unpredictable.

Canterbury

Join the throng in the cradle of Christianity.

Canterbury seems tailor-made for a weekend break. As well as being a manageable size, it offers stunning buildings, diverting museums, a fair range of food and drink, and a romantic aura forged by its narrow streets, meandering streams and scented gardens. Indeed, while the city may no longer have the spiritual draw it enjoyed in the Middle Ages, it retains much of its magneticism for the secular and the religious traveller. The principal attraction is, of course, the **Cathedral**, a majestic edifice that dominates the city and its history. But beware, for 1,000 years as the cradle of Christianity mean that Canterbury is the mecca for awaydays from the Continent as much as from the capital (three million visitors a year). Come off-season if you want to avoid the hordes.

Way back when...

Canterbury as a settlement dates back to pre-Roman times, for it has always been a significant crossing point of the River Stour en route inland from the east Kent coast. However, it became a substantial town under the Romans when Durovernum ('the stronghold amidst alders') grew by virtue of being on the road to London from the then coastal port of Richborough. The size of the town warranted an amphitheatre and two public baths, all within the city walls, which formed the basis for later medieval town planners, and which still exist.

Although early Roman Christians certainly practised here, it wasn't until the sixth century and the arrival of St Augustine that Christianity became firmly established. In 561 Ethelbert became King of Kent, and established his capital at Cantwarabyrig ('the township of the men of Kent'). Despite his pagan upbringing, the influence of his Frankish bride Bertha and the papal emissary Augustine resulted in the founding of an abbey and cathedral in the name

Canterbury Cathedral. *See page 19.*

of Christianity. The history of the city has thenceforth been one of successive assaults as much as the centre of the struggles between Church and State. It was sacked by the Vikings twice in the sixth century, occupied by William I following the Norman Conquest and by Wat Tyler and his rebels in 1381, stripped of its ecclesiastical wealth by Henry VIII in 1538, and more recently was the target of Hitler's 'Baedeker Raids' in June 1942 when he attempted to destroy the heritage sites of England (Oxford excepted). And now, of course, the city is invaded by tourists on an annual basis…

That was then...

Canterbury has been the destination for pilgrims since Thomas Becket's murder within the Cathedral in 1170 (*see page 17* **Becket kicks the bucket**). Immortalised in the first great work of English prose, Chaucer's *Canterbury Tales,* the journey need not take so long today,

By train from London

Trains to **Canterbury East** leave **Victoria** hourly (journey time **1hr 25mins**). Trains to **Canterbury West** leave **Charing Cross** every half an hour (journey time **1hr 45mins**).

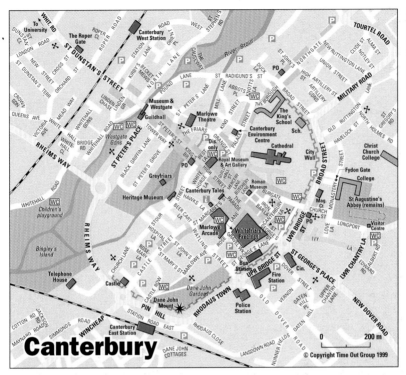

nor need you endure lengthy anecdotes along the way, although once in the town you will no longer be able to avoid Chaucer's contribution to the city's reputation. However, despite its medieval legacy and the prevalence of the heritage industry, Canterbury is still home to some 35,000 people. Most of the high street stores are here; some, but not too many, kitsch tourist boutiques; and some charming second-hand bookshops. Wandering streets such as Palace Street, punting along the Stour, or exploring the western corner around St Mildred's Church and Stour Street offer havens from the frenzy of the high street and the Buttermarket. A final point worth noting: for a city, Canterbury is surprisingly child-friendly. Extensive pedestrianisation, plentiful greenery, some fun museums and a cathedral that can't fail to impress, all combine to give plenty of running, learning and gawping opportunities.

Where to stay

There is little beyond the city walls in Canterbury that is worth the trek. Besides, the best way to see Canterbury is on foot, so try to stay within walking distance of the centre (you pay for this, of course).

That said, classy hotels and characterful B&Bs are not Canterbury's speciality. If you have your own transport, it might be preferable to stay in the better accommodation available in **Whitstable** (*see page 7*) on the coast, seven miles north of the city.

Cathedral Gate Hotel

36 Burgate, CT1 2HA
(01227 464381/cgate@cgate.demon.co.uk).
Rates (B&B) *single* £22-£51; *double* £40-£76; *triple* £58-£87.50; *family* £87.50-£97.50. **Rooms** 10 single (5 en suite); 8 double (4 en suite); 3 triple (1 en suite); 2 family (en suite). **Cards** AmEx, DC, Debit, MC, V.

Located by Christ Church Gate at the entrance to the Cathedral grounds, this rambling medieval building is the most charming hotel in the city. OK, so you may have to share a bathroom, and you won't marvel at the décor, but what the rooms lack in modern comforts, the creaking, groaning corridors make up for in history. In the summer you can take breakfast on a roof terrace under the shadows of Harry Bell Tower. The rooms 'Daybreak', 'Cathedral' and, best of all, 'Joy' all look directly on to the Cathedral. Children and dogs are welcome.

Canterbury

Canterbury

Time Out Weekend Breaks **15**

County Hotel

High Street, CT1 2RX (01227 766266/
info@county.macdonald-hotels.co.uk/
www.macdonaldhotels.co.uk/county-hotel).
Rates *single* £86; *double/twin* £102.50;
four-poster/deluxe £118. Special breaks.
Breakfast £9.50 (Eng), £7.50 (cont).
Rooms (all en suite) 15 single; 30 twin; 16 double;
4 four-posters; 8 deluxe. **Cards** AmEx, DC, Debit,
MC, V.

A huge operation on the High Street, the County thinks
of everything, in a slightly anonymous, corporate kind
of way. The rooms are comfortable, spacious and smart,
and those in the older part display some signs of the
building's Tudor and Georgian history, but there is little quirkiness. A large roof terrace is planned. The
restaurant, **Sully's**, is popular with residents and
locals. Children are welcome and non-smoking rooms
are available.

Ebury Hotel

65-67 New Dover Road, CT1 3DX (01227 768433).
Rates (B&B) *single* £50; *double/twin* £75; *family*
£85-£95. **Rooms** (all en suite) 2 single; 3 twin;
7 double; 3 family. **Cards** AmEx, DC, Debit, MC, V.

A grand hotel that is also good for families. A huge family room sleeps five, and the large garden and heated
swimming pool are great for unfettered frolicking. The
rooms are large, light and comfortable, and those at the
back overlook the extensive lawn, bungalows and swimming chalet. The restaurant is a good cut or two above
the hotel average. This family-run hotel is a thoroughly professional operation, the best on the New Dover
Road. Unfortunately, this main spur from the centre is
busy and bland, giving guests a charmless 15-minute
walk to the centre.

Falstaff Hotel

8-10 St Dunstan's Street, CT2 8AF
(01227 462138/fax 01227 463522).
Rates *single* £85; *double/twin* £95; *four-poster/
family/suite* £105. Special breaks. Breakfast £9.25
(Eng), £6.25 (cont). **Rooms** (all en suite)
7 single; 14 double; 1 suite; 3 four-poster; 2 family.
Cards AmEx, DC, Debit, MC, V.

A warren of rooms creak behind this fifteenth-century
house that lies just beyond the Westgate. The overhanging front displays lead-lined windows; inside panelled corridors undulate and creak with age. Period
details appear in most rooms, if only in the irregularity
of the shape. Room 27 at the front is spacious and lined
in ancient oak; but to avoid overlooking the busy street
go for the four-poster in Room 9. An award-winning
restaurant and pleasant bar overlook a courtyard at the
back, and the large lounge and roaring fire ensure comfort. Building is under way to add 15 more rooms.
Children welcome. Non-smoking rooms available.

Greyfriars

6 Stour Street, CT1 2NR (01227 456255/
fax 01227 455233/www.greyfriars-house.co.uk).
Rates *single* £25-£35; *double/twin* £45-£55;
family £55-£75. **Rooms** (all en suite) 7 single;
14 double/twin; 2 family. **Cards** Debit, MC, V.

The simplest, but cheapest, of our recommendations
within the city walls. As is a feature of accommodation
in Canterbury, no rooms are entirely level or regular in
shape. All are clean and simply decorated and furnished. The family room is large and welcoming,
although it's not really a place to lounge around. But
Greyfriars' proximity to the centre, simple efficiency
and friendly hosts make it a good value choice. Children
and dogs are welcome.

Indulge in four-poster frolics at the central **Falstaff Hotel**.

Becket kicks the bucket

'Touch me not, Reginald; you owe me fealty and subjection; you and your accomplices act like madmen.' So said Thomas Becket in the north transept of the Cathedral before sword blows rained down on him as he prayed to the blessed St Denys. On 29 December 1170, Reginald and three other knights murdered the Archbishop out of loyalty to Henry II, against whom Becket had been battling in order to preserve the privileges of the Church from being overwhelmed by the power of the State.

As the aptly named Edward Grim wrote, the knights severed the crown of his head 'so that the blood white with the brain and the brain red with blood, dyed the surface of the virgin mother Church with the life and death of the confessor

and martyr in the colours of the lily and the rose.' Grim had tried to protect Becket, but almost lost an arm in the process. Becket fell on his knees and spoke in a low voice: 'For the name of Jesus and the protection of the Church I am ready to embrace Death.' The location and horrific manner of the cleric's death earned him martyrdom. As word spread through Christendom, Canterbury became a source of pilgrimage, and Becket's relics were imbued with healing powers. Such was his status that in 1174 a guilt-ridden and remorseful Henry II came to Canterbury to be scourged by the monks at the martyr's tomb. Today the Altar of the Sword's Point marks the place where this miller's son finally met his maker.

Magnolia House

36 St Dunstan's Terrace, CT2 8AX (tel/fax 01227 765121/www.smoothhound.co.uk/hotels/magnoli.html).
Rates (B&B) *single* £38-£45; *double/twin* £72-£84; *four-poster* £95. **Rooms** (all en suite) 1 single; 4 double; 1 twin; 1 four-poster. **Cards** AmEx, DC, Debit, MC, V.

They treat you well at the Magnolia. The rooms are mostly small, with the notable exception of the very grand Garden Room (with a four-poster bed and Jacuzzi), but they are all well maintained and offer everything you might want. The garden is small but pleasing, and the breakfast wholesome and plentiful. Magnolia House's greatest bonus is that, although it's a good ten minutes from the centre on foot, and in a quiet residential area off St Dunstan's Street, the walk to and from the centre can take you through Westgate Gardens, past the Lord Mayor's Parlour, Greyfriars and the River Stour – a lovely, peaceful introduction to the city. All rooms are non-smoking.

Thanington Hotel

140 Wincheap, CT1 3RY (01227 453227/fax 01227 453225/thanington-hotel@compuserve.com/www.thanington-hotel.co.uk).
Rates (B&B) *single* £48-£52; *double/twin* £68-£72; *four-poster* £88; *family* £95. **Rooms** (all en suite) 8 double; 3 twin; 2 four-poster; 1 family.
Cards AmEx, DC, Debit, MC, V.

Although outside the city walls, and a tad overfloral in its décor, this is perhaps the best place in Canterbury for children. It has a large family room, a swimming pool, a snooker room (half-size table) and a small garden. Across the road, a small walled park holds climbing frames and running-about space. The friendly hosts take pride in their premises, from the slightly cramped four-poster

rooms in the Georgian main building fronting the main road to the quieter chalet rooms at the back. Although not particularly beautiful or romantic, this B&B is a pleasant and smart place, ten minutes' walk from the centre. Children welcome and non-smoking rooms available.

Zan Stel Lodge

140 Old Dover Road, CT1 3NX (01227 453654).
Rates (B&B) *single* £30-£42; *double/twin* £42-£52; *triple* £60-£69. **Rooms** 1 double (en suite); 2 twin/double; 1 triple (en suite).

Zan Stel Lodge has a friendly, family feel, with light and airy rooms and a charming garden that looks on to the County Cricket Ground (you can see the famous tree standing within the boundary). Opposite is the pleasant Bat & Ball pub, so if you're a cricket nut, then you won't have to move more than 20 yards all weekend. Unfortunately, the parking's not great as the Lodge is on a steep hill, and it's a good 15-minute walk to the centre, but the homely atmosphere offers its own rewards. All rooms are non-smoking.

Where to eat & drink

There's no shortage of eating and drinking opportunities in Canterbury. However, while the range may be impressive, the quality of them is rarely high. The standard offerings are all there: **Pizza Express** (5A Best Lane; 01227 766938); **Café Rouge** (53 St Peter's Street; 01227 763833); **Caffé Uno** (49A St Peter's Street; 01227 479777), and **Fatty Arbuckles** (45 St Peter's Street; 01227 784770).

Some of the hotels mentioned above, such as the Falstaff and the Ebury, have decent menus but rather bland dining-rooms; other cafés and pubs provide a livelier atmosphere: **Beaus Crêperie** (59 Palace Street) has a wide range of crêpes, and a light and airy setting; **Oranges** (14 St Peter's Street) has an impressive sandwich menu; and the **Thomas Becket** pub (21 Best Lane) serves roasts in the restaurant at the back, while farmers nurse pints under heavy wooden beams around the front bar.

Since the opening of a bar/club on the University campus, the city centre is quieter than it used to be on weekend evenings. The busiest pubs are, depressingly, the **Franklin & Firkin** outside Christ Church Gate, and the **Thomas Ingolsby**, a Wetherspoon's of unparalleled blandness on Burgate. Nevertheless, the **Three Tuns** on Castle Street is young and lively, and the **Bell & Crown** in Palace Street and the **Bishop's Finger** on St Dunstan's Street are both busy and authentic. If you're looking for a live music dive, the **Cardinal's Cap** on Rosemary Lane is as smoky and dingy as they get and, just up St Margaret's Street, **Alberry's** will have them queuing outside after closing time as it's the only venue within the city walls with a late licence. Beyond the walls, a nightlife of sorts centres around the **Churchill** and the **Works** nightclubs, but the city is really more a place for silent contemplation than raucous revelry.

Bistro Vietnam

72 Castle Street, CT1 2QD (01227 760022).
Food served noon-2pm, 7-10pm, Tue-Sat; 7-9.30pm Sun. **Cards** AmEx, DC, Debit, MC, V.

This small, narrow restaurant is pleasantly low-key. The kitchen is visible at one end of the room, where explosions of flame signal the preparation of another hot and spicy noodle dish. Downstairs, a brick-lined room is ideal for smallish parties. The Bistro has plenty of regulars, perhaps drawn by the laid-back service and the huge noodle and braised meat dishes (such as mixed meat or prawn noodles, £6.95; and braised spice lemongrass chicken, £5.95). Beware: the spicing takes no prisoners.

La Bonne Cuisine

Canterbury Hotel, 71 New Dover Road (01223 351880).
Food served noon-1.45pm, 7-9.45pm, daily.
Cards AmEx, DC, Debit, MC, V.

The Canterbury Hotel is a huge, imposing, lavishly decorated Victorian building, and the cooking in its restaurant is suitably grand, and very French. There's a Mediterranean bias in carefully assembled dishes such as a home-smoked eel, salmon and swordfish platter (a starter, £7.50); mains include roast seabass with fennel and Nantais-style butter and thyme (£12.50) and pan-fried Aberdeen Angus beef fillet with five pepper sauce (£15.50). Not a place to come, perhaps, for a chilled evening, but great if you fancy a posh blow-out.

Café des Amis du Mexique

95 St Dunstan's Street (01227 464390).
Food served noon-10pm daily. **Cards** AmEx, Debit, MC, V.

This bright, light and breezy Mexican diner is one of the most popular restaurants in Canterbury. And rightly so. With the brass beat and guitar strains of the homeland as background music, ochre walls and large windows, there's an upbeat feel to the place. Young staff serve a youngish crowd a fine collection of Mexican dishes: vatapa de peixe (salmon and prawns with ginger, coconut milk and lime sauce, £9.95); pato con mole (crispy duck 'burger' with mole sauce, mango salsa and sour cream and chive mash, £8.95); and a fine pollo verde in a spicy almond sauce (£7.95). And don't miss the dangerously seductive chocolate puds. Book in advance.

Marlowe's

55 St Peter's Street
(01227 462194/www.cantweb.co.uk/marlowes).
Food served 11am-10.30pm daily.
Cards AmEx, Debit, MC, V.

Marlowe's has a cosy feel. Black beams, orange walls (green upstairs) and muted lighting allow you to snuggle up and enjoy a langorous candle-lit dinner overseen by innumerable film stars (well, by their pictures lining the walls). It's a bring-your-own-wine venue, so prices are kept to a reasonable level. The menu is extensive, and has plenty of choice for vegetarians – perhaps warmed goat's cheese salad (£5.95), Archbishop's Medley (a vegetable, nut and breadcrumb bake, £6.95) or Pilgrims Pie (soya and tomatoes under puff pastry, £6.95). A number of Mexican dishes add to the imaginative repertoire.

Tuo e Mio

16 The Borough (01227 761471).
Food served 7-10.45pm Tue; noon-2.30pm, 7-10.45pm, Wed-Sat; noon-2.30pm, 7-10pm Sun.
Cards AmEx, DC, Debit, MC, V.

This smart black-and-white-decorated restaurant is among the best in Canterbury. White Artexed walls, starched linen and black trimmings give the premises a smart professional feel, endorsed by the smooth and stylish service. The food itself matches the surroundings – the menu includes the likes of halibut with salsa verde (£12.50), pollo Genovese with brandy, basil and mushrooms (£7.50) and a signature dish of tender and rich filetto tuo e mio (beef with cream brandy and mushrooms, £14.50). The dessert trolley is a virtual pâtisserie. Book in advance.

What to see & do

Tourist information centre

34 St Margaret's Street, CT1 2TG (01227 766567/www.canterbury.co.uk). **Open** July, Aug 9.30am-5.30pm daily; Sept-June 9.30am-5pm Mon-Sat.

Canterbury Castle

Castle Street (tourist info 01227 766567).
Open 8am-dusk daily. **Admission** free.

This huge Norman stone keep, built successively by William the Conqueror and William Rufus, retains some fine brickwork, giving clues to where the various doorways, dungeons and staircases once stood. The three floors have long since gone, but the remaining edifice is evocative of the once-great castle that was attacked by Wat Tyler and his revolting peasants in 1381.

The perfect way to avoid the summer crowds: punting by the **Westgate Gardens**.

Canterbury Cathedral

The Precincts (01227 762862).
Open *cathedral Easter-Sept* 8.45am-7pm Mon-Sat;
12.30-2.30pm, 4.30-5.30pm, Sun; *Oct-Easter* 8.45am-
5pm Mon-Sat; 12.30-2.30pm, 4.30-5.30pm, Sun. *Crypt*
10am-4.30pm Mon-Sat; 12.30-2.30pm, 4.30-5.30pm,
Sun. **Admission** £3; £2 5s-17s, OAPs, students.

The centrepiece of the city, and justifiably so. From the
splendour of the sixteenth-century Christ Church Gate,
which serves as the entry point, the Cathedral rises up
before you, with Bell Harry tower soaring heavenward
some 250 feet. Augustine first established a cathedral
here in 602; the current incarnation was begun by
Archbishop Lanfranc in 1070. To see what remains,
descend to the huge crypt to view the fine pillars with
intricate capitals and carved columns. On reappearing
in the north transept, note the Altar of the Sword's Point,
the site of Becket's gruesome end (*see p17* **Becket
kicks the bucket**). The main nave dates from around
1400; its intricate lierne vaulting (a complex form of
ribbed vaulting) is its finest feature, although this is
more than matched by the magnificent fan vaulting
beneath Bell Harry. Other essential viewing includes the
fifteenth-century quire screen, the tombs of the Black
Prince and Edward the Confessor in the Trinity Chapel
at the eastern end of the Cathedral, and, outside, the
magnificent cloisters and Green Court overlooked by
King's School. The Cathedral is at its most magical just
before dusk, with a recital reverberating from within,
and the coach parties long gone.

Canterbury Tales

St Margaret's Street (01227 479227).
Open *mid-Feb-June* 9.30am-5.30pm daily; *July-Oct*
9am-5.30pm daily; *Nov-mid-Feb* 9.30am-4.30pm daily.
Admission £5.25; £4.25 5s-15s; £4.50 OAPs,
students; £16.50 family.

Chaucer's tales, adapted, abridged and brought to life
by waxwork models, mechanical movements and
Bernard Cribbins reading through your headset. It
might be your scene, or it may enduce you to throw yourself on the 'grissly rokkes blackes'. Lasts 45 minutes.

Chaucer Centre

22-23 St Peter's Street (01227 470379).
Open 10am-5.30pm Tue-Sat. **Admission** free.

An interesting and concise exploration of the poet's life
and works, although not the most impressively housed
exhibition space. Suitable for all ages.

Dane John Garden

entrance at Watling Street.

The title of this garden and motte is a corruption of the
Norman French 'donjon', meaning motte, and while
there is only a simple mound to testify to its earlier use,
the city council has created a gentle garden with children's maze and play area; while the walk along the ramparts allow commanding views of, er, the ring road.

Eastbridge Hospital

High Street (01227 471688).
Open 10am-4.45pm Mon-Sat.
Admission £1; 50p 5s-16s; 75p OAPs.

Founded to meet the growing kipping needs of pilgrims
in the wake of Becket's murder in 1170, this small but
ancient 'spital' retains the smell and damp of ages past.
The display boards are a bit DIY, but the undercroft
with its tilting arches and the chapel with its thirteenth-
century mural and crown-post roof are wonderful.

Greyfriars

entrance on Stour Street (01227 462395).
Open *mid-May-Sept* 2-4pm Mon-Sat.
Admission free; donations welcome.

This thirteenth-century Franciscan building spans the
River Stour on the edge of a field of wild flowers.

Heritage Museum

Stour Street (01227 452747).
Open *Nov-May* 10.30am-5pm Mon-Sat;
June-Oct 10.30am-5pm Mon-Sat; 1.30-5.30pm Sun.
Last entry 4pm. **Admission** £2.30; £1.15 5s-18s;
£1.50 OAPs, students.

The best museum devoted to the history of Canterbury.
It begins with the early Roman settlement through to the

Keep it in the family – **Canterbury Castle**, *built by William I and his son. See page 18.*

city's emergence as the centre of English Christianity, all clearly presented in a series of well laid-out rooms. The 30-minute video on Becket's life and death is entertaining and informative, and the huge vaulted hall in this former Poor Priests' Hospital is worth the entrance fee in itself. The Rupert Bear room, in honour of its creator, Canterbury-born Mary Tourtel, is slightly overdone – more on Joseph Conrad (who lived in Canterbury and wrote most of his books here), and Christopher Marlowe (who was born in the city), would have been more apt.

Roman Museum

Butchery Lane (01227 785575).
Open *Nov-May* 10am-5pm Mon-Sat; *June-Oct* 10am-5pm Mon-Sat; 1.30-5pm Sun. Last entry 1hr before closing. **Admission** £2.30; £1.15 5s-18s; £1.50 OAPs, students.

An in-depth record of Durovernum, this carefully constructed museum focuses as much on the archaeological process as the finds themselves. Built around the undulating mosaic floor of a Roman townhouse, it features interactive computer displays, speculative reconstructions and a 'hands-on' area, where children and adults can weigh up reproduction artefacts.

Royal Museum & Art Gallery

High Street (01227 452727).
Open 10am-5pm Mon-Sat. **Admission** free.

Porcelain, silver, medallions and paintings take up the first floor of this Victorian monument. Most notable is a fine collection of Thomas Sydney Cooper's cattle portraits – the huge bull on the staircase is magnificent.

St Augustine's Abbey

Longport (01227 767345).
Open *Apr-Sept* 10am-6pm daily; *Oct* 10am-5pm daily; *Nov-Mar* 10am-4pm daily. **Admission** (EH) £2.50; £1.30 5s-16s; £1.90 OAPs, students.

The remains of this historic abbey are laid out in a park just outside the walls (Christian tradition forbade burials within city walls). In 597 St Augustine was sent to England by Pope Gregory to reintroduce Christianity to the island and, following his conversion, King Ethelbert duly gave land to the Benedictine monk to found this abbey. Archbishop Lanfranc rebuilt the abbey in the eleventh century, and it flourished until Henry VIII dissolved it in 1538 and converted the buildings into lodgings for Anne of Cleves. Subsequent uses have included a brewery and missionary college; it's now part of King's School. An audio tour takes you around the site, drawing a picture of the abbey in its prime.

St Martin's Church

North Holmes Road (01227 459482).
Open phone for details. **Admission** free.

This beautiful small church is reputed to be the oldest parish church in continuous use in England. It is thought to have been established in the sixth century, when Bertha, the Christian wife of the Anglo-Saxon King of Kent, Ethelbert, sought a place to worship. What now remains is mainly thirteenth- and fourteenth-century – look out for the font and the replica Chrismatory. The stepped graveyard holds the tombs of Mary Tourtel (the creator of Rupert Bear) and T Sydney Cooper (artist).

Westgate Museum

St Peter's Street (01227 452747).
Open 11am-12.30pm, 1.30-3.30pm, Mon-Sat. **Admission** £1; 50p 5s-18s; 65p OAPs, students.

Although there's been a gate on this site since the third century, the current twin towers were erected in the late fourteenth century. Fear of a French invasion prompted a powerful construction, much of which still stands today. The museum of weaponry and armaments on the first floor is small but informative, and the prison cells and the view from the roof are worth a gander.

Sandwich to Sandgate

Britain's historical frontline bristles with castles and cliffs.

It is with good reason that Dover's white cliffs have been immortalised in song, for not many places can boast such a rich heritage as this historically vital stretch of coastline. The Classis Britannica (the Roman fleet) was stationed here to defend the Channel, and the remains of the lighthouse, fort and vicus (hotel) are still in evidence. In the Middle Ages, this area was the heart of the curious federation of the **Cinque Ports** (*see page 25* **That Cinque-ing feeling**), which provided England's first line of defence against the beastly continentals.

All along the watchtowers

At the north end of this region is **Sandwich**. Sitting on the River Stour, this now-landlocked former port is still very much a small medieval town with half-timber-framed houses lining the narrow streets – Strand Street being a particularly fine example. Overlooking the grassy banks of the Stour is the town's most celebrated building, the fine sixteenth-century Barbican. Not far away are the golden sands and

By train from London

Trains for **Sandwich** leave **Charing Cross** hourly, passing through **Dover** (journey time **2hrs 10mins**). Trains to **Dover** also run from **Victoria** at least every hour (journey time **1hr 40mins**).

famous Royal St George golf course of Sandwich Bay. A couple of miles north of the town, set in the bleakly unappealing Pegwell Bay, are the remains of **Richborough Roman Fort**, one-time sentinel over the southern entrance to the Wantsum Channel, which formerly cut off the Isle of Thanet from the rest of Kent.

Moving south, the contiguous low-key resort towns of **Deal** and **Walmer** are notable chiefly for their Tudor castles (Henry VIII added both to the list of Cinque Ports). It's a fine 45-minute coastal walk between the two of them. Deal's winding streets, lined with antique emporiums, hardware stores, an old-fashioned sweet shop

Quirky, Tudor rose-shaped **Deal Castle**. *See page 26.*

and an excellent second-hand bookshop, bring to mind its considerable reputation as a one-time smugglers' den.

Don't pass the ports

During World War II, **Dover**'s cliffs concealed the wartime operations unit where Admiral Ramsey and Winston Churchill planned the Dunkirk evacuation. The tunnels beneath the striking Castle can be explored and, together with the White Cliffs Experience, represent two of the area's most worthwhile attractions, particularly for children. Next door to the latter, the Dover Museum (01304 201066) traces the history of the town from the Bronze Age to the present day with dioramas, paintings, models and artefacts. Close by, the Roman Painted House (New Street; 01304 203279), discovered in 1970, is impressively well preserved with chunks of frescoed walls, hypocaust heating system and brickwork. Also worth a visit is Old Town Gaol (Biggin Street; 01304 242766), where they'll happily let you try out a cell and lock the door. Despite these historical attractions, the town has a decidedly down-at-heel feel and is notably lacking in charm. It does, though, at least have some decent shopping at De Bradelei Wharf (01304 226616).

Away from the coast, the villages are few and scattered, dotted amid orchards and prime fruit-picking country. **Temple Ewell**, near Dover, was used as a stopping off point for the Knights Templar on their way to the crusades, while **Kearsney Abbey**, near River on the road between Dover and Folkestone, is a delightful spot for walks, with its sizeable duck pond and café in the remaining portion of the house (which incidentally had no ecclesiastical pretensions at all, having been built for the Dover banker John Minet Fector in 1820).

Folkestone and **Sandgate** are virtually one and the same, though Sandgate is markedly more well-to-do. After the crippling decline of its ferry crossings, and despite the proximity of the entrance to the Channel Tunnel, Folkestone is still struggling to get its economy back on track. The Bayle area is rapidly filling up with shops, the best of which is the long-serving Moon Palace, a fantastic Aladdin's cave of beads, decorated boxes, china, dolls' house furniture and cards. Just around the corner on the cobbled Old High Street is the Rock Shop, selling old-fashioned humbugs, sweet pebbles and aniseed twists, and where the rock is still rolled out and cut to the delight of sweet-toothed kiddies. At the bottom of the Old High Street, go through the harbour arches for a well-stocked shell and mineral shop, grab a pint of prawns on the seafront, and head for the sandy beach. The water, however, is best avoided…

Where to stay

There are hundreds of B&Bs along the coast. Wear Bay Road in **Folkestone** is the main drag for comfy accommodation, while the ship-shaped **Hotel Burstin** in the harbour ('Britain's biggest entertainment hotel' boasts the leaflet) is crawling with OAPs down for a country and western extravaganza by the sea. **Dover**'s waterfront area offers the best sea views and standards in the town – but be warned, there are some grotty dives if the good ones are full; **Deal** is an attractive alternative.

For something out of the ordinary try the **Woodville Hall Country House Hotel** (London Road, Temple Ewell; 01304 825256). It's a magnificent Georgian country house set in 25 acres of woodland and nature reserves, well worth a special break, but it only has three suites (£95-£120 per night), so book early.

The Churchill

The Waterfront, Dover, CT17 9BP (01304 203633/216320).
Rates *single* £59-£67; *double/twin* £79-£87; *family room* £92. Breakfast £10 (Eng/cont). **Rooms** (all en suite) 6 single; 37 double; 20 twin; 5 deluxe; 4 family. **Cards** AmEx, DC, Debit, MC, V.

Reminiscent of the Royal Crescent in Bath, this curving terrace of Regency townhouses was built in 1834 for visitors wishing to indulge in the new craze for sea-bathing. After World War I, a number of apartments were converted into hotels, which promptly closed at the outbreak of World War II. Reopened in peacetime and renamed the Churchill in recognition of the wartime PM's associations with the town, the exterior of the building has been sympathetically restored to the style of its '20s art deco heyday, while the interior is spotless and comfortable, though largely uninspiring. It is affordable, however, and offers good value weekend breaks.
On seafront between hover port and Eastern dock.

Dunkerley's Hotel

19 Beach Street, Deal, CT14 7AH (01304 375016/fax 01304 380187).
Rates (B&B) *single occupancy* £45-£65; *double/twin/family room* £35pp; *four-poster/suite* £50pp. Special breaks. **Rooms** (all en suite) 5 double; 7 twin; 1 four-poster; 1 suite; 2 family. **Cards** AmEx, DC, Debit, MC, V.

Right on the seafront, and just within staggering distance of the **King's Head**, Dunkerley's has 16 well-sized en suite bedrooms with satellite TV, some of which also have Jacuzzis. The unusual Romanian furniture adds a pleasantly rustic air and the sea views are utterly unspoilt. Ask about special break prices, which include dinner at the hotel's excellent restaurant.

King's Head

Beach Street, Deal, CT14 7AH (01304 368194/fax 01304 364182).
Rates (B&B) *single occupancy* £38; *double/twin* £25pp; *family room* £65. **Rooms** (all en suite) 8 double/twin; 6 family. **Cards** Debit, MC, V.

Oh, I do like to stroll along the Leas, Leas, Leas

Folkestone, to put it kindly, is not overwhelmed with attractions. The town is, though, justly proud of **The Leas**, its magnificent Edwardian promenade. At its far end rise the majestic frontages of the Metropole and the Grand Hotel. The former now houses an arts centre offering brilliant children's activities and events (01303 255070); the latter was once the seaside love nest of Edward VII and Lily Langtree; both are now mainly divided into flats.

Further down the prom's sweeping expanse of ironwork and regimented flower borders is the tile-fronted Leas Club (now a glorified pool hall), the bandstand, which accommodates all manner of musical happenings from jazz to rock, and The Leas Cliff Hall (01303 253193),

where the big-name touring concerts, exhibitions and comedy acts call in when they're in town. Not far away, to the seaward side, are the red railings of the water-powered chair lift (01303 251573), which delivers passengers quirkily yet safely down the sheer rockface on to the pebble beach below. Dominating this particular patch of shoreline is the Rotunda (01303 245245) – a sprawling '50s amusement complex that even in the height of summer resembles the abandoned set of a decidedly low budget B-movie. It's hugely popular with locals and visitors, the rides posing no great threat to the nervous system of small children, and rousing the curiosity of older generations who believed these kind of attractions had long since ceased to exist.

Add to this the colourful mass of the regular Sunday market – with its off-the-back-of-a-lorry air, teeming with bargain hunters and ringing with the patter of Kent Coast diamond geezers – and it's not hard to see why the area continues to exude considerable charm. With the injection of a £1m investment in the Lower Leas coastal park (including formal gardens, sculpture and a play area; project due to open in 2001), this is only likely to increase.

Overlooking the sea, this attractive red-brick hostelry was once a smugglers' haunt. The quaint cottage-style bedrooms are all en suite, and competitively priced. Good pub food is available; kids are not allowed in the bar area, but there are plenty of tables out on the front. Children and dogs welcome.

On seafront opposite Deal pier.

Loddington House

East Cliff, Marine Parade, Dover, CT16 1LX (tel/fax 01304 201947).
Rates (B&B) *single* £35-45; *double* £52-£56; *family room* £75-£90. **Rooms** 1 single (en suite); 5 double (3 en suite). **Cards** AmEx, MC, V.

Loddington House backs right on to the cliffs, giving you a breathtaking sight every time you come in and out of the front door. Ask for rooms facing away from the sea if you want to gaze up at the chalk face; these are also quieter because at this far end of the Parade the road is the main thoroughfare from the ferry terminal – just 200 yards down the road – with its predominant traffic of heavy goods lorries. Rooms are basic and clean

with small portable-style TVs and rudimentary facilities (shower, bar of soap, shampoo sachets). Not the romantic love nest of your dreams maybe but an attractive and friendly option for a whistle-stop all the same.

Sandgate Hotel

The Esplanade, Sandgate, CT20 3DY (01303 220444/fax 01303 220496).
Rates (B&B) *single* £44; *double/twin* £56-£64; *deluxe* £74. Special breaks. **Rooms** (all en suite) 2 single; 9 double/twin; 4 deluxe. **Cards** AmEx, DC, Debit, MC, V.

Though all the rooms in this very tall, elegant hotel are clean and bright (if smallish), the best ones are those with beflowered balconies overlooking the sea. The lounge is elegant and restful, with good views of the coastline from the terrace, and the pebble beach is just across the road. The French restaurant **La Terrasse** is highly recommended, though there's limited space, so be sure to reserve a table when you book a room. Note that the hotel is closed on Sunday evenings.

On seafront between Sandgate and Hythe.

*First-rate coastal rambling on **the Warren**, just outside Folkestone. See page 26.*

Wallett's Court

Westcliffe, St Margaret's at Cliffe, CT15 6EW
(01304 852424/fax 01304 853430/wallettscourt@
compuserve.com/www.wallettscourt.com).
Rates (B&B) *single occupancy £70-£90; double/twin*
£65-£80; four-poster £100; *suite* £130; *family room*
£80-£100. **Rooms** (all en suite) 7 double; 2 twin; 2
deluxe; 2 four-poster; 3 suites. **Cards** AmEx, DC,
Debit, MC, V.

Former home of William Pitt the Younger, this family
residence is a jewel in the East Kent countryside. The
main accommodation is in the substantial whitewashed
farmhouse where Queen Eleanor of Castile and Edward
the Black Prince still lay claim to the rooms through
plaques on the doors. Indeed, the rather lumpy mattress
seems an authentic souvenir of their stay, but overall
the experience is quite magical, with beautiful antique
dressers, cavernous baths and carved wooden four-
poster beds. Outside in the grounds is a sauna, steam
room, heated pools and spa, further chalet-style rooms,
a wooden treehouse and a bench swing affording fine
views of the voluptuous sheep-grazed hills.
A2 from Canterbury; take A258 towards Deal for 0.5 mile;
1st right after Swing Gate pub; Wallett's Court is opposite
church on right.

Where to eat & drink

Though this particular part of the East Kent
coast is not exactly overflowing with high-
quality eateries (or classic pubs), there's many a
value for money mid-range establishment to be
found in most of the towns – the recently
opened **Lemongrass** (High Street, Deal; 01304
367707) makes good use of the abundance of
fresh fish and seafood in the area. The
Griffin's Head at Chillenden (between Deal
and Canterbury; 01304 840325) has great
wholesome pub grub in the authentic setting of
a one-time medieval timber-frame house,
complete with inglenook fireplaces and exposed
beams. *See also page 23* **Sandgate Hotel**.

Dunkerley's

Beach Street, Deal (01304 375016).
Food served *bistro* 11am-10.30pm daily;
restaurant noon-3pm, 6-10.30pm, Tue-Sun.
Cards AmEx, DC, Debit, MC, V.

Specialising in seafood dishes, Dunkerley's offers both
bistro and restaurant dining. Dishes are inventive but
not gimmicky, with starters (between £2.75 and £5.50)
including crab perfumed with tarragon, mussel and saffron broth, and caramelised scallops with a Vermouth
butter sauce. Main dishes (from £11.95) take in haddock,
skate, Dover sole, roasted sea bass and whole lobster.
Meals in the bistro are less fancy and can be slow to
arrive when the restaurant is busy. The salmon with
honey mustard on a jacket potato (£6.95) and the linguini with spicy tomato sauce (£5.95) are, however,
worth the wait.

The Moonflower

High Street, Dover (01304 212198).
Food served noon-2.30pm, 5-11.30pm, Mon-Sat.
Cards AmEx, DC, Debit, MC, V.

A friendly family-style Chinese with plenty of choice,
including Malaysian specialities like mee goreng – meat,
seafood and vegetables cooked in chilli sauce and served
with noodles – as well as nostalgic 1970s dishes like foo
yung and chop suey. For vegetarians, the set meal for
two is extremely substantial and includes delicious bean
curd and cauliflower dishes, and crispy noodle nests
filled with stir-fried vegetables. Prices are low (between
£10 and £15 for three courses).

Park Inn

1-2 Park Place, Ladywell, Dover (01304 203300).
Food served 11am-10pm Mon-Sat; noon-10pm Sun.
Cards AmEx, Debit, MC, V.

Sister to the more remote **Crown Inn** at Finglesham
(01304 612555) – with its oak beams, sixteenth-century
restaurant, real ale and outdoor children's play area –
the Park offers the same excellent food and variety of
beers in a Victorian drawing-room setting. As it's located in the centre of Dover, there is no garden and clientele are more of a mixed bag, but children are very

welcome and the interior is spacious and quieter than most. Starters (from £2.85) include prawns in sherry and cream sauce, deep-fried cheeses and New Zealand green-lip mussels. Among the main courses are baked local crab, mushroom and cranberry Wellington in puff pasty with Stilton and port sauce, and citrus halibut steak with orange and dill sauce (£5.95-£7.65). Finish off, if you dare, with hot black cherries in cherry brandy with ice-cream (£3.25).

La Terrasse

The Esplanade, Sandgate (01303 220444).
Food served 12.15-1.30pm, 7.15-9.30pm, Tue-Sat; 12.15-1.30pm Sun. **Set meals** *lunch & dinner* £20.50 Tue-Fri lunch, £29.50 Fri dinner-Sun lunch.
Cards AmEx, DC, Debit, MC, V.

Rather affected and overpriced, perhaps, but if you want all the pomp and circumstance of a French auberge where dinner is a leisurely affair, then this is the place to come. Hors d'oeuvres are served in the lounge with drinks, and the starter and main course are punctuated by a light salad to freshen the palate; freshly baked bread rolls circulate with regularity. Portions are generally diminutive but exquisite with a predominance of fish – salmon, crab, scallops and local lobster, plus delicacies such as duck foie gras, Romney Marsh lamb, and baby eels with crushed garlic potatoes. Vegetarians and children will have a hard time of it here. Starters are from around £12, mains £16-£22, desserts £7.50.

Wallett's Court

Westcliffe, St Margaret's at Cliffe (01304 852424).
Food served noon-2pm Mon-Fri, Sun; 7-8.30pm daily. **Cards** AmEx, DC, Debit, MC, V.

Unique, largely French-biased cuisine with a Jacobean influence that fits harmoniously with the house (*see* *p24*). Meals are finely presented but not lacking in substance. Enjoy local monkfish, breast of duck, or hunks of sizzling steak accompanied with crisp, fresh farm-grown vegetables. The champagne dessert is a must – a champagne torte served in champagne sauce with a glass of champagne to wash it all down. The dining hall looks out on to the garden where classical statues peer out at you between the fronds of exotic plants. Stay for breakfast to enjoy fresh bacon and sausages from Barret's the Butchers in St Margaret's and eggs from the family farm in Coldred. The owners of Wallett's Court are related to the family who ran the hugely successful Coldred Court Farm and who now do a superior taxi service in white Mercedes cars, and are happy to give a bit of a guided tour to visitors at reasonable rates. (Call Merc'ury Cars on 01304 852884/0410 591217 for details).

What to see & do

Tourist information centres

Town Hall, High Street, **Deal**, CT14 6BB (01304 369576).
Open *June-Aug* 9am-2pm; *Sept-May* 9am-5pm Mon-Fri.

Townwall Street, **Dover**, CT16 1JR (01304 205108/www.doveruk.com).
Open *July-Aug* 8am-7.30pm, *Sept-June* 9am-6pm, daily.

Harbour Street, **Folkestone**, CT20 1QN (01303 258594/www.shepway.gov.uk).
Open *Easter-June* 9am-5.30pm daily; *Jul-Aug* 9am-7pm daily; *Oct-Easter* 9am-1pm, 2-5.30pm, Mon-Sat; 10am-1pm, 2-4pm, Sun.

Guildhall, **Sandwich**, CT13 9AH (01304 613565).
Open *Apr-Sept* 9am-4pm daily.

That Cinque-ing feeling

As the stretch of the English coast closest to mainland Europe, this part of Kent has long been key for the country's trade with and defence from the rest of the Continent. Before Henry VIII's founding of the Royal Navy, the monarchy had to rely on the individual ports to furnish ships and men for the nation's defence, in return for which they were granted a range of privileges. The initial five ('cinq' in French, although pronounced, in a proudly philistinic English way, 'sink'), **Hastings**, **New Romney**, **Hythe**, **Sandwich** and **Dover**, were probably first associated during the reign of Edward the Confessor (1042-66) but were later joined by more than 30 other Kent and Sussex towns (most not on the coast).

The ports were first granted liberties by charter in 1278 and reached their peak of privilege and influence during the thirteenth and fourteenth centuries. Thereafter, they lost their monopoly and gradually declined; some, such as Rye and Sandwich, had the indignity of suffering such severe silting that they are no longer even on the coast. Most of their privileges were officially abolished in 1855; only Dover remains a significant port. Yet their memory lives on in one of the Queen Mother's honorary titles – Lord Warden of the Cinque Ports – which conjures up the lovely image of the ever-vigilant Queen Mum crouching behind the battlements at Walmer Castle, scouring the oceans with her binoculars for signs of the approach of the dastardly Frenchies.

Bike hire

Deal Prams & Cycles 30 Mill Hill (01304 380680).
One mile from the rail station.

Caesar's Camp & the Warren

These marvellous chalk downs at Folkestone were once accessible from the town on foot by passing through the golf course on to fields grazed by sheep. Now, access is via a major road, which passes straight through the hillside, somewhat lessening the ambience of Caesar's Camp and Sugarloaf Hill. Nevertheless, the rocky, craggy wilds of the Warren are still great for walking, affording spectacular views of France on a clear day and access to lesser-known beaches. *See picture p24.*

Deal Castle

Victoria Road, Deal (01304 372762).
Open *Apr-Oct* 10am-6pm daily; *Nov-Mar* 10am-4pm Wed-Sun. **Admission** (EH) £3; £1.50 5s-16s; £2.30 OAPs, students.

Built by Henry VIII in the shape of a Tudor rose, the castle is a warren of dank, spooky corridors that seem to go on for miles. In the centre is a fine display of the castle's history and that of the other coastal fortifications. *See picture p21.*

Deal Maritime Museum

St George's Road, Deal (01304 372679).
Open *Easter-Sept* 2-5pm daily.
Admission £1.50; 50p 5s-15s; £1 OAPs, students.

The main gallery depicts the life and times of local sailors on this famously treacherous stretch of coast where the Goodwin sands have claimed many a vessel. There are also displays on aspects of local history, including Deal's military importance and naval yard.

Dover Castle

Dover (01304 211067/www.english_heritage.org.uk).
Open 10am-6pm daily. **Admission** (EH) £6.90; £3.50 5s-15s; £5.20 OAPs, students; £17.30 family.

Dover Castle offers great value for money. The grounds house the miraculously preserved Roman lighthouse, while in the castle itself there's a new exhibition looking at the preparations made here for the reception of Henry VIII in March 1539; run your fingers over fine furnishings and hear the royal servants at work. Prices include a guided tour of the secret wartime tunnels (the highlight for many people), and admission to the keep and its environs. Great for kids.

East Kent Railway

Station Road, Sheperdswell, nr Dover (01304 832042).
Open phone for details. **Tickets** £4; £2 3s-14s; £3.50 OAPs.

Enjoy a four-mile round trip on this former colliery railway. Each ticket buys the passenger two rides. Themed events run throughout the year.

Macfarlanes Butterfly & Garden Centre

A260 Swingfield, nr Folkestone (01303 844244).
Open *Apr-Sept* 10am-5pm daily. **Admission** £2; £1.25 3s-16s; £1.50 OAPs, students; £5.50 family.

Extensive garden centre with tropical greenhouses and many varieties of free-flying butterflies.

Richborough Roman Fort

Richborough Road, Sandwich (01304 612013).
Open *Apr-Oct* 10am-6pm daily; *Nov, Mar* 10am-4pm Wed-Sun; *Dec-Feb* 10am-4pm Sat, Sun. **Admission** (EH) £2.50; £1.30 5s-15s; £1.90 OAPs, students.

Site of Britain's first Roman fortress, which marks the likely spot of the AD 43 landing. The invasion of Britain was orchestrated from here. Not much remains now but the ruins of the massive triumphal arch built to signal the might of the Roman forces are still visible.

St Margaret's Museum & Pines Garden

Beach Road, St Margaret's Bay, Dover (01304 852764).
Open *pines garden* 10am-5pm daily; *museum May-Sept* 2-5pm Wed-Sun. **Admission** £1.50; 35p 5s-16s; free under-16s.

Just past the sleepy village of St Margaret's, on the road down to the bay, this somewhat bizarre yet imaginative six-acre garden was created in 1970, and includes a lake with waterfall, Romany caravan, wishing well and Oscar Nemon's statue of Churchill. The museum opposite is equally eclectic, with a large collection of maritime objects and local curios.

South Foreland Lighthouse

Beach Road, St Margaret's Bay, Dover (01304 852463).
Open 12.30-5pm Sat, Sun, bank hols.
Admission (NT) £1.50; 75p 5s-12s.

Right up on the cliff, the South Foreland Lighthouse gives an illuminating account of the history of lighthouses and apparently will be the first place in Britain to see in the new millennium.

Walmer Castle & Gardens

Kingsdown Road, Walmer, Deal (01304 364288).
Open *Apr-Oct* 10am-6pm daily; *Nov-Mar* 10am-4pm Wed-Sun. **Admission** £4.50; £2.30 5s-16s; £3.40 OAPs, students.

The most attractive and well preserved of the Cinque Ports fortifications, Walmer is still official home to the Lord Warden (*see p25* **That Cinque-ing feeling**); past encumbents include William Pitt the Younger and the Duke of Wellington (whose life is celebrated inside) and now looks more stately home than castle. It apparently provided the inspiration for Evelyn Waugh's *Brideshead Revisited*, and the gardens were redeveloped a few years ago to create a Queen Mother's Garden in celebration of the current Lord Warden's 95th birthday.

White Cliffs Experience

Market Square, Dover (01304 214566).
Open *Apr-Mar* 10am-5pm, *Nov-Mar* 10am-3pm, daily. **Admission** £5.75; £3.95 4s-14s; £4.60 OAPs, students; £17.95 family.

Easily the most exciting attraction in Dover if you're visiting with kids, it covers aspects of the town's history from the Roman invasion, the maritime heyday and war years, all brought to life with projection displays and hands-on exhibits, including a full-scale reconstruction of a street during World War II complete with bombed-out houses and air raid shelter. The animatronic puppet show is a must for younger viewers, while seasonal food and drink tastings and events should keep the older members of the household happy.

North Kent Downs

Ramble or ride your way through some of Kent's finest countryside.

To look at a road map of north Kent and see how the M2 and M20 motorways slash through the county to the ferry terminals of Dover and Folkestone, you'd think there'd be little left of the surrounding countryside to savour. Yet, surprisingly, once off the tarmacked track, a cyclist or walker can be so swallowed up by the chalky escarpments of the North Downs that the swish of fast-moving traffic feels a million miles away.

The major roads are testament to the fact that this area has been a main thoroughfare since Neolithic times: tracks along the Downs enabled walking travellers to stick to higher, drier ground on their journeys between the important centres of Stonehenge and Dover. Some of this route was dubbed the 'Pilgrim's Way' in the Victorian era, and this name has stuck for the section of path from Winchester to Canterbury. It's associated with the journey taken by the fictional pilgrims of Chaucer's *Canterbury Tales* between the two cathedral cities; the notion is encouraged by the numerous inns in the vicinity that have adopted the names of the pilgrims' tales as their own. Walkers are well-catered for, with bridleways and footpaths clearly signposted.

Beyond the temptation of local food and beer at a country pub after the physical and soul-soothing satisfaction of walking the Downs, there is little in this area of Kent to draw you indoors. Two historic highlights are just outside the county seat of Maidstone, at the foot of the North Downs: the fairytale **Leeds Castle** is one of Kent's main tourist attractions and, two miles further west, is the lesser-known **Stoneacre**, a delightful yeoman's house buried in the heart of orchard country.

By train from London

Trains to **Maidstone East** leave **Victoria** every half an hour (journey time approx **1hr**). Trains to **Ashford** leave **Victoria** hourly and pass through **Lenham** and **Charing** (journey time to Ashford **1hr 25mins**). Trains to **Faversham** leave from **Victoria** every 25 mins and pass thorough **Chatham** and **Sittingbourne** (journey time to Faversham is between **1hr** and **1hr 30mins**).

Village people

The area may not be bursting with major visitor draws, but what it does have is plenty of lovely villages. Handily, the majority of the most appealing are stretched along an axis that follows the North Downs Way (and, to the south, the M20) between Maidstone and Ashford; a country tour, taking in a handful of them, is as enjoyable a way as any to pass a leisurely day.

Despite the heavy traffic traversing it, the centre of **Lenham** (nine miles south-east of Maidstone) has retained its village character. On its large, pretty square is the Dog and Bear Hotel (01622 858219), built in 1602 as a coaching inn, which once boasted stables for 'six pairs'. Queen Anne stayed at the hotel in 1704, a visit commemorated by the royal coat of arms above the main entrance.

A few miles further south-east is **Charing**, not so much a village as an attractive tiny town with a twisting high street lined with mellow walls and roofs. An archbishop's palace was built here in 1333, the last in a chain that started at Otford, and the final resting place for travellers en route to Canterbury. The ivy-covered ruins of this palace can still be seen by the parish church of SS Peter and Paul. The barn to the east of these ruins was built in the fourteenth century as the archbishops' great hall. Henry VIII stayed overnight here on his way to the famous meeting with the French king Francis I at the Field of the Cloth of Gold near Guisnes in 1520. The block upon which St John the Baptist's head fell is said to have been kept in the church – a present from Richard the Lionheart that was later removed during the Dissolution of the monasteries.

Another mile or so south-east is **Westwell**, nestling beneath the Downs in the middle of luscious, pastoral countryside. Although not far from the M20, it feels well off the beaten track and from higher on the Downs is hidden from view by its towering horse chestnut trees. The one place for refreshment is the 250-year-old Wheel Inn (01233 712430), which has three cosy rooms and a huge beer garden.

About the same distance south-east again, you can walk to **Eastwell** and **Boughton Lees**. En route is the bomb-damaged, fifteenth-century church of St Mary's, which remains sacred ground despite being in ruins. The churchyard contains a number of impressive tombs, including that of Richard II's bastard son, who fled to Kent after his father's death at the Battle of Bosworth.

Two miles to the east of here is **Wye**, probably best known nowadays for its agricultural college, affiliated with the University of London. A college was founded here in 1428 by Archbishop John Kempe as a seminary college for priests, but was surrendered to the Crown during the Dissolution. On the hillside to the north of the town is a white chalk crown, carved into the hillside for the coronation of Edward VII in 1902 by students of Wye College. Wye is a charming village, though not essentially Kentish: it has a remarkably Georgian look, with many of its seventeenth-century houses unusually uniform and small in scale, radiating out from the thirteenth-century church. At the bottom end of Bridge Street is the Tickled Trout (01233 812227), an attractive riverside pub, perfect for al fresco imbibing.

As proud possessor of what could well be the prettiest village square in Kent, **Chilham** (eight miles north-east of Ashford) is probably one of the most visited villages in the entire country. A number of narrow lanes lead up to the square, framed with time-warp half-timbered Tudor houses.

Where to stay

Barnfield

Charing, nr Ashford, TN27 0BN (tel/fax 01233 712421). **Rates** (B&B) single £23-£28; double £42-£46; triple £56. **Rooms** 2 single; 2 double; 1 triple.

Almost halfway between Charing and Egerton is this fifteenth-century house in 30 acres of sheep-farming land, where Martin and Phillada Pym manage a cosy home from home. The property has been in the Pym family for over 60 years. There are five bedrooms, each with its own washbasin and facilities for making hot drinks, but guests share a small bathroom. There are no-smoking rooms and children of all ages are welcome. Guests can also use the tennis court and the comfortable, book-lined lounge.
Leave A20 at Charing roundabout; exit to Lenham; first left down Hook Lane; 2.5 miles on left.

Chilston Park `Offer`

Sandway, Lenham, ME17 2BE
(01622 859803/fax 01622 858588).
Rates (B&B) double £125-£180; four-poster £180-£195; suite £195-£250. **Rooms** (all en suite) 37 double; 12 four-poster; 4 suites. **Cards** AmEx, DC, Debit, MC, V.

Chilston Park prides itself on being something out of the ordinary. As soon as you arrive, you get the feeling that you're walking into some period stage set: liveried staff, elaborate décor and, if you arrive after dark, candlelight. All the accommodation is within the Grade I-listed thirteenth-century mansion, set in acres of exquisite parkland, overlooking a lake. The house was restored by Martin Miller (author of the antiques guides). The hotel

*Chilling in **Chilham**, the perfect way to pass a lazy summer's day.*

Medway awayday

OK, so you're not *that* likely to want to spend a weekend in *La Kent profonde* and then trek north to the frankly rather grim Medway towns (Rochester, Chatham, Gillingham) for the afternoon. But lovers of Dickens and matters nautical will find rich pickings in this otherwise rather down-at-heel conurbation.

Charles Dickens Centre

Eastgate House, High Street, Rochester (01634 844176).
Open 10am-5.30pm daily. Last entry 4.45pm. **Admission** £3.50; £2.50 5s-15s, OAPs, students; £9.50 family.

Dickens spent his youth in Rochester and, although he was not overly impressed with the place, it appeared in a number of his works (unflatteringly disguised as 'Mudfog' and 'Dullborough'); his last, unfinished novel, *The Mystery of Edwin Drood*, was set here. This entertaining centre elaborates on Boz's local connections.

Fort Amherst

Dock Road, Chatham (01634 847747).
Open *Mar-Oct* 10.30am-5pm, *Nov-Feb* 10.30am-4pm, daily. Last tour 90mins before closing.
Admission £4; £2 4s-16s, OAPs, students; £10 family.

Built to defend Chatham dockyard in the mid-eighteenth century and extended during the Napoleonic Wars, Fort Amherst contains batteries, barracks, tunnels and even, surprisingly, nature trails. Phone for details of the occasional military re-enactments. Visitors can wander round at their own pace or take a guided tour.

Gad's Hill Place

Gravesend Road, Higham, nr Rochester (01474 822366).
Open *Easter-Oct* 2-5pm 1st Sun in month, bank hol Sun. Last entry 4pm. **Admission** £2.50; £1.50 6s-14s.

Charles Dickens lived at this house from 1857 until his death in 1870 and it has been evocatively preserved as he left it.

Rochester Castle

The Keep, Rochester (01634 402276).
Open *Apr-Sept* 10am-6pm, *Oct-Mar* 10am-4pm, daily. Last entry 30mins before closing.
Admission (EH) £3.50; £2.50 5s-15s, OAPs; £9.50 family.

Rochester's massive keep (*see picture*) commands a wide bend on the River Medway and overlooks the town's small but beautiful cathedral. Built in the late eleventh century by the architect of the Tower of London, this is one of the finest Norman castles in England. Its early history was particularly lively, including occupation by Wat Tyler and his ragged-trousered forces in the Peasants' Revolt of 1381. Rochester's Guildhall Museum on the High Street (01634 848717) makes the most of the town's history.

World Naval Base

The Historic Dockyard, Chatham (01634 823800).
Open *Apr-Oct* 10am-5pm daily; *Feb, Mar, Nov* 10am-4pm Wed, Sat, Sun. Last entry 1hr before closing. **Admission** £8.50; £5.50 5s-15s; £6.30 OAPs; £22.50 family.

Founded by Henry VIII, Chatham had become England's biggest naval base within 100 years. Not surprisingly, the town's major attraction is the restored Georgian river dockyard. Vessels to explore include restored sloops, gunships and paddle steamers.

---

is also blessed with an award-winning restaurant (*see p30*). Children and small dogs are welcome.
A20 S from J8 off M20 towards Ashford; right into Lenham; right; pass Lenham station; left into Boughton Road; over crossroads and M20; Chilston Park is on left.

Eastwell Manor

Eastwell Park, Boughton Lees, TN25 4HR (01233 219955/reservations 0500 526735/ fax 01233 635530/eastwell@btinternet.com/ www.prideofbritainhotels.com).
Rates (B&B) *double* £180-£230; *suite* £250-£340. *Cottages* (self-catering) £500-£900 per week.
Rooms (all en suite) 18 double; 5 suites. *Cottages* 4 one-bed; 10 two-bed; 5 three-bed.
Cards AmEx, DC, Debit, MC, V.

Entering the grand gateway in what must be one of the longest stretches of wall in England, and driving up the gravel drive to the ivy-clad Jacobean-style buildings of Eastwell Manor, you could easily be in a historical time warp. Looks are deceptive: while a house on this site was mentioned in the Domesday Book, most of what you see is less than 100 years old. Inside, the illusion is further compounded, with lashings of antique furnishings, chandeliers, red leather Chesterfields, massive stone fireplaces and wood panelling. Owned by the Parrett family, the four-star hotel has 23 luxurious, individually decorated bedrooms, and 19 one- to six-person self-catering cottages have recently been built on Eastwell's 62 acres. There's a billiards room, croquet lawn, an outdoor heated pool and tennis courts as well as a restaurant (*see p31*). The epitome of luxury. Children and dogs welcome. Non-smoking rooms available.

J9 off M20; take A28 towards Canterbury, then A251 towards Faversham.

Harrow Hill Hotel

Warren Street, nr Lenham, ME17 2ED
(01622 858727/fax 01622 850026).
Rates (B&B) *single* £39.50; *double/twin* £49.50;
under-14s sharing with parents £5. **Rooms** 6 double
(5 en suite); 3 twin (all en suite); 5 family rooms
(all en suite). **Cards** Debit, MC, V.

The hamlet of Warren Street couldn't be more different from its olde worlde namesake. Formerly a forge, the Harrow Hill has been converted into a labyrinthine hotel with a long bar lounge and restaurant on the ground floor. What it lacks in country charm (the pub is very 'olde worlde', but elsewhere the décor is straightforward, with all mod cons) it makes up for in convenience: having the bar and restaurant under the same roof as your bedroom is kind to reluctant drivers and late arrivals. Children welcome. Non-smoking rooms available.

J8 off M20; A20 for 6 miles turn left into Warren Street; first house on right.

Leaveland Court

Leaveland, Faversham, ME13 0NP
(01233 740596/fax 01233 740015).
Rates (B&B) *single occupancy* £30; *double/twin* £40-
£50. Closed Dec, Jan. **Rooms** (all en suite) 2 double;
1 twin. **Cards** Debit, MC, V.

This enchanting family home is not the easiest place to find, hidden away from view of the road, amid woodland behind Leaveland's thirteenth-century church. Once there, you'll be welcomed by Corrine Scutt, who owns and runs the accommodation side of things on this working farm. Her timbered house has a sedate, genteel air about it, with private gardens, complete with a small heated swimming pool. For once, no one has gone overboard with floral prints in the clean, fresh bedrooms, which all have TV and tea- and coffee-making facilities. Children welcome. All rooms non-smoking.

J6 off M2; A251 towards Ashford; first right after turning for Belmont House; next to church on right.

Stowting Hill House

Stowting, nr Ashford, TN25 6BE
(01303 862881/fax 01303 863433).
Rates (B&B) *single occupancy* £30; *twin* £50.
Rooms 3 twin (2 en suite).

You become part of the family when you stay at Stowting Hill House. Guest rooms may have been vacated by the Latham children, but their photos and books still adorn the walls and shelves. Unfortunately, the Lathams have not replaced any of the single beds with doubles, so this isn't the place to come for a romantic weekend. Breakfast is served at a dark wood dining table in a room lined with blue floral-print fabric, lending it a soft, refined, yet informal feel. In addition to the huge shared lounge, there's a lovely airy conservatory to the rear, where new arrivals take tea or coffee, looking out over thoroughly groomed gardens. Children welcome. All bedrooms non-smoking.

J11 off M20; take B2068 N towards Canterbury; after 4.5 miles take left turn opposite BP garage; house is 1.7 miles further on left.

Wife of Bath

4 Upper Bridge Street, Wye, TN25 5AW
(01233 812232/812540/fax 01233 813630/
john@w-o-b.demon.co.uk/www.w-o-b.demon.co.uk).
Rates (B&CB) *single* £40; *double* £50-£80;
family room £55. Breakfast £5 (Eng).
Closed 2 weeks after Christmas.
Rooms (all en suite) 3 double; 2 twin; 1 family room.
Cards AmEx, DC, Debit, MC, V.

A few minutes' walk from Wye train station, this pretty village house is ideal if you plan to explore the Kent countryside on foot or by bike. Each bedroom is different and named after a different character in Chaucer's *Canterbury Tales*. The Knight's and the Miller's rooms are in converted stables and share a small kitchen. The Yeoman's room, painted in dark pink, boasts a splendid four-poster bed; all six rooms have their own bathroom, although one of them (the Franklin's) is across the corridor from the room. As well as the accommodation, John Morgan also manages a restaurant under the same name (*see p32*). Non-smoking bedrooms available.

J9 off M20; take A28 towards Canterbury; 4 miles after Ashford follow signs to Wye on right.

Worten House

Great Chart, nr Ashford, TN23 3BU
(01233 622944/fax 01233 662249).
Rates (B&B) *single occupancy* £30; *twin* £45-£50.
Rooms 2 twin.

There has been a house on this site since the time of the Domesday Book, but most of the red-brick and stone farmhouse that stands here today dates back only as far as the eighteenth century. The two large twin-bedded rooms are trimmed out in white broderie anglaise and have washbasins and facilities to make hot drinks, but they share a bathroom. The family pets – two cats and a puppy – are never allowed upstairs, and their presence means that, while visitors and children are made to feel more than welcome, guests' pets are not invited in. The Wilkinsons serve breakfast in a large elegant room looking on to the secluded garden at the back of the house; evening meals can be provided if requested in advance. Children welcome. Both bedrooms non-smoking.

J9 off M20; then A20 towards Charing; after 1 mile take left into Goddinton Lane; after 2 miles past cottages on left, Worten House is second turning on right.

Where to eat & drink

Chilston Park

Sandway, nr Lenham (01622 859803).
Food served noon-2.30pm, 7-9.30pm, daily.
Set meals *lunch* £17.50 (3 courses); *dinner* £29.95
(3 courses). **Cards** AmEx, DC, Debit, MC, V.

An evening meal at Chilston Park is quite an experience and you should dress smartly if you want to make the most of it. The 40-seat restaurant is lit with hundreds of candles and you are waited upon by staff wearing period costume. Chef Simon Hagen prepares an innovative range of dishes, such as, rack of lamb with pan-fried polenta, scented with garlic rosemary, with vegetable barrel and tomato coulis, from the set menu, and there's a pleasantly surprising choice of vegetarian meals. The fact that the menu changes with the seasons reflects Hagen's insistence on the finest quality ingredients from local sources wherever possible. Three courses à la carte without drinks comes to around £35 per person. If you really want to push the boat out, book a room for the night as well (*see p28*).

Eastwell Manor

Eastwell Park, Boughton Lees (01233 219955). **Food served** noon-2.30pm, 7-9.30pm, Mon-Thur; noon-2.30pm, 7-10pm, Fri, Sat; noon-3.30pm, 7-9.30pm, Sun. **Cards** AmEx, DC, Debit, MC, V.

If your budget doesn't stretch to the extravagance of a night here (*see p29*), take heart in the fact that the hotel restaurant is open to non-residents and that its combined menu of English and French cuisine is quite amenable (though the wine list doesn't exactly cater to those on a budget). Ingredients are top-quality: game comes from the Eastwell estate and organic pork from a local producer. Some of the desserts exploit another local product: the Cox's apple soup and cider sorbet are both scrumptious options. A three-course meal without drinks will set you back about £45 per person.

Flying Horse

Boughton Lees (01233 620914). **Food served** noon-2.15pm, 7-9.15pm, daily. **Cards** Debit, MC, V.

Since it's right on the Pilgrim's Way, it's not surprising that this lovely old pub and restaurant is popular with walkers. On a fine day, ramblers take a pew outside, either at the front, looking over the village green or in the beer garden at the back, and wash down sandwiches (the landlord seems to turn a blind eye to the fact that these have been drawn out of their rucksacks) with a cracking pint of Old Speckled Hen. Pub lunches, both contemporary (baked avocado with prawns and spinach, £7.75) and of a more traditional bent (sausage and mash, £6.50), are served. There's a no-smoking room at the back of the pub, where you can peer down through reinforced glass into two ancient spring water wells. The pub is on the cricket green in Boughton Lees.

Lime Tree

8-10 The Limes, The Square, Lenham (01622 859509). **Food served** 7-10pm Mon, Sat; noon-2pm, 7-10pm, Tue-Fri; noon-2pm Sun. **Cards** AmEx, Debit, MC, V.

On the side of Lenham's lovely main square is this hotel (doubles from £65) and restaurant, owned and managed by husband and wife team Musa and Anita Kivrak. It's smart in the extreme, so it's advisable to dress for the occasion of an evening meal here. The menu is mainly French in flavour, and pricey with it (seabass with chorizo oil, aubergine caviar, basil and fennel, £17.50, is one example) and, while the chef must be complimented on his cooking skills and choice of ingredients, the portions tend to err on the small size and the service is not always all it could be.

George Inn

Newnham (01795 890237). **Food served** noon-2pm, 7-9.30pm, Mon-Thur; noon-2pm, 7-10pm, Fri, Sat; noon-2pm, 7-9pm, Sun. **Cards** Debit, MC, V.

Just down the road from Doddington Place Gardens (*see p32*) is this wonderful country pub with a large beer garden set back from the road. It has served as the village brewhouse since the sixteenth century and formally became an inn in 1781, before Shepherd Neame got its hands on it in 1841. These days its extensive range of home-cooked food and cheery atmosphere still draw people from miles around. It can get extremely busy on Sunday lunchtimes (an early arrival is recommended). Book in advance for evening meals (a three-course dinner without drinks is around £22): food is along the lines of honey roast half shoulder of lamb with port and thyme gravy, £11.95. Across the road is the charming Periwinkle Press picture framers and tiny bookshop, which operates as the local newsagent/ sweetshop, and has a good selection of local maps and guidebooks.

The Pepperbox

Fairbourne Heath, nr Ulcombe (01622 842558). **Food served** noon-1.45pm Mon; noon-1.45pm, 7-9.45pm, Tue-Sat. **Cards** Debit, MC, V.

A few miles south of Leeds Castle, the Pepperbox is virtually the only place to mark Fairbourne Heath on the map. High up on Windmill Hill, it commands wonderful views across the Downs and the Weald. Work up an appetite for a slap-up pub lunch here with a walk or cycle up from Headcorn. The food and the beer are worth the effort, as local Morris dancers can confirm: they stop here for sustenance (or Dutch courage) before heading off to Leeds Castle to perform. There's a choice of different fresh breads with sandwich, soup and salad orders, or you could opt for one of the specials: beef and ale pudding (£6.95) or chicken with char-grilled pepper and tomato sauce (£8.50), for example. On fine days you

*Hit the bottle at the **Wife of Bath**.*

can absorb the views from the outdoor tables beneath the pergola; on not-so-fine days, it's lovely and cosy indoors by the fireplace.

Wife of Bath

4 Upper Bridge Street, Wye (01233 812232/812540). **Food served** noon-2.30pm, 7-10.30pm, Tue-Sat. **Set meals** lunch £10 (2 courses); dinner £23.75 (3 courses). **Cards** AmEx, DC, Debit, MC, V.

The pre-dinner drinks bar may be a little pokey and its stone floor and bench seats are not especially welcoming, but chef Robert Hymers's regularly changing menu makes up for this, drawing on a wide variety of sources for inspiration. Tempting dishes include Japanese-flavoured starters of crab spring rolls served with wasabi mayonnaise (£4.25) and smoked fish terrine with chervil mayonnaise (£5), and, as a main course, lamb cutlets with chestnut and aubergine (£13.95). The restaurant itself is housed further back, over two interconnecting low-ceilinged rooms. Service strikes the right balance between informal and efficient.

What to see & do

Kent County Council produces a catalogue containing over 100 routes to explore the county. For a free copy phone 01622 696730.

Tourist information centres

18 The Church Yard, **Ashford**, TN23 1QG (01233 629165/fax 01233 639166/ abc.media@easynet.gov.uk). **Open** Easter-Oct 9.30am-5.30pm Mon-Sat; Nov-Easter 9.30am-5pm Mon-Sat.

The Gatehouse, Palace Gardens, Mill Street, **Maidstone**, ME15 6YE (01622 602169/ fax 01622 673581). **Open** Easter-Oct 9.30am-5pm Mon-Sat; 10am-4pm Sun; Nov-Easter 9.30am-5pm Mon-Fri; 9.30-2pm Sat.

The Fleur de Lis, Preston Street, **Faversham**, ME13 8NS (01795 534542). **Open** Easter-Oct 10am-4pm Mon-Sat; 10am-1pm Sun; Nov-Easter 10am-4pm Mon-Sat.

Bike hire

Ken James Ltd 22A Beaver Road, **Ashford** (01233 634334). Close to the rail station.

Belmont

Belmont Park, Throwley, nr Faversham (01795 890202). **Open** Easter Sun-Sept tours 2-5pm Sat, Sun, bank hols. Last entry 4.30pm. **Admission** house & gardens £5; £2.75 5s-16s; £4.50 OAPs, students; gardens only £2.75; £1 5s-16s.

This beautiful Georgian mansion, the work of Samuel Wyatt, commands stunning views of Kent. It was bought by General George Harris in 1801 with the proceeds from his successful military career in India. In 1815 he was made Lord Harris for his victory over Tipoo Sultan at the Battle of Seringapatam, and inside are mementoes from the family's history and travels, including paintings of the West Indies by Michel Jean Cazabon, Indian silverware and the finest and most extensive private collection of clocks in the country.

Doddington Place Gardens

Doddington, nr Sittingbourne (01795 886101). **Open** May-Sept 11am-6pm Wed, bank hols; 2-6pm Sun. **Admission** £2.50; 25p children.

There were Roman settlements in the area around Doddington (four miles south-east of Sittingbourne). Today, during the summer, this private Victorian mansion throws open to the public its landscaped gardens and ten acres of grounds surrounded by gently rolling wooded countryside, including a woodland garden; a large Edwardian sunken rock garden with pools; a formal sunken garden (best in late summer); and a flint and brick folly. Kids love to walk inside the impressive clipped yew hedges that line the extensive lawns. There's also a café here.

Adjacent to Doddington Place is an enchanting and well-maintained church, one of two in England dedicated to the Beheading of St John the Baptist. A reference is made to a church on this site in the 1086 Domesday Book, though it's likely there has been one here since Saxon times. Inside, notice the double squint, which allows views from the lectern into both the chancel and the south chapel. On the left, towards the front of the church, is an unusually low window, thought to have been used for administering Holy Communion to plague- or leprosy-sufferers standing outside.

Leeds Castle

Broomfield, nr Maidstone (01622 765400/ www.leeds-castle.co.uk). **Open** Mar-Oct 10am-6pm daily; Nov-Feb 10am-4pm daily. Last entry 1hr before closing. **Admission** castle & park £9.30; £6 under-15s; £7.30 OAPs; £25 family; park only £7.30; £4.50 under-15s; £5.80 OAPs; £20 family.

Stunningly sited on two small islands in the middle of a lake, Leeds was built by the Normans nearly 900 years ago (on the site of a Saxon manor house), converted into a royal place by Henry VIII and now contains a mishmash of medieval furnishings, paintings, tapestries and, bizarrely, the world's finest collection of antique dog collars. The castle's greatest attractions, however, are external. Apart from the flower-filled gardens, there's the Culpeper Garden (an outsize cottage garden), a duckery and an aviary containing over 100 rare bird species and, best of the lot, the maze, which centres on a spectacular underground grotto adorned with stone mythical beasts and shell mosaics. Facilities for disabled visitors are good (a leaflet is available in advance). Special events are held throughout the year (phone for details).

Stoneacre

Otham, nr Maidstone (01622 862871). **Open** Apr-Oct 2-6pm Wed, Sat. Last entry 5pm. **Admission** (NT) £2.50; £1.25 5s-16s.

At the north end of Otham village, three miles south-east of Maidstone, is this National Trust property – a half-timbered yeoman's house. It is tucked away down a narrow winding road, so if you're coming by car, you're advised to use the village car park and walk the 100m down to the house. Stoneacre's attractions include a great hall and crownpost, dating from the late fifteenth century, and the delightful, recently restored cottage garden surrounding the house. There's also a children's trail in conjunction with Kent Gardens Trust.

Rye, Dungeness & Romney Marsh

Tweeside town, bleak coast and smugglers' marshland.

Rye is a tourist honeypot and a perennially popular weekend destination for break-seekers. The appeal of the town is chiefly the diversity and state of preservation of its architecture, from Norman to Tudor to Georgian; it's a tremendously pretty place, now liberally scattered with tearooms and antique shops. Hilly, cobbled Mermaid Street is perhaps Rye's most photographed spot, and it's here that you will find Lamb House, where novelist Henry James passed his last years. Other notable literary past residents include EF Benson and Captain Pugwash. Apart from simply wandering the streets, ancient St Mary's Church (dating originally from 1150), Rye Art Gallery, the medieval Landgate gateway (built 1329) and the sturdy thirteenth-century Ypres Tower are worth a peek. Thursday is market day.

Much of Rye's past prosperity stems from its former status as one of the **Cinque Ports** (*see page 25* **That Cinque-ing feeling**). Over the centuries the sea receded and the River Rother silted up, and the town is now marooned two miles inland.

Winchelsea, a couple of miles south-west of Rye, was another of the (late-joining) Cinque Ports. Built on a never-completed medieval grid pattern, it is an appealing retirement village today, and so quiet that it seems like a ghost town in comparison to its neighbour. The evocatively ruined church of St Thomas à Becket (looted and destroyed several times by the French during the thirteenth and fourteenth centuries) adds to the impression. A further mile or so south-east of here is pebbly Winchelsea beach, which is pleasantly sandy at low tide.

More popular for seaside frolicking is the extensive stretch of (often rather windswept) **Camber Sands** stretching east from Rye towards Dungeness Point. The sand's lovely, but be warned that in fine weather it's overrun by the families who stay at the many caravan parks and holiday lets that litter this stretch of the coast.

And now for something completely different...

It's hard to imagine a greater contrast to the people-packed cutesy-ness of Rye than desolate **Dungeness**, only a few miles to the east. A thousand years ago Dungeness Point didn't even exist. Longshore drift has built up huge banks of flint shingle, some of them 17 metres

Dungeness: *shingle, shingle everywhere.*

By train from London

Trains leave for **Rye** from **Charing Cross** hourly. They also pass through **Waterloo East** and **London Bridge**, and passengers have to change at **Ashford** (journey time **1hr 40mins**).

deep, which stretch miles out into the sea in a unique promontory. There are currently over 40 square miles of this undulating giant's sandpit, making it the largest accumulation of shingle in the world, with only one-third of it covered in vegetation; the rest is either bare or in the early stages of ecological succession. The light on this remote, gloriously bleak promontory is odd, reflected from the sea on both sides. The surreal quality of the landscape is enhanced by the presence of a massive nuclear power station with a hum that's audible for miles around. Until recently few visitors came here, but the publication of Derek Jarman's book *The Garden* put Dungeness Point on the (specialist) tourist trail (*see page 37* **Derek Jarman's garden**).

The power station is linked to the seaside developments straggling away to the north towards Folkestone by the dinky **Romney, Hythe & Dymchurch Railway**. Out of season (ie most of the year) these windswept coastal villages and towns look forlorn, although they do have a certain curiosity value. Plucky little **Dymchurch** ('Children's Paradise' say the ever-optimistic signs) has an extensive sandy (if frequently wind-whipped) beach and a fine example of a **Martello Tower** (topped by a restored 26-pounder gun). This part of the coast is littered with these relics of the

Napoleonic War coastal defences. Dymchurch also boasts a swashbuckling eighteenth-century vicar-turned-smuggler, brought to screen in 1963's *Doctor Syn, Alias the Scarecrow* (starring Patrick McGoohan and George Cole) and still celebrated in the village's annual 'Day of Syn' knees-up. Further north, **Hythe** boasts a cuteish, largely traffic-free High Street and the tardis-like eleventh-century Church of St Leonard, complete with bone-packed crypt.

Most visitors hug the coastal route, but a short detour into **Romney Marsh** is more rewarding. The traffic disappears as the narrow roads snake their way around the fields and drainage ditches, and the flat landscape teems with wildlife, especially plovers. There's also plenty of evidence of the culinarily-prized Romney Marsh lamb. At one time Romney Marsh was a haven for smugglers, and to this day Kent folk view Marshmen with some suspicion. A tourist trail (clearly signposted from Rye, New Romney and many junctions en route) guides you past many well-preserved Saxon, Norman and medieval churches (EM Nesbit is buried in St Mary in the Marsh) and quite a few excellent country pubs. One diversion worth making is into the village of **Appledore**, which used to be a Jute and then Norman port on the English Channel; now it's around six miles inland. **Lympne Castle** is also worth a short stop; there are wonderful views down towards the coast from the neighbouring churchyard. And kids will love the **Port Lympne Wild Animal Park**.

Arcing round from Hythe to the River Rother near Rye, the **Royal Military Canal** skirts the edge of the Marsh. It was built to provide a back-up defence against possible Napoleonic invasion but, like the Martello Towers, was never actually needed. There are some pleasant walks along its banks.

Where to stay

Most of the good accommodation is clustered around Rye and Winchelsea; all the best places tend to be booked out weeks ahead. If the options below are full, try **Playden Cottage Guesthouse** (01797 222234) just outside Rye.

Cleveland House Offer

Winchelsea, TN36 4EE (01797 226256/ fax 01797 226256/sarah.jempson@virgin.net). **Rates** (B&B) *single occupancy* £40; *double/twin* £60. **Rooms** 1 double; 1 twin (en suite). **Cards** MC, V. A modernised eighteenth-century house in the centre of Winchelsea. Its prime attraction is the wonderful one-and-a-half-acre garden, which offers views into the coastal haze, a secluded heated outdoor swimming pool in the summer, and a well-tended walled garden (complete with obelisk). The house is light inside and strewn

*View from Dungeness's **Old Lighthouse**.*

with antique furniture. Children and dogs welcome. Both bedrooms non-smoking.

A2070 to A259 through Rye; in Winchelsea, Cleveland House is the large white building facing out to sea.

Jeake's House

Mermaid Street, Rye, TN31 7ET (01797 222828/ fax 01797 222623/jeakeshouse@btinternet.com/ www.s-h-systems.co.uk/hotels/jeakes.html).
Rates £24.50-£44.50pp. **Rooms** 1 single; 10 double (all en suite); 1 four-poster (en suite). **Cards** MC, V.
Probably the loveliest and most atmospheric small hotel in Rye, and consequently very busy. Pink and chintz are the dominant looks, but in a building this quaint – it was built as a wool store in 1689 – they can get away with it. The rooms are lovely, have all the amenities you could want, and there is a decent selection of vegetarian dishes for breakfast.

Little Orchard House

West Street, Rye, TN31 7ES (tel/fax 01797 223831).
Rates (B&B) *single occupancy* £45-£65; *double/twin/four-poster* £64-£84. **Rooms** (all en suite) 1 double/twin; 2 four-posters. **Cards** Debit, MC, V.
Sara Brinkhurst's appealing Georgian townhouse in the centre of Rye has retained many original features, such as a pretty walled garden and a watchtower. Open fires and antique furniture enhance the period feel. There's a four-poster in the largest room, or you could stay in panelled Lloyd George's Room where the Liberal PM once kipped. All rooms non-smoking.

Old Vicarage

66 Church Square, Rye, TN31 7HF (01797 222119/ fax 01797 227466).
Rates *single occupancy* £42-£52; *double/twin* £24-£32; *family room* £86. **Rooms** (all en suite) 5 double/twin; 1 family.
A Georgian detached house, which faces on to the lovely square surrounding St Mary's at the top of Rye. The sitting room and dining room have exposed beams, and most of the bedrooms (heavy on the Laura Ashley) have views across the rooftops of Rye. The breakfasts, making the most of excellent local produce, are legendary. All bedrooms non-smoking.

Romney Bay House

Coast Road, Littlestone-on-Sea, New Romney, TN28 8QY (01797 364747/fax 01797 367156).
Rates (B&B) *single occupany* £60-£85; *double/twin* £75-£120; *four-poster* £115. **Rooms** (all en suite) 2 twins; 6 doubles; 2 four-poster. **Cards** Debit, MC, V.
The only really good place to stay on the Dungeness peninsula. Helmut and Jennifer Görlich have painstakingly renovated this beach house – designed by Sir Clough Williams-Ellis, who built Portmeirion – into an 11-room hotel. Helmut is a witty host who quickly puts guests at ease; Jennifer prepares the excellent home cooking (*see p36*). The rooms are spotless, the house filled with antique furniture in country home style, and there's a lookout (with telescope) for windy days. Superb value, and well worth the price as it's a delight to stay indoors here if the weather is inclement, which it often is on the Ness. All rooms non-smoking.

Littlestone-on-Sea is on the B2071 off the A259 at New Romney.

One on its own: **Romney Bay House**.

Where to eat & drink

Good food isn't a strong point of this part of Kent; the local speciality seems to be the deep-fryer. However, there is a decent range of interesting pubs with fine beers, and the quality of locally caught fish is excellent. If you arrive before noon on a Saturday get your fresh and smoked seafood from **Griggs of Hythe** (Fisherman's Landing Beach, Range Road); many Chinese restaurateurs drive here from London to make their selections. You need to book well ahead for the area's two really good places to eat: **Landgate Bistro** and **Romney Bay House**.

Apart from the pubs mentioned below, the cottage **Peace & Plenty** in Playden (15 minutes' walk from Rye along a busy main road; 01797 280342) and the **Ypres Castle** in Rye (with a splendid setting near the thirteenth-century Ypres Tower; 01797 223248) offer decent food and good beer. The **Red Lion** in Snargate, between Appledore and the Ness, lacks food but has bags of character (it was built 450 years ago and last modernised in 1890), a superb beer and farm cider selection and a beautiful garden.

Appledore Tea Rooms

8 The Street, Appledore (01233 758272).
Food served 10.30am-5.15pm Wed-Sun.
Appledore is an interesting small village with a few antique shops and pubs; this tearoom is the best place for a light lunch. Cream teas cost £4.10, sandwiches range from £2 to £2.70, and there is a wide selection of cakes at £1.85 each. Popular with the locals is the wonderfully named Black Sheep Gateau, which consists of fruits soaked in Black Sheep Beer (a North Yorkshire Ale) and is worth trying if only for curiosity value.

Britannia

Dungeness Point (01797 321959).
Food served noon-2.30pm, 6-9pm, Mon-Fri; noon-9pm Sat, Sun. **Cards** Debit, MC, V.

Derek Jarman described the nearby Pilot Inn as having 'the best fish and chips in England'; but since then it has changed hands, and you're better off at this free house, between the Point's two lighthouses, for huge portions of excellent, freshly caught cod and chips for around £5.

Landgate Bistro

5 Landgate, Rye (01797 222829).
Food served 7-9.30pm Tue-Fri; 7-10pm Sat.
Cards AmEx, DC, Debit, MC, V.

The best restaurant in Rye. The dishes are Modern European in style, and London in price (ie high). Great emphasis is placed on locally produced, seasonal ingredients, so expect to find Romney Marsh lamb (with butter, bacon and basil for £11.70), fur and feathered game, and local seafood (cod with ginger and spring onions, £8.90) – even the local salad leaves are superb.

Mermaid

Mermaid Street, Rye (01797 223065).
Food served noon-2.15pm, 7-9.15pm, daily.
Set meals *lunch* £13.50 (2 courses), £16 (3 courses); *dinner* £29 (4 courses). **Cards** AmEx, DC, Debit, MC, V.

This historic coaching inn (c.1420) is perpetually thronged with visitors who go for olde-worlde character. There is a pricey bistro and restaurant – it's worth splashing out for the likes of French onion and cider soup (£5) and roast best end of English lamb (£14.50) – and a small public bar, just off the courtyard. An appealing place for a pint in front of the real fire on a cold day.

Snoozing at **Port Lympne Wild Animal Park.**

Romney Bay House

Coast Road, Littlestone-on-Sea (01797 364747).
Food served *dinner* phone for details.
Cards Debit, MC, V.

This exemplary hotel (*see p35*) also serves food to non-residents. Superb four-course meals cost a set price of £28 per head (excluding wine). Booking is essential, but you can just drop in for breakfast (£10.50), lunch (from £6) or all-day coffee or afternoon tea (£3.50) – all are of a high standard. Lunch specials might include fresh crab salad with shellfish; dinner might be a selection of game with fresh vegetables and cheeses, fruits and chocolate terrine.

Woolpack Inn

Brookland (01797 344321).
Food served noon-2pm, 6-9pm, daily.
Cards Debit, MC, V.

Local people like their portions large and the prices low, and the Woolpack is first choice with nearby villagers who come here for simple but very filling evening meals such as mixed grill (£9.50) and grilled trout (£5.95).

What to see & do

Tourist information centre

Rye Heritage Centre, Strand Quay, **Rye**, TN31 7AY (01797 226696/www.rye.org.uk).
Open *Mar-Oct* 9am-5.30pm, *Nov-Feb* 10am-4pm, daily.

Contains the tourist information centre, the **Heritage Exhibition** and the **Story of Rye**, a 20-minute sound and light show (£2; £1 4s-16s; £1.50 OAPs, students). An audio tour of the town is available from the centre (£2; £1 4s-16s ; £1.50 OAPs, students).

Bike hire

Rye Hire 1 Cyprus Place, Rye (01797 223033).
A few minutes' walk from the station.

Dungeness Nuclear Power Station

Dungeness Point (01797 321815/www.bnfl.co.uk).
Open *Apr-Sept* 10am-4pm daily. **Admission** free.

From the eastern edge of the Weald of Kent across Romney Marsh, a huge building dominates the horizon; at night the illuminations make it look like the Pompidou Centre. This is Dungeness nuclear power station, sited almost on the tip of Dungeness Point. The hum is audible for miles, and was used as a backing soundtrack for Derek Jarman's film *The Garden*. The slickly presented visitor centre has displays about the area and information on 'harnessing nature's forces'.

Dungeness RSPB Nature Reserve

Dungeness Road, Lydd (01797 320588/www.rspb.org.uk).
Open *nature reserve* 9am-dusk, *visitor centre Mar-Oct* 10am-5pm, *Nov-Feb* 10am-4pm, daily
Admission £2.50; 50p 5s-16s; £1.50 OAPs, students; £5 family.

The best place to see the fragile ecology of Dungeness Point. This reserve is built around huge gravel pits; from the hides you can see scores of wildfowl species, and in late spring, terns, reed and sedge warblers, whitethroats

Derek Jarman's garden

A visit to the late Derek Jarman's garden has become a pilgrimage for nature lovers. It is the book *The Garden* that put Dungeness on the map for many people; Jarman's deep love of nature and gardening is best expressed in this book, and he writes lyrically and evocatively about the strangeness of the landscape around Dungeness Point. Howard Sooley's photographs also convey beautifully the surreal quality of both the Ness and the garden.

The small garden that surrounds Prospect Cottage (Coast Road, Dungeness Point) has no boundaries – Jarman loathed the idea of fencing it off. Respectful visitors are tolerated by the present occupier, but within reason. Bank holidays and sheer numbers of visitors sometimes result in day-trippers walking across the garden or even pressing their noses to the glass. It's not a museum, it's someone's home; respect his privacy.

and yellow wagtails migrating north. There are also scores of unusual moths and butterflies, with journals devoted to the subject sold at the bird sanctuary. It costs £2.50 for the hour-long walk around the reserve; there's no charge to look around the hide than constitutes the visitors' centre. There are regular events such as introductions to bird-watching or Dungeness plant life, guided by experts.

Lamb House

West Street, Rye (01797 224982).
Open *Apr-Oct* 2-6pm Wed, Sat.
Admission (NT) £2.50; £1.25 5s-14s.

The house where novelist Henry James once lived is now a small museum devoted to the man. Novelist EF Benson lived there after him.

Old Lighthouse

Dungeness Road, Dungeness (01797 321300).
Open & **Admission** phone for details.

No longer operational, but there are fine views from the top over the power station and the Ness.

Port Lympne Wild Animal Park

Lympne, nr Hythe (0891 800605).
Open 10am-dusk daily. Last entry 4pm.
Admission £8.90; £6.90 4s-16s, OAPs.

A combination animal-historic house experience. Peruse Sir Philip Sassoon's mansion (complete with rather garish wildlife murals and a fine muralled room by Rex Whistler), which was built in 1915 by Sir Herbert Baker, then commune with the beasts. The site is extensive – much is in sheltered woodland and features a particular-

ly impressive gorilla enclosure, some fearsome big cats and the largest breeding herd of black rhino in the UK.

Romney, Hythe & Dymchurch Railway

New Romney Station (01797 362353/ www.rhdr.demon.co.uk).
Times & **Tickets** phone for details.

A miniature railway runs from Dungeness Point to Hythe, stopping at the small beach towns along the coast. At one-third proper size, it was built by a (presumably barking) Captain Howey in 1927, and the steam locomotives provide a useful coastal service for weary walkers. It runs from March to October, but only on a daily basis from April to September.

Rye Art Gallery

107 High Street, Rye (01797 222433).
Open 10.30am-1pm, 2-5pm, daily. **Admission** free.

A constantly changing series of events, which are usually worth seeing. Past exhibitions have included the photography of Michael Ward, chief photographer of *The Times*, and 'Designs on Life: Edward Bawden'. Phone for details of current attractions.

Ypres Tower/Rye Castle

Gun Garden, Rye.
Open *Apr-Oct* 10.30am-5.30pm daily; *Nov-Mar* 10.30am-4.30pm Sat, Sun. **Admission** £2; 75p 7s-16s; £1.50 OAPs, students; £4 family.

More than 700 years old, this stark mini-castle was once used as the town jail.

The Heart of Kent

Where once the hop flourished, now grows the grape.

The sort of timeless Kentish countryside that brings a lump to the throat of city-dwellers.

The very heart of the Garden of England and the easternmost part of the Weald is where the gentle rolling hills and valleys of west Kent continue eastwards until they reach the flatlands of Romney Marsh. This enticing landscape of small towns, villages, farmland and forests has remained essentially unchanged for centuries. Countless listed buildings dot the landscape – from late medieval cottages to picture-postcard windmills.

The region began to prosper in the fourteenth century when Edward III invited Flemish weavers to settle in the area to teach the English a thing or two about producing good-quality cloth. It was a great success, and the area became the centre for the manufacture of broadcloth, the export of which was greatly helped by the close proximity of sea ports. The towns of Cranbrook and Tenterden and their

surrounding villages thrived for the next 350 years until the silting up of many of the Channel ports led to a decline in the industry.

Agriculture took over, especially hops and fruit, although today there are fewer hop gardens and orchards than there used to be, and many oasts, with their distinctive white cowls, have been transformed from dried hop storage to quirky homes (*see page 49* **A toast to the oast**). This part of the county has some of the most promising vineyards in south-east England (*see page 43* **Grape expectations**).

Into the heartland

Perhaps quieter and attracting fewer tourists than the western Kent Weald (*see page 44*), the Heart of Kent is an ideal area for walking, biking or touring by car. A circular tour of the region is probably the best way to take in the varied sights.

The attractive town of **Cranbrook** is dominated by its array of Wealden architecture, particularly the Union Windmill. The Cranbrook Museum provides an excellent introduction to local history. To the north-east lies the pretty white weatherboarded village of

By train from London

Trains to **Headcorn** leave **Charing Cross** about every 30 minutes; the journey time is just over **1hr**.

Sissinghurst, known nationwide for the splendour of **Sissinghurst Castle Garden** on its outskirts. Directly north, between peaceful Frittenden and Staplehurst, is **Iden Croft Herbs**, a fascinating and unusual garden for cooking and herbal enthusiasts.

East of Staplehurst is **Headcorn**. Formerly one of the area's major cloth-making centres, today's town has little to offer visitors except the conveniences of a train station, a supermarket, a cash dispenser and a bicycle shop, which does repairs but not hire. It's a good base from which to explore, whatever mode of transport you use.

Around here, the fabulous rolling countryside begins to flatten out; heading south on the A274 you come to a series of beautiful villages, which include unspoilt **Biddenden**, home to Kent's oldest commercial vineyard (*see page 43* **Grape expectations**). Further east and north-east are Smarden, Bethersden and **Pluckley**, which rises high above the surrounding countryside and is reputed to be the most haunted village in the South-East. Pluckley has a dubious claim-to-fame as the Dering windows capital of Kent – many of the village's houses feature this arched style of window, so called because a member of the Dering family is said to have escaped from the Roundheads during the Civil War through a window this shape. On a more familiar note, Pluckley is also known as the place where much of *The Darling Buds of May* series was filmed. Its welcoming pub, the Black Horse, boasts a large, peaceful beer garden where you can enjoy home-cooked food and cask ales.

The delightful market town of **Tenterden**, south of Biddenden, with its busy wide tree-lined thoroughfare, is filled with antique shops. The station in, logically enough, Station Road, is the main jumping-on point for the Kent & East Sussex Steam Railway. Trains currently run from Tenterden to Northiam, East Sussex, but will soon journey on to the moated thirteenth-century **Bodiam Castle** (*see page 56*). Younger children should also enjoy a visit to the **South of England Rare Breeds Centre** at nearby Woodchurch.

Leaving Tenterden to the south, the hills gradually descend with the approaching marshlands. Arriving at the village of Small Hythe, you'll find the charming sixteenth-century country house **Small Hythe Place**, once home to the actress Ellen Terry. Wine tastings, tours and tea can be had at **Tenterden Vineyard Park** across the road.

Just over the border with East Sussex at Northiam is the beautiful house and gardens of **Great Dixter** (*see page 56*). Returning towards Cranbrook, **Sandhurst Vineyards** and **Rowenden Vineyard** are well worth a tasting or two, while the eccentric collection of vehicles at **CM Booth Collection of Historic Vehicles** in **Rolvenden** is an added attraction in the pretty village.

Between Rolvenden and the tranquil village of Benenden is **Hole Park** (Rolvenden, Cranbrook; 01580 241251); phone before visiting as opening times are restricted), a fabulously peaceful garden.

Where to stay

The area is awash with hundreds of B&Bs of varying standards; the best of them provide better and more interesting accommodation than the hotels in the region, many of which seem stuck in a 1950s time warp.

Bettmans Oast

Hareplain Road, Biddenden, TN27 8LJ (tel/fax 01580 291463).
Rates (B&B) *double/twin* £45-£50. **Rooms** 2 double/twin (both en suite); 1 twin. **Cards** Debit, MC, V.

This carefully restored listed oast house and converted barn has two massive high-ceilinged double rooms at ground level. Located conveniently close to Sissinghurst and within staggering distance of the excellent Three Chimneys pub, this agreeable and relaxing home has beams and character aplenty and guests have the use of a sitting room with fireplace. There are more than ten acres of grounds at the back of the house, which are patrolled by free-ranging chickens, which supply the eggs for the morning fry-up. All rooms are no smoking.
A274 or A262 to Biddenden, then A262 towards Sissinghurst. After 1 mile, turn right at Three Chimneys pub past phone box; Bettmans Oast is 0.5 miles on right.

Bishopsdale Oast [Offer]

Biddenden, TN27 8DR (01580 291027/292065/fax 01580 292321/bishopsdale@pavilion.co.uk/www.users.globalnet.co.uk/~mist/bishopsdale).
Rates (B&B) *double/twin* £50-£60.
Rooms 4 double/twin (3 en suite). Min 2-night stay peak Fri, Sat. **Cards** Debit, MC, V.

Fresh ingredients from the garden are a wonderful organic touch to the optional evening meal in this comfortable converted oast house tucked down a lane in the heart of the Weald. With so many attractions nearby, this makes an ideal base for touring. In summer you can eat outside by the wild flower garden or, in winter, lounge by the roaring log fire. The decent-sized rooms retain the original beams, while at the same time are kept reassuringly up to date with a TV and other mod cons. All rooms are no-smoking.
A28 from Ashford to Tenterden; right at Cranbrook Road; after 2.5 miles, follow sign for Bishopsdale Oast.

Folly Hill Cottage

Friezley Lane, Hocker Edge, Cranbrook, TN17 2LL (01580 714299/decarlej@aol.com).
Rates (B&B) *single occupancy* £26-£30; *double* £40-£46. Min 2-night stay Fri, Sat.
Rooms 2 twin/double (1 en suite).

A great place to unwind. At the end of a narrow private lane in the heart of a wooded valley, this idyllic nineteenth-century house has all the necessary comforts for a relaxing stay in the country. One twin room has a small balcony overlooking the outdoor (unheated) swimming pool. The rooms, though not particularly big, are modern rather than period in style, with private bathrooms (one even has its own fridge), and the owners are friendly and accommodating. Guests have use of the small communal TV lounge. No smoking throughout.

N of A262 between Goudhurst and Sissinghurst.

Kennel Holt Hotel **Offer**

Goudhurst Road, Cranbrook, TN17 2PT (01580 712032/fax 01580 712495/www.kennelholt.co.uk).
Rates *single* £85; *single occupancy* £110; *standard double/twin* £135; *superior double/twin* £165; *four-poster* £135-£165. **Rooms** (all en suite) 2 single; 6 double/twin; 2 four-poster. **Cards** Debit, MC, V.

A wonderful place for romance. This small and exclusive country hotel is set in a beautiful Elizabethan manor house with five acres of gardens. Each room is unique – the King Henry VIII room is massive and full of character, with oak beams, a large fireplace and a great view over the gardens. Breakfast in bed is the only way to go. The pricey hotel restaurant is rather hit and miss and the luxurious surroundings can't quite make up for the variable quality of the cooking. Children are welcome.

On A262 between Goudhurst and Sissinghurst.

Little Hodgeham

Bull Lane, Bethersden, TN26 3HE (01233 850323).
Rates (B&B) £36.50pp. **Rooms** (all en suite) 1 double; 1 twin; 1 four-poster.

This picturesque Tudor cottage is surrounded by a pretty, mature garden complete with stream and swimming pool for the use of guests. Inside the house, the cosy rooms are spotless and filled with gleaming antiques. One room has a four-poster and a raised loft with two single beds. The chatty owner Erica Wallace is a great cook – her dinner parties (held most nights; £15.50 per person) are worth staying in for. Children welcome.

In Bethersden, take right at Bull pub; Little Hodgeham is 2 miles towards Smarden.

Maplehurst Mill

Mill Lane, Frittenden, TN17 2DT (01580 852203/fax 01580 852117/maplehurst@clara.net).
Rates (B&B) *single occupancy* £48; *double/twin/four-*

*Top trysting spot: the **Kennel Holt Hotel**.*

poster £76. Min 2-night stay Fri, Sat. **Rooms** 4 double/twin (3 en suite); 1 four-poster (en suite). **Cards** MC, V.

An exquisite thirteenth-century mill oozing character; you'd be hard-pushed to find a more romantic hideaway. Every antique-filled room has its own charm and individuality – whether you like to sleep with the soothing sounds of the millstream, or prefer views over the extensive gardens and meadows beyond, or even the decadence of a four-poster bed. Kenneth and Heather Parker are welcoming hosts and their candlelit dinners are imaginative, with an emphasis on home-grown produce and herbs. There is the added bonus of a heated outdoor swimming pool in summer. No smoking and children over 12 only are accepted. There are also disabled rooms.

A229 towards Hastings; turn left at Frittenden Road after Staplehurst; after 1.25 miles, turn right down narrow lane opposite big white house, turn right at end of lane, through woods; Mill is on right.

White Lion Inn

High Street, Tenterden, TN30 6BD (01580 765077/fax 01580 764157).
Rates (B&B) *single occupancy* £54; *double* £74; *four-poster* £94; *family room* £84. **Rooms** (all en suite) 10 double; 1 twin; 1 four-poster; 2 family. **Cards** AmEx, Debit, MC, V.

The White Lion is a recently renovated coaching inn, convenient for many of the attractions in the area, from Sissinghurst to the north, down to Small Hythe in the south, as well as being a short drive from many of Kent's best vineyards. Rooms are modern but spacious, clean and of a good standard – several have four-poster beds. The heavily beamed bar and restaurant downstairs make up for the lack of character in the rooms. This is a good choice for those who prefer a more lively town location. Children welcome.

Wittersham Court

Wittersham, Tenterden, TN30 7EA (tel/fax 01797 270425).
Rates (B&B) *single occupancy* £50; *double/twin* £75. Min 2-night stay Fri, Sat. **Rooms** 2 double (1 en suite); 1 twin. **Cards** MC, V.

This eighteenth-century listed house has beams and comforts at every turn. Attention to detail is evident throughout, with extras like towelling robes, all manner of lotions and a tennis court for the energetic. In winter, log fires and electric blankets add to the warmth of this home from home. Guests have the run of the place, from the book-lined drawing room to the cosy TV room, with its imposing fireplace. This is great walking country and the sea is only six miles away. No smoking in rooms.

B2082 from Tenterden to Wittersham and Rye; right at war memorial in Wittersham; entrance on left before church.

Where to eat & drink

Dining out in the area can be something of a lottery – there are some good places, but there are also plenty of restaurants with pretensions that the kitchen staff can't live up to. This is, though, a fertile hunting ground for the pub lover and there are a number of hostelries offering seriously good food. Among the rural pubs worthy of a journey are the unpretentious, friendly **Woodcock** at Iden Green (south of Benenden), the ancient sixteenth-century **Bell** at Smarden and the **Oak & Ivy** just outside of Hawkhurst. The town pubs in this region pale by comparison but if you are staying in or near Tenterden then head down to the inviting **William Caxton**. Biddenden's small **West House Restaurant** (28 High Street; 01580 291341) offers Conran-influenced Med food. Tenterden also has an Indian (**Badsha**, 10 West Cross, Tenterden; 01580 765151), and a traditional Italian (**Il Classico**, 75 High Street, Tenterden; 01580 763624); for a meze fix try the popular Turkish **Ozgur Restaurant** (126 High Street, Tenterden; 01580 763248).

Dering Arms

Station Road, Pluckley (01233 840371).
Food served noon-2pm, 7-9.30pm, Tue-Sat; noon-2pm Sun. **Cards** AmEx, Debit, MC, V.

Superb seafood can be found in this wonderfully old and atmospheric coaching inn replete with flagstones, wood floors, high ceilings and more of those Dering windows. Locals and visitors stream in to enjoy excellent dishes such as the house speciality (monkfish with bacon, orange and cream, £12.95), and wines from the extensive list. If you overindulge, there's simple accommodation upstairs (around £40 for a double room).

Rankins'

High Street, Sissinghurst (01580 713964).
Food served 7.30-8.30pm Wed-Fri; 7.30-9.30pm Sat; 12.30-2pm Sun. **Set dinner** £21.50 2 courses, £25.50 3 courses. **Cards** MC, V.

Looking out over the local chapel, the restaurant in this white wood-fronted house may be kitted out with slightly dated '60s furniture inside but the cooking is entirely du jour. The menu is short; a meal might start with red pepper mousse and artichoke salad followed by duck breast with mustard, calvados and apple sauce (£14). The wine list is a decent mix of French and New World, with a good selection of half bottles. This is a small, friendly place, run by the husband and wife team of Hugh and Leonora Rankin. Starters cost around a fiver, while mains go for about £12 to £15.

Soho South

23 Stone Street, Cranbrook (01580 714666).
Food served 11am-2.30pm, 6.30-9.30pm, Wed-Sat. **Cards** Debit, MC, V.

Old-world atmosphere with new-world cuisine. The confident and assured cooking in this rustic restaurant will keep even the most homesick Londoner content. The name is not a gimmick: the owners ran L'Epicure on Soho's Frith Street for many years. At lunch, the stripped-pine tables are left bare, while white tablecloths and candles appear in the evening. Ingredients are admirably fresh and the attention to detail is evident. The fusion cooking works well and might include Thai green curried guinea fowl with turmeric rice or Rye Bay scallops and butterfly prawns. Starters cost around £5; main courses are about £11. There's also a bistro menu at lunchtimes. Booking recommended.

Chin-wagging at the **Three Chimneys**.

Three Chimneys

just off the A262, west of Biddenden (01580 291472).
Food served noon-2pm, 6-10pm, Mon-Fri; noon-2.15pm, 6-10pm, Sat; noon-2.15pm, 7-10pm, Sun.
Cards Debit, MC, V.

The three rooms at the front of this atmospheric and rambling country pub look like they haven't changed in centuries. Flagstoned floors, low oak beams and big fireplaces provide a comforting background for quaffing well-kept beers straight from the cask. The back of the pub is more devoted to food than booze. Sautéed king prawn tails in white wine and garlic (£5.25) followed by pan-fried lamb's liver and bacon with red onion gravy (£8.50) are typically simple but assuredly executed dishes from the short menu. Booking is recommended.

What to see & do

Tourist information centres

Cranbrook Vestry Hall, Stone Street, **Cranbrook** (01580 712538). **Open** *Apr-Oct* 9.30am-5.30pm Mon-Fri; 9am-5.30pm Sat.
Tenterden Town Hall, High Street, **Tenterden** (01580 763572). **Open** *Apr-Oct* 9.30am-1.30pm, 2-5pm, Mon-Sat.

CM Booth Collection of Historic Vehicles

63 High Street, Rolvenden (01580 241234).
Open 10am-6pm Mon-Sat. **Admission** £1.50; 75p 4s-13s.

A small but eclectic private collection housed in an antique shop in the attractive village of Rolvenden. Inside are three-wheeled classic Morgans, a wealth of automobile memorabilia plus toy and model cars.

Cranbrook Museum

Carriers Road, Cranbrook (01580 712020/ freeweb.digiweb.com/pages/cranbrookmuseum).
Open *Apr-Sept* 2-4.30pm Tue-Sat; *Mar, Oct, Nov* 2-4.30pm Wed, Thur, Sat. **Admission** £1.50; 50p 4s-15s.

Housed in a building that is older than some of the exhibits, this diverting local museum features such delights as the Barking Spud, an agricultural implement essential for keeping out intruders, and displays recounting tales of the Frittenden Forgers – a group of men who made coins out of syphon tops stolen from local pubs.

Cranbrook Union Windmill

Mill Hill, Cranbrook (01580 712256/712984).
Open *Apr-mid-July, late Aug-Sept* 2.30-5pm Sat,
bank hols; *mid-July-Aug* 2.30-5pm Sat; 2-5pm Sun.
Admission free, donations welcome.

A local landmark, the Union Windmill is the largest and
one of the country's best-preserved smock mills, so
called because they were originally said to have resem-
bled the shape of a farmer's smock, from a distance. This
engineering marvel is run by volunteer enthusiasts and
still produces freshly milled flour, which can be purchased near the entrance. More windmills can be found
in nearby Rolvenden (no phone), Woodchurch (01233
860043) and Wittersham (01797 270295).

Great Maytham Hall

Rolvenden (01580 241346).
Open *May-Sept* 2-5pm Wed, Thur. Last entry
4.30pm. **Admission** £3.50; £1.75 5s-15s; *gardens
only* £2; £1 5s-15s.

Eighteen acres of parkland back on to this Luytens-
designed mansion house. The more formal gardens
include a walled garden, which inspired Frances
Hodgson Burnett to write *The Secret Garden.*

Headcorn Aerodrome

off A274 south of Headcorn, Ashford (01622 890226).
Open 9am-sunset daily.

Looking at old buildings and gardens at ground level
may not appeal to the adrenaline junkie, who might prefer to skydive at the Headcorn Parachute Club (01622
890862), have flying lessons with Weald Air Services
(01622 891539) or a trip in a Tiger Moth with the Tiger
Club (01622 891017). This could be the most different
and exhilarating way of exploring the heart of Kent.

Iden Croft Herbs

Frittenden Road, Staplehurst (01580 891432/
www.oxalias.co.uk/ic.htm).
Open *end Sept-Feb* 9am-5pm Mon-Sat; *Mar-end Sept*
9am-5pm Mon-Sat; 11am-5pm Sun, bank hols.
Admission £1.50; 50p 5s-15s.

Every herb imaginable can be found in this unique and
fascinating garden set in and around an ancient walled
garden. An extensive array of herbs is on sale for cooking and medicinal uses.

Kent & East Sussex Railway

Tenterden & Northiam stations (01580 765155/
www.seetb.org.uk/kesr).
Times phone for details. **Tickets** *return* £6.80;
£3.40 3s-15s; family £18.50.

Chug back into the past with a journey on a steam train
between Tenterden and Northiam. Throughout the year
there are special events geared for all members of the family, which might include a Thomas the Tank Engine fun
day or a themed dinner evening. From April 2000, the service will continue to Bodiam station, near the castle.

Sissinghurst Castle Garden

Sissinghurst, Cranbrook (01580 712850).
Open *Apr-mid-Oct* 1-6.30pm Tue-Fri; 10am-5.30pm
Sat, Sun. Last entry 30mins before closing.
Admission (NT) £6; £3 5s-15s.

The most popular attraction in the area, Sissinghurst is
famous not only for its wonderful, inspirational gardens
but also for its celebrity creators, poet and novelist Vita
Sackville-West and her husband Harold Nicolson, a
historian and diplomat. There's tremendous individuality evident in the varied gardens, which have something to offer whatever the season. Visitors can also visit
the fifteenth-century long library and tower.

Uncover the fiendish Frittenden Forgers at the diverting **Cranbrook Museum**. *See page 41.*

Grape expectations

You don't have to trek into Europe or fly to Sydney or San Francisco for a wine-tasting tour. Incredibly, there are more than 400 vineyards across Britain, many of which are located in the South-East. Though hardly a recent phenomenon – English winemaking goes back as far as Roman times – it's only in the last 50 years or so that the industry has been revived, and is now undergoing something of a renaissance. That's not to say that traditional stumbling blocks have gone away: to put it mildly, English wines have never been the most trendy tipple in the world, and, because of unreliable harvests due to a relatively cold climate, English producers have generally been unable to offer their best bottles at prices to match foreign makers. Nevertheless, gradually, the industry is gaining more and more respect, and many vineyards are only too happy to offer tastings to the public. As a general rule, whites are usually more refined than reds, though it's always good to taste as many as possible (all in the interests of research, of course). The best time to visit vineyards is September and October, when the vines are full and harvesting begins. Be sure not to confuse English wine with British wine, which is made from imported reconstituted grape juice.

For **Sedlescombe Vineyards**, near Battle, *see page 56*. Note that all the following vineyards do tastings, and though admission is free, some may charge for guided tours and/or tastings.

Biddenden Vineyards & Cider Works

Little Whatmans, Biddenden (01580 291726).
Open 10am-5pm Mon-Sat; 11am-5pm Sun, bank hols.
Kent's oldest commercial vineyard is also home to some CAMRA award-winning ciders.

Harbourne Vineyard

Wittersham, Tenterden (01797 270420/ www.users.globalnet.co.uk/~harvin).
Open 2-6pm daily.
A small vineyard that even produces wine that's acceptable for vegans and vegetarians.

Rowenden Vineyard

Sandhurst Lane, Rolvenden (01580 241255).
Open 10am-6pm Tue-Sun.
This vineyard may be relatively small but it produces a number of excellent wines. Christopher Lindlar has a reputation for being one of the UK's best winemakers.

Sandhurst Vineyards & Hop Farm

Hoads Farm, Crouch Lane, Sandhurst (01580 850296).
Open *Apr-Dec* 2-6pm Mon-Fri; 11.30am-6pm Sat; noon-3pm Sun.
A friendly family-run vineyard with some award-winning wines. The owners also run an agreeable B&B within their beautifully restored sixteenth-century farmhouse.

Tenterden Vineyard Park

Small Hythe, Tenterden 01580 763033/www. chapeldownwines.co.uk/tenterdenvineyardpark).
Open 10am-5pm daily; tours Apr-Oct.
Tenterden is the second largest winery in the UK and home to Chapel Wines. The park has the further attractions of a small museum, a plant centre and a herb garden.

Small Hythe Place

Small Hythe, nr Tenterden (01580 762334).
Open *Apr-Oct* 1.30-6pm Mon-Wed, Sat, Sun.
Admission £3; £1.50 5s-17s.
An idyllic timber-framed house, built in the early 1500s, which was once the home of Victorian actress Ellen Terry, who lived here from 1899 until her death in 1928. It is now a fascinating theatre museum that depicts the life and times of one of the most famous board-stompers of her generation. There is a small theatre in the garden, where plays are still staged. Surprisingly isolated, Small Hythe Place is surrounded by wonderful walking country.

South of England Rare Breeds Centre

Highlands Farm, Woodchurch (01233 861493).
Open *Apr-Sept* 10.30am-5.30pm daily;
Oct-Mar 10.30am-4.30pm Tue-Sun.
Admission £3.25; £1.90 3s-15s; £2.75 OAPs.
Very much a petting farm and an ideal attraction for families with small children, the South of England Rare Breeds Centre has far more than just a few piglets, lambs and cows. Among the more interesting fauna on view is an ancient breed of goat, brought to this country by the Crusaders, and Lincoln Longwool sheep, dating back to Roman times.

The Kent Weald

'Kent, sir – everybody knows Kent – apples, cherries, hops and women.' (*The Pickwick Papers*)

When the non-Kentish think of Kent, it is not the sprawling Medway towns, the superannuated resorts like Margate or the otherworldly Romney Marsh wildernesses that come to mind, but an idyllic, preserved-in-aspic, oast house-heavy landscape of small villages tucked within the neat folds of cosy wooded valleys, of hop gardens and fruit orchards, of ancient half-timbered pubs. What these people are actually thinking of is the Weald. And the Weald is actually like that.

Although the Weald is often thought of as specifically Kentish, the term does, in fact, refer to the entire basin between the North and South Downs and, thus, stretches from the South Kent coast all the way through Sussex, even spilling over into Hampshire. This break only covers part of the Kent Weald (for the more southerly section, *see pages 38-43* **The Heart of Kent**; for the Sussex Weald, *see pages 57-62* **The Ashdown Forest**).

The term 'weald' – meaning 'forest', from the Anglo-Saxon 'wald' – refers back to the immense swathe of oak and beech that once stretched from Hythe to Winchester. It was formidable enough that when Julius Caesar first landed on the south coast he chose to skirt around the forest rather than try to cross it. The Anglo-Saxons, searching for hog pastures, were the first to establish permanent settlements within the Weald. Anglo-Saxon terms are the most frequent suffixes on Wealden place names – '-hurst' is a wooded knoll, '-den' a clearing in a wood, '-ley' a meadow and '-ham', a small homestead. By the early fourteenth century, much of the forest had been cleared and the familiar landscape of hedged, cultivated fields punctuated by small, vestigial woods had been established.

By train from London

Trains to **Tunbridge Wells** and **Tonbridge** leave from London's **Charing Cross** about every 30 minutes, and pass through **Waterloo East** and **London Bridge** (**55mins** journey time). Trains to **Edenbridge** leave from **London Bridge** hourly or half-hourly and take **45mins**.

Surprisingly, perhaps, the Weald became the major manufacturing area of the country from the Middle Ages until the eighteenth century, and was renowned for its iron ore and sheep-rearing. Happily for us today, these industries both declined just as industrialisation got seriously ugly, leaving the Weald with an unparalleled collection of sizeable late medieval and Tudor buildings. Weather-boarded and tile-hung houses are another distinctive man-made feature of the landscape, as are the ubiquitous oast houses.

'Disgusted'?

Tunbridge Wells (more properly and pompously known, since 1909, as Royal Tunbridge Wells) exists chiefly in the public imagination as the staid, upright home of conservative *Times*-letter writers. It's actually a rather appealing town, if a touch staid, basking in a typically Wealden wooded valley, and makes an excellent base for exploring the region. As Kentish towns go, it's something of an upstart, dating back only to the seventeenth century, when Lord North discovered the Chalybeate Spring in 1606, declared himself cured of consumption and set in train a development that left the town second only to Bath in the fashionable spa circuit. The spring, at the end of the Pantiles, the town's most famous street (and attraction), still draws tourists today, who come to drink a glass of the iron-bearing, apparently revolting-tasting waters. The Pantiles were once described by John Evelyn as 'a very sweet place... private and refreshing'. This colonaded late seventeenth-century shopping street is still rather sweet and not yet totally overwhelmed by tacky trinket shops.

A favourite short family outing from here is to the **High Rocks**, a couple of miles south-west of the town. This series of sandstone rocks, linked by 11 bridges and set in a wooded valley, is a lovely spot for a stroll and a picnic. It isn't exactly undiscovered, though – the steam-powered **Spa Valley Railway** (01892 537715; leaving from West station close to the Pantiles irregularly from March to October; phone for details) passes by and there's a pub, restaurant and banqueting complex here.

All around the Weald

The Weald is perfect country for gentle touring, either by car or bike (although parts are hilly), and walking. There are marked cycle and motoring routes and a plethora of walking trails (leaflets are available at tourist information centres). Brief highlights follow.

Between Tunbridge Wells and Sevenoaks is the workaday town of **Tonbridge** (not to be confused with its more upmarket near-namesake), with its striking ruined Norman castle. West of here is **Chiddingstone**'s much-photographed single street (entirely owned by the National Trust) – virtually an open-air museum of fifteenth- and sixteenth-century domestic architecture. Neighbouring **Penshurst** is also exceptionally pretty and has the added attractions of **Penshurst Place & Gardens** and **Penshurst Vineyard**. Also close by is exquisite (and ultra-popular) **Hever Castle**.

South of Tunbridge Wells, on the border with East Sussex, is the equally well-patronised **Groombridge Place Gardens**, with its award-winning kid-paradise 'Enchanted Forest'. East of here lies **Bewl Water**, the largest body of water in the South-East. It's actually a reservoir, and a popular spot for watersports, fishing, walking and horse- and bike-riding. Bikes can be hired from the visitors' centre (bicycle hire 01323 870310) off the A21 between Lamberhurst and Flimwell. Nearby is the evocative ruined medieval **Bayham Abbey** (01892 890381), the extensive keyboard collection at **Finchcocks** and the effortlessly romantic **Scotney Castle Gardens**.

At the point north-east of Tunbridge Wells where the High Weald tumbles down into the Low (also known as the Vale) are a clutch of stunning little villages, such as **Goudhurst**, **Horsmonden** and **Matfield**. At **Beltring**, Whitbread has assembled the biggest collection of oast houses in the county (20). Alas, hops are no longer dried in these distinctive buildings anywhere in Kent, but you can at least see how it used to be done at the **Hop Farm Country Park**. (*See also page 49* **A toast to the oast**.) The country gently flattens towards where the Medway flows down towards Maidstone. Nearby **Leeds Castle** (*see page 32*), more remarkable for its setting than interior, is a major draw.

On the flanks of the greensand ridge that runs from Maidstone to Sevenoaks and beyond are yet more cutesy villages (such as **Plaxtol**) and yet more fine noble piles and gardens, chief among them the medieval/Tudor manor house of **Ightham Mote** and the vast Sackville family gaff of **Knole**.

Hoath House

Chiddingstone Hoath, nr Edenbridge, TN8 7DB (01342 850362).
Rates (B&B) *single occupancy* £25; *double/twin* £45; *family* £60. Min 2-night stay Fri, Sat. **Rooms** 1 double (en suite); 1 twin; 1 twin/family room.

The relaxed, friendly Streatfeild family have lived in exquisite Chiddingstone village (three miles away) for 400 years and their extraordinary current home – a mish-mash of architectural styles from Tudor onwards – is as far from a typical B&B as its possible to imagine. Guests are housed in the Edwardian wing but eat breakfast in the oak-beamed and panelled Tudor dining room and can lounge in the neighbouring beamed sitting room with its wood-burning fire. Decent food is available in nearby pubs.

North Tonbridge exit on A21; follow signs to Penshurst Place & Vineyard; pass vineyard; right at T junction towards Edenbridge; bear left in village; house 0.5 miles on left.

Hotel du Vin & Bistro

Crescent Road, Tunbridge Wells, TN1 2LY (01892 526455/fax 01892 512044/reception@tunbridgewells. hotelduvin.co.uk/www.hotelduvin.com).
Rates *double/twin/single* £75-£109 (£10 supplement Fri, Sat). Breakfast £9.50 (Eng); £6.50 (cont).
Rooms (all en suite) 14 double; 18 double/twin.
Cards AmEx, DC, Debit, MC, V.

Why can't all hotels be like this? This sister establishment to the original Hotel du Vin in Winchester (*see p104*) opened in late 1997 and repeats the same unbeatable formula. Each room (in the eighteenth-century house where Princess Victoria once summered) is sponsored and named after a wine company – all are immaculately decorated in chic, muted tones and distinguished by classy touches such as hi-fis, fresh milk in the mini-bar and Molton Brown toiletries. Those at the back of the house enjoy fine views over the town and Calverley Park. Good, unobtrusive taste continues in the public rooms – the warming Burgundy Bar, the latino-themed

The estimable **Hotel du Vin & Bistro.**

Havana Room (where billiards, cigars and armagnac can be decadently enjoyed) and the top-notch bistro (*see p47*). Children are welcome.

A21 to Tunbridge Wells, A264 exit; right at traffic lights towards town centre to small roundabout; left into Crescent Road; hotel is on left.

Jordans

Sheet Hill, Plaxtol, TN15 0PU (01732 810379).
Rates (B&ContB) *single* £38; *double* £66. Breakfast £3 (Eng). **Rooms** 1 single; 2 double.

This gorgeous fifteenth-century cottage surrounded by rambler roses and lovely gardens makes a great base for Ightham Mote and the other Kentish houses and gardens nearby. Ancient beams, inglenooks and leaded windows predominate and all bedrooms have en suite facilities. Note that check-in is not until 6pm, the house is no-smoking and only children over 12 are welcome.

Take A227 off A25 towards Tonbridge; sign to Plaxtol on the left; turn left by church on to Tree Lane; after 0.5 miles road becomes Sheet Hill; Jordans is on the left-hand side.

Newbarn

Wards Lane, Wadhurst, TN5 6HP (tel/fax 01892 782042/williscpuk@aol.com).
Rates (B&B) *single/single occupancy* £25-£38; *double/twin* £50; *cottage* £185-£495 per week. **Rooms** 1 single; 1 twin; 1 double; 2 cottages.

The setting's the thing at Newbarn. Clinging to a hillside overlooking Bewl Water reservoir, this eighteenth-century farmhouse is blessed with jaw-dropping views of the Kent-Sussex borderlands. Christopher and Pauline Willis have renovated the house skilfully, bringing light, flowery decorative schemes to the three bedrooms. There are also two self-catering cottages close by (one sleeps two, the other sleeps four or five), which are available for weekly hire. The garden descends to the water's edge and there are watersports, horse-riding and bike hire nearby plus a 13-mile footpath around the reservoir. Children welcome. Non-smoking throughout.

A21 to Lamberhurst; B2100 S to Wadhurst; take B2099 towards Ticehurst; after 1.5 miles turn left on to Wards Lane; house is on left after 1.5 miles.

Old Parsonage

Frant, TN3 9DX (tel/fax 01892 750773/oldparson@aol.com).
Rates (B&B) *four-poster/twin* £72. **Rooms** (all en suite) 2 four-poster; 1 twin. **Cards** MC, V.

Tony and Mary Dakin's sturdy, handsome Georgian house offers a higher class of B&B. The plant-filled public rooms are kitted out with antiques and chandeliers and the huge atrium floods the centre of the house with light. Bedrooms are beautifully clean and have good-sized bathrooms. Three acres of gardens provide plenty of scope for leg-stretching. Children over the age of seven and dogs welcome. All bedrooms are no-smoking.

2 miles S of Tunbridge Wells off A267; Old Parsonage is next to church at Frant.

Scott House

37 High Street, West Malling, ME19 6QH (01732 841380/fax 01732 522367).
Rates (B&B) *single occupancy* £49; *double/twin* £69. **Rooms** (all en suite) 1 twin, 2 double. **Cards** AmEx, DC, Debit, MC, V.

West Malling's an agreeable little town and Scott House, perched above an antiques shop on the high street, is a more than passable overnight stop. The three cute bedrooms in the Grade II-listed building are compact; the biggest boasts a half-tester bed. This is a good choice if staying in deep countryside brings out the agoraphobic in you. There's a decent selection of pubs and restaurants in town. No smoking throughout.

J4 off M20; West Malling is off A228.

Tanyard Hotel

Wierton Hill, Boughton Monchelsea, Maidstone, ME17 4JT (01622 744705/fax 01622 741998).
Rates (B&B) *single* £65; *single occupancy* £85-£90; *double* £115; *suite* £155. **Rooms** (all en suite) 1 single; 2 double; 2 twin; 1 suite. **Cards** AmEx, Debit, MC, V.

This gem of a house, parts of which date back to around 1350, now holds six eccentrically shaped, beam-heavy guest rooms of varying sizes. There are, perhaps, one too many floral flounces in the soft furnishings, but the out-of-kilter walls and floors detract the attention, as do the lovely setting and views. The small, low-lit sitting room and bar, both dominated by huge log-burning fireplaces, and the good if pricey restaurant and cheery service are further attractions. Children over six welcome.

J8 off M20; follow signs to Leeds Castle; pass entrance and continue on B2163 for 3 miles; at Plough pub at the staggered crossroads, cross over to Plough Wents Road; after 1.7 miles follow signs for hotel.

Where to eat & drink

There's a shortage of top-notch restaurants in this area (Tunbridge Wells represents the richest pickings), but this is compensated for by some cracking pubs, many serving decent food. Try the **Wheatsheaf Inn** (Hever Road, Bough Beech), a former hunting lodge renowned for its ales; the stereotypically picturesque **Crown Inn** (Groombridge, nr Tunbridge Wells); the rambling **Castle Inn** (Chiddingstone), which boasts the village's own-brewed Larkins Traditional; the creeper-clad **Harrow Inn** (Common Road, Ightham Common) and the **Bottle House Inn** (Coldharbour Lane, Smarts Hill; 01892 870306) in Penshurst, which offers particularly good grub. Also in Penshurst is the **Spotted Dog** (Smarts Hill), which is blessed with amazing views from its garden.

The Bull

Dunster Mill Lane, Three Legged Cross, Ticehurst (01580 200586).
Food served noon-3pm, 6.30-10.30pm, Mon-Sat; noon-3pm, 7-10pm, Sun. **Cards** Debit, MC, V.

This large, family-friendly pub is a good place to take kids: there's a garden with a sandpit and climbing frames, a restaurant area separate from the pub, and a non-scary menu: plaice and chips (£6), ciabatta pizza (£6.50), rabbit casserole (£6). As a result of this, the garden is swarming with little terrors, and if it all gets too much, the adults-only bar, with its rough wooden floors, low ceilings, and locals drinking pints of Harveys bitter (£2) has a far less wholesome feel.

The Hare

Langton Road, Langton Green, Tunbridge Wells (01892 862419).
Food served noon-9.30pm Mon-Sat; noon-9pm Sun.
Cards AmEx, Debit, MC, V.

There's a civilised, almost gentleman's club charm to the Hare's dining rooms, but the attitude is anything but stuffy. The long menu is ambitious and might include poshed-up black pudding with apple and sage purée and mustard sauce or fillet of trout with a light mushroom sauce (plus trad roasts on Sundays). In fine weather you can dine al fresco overlooking a perfect village green.

Hotel du Vin & Bistro

Crescent Road, Tunbridge Wells (01892 526455).
Food served noon-1.30pm, 7-9.30pm, Mon-Sat; 12.30-2pm, 7-9pm, Sun. **Cards** AmEx, DC, Debit, MC, V.

The Hotel du Vin's winning combination of restraint and flair is echoed on the menu of its equally stylish restaurant. In a smart yet thoroughly unstuffy candlelit setting, you can enjoy quality classics such as home-potted shrimps with toasted brioche (£6.25) and pan-fried calf's liver and bacon with mash (£11.75). As you might expect, the wine list is oenophile heaven. *See also p45.*

Thackeray's House

85 London Road, Tunbridge Wells (01892 511921).
Food served 12.30-2pm, 7-10pm, Tue-Sat; 12.30-2pm Sun. **Cards** Debit, MC, V.

The one-time home of the author of *Vanity Fair* has long been known as a Wealden gastronomic beacon. In the civilised, beamed dining room you can enjoy the likes of red mullet and monkfish ceviche, mussels and chilli (£7.50) followed by saddle of rabbit, crushed sweet potato and red cabbage (£16.50). The two-course lunch menu

(£13.50) is excellent value. The cheaper, less formal bistro is also recommended.

The phrase 'embarrassment of riches' scarcely does justice to the wealth of Wealden diversions. In addition to those listed below, other fine gardens in the area include **Marle Place Garden** near Brenchley (01892 722304), **Great Comp Garden** at Platt (01732 886154) near Sevenoaks, **Owl House Gardens** in Lamberhurst (01892 890230), **Stoneacre** at Otham (01622 862871) near Maidstone, **Broadview Gardens** at Hadlow (01732 850551) and the world's finest collection of conifers at the **Bedgebury National Pinetum & Forest Gardens** near Goudhurst (01580 211044).

Tourist information centres

Edenbridge TIC, Edenbridge Stangrove Park, **Edenbridge**, TN8 5LU (01732 868110).
Open 10am-3pm Mon-Fri; 10am-5pm Sat, Sun.
The Gatehouse, Palace Gardens, Mill Street, **Maidstone**, ME15 6YE (01622 602169).
Open *Apr-Oct* 9.30am-5pm Mon-Sat, 10am-4pm Sun; *Nov-Mar* 9.30-5pm Mon-Fri, 9.30am-2pm Sat.
Buckhurst Lane, **Sevenoaks**, TN13 1LQ (01732 450305). **Open** phone for details.
Old Fish Market, The Pantiles, **Tunbridge Wells**, TN2 5TN (01892 515675). **Open** *Sept-May* 9am-5pm Mon-Sat; *Jun-Aug* 9am-6pm Mon-Sat; *May-Sept* 10am-5pm Mon-Sat; *Oct-Apr* 10am-4pm Sun.

Groombridge Place Gardens – *the perfect destination for a family day out. See page 48.*

Bike hire

Secret Garden Cycles 113 Barden Road, **Tonbridge** (01732 367233). As this guide went to press, there were plans to move from the present location, about 400 yards from the train station, to premises inside the station; phone to check.

Finchcocks

Riseden, nr Goudhurst (01580 211702/ www.argonet.co.uk/finchcocks).
Open *Easter-July, Sept* 2-6pm Sun, bank hols; *Aug* 2-6pm Wed, Thur, Sun, bank hols. **Admission** £6; £5 OAPs; £4 6s-15s; £14 family; *garden only* £2.

Here's one for music lovers. This pert early Georgian mansion is named after the thirteenth-century owners of a previous house on the site but is now renowned as the home of Richard Burnett's superb collection of around 90 early keyboard instruments. From the end of August to the end of September you can hear the instruments in action during the excellent Finchcocks Festival.

Groombridge Place Gardens

Groombridge Place, Groombridge, nr Tunbridge Wells (01892 863999/www.groombridge.co.uk).
Open *Easter-Oct* 9am-6pm daily.
Admission £6.50; £5.50 3s-12s, OAPs; £20 family.

One of the most popular day's out in the area – and deservedly so. The seventeenth-century house (on a medieval site) may be closed to the public, but the wonderful gardens and surrounding parkland have inspired artists and writers over the centuries (including filmmaker Peter Greenaway and Sir Arthur Conan Doyle for *The Valley of Fear*). With a walled garden, walks through the award-winning 'Enchanted Forest', spring-fed pools and waterfalls giving way to dramatic views over the Weald, the possibilities for waxing lyrical are endless. A variety of events are held most weekends from spring to autumn. Great for kids.

Hever Castle

Hever, nr Edenbridge (01732 865224/ www.hevercastle.co.uk).
Open *Mar-Nov* noon-6pm, *Dec-Feb* 11am-4pm, daily; *gardens* 11am-6pm daily. Last entry 1hr before closing. **Admission** *castle & gardens* £7.30; £4 5s-16s; £6.20 OAPs; £18.60 family; *gardens only* £5.80; £3.80 5s-16s; £4.90 OAPs; £15.40 family.

Henry VIII is said to have courted Anne Boleyn in the magnificent gardens of this enchanting, double-moated thirteenth-century castle. The ill-fated queen reputedly spent much of her childhood here. Most of the furniture, paintings and objets inside are the legacy of William Waldorf Astor, who invested a packet in restoring the place in the early twentieth century. The grounds now boast splendid Italianate gardens, as well as a large lake and rose garden. One of Hever's most popular attractions is a 'splashing water maze' (open Apr-Oct), which invites bravehearts to reach a folly in the middle of a large pond by means of stepping stone paths, while avoiding jets of water. There's also a Yew maze (open May-Oct) and the Guthrie Miniature Model Houses Collection, which depicts country house living from medieval to Victorian times. During the summer there are regular weekend events such as jousting and long-bow demonstrations.

Hop Farm Country Park

Maidstone Road, Beltring, Paddock Wood (01622 872068/events hotline 01622 871577).
Open *Mar-Oct* 10am-5pm, *Nov-Feb* 10am-4pm, daily. Last entry 1hr before closing.
Admission *Mar-Oct* £5.50; £3.50 4s-15s, OAPs; £16 family; *Nov-Feb* £2.50; £1.50 4s-15s, OAPs.

The largest surviving collection of Victorian oast houses is the centrepiece of this multifaceted family attraction. Shire horse displays, the Hop Story Exhibition, the Animal Farm, the Shire Pottery (participation encouraged) and an adventure playground are further attractions, and there are also regular events.

Ightham Mote

Ivy Hatch, Sevenoaks (01732 810378/ infoline 01732 811145).
Open *Apr-Oct* 11am-5.30pm Mon, Wed-Fri, Sun, bank hols. Last entry 4.30pm.
Admission (NT) £5; £2.50 5s-18s; £12.50 family.

Set in a wooded valley, Ightham (pronounced 'eye-tam') Mote is a gorgeous Tudor and medieval manor house. Its restoration was the largest ever undertaken by the National Trust on a house of this age – an exhibition charts its progress – and the result is a treat. There are also fine gardens and woodland walks.

Knole

Sevenoaks (01732 450608).
Open *Apr-Oct* noon-4pm Wed-Sat; 11am-5pm Sun, bank hols; *garden Mar-Sept* noon-4pm 1st Wed of month. Last entry 30mins before closing.
Admission (NT) £5; £2.50 5s-17s; £12.50 family; £2.50 parking; *gardens only* £1.

The vast noble pile of Knole was largely created by Archbishop of Canterbury Thomas Bourchier in 1456 and carefully planned to be in harmony with the calendar (seven courtyards, 12 entrances, 52 staircases, 365 rooms – only 13 of which are open to the public). Knole was again remodelled by the Sackville family in 1605 and been in the family ever since. Deer roam the grounds.

Museum of Kent Life

Lock Lane, Sandling, nr Maidstone (01622 763936).
Open *May-Oct* 10am-5.30pm daily. Last entry 4.30pm.
Admission £4.20; £2.70 5s-15s, OAPs; £12 family.

This thoroughly entertaining award-winning open-air museum includes examples of a traditional oast, granary, hopper's hut and farmhouse. There are also herb, hop and kitchen gardens, a livestock centre and an adventure playground.

Penshurst Place & Gardens

Penshurst, nr Tonbridge (01892 870307/ www.seetb.org.uk/penshurst).
Open *house late Feb-late Mar* noon-5.30pm Sat, Sun; *late Mar-Oct* noon-5.30pm daily; *grounds* 11am-6pm daily. Last entry 5pm. **Admission** phone for details.

The Penshurst estate was founded by merchant Sir John de Poultney in 1341, and has been in the hands of the Sidney family since 1552. The highlight of the interior is the fourteenth-century Baron's Hall; outside, the grounds include an intricately laid-out Italian garden and an adventure playground, nature trail and toy museum for children. Phone for details of special events.

A toast to the oast

The modern hop, which endows your beer with bitterness and flavour, was brought from Flanders to England in the sixteenth century. Since then, the hop has prospered as an agricultural crop to become a valuable commodity and contributor to the local economy. At one time, more than 30,000 acres of Kent countryside were devoted to growing hops; today that acreage is significantly less, and not one of Kent's oast houses is still used for its original purpose of pressing and drying freshly harvested hops. Even the oast houses of Britain's oldest brewer are now redundant: Faversham-based Shepherd Neame no longer grows and dries its own hops and hasn't done so for about 15 years. While the hops it uses now are still grown in Kent, they arrive at the brewery, less appealingly, in dried pellet form, which makes them easier to store and lasts longer.

Before mechanisation began to change the face of agricultural activities in the early 1960s, hopping was an extremely labour-intensive business – from the cutting of 15-foot poles from chestnut trees up which the vines would grow, through planting, to harvesting. Such arduous tasks were carried out by all manner of casual labour. It wasn't long ago (until about 1940) that hundreds of Londoners would make a trip to Kent to stay on the hop farms for about three weeks' 'annual holiday', during which time they'd be paid to pick hops. The accommodation in those days was a basic wooden hut; 60 years on, 'working' and 'holiday' are mutually exclusive terms; nowadays people pay to stay in the converted oast houses – their white, lopsided cone-shaped cowls a reminder of the county's heritage.

The oast houses pictured above can be seen in the excellent **Museum of Kent Life**. If you fancy staying in an oast house, try **Bettmans Oast** and **Bishopsdale Oast**, both in Biddenden (*see page 39*).

Scotney Castle Gardens

Lamberhurst, nr Tunbridge Wells (01892 891081). **Open** *garden Apr-Oct* 11am-6pm Wed-Fri; 2-6pm Sat, Sun; *castle May-mid-Sept* 11am-6pm daily. Last entry 1hr before closing. **Admission** (NT) £4.20; £2.10 5s-16s; £10.50 family.

Undeniably romantic gardens surrounding a fourteenth-century moated castle ruin. Even out of peak season, Scotney has plenty to offer, including a dinosaur footprint, a Henry Moore sculpture and plenty of walks.

Tonbridge Castle

Castle Street, Tonbridge (01732 770929). **Open** 8.30am-5pm Mon-Fri; 9am-5pm Sat; 10.30am-5pm Sun, bank hols. Last entry 4pm. **Admission** £3.45; £1.70 5s-16s, OAPs; £8 family.

Perched perkily just off Tonbridge high street, this impressively ruined Norman motte and bailey castle can be perused in the company of an audio guide, which attempts to recreate the atmosphere of thirteenth-century castle life. Note that the interior of the castle will be closed until at least July 2000.

Yalding Organic Gardens

Benover Road, Yalding (01622 814650). **Open** *Apr, Oct* 10am-5pm Sat, Sun; *May-Sept* 10am-5pm Wed-Sun, bank hols. **Admission** £2.50; £1.25 5s-15s; £2 OAPs.

Opened in 1995, these 14 separate gardens have been imaginatively designed to take the horticulture lover through the history of garden design from the thirteenth century to the present day.

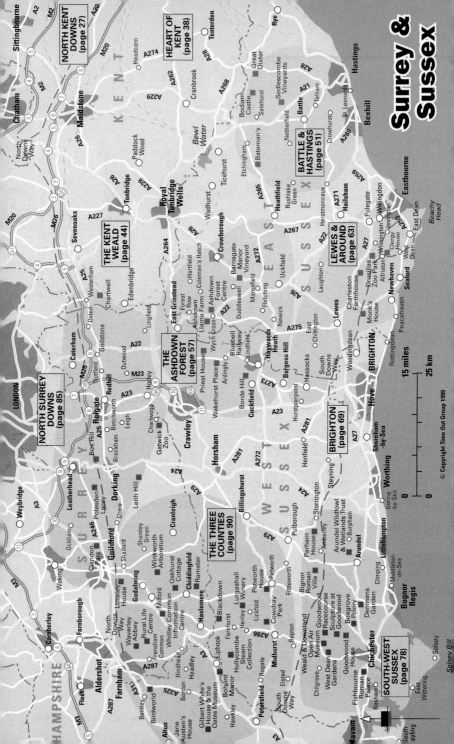

Battle & Hastings

Remembrance of invasions past.

East Sussex has seen its fair share of
bloodshed. Most famously, it was here that
the Norman hordes laid waste to thousands of
Saxons on 14 October 1066. These days it is a
much more peaceful place, dotted with quaint
villages, genteel tea shops, lots of pubs and
country house hotels set within acres of wildlife-
infested countryside, and the most violence you
are likely to encounter is from a blue-rinsed old
lady telling you off for walking in the wrong
direction in a National Trust property.

Into Battle

Battle should be the first port of call for
anyone coming to this part of the country for
the first time; there's enough history here to fire
up the dullest of imaginations. The beautiful
medieval town is dominated by the remains of
the **Abbey** that William the Conqueror built in
1067 at the very spot where his troops defeated
Harold's army. Although Battle today consists
of little more than a winding high street filled
with tea shops, pubs and retired couples taking
their daily constitutionals, there's enough here
to while away a good few lazy hours. One of the
most pleasant walks is around the battlefield
itself, taking in the fourteenth-century **St
Mary's Church** and ending up at the
Chequers Inn on Lower Lake for a pint of the
local brew. Also worth a visit is **Battle
Museum of Local History**, a few minutes'
walk away from the Abbey and presided over
by an extremely talkative old man, who will
make you realise how remarkably little has
happened here in the 900-odd years since
William took over.

Around Battle

Close by are a range of villages in varying
degrees of cutesy-ness, many with Victorian
terraced houses filling tiny winding streets that
look like they haven't changed much since the

Battle Abbey. *See page 55*.

last war. Five miles north of Battle is the
village of **Salehurst**, worth a look at after
visiting the wonderfully medieval **Bodiam
Castle** or the fifteenth-century manor house of
Great Dixter. At the heart of the South
Downs is **Netherfield**, a couple of miles
north-west of Battle and home to a profusion of
foxes, deer and water birds. Much of the land
around this village is owned by the forestry
commission, and there are many public
bridleways to ensure that no irate farmers will
pepper your bottom with blunderbuss pellets.
A few miles further on, just off the A265 at
Burwash, is **Bateman's**, long-time home of
Rudyard Kipling.

Hastings

Hastings could not be more different. It was
once a Cinque Port (*see page 25* **That Cinque-
ing feeling**), providing the Crown with naval
craft before the Royal Navy existed, and then a

By train from London

The fastest trains from **Charing Cross**
(leaving approximately every half hour)
take around **1hr 10mins** to reach **Battle**
and **Hastings**. There are some
additional trains from Cannon Street.

smugglers' base in the early nineteenth century. The grand Victorian façades along the seafront, known as the **Stade** (old English for 'landing place'), suggest that Hastings was once the pride of the South-East, but it has long since fallen into decline and now feels like a poor man's Brighton. The pier is a case in point, being rather rundown and looking like it hasn't had a new lick of paint since mods and rockers last threw deckchairs at each other here.

Further along the seafront and half a dozen dilapidated amusement arcades later, the **Rock-a-Nore** area (thought to mean 'Rock of the North' or 'Black Rock', named after the nearby cliff) is more interesting. The beach is filled with enough go-kart tracks and dodgems to keep the kids happy, and the cluster of windowless fishermen's net huts that stand at the bottom of the East Hill cliff face give this section of the Stade its own charm. These wooden sheds, first built in 1834 to house fishing gear, were only allowed to occupy eight or nine square feet each, so as the fishermen bought more nets they built their sheds upwards, resulting in multi-storey huts of differing height, many leaning dramatically to one side. The steepest funicular railway in Britain traverses the cliff face, and on Rock-a-Nore Road you'll find the award-winning **Shipwreck Heritage Centre** (01424 437452; free but donations welcome), the **Sea Life Centre** (01424 718776; £5.50, £3.50 under-14s), the **Fishermen's Museum** (01424 461446; free) and local fishermen selling their catches from the black-painted net huts – a reminder that despite the tourist tat, the Stade is still a working beach. A miniature railway can take you back along the seafront towards the centre of town.

Hastings is famed for its cluster of antique shops in the Old Town, along George Street and the High Street. Here you will find all kinds of oddities, ranging from seventeenth-century sea chests to '60s furniture, at much lower prices than you would in London or Brighton. In Courthouse Mews the prices hit rock bottom, with little shacks selling second-hand records, military gear, and more often than not what looks like the contents of somebody's attic.

From George Street the West Hill Cliff Railway travels up to St Clement's Caves, home of the **Smugglers Adventure**. What is left of **Hastings Castle**, which William the Conqueror built soon after defeating the Saxons, is a short walk away. The **Hastings Museum & Art Gallery** (Cambridge Road; 01424 781155; free) is worth a look for its spectacular Durbar Hall, built for the Indian and Colonial Exhibition of 1886.

Where to stay

The best places to stay are situated in little villages outside Battle and Hastings. If you don't have a car, the **Abbey View** (01424 775513; double £50) in Battle is, logically enough, very close to the Abbey, and **Parkside House** (01424 433096; double £50) in Hastings is in a quiet residential area away from the tacky seafront.

Brakes Coppice Farm

Forewood Lane, Crowhurst, nr Battle, TN33 OSJ (01424 830347/fax 01424 830067).
Rates (B&B) *single occupancy* £35; *double/twin* £50.
Rooms (all en suite) 2 double; 1 twin.

No one could accuse this farmhouse B&B of slovenliness – even the glasses by the bedroom sinks are wrapped in cling film. This apparent fear of dirt results in rather characterless, though well-kept, rooms, and a slightly precious atmosphere. That said, the views are stunning, and the mile walk into Battle (said to have been used by the Saxon soldiers in 1066) is very pleasant. Non-smoking throughout.
From centre of Battle, 2 miles on A2100 towards Hastings; immediately after the end of the 40mph limit turn right towards Crowhurst; entrance to farm 1 mile on left.

Fox Hole Farm

Kane Hythe Road, Battle, TN33 9QU (01424 772053/fax 01424 773771).
Rates (B&B) *single occupancy* £39; *double* £49.
Rooms (all en suite) 3 double. **Cards** AmEx, MC, V.

One of the best mid-range guesthouses in the area. Paul and Pauline Collins run their converted eighteenth-century woodcutter's cottage with a relaxed charm, and the rooms feel like they belong in someone's home rather than a hotel. Hidden away at the end of a long dirt track, this is as secluded as it gets, with the only neighbours being foxes, deer, chickens, geese and moorhens. The Collins have a natural way with people, and the lazy dogs usually found slumbering by the hearth add to the down-home feel. Children and dogs are welcome.
Take first right on A271 W of Battle on to B2096. Farm is 0.75 miles on right.

Great Crouch's

Rushlake Green, Heathfield, TN21 9QD (01435 830145).
Rates (B&B) *double* £60; *suite* £75.
Rooms (both en suite) 1 double; 1 suite.

Rushlake Green is a corking little village and Ruth Thomas's friendly B&B in a listed building is an agreeable base for seeing the area. There are beams and antiques aplenty plus huge gardens to explore and the luxury of an indoor swimming pool.
Take B2096 from Heathfield to Battle; follow signs to Rushlake Green.

King John's Lodge

Sheepstreet Lane, Etchingham, TN19 7AZ (01580 819232/fax 01580 819562).
Rates (B&B) *double/twin* £60-£70.
Rooms (all en suite) 3 double; 1 twin.

The King John in question is the fourteenth-century French monarch and he didn't so much lodge here as

One of East Sussex's finest hotels: **Stone House** *in Rushlake Green.*

be kept prisoner – it gives an idea of the historical pedigree of this wonderful house. Almost every architectural style from medieval to Victorian is represented somewhere, and the garden is as much of a treat. As might be expected, the bedrooms vary immensely in size and shape but all are packed with beamy character. Kids are welcome (and one of the double bedrooms has an annexe for children – £20-£25 per child). All rooms are no smoking.

A21 Flimwell then B2087 to Ticehurst. In Ticehurst, take first left after church on to Sheep Street. King John's Lodge is about 1 mile along on right.

Little Hemingfold

Telham, Battle, TN33 OTT (01424 774338).
Rates (B&B) £38-£44pp. Special breaks.
Rooms (all en suite) 8 double; 4 twin; 1 four-poster.
Cards AmEx, DC, Debit, MC, V.

The setting, close to a trout lake within 40 acres of grounds, is lovely, as is the building, parts of which date back to the seventeenth century. Bedrooms are decorated fairly sparingly but some are of a good size and have log fires – you're unlikely to be spending too much time in them anyway with fine walks, fishing, rowing, tennis and other activities on tap. An excellent four-course dinner is available at £22.50. Children and dogs are welcome.

1.5 miles S of Battle on A2100; follow sign for hotel by sharp right road sign; Little Hemingfold is up short track.

Powdermills

Powdermill Lane, Battle, TN33 OSP (01424 75511/fax 01424 474540/powdc@aol.com/www.powdermills.co.uk).
Rates (B&B) *single* £70; *double/twin* £85-£115; *suite* £150. **Rooms** (all en suite) 7 twin; 14 double; 6 suites. **Cards** AmEx, DC, Debit, MC, V.

This grand eighteenth-century country house, once a gunpowder works, sits in well-maintained grounds backing on to those of Battle Abbey. Powdermills benefits from having owners who are keen antiques collectors and have decorated the house along traditional lines. The Wellington suite, where the famous Duke once stayed, is very impressive and ideal for a romantic weekend, with its sunken oyster bath and four-poster bed, but the garden rooms are more basic. Staff are very attentive without being overbearing. Children and dogs are welcome.

Powdermill Lane is opposite Battle rail station; Powdermills is 1 mile along on right.

Stone House

Rushlake Green, Heathfield, TN21 9QJ
(01435 830233/fax 01435 830726).
Rates (B&B) *double* £95-£127; *twin* £105-£127; *four-poster/suite* £150-£195. **Rooms** (all en suite) 4 double/twin; 2 four-poster; 1 suite.

The jewel in the crown of the East Sussex country hotels. The Dunn family, who have occupied this stately home for over five centuries, have changed little about it since opening it up as a hotel (first in 1984; the house was destroyed in the 1987 hurricane and rebuilt thereafter): oil portraits of family members line the walls; the Elizabethan staircase is still in use; televisions are hidden so as not to infringe on the period charm. Stone House feels far more relaxed than most hotels, with priceless antiques casually inhabiting corners of rooms, and a library, a billiards room and a thousand acres of private land at the guests' disposal. Dogs are welcome.

B2096 from Heathfield to Battle; take 4th turn on right to Rushlake Green. Take first left by village green (keep green on your right) to crossroads; signpost for house here.

Where to eat & drink

Battle itself isn't particularly good for eating out. **Blacksmith's** (43 High Street; 01424 773200) looks like a '70s throwback, with a half-timbered interior and somewhat pretentious-sounding dishes such as smoked ostrich with ripe melon and mussel vol-au-vents in dill sauce. The best of the tea shops is the **Pilgrims Rest** (1 High Street) opposite the Abbey.

On the other hand, there's no shortage of pubs scattered throughout the region. Along with the ones mentioned below, **Chequers Inn** (Lower Lake, Battle; 01424 772088) has trad country cooking and an intimate atmosphere, while the **Bell** on the High Street in Burwash (01435 882304) serves a good local ale and dishes such as ham off the bone, egg and chips and a seafood basket. There's a large fireplace and every inch of wall space is taken up by bizarre farming implements, pots and pans and clocks. **Jack Fuller's** at Robertsbridge (nr Brightling; 01424 838212) is more family-oriented, with a log fire, a garden terrace and very good steak and kidney puddings.

Mermaid Restaurant
2 Rock-a-Nore Road, Hastings (01424 438100).
Food served 7am-7.30pm daily.

On the seafront and facing the rows of black wooden fishermen's net huts, the tiny Mermaid has built itself a reputation as one of the best restaurants for fish and chips in Britain. It is an unassuming place, more of a café than a restaurant, and very good value – cod or plaice and chips is £3.85/£4.15; skate and chips is £4.75/£5.15. It lives up to its reputation, with crisp batter and briney, tender fish that couldn't be fresher.

Netherfield Arms
Netherfield Road, Netherfield, NW of Battle (01424 838282).
Food served noon-2pm, 6.30-9.30pm, Mon-Sat; noon-2pm Sun. **Cards** Debit, MC, V.

Fifteen minutes' stroll from Fox Hole Farm (*see page 52*) is this friendly pub-restaurant, which attracts a healthy mix of villagers and visitors who come here for good staple dishes and a laid-back atmosphere. The fish is local and very fresh, with lemon sole (£7.50), dover sole (£11.95) and salmon, prawn and scallop tartlets (£8.95) all served with salad or vegetables and chips or new potatoes. There is also a vegetarian menu and a good wine list.

The Orangery at Powdermills
Powdermill Lane, Battle (01424 775511).
Food served noon-2pm, 7-9pm, daily.
Set meals £22.50 (2 courses), £25.50 (3 courses).
Cards AmEx, DC, Debit, MC, V.

The restaurant of this country house hotel is smart but relaxed, with wicker chairs, white marble walls and a grand piano lending it a rather agreeable 1920s feel.

The set course dinner is excellent value and might offer crostini of local wood pigeon, breast of pheasant with savoy and chestnut ragoût for the main course, and blanc on neige (a meringue ball served with crème anglaise) and crystal redcurrants. Having the hotel's grounds at your disposal for an after-coffee walk round the lake is a real bonus.

Röser's
64 Eversfield Place, St Leonards on Sea, Hastings (01424 712218).
Food served noon-2pm, 7-10pm, Tue-Fri; 7-10pm Sat. **Set Meals** *lunch* £19.95 (3 courses); *dinner* (Tue-Fri) £22.95 (3 courses). **Cards** AmEx, DC, Debit, MC, V.

An unassuming façade and a small room with simple rows of banquette seating belie the quality of chef Gerald Röser's traditional French/European cooking – and the prices. Mains include roast guinea fowl with a confit of shallots and wild boar bacon (£18.95), and char-grilled fillet of sea bass Mediterranean-style (£19.50). The set meals are a more affordable way to sample food that is simultaneously refined yet free from pointless gimmickry.

Salehurst Halt
Church Lane, Salehurst, Robertsbridge (01580 880620/www.villagenet.co.uk).
Food served noon-3pm, 7-11pm, Tue-Sat; noon-3pm, 7-10.30pm, Sun. **Cards** Debit, MC, V.

The super-quaint village of Salehurst is home to this small, low-ceilinged, heavy-beamed country inn, which is frequented predominantly by locals who come here to sup the excellent real ales (including local brews) and robust, well-cooked dishes such as lemon sole with new potatoes and vegetables (£7.95) and steak and chips

The ruins of **Hastings Castle**, the first Norman castle in England. See page 56.

1066 and all that

The problems started in 1016, when the Saxon king **Ethelred** died, leaving his son **Edmund** on the throne. The marauding Dane **Cnut** took advantage of Edmund's tender years, defeated him in battle, proclaimed himself King of England, married Ethelred's widow and made an ally of the powerful Saxon leader **Godwin**. Meanwhile, Ethelred's surviving sons, Edward and Alfred, had fled to Normandy, where they were looked after by their cousin **Duke William**. In 1035 Cnut died, and in 1042 Ethelred's son **Edward** ('The Confessor') returned to England after 25 years of exile in Normandy to become king.

But the question of succession was raised once more, when it was clear that Edward's wife was never going to bear a child. To complicate matters, Godwin's son **Harold** visited Duke William of Normandy in 1064. Norman historians have since claimed that Harold went as ambassador to swear an oath confirming an earlier promise of the English Crown to William, but another explanation, and the one held by the artists of the Bayeux Tapestry, was that Harold fell into William's hands and was forced into swearing the oath.

In any event, on 5 January 1066 Edward died, and Harold was accepted as king by the English nobles. In September, the King of Norway attacked England, but was defeated by Harold's army at Stamford Bridge near York. Harold and his Saxons then had to march down to what is now East Sussex, knowing that Duke William would not be entirely happy about Harold's succession. They were right. William landed at Pevensey on 28 September 1066, and on the morning of 14 October the two armies met. By the afternoon, Harold fell on the spot marked by the high altar of Battle Abbey, and on Christmas Day 1066 William the Conqueror was proclaimed King of England in Westminster Abbey.

(£8.95). Despite an amiable atmosphere, service can be extremely haphazard – on a recent visit, staff seemed more concerned with chatting to their mates than looking after diners. Probably better just to come here for a drink after a visit to nearby Bodiam Castle (*see page 56*). Booking advisable.

Sundial

Gardner Street, Herstmonceux (01323 832217).
Food served noon-2.30pm, 7-9.30pm, Tue-Sat; noon-2.30pm Sun. **Set meals** *lunch* £15.50 (2 courses), £19.50 (3 courses); *dinner* £19.50 (2 courses), £27.50 (3 courses). **Cards** AmEx, DC, Debit, MC, V.
A very traditional village restaurant occupying a seventeenth-century auberge, which has been serving classic French cuisine with a strong emphasis on seafood for over 30 years. Starters include chevreuil (roe) pâté, stuffed mushrooms and stuffed mussels; mains include fried langoustines with tartar, poached Scotch salmon with lobster sauce, and fillet of sea bass with olive oil, lemon vinegar and carrot purée. The clientele are well-to-do and well heeled: a meal here is likely to come to around £50 a head.

What to see & do

Tourist information centres

88 High Street, **Battle**, TN33 OAQ (01424 773721/battletic@compuserve.com/www.battletown.co.uk).
Open *Apr-Oct* 10am-6pm daily; *Nov-Mar* 10am-4pm Mon-Sat; 10am-2pm Sun.

Queens Square, Priory Meadow, **Hastings**, TN34 ITL (01424 781111/hic_info@hastings.gov.uk/ www.hastings.gov.uk).
Open *Apr-Oct* 9.30am-6pm Mon-Sat; 10am-4.30pm Sun; *Nov-Mar* 9.30am-6pm daily.

Bike hire

Hastings Cycle Hire St Andrew's Market (01424 444013). A few minutes' walk from the station.

1066 Battle of Hastings – Battlefield & Abbey

High Street, Battle (01424 773792/www.english-heritage.org.uk).
Open *Apr-Sept* 10am-6pm, *Oct* 10am-5pm, *Nov-Mar* 10am-4pm, daily (last entry 1hr before closing).
Admission (EH) £4; £2 5s-16s; £3 OAPs, students; £10 family ticket.
This is where it all happened – here is the field that saw the epic battle between the Normans and the Saxons and the remains of the Abbey that William built soon after to mark his victory. English Heritage has done an excellent job with the site: the visitor is allowed to wander freely through the buildings and the grounds, and audio tours recall the events of 1066 from the perspective of a bitter Saxon foot soldier, a Norman officer or Harold's widow. In the gatehouse is an exhibition that documents the progress of the battle as well as the history of the Abbey since then, and there are all kinds of winding turrets and hidden rooms to explore that keep this from being merely an educational experience.

1066 Country Walk

Pevensey to Rye leg is 31 miles in total (Battle tourist info 01424 773721/www.1066country.com).

Duke William of Normandy and his army landed at Pevensey and marched to what is now Battle, and you can, too. Whether he continued all the way to Rye is debatable, but this country walk retraces William's route and takes in some of the most beautiful areas of the East Sussex Downs as well as marshlands that are host to herons, warblers, grebes, wagtails and other water birds. You will need an Ordnance Survey map, some stout boots and several days to undertake the entire journey; there are 17 pubs along the route and a number of guesthouses. Walkers can continue on to Bexhill or Hastings: phone the above number for details.

1066 Story in Hastings Castle

Castle Hill Road, West Hill, Hastings (01424 781112). **Open** *Apr-Sept* 10am-5pm, *Oct-Mar* 11am-3.30pm, daily. **Admission** £3; £1.95 5s-15s; £2.40 OAPs, students; £8.75 family.

A multimedia exploration of the events leading up to the big battle within the ruins of Britain's first Norman castle. There are also dungeons and 'whispering chambers' to explore.

Bateman's

Burwash (01435 882302).
Open 11am-5pm Mon-Wed, Sat, Sun (last entry 4.30pm). **Admission** (NT) £5; £2.50 5s-14s.

The family home of Rudyard Kipling has been maintained as it was in his day, even down to his 1928 Rolls-Royce in the garage. The gardens and the house are very beautiful, but this is a National Trust property, which means high admission charges, much of the house cordoned off with 'DO NOT TOUCH!' signs on everything, and old ladies in every room making sure that your tour of the house follows exactly the same pattern as everybody elses. Such an enquiring mind as Kipling's would surely have been outraged at such strictures.

Bodiam Castle

Bodiam, Robertsbridge (01580 830436/
www.nationaltrust.org.uk).
Open *mid-Feb-Oct* 10am-6pm/dusk daily;
Nov-mid-Feb 10am-4pm/dusk Sat, Sun (last entry 1hr before closing). **Admission** (NT) £3.60; £1.80 5s-15s; £9 family.

A fourteenth-century castle that looks as if it has risen out of the pages of Arthur Rackham's *Fairy Tales*, with its four round towers and ramparts reflected dramatically in the moat below. There is a museum charting the castle's history and beautiful grounds surrounding it set on the banks of the River Rother, but unfortunately your movements inside the castle are limited. Very popular with kids.

Great Dixter House & Gardens

Northiam (01797 252878).
Open 2-5pm Tue-Sun, bank hols. **Admission** £5 (£4 gardens only); £1.50 5s-16s (£1 gardens only).

The main part of this stunning late medieval house dates back to the fifteenth century, while the rest of the building is new by comparison. In 1911 the Lloyd family commissioned the soon-to-be-famous architect,

Short, sharp shock at **Smugglers Adventure**.

Edwin Lutyens, to enlarge the property. Using materials from derelict homes, Lutyens seamlessly blended the new house into the old. The gardens are magnificent, too, with unusual use of bold and some immaculate topiary.

Herstmonceux Castle

Herstmonceux, Hailsham (01323 834444/
www.seetb.org.uk/herstmonceux).
Open *Easter-Oct* 10am-6pm daily.
Admission *grounds* £3; £2 5s-14s; £2 OAPs; £8.50 family; *castle tours* £2.50; £1 5s-14s; £2.50 OAPs.

This fifteenth-century brick-built moated castle is now used as a study centre and a venue for numerous weddings and functions, and is only open to the public on guided tours (Sun-Fri), but the 500 acres of Elizabethan garden surrounding it are worth a visit in themselves. Open-air concerts with fireworks are held here in the summer; phone for details. Note that the castle is sometimes closed when weddings and conferences are held there: phone to check.

Sedlescombe Vineyards

Cripps Corner, Sedlescombe (01580 830715/
www.tor.co.uk/sedlescombe).
Open 10am-6pm daily. **Admission** £2.50; free under-16s; £1.50 students, OAPs.

Visitors can taste a range of English wines and fruity drinks at this vineyard, which proudly bills itself as 'England's premier organic vineyard'. There's also a nature trail. For other vineyards in the area, *see p43* **Grape expectations**.

Smugglers Adventure

St Clement's Caves, West Hill, Hastings (01424 422964).
Open *Easter-Sept* 10am-5.30pm, *Oct-Easter* 11am-4.30pm, daily. **Admission** £4.50; £2.95 5s-15s; £3.75 OAPs, students; £12.95 family.

A labyrinth of tunnels filled with menacing-looking smugglers, rotting corpses chained to walls, skeletons with daggers lodged between their ribs, and, on a rather different note, a tea shop.

The Ashdown Forest

Gardens galore, heavenly heathland and plenty of Pooh.

The arboreally challenged expanse of **Ashdown Forest**.

The massive sweep of gently rolling Wealden countryside, lying between the North and South Downs, spans four counties: Kent, Sussex, Surrey and Hampshire. (For more on the Kent Weald, *see page 44*). The Sussex portion is home to large towns such as Crawley, East Grinstead and Haywards Heath, which, with the arrival of the railways connecting London with the south coast, grew up from small rural villages to thriving market towns, and have now become major London commuter centres.

By train from London

Trains for **East Grinstead** leave **Victoria** about every half hour (journey time **52mins**). Trains to **Uckfield** leave **Victoria** and **London Bridge** every hour (journey time **1hr 30mins**). Trains to **Haywards Heath** leave from **Blackfriars**, **King's Cross**, **London Bridge** and **Victoria** about every quarter of an hour (journey time **45mins** to **1hr 10mins**).

But between these dull conurbations lie thousands of acres of prime countryside and hundreds of historic houses and lost-in-time villages. Yet, despite the windmills, trugs, gardens, heathland and cream teas, this part of the Weald is not a major visitor destination – all the better for a quiet weekend away.

When is a forest not a forest?

The main draw in this part of the Weald is the **Ashdown Forest**, a relatively unknown and hence unspoiled area of ancient heathland. Once part of one of the largest areas of forest in England (it was said that a squirrel could travel from tree to tree from one end to the other), medieval deforestation has transformed this into the largest area of heathland in the South-East. It stretches over 6,000 acres, broken up by the odd wooded valley and copse, and offers countless miles of gorse-lined walks. Cycling and horse-riding are also popular. The Forest itself does not have an identifiable centre, although the **Ashdown Forest Centre** near Wych Cross is a good place to start.

Pooh's company

One of the main magnets for nostalgic visitors are the parts of the Forest around **Gill's Lap**, immortalised by AA Milne in his *Winnie the Pooh* stories. Most of the Pooh tourist traffic is centred on the shops of **Hartfield** – it seems people are keener to stock up on Pooh knick-knacks than visit the Forest locations themselves, although **Poohsticks Bridge** is a major exception. (*See page 59* **Pooh country**.)

Nutley Windmill (off the A22) is a far less commercial destination, located in a quiet part of the Forest where sheep graze by the roadside. Another more restful site is the **Airman's Grave**, a memorial marking the spot where a Wellington bomber crashed on its return from a bombing raid to Cologne in 1941. The grave is about a mile south of the village of Marlpits, which is on Danehill Road west of the B2026 just north of Duddleswell.

For children, the **Ashdown Llama Farm** is definitely worth a visit, and the **Bluebell Railway**, which runs from Sheffield Park to East Grinstead, will appeal to little boys of all ages. Even if you are not into trains, the views of the countryside are well worth the fare.

Smugglers' blues

Many of the surrounding villages breathe their history. The former Tiger Inn (now Church House), a meeting place for the old church next door) in the cute village of **Lindfield**, just outside Haywards Heath, once played host to smugglers, who would sail their contraband up the River Ouse from the Cuckmere Valley to hide it in false graves in the neighbouring churchyard. The village is now better known for its coffee houses and antique shops. A few miles north of Lindfield, the nearby village of **Ardingly** (pronounced 'Arding-lie') is the home of the South of England showground, which hosts events throughout the year. Ardingly is also the closest village to **Wakehurst Place** (*see page 61*), one of many houses and gardens in the area open to the public.

The grand **Gravetye Manor**. See page 60.

Where to stay

Accommodation varies from a small selection of expensive hotels, to a plethora of bed and breakfasts, with not a lot in-between. In addition to the places listed below, **Ockenden Manor** in Cuckfield (01444 416111; £120 double) and **Gravetye Manor** near East Grinstead, an Elizabethan house set in vast gardens (01342 810567; £175-£270 double; *see also page 60*), are both luxurious choices if money is no object. Both also have notable restaurants. If, on the other hand, cash is a very large object, a couple of additional suggestions are **Stairs Farmhouse** (01892 770793; £45 double) and **Bolebroke Mill** (01892 770425; £59 double), both in Hartfield.

Ashdown Park Hotel

Wych Cross, Forest Row, RH18 5JR (01342 824988/ fax 01342 826206/reservations@ashdownpark.co.uk/ www.ashdownpark.co.uk).
Rates (B&B) *single* £115-£285; *double/twin* £145-£305. **Rooms** (all en suite) 8 single; 87 double/twin.
Cards AmEx, DC, Debit, MC, V.

A Victorian mansion set in 186 acres of landscaped gardens right in the middle of the Forest, Ashdown Park is one of the area's most formal places to stay – no jeans in the public rooms after 7pm – but if you want to spoil yourself, this is definitely the place to come. Service is excellent, and the hotel is particularly noted for its restaurant, the Anderida. Prices start at £33 per head for dinner, but £60 is more of a typical average. The facilities – indoor swimming pool and fitness rooms, health and beauty clinic, golf course, putting green, squash and tennis courts – are top drawer, and the grounds themselves worthy of a leisurely exploration. Children welcome.
A22 S through East Grinstead; turn left at Wych Cross traffic lights; Ashdown Park on right after 0.75 miles.

Birch Hotel

Lewes Road, Haywards Heath, RH17 7SF (01444 451565/fax 01444 440109).
Rates (B&B) *single* £75-£80; *double* £113; *family room* £123-£133. **Rooms** (all en suite) 9 single; 10 twin; 29 double; 3 family.
Cards AmEx, Debit, MC, V.

A medium-size country house hotel, the Birch is on the very edge of Haywards Heath, within easy reach of the A23 and all the area's attractions. The hotel caters mainly for the mid-week business traveller, and is fairly quiet at the weekend. Although the Birch has its own restaurant, it is less than two miles away from the Broadway, where most of the town's eating places are located. For a great pub meal and local Sussex beers, try the nearby **Snowdrop Inn** down Snowdrop Lane (01444 412259), one of the narrow country lanes connecting Haywards Heath with the beautiful village of Lindfield. Children welcome in the hotel. Non-smoking rooms available. There is also a twin-bedded room for disabled guests.
A272 S through Haywards Heath; follow signs for Princess Royal Hospital; Birch Hotel is behind Shell garage.

Sussex & Surrey

Pooh country

'*They walked on, thinking of This and That, and by-and-by they came to an enchanted place on the very top of the Forest called Galleon's Lap – Sitting there they could see the whole world spread out until it reached the sky, and whatever there was all the world over was with them in Galleon's Lap.*'

(The House at Pooh Corner *by AA Milne*)

If you think Winnie the Pooh was invented by a Disney cartoonist and lives in a wood somewhere near Hollywood, give yourself a slap on the wrist and get yourself over to Hundred Acre Wood in the heart of the Ashdown Forest. Written for his son Christopher Robin, AA Milne wrote the Pooh stories during the 1920s while at the family's holiday home, just north of the Forest. All the places familiar to us in the stories – **Galleon's Lap**, the

Enchanted Place, **North Pole** and **Roo's Sandypit** – are within easy walking distance of **Gill's Lap** car park, one of the highest points on the Forest, just off the B2026 (on an un-numbered road towards Coleman's Hatch). A memorial stone and plaque to AA Milne and EH Shephard, illustrator of the stories and poems, is a short walk from the car park along the ridge.

Further north, between Marsh Green and Chuck Hatch, is **Poohsticks Bridge**, a popular pilgrimage destination for Pooh fans. The bridge itself is less magical than you would expect, and is usually crowded, but the fairly lengthy walk through the woods from the car park is pleasant enough. If you want to play Poohsticks, pick up sticks along the way. If you wait until you reach the bridge, you will find it difficult to find sticks, other than those already thrown that now form a massive dam across the stream! The car park for Poohsticks Bridge can be difficult to find, so make a visit first to **Pooh Corner** in **Hartfield**. Pooh Corner is a 300-year-old, low-ceilinged shop where Christopher Robin used to go shopping with his nanny. Now packed with (Disney-esque) 'Pooh-phernalia' and an inordinate number of tourists, the shop displays clear directions to the bridge and provides free local maps. It's open 9am-5pm Mon-Sat; 1.30-5pm Sun, bank hols.

Copyhold Hollow

Copyhold Hollow, Copyhold Lane, Borde Hill, Haywards Heath, RH16 1XU (01444 413265).
Rates (B&B) *single* £30; *twin* £50; *double* £55.
Rooms (all en suite) 1 single; 1 twin; 1 double.
Copyhold Hollow is a sixteenth-century cottage with an idyllic country garden set in a beautiful wooded hollow,

carpeted with thousands of bluebells in springtime. There are exposed beams and low ceilings throughout the house, and a huge inglenook fireplace in the private lounge, where the owner Frances Druce encourages her guests to relax and make themselves at home. And that's what Copyhold Hollow is: an extremely relaxed and welcoming home, which just happens to take in guests.

Dinner is available at an additional £12 per person for two courses. Copyhold Hollow is not licensed, so feel free to bring your own drink. Children and dogs are welcome. All bedrooms are non-smoking.

M23/A23 S; after Crawley, follow signs to Cuckfield, then to Borde Hill Gardens; take first right signposted Ardingly.

Griffin Inn `Offer`

Fletching, nr Uckfield, TN22 3SS (01825 722890/fax 01825 722810).

Rates (B&B) *single occupancy* £55-£70; *twin* £70-£85; *four-poster* £75-£85. **Rooms** (all en suite) 1 twin; 7 four-poster. **Cards** AmEx, Debit, MC, V.

If you're after a bit of peace and quiet, go to Fletching. This tiny village is a short drive away from most of the Forest's attractions, and boasts two cosy and welcoming pubs, but not a lot else. The Griffin has eight rooms, four above the pub, and four in the adjoining coach house. Eat either at the Griffin, or at the neighbouring Rose and Crown (01825 722039), both of which serve a good selection of bar and restaurant food. Children and dogs are welcome. Non-smoking rooms are available. In summer, weather permitting, the Griffin does a spit roast on the lawn and, on Sundays, live jazz on the terrace.

A22 to Nutley; then follow signs to Fletching.

Hooke Hall

250 High Street, Uckfield, TN22 1EN (01825 761578/fax 01825 768025).

Rates *double* £65-£85; *single occupancy (Mon-Thur only)* £50-£55; *suite* £105 & £120; *single occupancy (Mon-Thur only)* £85-£95. Breakfast £7.50 (Eng); £5.50 (Cont). **Rooms** (all en suite) 8 double; 2 suites. **Cards** AmEx, MC, V.

On entering Hooke Hall, you'd be forgiven for thinking you'd walked into someone's home – you have. Recently restored by its owners, this Queen Anne townhouse has an extremely relaxed and homely atmosphere. Guests are free to help themselves to the honesty bar in the lounge. Refreshingly or naively, depending on your viewpoint, there are no room keys – guests are given a code to open the front door. The rooms on the first floor (all named after famous lovers!) are large and airy, while the (boringly, numbered) rooms tucked away under the eaves are much smaller. Disappointingly, the Italian restaurant for which the hotel became noted has closed, and the only option is to wander down the High Street in search of a place to eat. But don't worry, the owners are more than happy to help you find somewhere. Children welcome.

Where to eat & drink

Eating out in and around the Ashdown Forest means either an expensive meal at a top hotel or restaurant, or relaxing in the cosy surroundings of a pub or tearoom. After a day walking in the Forest, a meal with a pint of the local brew in a rural country pub is highly recommended, but be warned that most pubs stop serving food fairly early in the evening. For a wider choice of restaurants, your best bet is to drive out of the Forest into one of the many small towns in the surrounding area. Although hardly picturesque, the Broadway in Haywards Heath is lined with many restaurants, from small independent bistros, to the usual chains such as Café Rouge.

Barnsgate Manor Vineyard

Herons Ghyll, nr Uckfield (01825 713366).

Open *tearoom, vineyard & shop* 10am-5pm daily. **Food served** *restaurant* noon-2.30pm daily. **Cards** Debit, MC, V.

Surrounded by fields of grapevines and woodland, Barnsgate Manor and its collection of converted barns and outhouses has a view over the Forest that stretches for miles. Sit outside on the patio, or in the old manor house, and choose either from the tearoom or restaurant menu, both of which offer a good choice of standard English fare. Prices start at around a fiver for a baked potato with various fillings, plenty of salad and bread. While you're there, indulge in a glass or two of the white wines made at the vineyard, or buy a few bottles from the wine and gift shop. The apple wine is also well worth tasting. After all that wine, if you see a llama, don't worry, you're not hallucinating. It's just a visitor from the owners' main herd from the nearby Ashdown Llama Farm.

Duddleswell Tea Rooms

Duddleswell, Fairwarp (01825 712126).

Open *Feb-Nov* 10am-5pm Tue-Sun, bank hols.

A twee roadside cottage in the middle of the Forest, with tables spilling out on to the grass in front. Lunch is served noon-2pm, with the teacakes, scones and cream teas available all day. Cakes are not a strong point, but this tearoom is well known for its 'naughty puddings', which cost a reasonable £2.30. A cream tea will set you back around £3.90.

Gravetye Manor

Vowels Lane, East Grinstead (01342 810567/fax 01342 810080/gravetye@relaischateaux.fr)

Food served 12.30-1.45pm, 7-9.30pm, Mon-Sat; 12.30-1.45pm, 7-9pm, Sun. **Cards** Debit, MC, V.

An Elizabethan country house hotel set in vast woodlands, Gravetye Manor has a reputation for its highly polished service, excellent food and well-stocked wine cellar (over 400 wines). At around £40 for dinner, excluding wine, it's not cheap, but as a member of the independent French hotel consortium, Relais et Châteaux, it comes highly recommended. The menu offers a mix of British and French cuisine, utilising herbs and vegetables grown in the hotel's gardens. The hotel also smokes its own salmon and uses water from its own spring. Gravetye is between Turner's Hill and West Hoathly.

Hatch Inn

Coleman's Hatch, nr Hartfield (01342 822363).

Food served noon-2.30pm Mon, Sun; noon-2.30pm, 7.30-9.15pm, Tue-Sat. **Cards** Debit, MC, V.

A picturesque inn dating back to 1430, not far from Hartfield and Winnie the Pooh country. Reputed to be an old smugglers' haunt, the pub is small and dark on the inside. Even in summer, candles are used to light the rooms. Outside, there are two lovely gardens with vistas on to the Forest. Food is inventive and varied (example dishes include chicken and mango salad with honey

In an English country garden

Sussex is a garden lover's paradise. The quality of the soil and temperate year-round climate make the county an ideal location for growing certain species of trees, plants and flowers that would be difficult to cultivate elsewhere in Britain. As a result, the area boasts a remarkable number of grand houses and impressively stocked gardens.

One of the most spectacular places to view exotic redwoods, Japanese maples and orchids is **Wakehurst Place** near Ardingly, an outpost of the Royal Botanic Gardens at Kew. Home to the National Lottery-funded Millennium Seedbank, Wakehurst Place is an imposing Elizabethan mansion set in 170 acres of grounds, which includes walks through rough valley terrain, to more gentle ornamental gardens and lakes. Wakehurst is one of several National Trust properties in the area. Others include **Nymans** at Handcross and **Sheffield Park** near Uckfield, both home to acres of beautiful gardens and woodland containing foreign and native plants, shrubs and trees. Sheffield Park's Capability Brown-designed gardens, based around a series of landscaped ponds, are particularly impressive during spring when its rhododendron collection is in full bloom. Nymans is the work of designer Ludwig Messel; its highlight is probably its wonderful walled garden.

Borde Hill (near Haywards Heath) is also well known for its rhododendrons, camellias and magnolias, and has a classic English rose garden. Borde Hill also puts on a number of events throughout the year, including horse trials, classical and popular music concerts, plays and family events. Last but not least, **Leonardslee** at Lower Beeding has been described as the most beautiful garden in Europe. It offers miles of walks through steep wooded valleys, gentle lakeland and sloping banks of brightly coloured azaleas. Wallabies live in semi-captivity in part of the garden, and deer roam the parks. There is also an excellent collection of bonsai trees that will have you itching to get your hands on a pair of clippers.

*Blazing flowerbeds at **Leonardslee**.*

Borde Hill Gardens Balcombe Road, Haywards Heath (01444 450326/www.bordehill.co.uk). **Open** *Mar-Oct* 10am-6pm, *Oct-Apr* 10am-dusk, daily. **Admission** £4; £1.50 3s-16s; £10 family.

Leonardslee Gardens Lower Beeding, nr Horsham (01403 891212/www.rhododendrons.com). **Open** *Apr-Oct* 9.30am-6pm daily. **Admission** phone for details.

Nymans Garden Handcross, nr Haywards Heath (01444 400321). **Open** *Mar-Oct* 11am-6pm/sunset Wed-Sun; *Nov-Mar* 11am-4pm Sat, Sun. **Admission** (NT) £2.50-£5; £1.25-£2.50 5s-18s (depending on season).

Sheffield Park Garden Sheffield Park (01825 790231). **Open** *Jan, Feb* 10.30am-4pm Sat, Sun; *Mar-Oct* 10.30am-6pm Tue-Sun; *Nov, Dec* 10.30am-4pm Tue-Sun. Last entry 1hr before closing/dusk. **Admission** (NT) £4.20; £2.10 5s-17s; £10.50 family.

Wakehurst Place Ardingly (01444 894066). **Open** *Feb* 10am-5pm, *Mar, Oct* 10am-6pm, *Apr-Sept* 10am-7pm, *Nov-Jan* 10am-4pm, daily. **Admission** (NT) £5; £2.50 5s-16s; £3.50 OAPs, students.

mustard dressing, £8.25, and char-grilled Thai salmon on a bed of red chard and baby spinach, £14.95), but has become something of a victim of its own success: be prepared to wait up to an hour to eat on busy days. Owner Nick Drillsma recommends you book in advance for all evening food and to arrive before 12.30pm for Sunday lunch. But don't be put off by the crowds – it's well worth a visit.

Newick Village Tandoori

7-9 Church Road, Newick (01825 723738).
Food served noon-2.30pm, 6-11pm, Mon-Thur, Sun; noon-2.30pm, 6-11.30pm, Fri, Sat.
Cards AmEx, DC, Debit, MC, V.

One of the best places in the area for a curry. Prices start at around £5 for a main course, and the portions are usually big enough for two. Though it's big, it's extremely popular with the locals, so it's best to book at weekends.

Stairs Farmhouse

High Street, Hartfield (01892 770793).
Food served 10.30am-5.30pm Mon, Wed-Sun.
Cards Debit, MC, V.

Once you've fought your way out of the crowds at Pooh Corner, cross over the road to refuel at seventeenth-century Stairs Farmhouse. Portions are huge, and use local produce where possible. Try the Pooh Bear Cream Tea at £3.95 – a feast for bears who like honey. This is also a great place for a traditional, slap-up Sunday lunch (£5.95-£6.95) – and a very popular one, so you're advised to book. Stairs also has a farm shop that sells a variety of local produce, including wine, honey, cheeses and meats. Bed and breakfast is available in the farmhouse (*see p58*).

see p58

What to see & do

Tourist information centres

There are 48 tourist information offices in Kent and East and West Sussex, but, surprisingly, none of them is located in or very close to the Ashdown Forest. The nearest offices are in **Burgess Hill** (01444 247726), **Lewes** (01273 483448) and **Tunbridge Wells** (01892 515675). If you're looking for additional accommodation not listed in this guide, call up before you set out or have a look at the website: www.sussex-countrytourism.co.uk.

Bike hire

Future Cycles Friends Yard, London Road, Forest Row (01342 822847). Two miles from East Grinstead station.

Ashdown Forest Centre

Wych Cross, Forest Row (01342 823583).
Open *Oct-Mar* 11am-5pm Sat, Sun, bank hols; *Apr-Sept* 2-5pm Mon-Fri.

A great place to start if you want to find out about walks in the Forest – a number of guidebooks and pamphlets are on sale. The centre also displays information on the Forest's history, its flora and fauna, and conservation efforts. There is also an art gallery displaying the work of local artists.

Ashdown Llama Farm

Wych Cross, nr Forest Row (01825 712040).
Open *Apr-Sept* 11am-5pm Tue-Sun, bank hols; *Oct-Mar* 11am-4pm Sat, Sun. **Admission** £2.50; £2.25 3s-16s, OAPs.

If you've got kids, the llama farm is a great place to visit. If you haven't, once you've seen one llama, you've seen them all. The 'World of Wool' museum is fairly interesting, but the walk around the eighteenth-century barns and fields is likely to appeal more to the younger generation. The llamas and alpacas are not particularly sociable animals – the angora and cashmere goats are far friendlier. The farm also has a play park and gift shop, with self-serve tearoom.

Bluebell Railway

Sheffield Park Station, on A275 between Lewes & East Grinstead (01825 723777/talking timetable 01825 722370/www.visitweb.com/bluebell).
Operates *May-Sept* daily; *Oct-Apr* Sat, Sun, school hols, bank hols. **Tickets** £7.40; £3.75 3s-15s; £6 OAPs; £19.90 family.

Not just for trainspotters, the Bluebell Railway is a delightful retro trip to the days of steam. The line runs for nine miles from Sheffield Park via Horsted Keynes (pronounced 'kanes') to Kingscote, where a bus service connects you to the Connex South Central station at East Grinstead while the rail link is being extended (work isn't due to end before 2001). Each station has been restored and takes you through the ages of steam from Victorian days to the 1930s and finally in to the 1950s. There are two museums, and a permanent locomotive collection. Special events run throughout the year, such as a Thomas the Tank Engine weekend for children in June, plus a Santa Special at Christmas. If you've secretly harboured trainspotting tendencies, come out of the closet and sign up for a course on how to fire and drive a steam engine (phone 0181 656 9376 for details).

Nutley Windmill

Crowborough Road, nr Nutley (01435 873367).
Open *Easter-Sept* 2.30-5.30pm last Sun of month.
Admission free.

Nutley Windmill is the oldest working trestle post windmill in Sussex. Park in the car park a third of a mile up the road past the windmill, then walk back. The windmill itself isn't often open, but you can get a good view of it at any time. The car park at Friend's Clump is also a great starting point for walks over the Forest and a good place for a picnic. As you'd expect, this part of the Forest is quite elevated, so there are great views.

Priest House

North Lane, West Hoathly (01342 810479).
Open *Mar-Oct* 11am-5.30pm Mon-Sat; 2-5.30pm Sun.
Admission *house & garden* £2.30; £1.10 5s-15s; £2.10 OAPs; *garden only* £1.

This lovely fifteenth-century timber-framed farmhouse and traditional English country garden in a quiet village seems lost in time. The beamed rooms have housed a museum since the beginning of the century, and display a collection of seventeenth- and eighteenth-century furniture, needlework and household items. Rather quiet, but interesting if you're into that kind of thing.

Lewes & around

In contrast to nearby big, brash Brighton, Lewes offers a quieter escape, with plenty to interest literature lovers.

Lewes, the county town of East Sussex, sits just east of Brighton, nestled between the hills and chalk cliffs of the South Downs where the River Ouse is crossed by an ancient east-west land route. Due to the area's close proximity to Normandy, William the Conqueror divided his Sussex estates among his most trusted lieutenants. The lands around Lewes were granted to William de Warenne who, with his wife Gundrada, constructed the Castle and the Priory of St Pancras, which has since been demolished.

Lewes remains steeped in history, parts of it virtually untouched since medieval and Tudor times. Like all old towns, its buildings are constructed from an amalgamation of features from the local landscape: no stone, but English oak, clay, chalk and flint. Its focal points are its steep **high street**, with its speciality shops, and **castle**. The Saxons founded the town, calling it 'Hlaew' or hill, and the high street

By train from London

Direct trains from **Victoria** to **Lewes** leave approximately every half hour and the journey takes just over **1hr**.

follows one of their cross-country trading routes. Today, this is where many of Lewes's most impressive original timber-framed buildings can be seen.

You can spot the town's mix of architectural styles by the lines of uneven rooftops: cranky, bent timber-framed buildings of the fifteenth century, some with original fronts, others with Georgian façades, sit alongside great Georgian townhouses. Despite its attractiveness, Lewes is not a particularly touristy town, other than during the opera season (May-August; for details phone 01273 812321) at nearby Glyndebourne. Residents are proud of their

*The approach to the **Barbican House Museum** and **Lewes Castle**. See page 68.*

heritage and keen to keep their town as much of a secret as possible. Other festivals in Lewes include the imaginatively named Lewes Festival, and Artwave; for details of both phone the local tourist information office.

Downs but not out

Surrounding Lewes is surprisingly varied countryside. In addition to the nearby attractions of Brighton and the coast, there's forest, farmland, great walking on the South Downs and charming villages, sleepy, peaceful, and proud of their flint buildings and churches.

Most of the main draws near Lewes lie between the A27 and the sea, east of the town. One of the oldest (founded in Saxon times) and prettiest of the local villages is **Alfriston**, a once-important river port and market town and, in the eighteenth century, a centre of smuggling. Well preserved, today it's a maze of narrow streets and cottages, and home to the Clergy House (a fourteenth-century timber-framed house), and a beautiful church, St Andrew's, commonly known as the 'Cathedral of the Downs'.

Nearby is **Wilmington**, worth a visit if only to see the 226-foot-high 'geoglyph' of a man carrying a staff in each hand – the Long Man of Wilmington – carved into Windover Hill's chalky side. Its origins are a mystery; no one knows who created it or why or when, but theories suggest it is a figure of a pilgrim, a

*Lewes's quirkiest accommodation: **Millers**.*

Saxon chieftain or even the 'Midsummer Man' of pagan folklore. A quarter mile-long footpath leads up to the site. The smaller village of **Firle**, a few miles north-west, offers stunning views from the top of Firle Beacon – at 712 feet, it's one of the eastern South Downs' highest points.

The area around Lewes is also Bloomsbury Group territory, with **Monk's House** south of Lewes, and, a couple of miles east of the town, **Charleston** farmhouse (*see page 67* **The Bloomsbury bunch**). Of greater appeal to kids will be the long-serving but still fresh **Drusillas Zoo Park**, a little further east.

It's also worth travelling down to **Beachy Head** (three miles west of Eastbourne – the town itself is an unexciting place), an imposing white chalk cliff (over 500-foot drop) that marks the eastern end of the South Downs. It's a great place for a picnic, to fly a kite or do a spot of hang-gliding, and the views are magnificent: looking to the east you can see as far as Dungeness, to the west, Selsey Bill and the Isle of Wight. To shippers the coastline was once known as the 'Devil's Cape' and to this day the lighthouse acts as a deterrent to warn ships from coming too close to the coastline.

Where to stay

Crossways

Lewes Road, Wilmington, nr Polegate, BN26 5SG (01323 482455/fax 01323 487811/ crossways@fastnet.co.uk).
Rates (B&B) *single* £48; *double/twin* £72-£76.
Rooms (all en suite) 2 single; 3 double; 2 twin.
Cards Debit, MC, V.

Though situated on the busy A27, Crossways makes a well-priced, double-glazed pit stop within easy reach of Lewes and most of the area's attractions, including the South Downs Way. Rooms are decorated in unassuming colours with comfortable beds and the usual facilities (mini-fridge with fresh milk, TV, hairdryer), with little details like homely mugs on the tea tray and pot pourri that make for a country feel. The restaurant is open for dinner and offers good-quality, substantial food made with local ingredients. In warmer months, guests can enjoy gazing at the duckpond and the frolicking rabbits in the garden.
On A27, 2 miles W of Polegate.

Millers

134 High Street, Lewes, BN7 1XS (01273 475631/ fax 01273 486226/millers134@aol.com).
Rates (B&B) *single occupancy* £47; *double* £52.
Rooms (both en suite) 2 double.

You wouldn't know of the exceptional interior of this discreet B&B by looking at its standard Georgian façade; being greeted by the charming hosts Teré and Tony Tammar and ushered into Millers is like entering another world. The building is actually sixteenth-century, but the most striking feature is the beautiful pine panelling of the hall and dining room. It's a family house, with only two double bedrooms for visitors: the Rose room, decked out with Victorian furniture and a mahogany four-poster, and the Studio, originally the workroom of 'The Ladies of Millers', two artists who lived in the house and had a close affiliation to the Bloomsbury Group – its shower-room is reputed to have once been a priest hole (where priests would hide during the reign of Elizabeth I because of Catholic persecution). Breakfast is a treat: fresh strawberries and cereal served before a perfectly cooked fry-up. Not appropriate for children. No smoking throughout.

Old Parsonage
Westdean, nr Seaford, BN25 4AL (tel/fax 01323 870432/raymond.woodhams@virgin.net).
Rates (B&B) *double* £55-£65; *four-poster* £70.
Rooms (all en suite) 2 double; 1 four-poster.
A beautifully preserved medieval house (built by monks in 1280) with thick stone walls, mullioned windows, oak beams and stone fireplaces. There are only three bedrooms for guests: the four-poster Old Hall, the Solar and the Middle Room. Owners Raymond and Angela Woodham have gone to great lengths to make guests comfortable with little details like fresh flowers and biscuits in each room and home-made jams and fruit from

the garden for breakfast. All rooms have a private bathroom, and one is reached down a spiral stone staircase. No smoking throughout.
Off A259, about 1 mile E of Seaford.

Shelleys
137 High Street, Lewes, BN7 1XS (01273 472361/ fax 01273 483152).
Rates (B&B) *single* £56-£167.50; *double/twin* £116- £245. **Rooms** (all en suite) 1 single; 18 double/twin.
Cards AmEx, DC, Debit, MC, V.
Former home of the Earl of Dorset and members of the literary Shelley family, this building dates in part from the sixteenth century, when it started life as an inn. The façade, which could do with a lick of paint, belies the treasure-filled interior. The large hall is decked out with fine antiques, and the rooms are large and true to their age, with crooked ceilings and wood panelling. Some rooms have walk-in wardrobes, while bathrooms are tiled from head to foot in stark blue and white. Being part of the Thistle group, the hotel does have a chain feel to it, but thankfully this doesn't override its old-style charm. Staff are professional and the food is among the best to be found in Lewes. Children and dogs welcome. Non-smoking rooms available.

All fired up

Perhaps one of the biggest surprises for the visitor to Lewes is that this peaceful heritage town is also home to the largest and liveliest Bonfire Night celebrations in Britain. Back in 1605 when the gunpowder plot against Protestant King James I was foiled, it seems staunchly Protestant Lewes celebrated the news with great enthusiasm.

Over the years to follow, Bonfire Night, declared a public holiday, became a grand and anarchic event with the Lewes Bonfire Boys, as they came to be known, dragging or rolling barrels of blazing tar through the streets, letting off fireworks indiscriminately and burning effigies of Guy Fawkes and the Pope.

Things came to a head before the festivities in 1847 when Lord Chichester read the revellers the Riot Act from the steps of the county hall, backed up by 100 bobbies from London. Many were injured in the subsequent fighting but order finally prevailed. Thereafter, the celebrations became more restrained, with the formation, in 1853, of the first two bonfire societies, from which the modern day event has evolved. The societies still paraded effigies of Fawkes and the Pope in torchlit processions

through the town, to be tossed on bonfires, but each had its own marching route and bonfire location. Opposition from some townsfolk towards the event led to the creation of a county council sub-committee charged with regulating the event. Bonfires, previously built within the town streets, were moved to the outskirts.

In the last 100 years the night has evolved into a spectacular pageant, with the anti-papist sentiments reduced to a historic role. Proof of this came when the Reverend Ian Paisley arrived one 5th November to try to make political hay but was sent packing.

Today, six societies march and hold firework displays at their respective bonfires. Prayers are said, wreaths laid and the Last Post played at the war memorial atop School Hill, in memory of the bonfire boys who died in the two world wars. Cliffe Society holds a race with two teams competing to drag a blazing tar barrel around the town. The once-charged and wild atmosphere is today more regulated and subdued but still a colourful and exciting reminder of the days when religious bigotry was a part of everyday life.

Stone Cross Farm

Laughton, nr Lewes, BN8 6BN (tel/fax 01323 811500/ mobritain@aol.com).
Rates (B&B) *twin* £40. **Rooms** 2 twin.

This family-run converted Tudor barn and farm, complete with horses, dogs, chickens and ducks, makes an ideal stop if you're on your way to Glyndebourne (a couple of miles away). There are no en suite facilities but a guest bathroom and dressing gowns are supplied. Though Stone Cross is an active family house, owner Julia Fenton is keen to promote a relaxed feel. The farmhouse breakfast consists of cereals and a full fry-up. Children welcome. No smoking throughout.

S side of B2124 about 0.5 miles E of Laughton at a minor crossroads; entrance is under a line of horse chestnut trees.

White Lodge

Sloe Lane, Alfriston, BN26 5UR (01323 870265/fax 01323 870284/www.scoot.co.uk/white.lodge.ho).
Rates (B&B) *single* £50; *single occupancy* £80-£100; *double/twin/family* £100-£130; *four-poster* £110; *suite* £146. Special breaks. **Rooms** (all en suite) 3 single; 11 double/twin; 2 four-poster; 1 suite.
Cards AmEx, DC, Debit, MC, V.

Set in five acres of land, this country hotel is a great out-of-town retreat but within easy access of the lovely village of Alfriston. It's a quirky place with somewhat dated flocked wallpaper (its conversion was in 1983) and a combination of individually decorated rooms, all with en suite facilities. Choose a room at the front overlooking a grand patio and stairwell leading to the garden. The restaurant offers a set menu at £18.95, with the likes of seafood ragoût served with a lime and herb sauce, and a choice of home-made desserts and cheeses. Children and dogs welcome. Non-smoking rooms available.

From A27 turn S at roundabout on to B2108; after 1.5 miles hotel sign on right; 250m past sign take sharp right into narrow lane.

Where to eat & drink

There's a decent range of places to eat in the area, from swanky hotel dining rooms (such as **Shelleys**, *see page 65*), to modern restaurants, to upmarket pubs. In addition to the places listed below, the **Pugin Restaurant** at Horsted Place Hotel, Little Horsted (01825 750581), serves up excellent global-influenced cuisine in posh surroundings, and bow-fronted **Quincy's** in Seaford's old town (01323 895490) offers interesting, accomplished dishes such as roast saddle of venison with mushrooms, bacon and a red wine sauce (two courses £21; three courses £25.50).

Of the local pubs, basic grub and good drinking can also be had at a gaggle of places within a few miles of each other: the **Lamb Inn** at Ripe and the characterful **Six Bells** in Chiddingly, both north of the A27; and, south of the A27, **Rose Cottage** in Alciston, the **Tiger Inn** in East Dean, the no-frills **Ram Inn** at Firle with its large garden, and the **Cricketers**

Arms in Berwick, which also has a lovely garden. Other top-notch drinking holes include the trendy **Snowdrop Inn** on South Street, Lewes, which stands on the spot where an avalanche killed eight people on Christmas Day, 1836, and the **Anchor** at Barcombe, a few miles north of Lewes.

Badger's Tea Room

13 North Street, Alfriston (01323 870849).
Food served 11am-5.30pm Mon, Tue, Thur-Sun.

A sweet place with low ceilings, crooked doors and plenty of oak beams on which to whack your head. Try the Badger set tea (choice of tea, cucumber, egg and cress sandwiches, scone with jam and cream plus cake, £4.75).

George Inn

High Street, Alfriston (01323 870319).
Food served noon-2pm, 7-9pm, Mon-Thur; noon-2.30pm, 7-9.30pm, Fri-Sun. **Cards** Debit, MC, V.

Opposite the Star Inn, the George promotes itself as a walkers' pub – a sign on the door informs ramblers to remove their boots, and food served during the day is hearty and wholesome (hiker's lunch: home-cooked ham, fried egg and fries, £5.25). The restaurant is open in the evening with an à la carte menu and a global wine list. The building dates back to the fourteenth century, and is often quoted as the Alfriston Smugglers' meeting place. Guest rooms are also available (double £60, including a three-course breakfast).

Giant's Rest

Wilmington, nr Polgate (01323 870207).
Food served noon-2pm, 7-9pm, daily.
Cards AmEx, Debit, MC, V.

A pub of the converted gastro variety, the Giant's Rest serves an eager local crowd of twenty- and thirtysomethings, who sit snug at the chunky wood tables playing Jenga and Connect Four by candlelight or eat well-cooked food. The menu is chalked on a blackboard and offers a big choice for vegetarians, including imaginative dishes such as cream cheese and cashew nut pâté (£4) and halloumi cheese salad (£5). Fish and meat eaters are sufficiently catered for, too, with choices like steak and mushroom pie with bubble and squeak (£6.50) and grilled skate wings with salad and quail's eggs (£9).

Hungry Monk

Jevington, nr Eastbourne (01323 482178).
Food served 7-10.45pm Mon-Sat; noon-2pm, 7-10.45pm, Sun. **Cards** AmEx.

A fifteenth-century building with an interior dominated by dark wood and comfortable furniture. Service is impeccable, with the whole evening structured to give diners the most relaxing and pleasant time possible. Drinks and savouries are served in the lounge while you muse over the set-price menu (£24.95, three courses). There's a good choice of meat and fish dishes (such as lamb with rösti potato; monkfish with red pepper purée sauce and spinach), though not much in the way of veggie dishes. Banoffee pie is said to have been invented here, and it's definitely a strong point. Finishing off with coffee and chocolates would satisfy the biggest of appetites. An exclusive treat.

Sussex & Surrey

The Bloomsbury bunch

The centre of gravity of what was later to be known as the **Bloomsbury Group** moved from London to East Sussex in 1916 when Virginia Woolf discovered **Charleston**, a beautiful farmhouse situated east of Lewes on the road to Eastbourne. At the time she and Leonard Woolf were living at Asheham House, five miles west of Charleston; Virginia decided that it would be the perfect house for her sister **Vanessa Bell** who had been living in Suffolk with the artist **Duncan Grant**, novelist **David Garnett** and her two sons.

Charleston became the centre of Bell and Grant's art and the subject of many paintings; they lived here for the rest of their lives (she died in 1961, he in 1978) producing the most stunning decorative works, ceramics and textiles in the bold colourful style, much influenced by the French Post-Impressionist movement, that made their name. Today the house stands as a living tribute to their work, and although it has undergone a huge restoration project, it gives a strong sense of how their life must have been. Almost every surface, whether wall or furniture, has been painted (Morpheus, the god of sleep, lives on a bedhead; Italian fresco-influenced figures occupy the fireplace and door panels). Chair and window seats and curtains and carpets are designed and made by the group and an abundance of paintings hang from the walls, whether executed by the Bloomsbury gang, their friends or famous names such as Cézanne, Sickert, Pissarro and Picasso. Every year, in late May, the **Charleston Festival** brings together prominent writers, artists and

*The Garden Room at **Charleston**.*

historians to discuss contemporary art and literature (phone 01323 811626 for details).

Though more classical and understated, **Virginia** and **Leonard Woolf**'s country retreat from 1919, **Monk's House**, is also worth a visit. Where Charleston is overwhelmed with imagery, Monk's House is a house of writers: peaceful, introspective and packed with books. Close by is the desolate spot on the River Ouse where Virginia drowned herself in 1941, walking into the water, her pockets full of stones.

Charleston (01323 811265/www.inn-quest.co.uk\charleston) signposted off A27 halfway between Brighton and Eastbourne, between Firle and Selmeston.
Open *Apr-June, Sept-Oct* 2-6pm Wed-Sun, bank hols; *July, Aug* 11.30am-6pm Wed-Sat; 2-6pm Sun, bank hols. Last entry 1hr before closing.
Admission £5.50; £3.50 5s-16s, OAPs, students; *garden only* £2; £1 5s-16s, OAPs, students.
Monk's House Rodmell (01892 890651).
Open *Apr-Oct* 2-5.30pm Wed, Sat.
Admission (NT) £2.50; £1.25 5s-16s.

Jolly Sportsman
Chapel Lane, East Chiltington (01273 890400).
Food served noon-2pm, 6-9.30pm, Tue-Thur; noon-2pm, 7-10pm, Fri; noon-2.30pm, 7-10pm, Sat; noon-3pm Sun. **Cards** Debit, MC, V.
A smart converted country pub with a separate dining area and a sophisticated menu, at prices to match – perfect for the well-heeled locals. Floors are stripped pine and the tables unadulterated wood with slants and cracks to prove it. The likes of Irish oysters with a garlic shallot vinegar (£5.85) and compote with pigeon breast (£4.95) for starters, and skate wing with salmon caviar (£11.95) and John Dory and scallop fricassée with seed mustard (£11.25) for mains. All dishes are beauti-

fully executed and cooked, and served by charming young waiters and waitresses. The wine list features some interesting bottles, all priced at around the £16-£18 mark, and home-made rhubarb and ginger ice-cream and meringue (all desserts are £4.85) is a splendid way to finish a meal.

Star Inn
High Street, Alfriston (0870 4008102).
Food served 7-9pm Mon-Sat; 12.30-2pm, 7-9pm, Sun. **Cards** AmEx, DC, Debit, MC, V.
The tankards on the wall, the low ceilings and uneven timbers carved with animal figures take you back a century or few as you drink in the Star Inn, one of England's

oldest inns, which was built in the thirteenth century and modernised in 1450. It's an amazing place, with a tiny bar and a mix of locals sitting at the big oak benches and settling into the comfy velvet chairs.

What to see & do

Tourist information centre

187 High Street, **Lewes**, BN7 2DE (01273 483448/ fax 01273 484003/www.lewes.gov.uk).
Open *Apr-Sept* 9am-5pm Mon-Fri; 10am-5pm Sat; 10am-2pm Sun; *Oct-Mar* 9am-5pm Mon-Fri; 10am-2pm Sat, bank hols.

Ann of Cleves House

52 Southover High Street, Lewes (01273 474610/ www.sussexpast.co.uk).
Open 10am-5pm Mon-Sat; noon-5pm Sun.
Admission £2.30; £1.10 5s-15s; £2.10 OAPs, students; EH members half price.
This sixteenth-century Wealden 'hall' house formed part of Henry VIII's divorce settlement with his fourth wife Ann of Cleves, though it is thought she never occupied the building. Its structure has changed considerably over the centuries: the kitchen and the bedroom are a re-creation of the house's early years, with original furniture to boot, while other rooms display archaeological finds of local interest, Wealden ironwork and exhibitions illustrating the post-medieval social and economic history of Sussex. Well worth a visit.

Clergy House

Alfriston (info 01323 870001).
Open *Mar-Oct* 10am-5pm (or dusk) Mon, Wed, Thur, Sat, Sun. Last entry 4.30pm. **Admission** £2.50; £1.25 5s-16s.
Situated on the southern edge of the green (the Tye), the Clergy House is a thatched fourteenth-century house with sourmilk and chalk flooring and original wattle and daub walls. And the first building (and second property) to be bought by the National Trust, in 1896, for the sum of £10. Today the house holds an interesting exhibition on medieval construction techniques and the history of many of the local historic buildings. The garden is a stunner, with some of the rarer plants dating back to Roman times.

Drusillas Zoo Park

Alfriston (01323 870656/www.drusillas.co.uk).
Open *Apr-Oct* 10am-5pm, *Nov-Mar* 10am-4pm, daily. **Admission** £6.95; £5.75 3s-12s; £5.25 OAPs.
This deceptively large wildlife park is clean, impressive and imaginatively designed. Children and agile adults can scramble through tunnels to re-emerge in minidomes amid meerkats and rats. There's also a huge playground with (free) activities including gargantuan slides and train rides.

Glynde Place

Glynde, Lewes (01273 858224).
Open *house & gardens June, Sept* 2-5pm Wed, Sun, bank hol Mon; 2-5pm Wed, Thur, Sun, bank hol Mon; *gardens Apr, May* 2-5pm Sun, bank hol Mon.
Admission £4; £2 4s-14s.
A handsome example of Elizabethan architecture and

*Hanging around at **Drusillas Zoo Park**.*

home to some fine family portraiture. A whole room is dedicated to Sir Henry Brand, speaker at the House of Commons (1872-84), and there's a collection of eighteenth-century Italian works.

Lewes Castle & Barbican House Museum

169 High Street, Lewes (01273 486290/ www.sussexpast.co.uk).
Open 10am-5.30pm/dusk Mon-Sat; 11am-5.30pm/dusk Sun, bank hols. **Admission** £3.50; £1.80 5s-15s; £3 OAPs, students; £10 family; EH members half price.
William de Warenne, a leading Norman noble, had Lewes Castle built after the Battle of Hastings as his stronghold in Sussex. The structure was altered and extended over the following 300 years, and now offers some of the most beautiful views across Lewes and the South Downs. Barbican House, close to the Castle gate, stands as a museum of local history, run by the Sussex Archaeological Society. It houses an interesting display of remains, tools and artefacts and explores the impact of invasion by the Romans, Saxons and Normans.

Parish Church of St Andrew

The Tye, Alfriston (01323 870376).
Open 9am-6pm/dusk daily.
Known as the 'Cathedral of the South Downs', Alfriston is rightly proud of this wonderful thirteenth-century church set behind the village next to the Cuckmere River on a hilly green known as the Tye. It's a surprisingly tall and spacious structure with a stunning oak-beamed ceiling, built in the shape of a Greek cross, with local square-knapped flints and greenstone.

Brighton

Be who you want to be in London-by-the-sea.

*Pneumonia-inducing sea? Blister-enhancing pebbles? It can only be **Brighton Beach**.*

'Brighton looks like a town that is constantly helping the police with their enquiries,' said Keith Waterhouse, and it is as a roguish, flamboyant, even tarty city that Brighton has come to be known. Its proximity to London helps foster this – this is where the capital's hard-working sophisticates come to let their hair down, and the place is full of temptations and opportunities for you to misbehave by the sea.

From political party conference delegates to dirty weekenders (and those who manage to be both), Brighton looks after its visitors well. It has endless hotels, guesthouses and

restaurants, a vast array of intriguing shops and a vibrant and sophisticated cultural scene and nightlife that thrive on close connections to the capital, just an hour away by train.

The energy of the place is heightened by a large (and affluent) student population and a gay scene entrenched enough to bring the city the nickname of Miami Beach UK. And with all the gaudy fun of a relatively sunny British beach-town (even if the shoreline is full of uncomfortable pebbles rather than sand), there's a year-round influx of coach parties and day-trippers here to soak up some beer, buy a stick of Brighton rock and play on the dodgems on the pier.

Brighton began life as a village called Bristmestune, and later Brighthelmstone, which augmented its fishing income with a good deal of smuggling. It continued pretty much undisturbed save for the occasional French sortie, until 1750 when a Dr Richard Russell invented the seaside. Russell proclaimed that sea water had amazing restorative benefits, encouraging fashionable

By train from London

The fastest train to **Brighton** leaves **Victoria** every half an hour (journey time **45mins**). There are also trains from **King's Cross** that leave every 15 minutes and pass through London Bridge and Blackfriars (journey time **1hr 5mins**).

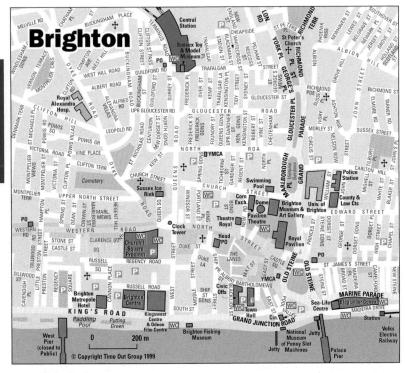

London to rush down to the coast with bucket and spade. Brighton was suddenly the cool holiday destination and there was a booming industry in hotels and bathing machines – covered wooden wagons that allowed bathers to enter the sea without having to worry about waxing their bikini line. 'Dippers' stood by, helping the gentlefolk to enjoy the salt water to the full by ducking them into it.

Things really took off in 1783 when the Prince Regent (later George IV) endorsed the delights of Brighton by renting a farmhouse here. As time went by and his crazy old father George III refused to die, the younger George became the centre of a hip and happening court-in-waiting. Kept from the throne for so long, he filled his time not by talking to plants and prognosticating about architecture, but by building a fabulous pleasure palace and inviting all the country's creative, beautiful and ambitious young things to join him there. This was the Pavilion (*see page 73* **The far-fetched Pavilion**). Thanks largely to its place at the centre of recreational Regency England, the town's population expanded from 3,500 in 1780 to 40,500 in 1831.

Today, Brighton is still a seaside resort first and foremost (and there are seven miles of uninterrupted coastline here), but there is plenty to do away from the beach. Shopping is exciting, with a concentrated area of clothes, records and gift shops, all with a knowing trendiness about them; drinking and dining is an ever-present option, and with a brash nightlife and a constant flow of thousands of lusty arrivals, you can always be sure that in Brighton mischief awaits.

Where to stay

Brighton certainly has the quantity, but is remarkably lacking in quality. Still, it's as well to book ahead during the summer. The tourist information centres operate a reservation service, so if the places mentioned below are full, they'll suggest alternatives. Beware, though: many places insist on a minumum occupancy requirement of two or even three nights. And if Brighton's full, try Hove, which is so close it's practically the same town. B&Bs are everywhere, and some of the best are to be

Only here for the piers

A moment's pause will tell you that a pier is a strange concept indeed. Unless you're using it to get on a boat, what's the point of walking a few hundred feet seawards on a wooden deck? Well, the Victorians, who were pier-mad, thought it was a good way of maximising the amount of sea air entering the lungs, of enjoying all the health-giving properties of a maritime excursion without the usual mortal danger and seasickness. Piers were also a chance for gentleman engineers to show off the latest marvellous iron technology. Plus, though they'd be loath to admit it, they provided a great excuse for the lads to go out and look at girls (and vice versa).

Brighton has two piers, the **Palace Pier**, a thriving jumble of fish and chip joints, bingo, amusement arcades and fairground rides, and the **West Pier**, a derelict hulk of a thing that hasn't been open for a quarter of a century. Not surprisingly, while the Palace Pier is the choice of thousands of video-gaming, candy-floss-eating, rollercoaster-riding funsters, it's the latter that is far more interesting.

Although it was damaged in the war, closed completely in 1975 and severed from the shore by the fierce storms of the 1980s, the West Pier is a Grade I-listed building (the only pier in the country to receive such status). Lottery-funded restoration work has now reached the point where it's possible, provided you put on a safety harness and a hard hat, to venture on to the crumbling structure, and guided tours take place fairly regularly throughout the year (*see below*).

Though there is much work to be done, you get to see the elegance of the architecture, unchanged since 1916, with the magnificent theatre and concert hall at the far end, and learn a little about the problems of restoring such a complex structure. And about the bizarre mobile pier, Brighton's 'Daddy Longlegs' railway on stilts, which lasted until the under-sea tracks rusted. Guides will also tell you about Brighton's first pier, the 1823 Royal Suspension Chain Pier, a row of four huge iron towers from which a platform was suspended by chains. This was used for boarding ferries to Dieppe and stood where the Palace Pier is now.

And after you've been wowed by the rusting grandeur of the West Pier, you can nip over to the Palace, gorge yourself on chips and dressed crab, play on the latest arcade games, make a fool of yourself in the karaoke bar and have a romantic snog on the Whirlitzer.

West Pier guided tours *Apr-Oct* 3pm Mon-Fri; 1.30pm, 3pm Sat; noon, 1.30pm, 3pm Sun; *Nov-Mar* 3pm Wed; 1.30pm, 3pm Sat, Sun.
Tickets £10 per person. No children under 16. Call 01273 321499 to book or visit the West Pier Trust's little kiosk at the head of the pier itself.

found slightly away from the seafront. For a handy location and reasonable prices try the secluded Russell Square, where almost every house offers accommodation.

Adelaide

51 Regency Square, BN1 2FF
(01273 205286/220904/adelaide@pavilion.co.uk).
Rates (B&B) *single* £41-£60; *double/twin* £65-£82; *family* £80-£85. **Rooms** (all en suite) 3 single; 8 double/twin. **Cards** AmEx, Debit, MC, V.

For the ultimate in – fnarr, fnarr – 'weekend breaks', head to the Adelaide and book into its grand Regency Room, complete with four-poster bed. Although the Adelaide is close to the front, it doesn't actually face the sea, but the prettily functional rooms more than make up for the less than panoramic views. Service is friendly and informal but ruthlessly efficient, and breakfast, which is included, is tip top, served in a fine old dining room. Children welcome.

Brighton Backpackers

75-76 Middle Street, BN1 1AL (01273 777717/ fax 01273 887778/backpackers@fastnet.co.uk/ www.stay@brightonbackpackers.com).
Rates £10-£12.50pp. **Rooms** 3 double; 28 dorms.

A bargain for clean and friendly accommodation, right in the centre of Brighton. Part of a network of independent hostels, the Backpackers is filled with kindred spirits and run by experienced travellers who also know the city very well. The hostel operates a policy of not taking too many reservations, but usually has room around 11am when people have moved on. As well as dorms, there are several double rooms available, many with a sea view. There's a nice breakfast/hangout room, a free pool table, and, best of all, no curfew.

The Grand

King's Road, BN1 2FW (01273 321188/fax 01273 202694/reservations@grandbrighton.co.uk/ www.brighton.co.uk/hotels).
Rates *single* £155; *double/twin* £195-£220; *deluxe double/twin* £285; *suite* £600. **Rooms** (all en suite) 8 single; 145 double/twin; 42 deluxe double/twin; 5 suites. **Cards** AmEx, DC, Debit, MC, V.

The Grand still maintains its reputation as Brighton's poshest hotel, and if you are careful about when you book, it's only twice as expensive as most of the lesser hotels in town. Rooms are large and filled with light, and

The Grand – *by name, and by tariff.*

the décor is a careful medium between good solid hotel blandness and twee Laura Ashley frills. The King's Restaurant is excellent, and an evening spent hanging out at the Victoria Lounge, sipping cocktails and listening to corny piano music, has all the trappings of a real luxury experience. Children and dogs are welcome.

The Twenty One

21 Charlotte Street, BN2 1AG
(01273 686450/fax 01273 695560).
Rates (B&B) *single* £35; *double* £60-£65; *four-poster* £75; *four-poster twin* £75. **Rooms** (all en suite) 1 single; 3 double; 1 four-poster; 2 four-poster twin. **Cards** Debit, MC, V.

Not for nothing is this universally recommended. Located in the quiet Kemptown conservation area, not too far from the seafront, in an early Victorian house, The Twenty One is a well-run bed and breakfast establishment with particular attention to detail. The finest rooms have period Victorian furniture; all of the others are designed individually with a sharp eye for cosiness and comfort, and plenty of flouncy floral fabrics to remind you you're staying in a guesthouse. Breakfast is a tour de force, with everything on offer from superhealthy organic vegan options to an all-English artery-busting fry-up.

Regency Hotel

28 Regency Square, BN1 2FH
(01273 202690/fax 01273 220438).
Rates (B&B) *single* £45-£50; *double* £68-£80; *twin* £85; *suite* £110. **Rooms** (all en suite) 2 single; 4 double; 2 twin; 1 suite). **Cards** AmEx, DC, Debit, MC, V.

At the head of Regency Square, up on the hill overlooking the sea and the beautifully wrecked West Pier, the Regency is a classy establishment, with an elegant dining room and drawing room. Most bedrooms are of a very high standard. However, some of those at the top are less than glamorous, with very poor sound insulation and extremely basic shared bathrooms. And don't bother with the in-room hairdryers: they make more noise than Concorde. Children are welcome and all bedrooms are non-smoking.

Valentine House Hotel

38 Russell Square, BN1 2EF
(01273 700800/fax 01273 707606).
Rates (B&B) *double/twin* £40-£50. **Rooms** (all en suite) 8 double; 2 twin. **Cards** MC, V.

As the name suggests, this is a romantic little hotel, situated in Russell Square, just up from the seafront. Their 'ideal for a romantic short break' suggestion hints at the level of privacy you'll receive, and most rooms – which are airy and clean and very prettily decorated – even have a little balcony for some Romeo and Juliet adventures. Breakfast is included and is delicious, with a fairly wide menu including vegetarian options.

Where to eat & drink

Food in Brighton is never far away, though when it's busy the best places fill up for dinner fast, and booking is advised. Not surprisingly for a seaside town, fish and chips are here in

The far-fetched Pavilion

George IV, in his days as rock 'n' roll Prince Regent, ordered the country's finest craftsmen to build him a beach-house and fill it with outrageous furniture and décor. The result is a playful, opulent and, at times, extremely camp collection of rooms and objects, all contained in a building that would look at home next to the Taj Mahal. Even if you hate tramping around old buildings, there is plenty here to amuse and astonish.

The Pavilion was transformed by architect John Nash, from a rather non-descript farmhouse into the oriental fantasy it is today, between 1815 and 1822. To allow such a dramatic overhaul, an iron exoskelton was erected over the original structure; this supports the weight of the various domes and towers. Inside, no expense was spared as acres of hand-woven carpets and fabric, amazing chandeliers and richly carved gilded furniture, predominantly in a Chinese-inspired style, were crafted for the place. George spent many years here, first as Prince Regent and then as King, entertaining his mistresses away from the gossip of London, and inviting a revolving group of influential folk down for parties by the sea. In later years it was used by Queen Victoria, who chucked out some of the gaudier furniture and complained about the lack of privacy.

Over the years, £10 million has been spent to restore the Pavilion to its former glory after general neglect and a damaging arson attack in 1975. And the Queen has graciously lent back many of the items that Victoria had removed to other royal dwellings. At night, it's all lit up like a fantasy playhouse; a visit to Brighton wouldn't be complete without a breeze through this surreal treasure.

The guided tours are the best way to see the place, as the guides treat the exercise with a good level of tongue-in-cheek fun-poking, dropping in all manner of quirky facts about the chic world of Regency society. For example, the amazing gold leaf psychedelic design of the music room makes all the more sense when described as an 'early nineteenth-century private disco', and you won't forget such details as the fact that the ladies of the time wore mouse-skin eyebrows to solve the problem of their own dropping off thanks to lead-based make-up.

Brighton Pavilion (01273 290900). **Open** *June-Sept* 10am-6pm daily; *Oct-May* 10am-5pm daily. **Admission** £4.50; £2.75 5s-16s; £3.25 OAPs, students. Guided tours (an extra £1) 11.30am, 2.30pm daily.

abundance – **Bardsley's** (22-23A Baker Street) is reckoned to be the best. For traditional seaside fare, visit the **Regency** (King's Road; 01273 325014), one of the oldest seafront restaurants, or **Wheelers of St James** (17 Market Street; 01273 325135), one of the classier seafood joints in a city with many. For big fry-ups and no end of post-club freaks and weirdos, head to the 24-hour **Market Diner** (Manchester Street), home of the original full works. **Grubbs Burgers** (St James Street) has three other locations and serves up a vast selection of quality burgers, available in both carnivorous and herbivorous incarnations. **Blind Lemon Alley** (41 Middle Street; 01273 205151) has rib-ticklin' Southern American cuisine; for Thai food, head to **Muang Thai** (77 St James Street; 01273 605223); for the best Chinese, try **Gars** (19 Prince Albert Street; 01273 321321).

Coffee bars are plentiful in town. The **Good Bean** (Bond Street & Albert Street) offers decent food and drink but rather blasé service. A better bet is **Disco Biscuit** (14 Queen's Road), which looks like a techno crusty hang-out but isn't.

Brighton's not short of pubs, but doesn't have many great ones. The **Pump House** (45 Market Street) is probably the best.

Black Chapati

12 Circus Parade, New England Road (01273 699011).
Food served 7-10pm Tue-Fri; 6.30-10pm Sat.
Credit AmEx, Debit, MC, V.

One of Brighton's finest, the Black Chapati serves a faultless pan-Asian menu in the shadow of a big concrete office development. The décor is not so much minimal as hardly present, and service can be rather joyless, but the food is undoubtedly excellent. Start, perhaps, with lamb patties and chutney (£5.25), before moving on to roast cod with shrimp and a coconutty lime leaf sauce (£11.50), or steamed guinea fowl in rice wine sauce with Chinese cabbage and dumplings (£12.50).

Casa Don Carlos

5 Union Street, The Lanes, Brighton (01273 327177).
Food served noon-3pm, 6-11pm, Mon-Fri; noon-11pm Sat; noon-10.30pm Sun. **Cards** AmEx, DC, Debit, MC, V.

In the bustle of The Lanes, this rustic Spanish tapas restaurant is undoubtedly the real thing. There are few pretensions, and it's not exactly spacious, but the food is great and reasonably priced. Paella is a speciality and it's excellent, as is the seafood soup. Expect to pay between £10 and £15 for three courses without drink.

Food for Friends

17 Prince Albert Street (01273 202310).
Food served 8am-10pm Mon-Sat; 9am-10pm Sun.
Cards Debit, MC, V.

This terrific vegetarian cafeteria is the kind of place where you may have to wait while someone in the queue analyses every last ingredient and then asks, 'Have you got any sugar-free puddings?', but the place isn't nearly as cranky as its customers, and it serves that rarest of cuisines – vegetarian food with real flavour. Try their curries or their Dutch stack (a sort of pancake lasagne), or stop by for a Big Breakfast complete with bottomless cappuccino. Three courses don't come to much over £10.

La Fourchette

101 Western Road (01273 722556).
Food served 6.30-10.30pm Mon; noon-2.30pm, 6.30-10.30pm, Tue-Fri; noon-3pm Sun.
Cards AmEx, DC, Debit, MC, V.

New in 1999, this cracking French restaurant has already established quite a reputation for itself. Mercifully pitching itself at the IKEA-minimal, cool and relaxed end of the spectrum (rather than the chintz and lugubrious formality end), the food is nevertheless classic Gallic. Such dishes as sea bass with sauce vierge and nage de poissons are executed with great care and flair. Main courses are around the £11 mark.

One Paston Place

1 Paston Place (01273 606933).
Food served 12.30-2pm, 7.30-10pm, Tue-Sat.
Cards AmEx, DC, Debit, MC, V.

Assured, well-rounded, French-biased cooking is what to expect from Mark Emmerson's rightly popular restaurant. There are no pointless decorations and superfluous ingredients, just classy belly-warmers like canon of lamb with mint and rocket pesto (£21), and turbot and lobster with lemon, thyme and coral jus with pommes boulangères (£22). Service is relaxed, yet as confident and professional as the food.

Terre à Terre

71 East Street (01273 729051).
Food served 6-10.30pm Mon; noon-11pm Tue-Sun. **Cards** MC, V.

Terre à Terre manages to be a vegetarian restaurant that doesn't scare off carnivores. Instead of gag-enducing nut-cutlet-and-tofu-type concoctions, this place serves proper, modern food that just happens not to include meat. Examples inclue borjak (£4.90) – little pasties filled with celeriac and lovage purée, served on a vodka and beetroot borscht – and split pea pikelets with mint pesto (£7.90). Not everything works, and service can be variable, but no visiting veggie will want to pass over the chance to give it a whirl.

What to see & do

Tourist information centres

10 Bartholomew Square, **Brighton** (01273 292599/www.brighton.co.uk).
Open *July, Aug* 9am-6.15pm Mon-Fri; 10am-6pm Sat; 10am-4pm Sun; *Sept-June* 9am-5pm Mon-Fri; 10am-5pm Sat; phone to check Sun.
Hove Town Hall, Church Road, **Hove** (01273 292589).
Open 9am-5pm Mon-Fri.

Booth Museum of Natural History

194 Dyke Road (01273 292777).
Open 10am-5pm Mon-Wed, Fri, Sat; 2-5pm Sun.
Admission free.

The Lanes

This tangled network of narrow cobbled alleyways (between East, North and Prince Albert streets) – not for the geographically challenged – marks the extent of the early town of Brighthelmstone; as late as 1635 this small square of buildings was all there was of Brighton. Here were situated fishmongers, bootmakers, bakers and no end of taverns filled with salty dogs returned from smuggling expeditions. After the town started to expand as a result of the trend for the 'sea-water cure', the Lanes fell into disrepair and were for many years little more than slum cottages. Now they form a charming area of shops, pubs and restaurants, where you'll find a good deal of interesting antiques and collectors' shops, jewellers, fashion stores and all manner of eats and drinks. At night the atmosphere gets increasingly festive as the tiny streets echo to the sound of drunken merrymakers.

Shopping is even more rewarding in the associated area, the North Laine, a series of streets, some pedestrianised, which offer a range of fantastically stocked shops. You'll find lovingly catalogued record stores, with an abundance of (pricey) rarities, boutiques selling clothes – both new and trendily vintage – and such style-friendly emporiums as a very adult-oriented toyshop selling Star Wars figures and '70s retro games, a mod shop with a Lambretta in the window and a period furniture store boasting a cosmic 'Lost In Space' jukebox.

Its fine efforts at more modern presentation and hands-on educational involvement can't hide the fact that at heart this is a beautifully old-fashioned collection of stuffed, mounted and skeletonised flora and fauna, most of which will have spent the bulk of their lives in Victorian glass-fronted boxes. Over half a million specimens are here, including a whale and the obligatory dinosaur bones, with a particularly well-stocked display of British birds shown in re-creations of their natural habitats.

Brighton Fishing Museum

201 King's Road Arches, on the lower prom between the piers (01273 723064).
Open 10am-5pm daily. **Admission** free.
Brighton wasn't always about ice-cream and sunburn, and to get an idea of its maritime history this museum is well worth a quick pop in while you're strolling along the front. It's a small exhibit centred around a pristine example of a clinker-built Sussex beach fishing boat. There are limited displays describing the history of the local fishing industry, and one explaining the origins of 'all aboard the Skylark' – the name of the first pleasure boat that operated from here. This is also where the last of Brighton's traditional fishermen ply their trade, occasionally bringing home a catch for sale from one of the adjoining arches. You can buy fresh fish and have it cooked at a nearby restaurant. If the fisherfolk aren't headed out to sea, you'll be able to watch them mend their nets. In addition, some of the arches around about are used by local artists and craftspeople, and

many are open to the public. This area is ambitiously called the 'Artists' Quarter'.

Brighton Marina

(01273 693636/www.brightonmarina.co.uk).
Without actually venturing out to sea in an open boat, few things show off the elemental power of the ocean as much as a simple walk down the concrete breakwater arm of the Marina (although it's closed in really rough weather). When you turn to look inshore you'll see a teeming school of condoms. Of course, there's far more to Brighton Marina than that, and nautical types can pass hours here looking longingly at the beautiful, expensive – and occasionally historic – boats that are moored in what is the UK's largest marina. And once you've tired of imagining life on the ocean wave, you can actually attempt it, by going out in one of the many sailing, fishing or diving boats to be found here. For fishing and diving trips, call 01273 693400; for sailing trips call 01273 818237.

If you haven't found your sea legs yet, there are all the meretricious attractions of ten-pin bowling, an eight-screen cinema, a series of off-the-shelf bars and restaurants (a Chef & Brewer pub, a Fatty Arbuckle's) and a place called the Octagon Village Square, which is a twee name for a shopaholic's dream/nightmare – a series of factory outlets selling everything from branded fashion to seconded chinaware. To find the Marina, just walk east along the beach or promenade. You'll pass some naked wrinklies (the nudist beach) and then, ahoy, thar she blows.

It is possible to find some sand on Brighton beach if you know where to look.

Brighton Museum & Art Gallery

Church Street (01273 290900).
Open 10am-5pm Mon, Tue, Thur-Sat; 2-5pm Sun.
Admission free.

An excellent and very diverse collection, taking in every-thing from Alma-Tadema's pre-Raphaelite beauties to Salvador Dali's much-reproduced lips sofa. There are non-Western arts such as Yoruba masks and Burmese textiles; even such historic artefacts as Egyptian tomb relics (including a mummy). There is a particularly strong showing of art nouveau and art deco from Gallé to Clarice Cliff, and a well-curated series of temporary and touring exhibitions.

British Engineerium

Nevill Road, Hove (01273 559583/
www3.mistral.co.uk/engineerium).
Open 10am-5pm daily. **Admission** £3.50;
£2.50 5s-16s, OAPs, students; £10 family.

This, to give it its full title, is the Museum of Steam and Mechanical Antiquities, and it was originally a Victorian pumping station serving up 150,000 gallons of water an hour to the surrounding area. Big lumps of polished metal abound and as well as the huge working beam engine that powered the pumps and its immense under-ground boilers, there are traction engines, locomotive models, vintage motorbikes, a horse-drawn fire engine, plus hands-on educational exhibits explaining the sci-entific principles at work. If you visit on the first Sunday in the month or on bank holiday Sundays and Mondays, you'll see everything fired up in full steam.

National Museum of Penny Slot Machines

250C King's Road Arches, Lower Esplanade, opposite the end of East Street (01273 608620).
Open *Easter-June* 11am-6pm Sat, Sun, school hols;

July-Sept 11am-6pm daily; *Oct-Easter* 11am-6pm Sun (weather permitting). Last entry 5.30pm.
Admission free.

Don't laugh. At this charming little diversion near the fishing museum, you get to see rows of the once-raunchy hand-driven film viewers full of Edwardian 'What the butler saw' naughtiness, and several other non-electric entertainments dating from the 1890s. You buy old pen-nies to work them. As their motto says, 'Old-fashioned fun at old-fashioned prices.'

Preston Manor

Preston Drove (01273 290900/292770).
Open 1-5pm Mon; 10am-5pm Tue-Sat, bank hols;
2-5pm Sun. **Admission** £3.10; £1.95 5s-16s; £2.60 OAPs, students; £5.05-£8.15 family.

Compared to the off-kilter splendour of the Royal Pavilion, Preston Manor is a lesson in normality. The building itself dates back to 1250 but has been restored and furnished as it stood in Edwardian times, with sumptuous family rooms and rather more basic ser-vants' quarters, exactly as they would have been in around 1905. Twenty or so rooms are open to the pub-lic, over four floors, containing a wealth of family heir-looms from furniture and paintings to silverware and fine china. Two miles north of Brighton on the A23, the Manor is accessible by train to Preston Park station, but if you're not driving, the best way is to get a cab.

Sea-Life Centre

Marine Parade (01273 604234/recorded info
01273 604233/www.sealife.co.uk).
Open 10am-6pm daily. Last entry 5pm. **Admission**
£5.95; £3.95 4s-14s; £4.25 OAPs; £3.95 students.

In days gone by this was the Brighton Aquarium and all manner of cooped-up fishes entertained visitors amid the Victorian columns, while the city's rollerskaters practised on the roof. Now it's part of a massive Europe-wide chain of Sea-Life centres (many euphemistically called 'sanctuaries') and its prime concern is supposedly environmental protection. Good intentions aside, in what is the oldest aquarium in Europe, the very best thing is the 60-foot undersea tunnel, which allows you to get up close and personal to sharks, rays and conger eels. But the sea-horse exhibit, albeit on a much smaller scale, is equally fascinating, as you watch these rather unlikely creatures go about their sedate business. Kids will love the 'Adventures at 20,000 Leagues' exhibit, a mock-up of Captain Nemo's submarine complete with animatronic attack by giant squid, but they can be kept pacified for far longer with the education packs that are doled out. Re-entry is allowed, so have a look at everything and return for feeding time.

Volks Electric Railway

(01273 292718). **Open** *Easter-mid-Sept* 11am-5pm daily. **Tickets** £1; 50p 5s-15s.

Running along the seafront between the Marina and the Sea-Life Centre, this is the oldest electric railway in Britain, built in 1883.

Dance, dance, dance

Perhaps it's because it's so close to London, or maybe it's because there are so many students here who fancy themselves as Mr Bigstuff promoters, or maybe it's simply that there's a constant flood of drunken youngsters who need entertaining after the pubs shut, but Brighton has more clubs than an iceberg full of seal-hunters. When planning your campaign, arm yourself with a copy of *The Latest*, Brighton's monthly entertainment guide (30p from newsagents). Here you'll find over a hundred nights listed, with basic descriptions and DJ line-ups. *Mixmag* is also a good source of info with at least 20 of the biggest Brighton nights listed, and you'll find thousands of flyers in boutiques, record stores and pubs all around town.

Your adventure starts in one of the many pre-club bars, such as **The Squid**, **The Escape Bar**, or any of the other raucous places along the seafront filled with DJs and continual drinks promotions. While here, don't forget to look out for money-off vouchers for the next stage of your evening.

As in London, most venues are musically fairly flexible, hosting a revolving series of nights, although banging funky house is the main ingredient, certainly at the weekends, when plenty of big-name DJs drop by to play. The most popular clubs are **The Zap** (King's Road Arches; 01273 821588), **The Honey Club** (King's Road Arches; 01273 202807), **The Escape** (Marine Parade; 01273 606906), and **The Beach** (King's Road Arches; 01273 278326), all of which are on or near the seafront.

The **BN1 Club** (Preston Street; 01273 323161) has quite wide-ranging tastes and hosts drum 'n' bass nights on both

Thursdays and Saturdays, with everything from NuNRG to funky garage on other nights. **The Jazz Place** (Ship Street; 01273 328439) is a swinging cellar with grooves along the jazz hip hop, funk and soul vibe. Other venues with plenty of good nights include the much-respected **Sussex Arts Club** (Ship Street; 01273 727371), **The Enigma** (Ship Street; 01273 328439), **The Tavern** (North Street; no phone) and **The Volks** (Madeira Drive; 01273 682828).

Look to listings and flyers to find out about the many one-off events, but individual nights worth seeking out include 'Bubble Funk', a great technoey breakbeat occasion fortnightly Fridays at The Escape, and 'Sunset Sundays', a free Balearic early evening shindig from 7pm to 11pm at The Beach. That Brighton institution, the famous 'Big Beat Boutique', you'll find on Fridays at The Beach, although it's now just called 'The Boutique'. Norman Cook still makes fairly regular guest appearances, although his DJing presence is rarely advertised in advance.

Gay Brighton is concentrated in two areas – around Regency Square and Preston Street, and in the area east of the Pavilion. Here you'll find club-bars like **Zanzibar** (St James Street; 01273 622100), **Secrets** (Steine Street; 01273 609672) and **The Revenge** (Steine Street; 01273 606064). Many of the London gay papers, especially *boyz*, have listings for Brighton bars and clubs.

Be aware that few nights in Brighton go on very late, with 2am and 3am being the norm. However, you all-nite party people should have no trouble locating like-minded locals, and these will no doubt let you in on a little after-hours party they happen to know about...

South-west Sussex

Cathedrals and coast, ancient sites and art, horse racing and horticulture – this corner of Sussex has it all.

MALTRAVERS STREET

*Charmingly retro **Arundel**.*

There's a lazy voluptuousness to this part of the South Downs – in the dips and folds of the shallow valleys, the slow curve of the hills, in the deep forest greens and sandy yellows. A rash of unappealing time-warp seaside resorts spatter the pebbly coastline, but the greater attractions lie inland. There are the cutesy and cultural diversions of the towns, particularly Arundel and Chichester, a slew of fine country houses, neatly scrubbed villages, wonderful walking on the Downs and a number of ancient sights – and a couple of notable sporting events, too.

Arundel

Crouching meekly beneath its immense, sprawling castle, **Arundel** is a small, quiet (tourists aside) charming place with tiny side streets lined with furniture and bric-a-brac stores, coffee shops and homely places selling country jams and the like. The town was a working port as late as the 1920s and, for a small town, there is a whiff of the cosmopolitan about it: there are good food shops and a French affinity that gives it *un peu de panache*.

Arundel Castle, built in the eleventh century by Roger de Montgomery and now the seat of the Dukes of Norfolk and Earls of Arundel, is well worth exploring for its fine paintings and furniture, and the gorgeous Fitzalan Chapel. The town's other main cultural attraction is **Arundel Cathedral** – the beautiful, imposing building is the nineteenth-century version of French Gothic. After your fill of history, take a cruise on the river – Skylark Cruises (0378 438166) runs an enjoyable trip up to Amberley.

Chichester

Chichester is the kind of place that Miss Marple would happily retire to: it's busy but restrained and has all the qualities of a classic English market town. It was founded in AD 70 by the Romans, who laid out the main street plan and built the original city walls (rebuilt in flint in medieval times). You can walk along the surviving walls accompanied by an audio tour available from the tourist information centre. The main north-south and east-west streets of the city (called, unimaginatively yet logically, North, South, East and West streets) slice it neatly into four areas, with the Cathedral dominating the south-west sector and the finest of the Georgian buildings in the south-east in the streets called the Pallants. **Pallant House** on North Pallant contains some good modern British art. The town is at its most lively during the excellent arts-oriented **Chichester Festival** in July (01243 785718).

There are two small but interesting museums: **Chichester District Museum** (Little London; 01243 784683), focusing on the

By train from London

Trains to **Chichester** leave **London Victoria** hourly (journey time about **1hr 45mins**). This train passes through **Arundel** (**1hr 30mins**).

district's geology, archeology and social history, while the **Guildhall Museum** (Priory Park; 01243 784683), where William Blake was tried for sedition during its days as a courthouse, contains some medieval frescoes.

The town's main draw, however, is its **Cathedral**. It's a stunning structure, best known for its soaring spire (a landmark for miles around) and a Marc Chagall stained-glass window. A leisurely mooch here, followed, perhaps, by a walk in the park with its cricket ground, bowling green and a curious pen with love birds is a relaxing way to spend a few hours. To be frank, though, the town's gentle fogeyism will probably start to grate after a while, and you'll be keen to head out towards the coast or up on to the Downs.

A shore thing

George V wasn't overly impressed with the seaside hereabouts, and you'll be tempted to join him in saying 'Bugger Bognor' (unless a monster Butlins is your idea of fun). If, on the other hand, you do need a fix of freeze-the-flesh-off-your-bones English Channel, then head for the unspoiled stretch of coast at **Climping**, a couple of miles east of Bognor. The shoreline is of the steeply shelved, pebbly variety (à la Brighton) but it's pleasant nonetheless and mercifully free of development.

The other waterside spot worth visiting in these parts is **Bosham** (pronounced 'Bozzum'), two miles west of Chichester. Peppered with thatched-roofed cottages and handsome houses, this is a choc-box English country village. Well known as a sailing village with a history as a fishing port that dates back to Roman times (the Emperor Vespasian allegedly had a residence here), Bosham is the most attractive of all the villages on the shores of Chichester Harbour. This is, according to legend, the spot where King Canute tried to turn back the tide. Bosham seems to have accepted the power of the sea these days and the village extends right down to the water's edge where at high tide the water laps against the stone walls of the houses. One of the village's other claims to fame is its small but perfectly formed Saxon church (which includes stones from the original Roman basilica). This is a beguiling and thoroughly relaxing (although hardly undiscovered) place to stay, and ideal for a romantic weekend.

And now the Down-side

As the flat coastal plain rises gently into the bosom of the South Downs, a host of attractions reveal themselves. There are the two important Roman sights – **Fishbourne Roman Palace** near Chichester and the smaller, but perhaps more evocative, **Bignor Roman Villa**; Elizabethan **Parham House**; the gardens of **Denmans** and **West Dean**; multifarious birdlife at the **Arundel Wildfowl & Wetlands Trust**; the imaginative and educational **Weald & Downland Open Air Museum**; and the quadruple attractions of **Goodwood** (*see page 80* **The four glories of Goodwood**).

Where to stay

There are plenty of hotels and B&Bs in all price brackets in the area. Note that prices rise significantly during the Festival of Speed (June) and Glorious Goodwood races (July), so avoid these weekends if you don't want to get stung.

Amberley Castle

Amberley, BN18 9ND (01798 831992/ fax 01798 831998/info@amberleycastle.co.uk). **Rates** (B&B) *double/twin* £145-£195; *four-poster* £195-£300; *suite* £240-£260. **Rooms** (all en suite) 9 double/twin; 6 four-poster; 5 suites. **Cards** AmEx, DC, Debit, MC, V.

For a full-on luxury experience, a weekend at Amberley Castle is hard to beat. The drive up to the castle is a stunner and not a little imposing – a sign discourages visitors who haven't booked and you are greeted by shrieking peacocks. The bedrooms are luxurious, furnished with antiques and trad fabrics. Many of the rooms have four-poster beds and en suite Jacuzzis. If you feel like playing at royalty for the weekend, then this is the perfect location. A 'castle break' starts at £380 for two nights including bed, breakfast and dinner. All bedrooms non-smoking.

B2139 SW from Storrington; turning on right after Amberley turning.

Bailiffscourt

Climping Street, Climping, nr Littlehampton, BN17 5RW (01903 723511/fax 01903 723107/ bailiffscourt@hshotels.co.uk/www.hshotels.co.uk). **Rates** (B&B) *single* £130; *double* £145; *deluxe double/twin* £185-£230; *four-poster* £185-£270; *suite* £315. **Rooms** (all en suite) 1 single; 7 double/ twin; 11 deluxe double/twin; 13 four-poster. **Cards** AmEx, DC, Debit, MC, V.

Amberley Castle: *not your average B&B.*

Bailiffscourt is an extraordinary faux medieval house (actually built in 1927), perfect for an indulgent summer sojourn. The house, packed with stone-flagging, tapestry-hung walls, oak beams and carved doors, is set in 22 acres of pastureland with walled gardens, and is only 200 metres from Climping beach. There are facilities aplenty including a swimming pool, tennis court, croquet lawn and even a helipad. Many of the 32 bedrooms have four-poster beds. Children and dogs welcome.

Hotel is signposted off A259 between Bognor and Littlehampton.

Burpham Country Hotel

Burpham, nr Arundel, BN18 9RJ (01903 882160/ fax 01903 884627).
Rates (B&B) *single* £40; *double/twin* £41-£45; *four-poster* £50. **Rooms** (all en suite) 1 single; 9 double/twin. **Cards** AmEx, MC, V.

Not the huge country house hotel you might expect from the name, but a very pleasant B&B situated in the cute village of Burpham, a mile north-east of Arundel. The bedrooms are clean and decorated in classic English fashion with floral prints and gentle colours; many have good views of the surrounding countryside. There's a lounge and dining room for the use of guests, or it's only a quick stroll up the road to the excellent food and drink at the George & Dragon (*see page 83*). All bedrooms non-smoking.

Heading out of Arundel towards Worthing on A27, take left after railway bridge towards Burpham; hotel is 2.5 miles on right.

Critchfield House

Bosham Lane, Old Bosham, PO18 8HG (tel/fax 01243 572370/janetta@critchfield.demon.co.uk).
Rates (B&B) *single occupancy* £40; *double/twin* £60; *four-poster cabin* £70. **Rooms** 3 double (2 en suite); 1 four-poster cabin (en suite).

A light, airy B&B, in a Queen Anne house with a pretty garden that's kitted out with more than the standard bits and bobs including herbal teas, biccies and fresh fruit. Beds are comfy and the breakfast is up there with the best of them. Bosham is a peach of a village.

Bosham is four miles W of Chichester off A259; house is in centre of village by a garage.

The four glories of Goodwood

Few spots in South-East England can have as wide an appeal as **Goodwood**, a couple of miles north-east of Chichester.

First up, there's **Goodwood House**. Home for more than 300 years to the Dukes of Richmond, this wonderful Regency mansion has been restored in recent years to its original glory. There's plenty of priceless stuff to gawp at inside the house, including Gobelin tapestries, an extensive collection of Sèvres porcelain, paintings by Canaletto, Stubbs and Van Dyck, and furniture that includes Napoleon's campaign chair.

Secondly, there's the unexpectedly brilliant **Sculpture at Goodwood** (*see opposite*). The £10 admission fee may be offputting (and you have to be buzzed through a gate to gain entry), but noone interested in modern art should pass up the chance to stroll around the 40 or so exhibits of this stunning collection of contemporary sculpture, set in 20 acres of woodland. Around 12 new pieces are commissioned each year, so the collection is ever-changing. Among those who have contributed in the past are Elizabeth Frink, Anthony Caro, Andy Goldsworthy and David Mach.

Goodwood's other two major draws are sporting. Enjoying one of the loveliest situations of any horse-racing course in the country, the May to September season centres around the five-day July festival meeting, popularly known as **Glorious Goodwood**. The meeting has been a key sporting and social event since its introduction by the 4th Duke of Richmond in 1814.

Even more unusual is the three-day **Festival of Speed** in June, possibly the greatest gathering of motor cars and stars in the world. Highlights in 1999 included Emerson Fittipaldi driving the 228mph Penske PC23 and Sir Jack Brabham celebrating the fortieth anniversary of his first world championship behind the wheel of his 1959 Cooper T5I. There's also another race meeting in September.

Goodwood House (01243 755048/recorded info 01243 755040/www.goodwood.co.uk).
Open *Apr-July, Sept* 1-5pm Sun, Mon; *Aug* 1-5pm Mon-Thur, Sun. **Admission** £6; £3 12s-18s.

Goodwood Festival of Speed Goodwood Motor Circuit (01243 755055/www.goodwood.co.uk). **Admission** from £10 per day.

Goodwood Racecourse (0800 018 8191/01243 755022/www.gloriousgoodwood.co.uk). **Admission** from £7 per day.

Sculpture at Goodwood east of Goodwood House (01243 538449/www.sculpture.org.uk). **Open** *Mar-Oct* 10.30am-4.30pm Thur-Sat. **Admission** £10; £6 students; free under-6s.

Four facets of the stunning works on display at the outdoor **Sculpture at Goodwood**. See opposite.

Forge Cottage

Chilgrove, Chichester, PO18 9HX (01243 535333/ fax 01243 535363/forgecottage@btinternet.com/ www.scoot.co.uk/forge_cottage).
Rates (B&B) single £35; double/twin £79.
Rooms (all en suite) 1 single; 4 double/twin.
Cards AmEx, DC, Debit, MC, V.

This is a gem of a B&B, with plenty of home comforts and characterful surroundings. Watch out if you're tall – the seventeenth-century cottage has very low ceilings, but it's worth stooping to enjoy the charming, clean, well-furnished rooms. Many have lovely views, and there's a garden to lounge in, too. Breakfast is served hot from the Aga. A bonus is that the excellent White Horse Inn (*see page 83*) is literally over the road. One room is equipped for wheelchair users or those with limited mobility. Dogs welcome. All bedrooms non-smoking.
From A286 N of Chichester, take B2141 towards Petersfield; turn right to Chilgrove; Forge Cottage is next to White Horse pub in village.

Little Thakeham

Merrywood Lane, Storrington, RH20 3HE (01903 744416/fax 01903 745022).
Rates (B&B) single occupancy £129.25; double/twin £176.25-£235. **Rooms** (all en suite) 9 double/twin.
Cards AmEx, DC, Debit, MC, V.

Pricey, but a stunner. This 1902-3 Tudor-style manor is one of Edwin Lutyens's finest constructions (he called it 'the best of the bunch') and glories in its lofty proportions, expanses of stonework and antique strewn interior. The centrepiece is the wonderful soaring sitting room complete with minstrels' gallery and a huge fireplace. Bedrooms are equally grand in scale and décor, yet the hotel manages to feel wonderfully relaxed and indulgent. The Gertrude Jekyll-style gardens are a further attraction. Children are welcome.
A24 from Horsham towards Worthing; all the way round Washington roundabout (back to A24); turn left on to Rock Road (slip road); after 1 mile turn right at staggered crossroads into Merrywood Lane; the hotel is 300m on the right.

Millstream Hotel & Restaurant

Bosham, Chichester, PO18 8HL (01243 573234/ fax 01243 573459).
Rates (B&B) single £69; double/twin £112; four-poster £112. Children £10 per night.
Rooms (all en suite) 5 single; 27 double/twin; 1 four-poster. **Cards** AmEx, DC, Debit, MC, V.

This hotel is set in the idyllic waterside village of Bosham within a converted eighteenth-century malthouse cottage. It's a warm and welcoming place, although the bedrooms lack character. Facilities are good, however, and the staff are notably pleasant and helpful. Phone for details of special breaks including dinner at the hotel. Very popular, so book well in advance. Children and dogs welcome. Non-smoking rooms available.
Take A259 from Chichester W to Bosham; turn left at Bosham roundabout and follow signs to Bosham church and Millstream Hotel.

Ship Hotel

North Street, Chichester, PO19 1NH (01243 778000/ fax 01243 788000).

Rates (B&B) single £73; double/twin £109; four-poster £145; suite/family room £125. **Rooms** (all en suite) 6 single; 26 double/twin; 1 four-poster; 3 suite/family. **Cards** AmEx, DC, Debit, MC, V.

This small, efficiently run hotel (one-time home of Admiral Sir George Murray) is very conveniently situated if you're travelling to Chichester by train. The building's an appealing, red-brick Georgian affair, and all the clean, spacious rooms have been newly refurbished in a traditional, pleasant, if slightly anonymous generic hotel style. The larger First Sea Lord Room and those with four-posters come at a premium, but they're a nice treat. Children and dogs welcome. A cheaper alternative in town is **Suffolk House Hotel** (01243 778899; double from £88).

Swan Hotel

27-29 High Street, Arundel, BN18 9AG (01903 882314/fax 01903 883759/info@swanhotel.co.uk/ www.swan-hotel.co.uk).
Rates (B&B) single £55; double £60-£85; twin £75; triple £95. **Rooms** (all en suite) 1 single; 12 double; 1 twin; 1 triple. **Cards** AmEx, DC, Debit, MC, V.

The Swan feels more like a pub with rooms rather than a bona fide hotel, but you can't beat its central location and very reasonable rates. Bedrooms are brightly decorated and kitted out with all necessary comforts. A good choice if you're planning on visiting Arundel by train. Children welcome. All bedrooms non-smoking.

Where to eat & drink

Arundel and Chichester have a decent spread of pubs and (largely chain) restaurants between them. The best grub, though, is out of the urban centres. In addition to the places below, it's worth journeying eight or so miles west of Chichester to sample Ramon Farthing's classically influenced yet inventive cooking at **36 on the Quay** (01243 375592) in Emsworth. **Spencers** (01243 372744), also in Emsworth, is another good option.

Decent food is also available at a number of the area's pubs. The best bet in Amberley is the friendly **Bridge** (01798 831619), although the pretty **Black Horse** (01798 831700) and **Sportsmans** (with its lovely views; 01798 831787) are also worth a look. Other agreeable drinking holes in the area include the **Old House at Home** in Chidham (01243 572477), Donnington's **Blacksmiths Arms** (01243 783999), the sixteenth-century **Woodmans Arms** in Hammerpot (01903 871240) and the thatched **Gribble** in Oving (01243 786893), just east of Chichester, which brews its own ales

Amberley Castle

Amberley (01798 831992).
Food served 12.30-2pm, 7-9pm, daily.
Set meals *dinner* £35 (3 courses); *Sun lunch* £25.50 (3 courses). **Cards** AmEx, DC, Debit, MC, V.

As with the setting, so with the food at Amberley Castle – grand, opulent and luxurious. The chef also goes to strenuous lengths to dig up some of England's long-forgotten recipes, so expect the odd olde English gem like pike in water souchy sauce among more modern offerings. If you can't stretch to dinner (which, by the way, is pricey, with starters and desserts around £10 and mains around £20), then Sunday lunch is a more affordable option. This is jacket and tie territory. Booking is strongly advised.

Comme Ça

67 Broyle Road, Chichester (01243 788724).
Food served noon-2pm Tue-Sun; 6-10.30pm Tue-Sat. **Set meals** *lunch* £14.75 (2 courses), £17.75 (3 courses). **Cards** AmEx, DC, Debit, MC, V.

This very popular restaurant is really a converted roadside pub. It's quite a way north of the city centre, but fairly close to the Chichester Theatre and offers pre- and post-theatre dinners. At weekends the place is packed to capacity and booking is essential. Its popularity is down to a combination of assured, interesting food (for example, roast breast of French guinea fowl with an apricot and raisin chutney sauce), an extensive wine list and friendly helpful service.

Fleur de Sel

Manleys Hill, Storrington (01903 742331).
Food served noon-2pm Tue-Fri, Sun; 7-9.30pm Tue-Sat. **Set meals** *lunch Tue-Fri* £12.50 (2 courses), £16.50 (3 courses); *dinner Tue-Thur* £16.50 (2 courses), £20.50 (3 courses). **Cards** AmEx, Debit, MC, V.

The Fleur de Sel (previously located in Haslemere) is run by the highly acclaimed, Michelin-starred Michel Perraud. Food is (of course) French-influenced – expect to experience the delights of dishes such as crab cakes with langoustines and hazelnuts or pan-fried fillet of Scottish salmon and scallops with tomato and orange concassé. The emphasis is on using the freshest of seasonal products cooked with flair and imagination – well worth a visit. Three courses from the carte comes to around £30. Another (more modern) eating option in Storrington is the **Old Forge** (01903 743402).

George & Dragon

Burpham, nr Arundel (01903 883131).
Food served *restaurant* 7-9.30pm Mon-Sat; *bar food* noon-2pm, 7-9.45pm, Mon-Sat; noon-2pm, 7-9pm (Oct-Easter), Sun. **Cards** AmEx, DC, Debit, MC, V.

This attractive country pub is set in the lovely hamlet of Burpham, just north-east of Arundel. The gourmet aspect of the place is most in evidence at weekends when the dining room is opened for an array of well-cooked dishes such as calf's liver with orange and red onion chutney in a Grand Marnier gravy (£12.50) and fillet of bream with chive butter (£11.50). Sunday lunch, too, is well worth a try. Burpham is north of the A27 east of Arundel.

Platters

15 Southgate, Chichester (01243 530430).
Food served noon-1.45pm, 7-9.30pm, Tue-Sat. **Cards** DC, Debit, MC, V.

This comfy, unstuffy restaurant offers a good range of French-style cooking with a smattering of Asian influences. Portions are hearty and main meals come with a selection of vegetables. There's no blow-your-socks-off

originality here, but the cooking is perfectly competent, the atmosphere relaxing and the wine list extensive and reasonably priced. Wild mushrooms find their way in to many dishes (such as fillet of roast English lamb carved over a bed of wild mushrooms with a port wine sauce, £15.95). You can reserve for post-theatre dinner.

White Horse Inn

Chilgrove (01243 535219).
Food served noon-2pm, 6.30-9.45pm, Tue-Sat; noon-2pm Sun. **Set meals** £20 (2 courses), £24.50 (3 courses). **Cards** AmEx, Debit, MC, V.

In the tiny village of Chilgrove (on the B2141 between Petersfield and South Harting) this highfalutin pub serves first-rate food with a French slant (roast halibut with a samphire beurre blanc; roast magret of duck with wild cherries and gingerbread sauce). The real highlight of the White Horse, however, is a spectacular wine list, which includes such glories as Pétrus and Domaine de la Romanée Conti, as well as more reasonably priced bottles from South Africa and Germany.

What to see & do

Tourist information centres

61 High Street, **Arundel**, BN18 9AJ (01903 882268/ fax 01903 882419/www.arun.gov.uk).
Open *Easter-Oct* 9am-5pm Mon-Fri; 10am-5pm Sat, Sun; *Nov-Easter* 10am-3pm daily.

29A South Street, **Chichester**, PO19 1AH (01243 775888/fax 01243 539449/www.chichester.gov.uk).
Open 9.15am-5.15pm Mon-Sat; 10am-4pm Sun (Apr-Oct only).

Bike hire

Hargroves Cycles 2 Christchurch Buildings, **Chichester** (01243 537337). Close to the station.

Arundel Castle

Arundel (01903 882173).
Open *Apr-last Fri in Oct* noon-5pm Mon-Fri, Sun. Last entry 4pm. **Admission** £6.70; £4.20 5s-15s; £5.70 OAPs; £18 family.

This wonderful, imposing pile has its origins in the eleventh century, but the original Castle was heavily damaged during the Civil War and extensively remodelled in the eighteenth and nineteenth centuries. Inside is a fine collection of sixteenth-century furniture and paintings by Van Dyck, Gainsborough, Reynolds and Mytens among others. Don't miss the gem-like fourteenth-century Fitzalan Chapel (it can also be spied through gates at the back of St Nicholas Church), home to a clutch of tombs to Dukes of Norfolk past, and mercifully showing no signs of the time when Cromwell used it as a stable.

Arundel Cathedral

Parsons Hill, London Road, Arundel (01903 882297).
Open 9am-6pm/dusk daily. **Admission** free.

When he wasn't designing cabs, Joseph Hansom liked to turn his hand to a spot of architecture. This Catholic cathedral, which opened in 1873, was his idea of French Gothic from around 1400 – its exterior is best viewed from a distance. There's a fine rose window over the west door and, inside, the shrine of St Philip Howard (the Cathedral of Our Lady & St Philip Howard is the church's full name). Howard's father, the 4th Duke of Norfolk, had been beheaded by Elizabeth I for his part in Mary Queen of Scots' intrigues. Howard converted to Catholicism and, in anti-papist hysteria following the defeat of the Spanish Armada, was arrested and sentenced to death in 1589, although he died in the Tower of London six years later.

Arundel Museum & Heritage Centre
61 High Street, Arundel (01903 882344).
Open *Apr-Sept* 10.30am-5pm Mon-Sat; 2-5pm Sun; *Oct* 10.30am-5pm Sat; 2-5pm Sun. Last entry 4.30pm. **Admission** £1; 50p 5s-16s, OAPs.
A smallish but nonetheless interesting museum devoted to the history of the town, with scale models and old photographs.

Arundel Wildfowl & Wetlands Trust
Mill Road, Arundel (01903 883355).
Open *Apr-Oct* 9.30am-5.30pm daily; *Nov-Mar* 9.30am-4.30pm daily. **Admission** £4.75; £2.75 4s-16s; £3.75 OAPs, students; £12.25 family.
One of the network of nationwide wildlife centres founded by Sir Peter Scott, the Arundel WWT extends over 60 acres of beautiful parkland and is visited by thousands of migratory birds including Bewick's Swans. This is a lovely place for a wander and great for kids.

Bignor Roman Villa
Bignor, nr Pulborough (01798 869259/www.pyrrha.demon.co.uk).
Open *Mar-May, Oct* 10am-5pm Tue-Sun, bank hols; *June-Sept* 10am-6pm daily. **Admission** £3.35; £1.45 5s-16s; £2.35 OAPs.
Enjoying a lovely Downland setting, this evocative and pleasingly low-key excavated Roman villa is notable chiefly for its wonderful mosaic floors, one of which is the longest stretch of mosaic (80ft) on display in Britain.

Boxgrove Priory
Church Lane, Boxgrove (01243 774045).
Open 7.30am-dusk daily. **Admission** free; donations welcome.
This beautiful, early English church has a sixteenth-century painted ceiling by Lambert Barnard, a plethora of Victorian stained glass and the ruins of a Benedictine monastery nearby.

Chichester Cathedral
West Street, Chichester (01243 782595).
Open *Easter-Oct* 7.30am-7pm daily; *Nov-Easter* 7.30am-5pm daily (visiting restricted during services and concerts). **Admission** free; donations welcome.
The Cathedral that dominates the town was started in the 1070s and, although modified in succeeding centuries, has remained largely unaltered since around 1300 (although the famous slimline spire is a nineteenth-century addition). There's plenty of interest inside, including Chagall's powerful stained-glass window and a huge altar-screen tapestry by John Piper. Also here is the tomb of Richard Fitzalan, Earl of Arundel (d.1376), and his Countess, which was the inspiration for a poem by Philip Larkin.

Denmans Garden
Fontwell, nr Arundel (01243 542808).
Open *Mar-Oct* 9am-5pm daily. **Admission** £2.80; £1.50 4s-16s; £2.50 OAPs.
The philosophy behind this unique twentieth-century garden is to explore the way plants grow in the wild. As such, it's a delightfully relaxing place to wander around.

Fishbourne Roman Palace
Salthill Road, Fishbourne, Chichester (01243 785859).
Open *mid-Feb-Mar, Nov-mid-Dec* 10am-4pm daily; *Apr-July, Sept, Oct* 10am-5pm daily; *Aug* 10am-6pm daily; *mid-Dec-mid-Feb* 10am-4pm Sat, Sun. **Admission** £4.40; £2.30 5s-15s; £3.70 OAPs, students; £11.50 family.
These are the most extensive remains of a Roman palace in Britain, and are particularly famed for their beautiful mosaic floors. Only the north wing of the palace has been excavated; it's likely that the original building contained around 100 rooms. There are also gardens recreated in their Roman pattern, and a Roman gardening museum.

Pallant House Gallery
9 North Pallant, Chichester (01243 774557).
Open 10am-5pm Tue-Sat; 12.30-5pm Sun, bank hols. **Admission** £4; free under-16s; £3 OAPs; £2 students.
Housed in a lovely Queen Anne townhouse, a diverting selection of modern British art (including works by Moore and Hepworth) is laid out within the period furnished rooms and garden.

Parham House & Gardens
nr Pulborough (01903 742021/www.parhaminsussex.co.uk).
Open *house Apr-Oct* 2-6pm, *gardens Apr-Oct* noon-6pm, Wed, Thur, Sun, bank hols. Last entry 5pm. **Admission** *house & gardens* £5; £1 5s-15s; £4 OAPs; £10 family; *gardens only* £3; 50p 5s-15s; £3 OAPs.
A rare example of mid-twentieth-century restoration ideas on a large Elizabethan manor. The result is wonderfully harmonious and includes the fine panelled Long Gallery and Great Hall plus 11 acres of exquisite gardens.

Weald & Downland Open Air Museum
Singleton, nr Chichester (01243 811363/www.wealddown.co.uk).
Open *Mar-Oct* 10.30am-6pm daily; *Nov-Feb* 10.30am-4pm Wed, Sat, Sun; (*26 Dec-1 Jan* 10.30am-4pm daily). **Admission** £5.20; £2.50 5s-16s.
One of the area's most worthwhile museums, this unusual collection of around 40 historic buildings scattered over a 50-acre site offers a fascinating historical journey through the region's architecture. There are regular events and plenty to amuse the kids. Phone for details.

West Dean Gardens
West Dean, nr Chichester (01243 818210/www.westdean.org.uk/gardens.html).
Open *Mar-Oct* 10.30am-5pm daily. **Admission** £4; £2 5s-15s; £3.50 OAPs; £10 family ticket.
A fantastic place to visit, with an outstanding working Victorian walled kitchen garden including 13 historic greenhouses, plus 35 acres of ornamental grounds set in the Downland landscape.

North Surrey Downs

Life beyond the 'burbs.

Box Hill: *the finest views in Surrey.*

Funny place, the North Downs. As you sweep out of south London you could be forgiven for wondering whether it exists, or had been devoured whole by the sprawling, voracious grey metropolis. And then suddenly, as you cross the M25, you reach the green: acres of farmland pitted with pretty villages to the east; rolling chalk hills thick with woodland to the west. But the contrast is relative: this swathe of Surrey and Kent has been seared by the T-shaped M25 and M23 motorways; practically the entire area from Guildford in the west almost to Sevenoaks in the east and south to

Gatwick has been to varying degrees colonised by commuters and suburbanites. At times, when you pull out of one of the main towns and off the main road, the sudden arrival of a stretch of countryside becomes oddly disorienting; if you look too hard, the fields of cows seem strangely and comically out of place, like eccentric accessories to the suburban garden.

Aside from the almost magically secluded uplands south-west of Dorking, this area is not a place you can easily lose yourself in. A main road, it appears, is never more than ten minutes away. Nor is it uniformly picturesque; in many villages it seems that for every romantic old orange brick Surrey cottage there are two incongruously vulgar 1970s villas. In this sense, the North Downs is perhaps best regarded as a series of elegant, self-contained set pieces, to enjoy before moving on to the next one. And for this small mercy one must be thankful for the National Trust. The area is studded with its properties, which range from country houses to that rare phenomenon of the South-East, the large tract of common heath and woodland.

By train from London

Trains to **Dorking** leave **London Waterloo** every half an hour (journey time **40mins**). Trains to **Reigate** leave **London Victoria** hourly – there is a change at **Redhill** (total journey time **45mins**). Trains to **Guildford** leave **London Waterloo** every quarter of an hour (journey time **35-55mins**).

Towns and country

The town of **Reigate** falls just west of where
the two great motorways intersect. Although
there are reminders of its rather unexciting
history going back to the Norman Conquest –
such as the castle, of which nothing remains but
an arch, and the eighteenth-century market hall
on the high street – this is principally a thriving
but rather dull commuter town. You can stock
up here and head off south and west to sample
a clutch of infinitely more rewarding villages in
the **Mole Valley**. **Betchworth**'s claim to fame
is the appearance of its church in the film *Four
Weddings and a Funeral*; St Michael's is an
impressively large building, parts of which date
back to Saxon times. **Leigh** (pronounced 'Lye')
is a useful stop-off point for a pint. **Brockham**
has won the Best Kept Village in Surrey award
on several occasions, and it is worth checking
out the village green. Heading east, **Outwood**
boasts the seventeenth-century Post Mill, built
in 1665, which is surrounded by acres of
National Trust-owned common land, ideal for
picnics and nature walks. **Godstone**, with its
splendid village green, and **Oxted** have their
moments, but these are essentially commuter
towns. South of Westerham, just over the
border in Kent, lies Churchill's old house,
Chartwell (*see page 89*). If you fancy a flutter,
why not spend a day at the races at **Lingfield**,
the country's busiest racecourse (01342 834800).

West of Reigate lies **Dorking**. Again, this is
a dull residential town, its value maintained by
its proximity to some of the most beautiful
parts of Surrey, preserved by green belt
policies, unfolding out west towards Guildford.
Box Hill is the site of the traumatic picnic in
Jane Austen's novel *Emma*; it is rather busier
these days, but a welcome oasis of greenery
nonetheless. Heading south and west into the
big patch of green on your map, you climb into
gorgeous woodland. The narrow, winding roads
here are bordered with lush, sprawling
rhododendrons, occasionally interrupted by
sections where the road passes under a thick
canopy of trees, temporarily plunging you into
a mysterious, ancient gloom. **Coldharbour** is
well groomed, with none of the suburban
naffness infecting many Surrey villages, and is
a convenient base camp for visiting nearby
Leith Hill.

Guildford, the bustling, ancient capital of
Surrey, has an old castle and a modern
cathedral – enough to detain you for half a day.
But your attention may well wander to the
array of attractions that peel off the A248 to the
east: manor houses, gardens and a couple of
picturesque villages, including the much-visited
Shere, which boasts a partly Norman church.

Where to stay

There's the usual range of grand converted
manor house hotels and cosy farmhouse B&Bs
along this part of the North Downs. Make sure
you get the owners to send a detailed route
map, particularly if you are staying in a smaller
place: they can be literally off the beaten track,
and not well signposted.

Bulmer Farm

Holmbury St Mary, Dorking, RH5 6LG
(01306 730210).
Rates (B&B) *single occupancy* £20-£32;
double/twin £40-£44. **Rooms** 3 double (all en suite);
5 twin (2 en suite). Min stay 2 nights (en suite rooms).
At the southern end of this pretty village, set in deep
countryside, this attractive seventeenth-century farmhouse B&B offers peace, quiet and privacy – some of the
rooms adjoin the main farmhouse allowing guests to
come and go freely. No children under the age of 12. Non-
smoking rooms available.
*A25 E of Dorking; turn left at Abinger Hammer on to
B2126; 3 miles to Holmbury St Mary; farm is on corner
opposite garage.*

Godstone Hotel

The Green, Godstone, RH9 8DT (01883 742461).
Rates (B&CB) *single occupancy* £39; *double/twin*
£55. **Rooms** (all en suite) 6 double; 2 twin.
Cards AmEx, DC, Debit, MC, V.
Don't be misled by the Moët & Chandon sun parasols
outside; this is a resolutely middle-brow affair. Its origins are sixteenth century and, while it has the low
beams and open fire, the place has a rather uninspiring
late 1970s ambience (though little in the way of kitsch
value). The domineering car park at the rear (which
overpowers the half-hearted attempt at a garden) suggests this is more motel than hotel. Children welcome.
*J6 M25; follow signs to Godstone; last building on left of
High Street (after village green).*

Herons Head Farm

Mynthurst, Leigh, RH2 8QD (01293 862475/
heronshead@clara.net/www.seetb.org.uk/heronshead).
Rates (B&B) *single occupancy* £45; *double/twin* £50;
family £75. **Rooms** (all en suite) 4 double/twin.
A Grade II-listed sixteenth-century farmhouse hidden
well away from the nearest road, this secluded B&B
offers astonishing value for money: cosy period bedrooms, some with a whirlpool, some with a dreamy view
over the pretty garden and nabe (haunt of the magnificent herons). The owners are relaxed, and happy to
uncover the outdoor heated swimming pool for guests,
who also have use of a tennis court. Children welcome.
Non-smoking throughout.
*Leigh is SW of Reigate and SE of Dorking; at crossroads in
Leigh take road S towards Norwood Hill; right turn after 1
mile (after sign to Mynthurst); farm is 0.5 miles on right.*

Langshott Manor

Langshott, nr Horley, RH6 9LN (01293 786680/
admin@langshottmanor.com/www.slh.com/langshot).
Rates (B&B) *double/twin* £155-£185; *four-poster*
£210; *suite* £210-£250. **Rooms** (all en suite) 10

double/twin; 3 four-poster; 2 suites.
Cards AmEx, DC, Debit, MC, V.

For all its reconditioned sixteenth-century splendour, it's hard to forget that a (thankfully sleepy) modern executive home estate is hidden just a few hundred yards away behind the walls of the garden of Langshott Manor. Isolated it ain't. But it is undoubtedly luxurious, if authentically and charmingly cramped, the staff are attentive and friendly, and – surrounded by a fast-maturing walled garden – it somehow exudes a country ambience. There's little, if any, noise from the nearby Gatwick jets.

A23 to Horley Chequers roundabout; take Ladbroke Road to Langshott; house is 0.75 miles on right.

Nutfield Priory

Nutfield, Redhill, RH1 4EL (01737 824400/nutpriory@aol.com.uk).
Rates *single* £120; *double/twin* £145; *four-poster* £225; *suite* £205-£285. Special breaks.
Rooms (all en suite) 8 single; 27 double; 11 twin; 5 four-poster; 9 suites. **Cards** AmEx, DC, Debit, MC, V.

Don't be put off by the horribly corporate entrance gates; this ex-folly, built for a Victorian MP in a Gothic-style meant to reflect the Palace of Westminster has real charm. The rooms are spacious and elegant; elsewhere, stained glass, cloisters and an impressive-looking library set a gentle, faintly scholastic tone. Do insist on a room on the south side, with its spectacular views rolling out across the Surrey countryside. Children and dogs welcome. Non-smoking rooms available.

In Redhill take A25; follow signs E to Godstone; hotel is 1.5 miles on right.

Mickleham's creeper-clad **William IV** *pub.*

Where to eat & drink

In the opinion of one twentysomething local, Reigate is 'buzzing at night' these days; but where drinking is concerned there's little out of the ordinary in the market towns. Out in the villages you will find a number of pubs offering decent ale, atmosphere, pub grub and no sign of rowdy, bored suburban teenagers. South of Reigate, the **Plough** in Leigh is a large, friendly pub with a rose-bordered beer garden, basic pub grub and King & Barnes ale. The **Dolphin** at Betchworth (01737 842288) serves Young's beer and offers a large menu and a small selection of wines by the glass; it's heaving at weekend lunchtimes and has the unusual attraction of a working blacksmith's forge across the road. South-west of Dorking, the **Plough Inn**, Coldharbour, offers nine real ales (Crooked Furrow, Tallywacker, et al) and boasts the Leigh Hill Brewery on site. If you've overdone it on the grog, take advantage of the fact it has accommodation (single occupancy £55; double £70). There's an extensive (reasonably priced) menu and wine list, and a garden to relieve the pressure in the front parlour. Around Box Hill, the **William IV** at Mickleham (01372 372590) has attracted plaudits for its mixture of fine dining, real ales

and panoramic views. West of Reigate, the **Fox & Hounds** on Tilburstow Hill (01342 893474) outside South Godstone is a warm, low-beamed pub offering expensive pub grub as well as sit-down restaurant fare. You can sup your Greene King ales in the beer garden, which overlooks meadowland to the rear. And if you fancy a bit of spice, **Le Raj** in Epsom Downs (211 Fir Tree Road; 01737 371371) offers Bangladeshi food of a standard that you'd be hard-pushed to beat in London. Recently, there has also been a rash of decent new restaurants in the market towns, including the following.

La Barbe

71 Bell Street, Reigate (01737 241966).
Food served noon-2pm, 7.15-9.45pm, Mon-Fri; 7.15-9.45pm Sat. **Cards** AmEx, Debit, MC, V.

A loud, fun, chaotic tribute to all things French, this is the place to come to enjoy a relaxed, unpretentious party atmosphere. The menu is equally straightforward: if you're in the Gallic mood, try the snails cooked in garlic butter; follow up with a choice of user-friendly meat and fish dishes. Expect to pay around £24.95 for the three-course dinner, with wine on top.

The Chapel at the Hautboy

Ockham Lane, Ockham (01483 225355).
Food served 7-9pm daily. **Set meals** £35 (3 courses); £42 (4 courses). **Cards** AmEx, DC, Debit, MC, V.

Sussex & Surrey

The Chapel is the centrepiece of this grand, self-proclaimed 'Gothic hostelry', with its vaulted ceiling, replica Tuscan frescoes and minstrel's gallery. The fish and meat-dominated menu offers the likes of roasted sea bass on a bed of fennel purée with caviar sauce. The four-course set menu will cost you £42 before wine. It's a popular choice for wedding receptions, so check in advance.

The Dining Room

59a High St, Reigate (01737 226650).
Food served noon-2.30pm, 7-10pm, Mon-Fri; 7-10pm Sat; noon-2pm Sun. **Cards** AmEx, DC, Debit, MC, V.

Gourmands come from all over to experience the pleasures of the Dining Room; its L-shaped, intimate layout and cream and gold décor may not appeal to all, but the menu's traditional English/Mediterranean fare – a lean, fleshy fillet of rabbit wrapped in parma ham, grilled baby fennel and fresh herb dressing perhaps – will satisfy anyone in search of high-class, rich comfort food. Dinner here will set you back around £50 a head.

Gurkha Kitchen

111 Station Road, Oxted (01883 722621).
Food served noon-2.30pm, 6-11pm, Mon-Thur; 6-11.30pm Fri, Sat; 1-10pm Sun. **Set meals** lunch Sun £7.50 (3 courses). **Cards** Debit, MC, V.

A genuine Nepalese restaurant in the heart of Surrey. The room is surprisingly elegant, with black steel chairs, floorboards and starched napery, and the food is first-rate and as far from bog-standard curry-house as it's possible to imagine. Try the bhutuwa (chicken livers stir-fried in Nepalese spices) or hariyo macha (fish wrapped in spinach) and expect to eat well for under £15.

Kinghams

Gomshall Lane, Shere (01483 202168).
Food served noon-2.15pm, 7-9.15pm, Tue-Sat; noon-2.15pm Sun. **Set meals** lunch Mon-Sat £11.95 (2 courses); dinner Mon-Thur £13.95 (2 courses). **Cards** AmEx, DC, Debit, MC, V.

This old, squat building on the main street of Shere has tiny windows and is rather dark and cosy. Carnivores will appreciate the rich, meaty emphasis – Guinea fowl filled with boursin marinated in red wine is typical. There's a long wine list, while post-prandial coffee can be taken out in the garden, weather permitting. The bill generally comes to around £30-£40 per head.

Langshott Manor

Langshott, nr Horley (01293 786680).
Food served 12.30-1.30pm, 7-9pm, daily.

This tiny, understated restaurant offers a fine mix of sophisticated English and continental cuisine in keeping with its luxurious hotel surroundings. The staff are friendly but discreet. Foodies can pig out on the seven-course gourmet menu at £45, washing it down with a little number chosen from the rather expensive wine list (£18-£110). Reservations are essential.

Tu Tu L'Auberge

Tilburstow Hill, South Godstone (01342 892318).
Food served noon-1.45pm, 7-9.30pm, Tue-Sat; noon-1.45pm Sun. **Set meals** £16.50 (3 courses) Mon-Fri; £18.50 (3 courses) Sat, Sun. **Cards** AmEx, DC, Debit, MC, V.

This eccentric restaurant (the name refers to the owners' ballet-dancing daughter) was once a crusty English manor house eaterie; it is now a bright, eclectic shrine to art deco and '50s French film stars, where the friendly, efficient staff wear (when the mood takes them) Hawaiian shirts. The sparky set menus (which change weekly) suggest good value for money: examples include honeyed duck confit and Szechuan pepper, and poached skate in a Thai red masala paste with saffron new potatoes. On a nice day you can eat al fresco. Check to ensure it hasn't been commandeered by a summer wedding party.

What to see & do

Tourist information centres

14 Tunsgate, **Guildford**, GU1 3QT (01483 444333/www.guildfordborough.co.uk).
Open Mar-Sept 9am-5.30pm Mon-Sat; 10am-4.30pm Sun; Oct-Feb 9am-5pm Mon-Sat.

Town Hall, Castlefield Road, **Reigate**, RH2 0SH (01737 276045). **Open** 9am-5pm Mon-Fri.

Clacket Lane Motorway Service Area, M25 Westbound, **Westerham** (01959 565615).
Open 9am-5pm daily.

Bike hire

Action Packs Box Hill Station, **Westhumble**, Dorking (01306 886944). Inside station booking hall.

Box Hill

Off A24, N of Dorking (01306 885502).

A steep, winding road leads you 172 metres up to the National Trust information centre car park just below the summit, where you can strap on your walking boots, and wander off with your picnic into 1,200 acres of woodland and chalk downland with some stunning views towards the West Sussex Downs. Box Hill is home to roe deer, and rare orchids, butterflies and bats.

Clandon Park

The Street, West Clandon (01483 222482/www.nationaltrust.org.uk).
Open house 11.30am-4.30pm Tue-Thur, Sun; gardens dawn-dusk daily. **Admission** (NT) £4.40; £2.20 5s-16s.

This sumptuous and elegant eighteenth-century Palladian mansion (located three miles east of Guildford off the A247) was built on a grand scale by the Venetian architect Leoni. The house is known for its stunning two-storey Marble Hall and the Gubbay Collection of porcelain, furniture and needlework. Capability Brown designed the garden.

Denbies Wine Estate

Off A24 N of Dorking (01306 742002).
Open 10am-5.30pm Mon-Sat; 11.30am-5.30pm Sun.
Admission £5; £2.50 5s-16s; £4.25 OAPs; £12 family.

England's biggest wine estate ('blessed with the same chalk soil structures as the Champagne region of France') produces 400,000 bottles of wine a year, and offers tours of the vineyards and the winery, and tastings in the cellar. There's also a restaurant and a shop.

Gatwick Zoo

Russ Hill, Charlwood (01293 862312/
www.cappuccino.co.uk/gatwickzoo).
Open 10am-5pm daily. **Admission** £4.95;
£3.95 3s-14s.

Penguins, wallabies, flamingos and monkeys are among
the inmates. Kids can burn off any excess energy in the
adjoining adventure playground.

Leith Hill

Off A24 SW of Dorking, 1 mile from Coldharbour.
(01306 711777).

The National Trust-owned Leith Hill is, at 965 feet, the
highest point in the south-east of England and almost
as popular as Box Hill with weekend walkers. At the
summit stands an eighteenth-century Gothic tower offering magnificent views, including a glimpse of the
English Channel on a clear day.

Outwood Windmill

The Old Mill, Outwood Common, nr Redhill (01342
843644). **Open** *Easter-Oct* 2-6pm Sun, bank hols.
Admission £2; £1 4s-14s; £1 OAPs.

Have a wander round the ground floor of Britain's oldest working windmill, which dates from 1665, and is set
among gorgeous scenery.

Polesden Lacey

Dorking Road, 2 miles S of Great Bookham off A246
nr Dorking (01372 452048). **Open** *Mar-Oct* 1.30pm-
5pm Wed-Sun. **Admission** (NT) £6; £3 5s-16s.

The Queen Mother spent part of her honeymoon at this
National Trust Regency villa. You can admire its extravagant Edwardian furnishings and its renowned herbaceous borders in the walled garden. If you're feeling
energetic, follow one of the extensive walks into the surrounding countryside, with its acres of parkland: it's
ideal for a picnic or game of cricket with the kids.

Churchill's Chartwell

You may be left cold by the appropriation
of Winston Churchill as the cigar-toting
totem of the reactionary right, but don't
let that put you off a visit to his country
pad, **Chartwell**. This is a gem of a house,
with a brilliantly original exhibition, and a
stunning garden thrown in. Churchill
bought Chartwell, then a crumbling and
gloomy Victorian mansion, in 1922. He
proceeded to renovate it – even building
some of the brick walls himself – with the
help of the architect Philip Tilden,
transforming it into a light, warm and
surprisingly unpretentious family home.
The house manages to avoid being yet
another tribute to Churchill's World War
Two exploits (he never stayed at Chartwell
during this period) but – a stroke of
originality – is 'preserved' in its 1930s
state when he was out of office, and
when the place served as a locus for anti-
appeasement plotters. The lack of pomp
and grandeur is striking: the elegant front
door, we are told, was discovered by
Tilden in a London junk shop. The
entrance hall is modest – look out for the
visitors' book, a fascinating who's who of
mid-century society, from Field Marshal
Montgomery to Churchill's best-known
portraitist, Graham Sutherland. A finely
chosen array of photographic prints are
hung around the house, charting
Winston's life from bowler-hatted Brighton
schoolboy to dashing, pencil-
moustachioed cavalryman, through both

wars to an endearing picture of him in
later years waddling along in what
appears to be an outsized Hawaiian shirt.
Make sure you see the dining room, with
its view to die for, and Churchill's study –
the engine room of the Churchill finances,
from which he dictated his copious output
of books and articles. On your way out
through the kitchen a simple, succinct
exhibition sets his life in context.

Outside, the gardens are trad English
country house in style but executed with
an informal and unselfconscious grace.
From here you can take in the magnificent
prospect of the Weald of Kent before
ambling downhill towards the two lakes
and the swimming pool.

This is no jingoistic shrine but a portrait
of the man in full; an affectionate and
subtle tribute to a political giant; a
complex man whose breadth of learning,
experience and interests has the effect of
making his political successors appear
dull and one-dimensional in comparison.

Note that admission to the house is by
timed ticket – if you have to wait before
you can enter, there's plenty to keep you
occupied (by way of the garden, Churchill's
studio and the inevitable shop).

Chartwell Westerham (01732 868381).
Open *house, garden & studio late July-Aug* 11am-
5pm Tue-Sun, bank hols; *Sept, Oct* 11am-5pm
Wed-Sun. Last entry 4.15pm.
Admission (NT) £5.50; £2.75 5s-16s. Guided
tours (min 20 people) 10am Wed (phone to book in
advance). Phone for details of special events.

The Three Counties

Greenery, scenery and gorgeous country houses.

The junction of Hampshire, Surrey and West Sussex provides one of the loveliest examples of countryside near London. The combination of gently rolling fields, lushly wooded areas and pretty villages makes it an attractive prospect, and the (many) signs of commuter life are easily hidden behind the greenery. The area near Guildford and Godalming is the most developed, but even here there are many wonderful pubs and villages – just ignore the A-roads and investigate the byways.

Of the small towns, **Farnham**, **Petersfield**, **Midhurst** and **Haslemere** are all handsome, relatively unspoilt places, but the glory of this area is the countryside. Walkers and cyclists are spoiled for choice – many of the walks in the *Time Out Book of Country Walks* are based in this region. The land between and around **Frensham Common** and **Hindhead** offers heath and woodland, including trails to the scenic **Devil's Punch Bowl**; sections of the **North** and **South Downs** top and tail the area; and there are wonderful gardens, ranging from the vast **Winkworth Arboretum** to the smaller **Ramster** (near Chiddingfold; 01428 654167). Much of the land is owned by the National Trust; its heathland management work is explained at **Witley Common Information Centre**.

Conversely, there aren't many stately homes in the Three Counties (although there's a wealth of interesting domestic architecture), but one gem is the late seventeenth-century mansion at **Petworth**. Also notable, especially if you have kids in tow, is **Loseley Park**, home of Loseley ice-cream. Homes worth visiting because of their literary associations are Gilbert White's house at **Selborne** and Jane Austen's in **Chawton**.

By train from London

Trains to **Farnham** leave **Waterloo** every half an hour to 1 hour (journey time between **45mins** and **1hr**). Trains to **Petersfield** leave **Waterloo** hourly (journey time just under **1hr**), the train also passes through **Haslemere** (journey time **40mins**). Trains to **Godalming** leave **Waterloo** every half an hour (journey time **40-45mins**).

Village life

In addition to the (well-signposted) sights, the towns and villages of the Three Counties reward investigation. The village of **Petworth** is stuffed with antiques shops (parking is difficult, but persevere). The big attraction is **Petworth House**, but to see how the other half lived, look at **Petworth Cottage Museum** (346 High Street; 01798 342100), based in an estate worker's cottage. Children may enjoy the **Dolls House Museum** (Station Road; 01798 344044). There's also an arts festival each summer (01798 343523 for details).

A few miles west is **Midhurst**, a picturesque town with a decent variety of cafés and restaurants, and the ruins of **Cowdray House** (a Tudor mansion that partly burnt down in the late eighteenth century); it's also handy for polo at **Cowdray Park** (01730 813257). Directly north is **Haslemere**, another handsome town, with a decent bookshop, an idiosyncratic museum, a quality cheese shop, a teashop and good restaurants (try the **Little Gem** – 01428 651462 – where the bargain set lunch is £8.50 for two courses, or the **Poacher's Pocket** – 01428 652625 – which is housed in an old bakery); the **Dolmetsch Festival of Early Music** is held here every July. Much of the surrounding countryside is owned by the National Trust; **Blackdown** (over 900 feet above sea level, the highest point in Sussex) offers wonderful views – Tennyson had a house on the slopes. Just before Haslemere is **Hindhead**, notable as the birthplace of Arthur Conan Doyle and home of **Drummonds Architectural Antiques** (01428 609444), a splendid architectural salvage yard.

Further north, **Farnham** has many Georgian buildings, a castle, a museum of local history with a walled garden, a range of places to eat (including Pizza Express and Café Rouge) and some interesting shops. Just outside Farnham is **Bentley**; this village featured in the fly-on-the-wall TV documentary *The Village*, and is worth visiting for the garden and teashop at **Bury Court** (01420 23202). Also near Farnham, on the B3001, is **Waverley Abbey**. These English Heritage-owned Cistercian monastery ruins are reached by a short lakeside walk.

West of Farnham is **Godalming**, a nice enough town worth visiting if you're interested in the Arts and Crafts movement (which was very active in Surrey). In the town museum there's a room devoted to the Gertrude Jekyll/Edwin Lutyens collaboration and a small courtyard garden reconstructed to a Jekyll design; and behind the parish church is a memorial cloister and Jekyll garden dedicated to local man Jack Phillips, the wireless operator on the *Titanic*. Outside Godalming, at **Hambledon**, is the National Trust-owned **Oakhurst Cottage**, which is furnished with items from the Gertrude Jekyll collection (open by appointment only; phone 01428 683207 for details). Slightly west of Hambledon (just outside Brook on the A286) is **Green Stop** (01428 682913), an exceptionally nice garden centre, with an enclosed play area and spacious café, that makes a great pitstop, especially if you have bored children in the car.

Where to stay

Crown Inn

The Green, Petworth Road, Chiddingfold, GU8 4TX (01428 682255/fax 01428 685736).
Rates (B&B) *single* £57; *double* £67; *four-poster* £90-£110. **Rooms** (all en suite) 1 single; 3 double; 4 four-poster. **Cards** AmEx, DC, Debit, MC, V.
A medieval timber-framed inn with rooms, a restaurant and a spacious bar. It's a mellow place that doesn't over-do the 'olde worlde' aspect, despite having more than its fair share of wood beams, open fires and four-posters. Decent food runs from bar meals (leek and potato soup, £2.75; cottage pie, £6.25) through cream teas (£3.75) to full meals. Don't leave without checking out the upholstered phone booth in the entrance hall. Children welcome.
Chiddingfold is on A283; inn is on right.

Mizzards Farm

Rogate, Petersfield, GU31 5HS (01730 821656/fax 01730 821655).
Rates (B&B) *double/twin* £54-£58; *four-poster* £62.
Rooms (all en suite) 2 double/twin; 1 four-poster.
As superior a B&B as you could hope for. Harriet and Julian Francis's sixteenth-century farmhouse stands in wonderful rolling countryside within two acres of gardens packed with enough amusements to fill a weekend, including a heated swimming pool, croquet lawn and outsize outdoor chess. Two of the bedrooms are smallish and not particularly distinguished but the master bedroom, complete with four-poster and kitschy marble bathroom, is a corker. An excellent breakfast is served in the imposing central hall. Children over eight welcome. Non-smoking throughout.
From A272 at Rogate, take turn to Harting/Nyewood; over humpback bridge; after 300m turn into lane on right; house is at end of lane.

Old Railway Station

nr Petworth, GU28 OJF (tel/fax 01798 342346/ mlr@old-station.co.uk/www.old-station.co.uk).
Rates (B&B) *single occupancy* £40-£60; *double/twin* £60-£84. **Rooms** (all en suite) 4 double; 2 twin.
Cards Debit, MC, V.
A beautiful and idiosyncratic B&B, in what was Petworth railway station and several converted Pullman

*Put your Nimzo-Indian defence through its paces while staying at **Mizzards Farm**.*

carriages. The bedrooms are simply but delightfully furnished; breakfast is served in what was the waiting room or, in summer, on the platform overlooking a banked garden. The Badgers, a real ale pub, is about two minutes' walk. A stylish but unfussy base at a very reasonable price. Book well ahead. No children under ten years old. All bedrooms non-smoking.

On A285 1 mile S of Petworth; pull into front of Badgers pub; take slip road leading to hotel.

Park House

Bepton, nr Midhurst, GU29 0JB (tel/fax 01730 812880). **Rates** (B&B) *single* £45-£75; *double/twin* £99-£130; *family room* £110-£140. **Rooms** (all en suite) 1 single; 12 double/twin; 1 family room. **Cards** AmEx, DC, Debit, MC, V.

A small, unassuming, family-run country house hotel with a great deal of charm. Amusements include two grass tennis courts, a pitch and putt course, a croquet lawn and a heated outdoor swimming pool. The relaxed atmosphere carries through to the bar – residents help themselves, at any hour, and pay later. Not a luxury venue, but a very nice one. Non-smoking rooms available.

On B2226, 2 miles S of Midhurst.

Spread Eagle Hotel & Health Spa

South Street, Midhurst, GU29 9NH (01730 816911/fax 01730 815668/ i.fleming@virgin.net/www.hshotels.co.uk). **Rates** (B&CB) *single occupancy* £95-£140; *double/twin* £125-£205; *four-poster/suite* £205. **Rooms** (all en suite) 32 double/twin; 5 four-poster; 2 suites. **Cards** AmEx, DC, Debit, MC, V.

This chichi hotel is located in the midst of Midhurst. Its health spa is newly built and features a pool, a gym, a hot tub, a sauna, a steam room and a beauty centre. Some of the pleasantly decorated bedrooms have four-posters (as befits a hotel established in 1430). This is one for those who want modern comforts with a certain amount of traditional charm. Midhurst's **Angel Hotel** (01730 812421) has the same owners, but a more old-fashioned, townhouse atmosphere; it also has two restaurants. Children and dogs welcome. Non-smoking rooms available.

Swan Inn

Lower Street, Fittleworth, RH20 1EN (01798 865429/865721). **Rates** (B&B) *single* £30; *double/twin* £60; *four-poster* £75. **Rooms** (all en suite) 3 single; 4 double; 2 twin; 2 four-poster. Special breaks. **Cards** AmEx, Debit, MC, V.

A large fourteenth-century coaching inn with a lovely garden, in a very pretty village. The interior has several low, oak-panelled bar rooms, hung with artworks 'painted by resident artists in the late nineteenth century in lieu of board and lodging'. An interesting menu lists open sandwiches (£4.75) alongside mains such as spinach and cream cheese dumplings (£7.50). The pub is opposite the River Arun and is surrounded by public footpaths, which are great for strolls in the country; in cold weather put your feet up with a pint and the papers in front of the open log fire. Children welcome. Non-smoking rooms available.

On B2138 between Pulborough and Petworth.

Where to eat & drink

There are some very characterful pubs in these parts; the problem is that most of them can only be reached by car. For atmosphere and a decent pint, we recommend the following: the **Sun** (Dunsfold; 01483 200242), which overlooks the village green; **Noah's Ark** (Lurgashall; 01428 707346), an attractive pub serving decent food – especially the sandwiches, where, pop trivia fans might like to note, Haircut 100 shot their video for *Fantastic Day*. The **Grantly Arms** (Wonersh; 01483 893351) is in a beautiful village, looks the epitome of English quaint (though the interior is a disappointment) and has a ten-pin bowling alley; just along the road is the **Villagers** (Blackheath; 01483 893152) – hidden away, it's not a typically pretty pub, but the staff are friendly and the food is a cut above average. The **White Horse** (Hascombe; 01483 208258) is a handsome inn adorned with beautiful tiles and biblical scripts; also good-looking is the **Chequers** (Well; 01256 862605) – drink outside on a vine-covered terrace. The attraction of the **Woolpack** (Elstead; 01252 703106) lies in the easygoing atmosphere, blackboard menu of crowd-pleasers, real ales and warren of low-slung rooms. For more formal dining, try the modish menu at the **Swan** (Chiddingfold; 01428 682073).

Duke of Cumberland Arms

Henley (01428 652280). **Food served** 11am-2pm, 7.30-9pm, Mon-Sat; noon-2pm, 7.30-9pm, Sun.

The pretty garden with trout ponds and a view over the Sussex/Surrey Weald to the North Downs are reasons enough to come to the Duke of Cumberland Arms, but the relaxed atmosphere and the unpretentious, first-rate food make it a must-visit. Excellent sandwiches, plough-man's lunches, own-made treacle tart and apple pie – all take a back seat to the daily changing array of seafood (dressed crab, £5.50). Indoor seating is restricted to one small wood-panelled, cream-painted bar. Children – who will love the garden – are made very welcome.

Hawkley Arms

Hawkley (01730 827205). **Food served** noon-2pm, 7-9.30pm, Mon-Fri; noon-2.30pm, 7-9.30pm, Sat; noon-2.30pm Sun. **Cards** MC, V.

One for London-based *Guardian* readers feeling stifled by the conservative nature of the country. The Hawkley Arms has a slightly hippy-ish atmosphere (prices are entirely Hampshire, however), well-cared-for real ales and simple but very appetising food. An excellent ploughman's (ham, Stilton, Cheddar) costs £5.85; salmon fish cakes are £8.95. At the back is a big garden with a solid wooden climbing frame for children.

King's Arms

Midhurst Road, Fernhurst (01428 652005). **Food served** noon-2.30pm, 7-10pm, Mon-Sat; noon-2.30pm Sun. **Cards** Debit, MC, V.

Watts: the story

George Frederick Watts (1817-1904) was a Victorian painter and sculptor, and sufficiently famous in his day to be nicknamed 'England's Michelangelo'. He occupied an unusual niche in that he belonged to no school but his own – although he had links with the Pre-Raphaelites and the Symbolists. He wished to do good through art – a very Victorian notion – and because of this insistence upon message his work seems very dated, but the best of it remains fascinating. He painted landscapes, social comment pieces, allegories and portraits; he also produced drawings and sculptures, but whatever he did, there was a moral dimension or social comment to his work. Many of his paintings have titles such as *Hope* (for many years one of the most reproduced pictures in the world) or *Found Drowned*. There are examples of all these genres in the **Watts Gallery** in Compton, as well as works by some of his contemporaries.

The building itself was opened in 1904 and has an Arts and Crafts homeliness that is instantly endearing; additions were made in 1906 and 1922. Anyone who enjoys idiosyncratic, non-formulaic museums or galleries will like it and it's small enough that children won't get bored.

Watts's life was devoted to art – he was not rich until the last decades of his life, but he lived in comfort thanks to a series of wealthy patrons. After an unconsummated marriage to the actress Ellen Terry in 1864 (he was 47, she was 30 years younger) he met his ideal match in Mary Fraser-Tytler (1849-1938), whom he married in 1886 at the age of 69. Also an artist, and a believer in good works, she was responsible for the other reason to visit Compton – the extraordinary **Watts Chapel**.

The need for a new chapel and graveyard came about because the burial ground in Compton was full; Mary Watts saw a way to combine the glories of art with her philanthropic instincts – the ideal Arts and Crafts project. Compton villagers attended evening classes under her guidance and learned to work in clay so as to decorate the chapel – so successfully that very soon they turned professional, becoming the Compton Potters' Arts Guild.

The Watts chapel (consecrated 1898) is a riot of symbolism, inside and out. The building is a blend of styles, but most strongly Byzantine – seeing it perched on a low hill in Surrey, surrounded by grazing livestock, is a thrill, even after several visits. The exterior is adorned with Christian Celtic geometric patterns mutated by art nouveau forms; attention to detail is amazing – everything, right down to the iron hinges on the main doors, is representative of an idea or a thing (and often both). The stunning, colourful interior is decorated with images depicting the Tree of Life. For a full appreciation of the chapel, take with you *Watts Chapel* by Veronica Franklin Gould (available from the Watts Gallery, £4.95). The graveyard also contains the Watts Memorial Cloister (1911), designed by Mary in memory of her husband.

End a trip to Compton with a visit to the Tea Shop. Savoury snacks, home-made cakes and a wealth of hot and cold drinks are served with a smile in a small hut-like room.

Watts Gallery Down Lane, Compton (01483 810235). **Open** *Apr-Sept* 11am-1pm, 2-6pm, Wed, Sat; 2-6pm Mon, Tue, Fri, Sun; *Oct-Mar* 11am-1pm, 2-4pm, Wed, Sat; 2-4pm Mon, Tue, Fri, Sun. **Admission** free.
Watts Chapel off Down Lane, Compton. **Open** 9am-dusk daily. **Admission** free.

A very popular dining pub where the ambitious menu has prices to match: warm salad of black pudding, new potatoes and poached egg (£5.50); braised lamb shank and savoy cabbage, aubergine purée and rosemary jus (£10.25). Snacks, sandwiches and ploughman's are also available – indeed, you don't have to do anything but drink, so bag a table in one of the comfortable, old-fashioned bars and take your pick.

Lickfold Inn

Lickfold (01798 861285).
Food served noon-2.30pm, 7-9.30pm, daily.
Cards AmEx, DC, Debit, MC, V.

A Hansel and Gretel-esque pub that's managed to maintain a certain amount of charm despite a recent high-class makeover. A herringbone-brick floor and antique furniture are a good backdrop for first-class food served in substantial portions. There are sandwiches, but more tempting is char-grilled scallops with sweet chilli butter (£8.50) and corn fritters with avocado and salsa with rocket and sour cream (£7.50), and no one should miss sticky toffee pudding with caramel sauce (£4.25).

Red Lion

Shamley Green, nr Guildford (01483 892202).
Food served noon-3pm, 6.30-10pm, Mon-Thur; noon-3pm, 7-10pm, Fri-Sun. **Cards** AmEx, DC, Debit, MC, V.

A welcoming pub with loads of tables outside and a beer garden at the back. The setting – overlooking the green – is charming; the locals are friendly and the staff helpful. An unassuming menu lists superior versions of old favourites such as salmon in pastry, king prawns and stuffed mushrooms; portions are pleasing and all mains

come with four vegetables. As a rough idea, starters and desserts cost around a fiver, mains £8-£15.

Three Horseshoes

Elsted (01730 825746).
Food served noon-2.15pm, 6.30-10pm, Mon-Sat; 7-9pm Sun.

Set beneath the South Downs, with an acre of tended garden, the Three Horseshoes is blessed with an idyllic location. Inside, there are brick floors and bespoke oak tables. Elevated pub grub, including a wide choice of seafood, is served here or outdoors. Good 'ole steak and kidney pie and braised lamb with apples and apricots are good value, at £8.95 each. The local brew, Gales, is on tap.

What to see & do

Tourist information centres

Council Offices, South Street, **Farnham**, GU9 7RN (01252 715109). **Open** 9.30am-5.15pm Mon-Thur; 9.30am-4.45pm Fri; 9am-noon Sat.

North Street, **Midhurst**, EU29 9DW (01730 817322). **Open** 9.30am-5.30pm Mon-Sat; 11am-4pm Sun; *Nov-Mar* 10am-5pm Mon-Sat.

Market Square, **Petworth**, GU28 OAF (01798 343523). **Open** *Mar, Oct* 10am-4pm Mon-Sat; 11am-3pm Sun; *Apr-Sept* 10am-5pm Mon-Sat; 10am-4pm Sun; *Nov-Feb* 11am-3pm Fri, Sat.

Bike hire

Aldershot Cycle World Alexander House, Station Road, Aldershot (01252 318790).
On the same road as the station (Aldershot is the stop before Farnham).

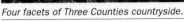

Four facets of Three Counties countryside.

Birdworld

Holt Pound, Farnham, GU29 9DW
(01420 22992/www.birdworld.co.uk).
Open *mid-Feb-Oct* 9.30am-5pm daily; *Nov-mid-Feb*
9.30am-5pm Sat, Sun. **Admission** £7.50; £3.95 3s-
14s; £5.95 OAPs, students.
Twenty-six acres of gardens, boasting all sorts of birds,
plus a children's farm, an aquarium, play areas and picnic sites, a restaurant and the inevitable gift shop.

Bohunt Manor

Liphook (01428 722208). **Open** 10am-6pm daily.
Admission £1.50; free under-14s; £1 OAPs.
Attractive woodland gardens owned by the Worldwide
Fund for Nature.

Gilbert White's House & the Oates Museum

The Wakes, Selborne, nr Alton (01420 511275).
Open 11am-5pm daily. **Admission** £4; £1 5s-15s;
£3.50 OAPs.
Reverend Gilbert White (1720-93), England's first ecol-
ogist, lived here for most of his life: the original manuscript of *A Natural History of Selborne* is on show. The
restoration of the beautiful garden to its eighteenth-
century form is almost complete – there are always
unusual plants for sale, and once a year in June (phone
for details) there's an unusual plants fair. Also here is
the Oates Museum, commemorating Captain 'I am just
going outside. I may be some time' Oates and his uncle
Frank Oates, a Victorian explorer. Further pluses are the
superior teashop and the engaging village itself. Walk
from the village on to Selborne Hill, 250 acres of which
are National Trust-owned.

Hollycombe Steam Collection

Hollycombe (01428 724900).
Open *Apr-June, Sept-mid-Oct* 1-6pm Sun, bank hols;
July, Aug 1-6pm daily. **Admission** £6.50; £5 2s-15s,
OAPs; £20 family.
One for families (and steam enthusiasts): attractions
include a steam fairground (occasionally open at night),
a steam railway and traction engine-hauled rides, plus
a farm (with animals and steam-driven machinery) and
woodland gardens. Once you've paid the entrance fee,
all rides are free.

Jane Austen's House

Chawton (01420 83262).
Open *Mar-Dec* 11am-4.30pm daily; *Jan, Feb* 11am-
4.30pm Sat, Sun. **Admission** £2.50; 50p 8s-18s;
£2 OAPs, students.
Jane Austen's last home, where she lived with her mother and sister, Cassandra, from 1809 until 1817. *Mansfield
Park*, *Emma* and *Persuasion* were written on a small
round table in the red-brick seventeenth-century house.
When you've worked your way through the letters and
memorabilia, retire to Cassandra's Cup across the road
for tea. Children and steam train enthusiasts should note
that just north of Chawton, in Alton, is the starting point
for the **Mid-Hants Watercress Line** (*see page 107*).

Loseley Park

nr Guildford (01483 304440/24-hour info 01483
505501). **Open** *house June-Aug* 2-5pm Wed-Sat, bank

Jane Austen's House *in Chawton.*

hols; *garden, shop & tearoom May-Sept* 11am-5pm
Wed-Sat, bank hols. **Admission** £5; £3 3s-16s;
£4 OAPs, students.
Home to the Loseley Jersey herd (yoghurts, ice-creams
and cream are all available from the gift shop), this is
an attractive Elizabethan mansion still lived in by the
More-Molyneux family. The grounds feature fountains
and rose, herb and flower gardens; tractor and trailer
tours of the estate are offered on Saturday afternoons
from May to September. There's also a tea room.

Lurgashall Winery

Windfallwood, Lurgashall (01428 707292/
www.lurgashall.co.uk). **Open** 9am-5pm Mon-Sat;
11am-5pm Sun. **Admission** free.
An award-winning producer, selling fruit and flower
wines, meads and liqueurs, plus honey, mead mustard
and chocolates. There's also a herb garden.

Petworth House & Park

Petworth (01798 342207). **Open** *Apr-Oct house* 1-
5.30pm Mon-Wed, Sat, Sun. Last entry 4.30pm; *park*
8am-dusk daily. **Admission** (NT) £5.50; £2.50 5s-17s.
A magnificent late seventeenth-century pile housing a
notable art collection. There are works by, among others,
Van Dyck, Reynolds, Titian, Blake and Turner (who spent
time here with his patron, the 3rd Earl of Egremont), plus
furniture, sculpture and limewood carving by Grinling
Gibbons. Phone for details of regular events.

Rural Life Centre

Old Kiln Museum, Reeds Road, Tilford
(01252 795571/www.surreyweb.org.uk/rural-life/).
Open *Apr-Sept* 11am-6pm Wed-Sun, bank hols.
Admission £3; £1.50 5s-16s; £2.50 OAPs.
Social history, agricultural implements, ploughs and
carts, crafts and buildings covering aspects of farming
and village life are displayed over ten acres of field, woodland and barns. There's a café and Sunday train rides.

Winkworth Arboretum

Hascombe Road, nr Godalming (01483 208477).
Open dawn-dusk daily. **Admission** (NT) £2.75;
£1.35 5s-16s.
A glorious display of over 1,000 different shrubs and
trees, spread over a hillside and around two lakes. It's
owned by the National Trust, which is particularly
proud of the bluebell and azalea displays in spring, and
the fabulous palette of colours in the autumn.

Around Newbury

Gambolling with the gee-gees.

Newbury is an unlovely town in the heart of Berkshire's commuter belt – a less than seething hotbed of auto-part centres, middle-management employees in Rovers, and sullen youth with gelled hair. But the town is also home to one of the best racetracks in the country, and the racing world's community of bookmakers, stablelads, jockeys and professional gamblers gives the area its real character. There are also patches of pretty, unspoilt countryside with some beautiful pubs and country houses sandwiched between the tangle of motorways, ill-conceived bypasses and A-roads, so even the blow of a betting disaster at the track can be softened by long walks, pints of local ale, and a soft bed within the accommodating walls of a local farmhouse.

Newbury itself offers few charms to the visitor beyond the track; the centre is dominated by the Kennet shopping centre, while the outskirts are made up of industrial estates and business parks, so it's best to hotfoot it out of town as soon as the races are over. Those with an interest in English history might wish to visit the museum (01635 30267; it also houses the tourist office), which gives a detailed account of the area's role in the Civil War. For details on Newbury's horse-racing calendar, the highlights of which include the Hennessy Cognac Gold Cup, call the racecourse (01635 40015).

All along the Ridgeway

Many people come to this area to explore the **Ridgeway**, the ancient wayfare that crosses the Lambourn Downs, purported to be the oldest road in Britain (for more on the Ridgeway, *see page 191*). Ex-editor of the *Independent* Andreas Whittam-Smith used to come walking here almost every weekend and made a point of writing about his exploits regularly in the newspaper. Equine enthusiasts

*Possibly Stanley Spencer's finest work: the **Sandham Memorial Chapel** at Burghclere.*

This sporting life

You can tell that you're in horseriding country around Newbury. Signs bearing the legend 'Please drive slowly – Valley Of The Racehorse' are littered throughout the Lambourn Downs, it is almost impossible to take a car journey without passing a horse on the road, and most of the pubs north of Newbury have dedicated themselves to equine culture. Lambourn is the centre of Britain's jump-racing industry, and racing attracts all manner of people, so the pubs have none of the gruff, suspicious attitude prevalent in so many places. Go into the **Hare & Hounds** in Lambourn Woodlands on a Saturday night and you could well spot Channel 4's racing correspondent John Franklin chatting to a stable lad by the bar while jockeys celebrate or rue the day's racing a few metres away.

For those really keen on learning about the sporting life, a 6am trip up on to Lambourn Downs will be rewarded by sightings of the horses and jockeys training on the open land. And finally, a word of warning: jockeys have made a career out of conquering their fears, and consequently they tend to drive their cars like maniacs. The Newbury area is infamous for serious car crashes.

---

have had a long relationship with the Lambourn Downs. Some of the earliest left their mark with an enormous chalk **White Horse**, near the village of Woolstone, which is also home to the characterful White Horse pub, a beautiful thatched cottage that the band Traffic once recorded a video in. Ex-Traffic lead singer Stevie Winwood still pops in for a pint every now and then.

Aimful ramblings

On the south side of Newbury the villages are prosperous and genteel. One of the most rewarding to visit is **Inkpen**, home to some of the most zealous ramblers in the country. These fearless defenders of the common person's right to go for a stroll have for 25 years run the Inkpen Rights of Way Committee, which ensure not only that the area's rights of way are kept public, but also that they are clearly signposted. As a result, two of the best walks in Berkshire originate from this humble village; rambles deep into the countryside that take in regular sightings of ducks, foxes, hares and the occasional hunting party. A leaflet detailing the particulars of the walks is available from the Swan and the Crown & Garter pubs.

Also worth a visit for a hearty stroll is the village of **Ashmansworth**, which is made up of little more than two working farms and a church, but is imbued with a plethora of public bridleways. It is close to the stunning **Sandham Memorial Chapel**, overlooking Watership Down (*see page 101* **Bright Eyes**) at Burghclere. Painter Stanley Spencer was a medical orderly during World War I and his experiences inspired the murals that fill the chapel's walls. Nearby is **Highclere Castle**, the stately family home of Lord and Lady Carnavon, and most importantly, an excellent pub called the Yew Tree in Highclere village, where there are two log fires and a decent restaurant.

If you stray further east towards Basingstoke, amid a tangle of country lanes and villages with 'Bramley' or 'Mortimer' in their names, are two more fine country houses: **Stratfield Saye** and **The Vyne**.

Where to stay

This is a well-to-do area and accommodation isn't cheap; it also may be difficult to come by at the last minute if a big race is on at Newbury. In addition to the places listed below, **Langley Hall Farm** (01635 248222; from £20 per person) at World's End is at the heart of horse-racing country and good value; **Rookwood Farm House** (01488 608676; doubles £60) is just outside of Newbury and has a heated outdoor pool.

*Are you to the **Esseborne Manor** born?*

Around Newbury

Beaumont House

4 St John's Road, Newbury, RG14 7LX
(tel/fax 01635 47858).
Rates (B&B) *single £27-£30; double/twin £60; four-poster £56; family £70.* **Rooms** 1 single; 1 double; 1 twin (en suite); 1 four-poster.

This is one of the best reasons to come to Newbury – a B&B in a beautiful family home run by a French woman who is mercifully free of the fussiness that characterises so many B&B proprietors. The rooms certainly have character: one has a four-poster bed, a library of books on China, and a black-and-white-tiled bathroom with, inexplicably, two sinks and no bath. Breakfast is served in a glass conservatory filled with tropical plants. Children welcome. All bedrooms non-smoking.
A34 towards Newbury; straight over 1st two roundabouts towards Winchester; right at 3rd roundabout; house is on right.

Dundas Arms

53 Station Road, Kintbury, RG17 9UT
(01488 658263/658568/info@dundasarms.co.uk/www.dundasarms.co.uk).
Rates (B&B) *single occupancy £60; double/twin £70.* **Rooms** (all en suite) 3 double; 2 twin. **Cards** AmEx, Debit, MC, V.

Don't expect the warmest of welcomes at this canalside inn – the staff don't go out of their way to make their guests feel at home. The taste in interior decoration is questionable, too, with avocado bathrooms and pottery ducks in the bar downstairs belonging to the set of an early Mike Leigh film, but the location is superb – at the confluence of a river and a barge-strewn canal, and Kintbury is a sweet village. Children welcome.
A4 towards Hungerford from Newbury; follow signs to Kintbury on left.

Esseborne Manor

Hurstbourne Tarrant, Andover, SP11 OER
(01264 736444/fax 01264 736725).
Rates (B&B) *single occupancy £88-£95; double/twin £95-£160; four-poster £135.* **Rooms** 8 double; 6 twin; 1 four-poster. **Cards** AmEx, DC, Debit, MC, V.

This country house hotel is good value. It has the trappings of a luxury hotel – tennis court, herb garden, overabundance of fluffy towel robes – but its prices are not astronomical and, unlike many hotels of this size, it has not given in to a corporate approach. While the rooms inside the house are awash with silks and spa baths, the converted stable rooms are less flashy and more relaxed, with simple pine furniture and cream walls. Children and dogs welcome.
A343 from Newbury; turn right at Highclere; house is on left after 7 miles.

Fishers Farm

Ermin Street, Shefford Woodlands, nr Hungerford, RG17 7AB (01488 648466/fax 01488 648706/mail@fishersfarm.co.uk/www.fishersfarm.co.uk).
Rates (B&B) *single occupancy £35; double/twin £50.* **Rooms** (all en suite) 1 double; 2 twin.

This is part of a working farm a long way down a dirt track, and entirely secluded, surrounded as it is by fields and woodland. Mary Wilson is good-natured and welcoming, although you might get told off if you splash too much in the indoor swimming pool. The rooms are kept simple with beamed ceilings, cream walls and pine furniture, and this feels like a good place to take kids: miles away from a road, awash with cats and dogs, and with the added advantage of the pool. Children welcome. All bedrooms non-smoking.
J14 M4; A338 N for 0.5 miles; left to B4000; farm is on right 400m after Pheasant pub.

Hollington House

Woolton Hill, nr Newbury, RG20 9XA (01635 255100/fax 01635 255075/hollington.house@newbury.net).
Rates (B&B) *single occupancy £105-£185; double £145-£195; four-poster/suite £275.* **Rooms** (all en suite) 19 double; 1 four-poster suite; 4 suites. **Cards** AmEx, DC, Debit, MC, V.

The interior design of this Edwardian country mansion might be a little over the top – there are the heads of 12-point bucks on the walls of the hall, the bedrooms all have a theme, from Japanese to nautical – but for the stressed urbanite wishing to indulge in a bit of luxury for the weekend, everything has been taken care of. There are en suite whirlpools surrounded by trompe l'oeil; 25 acres of land with a pool, croquet and tennis court; and a very good restaurant with an extensive New World wine list. Guests can even arrive by helicopter. Children welcome. Non-smoking rooms available.
M4 J13; A34 S; exit right at sign to Highclere; turn right to Woolton Hill after 0.5 miles; after 0.5 miles turn left by school; house is on left after 0.5 miles.

Where to eat & drink

The best places to eat in this area are country pub-restaurants, and a handful of very smart and very expensive stockbroker-magnet destination dining spots. In addition to those below, the **Café Blue Cobra** Indian restaurant in Theale (01189 304040) is well worth a visit; it has now doubled up as a Thai restaurant since a Thai mate of the owner turned up. The restaurant at **Esseborne Manor** (01264 736444) is also good, with a reasonably priced traditional British menu, including a gourmet evening every Wednesday at £25 per person. Another grand setting is **Hollington House** at Highclere (01635 255100), which agreeably

*The **Royal Oak**, a superior boozer. See p100.*

Time Out Weekend Breaks **99**

balances accomplishment with a laid-back attitude, and offers a stunning selection of Aussie bottles on its wine list.

The pubs are where the heart of horse-racing country lies. The **Star** at Sparsholt, near Wantage, is unique: this simple, low-ceilinged inn is run by an Irish couple and features locals like Edgar, who is at least 90 and rarely moves from his armchair, and a Foghorn Leghorn-type gardener called Bubbles. Then there's the **Hare & Hounds** in Lambourn Woodlands, where you'll be hard-pressed to find a regular who isn't in some way connected to the racing world. It is owned by trainer Henry Cecil's brother David. Close to the Ridgeway, and not far from the Thames at Goring, the fourteenth-century **Bell** at Aldworth is a great place to end a walk and offers superb-value grub. The **Pot Kiln** in Frilsham, Yattendon (01635 201366), stands out for its location: in the middle of rambling countryside, it's a lovely place to stop for a drink.

Crown & Horns

East Ilsley (01635 281205).
Food served noon-2.30pm, 6-10pm, daily.
Cards Debit, MC, V.

'Newbury was good to me today,' announced landlord Chris Bexx about that day's racing, and this pub, in the heart of horse-training country, is a mecca to all things equine. Copies of the *Racing Post* lie about, and horse prints line the walls. Stable lads and trainers come here for a huge range of real ales and good food including an excellent fish pie (£7.50) and Cumberland sausages and mash (£5.75). There is also a skittles alley, darts, pool, and a side bar with a television tuned to, you guessed it, the latest races.

Dew Pond

Old Burghclere (01635 278408).
Food served 7-10pm Tue-Sat. **Set meals** £25 (3 courses). **Cards** AmEx, DC, Debit, MC, V.

The Dew Pond's immensely cute knocked-together sixteenth-century cottages are a homey setting (with some wonderful views) for simple, hearty country dishes. Yet this is not what you get. There's a sound base in classic cooking, but Keith and Julie Marshall's popular restaurant can be bold and assured in its flavourings and ambitious with its ingredient combinations. An excellent, fairly priced wine list adds to the appeal. Main courses from the set menu might include roe deer with truffle sauce and confit of new season garlic, or pan-fried calf's liver with purée of potato and leeks with a lime sauce; desserts include the likes of bourbon vanilla crème brûlée with raspberries and compôte of spiced peaches.

Royal Oak

The Square, Yattendon (01635 201325).
Food served noon-2pm, 7-9.30pm, daily.
Set meals *lunch* £12 (2 courses); £15 (3 courses).
Cards AmEx, DC, Debit, MC, V.

The smartness of this country pub is indicative of the kind of people who live in the pretty village it occupies:

rich ones. It's not excessively expensive, just rather posh for a local. You won't find Betty's hotpot on the bar menu here – rather octopus salad, bresaola with mozzarella marinated in truffle oil, and crab salad with spicy tomato and spring onion salsa. Staff can be offhand, but there's no denying the quality of the menu here, or the allure of the log fire and locally brewed beers on tap. Starters cost around £5, while mains are about £11.

Swan

Craven Road, Lower Inkpen (01488 668326).
Food served noon-2.30pm, 7-9.30pm, Tue-Sun.

Although at first glance this sixteenth-century village pub looks a little characterless, it's worth a visit for its charming and welcoming owners, Mary and Bernard Harris, and their food, which only uses organic beef and vegetables from their farm. Mary does what she knows best, which is traditional country cooking like beef in beer in Yorkshire pudding (£6.25) and a delicious leek and mushroom crumble with salad and chips (£5.50). Locals congregate in the darts room and drink pints of Adnams and Butts bitter and a very dry but delicious local cider.

The Vineyard

The Vineyard at Stockcross, Newbury
(01635 528770).
Food served noon-2pm, 7-10pm, daily. **Set meals** *lunch* £15 (2 courses), £20 (3 courses); *dinner* £39 (3 courses). **Cards** AmEx, DC, Debit, MC, V.

The Vineyard, the pet project of millionaire industrialist Sir Peter Michael, is a shrine to wealth. Flames leap up from the lake by the entrance, commissioned sculptures occupy hidden corners, liveried doormen park your car. Inside there's a reasonably restrained country club feel, and Billy Reid's Modern British cooking is very impressive: the Fusion menu at £70 a head includes six courses and four matching wines, with such delicacies as crab risotto, champagne granita, fried scallops with cucumber, and fillet of sea bass. Many of the wines are Californian; Sir Peter just happens to own a vineyard in the Napa Valley.

Yew Tree

Hollington Cross, Andover Road, Highclere
(01635 253360/255035).
Food served noon-2.30pm, 6.30-10pm, daily.
Cards AmEx, DC, Debit, MC, V.

A smart 350-year-old pub and restaurant on the outskirts of a very well-to-do village, the Yew Tree attracts a fair few well-heeled locals who fill the car park with shiny Mercs and BMWs. The beamed restaurant serves dishes such as crispy duck salad, local pheasant, roast beef, and mozzarella and beef tomato salad, and the large fireplace by the bar makes a nice place to cradle a pint of ale. Starters are around a fiver, mains go from £8 to £13.

What to see & do

Tourist information centre

The Wharf, **Newbury**, RG14 5AS (01635 30267/ fax 01635 519562/www.westberks.gov.uk/ tourism@westberks.gov.uk).
Open *Apr-Sept* 10am-5pm Mon-Fri; 10am-4.30pm Sat; *Oct-Mar* 10am-4pm Mon-Sat. Closed bank hols.

Bright eyes

It's not only horses that the Newbury area is famous for – there are bunnies, too. Richard Adams's phenomenally popular 1970s tear-jerker *Watership Down* was set in the countryside just south of the town. Rabbits might not actually be able to chat to each other, but the country inhabited by Hazel, Bigwig, Fiver, Dandelion, Pipkin and chums is real enough.

The area in question largely falls between the A34 and A339, a few miles south of Newbury, and devotees should be able to locate a number of sites described in the book. There's the **Sandleford**

Warren, north-west of Newtown, **Newtown Churchyard**, which the rabbits passed through by moonlight, **Nuthanger Farm** (south of Echinswell) and **Watership Down** itself (a little south of the farm, around a mile from Kingsclere). The Down, rising 300 feet, is a popular spot for dog-walking and kite-flying, but come at dusk or dawn and you may just see fluffy tails bobbing out of the hillside warrens. Newbury tourist office has information about walks in the area, including the Wayfarers Walk, which passes through Kingsclere, where you can admire extensive views of Watership Down.

Barge cruising

Kennet and Avon Canal, on the Rose of Hungerford (01488 683389) from Hungerford, or the Avon (01635 44154) from Newbury, or the Kennet Valley (01635 44154) from Kintbury. **Tickets** *Rose of Hungerford* £3; £2 3s-16s, OAPs Wed, Sat, Sun; *Avon, Kennet Valley* £4-£5 Wed, Fri, Sun.

The Kennet and Avon Canal, which fell into disuse and lay dormant until 1990, is home to some of the most beautiful painted barges in the country. The canal passes through Berkshire's most unspoilt countryside, so a trip on one of these boats on a summer's day is nothing short of idyllic. The *Rose of Hungerford* often has jazz bands playing on Sunday afternoons, while the *Kennet Valley* is horse-drawn from the beautiful village of Kintbury.

Highclere Castle

Highclere, Newbury (01635 253210/ www.highclerecastle.co.uk). **Open** *July-early Sept* 11am-4pm Mon-Fri, Sun; 11am-2.30pm Sat. **Admission** *castle & grounds* £6; £3 4s-15s; £4.75 OAPs, students; *grounds only* £3; £1.50 4s-15s.

Kids looking forward to a turreted castle with a drawbridge and a dragon in the moat will be disappointed – this is more of a stately home. But those interested in Victorian architecture will be impressed; it was built by Sir Charles Barry, architect of the Houses of Parliament, and is quite similar in style. Inside, there are Egyptian relics brought over by the 5th Earl of Carnarvon in the 1920s, and the walled garden contains a Greek-style folly and a miniature temple. The grounds often host classic car rallies.

Stratfield Saye

Stratfield Saye (01256 882882). **Open** *house May, Sept* noon-3.30pm Sat, Sun, bank hols; *June-Aug* noon-3.30pm Mon-Thur, Sat, Sun; *grounds & exhibition May, Sept* 11.30am-4pm Sat, Sun, bank hols; *June-Aug* 11.30am-4pm Mon-Thur, Sat, Sun. **Admission** £5; £2.50 5s-16s.

The Duke of Wellington's present from the nation for beating Boney at Waterloo in 1815, Stratfield Saye is still home to his descendants and, unsurprisingly, it's packed with the Iron Duke's personal bits and bobs. The old stable building contains a well put-together exhibition of the Duke's exploits, and true Wellingtonians won't want to miss the grave of his venerable charger Copenhagen in the grounds.

The Vyne

Sherborne St John (01256 881337). **Open** *house Apr-Oct* 1.30-5.30pm Wed-Sun; *grounds Apr-Oct* 12.30-5.30pm Wed-Sun. **Admission** (NT) *house & grounds* £5; £2.50 5s-17s; *grounds only* £2.50; £1.25 5s-17s.

Architectural students can get their fill of styles at The Vyne. Started in the early sixteenth century for Henry VIII's Lord Chamberlain Lord Sandys, it was given a pioneering classical portico in the mid-seventeenth century. The interior is in a wonderful state of preservation, with much original oak panelling and bucketloads of antiques. Don't miss the Tudor Chapel containing Renaissance stained glass and the lovely walks in the grounds.

Wilton Windmill

Wilton, nr Burbage (01672 870266). **Open** *Easter-Sept* 2-5pm Sun, bank hols. **Admission** £2; 50p 5s-16s; £1.50 OAPs; £4 family.

This brick windmill, built in 1821 for the local millers, has not been used since 1920, but was restored to its former state in 1980 and is now fully working. Floodlit at night and standing on a chalk ridge 550ft above sea level, the windmill is a fun, low-key place to visit, and is within walking distance of the Kennet and Avon canal.

Winchester & around

The Millennium? – Winchester's seen it all before.

Winchester is a city that peaked a long, long time ago. An Iron Age settlement was established on St Catherine's Hill, just to the east, in about 450BC. The Romans moved the town down to its present site west of the River Itchen in around AD 70, when they created their city of Venta Belgarum. After a blip of a couple of centuries it became an important centre for the newly arrived Saxons, and the first Cathedral was begun in 648. In 871 Alfred the Great made Winchester capital of his kingdom of Wessex. It still enjoyed roughly equal status with London as joint capital of England during the two centuries after the Norman Conquest, and around 1150 Winchester's market was one of the most important in Europe. Then, from about 1250, it began a steady decline. The Bishops of Winchester remained wealthy and important figures, but Winchester itself fell into being a quiet, minor country town.

As a result Winchester today can sometimes seem to have its head in the past more than just about any other city in Britain. Its medieval core is still very much the heart of town, with winding lanes of enormous, archetypically English charm, neat, compact and very easy to wander around. Within it there is a remarkable range of ancient buildings – from one of the oldest and grandest of English cathedrals to hole-in-the-wall churches, fortified gates, the great hall of a royal palace and a fifteenth-century watermill. In 1382 Winchester acquired the last of its great medieval institutions, when Bishop William of Wykeham founded Winchester College (you're not supposed to call it a 'school'), and this public school remains peculiarly prominent in the life of the town, especially south of the Cathedral Close.

More recently, though, after centuries in the economic doldrums, Winchester has reached another peak of a sort. As a definitive green-field city of the 1980s it became very attractive to small, clean but prosperous hi-tech industries. At the same time, the city's old-world tranquillity and the postcard-prettiness of the surrounding villages made them magnets for commuters and second-home buyers. Consequently, Winchester and area is now frequently cited as having the highest standard of living in Britain. This is also evidenced by the showroom-loads of top-of-the-range four-wheel-drives and people-movers that ply the country lanes. One sideways effect of this affluence is that Winchester now has a notably high-standard range of restaurants.

Around Winchester

Some 16 miles to the north-west is **Andover**, under-loved ever since it was earmarked in the 1960s as a destination for 'London overspill'. Around it, though, are villages that seem lost in deep-green countryside, especially in the valley of the Test, which runs due south. This is one of the most renowned trout-fishing rivers in Britain; it also has a beautiful long-distance footpath, the Test Way, alongside it. Along the way there are characterful villages with pubs, especially **Wherwell**, **Longstock** and **King's Somborne**, from where another path (the Clarendon Way) leads to Winchester or Salisbury.

Shortly before the Test enters Southampton is the old market town of **Romsey**, the prime attractions of which (apart from some rather twee teashops) are the twelfth-century Romsey Abbey, one of the finest intact examples of Norman architecture in England, and King John's House, which, despite the name, is a non-royal but remarkably complete medieval house.

East of Winchester, beyond the barrier of the M3, the A31 road runs up to the valley of the Itchen. A turn south on to the A272 Petersfield road, around three miles from the city, will take you up to **Cheesefoot Head**, a giant ridge in the down where the road crosses the South Downs Way. The views are spectacular, and it

By train from London

Trains to **Winchester** and **Portsmouth** leave **London Waterloo** every 15 minutes. Journey time to Winchester is about **1hr**, and **1hr 30mins** to Portsmouth.

*The ancient city of **Winchester**, as seen from St Giles Hill.*

makes a good jumping off point for a shortish walk along the footpath. The main road runs after seven miles into **New Alresford**. A classically pretty old country town (the 'New' dates from the thirteenth century), it has a wide main street (laid out to house medieval sheep markets), a riverside walk, a quirky range of shops and a disproportionate number of pubs. A great many of its visitors, though, are railway buffs, drawn by the Watercress Line.

South of Winchester, beyond the **Marwell Zoological Park**, the main point of interest is **Bishop's Waltham**, a likeable, unprettified, mostly Georgian town. For nearly 1,000 years it was the property of the Bishops of Winchester, who built one of their many residences there, Bishop's Waltham Palace. A little further south is **Wickham**, birthplace of William of Wykeham of Winchester College. Although only a large village (or small town), it has a peculiarly large main square, created to fit a market fair in 1268. Surrounded by buildings from medieval through Georgian to Victorian, it gives Wickham an oddly grand, urban look. It's also a handy base for trips into Portsmouth.

Wickham stands at the southern end of the valley of the River Meon, another prestigious trout stream. It contains some of the most heart-of-England pretty, riverbank-and-hollyhocks villages in Hampshire, in **Droxford**, **Exton**, **West Meon** and others. A long-distance path, the **Wayfarers' Walk**, runs through Exton north to New Alresford and south to the coast.

Just north of Exton the A32 valley road crosses the **South Downs Way**, which you can use to climb Old Winchester Hill, a massive down with the remains of an Iron Age fort at its top.

As well as any specific destination, though, it can be as enjoyable just to wander between villages with no particular plan. Places like **Upham**, **Owslebury**, **Beauworth** (just off the South Downs Way) and **Cheriton** make particularly pleasant spots to lose a few hours, discovered between rolling downs or along meandering lanes that in summer can seem like tunnels beneath great arches of greenery.

Where to stay

The Guard House

Corner of Archery Lane, Southgate Street, Winchester, SO23 9EF (01962 861514).
Rates (B&B) *single occupancy* £50-£55; *twin* £60-£65. **Rooms** 2 twin (1 en suite).

The Guard House is what it says: the one-time guard house of the Army's Peninsula Barracks, imaginatively renovated by Mary and Andrew Dolman as a high standard B&B. The big, light, very comfortable bedrooms are decorated in a more contemporary style than is the norm in country B&Bs. Varied breakfasts are served at a big wooden table in a large, bright kitchen. The Guard House is in the middle of town, a few doors from the Hotel du Vin, but even so is easy to miss: look for the Archery Lane turning off Southgate Street. Non-smoking throughout.
M3 J11; follow signs to St Cross and Winchester along St Cross Road; after 0.75 miles it becomes Southgate Street; Archery Lane on left; house next to St Thomas' Church.

Fortitude Cottage

51 Broad Street, Old Portsmouth, PO1 2JD
(tel/fax 01705 823748/fortcott@aol.com).
Rates (B&B) *single occupancy* £27-£35;
double/twin £23pp. **Rooms** 1 double (en suite);
2 twin (1 en suite). **Cards** AmEx, DC, Debit, MC, V.

The name might suggest a hardy life before the mast,
but no fortitude is really required to stay in this cosy old
house on the main quayside street of Spice Island in Old
Portsmouth. The three charming rooms have very good
facilities (TVs, tea-making equipment and so on) and the
one non-en suite room has its own bathroom just outside. The very pretty breakfast room, the double and the
en suite twin all have harbour views; the non-en suite
room looks out from the back of the house. It's a short
walk from the harbour ramparts, plenty of pubs and
restaurants, and you can get the Waterbus across to the
Historic Dockyard. Non-smoking throughout.

*M27 into Portsmouth; follow English Heritage and IOW
signs; then follow signs for Old Portsmouth Cathedral; pass
Cathedral; turn right into Broad Street; hotel on left.*

Hotel du Vin & Bistro

14 Southgate Street, Winchester, SO23 9EF
(01962 841414/fax 01962 842458/admin@
winchester.hotelduvin.co.uk/www.hotelduvin.co.uk).
Rates *double/twin* £89-£99; *deluxe double/twin*
£115; *four-poster/suite* £185. Breakfast (Eng) £9.50;
(cont) £7.50. **Rooms** (all en suite) 6 double/twin; 15
deluxe double/twin; 1 four-poster/suite.
Cards AmEx, DC, Debit, MC, V.

Robin Hutson (hotelier) and Gerard Basset (sommelier)
opened Hotel du Vin in 1994. It's a fabulous blend of
comfort and style with an egalitarian atmosphere. All
are welcome at this red-brick Georgian house, and the
young, friendly staff put guests at their ease – no whispering necessary here, and no dress code either. The bedrooms (all different, each sponsored by a drinks
company or wine producer) have comfortable beds, big
baths, power showers, TVs, CD players and restrained
décor. The Bistro is equally user-friendly, and many
non-residents dine here. A modish menu – char-grilled
sardines with tomato tartlet and pesto (£5.50), calf's liver
with creamed polenta and pepper jus (£12.95) – is supported by a classy wine list. Children welcome. There's
another Hotel du Vin in Tunbridge Wells (*see p45*).

*M3 J11; follow signs to St Cross & Winchester; over 2
roundabouts; hotel is 2 miles along St Cross Road on left
approaching central Winchester.*

Malt Cottage

Upper Clatford, nr Andover, SP11 7QL
(01264 323469/fax 01264 334100/
info@maltcottage.co.uk/www.maltcottage.co.uk).
Rates (B&B) *single occupancy* £35; *double* £60; *twin*
£45-£60; *family* £105. **Rooms** (all en suite) 2 double;
1 twin/family.

Deep in the Test Valley countryside, the 250-year-old
Malt Cottage – in part a converted barn – makes a dis-
tinctively comfortable rural retreat. Owners Patsy and
Richard Mason are garden designers, and the six-acre
garden they have created, complete with huge pond, is
really spectacular; barbecues are cooked up there (on
request) in summer. When the weather drives you
inside, there's a very attractive sitting room with log fire.
Rooms are big and well equipped, and those that are not

The **Wykeham Arms** *– top board and food.*

en suite have adjacent sole-use bathrooms of equal standard. Many extras (a choice of fresh-produce breakfasts,
airport pick-ups, car hire bookings) are also available.
Upper Clatford is well situated for fishing on the Test
(which the Masons can arrange) and walking the Test
Valley. Children welcome. Non-smoking throughout.

*A303; turn S on to A3057 towards Stockbridge; first right
at bend after 0.25 miles; first left; right at T-junction into
Upper Clatford village; after 0.25 miles Crook & Shears pub
on left; private lane opposite; house at bottom of lane.*

Old House Hotel

The Square, Wickham, PO17 5JG
(01329 833049/fax 01329 833672).
Rates *single* £65; *single occupany* £70; *double/twin*
£75. **Rooms** (all en suite) 1 single; 7 double/twin.
Breakfast £12 (Eng); £7.50 (cont). **Cards** AmEx, DC,
Debit, MC, V.

The 'old house' is an impressive Georgian brick townhouse on Wickham's giant main square, and the current
base of renowned local chef Nicholas Ruthven-Stuart
(for the restaurant, *see p105*). Behind its rustic grand
portico are a bar, comfortable lounges with vaguely
Regency-style sofas and huge original fireplaces and a
walled garden. The rooms on the floors above have similarly understated character, with assorted original features such as beams, sloping ceilings and fireplaces and
a rather quirky mix of newish and slightly aged facilities. Prices are higher than the norm, particularly since
breakfast is charged separately, but the hotel has devoted fans. Children welcome.

M27 J10; A32 to Wickham Square; hotel is on right.

Priory Inn

Winchester Road, Bishop's Waltham, SO32 1BE
(01489 891313/896370).
Rates (B&B) *single occupancy/double/twin* £17.50pp;
family £40. **Rooms** (both en suite) 1 double; 1 twin.

An unfussy, friendly local's pub on the north-west road
out of Bishop's Waltham, the Priory has two light and
comfortable guest rooms with well-sized bathrooms (the
double more so), TVs and tea-making facilities. They're
not as striking as some B&B rooms in the area, but are
more accessibly priced. Breakfast is served in the bar;
at lunchtime and in the evenings, a big choice of pub
grub, including the odd Thai or Indian dish, is offered.
Children welcome.

*M3 J12; follow signs to Marwell Zoological Park; turn
left on to B2117; inn is on left on way into Bishop's
Waltham.*

Wykeham Arms

75 Kingsgate Street, Winchester, SO23 9PE
(01962 853834/fax 01962 854411).
Rates (B&B) *single* £45; *single occupancy* £69.50-
£99; *double/twin* £79.50-£95; *suite* £117.50.
Rooms (all en suite) 1 single; 9 double; 2 twin;
1 suite. **Cards** AmEx, DC, Debit, MC, V.

One of Winchester's most historic inns, open since 1755,
the Wykeham Arms has so much character you could
bottle it for export, with every wall of its nooks and crannies covered in sporting prints, military memorabilia
and other bits of old England. It stands in an ancient
lane surrounded by different parts of Winchester
College. Due to the quirks of the old building some
rooms, reached via up-and-down staircases, are quite
small, but inside them is a full range of modern comforts
and extras. For more space with a little less character
ask for one of the more expensive rooms (or the suite) in
the St George's annexe, an eighteenth-century house
across the street, which also have the use of a leafy garden patio with a fine view of the College buildings. The
Wykeham is also one of Winchester's most popular pubs
for drinking and eating (*see p106*). Dogs welcome. Non-
smoking rooms available.

*M3 J9; follow signs to Winchester over 3 roundabouts
into Garnier Road; right at T junction into Kingsgate;
pub is on left.*

Where to eat & drink

Winchester has a big choice of eating places. In
addition to those below, the **Hotel du Vin &
Bistro** (*see page 104*) is one of the top places in
town. For good-value breakfasts, lunches or
snacks the **Cathedral Refectory** (01962
857200; licensed) in the Visitor Centre is a good
bet (with plenty for vegetarians). Of the many
pubs, the tiny **Eclipse** on the Square (01962
865676), once the rectory of St Lawrence's
church, has reliable pub nosh: the **Old Vine**,
also on the Square (01962 854616), is bigger
and has a wider choice. Near the river, the
Mash Tun on Eastgate Street is a student
favourite, and the **Old Monk** is a big pub
with riverside garden.

In the Test Valley, pubs to look out for
include the **Royal Oak** in Goodworth Clatford
and the **Peat Spade** in Longstock. South and
east of Winchester among the most enjoyable
pubs are the **White Horse** in Droxford, the
historic old **Brushmakers' Arms** in Upham,
the 250-year-old **Milbury's** in Beauworth
(great for walkers), the **Globe** in Alresford and
the **Flower Pots** in Cheriton. The last of these
has the distinction of brewing its own prize-
winning beer, and selling it at bargain prices.
Wickham has a great local caff, the **Wickham
Tea House** (01329 835017; licensed), open for
breakfast and lunch every day and with tables
on the Square. Portsmouth, true to form, has a
clutch of high-quality (but well-priced) fish
and seafood restaurants.

Flounders at the American Bar

58 White Hart Road, Old Portsmouth (01705 811585).
Food served noon-2.30pm, 6.30-10pm, Mon-Sat;
noon-3.30pm, 6.30-9.30pm, Sun. **Cards** AmEx, DC,
Debit, MC, V.

A popular seafood restaurant/bar in Old Portsmouth,
decorated in a bright mix of English nautical and
American diner style. It's located right opposite the fish
market, so there's no problem with the freshness of the
main ingredient. The globetrotting menu combines the
likes of seafood chowder (£4.40), moules marinières
(£4.95-£6.95), char-grilled swordfish (£12.25), the 'ultimate fish and chips' (with monkfish and garlic mayonnaise, £11.95) and a catch of the day among other
choices; there are also sandwiches and baguettes (£3.95-
£5.25), and, for non-fish-eaters, some good meat and
vegetarian options.

Lemon Sole

123 High Street, Old Portsmouth
(01705 811303/www.lemonsole.co.uk).
Food served noon-2pm, 6-10pm, daily.
Set meals *lunch* £5.25 (1 course); *dinner* £7.95
(2 courses). **Cards** AmEx, DC, Debit, MC, V.

A seafood restaurant with a special 'pick-your-own' formula. A big range of market-fresh fish and shellfish is
displayed in a big ice cabinet. You select your fish, and
it's then cooked in the style of your choice. Starters are
chosen from a set list, which includes pan-fried prawns
in garlic butter (£6.95) and bang-bang chicken (£4.95).
You similarly pick your own wine, from big racks along
one wall. Non-fishophiles are catered for with a few meat
and veggie choices. The basement wine bar has an interesting, well-priced bar snacks list.

Old Chesil Rectory

1 Chesil Street, Winchester (01962 851555).
Food served noon-2pm, 7-9pm, Tue-Thur; noon-
2pm, 7-9.30pm, Fri, Sat. **Set meals** *lunch* £20
(3 courses), £16 (2 courses); *dinner* £32 (3 courses),
£28 (2 courses). **Cards** DC, Debit, MC, V.

The oldest house in Winchester, with massive half-
timbered gables and dating from 1459, now contains a
restaurant where chef-proprietor Philip Storey prepares
sophisticated modern food with a light touch. The frequently changing menu might include crab gazpacho
and a salad of parma ham and asparagus, and guinea
fowl tartlet with spinach and mustard sauce and duck
breast with pak choi in a spiced duck sauce. There's also
a daily choice of fresh fish dishes (roast sea bass with
fennel and artichokes in balsamic vinegar dressing), and
a vegetarian menu. To follow there's a luxurious range
of desserts; the wine list has been chosen with equal care.

Old House Hotel & Brasserie

The Square, Wickham (01329 833049).
Food served 7-9.30pm Mon; noon-2pm, 7-9.30pm,
Tue-Sat. **Set meals** *lunch* £13.50 (2 courses); £17.50
(3 courses); *dinner* £26 (2 courses); £30 (3 courses).
Cards AmEx, DC, Debit, MC, V.

Chef Nicholas Ruthven-Stuart has worked his way
around several different locations in Hampshire, and
his adventurous cooking has been widely praised (*The
Times*' Jonathan Meades is a particular admirer).
Ruthven-Stuart has an uncompromisingly definite

style, which you perhaps either like, or do not. Rich, strong flavours and liberal use of game are hallmarks; sauces are gutsily emphatic. In a salad of crispy duck, bacon and lentils with soy, honey and ginger dressing, the meat was delicate and very finely balanced; in roast seabass with fennel and an orange, vanilla and cardamom vinaigrette, on the other hand, the citrus sauce was too much for the (excellent) fish. Similarly non-minimalist no-prisoners-taken desserts like chocolate marquise with mascarpone ice cream complete the mix. A three-course dinner will come to around £30 (£25 at lunch).

Wykeham Arms

75 Kingsgate Street, Winchester (01962 853834).
Food served noon-2.30pm, 6.30-8.45pm, Mon-Sat.
Cards AmEx, DC, Debit, MC, V.

The influence of Winchester College extends inside the Wykeham Arms: many of the bar tables are old school desks, and College memorabilia figures heavily on the curio-drenched walls. At midday there's a varied, light-ish lunch menu, with good soups and sandwiches. The dinner menu is more substantial: Aberdeen Angus steaks are a speciality, but you may also find goat's

Old Pompey

Portsmouth, home of the Royal Navy and one of England's most angst-ridden football teams, does not enjoy the best of press. It often appears as a rather plain modern city, or maybe just a convenient ferry port. However, centuries at the centre of Britain's maritime life have left it with a distinctive character, and loads to see.

As well as all its naval attractions, it has a bit of old-fashioned seaside, on Southsea Esplanade, with a pier, shingle beach and fun-parks like the Sealife Centre and Pyramids Centre indoor waterpark. For wandering around the focus is Old Portsmouth, south of the main dockyard. Heavily bombed in World War II, it was rebuilt without much heritage-awareness, so calling it 'Old Portsmouth' can seem a tad misleading, but its streets still have plenty of harbour-town character, especially the headland known as Spice Island. In the days when Britannia ruled the waves and a Jack Tar was a Jack Tar this little knot of quayside streets had over 40 pubs. Today things are calmer and it has just three, but old inns like the Spice Island Inn and the Still & West Country House are still engaging

places with fine harbour views, and there's a good walk along the sea wall. Old Portsmouth is also home to the city's best fish restaurants (for two of the best, *see page 105*).

Charles Dickens Birthplace Museum

393 Old Commercial Road, Portsmouth (01705 827261).
Open *Apr-Oct* 10am-5.30pm daily; *29 Nov-19 Dec, 7 Feb* 10am-4pm daily. **Admission** £2; free under-13s; £1.20 14s-18s, students; £1.50 OAPs.

One Portsmouth attraction with only a sideways connection with the Navy, a little away from central Portsmouth near the ferry terminal. The great novelist actually had few memories of this house, since his father, a Navy clerk, moved the family on not long after Charles was born here in 1812, but it's a very charmingly preserved example of a modest early nineteenth-century house, and also has several relics of the writer's later life. Normally closed in winter, it opens specially on 7 February, Dickens' birthday.

Portsmouth Historic Dockyard (Flagship Portsmouth)

Porter's Lodge, 1/7 College Road, HM Naval Base, Portsmouth (01705 861512/www.flagship.org.uk).
Open *Mar-Oct* 10am-5.30pm daily; *Nov-Feb* 10am-5pm daily. **Admission** *each individual attraction* £5.95; £4.45 5s-14s; £5.20 OAPs; *all-ships ticket* £11.90; £8.90 5s-14s; £10.40 OAPs; £28.25 family.

Portsmouth's star historic attraction contains four main elements: Nelson's flagship HMS *Victory*, the world's first all-iron warship, HMS *Warrior*, the remains of Henry VIII's *Mary Rose*, preserved in a fascinating visitor centre, and the Royal Naval Museum. The old dockyard buildings are of interest in themselves, and with the 'all-ships' ticket you can return any time within two years to catch up on parts you have missed. Fans of the nautical and/or military naturally have many other places to choose from around Portsmouth, such as the D-Day Museum, the Royal Marines Museum, the Royal Navy Submarine Museum and more (for details, contact Portsmouth tourist office on 01705 826722).

cheese, basil and red pepper tart (£4.75), a fine ballotine of salmon wrapped in spiced spinach (£4.95) and rack of lamb with roast garlic and rosemary (£12.60). As well as local beers (Gale's) there's a Burgundy-oriented wine list. Beyond the labyrinthine rooms you'll find a garden at the back. Very popular, so always book for dinner. For the hotel, *see page 105*.

What to see & do

Winchester hosts several festivals, for which July is the peak month: the **Hat Fair Street Theatre Festival** occupies the first weekend, followed by the all-the-arts **Winchester Festival**; at the end of July there is the **Southern Cathedrals Festival**, with lashings of choral music in the Cathedral. In late September Winchester also hosts a **Literature Festival**.

There are plenty of enjoyable and (thanks to Winchester's sedate pace) peaceful walks within the city, and the tourist office offers guided walks and tours. Winchester is also a junction of long-distance footpaths. It is the westernmost point of the South Downs Way, which runs to Eastbourne, and the Pilgrims Way, to Canterbury. The Itchen Way runs south to join the Solent Way, to Southampton and Portsmouth, and the Clarendon Way goes west to Salisbury. Several guides are available to these paths, and the Winchester tourist office has local guides to these and other footpaths nearby. Andover and Romsey offices have guides to the Test Way.

Tourist information centres

Town Mill House, Bridge Street, **Andover**, SP10 1BL (01264 324320). **Open** *Apr-late July, Sept-late Oct* 9.30am-5.30pm Mon-Sat; *late July-Aug* 9.30am-5.30pm Mon-Sat; *late Oct-Mar* 10am-4.30pm Mon-Sat; 1-5pm Sun; *bank hols* 11am-4pm.
The Hard, **Portsmouth**, PO1 3QJ (01705 826722/www.portsmouthcc.gov.uk/visitor). **Open** *Apr-Sept* 9.30am-5.45pm daily; *Oct-Mar* 9.30am-5.15pm daily.
1 Latimer Street, **Romsey**, SO51 8DF (01794 512987). **Open** *Apr-July, Sept* 9.30am-5pm Mon-Sat; *Aug* 9.30am-5pm Mon-Sat; 2-5pm Sun; *Oct-Mar* 10am-4pm Mon-Sat.
The Guildhall, The Broadway, **Winchester**, SO23 9LJ (01962 840500/www.winchester.gov.uk). **Open** *June-mid-Sept* 10am-6pm Mon-Sat; 11am-2pm Sun; *mid-Sept-May* 10am-5pm Mon-Sat.

Bishop's Waltham Palace

Bishop's Waltham (01489 892460). **Open** *Apr-Sept* 10am-6pm daily; *Oct* 10am-5pm daily. **Admission** (EH) £2; £1 5s-14s; £1.50 OAPs, students.
This once-lavish residence of Winchester's medieval bishops was begun in the 1130s, and extended many times. It was destroyed during the Civil War in 1644,

Lemur at **Marwell Zoological Park**.

after it had been used as a Royalist stronghold. However, the surviving ruins, looming up in the middle of the town, are impressively atmospheric.

Hospital of St Cross

St Cross Road, Winchester (01962 851375). **Open** *Apr-Oct* 9.30am-5pm Mon-Sat; *Nov-Mar* 10.30am-3.30pm Mon-Sat. **Admission** £2; 50p 5s-14s; £1.25 OAPs, students.
The medieval almshouse of St Cross, about a mile south of Winchester town centre, is the oldest still-functioning house of charity in the country (founded in 1136). The towering Norman church is twelfth-century; most of the other buildings were added in the 1440s. They have a marvellous tranquillity, and make a beautiful end to a walk. St Cross still houses a religious community, and hungry visitors can ask at the Porter's Lodge for the 'Wayfarer's Dole', of free bread and ale.

Marwell Zoological Park

Colden Common, Winchester (01426 943163). **Open** *Nov-Mar* 10am-4pm daily; *Apr-Oct* 10am-6pm daily. **Admission** £8.50; £6 3s-14s; £7.50 OAPs; £27 family.
A family favourite, with some 1,000 animals living in 100 acres of parkland. The breeding and sustaining of endangered species is a park speciality, but there's also a kid's zoo, picnic areas, miniature railway and so on. Among the most popular attractions are 'World of Lemurs' and 'Penguin World'. It's off the B2177 road to Bishop's Waltham, seven miles south of Winchester. Phone for details of the regular special events.

Hampshire & Isle of Wight

Winchester Cathedral – *the city's glory.*

Watercress Line – Mid-Hants Railway

The Station, New Alresford
(info 01962 733810/www.watercress.line).
Tickets *unlimited travel for one day* £8; £5 5s-15s;
£6 OAPs; *single tickets* £4.50; £3 5s-15s, OAPs.

The ten-mile rural rail line between Alresford and Alton
was cast aside by British Rail in 1973, but has since been
kept going by determined local enthusiasm, with an all-
steam fleet. Trains run every Sunday and most
Saturdays from February to October, and almost daily
from June to August and during December. To appeal
to a wider public as well as the train-potty the line also
offers special trips such as silver-service dining-car
lunches, cream teas on the train, Thomas the Tank
Engine tours and so on. The line has played parts in
umpteen period TV shows.

Winchester Cathedral & Close

The Close, Winchester (01962 857200).
Open *cathedral* 7.15am-6.30pm daily; *Triforium &
library Easter-Oct* 10.30am-4.30pm Mon-Sat; *visitor
centre* 9.30am-5.30pm daily. **Admission** *expected
donation* £2.50; 50p 4s-18s; £2 OAPs, students; £5
family; *Triforium & library* £1; 50p 4s-18s.

Winchester's majestic Norman Cathedral was begun in
1079. To build it the Norman conquerors swept aside
the Saxon Old Cathedral, the outline of which can still
be seen in the Close. This cathedral contained the first
tomb of Saint Swithun, Bishop of Winchester 837-61; as
every book on Winchester has to remind you, if it rains
on his day (15 July), it's due to pour down for 40 days
thereafter. In the present Cathedral, the beautifully simple transepts are those of the eleventh-century building;
the huge Gothic nave was added in the fourteenth century and is the longest in Europe. Inside, the Cathedral
has too many treasures to detail here, among them
twelfth-century wall paintings in the Chapel of the Holy
Sepulcre, and the grave of Jane Austen. Don't pass over
the climb up to the Triforium, which gives you a spectacular view of the transepts, and contains a remarkable
collection of carvings in stone and wood; in the seventeenth-century Library the centrepiece is the Winchester
Bible, a dazzling illuminated manuscript begun in 1160.
Informative guided tours of the Cathedral are available;
ask at the information desk.

   The other buildings around the Close are almost as
historic. The Deanery dates from the thirteenth century; next to it, Dean Garnier's Garden contains the

remains of a Gothic cloister. The huge half-timbered
Cheyney Court, by the southern gate of the Close, was
originally the Bishops' courthouse. As a change from
the medieval, around the Close there is also now an interesting collection of entirely modern sculpture. Ask at
Cathedral information about tours of the Close buildings, most of which are not normally open to visitors.

Winchester City Mill

Bridge Street, Winchester (01962 870057).
Open *Mar* 11am-4.45pm Sat, Sun; *Apr-Jun, Sept, Oct*
11am-4.45pm Wed-Sun, bank hols; *Jul, Aug* 11am-
5.45pm daily. **Admission** £1; 50p 5s-14s.

Established since the fifteenth century and last rebuilt
in 1744, this grand watermill is a very impressive example of early technology and spectacular timbering, with
a riverside garden behind it. Run by the National Trust,
it also houses a video exhibition on the working of the
mill, a shop and Winchester's youth hostel.

Winchester Great Hall & Westgate

Great Hall Castle Avenue, Winchester (01962 846476).
Open *Apr-Oct* 10am-5pm daily; *Nov-Mar* 10am-5pm
Mon-Fri; 10am-4pm Sat, Sun. **Admission** free;
donations welcome.

Westgate Upper High Street, Winchester (01962
848269/www.winchester.gov.uk/heritage/heritage.htm).
Open *Feb-Mar, Oct* 10am-5pm Tue-Fri; 10am-1pm,
2-5pm, Sat; 2-5pm Sun; *Apr-Sept* 10am-5pm Mon-Fri;
10am-1pm, 2-5pm, Sat; 2-5pm Sun. **Admission** 30p.

One of Winchester's lesser-known gems, Henry III's
spectacular Great Hall (1222-35) is the last remaining
part of what was for 500 years one of England's principal royal palaces. Its most famous feature is the 'Round
Table' hanging on one wall, believed to have been made
in the thirteenth century and repainted for Henry VIII
in 1522. In the small museum in the Westgate there's a
sixteenth-century painted ceiling from Winchester
College, but all eyes are drawn to the seventeenth century graffiti, carved by prisoners locked up in the gate.

Winchester Military Museums

Peninsula Barracks, Romsey Road.
Winchester Gurkha Museum (01962 828536).
Light Infantry Museum (01962 828550).
King's Royal Hussars Museum (01962 828541).
Royal Green Jackets Museum (01962 828549).
Royal Hampshire Regiment Museum
(01962 863658).

Military buffs can spend the whole day in Winchester
going round the Peninsula Barracks, with the Gurkha
Museum to add a touch of the exotic. Admission times
and prices vary; phone the individual sights for details.

Wolvesey Castle

College Street, Winchester (01962 854766).
Open *Apr-Sept* 10am-6pm daily; *Oct* 10am-5pm
daily. **Admission** (EH) £1.80; 90p 5s-16s; £1.40
OAPs, students.

The twelfth-century main residence of the Bishops of
Winchester was one of the largest medieval palaces in
England, rivalling in size the royal castle to the west.
Like Bishop's Waltham it was mostly destroyed in the
1640s, and is now a rambling ruin.

The New Forest

Lose the crowds and commune with the ponies.

Edge-of-forest tranquillity on the Lymington River.

Ever since it was William the Conqueror's personal hunting ground, the New Forest has been a green and pleasant bit of land near enough to the capital for some decent R&R. The Norman king's son and successor, William Rufus, met his accidental end here, shot by an arrow while hunting – the Rufus Stone, near Fordingbridge, marks the spot – although the most danger you're likely to face in the New Forest today is being knocked down by hordes of kids racing for the ice-cream van. The historic towns and villages are often heaving with visitors, but it's still possible to get away from it all in the largest area of woodland left in the South, although you can't go far without meeting a pony. Tree-spotters will be in their element in the New Forest: among the types you'll come across in the 145 or so square miles are holly, yew, birch, Scots pine and ancient oaks and beeches. The best way to make the most of the scenery is to park the car and head off into the woods; the **Forestry Commission** (0131 314 6505) provides details of guided walks, camping and facilities for disabled people within the Forest. If you want to know more about the history of the Forest, or 'get up to date on Forest issues', visit the **New Forest Museum & Visitor Centre** in Lyndhurst (in the same building as the tourist information centre; 01703 283914).

By train from London

To properly explore the New Forest you'll need your own transport, but a healthy alternative to driving is to take the train and hire bikes. Trains to **Ashurst New Forest** leave **Waterloo** every other hour (journey time **1hr 30mins**). Trains to **Brockenhurst** leave **Waterloo** hourly (journey time **1hr 30mins**); change here for **Lymington** (which takes an additional 8 minutes).

The south coast

Of course, woodland isn't the only attraction of the area. The New Forest's proximity to the

Solent makes it a popular sailing destination, with many boats moored on the Lymington River. **Lymington** is an ancient port, famed for its saltworkings, and thanks to its *Howard's Way*-style affluence in recent years, remains pretty unspoilt – a quaint market town. Landlubber pursuits are gentle and genteel – **Lymington Antiques Centre** (76 High Street; 01590 670934) is worth a potter around, and **St Barbe Museum** (New Street; 01590 676969) has national and local art exhibitions. The town comes alive during the Saturday market. From the main street, you can walk down the cobbled passageway to the quay to watch local fishermen landing boxes of squid. The tiny street is lined with shops selling locally made ice-cream in imaginative flavours.

Lymington is a good centre from which to explore the Forest, but if you're looking for a little more seclusion, the village of **Sway** nestles right up in the open heathland section of the Forest, and you can drive, walk or cycle through beautiful open stretches of land teeming with flora and fauna (including Disney-like foals that you will want to take home).

In fact, if flowers and furry friends are your thing, you're in the right place. Gardens are a local mania – many hotels and guesthouses take as much pride in their grounds as their rooms and there are a number of open gardens to visit (**Spinners Garden**, Boldre, Lymington, 01590 673347; **Furzey Gardens**, Minstead, nr Lyndhurst, 01703 812464; **Exbury Gardens**, nr Beaulieu, 01703 891203; **Braxton Gardens**, Lymore Lane, Milford on Sea, 01590 642008), as well as the **New Forest Otter, Owl & Wildlife Conservation Park**.

Some of us, though, are content to lie back and think of England's birds and bees buzzing away by themselves while we sun ourselves on the beach. **Milford on Sea** in Christchurch Bay has a good beach for swimming and windsurfing, but the village is quieter than Lymington, but boasts the same Georgian-fronted buildings, little shops and pubs around the village green.

East side story

In the south-east corner of the Forest, **Beaulieu** (pronounced 'Bewley') is home to the Montagu family, who have managed to stave off selling their ancestral home by creating a popular and unprecious museum centre, and the village itself is tremendously pretty with thatched and red-roofed dwellings clustered around the Beaulieu River. It's a lovely stroll from here along the river to **Buckler's Hard**, the village where the historic shipyard that built Nelson's fleet was based. The **Maritime Museum** (01590 616203) charts the history of the

Chewton Glen: *serious luxury, serious prices.*

waterside village, and some of the cottages have been reconstructed to show how life would have been for those working for Nelson in 1793. The rest of the cottages make up the **Master Builder's House Hotel**, which serves good lunches and drinks out in the garden overlooking the river.

Further east, the banks of Southampton Water offer a collection of little villages known as the Waterside, the biggest being **Hythe**, from where the *Titanic* first sailed. **Fawley** and **Calshot** are also pretty and good walking and sailing areas, and **Lepe** has the best sandy beach, with views across the Solent.

Wheeling along

Perhaps the most civilised, and certainly the most leisurely, way to see the New Forest is using pedal power. There are cycle hire places in **Burley** (Burley Bike Hire, Burley Village Centre; 01425 403584), **Lyndhurst** (AA Bike Hire, Gosport Lane; 01703 283349) and **Brockenhurst** (New Forest Cycle Experience, 2-4 Brookley Road; 01590 624204), which are all places in the heart of the Forest with easy access to plenty of traffic-free routes and a good number of pub stop-off points. Brockenhurst is a particularly popular centre for hiring bikes, as it's lined with little tearooms, pubs and ice-cream places to reward yourself after all that exercise.

Where to stay

Restaurants and pubs often have a few rooms to let in this very tourist-oriented area. The **Thatched Cottage Hotel** in Brockenhurst (*see below*) has double rooms from £90 and the **Montagu Arms** in Beaulieu (Beaulieu; 01590 612324) are particularly good examples.

Burbush Farm

Pound Lane, Burley, BH24 4EF
(tel/fax 01425 403238/burbush-farm@excite.com).
Rates (B&B) £25-£30pp. **Rooms** (all en suite)
3 doubles. **Credit** Debit, MC, V.

The garden of this B&B, hidden at the end of a farm track, is particularly beautiful, and the Hayles' fondness for foliage seems to have spread into the house, where the bedrooms are a riot of frothy floral motif. It's pretty comfortable though, and the owners are warm and welcoming. There is a swimming pool in the garden, around which guests can lounge; bikes are for hire if anybody feels actively inclined, although it might be wise to wait awhile after one of Carol's enormous breakfasts before saddling up. The nervous and cack-handed should take note – there's more china, silver and crystalware on the breakfast table than the entire second floor of Harrods. The whole building is non-smoking.

M27/A31 towards Bournemouth; take left to Burley Street and Burley village; turn right at the Cross war memorial into Pound Lane; Burbush Farm is 0.5 miles on left.

Chewton Glen

Christchurch Road, New Milton, BH25 6QS (01425 275341/fax 01425 273310/reservations@ chewtonglen.com/www.chewtonglen.com).
Rates *single occupancy/double/twin* £230-£530; *suite* £430-£530. **Rooms** (all en suite) 33 double/twin; 19 suites. Special breaks. Breakfast £9-£17.50.
Cards AmEx, DC, Debit, MC, V.

When a hotel is voted one of the Top 20 in the world by numerous eminent travel publications, expectations are high. Chewton Glen is as super-luxurious as the articles and brochures make out. Whether your room is a standard or a suite, it has either a terrace or balcony, and the views over the gardens and parklands are tremendous. There is an outdoor pool, croquet lawn, health club with big indoor pool and golf course. The old house and grounds are beautiful and there are numerous touches, from sherry to huge bathrobes in the rooms, no less than one would expect for the price and, to be frank, the pervading feel is slightly corporate. Fine, if yours is the world of Eurotrash millionaires (in which case you probably won't be reading this), fantastic if you need some mega-pampering, but, to sum it up, this is the place where Alan Partridge would come to die.

M3/M27 towards Bournemouth; turn left (3 miles after J1) to Emery Down; at T-junction take A35 towards Christchurch; after 8 miles turn left at staggered junction; take 2nd left after Walkford into Chewton Farm Road; hotel is on right.

Mulberries

6 West Hayes, Lymington, SO41 3RL (01590 679549).
Rates (B&B) *single* £29pp; *double/twin* £29pp; *appartment* £175-£245 per week. **Rooms** (all en suite) 1 single; 1 double; 1 twin; 1 apartment.

If you haven't got a car, Mulberries is ideal as it's only a short walk from Lymington coach and train stations. The house is set in a 'select little cul-de-sac' as Hyacinth Bucket might say, but is mercifully spared the flouncy décor that is the usual realm of B&Bs. The two secluded rooms on the top floor are large, comfortable (especially the bed) and tastefully furnished with bits and pieces of antique china and a particulary good selection of books on the shelves. The garden is divided between lawns and herbaceous borders and there's a heated pool for summer use. Breakfast is an informal affair, and if you arrive in time for afternoon tea, you'll be lucky enough to sample some of owner Jan Messenger's homemade cake. The whole building is non-smoking.

J1 off M27; A337 to Lymington; in Lymington go under railway bridge; turn left into Marsh Lane; straight over into Gosport Street; straight over into Captain's Row; right into Grove Road; West Hayes is turning after 300m.

Nurse's Cottage

Station Road, Sway, SO41 6BA (tel/fax 01590 683402/nurses.cottage@lineone.net).
Rates (B&B) *single* £52.50; *single occupancy* £62.50; *double/twin* £90. **Rooms** (all en suite) 1 single; 1 double; 1 twin. **Cards** AmEx, Debit, MC, V.

Although the building in which the award-winning Nurse's Cottage is housed isn't much to write home about, owner Tony Barnfield has certainly made the best of what he's got. Thoughtful details and extras are abundant – the fridges in each room have fresh milk ('No horrid UHT here'), and fruit, chocolates and sherry, afternoon tea and daily papers are all included in the price. The bedroom phones even have modem connections should urban types feel that the forest seclusion is a bit too much for them and need some urgent downloading. The small dining room also serves as a (popular) restaurant, which makes use of local produce including freshly caught fish, farm eggs, English cheeses and Isle of Wight ice-cream – and there is an impressively extensive wine list, too. No smoking throughout the building.

J1 off M27; follow signs to Lyndhurst, then to Brockenhurst and Sway; the cottage is next to post office in Sway.

Westover Hall `Offer`

Park Lane, Milford on Sea, SO41 0PT (01590 643044/ fax 01590 644490/westover@lds.co.uk).
Rates (B&B) *single* £65-£85; *double/twin* £110-£140; *half-tester* £140; *family room* £150. Special breaks.
Rooms (all en suite) 1 single; 11 double/twin; 1 family room. **Cards** AmEx, DC, Debit, MC, V.

The owners of this luxurious Victorian mansion wanted a change from working in the fashion industry, so they bought a hotel. You don't have to be a media darling to appreciate this place, though – if you despair of country house hotel tweeness, Westover ('we don't do peach') Hall is for you. The house was lavishly built for the Siemens family and all the original features are still there, including the oak panelling and stained-glass windows. Furnished with a mix of antique and contemporary, each of the rooms has its own character: one has an ornate gilt bed; another a canopied half-tester; and many have sea views. The atmosphere is far from precious, and guests are treated as friends. Mum presides over reception and Arthur the cat, resplendent in his Gucci collar, presides over everything else. Both relaxed and funky, Westover is well worth splashing out on for a treat. Children and dogs welcome. *See also p113.*

J1 off M27; take A337 to Lymington; after Lymington follow signs to Milford on Sea and B3058; hotel is on clifftop after Milford on Sea.

Where to eat & drink

Chequers

Lower Woodside, Lymington (01590 673415).
Food served noon-2pm, 7-10pm, Mon-Fri; noon-2pm Sat; noon-2.30pm, 7.30-9.30pm, Sun.
Cards Debit, MC, V.

It's a pleasant walk to the Chequers from Lymington (about 15 minutes down tiny lanes) but it might be advisable to take a torch in the evening. Safely there, you'll find the pub couldn't be more lively, as it's a favourite with the local yachting fraternity, with much hearty, beer-fuelled hilarity going on. The restaurant is hugely popular at weekends, and it's best to book if you don't want to eat just before closing time. The menu makes good use of local seafood such as moules marinières (£4.25), grilled plaice (£8.75) and grilled sea bass (£10.50). Puddings are also tasty, although, on a recent visit, peach and mango cheesecake and treacle, apple and sultana tart (both £5) came drowned in a lake of cream.

Marryat Restaurant

Chewton Glen, Christchurch Road, New Milton (01425 275341).
Food served 7.30-9.30pm Mon; 12.30-2.30pm, 7.30-9.30pm, Tue-Sun. **Set meals** *lunch* £13.50 (2 courses), £18.50 (3 courses); *dinner* £45 (3 courses).

Even if you can't afford 500 quid for a bedroom at Chewton Glen, the Michelin-starred cooking of chef Pierre Chevillard is still available to all and the dining room of the Marryat, overlooking the hotel grounds, is just as good a way to experience a bit of luxury. Dinner could be double-baked Emmenthal soufflé served with a fondue sauce, followed by roasted local lobster with beurre blanc and herbs and hot chocolate fondant with home-made pistachio ice-cream or English and French farmhouse cheeses to finish. The menu is scattered with indications of healthy or vegetarian choices, and the chef's signature dishes.

Old Bank House

68 High Street, Lymington (01590 671128).
Food served noon-2pm, 7-10pm, Mon-Fri; 7-10pm Sat. **Set meals** *lunch* £7.95 (2 courses).
Cards AmEx, DC, Debit, MC, V.

A restaurant of the old school, the Old Bank House is the picture of the provincial upmarket eaterie. Don't expect anything too weird or fashionable: the menu mostly consists of '70s staples with a few modernist twiddles, but the upside is that the combinations are tried and tested. Starters include gravadlax (£6.50), warm pigeon breast, bacon and mushroom salad (£6) and sautéed squid with Greek salad (£6). Main dishes are just as safe: take salmon fishcakes (£9.95), roast monkfish wrapped in parma ham with mash (£14.95) and wild mushroom and rocket risotto with goat's cheese (£11) as examples.

Provence Restaurant at Gordleton Mill de Jean-Christophe Novelli

Silver Street, Hordle, nr Lymington (01590 682219).
Food served noon-2pm Mon, Sun; noon-2pm, 7-10pm, Tue-Sat. **Cards** AmEx, DC, Debit, MC, V.

In early 1999, the ubiquitous Novelli bought the hotel and restaurant where he started his UK culinary career. The seventeenth-century watermill is set in five acres of garden in the New Forest, so there's ample opportunity to walk off any indulgence. You can dine in a private room, in the (rather formal) restaurant or on the terrace overlooking the water. Novelli's superb French signature dishes include trout tartare, roast lamb cutlets with

soufflé of Roquefort cheese, and a hot and cold white and dark chocolate plate. The wine list concentrates on regional French specialities.

Red Lion

Rope Hill, Boldre (01590 673177).
Food served noon-2.30pm, 6.30-9.30pm, daily.
Cards AmEx, DC, Debit, MC, V.

A good place to stop if cycling through the Forest, the Red Lion is an archetypal country pub, well worth pedalling down winding lanes to get to. You can tick the requirements for authenticity off on a list here. Inglenooks, check; rustic whatnots on the wall, check; open fire (even when it's sunny outside), check; local girls behind the higgledy-piggledy bar, check. What's more, the food is a cut above the usual ye olde lasagne and chips fare. You can sit at the little clusters of tables outside to enjoy the local Websters Green label bitter, special New Forest game pie (£9.90), roast rabbit (£8.90), dressed crab salad (£7.90) and steamed lemon sponge (£3.20).

Royal Oak

North Gorley (01425 652244).
Food served noon-2pm, 6.30-9.30pm, daily.
Set meals £9.50/£10.50 (2 courses); £14 (3 courses).
Cards AmEx, DC, Debit, MC, V.

A thatched country pub in picturesque surroundings on the western edge of the Forest, where you can sit and watch the ducks on the pond while supping your pint from the local Ringwood Brewery, then play skittles in the skittle alley. There's also a playground for kids. Inside, the pub is surprisingly large and sprawling, but the best place to eat is the snug bar, which has its own entrance. Food is pretty standard pub grub, but the shepherd's pie (£5.75), and broccoli and stilton bake (£5.25) that we last tried were fine if not scintillating, and the sticky toffee pudding with ice-cream (£2.75) was exactly as described.

Thatched Cottage

16 Brookley Road, Brockenhurst, SO42 7RR (01590 623090).
Food served 12.30-2pm, 7.30-9.30pm, Tue-Sat; 12.30-2pm Sun; *afternoon tea* 2.30-5.30pm Tue-Sun.
Set meals *dinner* £30 (3 courses).
Cards Debit, MC, V.

The Thatched Cottage is just that, and you could imagine characters from an EM Forster novel taking tea in the little garden, with its dainty tables covered in lace cloths. Afternoon tea (£8.50) is a speciality, featuring astounding tiers of delicious finger sandwiches, scones and cream and luscious cakes, served with champagne to those who so wish. The tiny hotel/restaurant is run by the Matysik family and Martin Matysik, the chef, has come from a background of 'Michelin-starred restaurants', hence the overwhelmingly adventurous lunch and dinner menus. Flaked king scallop and crab wrapped in courgettes with provençal salsa and cocktail sauce followed by confit of potato with melting foie gras, sorrel and globe artichoke and spiced port wine reductions is an example of a typical grandiose-sounding meal. The dining room has an 'open-to-view country kitchen'. Should you wish to stay the night, the inviting bedrooms cost from £90 for a double.

A walk in the woods

You can't go far in the New Forest without bumping into a hiker with a knapsack on his back, but boy scout tendencies aside, the opportunities for a good tramp or even a little wander are seemingly inexhaustible, and because the Forest is bordered by rivers and coastland, the scenery is varied. Hardy types will pack a tent and march for days, but even the luxurious Chewton Glen will point you in the right direction if you feel perambulatorily-inclined. The conditions in the Forest are particularly good for walking as it's so sheltered, but it's a good idea to have waterproof shoes as the ground can get pretty boggy in places. Don't forget a drink as well, as there aren't any cafés or pubs in the more sparsely populated areas. Map-reading isn't easy in the Forest as there are few landmarks, so a compass is useful, and don't forget to follow the country code or you're likely to incur the wrath of a passing member of the Ramblers Association.

Most hotels will give you information about good walks in the area and the tourist offices have numerous books mapping out routes, which are handy for avoiding the M27 or landowners who greet trespassers with a twelve-bore. A good walk in the heart of the Forest is the Rufus Stone and Lower Canterton one, which is three miles and passes the Sir Walter Tyrell pub.

Westover Hall

Park Lane, Milford on Sea, SO41 0PT (01590 643044).
Food served noon-2pm, 7-9pm, daily.
Cards AmEx, DC, Debit, MC, V.

If you just fancy a day at the beach, Westover Hall is open to non-residents for lunch, drinks or afternoon tea in the pretty wood-panelled bar – painted a sunny yellow – or outside on the garden terrace. The restaurant in the dining room, which overlooks Christchurch Bay and has views of the Needles , has a daily-changing dinner menu for non-guests at £25 a head. The three courses could consist of paupiette of crab and smoked salmon with gazpa-

cho sauce to start, then chargrilled rack of lamb, parsnip crisps, honey roast garlic and rosemary sauce with an iced parfait of chocolate and mint with orange and strawberry salad to end the meal. *See also p111.*

What to see & do

Tourist information centres

New Street, **Lymington** (01590 6890000).
Open 10am-5pm Mon-Sat.
Main Car Park, **Lyndhurst** (01703 282269). **Open** *summer*10am-6pm daily; *winter* 10am-5pm daily.

Bike hire

(see page 110)

Hurst Castle Ferry

28 Park Road, Milford on Sea (01590 642344).
Times *Apr-Oct* departs Keyhaven Quay on the half hour from 10am and returns from Hurst Castle on the half hour until 5.30pm, daily. **Tickets** (EH) £2.80; £1.90 3s-16s; £2.60 OAPs.

Built by Henry VIII as one of a chain of coastal fortresses, Hurst Castle was where Charles I was once held prisoner and is now said to be haunted by the ghost of a priest incarcerated there in the eighteenth century. You can take a boat from Keyhaven to the castle, which is the nearest point to the Isle of Wight and has amazing views. There's good swimming and fishing around here too.

National Motor Museum

John Montagu Building, Beaulieu (info 01590 612123/ 612345/www.beaulieu.co.uk.).
Open 10am-5pm daily. Last entry 4.20pm.
Admission £9; £6.50 4s-16s; £7.50 OAPs; £29 family.

Palace House at Beaulieu has been in the Montagu family since 1538 and, to keep it that way, Lord Montagu has had to come up with a few visitor-friendly ideas. The result is a pretty-sussed operation, with lots to see and do. The National Motor Museum was started to indulge Montagu's own interests, and now there are over 250 vehicles to see, including the Bluebird. Not only that, but you can wander down a 1930s street and motor through time in a space-age pod. In the house itself, you can chat to Victorian characters about the price of fish (literally), or check out the exhibition of monastic life at the Domus of Beaulieu Abbey, dating from 1204, before switching centuries (again) for a ride on the monorail.

New Forest Otter, Owl & Wildlife Conservation Park

Longdown, Ashurst (01703 292408).
Open *summer* 10am-6pm daily; phone for winter times. **Admission** £4.95; £2.95 4s-14s; under-4s free.

Set in 25 acres of ancient woodland on the edge of the New Forest, the park is home to Europe's largest collection of multi-specied otters, owls and other indigenous wildlife. The tree-lined walks make the most of the park's location, and there's a tearoom to relax in afterwards.

New Forest Water Park

Hucklesbrook Lakes, Ringwood Road, Fordingbridge (01425 656868).
Open *Easter & Oct-mid-Nov* 10am-9pm/dusk Sat, Sun, bank hols; *May* 10am-9pm Wed-Sun, bank hols; *June-Sept* 10am-9pm daily. **Rates** waterskiing (per tow) from £14; aquarides £6; jetskiing £27.50-£30.

For the more active, the Water Park offers plenty of opportunies to get wet 'n' wild. A go at waterskiing gives you four laps around the lake; aquarides are on inflatable bananas or tyres; jetskis are solo stand-ups or two seater sit-downs and you can get tuition if you need it.

Paultons Park

Ower, nr Romsey (01703 814442).
Open & **Admission** phone for details.

If you haven't managed to palm the kids off for the weekend, you could do worse than to come to this family theme park. It's hardly Disneyworld, but it does have plenty to keep children amused, with attractions such as the Runaway Train, Dinosaurland and, for younger kids, Tiny Tots Town and animated nursery rhymes. Restaurants, shops and a picnic area complete the picture. The park is located off junction 2 of the M27.

Auto heaven at Lord Montagu's **National Motor Museum** *at Beaulieu.*

Isle of Wight

Savour the flavour of Little England.

Looking down from the top of **Tennyson Down**, named in honour of the poet who lived here and described the air as being 'worth sixpence a pint', the Isle of Wight lies before you like a child's drawing of an island. Shaped like a pair of bee-stung lips, to the north-west the River Yar flows out to the Solent past the castle that guards Yarmouth harbour; at the far western tip of the island, the jagged chalk line of the **Needles**, jutting from the sea, ends with a red-and-white lighthouse; to the south is the great crumbling sweep of **Compton Bay**, while further south the sheer cliffs fall dramatically into the Channel. Often described as encompassing the whole of southern England in miniature, the island's 147 square miles contain rolling farmland, marshy estuaries, castles, cliffs, vineyards, beaches, steam trains, Roman villas, dinosaur fossils, red squirrels and a whole clutch of manor houses.

During the 1800s, visitors poured in from all over Europe to enjoy the water, the sea air and the balmy climate. As well as Tennyson, whose home, Farringford, at **Freshwater**, is now a hotel, the poet Swinburne was born (and buried) in **Bonchurch**, where Dickens wrote *David Copperfield*; and the Russian writer Turgenev conceived his most famous novel, *Fathers and Sons*, while visiting **Ventnor** for the sea-bathing. Meanwhile at **Dimbola Lodge**, Tennyson's neighbour, the Victorian photographer Julia Cameron, was taking pictures of whoever she could persuade to sit still long enough. And of course, Queen Victoria

herself spent her summers with her family at **Osborne House** in East Cowes.

In the twentieth century, the island's star waned; in his novel *England, England* – in which the Isle of Wight has become a giant heritage theme park – Julian Barnes describes it as 'a mixture of rolling chalk downland of considerable beauty and bungaloid dystopia'. Today's grockles stick to the well-travelled coach routes from the tacky east coast resorts of **Sandown** and **Shanklin**, taking in the thatched tearooms of **Godshill**, **Blackgang Chine Fantasy Park**, the **Pearl Centre** (sadly not a local product harvested by nubile divers from the Channel's chilly waters) and the **Needles Pleasure Park**. All the better for the rest of us, as it leaves most of the island blissfully free of visitors even in the height of summer. There are actually far too many things to do here in a month, let alone a weekend, so unless it's raining stair rods, give the much-vaunted 'attractions' a miss and explore on foot or by bike. The island is a paradise for walkers and cyclists, boasting more footpaths per square mile than anywhere else in Britain – all meticulously signposted and maintained. Sailors can weigh anchor in the fine natural harbours of **Yarmouth**, **Cowes** and **Seaview**, surfers can brave the waves at Compton Bay, where fossil hunters admire the casts of dinosaurs' footprints at low tide. There is just one small drawback, however. The south-west of the island is disappearing into the sea, not inch by inch, but acre by acre. Every winter more cliffs collapse soufflé-like on to the beaches below, leaving fences and steps hanging suspended precariously in mid-air. In a thousand years the chalk spine that ends in the Needles could be all that remains. Better not put off your visit for too long.

By train (and boat) from London

There are trains from **Waterloo** to **Portsmouth** (approx **2hrs**), with a ferry crossing to **Ryde**, and from **Waterloo** to **Lymington** (**2hrs 15mins**), with a ferry crossing to **Yarmouth**. **Wightlink** (0990 827744) runs car and passenger ferries from **Portsmouth** to **Fishbourne** (crossing time usually **35mins**) and from **Lymington** to **Yarmouth** (**30mins**), while a catamaran runs from **Portsmouth** to **Ryde** (**15mins**).

Where to stay

George Hotel

Quay Street, Yarmouth, PO41 0PE (01983 760331/ fax 01983 760425/res@thegeorge.co.uk).
Rates (B&B) *single* £70-£95; *double/twin* £130-£175; *four-poster* £160. **Rooms** (all en suite) 2 single; 14 double/twin; 1 four-poster. **Cards** AmEx, Debit, MC, V.

The perfect hotel for a car-free weekend; disembark from the Lymington-Yarmouth ferry and the hotel is less than a minute's stroll away. The George is housed in the seventeenth-century former home of the island's governor,

*The effortlessly classy **Priory Bay Hotel.***

hard up against the wall of the castle, and all bedrooms are en suite, most with king-sized beds, satellite TV and phones. Situated on the old town square, the hotel has easy access to the shops and restaurants of this tiny port, and also boasts a great position from which to explore West Wight or follow the coastal path to Freshwater Bay. A private motor launch is available for charter. Children and dogs welcome. Non-smoking rooms available.

Two buildings away from terminal for Lymington-Yarmouth ferry.

Gottam Manor Bed & Breakfast

Gottam Lane, Chale, PO38 2HQ
(tel/fax 01983 551368/caroline.smith6@virgin.net).
Rates (B&B) £20-£24pp; *cottages* £250-£600 per week. **Rooms** (both en suite) 2 triple; 2 cottages (sleep 4-6).

This B&B is nestled under St Catherine's Down, where former manor resident Walter de Godeton was obliged to erect a lighthouse as penance for receiving smuggled goods. You'll need transport if you stay here, though – Gottam Manor is at the end of a long lane at the southern end of the island. One bedroom in the limewashed thirteenth-century annexe with wooden floors is reached by wooden steps and includes a discreetly screened cast iron bath. Home-made jams and local products make an appearance at breakfast. Self-catering accommodation is available in a converted barn for longer stays. Children welcome. No smoking throughout.

0.5 mile S of Chale Green on B3399; after village, turn left at Gottam Lane; hotel is at end of lane.

Kerne Farm Bed & Breakfast

Alverstone, Sandown, PO36 0EY
(01983 403721/403908).
Rates (B&B) £20pp; *cottages* £225-£520 per week. **Rooms** (both en suite) 1 triple; 1 four-poster; 2 cottages. Min 2 nights.

A character-packed, higgledy-piggledy sixteenth-century farmhouse crammed with antiques. Guests can read in the lovely conservatory or explore the garden. Right on the Bembridge Trail, the farm is criss-crossed by a network of bridleways and the owners will happily accommodate your horse, should you have one. Two self-catering cottages are also available for stays of a week or more. No children under 12. Bedrooms non-smoking.

From ferry terminal, head towards Ryde and Brading; follow signs to Adgestone Vineyard; pass vineyard to Alverstone village; turn right in village; Kerne Farm is straight ahead after 0.75 miles.

North Court Bed & Breakfast

Shorwell, PO30 3JG (01983 740415/fax 01983 740409).
Rates (B&B) £27.50pp. Special breaks.
Rooms (all en suite) 6 double/twin.

This imposing Jacobean pile set in 15 acres of gardens with brooks, terraces and shady woodland and exotic flowers is bliss. Around five miles south-west of Newport, it's an ideal stopping off point if you are walking across the island, or if you're feeling really energetic you could walk the 12 miles to the Needles and catch the bus back. Children and dogs welcome. No smoking in the house.

4 miles SW of Newport on Newport-Brighstone Road; hotel is in middle of Shorwell village.

Priory Bay Hotel Offer

Priory Drive, Seaview, PO34 5BU
(01983 613146/fax 01983 616539).
Rates (B&B) *single occupancy* £65-£127.50; *double/twin* £90-£182; *deluxe double/twin* £120-£212; *family suites/cottage suites* £125-£230.
Rooms (all en suite) 8 double/twin; 8 deluxe double/twin; 2 family suites; 7 cottage suites.
Cards AmEx, Debit, MC, V.

Opened by the genial Andrew Palmer (founder of the New Covent Garden Soup Company) in 1998, the Priory Bay has established itself as the chicest and most individual of the island's luxury hotels. Yet this is a thoroughly relaxed place, boasting a nine-hole golf course and an unheated outdoor pool among its facilities. The elevated position, surrounded by trees and overlooking the sea, is stunning, and to walk down through the woods, past the Oyster Seafood Café to the wide sweep of sandy beach, you'd swear you were in the Mediterranean rather on the Channel. All bedrooms are individually decorated with great panache – particularly appealing is the fresh, New Englandy room 11 in the eaves and the Chinese-themed room 20 with a roll-top bath in the bedroom. Self-catering accommodation, with limited room service, is available in 16 cottages in the grounds. The two restaurants are excellent, too. Who could want for more? Children and dogs welcome.

From Fishbourne ferry terminal follow signs to Ryde, then Nettlestone and St Helen's; through Nettlestone, after 0.5 miles turn left at sign to Prior Bay Hotel.

Royal Hotel

Belgrave Road, Ventnor, PO38 1JJ (01983 852186/
fax 01983 855395/royalhotel@zetnet.co.uk).
Rates (B&B) £50-£60pp. **Rooms** (all en suite) 5 single; 43 double/twin; 7 family. **Cards** AmEx, DC, Debit, MC, V.

A short stroll from the town centre and the beach (but not so close that it's likely to go the way of a rival establishment that slipped into the sea), this stately stone building has been refurbished to a high standard. The rooms are light and comfortable – in a grandish but not overly heavy country house style – with views over the garden, where there is a heated swimming pool. Children are catered for with early suppers, high chairs and baby listening, so parents can sit back and enjoy the excellent restaurant (*see p118*). Children welcome. Non-smoking rooms available.

Follow one way system in Ventnor; turn left at traffic lights; follow road up hill and bear left into Belgrave Road; hotel is at end of road on right.

Seaview Hotel `Offer`

High Street, Seaview, PO34 5EX (01983 612711/ fax 01983 613729/seaview.hotel@virgin.net).
Rates (B&B) *single* £55; *single occupancy* £55-£95; *double/twin* £70-£120; *family* £180.
Rooms (all en suite) 2 single; 13 double/twin; 1 family. **Cards** AmEx, DC, Debit, MC, V.

Described by its many regular guests as 'the perfect seaside hotel', the award-winning Seaview caters equally happily to families, romantic couples and old salts. A couple of steps from the beach, it's the social centre of the village. The hotel is very child friendly, with high chairs and baby listening; even dogs are welcome. Non-smoking rooms available.

Where to eat & drink

Beware: it is possible to eat very badly indeed on the Isle of Wight. One of the joys of the island is that it feels as if it is stuck in the 1950s but unfortunately this applies to the food as well: cappuccino has yet to make it across the Solent. Almost every pub claims to specialise in local seafood but it's often spoilt by having spent too long at the back of the fridge or by the sachets of salad cream and malt vinegar that are offered as the sole accompaniments. One tearoom within spitting distance of the sea cheerfully serves up a fisherman's platter that owes more to the freezer than the nearby Channel, while crab sticks surface in fish soup within sight of where the local fishermen unload their catch. Other local produce such as garlic, sweetcorn and honey rarely make their way on to menus, though Minghella ice-cream, still produced by the parents of film director Anthony, is easy to find. For afternoon tea in peaceful surroundings visit the gardens of one of the many manor houses or vineyards.

In addition to the pubs below, the **Fisherman's Cottage**, located at the bottom of Shanklin Chine, and the ultra-kid-friendly **Wight Mouse** at Chale are also worth a visit. The **Beach House Café** at Bonchurch Beach is excellent for classy snacks and can supply picnic baskets to order.

Burrs Restaurant

Lugley Street, Newport (01983 825470).
Food served noon-1.45pm, 7-9pm, daily.
Cards Debit, MC, V.

Located in an atmospheric old pub with log fires in winter, this bistro is popular with locals (tourists tend to give Newport a miss). Excellent fresh fish dishes change daily, and home-made puddings, such as marmalade bread and butter pudding, are a speciality.

Chequers Inn

Niton Road, Rookley (01983 840314).
Food served noon-10pm Mon-Sat; noon-9.30pm Sun. **Cards** Debit, MC, V.

Voted the UK Family Pub of the Year in the 1999 *Good*

Pub Guide, but don't let that put you off – local farmers still drink in the flagstoned public bar – this country pub combines real ale (Old Speckled Hen, £2 a pint) and an extensive menu, from avocado and prawn sandwiches (£3.95) to a seafood medley for two (£25). All this, plus views of the open country, and a large adventure playground and pony rides.

Crown Inn

Walkers Lane, Shorwell (01983 740293).
Food served noon-2.30pm, 6-9.30pm, daily.
Cards Debit, MC, V.

A stream with trout and ducks meanders through the garden of this pretty seventeenth-century inn where specials include sea bream with crab sauce and steak and kidney pie. Families are particularly welcome; high chairs and children's meals are available (scampi and chips, £3.25; half a roast dinner, £3.25).

George Hotel

Quay Street, Yarmouth (01983 760331)
Food served *restaurant* 7-9.45pm Tue-Sat; *brasserie* noon-3pm, 7-10pm, daily.

The only Michelin-rated restaurant on the island, with a menu strong on fish, featuring the likes of nage of monkfish with roasted scallops and pan-fried red mullet with baby squid, and also inspired dishes such as rack of lamb with a sea kale and sweetbread ravioli. The three-course set meal is £36.75. For simpler food in a less formal setting try the brasserie, where in summer you can sit outside and children can play on the pebbly private beach or watch the comings and goings of the ferry. Children under eight years old are not allowed in the restaurant but are welcome in the brasserie.

New Inn

Shalfleet (01983 531314).
Food served noon-3pm, 6-11pm, daily.
Cards AmEx, DC, Debit, MC, V.

A reputation for excellent food, which includes all kinds of fish and seafood dishes, makes this traditional seventeenth-century inn one of the most popular places to eat on the island. Shalfleet is between Newport and Yarmouth.

Red Lion

Church Place, Freshwater (01983 754925).
Food served noon-2pm, 6.30-9pm, Mon-Sat; noon-2pm, 7-9pm, Sun. **Cards** Debit, MC, V.

Popular with the yachtsmen who sail down the river from Yarmouth for lunch, this is a good place to stop off whether you are cycling or walking along the estuary towards Freshwater. Daily specials on the blackboard include soups (£3), seafood (£7.25-£10) and steak and kidney pie (£7.25).

Priory Bay Restaurant & Oyster Seafood Café

Priory Drive, Seaview (01983 613146).
Food served *restaurant* 12.30-2pm, 7.30-9.30pm, daily; *café* 9am-2pm, 3-6pm, 6.30-9.30pm, daily.
Cards AmEx, Debit, MC, V.

The Priory Bay Hotel's French-led kitchen knocks out some of the island's best cooking – perhaps foie gras wrapped in bacon, followed by melting rack of lamb.

The more recently opened café has simpler but equally good fare – salads, barbecued meats and seafood – which can be enjoyed al fresco in a wonderful woodland setting overlooking the sea.

Royal Hotel

Belgrave Road, Ventnor (01983 852186).
Food served *restaurant* 7-9.15pm daily;
bar noon-2pm daily. **Set meal** £22 (3 courses).
Cards AmEx, DC, Debit, MC, V.

A reliably classy if not ground-breaking restaurant, the Royal offers a three-course set dinner (£22) featuring Dover sole, lobster, steak and a daily special. Light lunches, including salads and omelettes (from around £8) are served in the bar and conservatory.

Salty's

Quay Street, Yarmouth (01983 761550).
Food served *mid-July-Aug* noon-2pm, 6.30-9.30pm, Mon-Sat; noon-3pm Sun; *Sept-mid-July* noon-3pm, 6.30-9.30pm, Thur-Sat; noon-3pm Sun.
Cards Debit, MC, V.

A popular local bar and restaurant right on the harbour, specialising in locally caught fish. Opening times can be erratic so phone before visiting.

Seaview Hotel

High Street, Seaview (01983 612711).
Food served noon-1.45pm, 7.30-9.30pm, Mon-Sat, bank hols. **Set meals** *Sun lunch* £13.95 (3 courses).
Cards AmEx, DC, Debit, MC, V.

The two dining rooms (smoking and non-smoking) are open to non-residents and serve up imaginative modern cuisine such as rack of lamb with couscous crust and caramelised onions (£15.95). You can have a superior bar snack (say, hot crab ramekin, £4.95) sitting under the umbrellas at the front and watch the world make its way down to the lovely little harbour below. *See also p117.*

Spy Glass Inn

Esplanade, Ventnor (01983 855338).
Food served *May-Aug* 10.30am-11pm Mon-Sat; 10.30am-10.30pm Sun; *Sept-Apr* 10.30am-3pm, 6.30-11pm, Mon-Fri. **Cards** Debit, MC, V.

Perched above the beach at Ventnor, this is the perfect place to have a pint of local ale and fresh seafood (caught by Blake, whose hut is a hundred yards down the beach). It's particularly good for parents, who can keep an eye on children playing on the beach. Note that it gets very crowded on summer evenings, so booking is advisable. Pianist or other live music most days.

Waterfront Freehouse & Restaurant

Totland Bay, Totland (01983 756969).
Food served noon-2.30pm, 6-9.30pm, daily.
Cards Debit, MC, V.

Situated right on the beach in West Wight, this is a wonderful place to watch the sun go down on a summer's evening, with boats bobbing out on the bay and Hurst Castle looming eerily out of the dusk. Stick to the grilled fresh fish (or the moules, £7.45) – the deep-fried battered variety tends to be jaw-breakingly hard. Live music and barbecues in the summer.

What to see & do

Many attractions are closed between the end of October and Easter so always phone first when planning a visit. For information on cycling and walking, call 01983 823741.

The long-standing but fast-disintegrating **Blackgang Chine Fantasy Park.**

The coastal path

The 77-mile walk around the island might be a tad energetic to attempt in a weekend, but if you want to get a taste of the coastal path skip the north-east section and take the train from Ryde to **Shanklin**. Here you can join the path as it climbs up from the sea before descending again through the beautiful ferny depths of the **Landslip** (so called because much of it fell into the sea in 1810). From there you can walk around **Wheelers Bay** to **Ventnor**. (Watch out around here: sea defence work might mean there's a diversion in these parts over the next year or so). Above the bay the newly opened **Coastal Path Visitors' Centre** has an exhibition about the path and sells maps and postcards.

The path continues along the beach at Ventnor before climbing the cliff behind the **Spyglass Inn** (a good place to stop for lunch; *see page 118*). You can continue along the cliffs past the Enid Blyton-cosiness of **Steephill Cove** (deckchairs and china teapots with cosies from the beach café) before climbing up to the **Ventnor Botanical Gardens** and then along the cliffs, past **Woody Bay** until the path turns inland towards **St Lawrence**. Although it's not actually on the coastal path, the area around **St Catherine's Lighthouse**, the southernmost tip of the island, is well worth exploring. It is quite off the beaten track and reminiscent of the wilder shores of a Greek island.

The walk from Shanklin to St Catherine's is about 9 miles (3-4hrs). From St Catherine's you can catch the 6 or 6A bus along the coast back to Shanklin, or take the 7 bus, which takes a more inland route.

Coastal Visitors' Centre Dudley Road, Ventnor, PO38 1EJ (tel/fax 01983 855400). **Open** *Mar-Oct* 9.30am-5pm Tue-Sat; 11am-4pm Sun; *Nov-Apr* 9.30am-5pm Tue-Fri; 9.30am-4pm Sat.

Tourist information centres

Western Esplanade, **Ryde**, PO33 2LW (01983 562905/www.isle-of-wight-tourism.gov.uk/post@isle-of-wight-tourism.gov.uk). **Open** phone for details.

8 High Street, **Sandown**, PO36 ODG (01983 403886). **Open** *Mar-Oct* 9am-6pm daily; *Nov-Feb* 10am-4pm Mon-Sat.

67 High Street, **Shanklin**, PO37 6JJ (01983 862942). **Open** *Apr-Aug* 9am-6pm daily; *Oct-Mar* 10am-4pm Mon-Sat.

Bike hire

Autovogue 140 High Street, **Ryde** (01983 812989). Ten-minute walk from the ferry terminal.

Isle Cycle Wavells Fine Foods, The Square, **Yarmouth** (01983 760219). Two-minute walk from ferry terminal.

Adgestone Vineyard

Upper Adgestone Road, Adgestone (01983 402503/www.englishwine.co.uk). **Open** phone to check. **Admission** free.

Drop in for afternoon tea here and, if the mood takes her, your hostess, no mean concert pianist, might treat you to an impromptu concert. The vineyard makes all types of wine (dry white starts at £5.85 a bottle) and a tour of the cellars costs £2.50

Blackgang Chine Fantasy Park

Chale (01983 730330). **Open** *Mar, Apr, mid-Sept-mid-Oct* 10am-5.30pm daily; *May-mid-Sept* 10am-10.15pm daily. **Admission** £5.50; £4.50 3s-13s; £5 OAPs; £18 family.

One of the country's oldest theme parks still clings to the edge of this crumbling coastline. The latest attraction is a waterslide with rubber boats hurtling down from the top of the cliff. The park may be closed for refurbishment, with probable opening in June 2000; phone to check.

Brading Roman Villa

Morton Old Road, Brading (01983 406223). **Open** *Apr-Oct* 9.30am-5pm daily. **Admission** £2.50; £1.25 5s-16s; £1.25 students.

There are fine mosaic floors to admire here (just north of Sandown) – look out for the figure representing winter whose British hooded cloak became a wardrobe must-have for expat Romans in chilly climes.

Carisbroke Castle

Carisbroke, near Newport (01983 522107). **Open** *Apr-Aug* 10am-6pm daily; *Sept-Mar* 10am-4pm daily. **Admission** £4.50; £2.30 5s-15s; £3.40 OAPs, students.

Charles I was held in this hilltop Norman castle before being taken back to London to be executed. The museum inside tells the story of his incarceration as well as that of other royal residents. There are wonderful views of the island from the battlements, and jousting and fayres in the summer months.

Dimbola Lodge

Freshwater Bay (01983 756814). **Open** 10am-5pm Tue-Sun. **Admission** £2.50; free under-16s.

Carisbrooke Castle: *Charles I's prison.*

The restored home of Victorian photographer Julia Cameron displays her work in its galleries along with contemporary exhibitions, a camera museum and a vegetarian café.

Dinosaur Farm

Military Road, nr Brighstone (01983 740401/07970 626456). **Open** 10am-5pm Tue, Thur, Sun. **Admission** £2; £1 4s-16s; £1.50 OAPs.

The Isle of Wight is a rich hunting ground for paleontologists, whose job is made easier by the natural slippage of the land. The Dinosaur Farm is a charmingly scruffy collection of barns where you can chat to the experts and enthusiastic amateurs as they patiently piece together the bones of a yet-to-be-named dinosaur found down the road in the cliffs above Compton Bay after a storm a couple of years ago. Book a place on one of the fossil walks along the foreshore at low tide. There are plans to build a flash hands-on Dinosaur Museum in Sandown in the near future.

Guildhall Museum

High Street Newport (01983 823366). **Open** 9am-4.15pm Mon-Fri; 10am-4.15pm Sat. **Admission** £1.80; £1 4s-14s; £1 OAPs, students; £4 family.

An imaginative hands-on history of the island, housed in the old town clock tower.

Isle of Wight Steam Railway

Havenstreet (01983 884343). **Open** *mid-Mar-Oct* 9.30am-5pm daily. **Tickets** £6.50; £4 4s-15s; £5.50 OAPs.

A five-mile line connecting with more prosaic electric trains at Ryde. Beautifully restored locos and a steam museum. The railway runs roughly every half hour from 10.30am to 4.15pm.

Museum of Smuggling History

Botanical Gardens, Ventnor (01983 853677). **Open** *Apr-Sept* 10am-5pm daily. **Admission** £2.20; £1.10 7s-16s.

Housed in the underground vaults of the lovely informral botanical gardens, this museum recounts the ingenious methods used by smugglers during 700 years of avoiding taxes.

The Needles Old Battery

Alun Bay (01983 754772). **Open** *Apr-Jun, Sept, Oct* 10.30am-4.30pm Mon-Thur, Sun; *Jul, Aug* 10.30am-4.30pm daily. **Admission** (NT) £2.50; £1.20 4s-18s; £6 family.

Not to be confused with the tacky pleasure park nearby, this Victorian fort enjoys spectacular views over the Needles, the Solent and the Channel. It's best viewed at the conclusion of a bracing walk over Tennyson Down from Freshwater.

Old Town Hall

Newtown (01983 741020). **Open** *Apr-Jun* 2-5pm Mon, Wed, Sun; *Jul, Aug* 2-5pm Mon-Thur, Sun. **Admission** (NT) £1.40; 70p 5s-16s.

Once a flourishing port and the former capital of the island, Newtown was one of the 'rotten boroughs', returning two Members of Parliament until 1832. The town hall was saved from ruin by a mysterious group of enthusiasts whose story is recounted here. The marshy estuary (on the island's north-west coast) has interesting walks and a hide for bird watchers.

Osborne House

East Cowes (01983 200022/ www.english-heritage.org.uk). **Open** *Apr-Sept* 10am-6pm daily; *Oct* 10am-5pm daily; *Nov-mid-Dec, Feb, Mar* 10am-2.30pm Mon, Wed, Thur, Sun (pre-booked tours only). **Admission** (EH) £6.90; £3.50 5s-15s; £5.20 OAPs, students; £17.30 family.

Built in the style of an Italian villa by Thomas Cubitt, this was the much-loved country retreat of Queen Victoria and has been maintained as it was at her death here in 1901. The Swiss Cottage, built as a playhouse in the garden for the royal children, is larger than many Londoners' flats. Pre-booking for guided tours (spring and autumn only) is essential.

Shipwreck & Maritime Museum

Sherbourne Street, Bembridge (01983 872223). **Open** *mid-Mar-Oct* 10am-5pm daily. **Admission** £2.50; £1.35 5s-16s; £1.75 OAPs, students.

On the far eastern tip of the island, Bembridge is worth a visit solely for its award-winning display of pirate gold, mermen and the story of a wrecked submarine.

Bournemouth & Poole

'Sexy' and 'Bournemouth' – two words that the local tourist department would have us believe are made for each other.

Being only 200 years old is quite a stigma in this country, where almost every hamlet and vale can trace its ancestry back to the Domesday Book. They feel it in America, they feel it in Australia, and yes, they feel it down in **Bournemouth**, too – a rootless, shifting sense of everything being transitory. In short, heritage guilt. The town dates back only to the early nineteenth century, when it was first settled as a summer holiday destination. Nothing has changed since then in that respect: in the height of summer, Bournemouth's extensive beaches are packed to capacity.

But the town is slowly making up for lost time. *Harpers & Queen* may have jumped the gun a little when they called it 'the next coolest city on the planet', and it will take a while to shrug off that tacky 'kiss me quick' image, but retail outlets touting surf labels and discount designer gear are becoming more common in among the chip shops and amusement arcades, and there is undoubtedly a lively club scene. The pier area in particular is on the up with a brand new IMAX cinema, with both 2- and 3-D screens, plus restaurants and bars.

Cooler in Poole?

Neighbouring **Poole** (which virtually runs into Bournemouth), on the other hand, can reel off a long list of smuggler's haunts and adventures on the high seas, its narrow, winding lanes and bustling quayside having seen centuries of trade. From its inception as a borough in 1342, Poole set up fishing links with Newfoundland, bringing prosperity to the area, as evidenced by

*The new, sexy face of **Bournemouth**?*

the magnificent merchant houses and quayside warehouses that still stand intact. These days the wharf buildings house the vast Poole Pottery offering shelf upon shelf of gifts and homewares, while for everything else you might need, the Dolphin shopping centre in the middle of town has over 100 shops, plus cafés, displays and touring exhibitions.

Escaping the crowds

It's true, when the Wurzels sang 'Dorset is beautiful wherever you go', they were not lying, it's just that you'll have to put up with the fact that everybody else wants to go there, too. Visitors wishing for a quiet break might find themselves better off further afield. The best beach in the area is the award-winning **Sandbanks** but beware crowds and money-spinning attractions; **Branksome Chine** is a nice location with a beach café and shop. On **Flaghead** and **Alum Chines** you can walk through the wooded chines to reach the sea. **Studland**, reached by car ferry, has a beautiful beach but it gets very popular in high season.

For a taste of old England, **Christchurch** is the nearest pretty village, the old town with its marketplace mostly unchanged since Saxon times. Places to visit include the substantial Priory Church, with its array of fine medieval carvings, and 'miraculous' beam supposedly fitted by the hand of God, which in itself

---

By train from London

Trains run from **Waterloo** to **Bournemouth** about every half an hour. The fastest train takes **1hr 45mins**. The station is about a mile east of the town centre, but there are frequent buses from the bus station, opposite the train station, into town.

---

brought about the current name of the town. The restored watermill and Georgian splendour of the Red House Museum & Gardens (Quay Road; 01202 482860), with its walled herb garden and dolls' house collection, are also of note. Bedecked in floral displays, Christchurch is a charming upmarket spot to spend the day with plenty of exclusive shops and ancient inns.

Where to stay

Bournemouth was built as a tourist attraction so there's no shortage of hotels, guesthouses or self-catering options to choose from, but some, naturally, are more amenable than others. The **Rockley Park Holiday Centre** in Poole (01202 679393/0345 753753) has fixed mobile homes (£133-£703 per unit per week, depending on the time of year). Facilities include indoor and outdoor heated swimming pools, children's play area, entertainment, cafés, bars; it's also an ideal spot for crabbing.

Chine Hotel

Boscombe Spa Road, Bournemouth, BH5 1AX (01202 396234/fax 01202 391737/ reservations @fjbhotels.co.uk).
Rates (B&B) £52-£65pp. Child supplement: £1.85 for each year of child's age when staying in family room. Special breaks. **Rooms** (all en suite) 6 single; 37 double; 35 twin; 13 family. **Cards** AmEx, DC, Debit, MC, V.

A wonderful family hotel with indoor and outdoor pools, pitch and putt and children's play equipment. It's set in three acres of grounds, with access to the lovely shady paths of Boscombe Chine leading down to Boscombe beach, which is a little less crowded than Bournemouth. Views to the rear are spectacular, looking over the tops of trees across to the glittering sea. The old Victorian lift with its open-link brass doors is worth the trip, too. Baby listening available, indoor soft play room. Children welcome. Non-smoking rooms available. *See also p124.*

The Inverness

26 Tregonwell Road, Bournemouth, BH2 5NS (tel/fax 01202 554968).
Rates (B&B) £20-£30pp. Special breaks. **Rooms** (all en suite) 1 single; 6 double; 1 twin; 2 family **Credit** Debit, MC, V.

An elegantly furnished Victorian-character hotel, close to the town centre, offering a very friendly and efficient service. There's a family-style lounge with bar, dining area and comfortable rooms with en suite showers. A very nice touch is the hotel's own recommended list of pubs and restaurants in the area with location map, and a review of entertainment throughout the year and local transport. The optional evening meal is £9 per person. Children over five welcome.

Langtry Manor Hotel

26 Derby Road, Bournemouth, BH1 3QB (01202 553887/290115/lillie@langtrymanor.com/ www.langtrymanor.com).

Rates (B&B) *single occupancy* £74.75-£119.75; *double/twin* £99.50-£199.50; *four-poster* £119.50-£139.50 (£10 child supplement). Special breaks.
Rooms (all en suite) 16 double/twin; 9 four-posters.
Cards AmEx, DC, Debit, MC, V.

You can't go very far along the south coast without encountering one of Edward VII and Lillie Langtry's love nests, but this one is particularly noteworthy as the house he built for her at the height of their tryst. The air of romance lingers as you walk up the gravel path flanked by immaculate lawns and trees to this charming gable-roofed Edwardian half-timber house. Stay in the suite the prince designed for his lover, or her four-poster room with heart-shaped corner bath. All rooms are individual, some with four-posters and Jacuzzis, and the dining hall has a wooden minstrels' gallery. Look out for the carved initials of you know who. Children and dogs welcome. Non-smoking rooms available.

The Mansion House

Thames Street, Poole, BH15 1JN (01202 685666/ fax 01202 665709/enquiries@themansionhouse.co.uk/ www.themansionhouse.co.uk).
Rates (B&B) *single* £87; *double/twin* £98-£118; *deluxe double/twin/four-poster* £118-£125; *family* £118-£135. Special breaks.
Rooms (all en suite) 9 single; 9 double/twin; 14 deluxe double/twin (1 four-poster); 2 family (1 four-poster). **Credit** AmEx, DC, Debit, MC, V.

Located behind the shopping and quayside area, this quiet and stately Georgian house boasts a fine dining area with cherrywood panelling and a spacious lobby leading to the sweeping open staircase. Rooms are individually designed and named after famous Georgians and Victorians. All feature antique furniture and rather dramatic drapes and table lamps. Apart from the main body of the hotel, there's also the Mill House mews apartments (non-smoking) just down the street, including a very frothy but sunlit and romantic honeymoon suite. The special occasion breaks are great value, with superior four-poster double, breakfast, three-course dinner, flowers and bottle of champagne. Children welcome. Non-smoking rooms available. *See also page 124.*

Redlands Hotel

79 St Michael's Road, West Cliff, Bournemouth, BH2 5DR (01202 553714).
Rates (B&B) £18-£20pp. **Rooms** (all en suite) 2 single; 10 double/twin. **Credit** MC, V.

A welcoming small hotel right in the centre of town. This characterful Victorian redbrick has a lovely flowering terrace at the front and bright and breezy rooms within, all recently decorated. Breakfast and evening meals (around £25 for three courses) are available in a pleasant, informal setting. Children and dogs welcome. Non-smoking rooms available.

Swallow Highcliff

St Michael's Road, West Cliff, Bournemouth, BH2 5DU (01202 557702/fax 01202 292734/ info@swallowhotels.com/www.swallowhotels.com).
Rates (B&B) *single occupancy* £105; *double/twin* £140; *deluxe double/twin* £170-£175; *family* £140-£230; *suite* £240. Special breaks. **Rooms** (all en suite) 64 double; 12 twin; 46 deluxe double; 23 deluxe twin; 9 family; 3 suites. **Credit** AmEx, DC, Debit, MC, V.

Brownsea Island

Sitting in Poole Harbour, Brownsea is a blissful getaway from the tourist-crush of the mainland. About half of the island is open to the public; the other part is a nature reserve, accessibly only on tours, where protected species of wildfowl glide on its tranquil lagoons, deer graze in the underbrush, and the reclusive red squirrel forages in forests of Scots pine. (Tours run daily April-June and in September; self-guided 10.30am-1pm; guided July/August only 2.45pm; for details, contact the warden at Canford Cliffs on 01202 709445/707744).

Currently owned by the National Trust, in part due to its importance as the founding site of Baden-Powell's scout movement, Brownsea has had a chequered past in terms of ownership. The remains of a pottery dating from the mid-1800s mark the ill-fated Colonel Waugh's failed get-rich-quick scheme; the fine church of St Mary and the vicarage are also part of his legacy. Under the fiefdom of Mary Florence Bonham Christie around a century later, the island was taken over by nature and Ms Christie defended its boundaries from invasion with a shotgun, her fear being that careless visitors might set the whole place ablaze. Despite her fervent efforts, however, fire did indeed break out in the '30s resulting in the creation of the reserve today.

There's also Brownsea Castle (originally part of Henry VIII's coastal defences), which isn't open to the public; it's used by the John Lewis Partnership as a holiday home for their staff.

The part of the island offering public access is beautiful but without amenities apart from the café and shop by the entrance, so take a picnic if you're venturing inland, and don't expect mile upon mile of golden sands; the beach is fairly coarse and surrounded by thick gloopy mud.

Ferries to Brownsea leave from Poole Quay (01202 680580), Bournemouth Pier (01202 558550), Swanage (01929 427659) and Sandbanks (01202 666226). Admission to the island is £2.50; £1.30 child; £6.30 family.

Just a stroll away from Bournemouth Pier and adjacent to the lift down to a Blue Flag beach, the Swallow affords magnificent views over the bay. Recently refurbished, this executive class hotel features two restaurants, a cocktail bar, plus its own spa, pool and sauna complex attached. Outdoor sports facilities include a golf practice net, floodlit tennis court and an outdoor sun terrace and pool overlooking the sea. Rooms are spacious with en suite bathrooms and come with fridge, towelling robes and satellite TV. Many of them have sea views (for which you pay a hefty supplement of £30-£35). Baby listening available, crèche in summer. Children and dogs welcome. Non-smoking rooms available.

Where to eat & drink

Still hotel restaurant dominated, Bournemouth is extending its repertoire to include modern European-style café-bars, including the recently opened **CH2** on Exeter Road (01202 296296). The happening **Slam Bar** on Firvale Road (01202 555129) is a new art deco-style brasserie and pre-club chill zone. Top of the pile is still the **Bistro on the Beach**, Solent Promenade, Southbourne (01202 431473), a café by day and gourmet delight by night. The proprietors formerly worked at the Waldorf Astoria and the Dorchester, which might account for the six-month waiting list for dinner. For a less formal pub setting try the intriguingly named **Goat & Tricycle** (01202 314220) in the town centre, which offers bar meals until 8.30pm, or the **Durley Inn**, West Cliff (01202 290480), overlooking the bay. If you're craving a Chinese, head down to award-winning **Mr Pang's** (234 Holdenhurst Road, 01202 553748).

Poole Quay has many places to eat including a plethora of fast-food joints. **Fatty Arbuckles** (01202 669747), **Da Vincis** (01202 667528) and **Oriel's** (01202 679833) are good for light lunches, and the accommodating **Warehouse Brasserie** (01202 677238) is great for local fish. The quay is also dotted with nautical pubs with tables outside – the **King's Head** on the High Street has a beer garden and excellent local Badger ale. **Splinters** on Church Street, Christchurch, is also recommended.

Carters

Poole Pottery, Poole Quay (01202 667556).
Food served 6.30-9.30pm Mon-Sat.
Cards DC, Debit, MC, V.

A stylish modern eaterie right on the seafront, with tables outside plus a lovely cool interior of tiles, chrome and shady blue paintwork. The bistro-style menu features starters from £3.50, including wild mushrooms flavoured with tarragon, marinated sweet pepper salad, and smoked Scottish salmon with mixed leaves. Follow on with pan-fried calf's liver or breast of duck with leeks in oriental sauce, chicken rolled in coconut with a mild curry sauce, salmon and monkfish served with basil pesto. Main courses are from £9.95. Puddings (from £2.25) are a speciality, with dark and white chocolate terrine with rum sauce or amaretto crème brûlée.

Chine Hotel

Boscombe Spa Road, Bournemouth (01202 396234).
Food served 12.30-2.30pm, 7-8.30pm, Mon-Fri, Sun; 12.30-2.30pm Sat. **Set meals** *lunch* £16.50; *dinner* £18.95 (3 courses). **Cards** AmEx, DC, Debit, MC, V.

Smart dress is required for this fine dining restaurant overlooking the hotel gardens. The cooking is artful with good steak and fish dishes including gravadlax or smooth liver parfait to start, followed by seared tuna, roast monkfish or escalope of turkey in savoury crumb. Vegetarian options are interesting, with pan-fried polenta medallions and sesame vegetables, warm mozzarella salad or goat's cheese pithivier. The side dishes of vegetables are exceptional – perfectly al dente and fresh; the wine list is notable. Children are not excluded from the evening meal and staff are more than happy to serve a simple dish like an omelette, or opt for the children's high tea served between 5pm and 5.30pm. *See also p122.*

Coriander

22 Richmond Hill, Bournemouth (01202 552202).
Food served noon-10.30pm Mon-Thur, Sun; noon-11pm Fri, Sat. **Set meals** *lunch* £5.95 (1 platter); *dinner* £9.75, £11.25 (2 courses). **Cards** AmEx, Debit, MC, V.

Friendly family-style Mexican dining at rustic tables, with crayons and paper for kids to design their own placemats, and plenty of mouth-watering cocktails to amuse the adults. Well-prepared dishes include nachos with a choice of dips to share with real hot salsa, chilli with cheese, and guacamole among them. The more adventurous, meanwhile, might like to sample Chicken Vesuvius, spicy chorizo and beans or a spiced vegetable chilli. Starter, main and dessert from £5.95.

Hot Rocks

Pier Approach, Bournemouth (01202 555559).
Food served 10am-midnight daily.
Cards AmEx, Debit, MC, V.

No up-and-coming seaside resort is complete these days without some kind of surfie hangout. Hot Rocks goes one step further, dubbing itself an 'American Surf

Bournemouth *beach and pier from East Cliff.*

Restaurant Complex'. This consists of informal café area on the ground floor and surf gear emporium, while upstairs is the bar and serious eating area. Arrive early as service doesn't exactly 'rock' and, if it's hot outside, try to nab the balcony over the entrance, which is the coolest spot to enjoy your sizzling feast. Portions are generous and the menu features starters like spicy onion rings, crispy cajun mushrooms, and marinated chicken wings. Mains include fajitas with a choice of steak, chicken or tiger prawns, walnut and cheeseburger, beef-burgers, plus fresh fish and pasta dishes. It's not cheap – lunch for two with drinks is around £20.

The Mansion House

Thames Street, Poole (01202 685666).
Food served noon-1.45pm, 7-9.15pm, Mon-Fri; 7-9.15pm Sat; noon-1.45pm Sun. **Set meals** *lunch* (Mon-Fri) £16.25 (3 courses); (Sun) £17.50 (3 courses); *dinner* £17.25 (2 courses). **Cards** AmEx, DC, Debit, MC, V.

Fairly formal dining with a smart/casual dress code in the evenings and for family lunch on Sundays. From the well-presented and original menu start, perhaps, with pan-fried sausage with a beurre blanc sauce, Caesar salad with char-grilled chicken and Parmesan crackling or twice-baked cheese soufflé. Main courses include loin of lamb in herb crust, Dover sole with mushroom, shallot and fish cream, or pan-fried scallops and a ravioli of Dublin Bay prawns. *See also p122.*

The Salad Centre

667 Christchurch Road, Boscombe (01202 393673).
Food served 11.30am-4.30pm Mon-Sat.

Traditional caff with a twist situated east of Bournemouth town centre. This vegetarian wholefood restaurant offers a wide range of quiches, salads and speciality dishes like cottage leek pie and lentil burgers, plus delicious home-made soups and bread. Save some room for the wide selection of cakes stuffed with fruit or coated in carob. Extremely good value for money. Three courses from just £3.50.

What to see & do

Every year from late July to the end of August the beaches in Bournemouth and Poole come alive day and night with fireworks, theatre, music, jugglers and beach games for both kids and adults. Also look out for the pioneering Kid Zone tagging system to make sure wandering youngsters don't get lost. Board and yacht sailing is available – contact Poole tourist office. If you're interested in hiring a beach hut, call the beach hut office on 01202 708181.

Being such popular summer destinations, Bournemouth and Poole are well geared up for families seeking a day out. Below is our pick of the best, though there are plenty more.

Tourist information centres

Westover Road, **Bournemouth** (0906 802 0234/ www.bournemouth.co.uk). **Open** *mid-Jul-Aug* 9.30am-7pm Mon-Sat; 10.30am-5pm Sun; *Sept-mid-July* 9.30am-5.30pm Mon-Sat.

Poole Quay, **Poole** (01202 253253/ www.poole.gov.uk). **Open** *Apr, May* 10am-5pm Mon-Fri; 10am-4.30pm Sat, Sun; *June, July, Sept* 10am-5.30pm Mon-Fri; 10am-5pm Sat, Sun; *Aug* 10am-6pm daily; *Oct-Mar* 10am-5pm Mon-Fri; 10am-3pm Sat; noon-3pm Sun.

High Street, **Christchurch** (01202 471780/ www.resort-guide.co.uk). **Open** *June, Sept* 9.30am-5.30pm Mon-Fri; 9.30am-5pm Sat; *July, Aug* 9.30am-5.30pm Mon-Fri; 9.30am-5pm Sat; 10am-2pm Sun; *Oct-May* 9.30am-5pm Mon-Fri; 9.30am-4.30pm Sat.

Alice in Wonderland Family Park

Merritown Lane, Hurn, Christchurch (01202 483444). **Open** 10am-6pm (last entry 4pm) daily. **Admission** £4.25; £3.75 3s-16s; £2.50 OAPs, students; £15 family.

Themed junior rides, indoor play area, massive mazes, farmyard animals, adventure playground, theatre shows and storytelling in summer. Mad Hatters Restaurant, plus picnic areas.

Compton Acres

Canford Cliffs Road, Canford Cliffs, Poole (01202 700778/www.comptonacres.co.uk). **Open** *Mar-Oct* 10am-6pm (last entry 5.15pm) daily. **Admission** £4.95; £1 5s-15s; £3.95 OAPs; £10 family.

Reputed to be the finest gardens in Europe, with rare plant species, Italian and Japanese formal gardens, sculpture garden, and a brasserie and gift shop.

Oceanarium

Pier Approach (next to the pier), Bournemouth (01202 311993). **Open** *mid-Feb-Oct* 10am-5pm daily; *Nov-mid-Feb* 10am-4pm daily. **Admission** £4.95; £3.75 3s-16s; £4.50 OAPs, students; £16.50 family.

Thousands of species of marine life including the giant gourami from the Ganges and lionfish from the Hawaiian coral reef, plus the Ocean Eye, where you can witness undersea environments close up. Café and shop.

Poole Aquarium & Serpentarium

Hennings Wharf, The Quay, Poole (01202 686712). **Open** *July, Aug* 9am-9pm, *Nov-June* 10am-5.30pm, daily. **Admission** £3.95; £2.95 4s-16s; £3 OAPs, students.

A thrilling array of dangerous beasties, from rattlesnakes and pythons to piranhas and sharks. Animal rescue centre, coffee shop, gift and model railway shop.

Poole Park

Close to the town centre with lots of attractions, Swan Lake Family Restaurant (01202 742842), complete with children's play area, Gus Gorilla's Jungle Gym (ball pool), crazy golf, boat hire and mini-train.

Splashdown

Tower Park Leisure Complex, Poole (01202 716000). **Open** *school summer hols* 9am-10pm Mon-Fri; 9am-6.30pm Sat; 9am-7pm Sun; *rest of year* 2-9pm Mon-Sat; 10am-7pm Sat, Sun. **Admission** *2hr session* £5.80; £2.50 2s-4s; £1 under-2s; £4.60 students; £20 family.

Perfect when the weather's good (though there are indoor rides as well). Have fun on the 140m Torpedo Run, Grand Canyon Tyre Ride, and Baron's Revenge, a near-vertical drop in total darkness. Sliders must be 1m tall. Although there's a paddling pool and interactive play zone for kids, there's no swimming pool for adults.

Upton Country Park

signposted from A3049 and A35 (01202 672625). **Open** *park* 9am-dusk daily; *heritage centre* 10.30am-4.30pm daily. **Admission** free.

A perfect spot for picnics, ball games and cycling. You can ride along the bike path beside Poole harbour to reach Upton through the woods. The Countryside Heritage Centre here has a café, exhibitions and information. There's a bird watching hide looking out across the estuary, and you can feed the ducks and the peacocks.

Vistarama Balloon

Lower Gardens, Bournemouth (01202 399939/ www.vistarama.co.uk). **Rides** 9.45-10pm daily (weather permitting). **Admission** £9.95; £5.50 4s-13s; £8.50 OAPs; £5.95 students; £24.95 family.

A tethered balloon ride rising to 500ft affording spectacular views. This is a once-in-a-lifetime experience – the ten or so minutes up in the clouds feel like hours. There's a fun pitch and putt course in the gardens, too.

Waterfront Museum

Old High Street, Poole (01202 683138). **Open** *Apr-Oct* 10am-5pm Mon-Sat; noon-5pm Sun. *Nov-Mar* 10am-3pm Mon-Sat; noon-3pm Sun. **Admission** £4; £2.85 5s-16s; £3.40 OAPs, students; £8.50-£11.50 family.

This maritime museum details the history of the area from Roman times, including plenty of spicy tales of smuggling raids in the locale, plus medieval cellars.

Up, up and away in the **Vistarama Balloon***.*

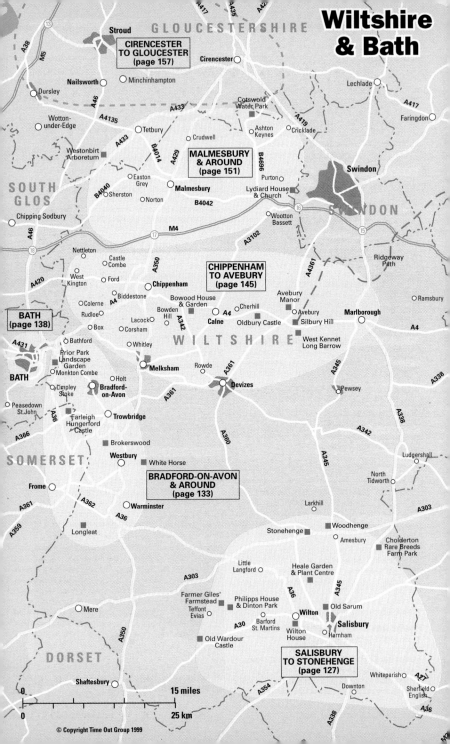

Wiltshire & Bath

CIRENCESTER TO GLOUCESTER (page 157)

MALMESBURY & AROUND (page 151)

CHIPPENHAM TO AVEBURY (page 145)

BATH (page 138)

BRADFORD-ON-AVON & AROUND (page 133)

SALISBURY TO STONEHENGE (page 127)

GLOUCESTERSHIRE

SOUTH GLOS

WILTSHIRE

SOMERSET

DORSET

Stroud
Nailsworth
Minchinhampton
Cirencester
Dursley
Lechlade
Wotton-under-Edge
Faringdon
Tetbury
Cotswold Water Park
Ashton Keynes
Crudwell
Cricklade
Westonbirt Arboretum
A419
Swindon
Easton Grey
Malmesbury
Purton
Sherston
Norton
Lydiard House & Church
Chipping Sodbury
Wootton Bassett
SWINDON
Nettleton
Castle Combe
Ridgeway Path
West Kington
Ford
Chippenham
Ramsbury
Colerne
Biddestone
Bowood House & Garden
Cherhill
Avebury Manor
Rudloe
Bowden Hill
Calne
Avebury
Marlborough
Box
Lacock
Oldbury Castle
Silbury Hill
Bathford
Corsham
Whitley
West Kennet Long Barrow
Prior Park Landscape Garden
Rowde
Pewsey
BATH
Monkton Combe
Melksham
Devizes
Limpley Stoke
Holt
Bradford-on-Avon
Peasedown St John
Farleigh Hungerford Castle
Trowbridge
Brokerswood
Ludgershall
Westbury
White Horse
North Tidworth
Frome
Larkhill
Warminster
Woodhenge
Stonehenge
Amesbury
Cholderton Rare Breeds Farm Park
Longleat
Little Langford
Heale Garden & Plant Centre
Farmer Giles' Farmstead
Philipps House & Dinton Park
Teffont Evias
Barford St Martins
Wilton
Old Sarum
Mere
Old Wardour Castle
Wilton House
Salisbury
Harnham
Shaftesbury
Whiteparish
Downton
Sherfield English

15 miles

25 km

© Copyright Time Out Group 1999

Salisbury & Stonehenge

Everybody must get stoned...

The elaborately carved choir of **Salisbury Cathedral**. See page 132.

(see page 130) It really isn't to slight Farmer Giles' Farmstead (*see page 130*), or even Salisbury Cathedral (*see page 132*), to recognise that **Stonehenge** is south Wiltshire's number one attraction by several million miles. Let's face it, it's Britain's number one attraction by several million miles. That said, **Salisbury** itself is eminently potterable – compact and historic, with plenty of crooked nooks to explore – and the westerly countryside of the Ebble and Nadder Valleys is just perfect for walking, pubbing or B&Bing for one of your overnight stays. Virtually every two- or three-dot village in these parts has a

By train from London

Trains to **Salisbury** leave from **Waterloo** approximately every hour; the fastest takes **1hr 20mins**.

cuddly name, a pub with good food and/or rated accommodation, and most likely a resident ghost or other time-honoured claim to fame thrown in.

North of Salisbury is the Iron Age hill fort of **Old Sarum**, around whose lofty castle and cathedral a thriving medieval settlement clustered before work was started on Salisbury Cathedral, on the water-meadows of the Avon, in the thirteenth century. Gradually – stone by stone in the case of the old cathedral – the whole town made the gradual move a mile-and-a-half south.

Salisbury Cathedral dominates the city to this day, and if this is the first time you've heard that the 404-foot fourteenth-century spire is the highest in England (and second highest in Europe), it certainly won't be the last. The walled **Cathedral Close** is a sizeable oasis of quiet in the midst of tight, traffic-clogged streets, gathering together many of the city's historic attractions, including the **Salisbury and South Wiltshire Museum**, **Mompesson House**, **The Wardrobe** and **Medieval Hall**. Of equal interest are the lovely lawns ranging out from the foot of the towering Cathedral – they're great for picnicking and lazing.

Make no mistake: this town is a major international tourist centre, visitors being drawn in by the Toytown architecture, sparkling cleanliness and senior citizens' lunchtime specials. Market day is Saturday – Tuesday, too, should you extend your trip into the week – and shows off good value local agricultural produce: goose eggs, venison sausages, piled-high veg and fresh fish. The local tourist literature describes the **Market Square**, a trifle immodestly and optimistically, as one of the loveliest in Europe. The narrow, pedestrianised Fish Row, Butcher Row and Salt Lane adjoin the market, their atmospheric, picturesque charms topped off by the stone-stilted **Poultry Cross**.

There are tinkling rivers, teashops and half-timbered inns aplenty in Salisbury. Indeed, if it weren't for the aimlessly tootling tourists and the occasional boy racer beating his way around the one-way system, Salisbury could almost be trapped in another time. One of the chief pleasures is a summer-evening stroll over the water-meadows south of the city. Take the town path to **Harnham** from the **Queen Elizabeth Gardens**, take time out for refreshment and take in a view of the city virtually unchanged since Constable famously froze it on canvas.

South Wiltshire

Six miles south of Salisbury, **Downton** is an idyllic, thatch-happy village on the Avon, replete with textbook village greens and Cuckoo Fair customs (first bank holiday Saturday in May). **The Moot** is a strange ancient monument, a reputed Saxon meeting place and parliament, featuring a medieval 'bailie' mound and amphitheatre in Grade I-listed eighteenth-century ornamental gardens.

Three miles west of Salisbury lies **Wilton**, the ancient capital of Wessex and home of Wilton carpets, the exquisite **Wilton House** and more antique shops than you can shake a big stick at. This is superior mooching country, with its startling Italianate church, ruined abbey and river walks along the Wylye.

Heading north to **Stonehenge** (*see page 131* **Stonehenge: Bronze Age power statement**) and the MOD's jealously razor-wired expanses of **Salisbury Plain**, the quiet market town of **Amesbury** offers B&Bs and

inns, but none of Salisbury's grander distractions. If only the rumbling mock-warfare were to halt on the Plain, Amesbury would be the ideal centre to trample southern England's most perfect, albeit accidental, nature preserve. As tends to be the case with chemical/biological weaponry, don't bother holding your breath.

Where to stay

There's an abundance of classy farmhouse B&Bs in south Wiltshire, while Salisbury itself is known for its conference-quality hotels, as well as decent guesthouses and inns with rooms. *See also page 130* **Old Mill Hotel**.

Howard's House Hotel

Teffont Evias, SP3 5RJ (01722 716392/ fax 01722 716820/paul.firmin@virgin.net/ www.howardshousehotel.co.uk).
Rates (B&B) *single occupancy* £75; *twin/double* £95-£125; *four-poster* £145; *family room* £175. Special breaks. **Rooms** (all en suite) 1 twin, 6 double, 1 four-poster, 1 family. **Cards** AmEx, DC, Debit, MC, V.

Seventeenth-century Howard's House sits in two acres of grounds, around ten miles west of Salisbury. Tranquillity, comfort and informality are the bywords here: it's hard to resist a quality hotel with the tag-line 'Children encouraged. No dress-code. No rules'. First-rate Modern British food from chef Paul Firmin pulls in non-residents to the restaurant, which warrants recognition by Michelin, among others. As Jonathan Meades wrote in *The Times*, 'This is a fine outfit and one to return to.'

A303 west; 8 miles after Stonehenge bypassing Wylye, turn left (0.25 miles after dual carriageway ends); after 0.25 miles turn left to Teffont Evias; turn right at sharp bend in village; follow signs to hotel.

Little Langford Farmhouse

Little Langford, SP3 4NP (01722 790205/ fax 01722 790086/helyer@littlelangford.u-net.com).
Rates (B&B) £24-£26pp. **Rooms** 1 double; 1 double/twin (en suite); 1 twin.

Set in the Earl of Pembroke's 1,400-acre estate just south of Salisbury Plain (and eight miles north-west of Salisbury), this imposing Victorian farmhouse is blessed with good-sized rooms, kitted out in a thoroughly trad style. Visitors can stroll around the farm, watch cows being milked and then pour the stuff on their cornflakes. A games room is available for guests' use. The whole building is non-smoking.

A36 from Salisbury to Bath; left at Stoford into Great Wishford; keep church on left; turn right at Royal Oak pub; after 2 miles follow sharp bend into Little Langford; house on right.

Newton Farmhouse

Southampton Road, Whiteparish, SP5 2QL (tel/fax 01794 884416/newton.farmhouse.b-b@lineone.net/ website.lineone.net/~newtonfarmhouse.b-b).
Rates (B&B) *single* £25pp; *twin* £19pp; *double* £22.50-£25pp; *additional people* £10 (5s-12s); £15 (12s-18s). **Rooms** (all en suite) 1 single; 1 double; 1 twin; 3 double/twin; 2 family.

Wiltshire & Bath

At eight miles south of the city, on the fringes of the New Forest, this sixteenth-century listed farmhouse is very much on the edge of the area covered by this break, but Salisbury is only a short drive away, and Newton Farmhouse's four-poster beds (there are no fewer than five of them), flagged floors and inglenook fireplace more than justify inclusion. Still in doubt? Brekkie includes home-made bread and preserves. And there's an outdoor swimming pool, which can be used when the weather's warm enough. Children welcome. No smoking throughout.

J2 M27; A36 past sign for Whiteparish; house is on left after 0.5 miles immediately before turning to Downton and Redlinch.

Old Bell Hotel

St Ann's Street, Salisbury, SP1 2DN (01722 327958/fax 01722 411485). **Rates** (B&CB) *single* £30; *double* £50; *twin* £45-£50; *four-poster* £75; *family* £60. **Rooms** 1 single; 3 double (all en suite); 3 twin (2 en suite); 2 four-poster (both en suite); 1 family (en suite). **Cards** MC, V.

A fourteenth-century inn right opposite St Ann's Gate, with a fish restaurant on the side and accommodation upstairs. The rooms are not all equipped with every conceivable luxury, but they're more than functional – and how often do you get the chance to stay in a fourteenth-century inn? Waking up with a scarred, ancient beam sagging over your head is wonderful. Children and dogs welcome. Non-smoking rooms available.

Onion Store

Sherfield English, nr Romsey, SP51 6DU (01794 323227). **Rates** (B&B) *suite* £52pp. **Rooms** (all en suite) 3 suites.

A wildly romantic hideaway, once part of the estate of Florence Nightingale's family. The three 'suites' (one in the wing of the main seventeenth-century 'cottage', and two in converted outbuildings) are chicly rustic yet comfy. An indoor swimming pool in the conservatory is open to guests from spring to autumn, and the barbie facilities are also a hit for summer dining. Not surprisingly, this is a hugely popular place, so you'll need to book months in advance.

Sherfield English is off A27, west of Romsey.

Red Lion

Milford Street, Salisbury, SP1 2AN (01722 323334/fax 01722 325756). **Rates** *single* £81.50; *double/twin* £101.50; *four-poster* £115; *family* £123. Special breaks. **Rooms** (all en suite) 14 single; 35 double/twin; 2 four-poster; 2 family. **Cards** AmEx, DC, Debit, MC, V.

Reputedly the oldest purpose-built hotel in the country, the Red Lion has had since 1230 to collect up its manifold knick-knacks, myths and enviable reputation. The 'skeleton and organ' clock and wattle-and-daub walls are just two of the conversation-starters. The lovely old creeper-clad courtyard is an oasis of peace just yards from the hectic traffic of the city centre. The bedrooms have extremely plush and chintzy décor. The restaurant is recommended. Now owned by Best Western. Children welcome. Non-smoking rooms available.

Two roads down from Market Square in Salisbury city centre.

Where to eat & drink

Virtually every pub in Salisbury serves food, and the genteel market dictates that it's generally far superior to the standard burgers and misjudged baltis; in this part of the world, the trick is to find a pub where your drinking isn't encroached upon by restaurant tables and plate-balancers. The **Moloko Bar** (5 Bridge Street) is a trendy diversion, offering a wonderful range of weird vodkas. Or try the **Wig & Quill** (1 New Street), a super old Wadworth's boozer, serving up a perfect pint of 6X, Henry's IPA, Tangle Foot and Forest Gold.

Tearooms are another local attraction: at **David Brown's** (31 Catherine Street) a hot roast beef baguette is irresistible, and £2.70; at the butcher's shop downstairs it's only £2, but you don't get to look down on shoppers' heads and read the papers. Other top tearooms include **Michael Snell** (8 St Thomas' Square) and **Berniere's Tea Room** and **Mompesson House**, both located in The Close. Picnickers heading for The Close or further afield: stock up first at the **Good Food Shop** (50 Winchester Street) and **Reeve the Bakers** (2 Butcher Row).

If you're looking for a real countryside pub, there are plenty to choose from: drive out west, deeper into Hardy Country, and enjoy the rural boozing idylls of **Ansty** (wahey – tallest maypole!), **Chilmark**, **Tisbury** and **Chicksgrove**, or try the pretty, secluded **Horseshoe Inn** in Ebbesbourne Wake.

Asia

90 Fisherton Street, Salisbury (01722 327628). **Food served** noon-3pm, 5.30-11.45pm, Mon-Fri, Sun; noon-midnight Sat . **Set meal** £12 (3 courses). **Cards** AmEx, Debit, MC, V.

An unexpected array of Indian specialities straddling the north-south divide: try naryal duck, an exotic southern treat suffused with coconut; or the kurzee lamb, a whole roasted leg for two (with 24 hours' notice), and the marinated vegetable sobzi mossala, all cooked with real care. Just gets the nod ahead of the nearby **Rajpoot** (01722 334795), despite the outrageous murals of Stonehenge and the Poultry Cross at the latter.

Barford

Barford St Martin (01722 742242). **Food served** noon-2.30pm, 7-9.30pm, Mon-Sat; noon-2.15pm, 7-9pm, Sun. **Set meal** £8 (3 courses) Mon. **Cards** DC, Debit, MC, V.

A sixteenth-century former coaching inn 'five miles from Salisbury, yet right in the middle of countryside'. Turn off the A30 at the most spectacular hairpin bend in all Wessex and use the mounting block in the courtyard to dismount from your trusty steed. Brilliant Badger brews fresh from Blandford Forum, beamy ceilings, great food courtesy of head chef Gino Babord: check out his Friday night meat-feast Israeli barbecues. Accommodation is available in the annexe (from around £40 to £55).

Wiltshire & Bath

Haunch of Venison

1-5 Minster Street, Salisbury (01722 322024).
Food served 11am-11pm Mon-Sat; noon-10.30pm
Sun. **Cards** AmEx, Debit, MC, V.

Venison steaks and pork chops with fluffy mash, crisp
veg and thick, no-nonsense gravy make the Haunch a
Salisbury must. It's an original, Dickensian chop-house,
with black wooden walls and floors every bit as twisted as Ebenezer Scrooge. Have a drink at one of Britain's
two remaining pewter bars, or squeeze into the minute
nobs' snug halfway up the cramped spiral staircase:
beware the mummified hand of a card sharp preserved
in a hole in the wall.

LX1X

67-69 New Street, Salisbury (01722 340000).
Food served noon-2.30pm, 7-10.30pm, Mon-Fri;
7-10.30pm Sat. **Set meal** lunch £10 (2 courses).
Cards AmEx, Debit, MC, V.

You'll need to book in advance to sample 69's fine wines,
exquisite escalopes/medallions/drizzles of hare, offal and
the like; but don't be intimidated: chef Rupert Willcocks
and front-of-house manager Andrew Grigg are every bit
as friendly as they are creative. Recommended sea bass
with sun-blushed tomato and red onion salad and
Rupert's gran's plum duff (expect to pay anything from
£20 to £35 for a three-course meal). Easily the post-
modernest Mod-Brit joint in Wiltshire.

Old Mill Hotel

Town Path, Harnham (01722 327517).
Food served 7-9.30pm Mon-Fri; noon-2.30pm,
7-9.30pm, Sat; noon-2.30pm Sun. **Set meal** dinner
£16.50 (3 courses). **Cards** AmEx, Debit, MC, V.

*The **Old Mill Hotel** at Harnham.*

Yes, it's an old mill on the River Nadder – and your final
destination on that summer stroll over the water-
meadows. Simple but good pub lunches are served in
the cosy bar – poached salmon; mushroom and spinach
lasagne; a choice of deeply sexy ploughmans. There are
also 11 bedrooms (single £45, double £75) in case you
like it so much you don't want to leave.

What to see & do

Tourist information centres

Redworth House, Flower Lane, **Amesbury**, SP4 7HG
(01980 622833). **Open** June-Aug 9am-5pm Mon-Sat;
Sept-May 9am-5pm Mon-Fri.

Fish Row, **Salisbury**, SP1 1ES (01722 334956).
Open May 9.30am-5pm Mon-Sat; 10.30-4.30pm Sun;
June, Sept 9.30am-6pm Mon-Sat; 10.30am-4.30pm
Sun; July, Aug 9.30am-7pm Mon-Sat; 10.30am-5pm
Sun; Oct-Apr 9.30am-5pm Mon-Sat.

Bike hire

Hayballs 26-30 Winchester Street, **Salisbury**
(01722 411378). A ten-minute walk from the station.

Cholderton Rare Breeds Farm Park

Amesbury Road, Cholderton (01980 629438).
Open mid-Mar-Oct 10am-6pm daily.
Admission £3.95; £2.80 2s-16s; £12 family.

Daddy, daddy! Take us to see the lop-eared bunnies, the
spotty percy porkers and the seaweed-eating sheep!
Tractor rides and pig-racing for parents, too.

Farmer Giles' Farmstead

Teffont Magna (01722 716338).
Open late Mar-early Nov 10am-6pm daily; early Nov-
late Mar 10am-dusk Sat, Sun. **Admission** £3.95;
£2.85 4s-16s; £3.50 OAPs, students; £13 family.

This 175-acre working dairy farm offers a variety of petting options for the kids. The farm is ten miles west of
Salisbury on the B3089.

Figsbury Ring

Just north of A30, 3 miles north-east of Salisbury.

Although commonly taken to be an Iron Age hill fort,
there's no evidence to support this view. A ritual site?
A settlement? A mystery. A vast circular earthwork
with a deep inner quarry ditch, atop a moody hill.

Heale Garden & Plant Centre

Middle Woodford (01722 782504).
Open 10am-5pm daily. Last entry 4.30pm.
Admission £3; free under-14s.

The beautiful gardens of Heale House (private) feature
a wide collection of roses, shrubs and plants amid
clipped hedges and mellow stonework. Unusual plants
for sale. Located four miles north of Salisbury.

Medieval Hall

The Close, Salisbury (01722 324731).
Open Apr-Sept 11am-6pm daily (presentations
hourly). Last entry 5pm. **Admission** £1.50; £1 5s-18s.

Follow a 30-minute slide-show and audiovisual presentation of the history of Salisbury in this impressively
beamed thirteenth-century hall.

Wiltshire & Bath

Stonehenge: Bronze Age power statement

'There it is!' – the very words that have tumbled from the mouths of pilgrims and passers-by for the past 3,500 years as they've popped over the rise in the A303, and into the bleak valley of Stonehenge.

There it is: just as you imagined, only now it's strangely real. It's impossible to mistake; smaller than you thought it was going to be, then you take the turning off the main road and it looms larger and larger. It truly is awe-inspiring, drawing you in, emanating a nameless, mysterious power.

Is it a clock? A solar calendar? A launch-pad? Was it built by the Romans (as argued in 1906)? By a travelling Mycenaean prince (1953)? Or perhaps by incursive Bretons (1997)?

In *The Modern Antiquarian*, his landmark dayglo exposition of prehistory, Julian Cope makes the point that Stonehenge is quite mistakenly used as a symbol of Britain's megalithic culture: it's totally unrepresentative, bearing zero resemblance to the rough-hewn sacred standing stones he charts so lovingly elsewhere. There's no natural harmony in Stonehenge: it was fashioned as 'a Bronze Age power statement' – an endpiece, a stunning trump – long after the golden era of Stone Age temple-building had passed.

Where other megalithic sites were built in awe of the earth, the sky, the sun, the stars, Stonehenge sought to master them. Constructed on an existing sacred site, the horseshoe of towering trilithons was made of the same sarsen stone as the earlier cathedral at Avebury, even including a dismantled temple of Welsh bluestones – 'an act of domination, rather than one of cameraderie or deference', Copey echoes visionary archaeologist Aubrey Burl. After 3,500 years, it comes as a surprise to recognise that the basis of Stonehenge's still-tangible power is political as much as it is spiritual.

Coming over the rise in the A303 today, that uncomfortable feeling of wonderment and insignificance is exactly the impact this extraordinary construction was designed to have over us impressionable, slightly backward natives.

By junction of A303 and A360, west of Amesbury (info line 01980 624715). **Open** *mid-Mar-May* 1.30-6pm daily; *June-Aug* 9am-7pm daily; *Sept-mid-Oct* 9.30am-6pm daily; *16 Oct-23 Oct* 9.30am-5pm daily; *24 Oct-mid-Mar* 9.30am-4pm daily. **Admission** £4; £2 5s-16s; £3 OAPs, students; £10 family.

Resisting the urge to run and touch and get in among the stones is hard. The audio-handset commentary can grind a bit; the roads are unfortunately close; yet it's still absolutely flipping marvellous.

To get to Stonehenge by public transport, catch the No.3 bus from the bus station on Endless Street or from Fisherton Street near the rail station. Buses leave on the hour, every hour, from 10am to 5pm and the journey takes 40mins. It's best to get an Explorer ticket rather than a return to Stonehenge (both cost £4.80 but the former also allows you free travel round Salisbury).

Julian Cope's The Modern Antiquarian *is published by Thorson's, £30.*

Wiltshire & Bath

Mompesson House

The Close, Salisbury (01722 335659).
Open *Apr-Oct* noon-5.30pm Mon-Wed, Sat, Sun. Last entry 5pm. **Admission** (NT) £3.40; £1.70 5s-18s.

An elegant eighteenth-century Queen Anne house, which featured in the award-winning film version of *Sense and Sensibility*. Attractions include the Turnbull collection of drinking glasses, period furniture and a walled garden.

Old Sarum Castle

1.5 miles north of Salisbury (01722 335398).
Open *Mar-Oct* 10am-6pm daily; *Nov-Feb* 10am-4pm daily. **Admission** (EH) £2; £1 5s-16s; £1.50 OAPs, students.

The knee-high remains of Old Salisbury, perched atop its atmospheric rise.

Old Wardour Castle

N of A30, near Ansty (01747 870487).
Open 10am-6pm daily. **Admission** (EH) £1.90; £1 5s-16s; £1.40 OAPs, students.

The unusual hexagonal ruins of this dreamy lakeside castle last saw bloodthirsty action in 1643 – argumentative picnics excepted. Landscaped grounds include an elaborate rockwork grotto.

Philipps House & Dinton Park

N side of B3089, Dinton (01985 843600).
Open *Apr-Oct* 1-5pm Mon; 10am-1pm Sun. **Admission** (NT) £2.

A graceful neo-classical house surrounded by inviting parkland, nine miles west of Salisbury.

Reach for the skies in the **Salisbury** *twilight.*

Salisbury Cathedral

High Street, Salisbury (01722 555120).
Open *June-mid-Sept* 7am-8.15pm Mon-Sat; 7am-6.30pm Sun; *mid-Sept-May* 7am-6.30pm daily. **Admission** free; £3 suggested donation.

Around 600,000 visitors each year take in the thirteenth-century Cathedral, hugely impressive both as a guiding beacon and a cold, grey diffuser of light. Highlights include the vaulted cloisters, wonderfully serene and cedar-shaded, plus the octagonal, bright and beautiful Chapter House, which houses one of four remaining originals of the Magna Carta. Hardy's Jude in *Jude the Obscure* worked here, at 'Melchester' Cathedral, as a stonemason. *Roy of the Rovers* was a later local literary hit.

Salisbury & South Wiltshire Museum

King's House, 65 The Close, Salisbury (01722 332151).
Open *July, Aug* 10am-5pm Mon-Sat; 2-5pm Sun; *Sept-June* 10am-5pm Mon-Sat. **Admission** £3; 75p 5s-16s; £2 OAPs, students.

This award-winning museum contains a Stonehenge Gallery and a designated archaeological collection of national importance, and includes the story of Keith Pitt-Rivers, founding father of modern archaeology. Also ceramics, costumes and surprise Turner watercolours.

The Wardrobe

58 The Close, Salisbury (01722 414536).
Open *Feb, Mar, Nov-mid-Dec* 10am-5pm Tue-Sun; *Apr-Oct* 10am-5pm daily. **Admission** £2.50; 50p 5s-16s; £1.90 OAPs, students; £5 family.

The local regimental museum is housed in a fine house dating from 1254, which was used by bishops in the fourteenth century to house clothing.

Wilton Carpet Factory

King Street, Wilton (01722 742733).
Open 9.30am-5.30pm Mon-Sat; 11am-5pm Sun. **Admission** £4; £2.50 4s-16s; £3.75 OAPs, students; £10 family.

Unravel the mysteries of Wilton and Axminster carpet-making, which dates back nearly 300 years. The Wilton factory outlet shop (plus fashion, textiles, sports equipment, etc) is in the **Wilton Shopping Village** on Minster Street (01722 741211).

Wilton House

Wilton (01722 746720).
Open *Easter-Oct* 10.30am-5.30pm daily. Last entry 4.30pm. **Admission** *house, exhibition & grounds* £6.75; £4 5s-15s; £5.75 OAPs, students; £17.50 family; *grounds only* £3.75; £2.50 5s-15s.

Built by Inigo Jones, Wilton House contains a fabulous art collection (heavy on Van Dyck, Rembrandt and two of the Brueghels) and also boasts a choccie-box Palladian bridge over the Nadder, 21 acres of landscaped parkland, a Victorian laundry and Tudor kitchen, and kiddies' adventure playground.

Woodhenge

off A345, just N of Amesbury.
Site of a covered wooden monument that predated Stonehenge, discovered in 1925. Concrete posts now mark the many excavated postholes. Enthusiasts only.

Bradford-on-Avon & around

Though it has always lived in the shadow of neighbouring Bath, this lovely town offers many similar charms, but without the hassle.

A quiet corner in **Bradford-on-Avon**...

As a tourist town, **Bradford-on-Avon** has been likened to a mini-Bath: architecturally elegant, built of the same distinctive honey-coloured stone, and packed with historic remnants. Thankfully, the two towns differ in one crucial area: crowds. In actual fact, Bradford is a worthy tourist attraction in itself; its dramatic topography alone is enough to create an impression, with steep terraces of houses rising up from the river, and excellent viewpoints

By train from London

There are roughly three trains a day that run from **Waterloo** to **Bradford-on-Avon** (via Warminster), with a journey time of just under **2hrs**.

and appealing areas to wander around. Added to which, Bath (*see page 138*) is still an option, just ten minutes to the north, and there are rolling tracts of countryside to explore to the south.

Bradford itself dates back to prehistoric times, having sprung up naturally around a handy crossing point along the River Avon. There was an Iron Age settlement here, and the tiny Church of St Laurence on Church Street is one of the best surviving remainders of Saxon architecture in the country. The 'broad ford' was spanned in the thirteenth century by a stone town bridge, which, in its seventeenth-century form with its characteristic lock-up halfway across, still forms the centre of the town today. Bradford grew to become a powerful centre for the woollen and cloth industries from the Middle Ages onwards, reaching a peak in the seventeenth century (hence the number of generously appointed merchants' houses surviving from that time). Terraced weavers' cottages were built on the steep hillsides to the north of the town, many of which still remain, along with the large mills that later sprang up in the centre of town. After a steady decline, the woollen trade had collapsed entirely by the 1840s but the town reinvented itself as a rubber manufacturer almost immediately afterwards, and the mills were retooled to this end. This trade also eased off, however, and today, the mills have all been converted into granny flats, and there is little industry to speak of apart from tourism. At the end of the twentieth century, Bradford is, by its own admission, 'a small town of 10,000 inhabitants that is looking for a new role in the post-industrial age'.

Out and about

Parts of the town still follow a cramped medieval street plan, but the further you travel out of the centre, the grander the architecture gets. When you get to the Baron Farm Country Park and the fourteenth-century Tithe Barn, half a mile south of the town bridge, it's open country. Surrounding buildings have been converted to craft workshops and tearooms.

... and another.

The country park is one of the best places for a stroll along the river.

As appealing as the countryside around Bradford is, it is a landscape that has been irrevocably altered over the years, particularly during the nineteenth century. As one form of transport succeeded another, the area became a comprehensive tangle of communication routes, requiring an inordinate number of bridges, viaducts and tunnels. Fortunately, these structures were built with a tremendous monumentalism, with the result that they have not only endured, usually in a magnificent state of semi-ruin, but have added undeniable character to the region, and found new leisure applications.

Frome sweet Frome

Heading out of town, tucked away in the Mendip Hills and the valleys of the Avon and the Frome rivers, are dozens of stately homes and gardens, plus all manner of prehistoric monoliths, medieval castles and historic villages. **Frome** is the next largest town in the area, though not in the same league aesthetically. Like Bradford-on-Avon, it formed around the river and prospered with the cloth industry (at one time it was more important than Bath). It also retains much of its architectural heritage: steep cobbled streets and a wealth of listed buildings, maintained with pride and so authentic that it frequently doubles as nineteenth-century London for TV purposes.

Go further east and you're heading towards Salisbury Plain and the heart of Wiltshire. The area around **Westbury** and **Warminster** is particularly pleasant countryside for walking and cycling, and includes the privately owned (but publicly accessible) ancient forest of **Brokerswood**.

Where to stay

For a touch of luxury, try the ultra-trendy **Babington House**, at Babington, north-west of Frome (01373 812266; doubles from £175).

Bradford Old Windmill

4 Masons Lane, Bradford-on-Avon, BA15 1QN (01225 866842/fax 01225 866648).
Rates *single occupancy* £69-£89; *double* £79-£99.
Rooms (all en suite) 3 double. **Cards** AmEx, DC, MC, V.

This converted mill perched on the hillside overlooking the town is eccentric, romantic and very popular (book two to three months ahead). The three rooms all have a character of their own. The cheapest, Damsel, features a waterbed and high conical ceiling, Great Spur has a round bed and a hanging wicker chair, and Fantail has its own lounge, plus a minstrels' gallery with a nine-foot-long box bed for kids. There's a spacious circular lounge on the ground floor, too, and exposed beams, mill-related ornaments and folkie décor throughout. Well-travelled owners Priscilla and Peter Roberts provide ethnic vegetarian evening meals (and carnivore-friendly breakfasts). Non-smoking throughout.

A363 S towards Bradford-on-Avon town centre; 100m after Castle pub turn left into private driveway; house is immediately before first roadside house (no sign or number).

Dundas Lock Cottage

Monkton Combe, nr Bath, BA2 7BN (tel/fax 01225 723890).
Rates (B&B) *single* £23.50; *double* £50; *family room* £70.50. **Rooms** 1 single; 2 double.

This former lock-keeper's house is perfectly situated for those in search of isolation at reasonable rates. Nestled in the Avon Valley, the rose- and honeysuckle-covered cottage stands at the intersection of two canals, one of which runs right through the well-tended garden. Inside, it's more like a home than a hotel; there are no great luxuries (no locks on the doors, not all of them have en suite bathrooms), but it's spacious and clean and there are good canal views from all the rooms. The friendly and experienced proprietors can provide plenty of local info. Children welcome. Non-smoking throughout.

A36 S from Bath; cottage is on left 500m before BP garage (turn around in garage and approach entrance from other direction for easier access).

Eagle House

Bathford, nr Bath, BA1 7RS (01225 859946/ fax 01225 859946/www.eaglehouse.co.uk).
Rates (B&ContB) *single/single occupancy* £36-£46; *double/cottage rooms* £46-£74. Breakfast £3.20 (Eng). **Rooms** (all en suite) 2 single; 4 double; 2 cottage rooms. **Cards** MC, V.

A handsome, refined Georgian house designed by Bath planner John Wood the Elder, in a charming conservation village. The elegant but unstuffy interiors include a large octagonal drawing room with marble fireplace overlooking the 1.5-acre terraced garden (with grass tennis court. The six rooms in the house itself, which are named after trees, vary in size, with good views, though the plumbing is not perfect. Even better are the two rooms in the cottage in the adjoining walled garden. Relaxed owners John and Rosamund Napier are the perfect hosts. Children and dogs welcome. Non-smoking rooms available.

A4 NE from Bath; after 3 miles turn right on to A363; after 100m take left fork into Bathford Hill; after 250m, take first right into Church Street; house on right after 200m.

Grey Lodge

Summer Lane, Combe Down, nr Bath, BA2 7EU (tel/fax 01225 832069/ www.visitus.co.uk/bath/hotel/grey_lodge.htm).
Rates (B&B) *single occupancy* £35-£40; *double/twin* £60-£65; *family suite* £85. **Rooms** (all en suite) 2 double/twin; 1 family suite.

A nineteenth-century house with well-maintained gardens, which feels like it's in the middle of nowhere but is actually less than ten minutes' drive from either Bath or Bradford-on-Avon. The house has fantastic views across the Down, which can also be seen from the two back rooms; one has the added attraction of a full-height window, the other has a small adjoining room that can sleep a third person (for a total of £85). The third room

overlooks the front garden and road but is just as quiet and private. All rooms are very comfortable, well co-ordinated and well equipped. Above all, the owners are genuinely warm and accommodating. Children welcome. Non-smoking throughout.

A36 S from Bath; after 5 miles turn right up hill at traffic lights by Viaduct Inn; first left to Monkton Combe; 0.5 miles after village, first house on left.

Priory Steps

Newtown, Bradford-on-Avon, BA15 1NQ (01225 862230/fax 01225 866248/priorysteps@clara.co.uk).
Rates (B&B) *single occupancy* £55; *double* £34-£38pp. **Rooms** (all en suite) 2 twin; 3 double. **Cards** MC, V.

A smart, family-run converted terrace of seventeenth-century weavers' cottages only a few minutes from the centre of town. All rooms have private, modern bathrooms, well-chosen antique furnishings and fine views across town and beyond (you can see the White Horse on a clear day). Healthy three-course set dinners (£19) are served every evening in the yellow communal dining room (book in advance); there's also a library and sunny terraced garden. Part of the Wolsey Lodge group. No smoking in the bedrooms. Children welcome.

Woolley Grange

Woolley Green, Bradford-on-Avon, BA15 1TX (01225 864705/fax 01225 864059/woolley@luxury-hotel.demon.co.uk/www.luxury-family-hotels.co.uk).
Rates (B&B) *single occupancy* £89.10-£234; *double* £99-£200; *suites* £170-£260; *family room* £250-£260. **Rooms** (all en suite) 17 double; 3 suites; 3 family. **Cards** AmEx, DC, Debit, MC, V.

If you've money to spare, this is the place to come for a good pampering. Woolley Grange is a hilltop, ivy-covered Jacobean mansion with stone balustrades, and some 15 acres of garden with a heated swimming pool, tennis court and croquet lawn. Inside, there's plenty of period detailing (oak panelling, parquet floors) alongside refurbished areas. The hotel is family run and family oriented; kids can stay free in parents' rooms, and have their own nursery and games rooms in separate buildings, with all-day childminders. Rooms vary in size (the smallest are pretty stingy) and location (some are in outbuildings) but all are well equipped, with luxury extras like fresh fruit and newspapers, and even in-room massages (for a fee). Good restaurants, too (*see p136*). Children and dogs welcome.

Where to eat & drink

If you want cosmopolitan dining, your best bet is to head into Bath (*see page 138*); apart from a few restaurants in Bradford itself, there's little beyond pub level in this area. Not that there aren't some fine pubs around, although most have earnt their popularity by way of location rather than cuisine. The **Canal Tavern** in Bradford (49 Frome Road; 01225 867426) has a pleasant canal-side setting and serves up a good selection of fresh fish. Further afield, try the **Seven Stars** in Winsley (01225 722204), the **George Inn** at Bathampton (01225 425079), the **Hop Pole** in Limpley Stoke (01225 723134), the

Creeper-clad **Bishopstrow House**.

Woolpack in Beckington (01373 831244), or the **Full Moon** in Rudge (01373 830936) for the best of local flavour – cuisine, ales and people.

Bishopstrow House

Warminster (01985 212312).
Food served 11am-9.30pm daily.
Set meals *dinner* £35 (3 courses).
Cards AmEx, DC, Debit, MC, V.

Close to Salisbury Plain, this Georgian house represents one of the best eating and accommodation options in the area. It's a classic country-house setting, with a good selection of meals to match: usually rich and rural, with a touch of Mediterranean. Toasted goat's cheese is a typical starter, with roasts and fish dishes given a twist here and there. Ornate desserts complete the picture. Starters are around £7.80, mains £19.50, desserts £5.

Bridge Tea Rooms

24A Bridge Street, Bradford-on-Avon (01225 865537).
Food served 9.30am-5pm Mon-Fri; 9.30am-5.30pm Sat; 10.30am-5.30pm Sun.

An attractively ramshackle seventeenth-century house next door to the Georgian Lodge and something of an institution. It's Victorian-themed, with sepia photos, lacy tablecloths, Victoriana and staff in period costume. The place is very good on the teas (nearly 30 different types), coffees and infusions, and home-made cream cakes positively sagging with richness (not to mention calories). Light lunches, including home-made soups, and main meals are also available, although the downstairs area is probably too cramped for comfortable dining. Tea for two costs £11.95.

Cross Guns

Avoncliff, nr Bradford-on-Avon (01225 862335).
Food served noon-2.30pm, 6.30-10pm, daily.
Cards Debit, MC, V.

A very popular local pub (often fully booked) in an excellent location by the river. The long seventeenth-century interior is fairly dark, with solid furniture and stone walls. Outside is a better option – weather permitting – with a floodlit, terraced garden descending to the river. There's a wide choice of standard pub fare, including fish, steaks and pies, plus a good selection of ales and malt whiskies. Makes for a pleasant walk from Bradford along the canal. As an idea, steaks cost around £8.50, desserts are about £3.50.

Georgian Lodge

25 Bridge Street, Bradford-on-Avon (01225 862268).
Food served varies; phone to check.
Cards AmEx, DC, Debit, MC, V.

Probably the best place to eat in town, a former coaching inn overlooking the bridge. The lower half of the split-level dining room has been recently updated in a bright, pared-down style, while the upper level has a more traditional white-tablecloth ambience. The menu tends towards strong Mediterranean flavours, but also takes in the local and the exotic, all to a consistently high standard. You can also choose from the good selection of daily specials and set options. Rooms are available here (£62-£78 for a double), a perfectly good accommodation choice for the centre of town. Starters are about £4.50, mains £12, desserts £3.95.

Thai Barn

24 Bridge Street, Bradford-on-Avon (01225 866443).
Food served 6-10.30pm Tue-Sun. **Set meals** £17.95 (2 courses). **Cards** DC, Debit, MC, V.

Authentic Thai cuisine at reasonable prices. The Thai Barn's curries are especially good, the pastes being made on the premises from fresh herbs and chillies. As the name suggests, the interior is a converted barn, and very spacious it is, too, with high ceilings and split-level dining area. Also does takeaway. Mains won't cost you more than a tenner.

Woolley Grange

Woolley Green, Bradford-on-Avon (01225 864705).
Food served noon-2pm, 7-9.30pm, daily.
Set meals *lunch* £15.50 (2 courses), £20 (3 courses); *dinner* £34.50 (3 courses). **Cards** DC, Debit, MC, V.

A highlight at the high end, with the best of country house cooking in an appropriately grand setting. The internal dining area is split into two rooms, plus an adjoining converted conservatory with a more casual tone. All serve the same set menu, with a three-course dinner plus coffee and canapés for £34.50. Ingredients are as local as possible (right down to the hotel's own garden), with dishes such as veal with ceps, oxtail dumplings and shallot and port sauce, or roasted guinea fowl with prunes, brandy and pancetta. Desserts (£4.50), cheeses and wines are equally sumptuous. Otherwise, main courses are pricey, at going on for £20.

Tourist information centres

34 Silver Street, **Bradford-on-Avon**, BA15 1JX (01225 865797). **Open** *Apr-Sept* 10am-5pm daily; *Oct-Mar* 10am-4pm daily.

2 Bridge Street, **Frome**, BA11 1BB (01373 467271). **Open** *Apr-Oct* 10am-5pm Mon-Sat *Nov-Mar* 10am-4.30pm Mon-Sat.

Central Car Park, **Warminster**, BA12 9BT (01985 218548). **Open** *Apr-Oct* 9.30am-5.30pm Mon-Sat; *Nov-Mar* 9.30am-4.30pm Mon-Sat.

Bike hire

Lock Inn Cottage Frome Road, **Bradford-on-Avon** (01225 868068). A five- to ten-minute walk from the station.

Barging through the country

Linking Bristol to the Thames at Reading, the Kennet & Avon Canal was one of the most ambitious waterway projects ever undertaken in Britain, and almost a complete waste of time. It was opened in 1810, but by the 1840s it was all but superseded by the Great Western Railway, which runs parallel to it, as though in open mockery. It fell into abandon in the 1950s until the 1980s when its recreational potential sparked a massive, still-ongoing, restoration plan.

There's plenty to do here, even without leaving the towpath, since the canal winds through some beautiful countryside and connects plenty of interesting places. With leisurely barges comprising the only motor traffic and no steep gradients, it's a very pleasant walking route, threading through some delightful woodland, country parks and historic architecture such as the Claverton water-

powered pumping station and the magnificent Dundas Aqueduct. On the way to Bath (about three hours' walk from Bradford), villages such as **Avoncliff**, **Limpley Stoke**, **Claverton** and **Bathampton** provide plenty of waterside watering holes.

The towpaths are also popular with anglers and cyclists. Bikes, trikes, tandems and trailers are available for hire from the **Lock Inn Cottage** in Bradford (01225 868068), which also serves a hearty boatman's breakfast to start the day. Canoes and self-drive day boats are also available for the more nautically inclined, and the nearby **Bradford-on-Avon Wharf** (01225 868683) runs 1½-hour narrowboat trips from April to October. Hiring a live-in barge is more appropriate for longer periods of time, but a quick paddle could whet your appetite for your next holiday.

The Courts Garden

Holt (01225 782340).
Open 1.30-5.30pm Mon-Fri, Sun.
Admission (NT) phone for details.

Seven acres of authentic English country garden run by the National Trust. Well maintained, with water features, yew hedges and unusual topiary.

Farleigh Hungerford Castle

Farleigh Hungerford (01225 754026).
Open *Apr-Sept* 10am-6pm, *Oct* 10am-5pm, daily; *Nov-Mar* 10am-4pm Wed-Sun. **Admission** (EH) £2.40; £1.20 5s-16s, £1.70 OAPs, students.

This large, semi-ruined castle in the Frome valley was once home to the Hungerford Lords, whose colourful deeds during the Middle Ages (explained in a free audio tour) add to the remaining architecture. There are battle re-enactments throughout the year (phone for details).

Iford Manor

off A36 8 miles SE of Bath (01225 863146).
Open *Apr* 2-5pm Sun, Easter Mon; *May-Sept* 2-5pm Tue-Thur, Sat, Sun, bank hol Mon; *Oct* 2-5pm Sun.
Admission £3; £2 OAPs, students, 10s-16s; free under-10s.

The residence of nineteenth-century architect Harold Peto, famed for its award-winning Italianate gardens. Peto plundered classical artefacts, as well as design ideas, from across Europe to create his architecture-and-plants vision of the perfect garden. The result is enchanting. There is a festival of classical music, jazz and opera every year, from mid-June to mid-August (call 01225 868124 for details). Children under ten are not allowed on weekends.

Longleat

Warminster (01985 844400/www.longleat.co.uk).
Open *house* 10am-5pm daily; *safari park Mar-Oct* 10am-5pm daily; *attractions Mar-Oct* 11am-6pm daily. **Admission** £13; £10 4s-14s, OAPs; *safari park only* £6; £4.50 4s-14s, OAPs.

Lord Bath's famous home has amassed an ever-expanding roll-call of attractions over the years: the safari park, giant cosmic-themed hedge mazes, Dr Who exhibition, Postman Pat village. Oh yes, there's a house here, too – an exquisite Elizabethan manor stacked with art treasures, historic exhibits and general relics of the aristocracy. Where there are attractions there are crowds, however, and on a hot summer weekend you may find yourself wishing you'd gone elsewhere.

Prior Park Landscape Garden

Ralph Allen Drive (01225 833422/info line 0891 335242/www.nationaltrust.org.uk).
Open noon-5.30pm Mon, Wed-Sun.
Admission (NT) £3.80; £1.90 5s-16s.

This hilltop eighteenth-century garden was built by one of Bath's founding fathers, Ralph Allen (with advice from poet Alexander Pope and Capability Brown). There are excellent views over Bath and the area, lakes and a grand Palladian bridge. No parking on the site.

Westbury White Horse

One of the oldest and largest in the country dating back to 878 but recut in the eighteenth century and concreted in the 1950s. Great views and hang-gliding from the top, if the urge should take you. Nearby is the Iron Age hill fort of Bratton Castle.

Bath

An open-air museum of Georgian architecture.

The Romans were the first people to properly tap the waters of Britain's only hot springs, building a bathhouse, which formed the gushing heart of Aquae Sulis. The Roman Baths flourished between the first and fifth centuries AD, and were finally excavated some 1,400 years later, actually missing out on Bath's Georgian heyday, when the nearby Cross Bath and Hot Bath were in use (*see page 143* **Bath time**).

Between-times, Edgar, the first king of England, was crowned at a Saxon monastery on the site of Bath Abbey in 973; the city's medieval menfolk were terrorised by Geoffrey Chaucer's earthy 'Wife of Bath', and the city saw Queen Elizabeth I slip out of her farthingale on a visit to the trendy Tudor bathing spa in the 1570s. In the eighteenth century, John Wood (first the elder, then the younger) constructed many of the city's landmark buildings and honey-stone streets, while the dandyish Beau Nash presided over a burgeoning social scene. The Pump Room adjoining the baths dates back to this Georgian era – when it was indisputably

By train from London

Trains leave **Paddington** for **Bath** approximately every half hour; the fastest takes a mere **1hr 13mins**.

the place to be seen – as do the luxurious arc of the Royal Crescent, The Circus, the Cross Bath and Hot Bath (these last two are currently undergoing renovation), the Assembly Rooms and the Italianate, shop-lined Pulteney Bridge over the River Avon.

Among the artists, writers and musicians inspired by Bath were Dickens, Scott, Gainsborough and Handel; but Jane Austen is the city's most famous literary resident by far. 'Oh, who can ever be tired of Bath?' sighed the heroine of *Northanger Abbey*, echoing the sentiment of many a social butterfly who flitted from the Pump Room to the new Theatre Royal, between the promenades, balls and assemblies which confirmed the city as high society's favourite watering hole in the 1800s.

The Circus – *John Wood the Elder's masterpiece, finished off by his son.*

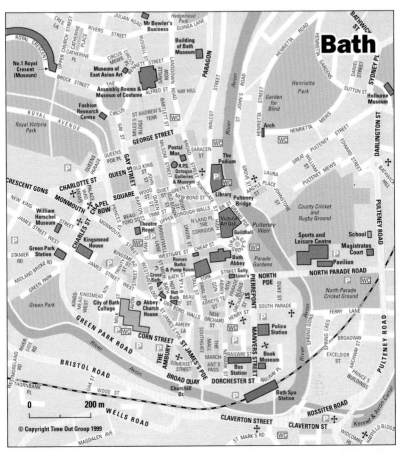

It wasn't until the 1880s when the cellars of Pump Room finally gave up their secret of the Great Roman Bath and temple to Minerva. Yet more ungodliness for Good Queen Victoria to contend with: she is said to have snapped shut the curtains of her carriage when she was being driven through the city. Clapping eyes on an decadent individual who had only recently stripped down to their final three layers of underwear could have risked a scandalised fit of the vapours.

Make no mistake: throughout its eighteenth- and nineteenth-century prime, Bath was synonymous with sex; or rather with an escape into subtle resort-town decadence, where social laws were fractionally relaxed. Even now that sexual contact between the comfortably-off routinely extends to more than fluttering eyelashes and heaving bosoms, this exclusive, costume-drama city still acts as something of a romantic magnet, where its possible to stroll hand-in-hand through the very fabric of a glamorous past.

Summon up eighteenth-century dandy, gambler and arbiter of fashion Richard 'Beau' Nash as your guide as you explore the Paragon. Window-shop for antiques and dusty tomes that mention your hotel. Try out the echo from the green in the middle of The Circus, and wonder at the throwaway fact that the constituent crescents have a diameter exactly matching that of Stonehenge. Gaze into the hypnotic horseshoe weir set before Robert Adam's Pulteney Bridge. Gourmandise. Quaff. Dip a toe into a splendid living museum. Immerse yourself in Bath.

Where to stay

Unlike the other towns and cities in the region, there are no pubs offering a good standard of accommodation anywhere near the centre of Bath. The genteel evolution of the city has given rise to two options: a relatively classy hotel near the centre, or a relatively classy guesthouse perched somewhere up on the rim of the bowl enveloping the golden city.

Apsley House Hotel

141 Newbridge Hill, BA1 3PT (01225 336966/fax 01225 425462/apsleyhouse@easynet.co.uk).
Rates (B&B) *single occupancy* £60-£70; *double/twin* £75-£95; *four-poster* £105; *additional person* £10-£15. **Rooms** (all en suite) 8 double/twin; 1 four-poster. **Cards** AmEx, Debit, MC, V.

David and Annie Lanz's stunning house was built for the Duke of Wellington in 1830 and is backed by beautiful gardens. It's as well to ask for a bedroom at the rear of the house to avoid possible traffic noise from the busy Newbridge Road. The atmosphere within the house is tranquil but warm, and the décor is antiquey and restrained. Children over 5 welcome.
1.5 miles W of city centre; on Newbridge Hill off Newbridge Road (A4).

Harington's Hotel

8-10 Queen Street, BA1 1HE (01225 461728/fax 01225 444804/post@haringtonshotel.co.uk/www.haringtonshotel.co.uk).
Rates (B&B) *single occupancy* £65-£75; *double/twin* £78-£98; *triple* £120. **Rooms** (all en suite) 10 double; 2 twin; 1 triple. **Cards** AmEx, DC, Debit, MC, V.

The best of the city-centre hotels within the (relative) budget bracket, Harington's is smack in the middle of the hubbub. Unload on the narrow, cobbled Queen Street, and then go around the one-way system to the nearby car park (£5 per 24 hours). All rooms are newly refurbished and have cable TV. There's a coffee-lounge/bar downstairs, and a decent fry-up for breakfast. Children welcome. No smoking in any of the bedrooms.

*The classy **Queensberry Hotel**.*

Haydon House

9 Bloomfield Park, BA2 2BY (tel/fax 01225 444919/haydon.bath@btinternet.com).
Rates (B&B) *single occupancy* £50-£60; *double/twin* £70-£90; *family* £100-£120. **Rooms** (all en suite) 5 double/twin; 1 family. **Cards** AmEx, MC, V.

Magdalene and Gordon Ashman-Marr ensure a warm, chatty welcome for guests at their flowery Edwardian guesthouse. Situated a good half-mile or so above the centre, it's all too tempting to spend time here in one of the five carefully ornamented bedrooms, amid the busy touches of the pink lounge or beautiful garden. The fried 'Bloomfield Breakfast' is served to guests at one large table, and nicely sidesteps the hushed, china-clinking misery to be endured at certain establishments. Children welcome. No smoking throughout.
Take A367 Wells Road S of centre; take right fork into Bloomfield Road; 2nd right into Bloomfield Park.

Holly Lodge

8 Upper Oldfield Park, BA2 3JZ (01225 424042/fax 01225 481138).
Rates (B&B) *single* £48; *double/twin* £79-£89; *four-poster* £85-£94. **Rooms** (all en suite) 1 single; 4 double/twin; 2 four-poster. **Cards** AmEx, DC, Debit; MC, V.

A high-standard B&B, and another one hovering vertiginously above the city – try and get a room with a view. Sit out in the floodlit gazebo or statue-strewn terraced garden when weather permits. Décor is plush (chandeliers, swagged curtains, antique furniture); proprietor George Hall is friendly and helpful; breakfast in the conservatory is worth writing home about. Children welcome. No smoking throughout.
Take A367 Wells Road S of centre; up hill, first right into Upper Oldfield Park; 100 yards on right.

Queensberry Hotel

Russell Street, BA1 2QF (01225 447928/queensberry@dial.pipex.com).
Rates (B&CB) *single occupancy* £100-£110; *double/twin* £120-£185; *four-poster* £210. Breakfast £7.50 (Eng). **Rooms** (all en suite) 28 double/twin; 1 four-poster. **Cards** MC, V.

Unashamed elegance and comfort in a Regency townhouse built for the Marquis of Queensberry by one of the John Woods – and expertly given a bold contemporary dash by interiors wizard Penny Ross. Bedrooms are kitted out in relatively simple style; ceilings lower the higher up the building you stay. The hotel's **Olive Tree** restaurant (*see p142*) is excellent, and the courtyard garden is a lovely spot to sip a G&T on a summer's evening. Children welcome.

Royal Crescent

16 Royal Crescent, BA1 2LS (01225 823333/fax 01225 339401/reservations@royalcrescent.co.uk/www.royalcrescent.co.uk).
Rates *double/twin* £190; *deluxe double/twin* £230-£290; *suites* £380-£695. **Rooms** (all en suite) 12 double/twin; 18 deluxe double/twin; 4 four-poster suites; 12 suites. Breakfast £16.50 (Eng); £13.50 (Cont). **Cards** AmEx, DC, Debit, MC, V.

Given its location, in the middle of the most famous architectural set-piece in the bottom left-hand quarter of England, you might expect the Royal Crescent hotel to be somewhat special. It is – even if you're 'relegated' to a room in one of the extensive rear garden's Georgian villas. Console yourself with a leisurely game of croquet. Take a Roman-style steam bath, or a swim. Go on a balloon trip. Flick through your room's hand-tooled Austens. Heck, stay the week and actually finish one. Above all, don't turn up here to pinch pennies: why spend two hundred quid on a night's sleep when it's perfectly possible to tick a few more options and splash out £695. Children and dogs are welcome. Non-smoking rooms available.

Where to eat & drink

Thought to have more restaurants per capita in the UK than any other city outside London, Bath offers plenty of choice between the premium, Georgian-housed award-winners and the less lavish. Second-honeymooners and those on expense accounts head for **Lettonie** (*see below*) or the **Brasserie** at the **Royal Crescent** hotel (01225 823333) or the excellent **Bath Priory** hotel (Weston Road; 01225 331922); otherwise, the wine bar/bistro **Moon & Sixpence** (6A Broad Street; 01225 460962), the **Circus** (34 Brock Street; 01225 318918) and the veggie-friendly **Demuth's** (2 North Parade Passage; 01225 446059) are more moderate. The vibrant **Green Street Seafood Café** (6 Green Street; 01225 448707) serves up the fish caught fresh by its own Cornish boat.

Perhaps unexpectedly, Bath is a city that's fairly hot on Indian/Asian food: even **Pimpernel's** (01225 823333) at the Royal Crescent hotel offers a downplayed, upmarket version of Thai/Chinese/Indian. Meanwhile, the **Rajpoot** (4 Argyle Street; 01225 466833) is very high class; the **Eastern Eye** (8a Quiet Street; 01225 422323) is cartoon opulent beneath its Georgian ceiling, but good fun, and **Mai Thai** (6 Pierrepoint Street; 01225 445557) deserves its good reputation.

Pub-wise, you're spoilt for cosy, cuddly-corner choice: for starters, check out the **Star** (The Vineyards), the welcoming **Bell** (Walcot Street; excellent thrice weekly free music and cracking real ales), the **Crystal Palace** (Abbey Green; nice courtyard), the **Coeur de Lion** (tiny, situated in quaint alley – Northumberland Place, off High Street, by WH Smith) and the **Cross Keys** (Midford Road – garden and aviary, good for kids); also the walkable canalside **George Inn** (Mill Lane, Bathampton, just outside outside of Bath).

Clos du Roy
1 Seven Dials, Saw Close (01225 444450).
Food served noon-2.30pm, 6-9.30pm, daily.
Set meals *lunch* £13.95 (3 courses); *dinner* £19.50 (3 courses); *pre-theatre* (6-7pm) £6.70 (3 courses).
Cards AmEx, DC, MC, V.

It's worth pointing out the pre-theatre and Sunday roast specials at this extremely French (French proprietor, French chef, French waiting staff) restaurant. Tucked away on the first floor of a pedestrian precinct, it scores low on Georgian loveliness, but high on comfort, tinkling piano tunes, and fresh, painstakingly simple contemporary classics. Fish. Lamb. Wine. Cream. Chocolate. You know the score.

Hullaballoos
36 Broad Street (01225 443323).
Meals 6-10.30pm Mon; noon-2pm, 6-10.30pm, Tue-Sat. **Set meals** *lunch* £5.99 (2 courses); £7.99 (3 courses); *dinner* £14.50 (2 courses); £17 (3 courses).
Cards AmEx, DC, Debit, MC, V.

This calm, quiet, well-designed and well-located restaurant is exceedingly welcome in a city where it can be hard to find decent food at reasonable prices. Operating a BYO policy helps what is already a well-priced menu offer even better value (BYO is for wine only – almost uniquely, the restaurant does actually have has its own alcohol licence; it just prefers to see its customers get the best deals available). The menu is Med-influence, extensive and sensibly not too ambitious – and the food is very good indeed. We have been particularly impressed by the marinated chicken with prosciutto and coriander dressing, and the grilled fillet of salmon with tomato, garlic and basil salsa.

Jamuna
9-10 High Street (01225 464631/ www.currypages.com/jamuna).
Food served 6pm-midnight daily.
Cards AmEx, Debit, MC, V.

Less ostentatious than some local Indian restaurants, the ever-popular Jamuna is the pick of the lot. Views of the Abbey opposite fill the tall first-floor windows in the bright, crescent-shaped dining-room. Some true specialities lurk amid established favourites, including spicy deep-fried cauliflower, broccoli and aubergine (£3.50 per dish); the fragrantly saucy chuka sabji dal (£4.50), and the gorgeous Goan lamb xacutti (£6.95). It's cooked with raw peanuts, egg yolk, grated coconut and fearsome dried bullet chillies.

Lettonie
35 Kelston Road (01225 446676).
Food served 12.30-2pm, 7-9pm, Tue-Fri; noon-2pm, 7-9.30pm, Sat. **Set meals** *lunch* £15 (2 courses); £25 (3 courses); *dinner* £44.50 (3 courses).
Cards AmEx, DC, Debit, MC, V.

Bath's only two-star Michelin restaurant is, as might be expected, a confident, virtuoso affair. In a spacious Georgian house, chef Martin Blunos creates the classiest of French dishes with distinctive Latvian touches, resulting in such mouthwatering delights as a starter of borscht terrine served with shredded beef piragi and soured cream, part of the set dinner menu. The restaurant also has rooms for the night (B&B £95-£150).

Moody Goose
7A Kingsmead Square (01225 466688).
Food served noon-2pm, 6-9.30pm, Tue-Thur; noon-2pm, 6-10pm Fri, Sat. **Set meals** *lunch* £10 (2 courses); *dinner* £20 (3 courses). **Cards** AmEx, DC, Debit, MC, V.

A cosy, highly regarded retreat for a well-deserved Mod-Brit pampering: try galantine of partridge stuffed with mushrooms and apricots; demand the old-fashioned rice pud with apple and cinnamon. Eat in the airy basement restaurant or more intimately in the small, vaulted dining room. Expect to pay around £15 for a main course.

Old Green Tree

12 Green Street (01225 448259).
Food served noon-2.15pm Mon-Sat.

Three small, wooden-floored and panelled rooms surround a well-stocked bar. Oddly, the Tree was a theme-pub and microbrewery long before the current crazes, being a 1920s recreation of a Golden Age Victorian pub, which used to boast its own backyard brewery. Hand-pumped RCH Pitchfork, Bath Spa and Brand Oak help ease the pain. Main courses cost around a fiver and are a mixture of tapas and pub grub (the chef is Spanish).

Olive Tree

Russel Street (01225 447928).
Food served noon-2pm, 7-10pm, Mon-Sat;
7-9pm Sun. **Set meals** *lunch* £12.50 (2 courses);
£14.50 (3 courses); *dinner* £24 (3 courses).
Cards Debit, MC, V.

The Queensberry Hotel's restaurant offers the best of contemporary fare – roast loin of lamb with spinach; sweet potato and caramelised onion gâteau – served up in informal surroundings with classical alacrity: 'the best place to eat in Bath', according to *The Times'* Restaurants of the Year in 1996. Starters begin at around a fiver; mains will set you back about £15.

Pump Room

Abbey Church Yard (01225 444477).
Food served noon-2.30pm daily. **Set meals** £14.50 (3 courses). **Cards** AmEx, Debit, MC, V.

When in Roman Baths, do what the Georgians did: see and be seen sipping steamy refreshments in the fashionable salon that has long been at the social heart of the city. Experiment with a glass of spa-water drawn from the fountain. Champagne breakfasts, tempting cakes and full meals are all served to the musical accompaniment of the Pump Room Trio.

What to see & do

Boredom is not likely to be a problem in Bath; the city is packed with museums (around 20), most of them excellent. And if the weather is fine, hire a boat at the Victorian **Bath Boating Station** (Forester Road; 01225 466407) or a bike.

Tourist information centre

Abbey Chambers, Abbey Churchyard (01225 477101).
Open *Oct-Apr* 9.30am-5pm daily; *May-Sept* 9.30am-6pm Mon-Sat; 10am-4pm Sun.

Bike hire

Avon Valley Cyclery, behind Bath Spa Station (01225 461880).

American Museum & Gardens

Claverton Manor (01225 460503).
Open *Apr-July, Sept, Oct museum* 2-5pm Tue-Sun; *gardens* 1-6pm Tue-Fri; noon-6pm Sat, Sun; *Aug museum* 2-5pm daily; *gardens* 1-6pm Mon-Fri; noon-6pm Sat, Sun. **Admission** £5.50; £3 5s-16s; £5 OAPs, students.

The American Way of Life transported from the seventeenth to nineteenth centuries, and over the big pond. American trees and shrubs; Native American, African-American and folk art, plus special events including

*Interiors of yore, in the **American Museum**.*

Bath time

For too long – over 20 years, now – the batho-centric, bath-crazy city of Bath has been up the creek without any prospect of a paddle. Thankfully, work has now started on the ambitious **Bath Spa Project**, which will see the city's two major Georgian baths renovated and reopened together with a new state-of-the-art complex by 2001.

A couple of minutes' walk from the Roman Baths (fed by the King's Spring), at the western end of collonnaded Bath Street, stand John Wood's **Hot Bath** and **Cross Bath**, named for the hot springs that serve them. Like the Roman Baths, which were used occasionally for special

events and toga-happy 'Roman Holidays', these baths saw their last use in the '70s, when a combination of health scares, dilapidation and the withdrawal of NHS funding made Bath a dry city.

Another famous old Bath building, the **Hetling Pump Room** (opposite the Hot Bath), is due for reinvention as the **Bath Spa Visitors' Centre**, while the Beau Street swimming baths – site of the Tepid Baths until the '20s – will be swept away for a smart new centre, custom-designed to offer bathing, water therapy and specialist complementary treatments.

At last, the City of Bath will once again be worthy of the name.

wartime (Civil, French and Indian, sorry, Native American) re-enactments. The reconstructed historical domestic interiors are fascinating, but, alas, Conkey's Tavern only serves up eighteenth-century Massachusetts gingerbread. Bus 18 runs from the centre of town to the museum on the outskirts of the city.

Bath Abbey
Abbey Churchyard (01225 422462/ www.bathwells.anglican.org/bathabbey).
Open *Easter-Oct* 9am-6pm Mon-Sat; *Nov-Easter* 9am-4.30pm Mon-Sat. **Admission** free; *cellars* £2; £1 5s-16s, OAPs, students.
At the heart of the city, by the Roman Baths, Bath Abbey is a Top Three target for visitors. Dating back to the fifteenth century, though incorporating parts of a ruined Norman predecessor, the Abbey is crammed full of monuments and memorials. Cleaning work has marvellously restored the heavenly colours of the spectacular fan vaulting. The 1,600-year history of the Abbey site is explained in the restored eighteenth-century cellars.

Bath Boating Station
Forester Road (01225 466407).
Open *Easter-Sept* 10am-6pm daily (weather permitting). **Admission** £4.50 per person for 1st hour (£1.50 per hour thereafter); £2.25 5s-13s (75p per hour thereafter); £5.50 all-day student ticket.
A unique surviving Victorian boating station with tea gardens and restaurant. Spend a family day messing about on the river, brandishing paddle or punt.

Bath Postal Museum
8 Broad Street (01225 460333).
Open 11am-5pm Mon-Sat; 2-5pm Sun. **Admission** £2.90; £1.20 (7s-15s); £1.95 OAPs, students.
The first-ever Penny Black was posted here in 1840. The museum includes a recreated Victorian Post Office, kids' activity room, film room, tea room and the history of written communication from 2000BC.

Book Museum at George Bayntun
Manvers Street (01225 466000).
Open 9am-1pm, 2-5.30pm, Mon-Fri; 9.30am-1pm Sat (closed bank hols). **Admission** £2; £1 4s-16s; £1 OAPs, students.
The eponymous bookbinder's skills revealed, plus a reconstruction of Dickens' study and 'Bath in Literature', featuring Jane Austen rarities.

Building of Bath Museum
The Countess of Huntingdon's Chapel, The Vineyards (01225 333895/www.bath-preservation-trust.org.uk).
Open *mid-Feb-Nov* 10.30am-5pm Tue-Sun.
Admission £3.50; £1.50 10s-16s; £2.50 OAPs, students.
Intelligent and witty, this exposition of how the Georgian city was built centres on a spectacular model of the city. 'No visitor to Bath should miss it' – *The Spectator*.

Holburne Museum & Crafts Study Centre
Great Pulteney Street (01225 466669/www.bath.ac.uk/holburne).
Open *Feb-mid-Dec* 11am-5pm Mon-Sat; 2.30-5.30pm Sun. **Admission** £3.50; £1.50 5s-16s; £3 OAPs; £2 students.
Stunning displays of silverwork, porcelain and glass presented alongside paintings by the likes of Turner, Gainsborough and Stubbs. Jane Austen lived opposite, at 4 Sydney Place, between 1801 and 1804.

Mr Bowler's Business
Bath Industrial Heritage Centre, Julian Road (01225 318348). **Open** *Apr-Oct* 10am-5pm daily; *Nov-Mar* 10am-5pm Sat, Sun.
Admission £3.50; £2.50 5s-16s, OAPs, students.
One hundred years-worth of collected ephemera from a Bath bottled-water firm provides insight and entertainment. Displays of Bath at work include cabinet making and the story of Bath stone.

*Get your teeth into **Sally Lunn's** buns.*

Museum of Costume & Assembly Rooms

Bennett Street (01225 477789/
www.museumofcostume.co.uk).
Open 10am-5pm daily. **Admission** £3.90;
£2.80 6s-18s; £3.50 OAPs, students; £11 family.

Four hundred years of costume are presented in an eye-opening, benchmark collection of bustles, paniers, pantaloons and fontages. The earliest complete costume in the museum is a formal cream silk dress woven with silver thread from the 1660s – a very rare survival. The chief impression left by the collection is invariably how much slighter people were in the past – even in the '50s and '60s.

Museum of East Asian Art

12 Bennett Street (01225 464640/
www.east-asian-art.co.uk).
Open *Apr-Oct* 10am-6pm Mon-Sat; 10am-5pm Sun;
Nov-Mar 10am-5pm Mon-Sat; noon-5pm Sun.
Admission £3.50, £1 6s-12s; £3 OAPs;
£2.50 students; £8 family.

This extensive collection of oriental fine and applied art features treasures from China, Mongolia, Japan, Korea, Thailand and Tibet, stretching from 5000 BC right up to the present day.

No. 1 Royal Crescent

1 Royal Crescent (01225 428126/
www.bath-preservation-trust.org.uk).
Open *mid-Feb-Oct* 10.30am-5pm Tue-Sun;
Nov 10.30am-4pm Tue-Sun. Last entry 30mins before closing. **Admission** £4; £3 5s-16s, OAPs, students; £8 family.

The corner townhouse in John Wood's famous crescent, designated a World Heritage Building, is restored, redecorated and furnished to appear as it might have done when it was built in 1786.

Roman Baths

Abbey Church Yard
(01225 477785/www.romanbaths.co.uk).
Open *Jan-Mar, Oct-Dec* 9.30am-5pm daily;
Apr-July, Sept 9am-6pm daily; *Aug* 9am-9.30pm daily.
Admission £6.75; £4 6s-18s; £6 OAPs, students; £17 family.

An excellent handset-guided tour takes you around the steamy bowels of the Roman Baths. Apart from the photogenic Great Bath, there are surprising complexes of indoor baths, the Minerva temple and bubbling King's Bath source, which produces 250,000 gallons of water a day, at a constant 46°C. Another highlight is the hot overflow waterfall. Great collections of temple sculpture, jewellery, pottery, wishing-spa coins and curses. A must-see.

Royal Photographic Society, Octagon Galleries & Museum

The Octagon, Milsom Street
(01225 462841/www.rps.org).
Open 9.30am-5.30pm daily. Last entry 4.45pm.
Admission £2.50; £1.75 7s-16s, OAPs, students.

Home of the world's foremost photographic society. The world's first ever snap is on display in the Octagon Galleries, along with hundreds of important and fascinating historical photographs as well as interesting contemporary works.

Sally Lunn's Refreshment House & Museum

4 North Parade Passage (01225 461634).
Open *restaurant* 10am-10pm Mon-Sat; 11am-6pm Sun; *museum* 10am-6pm Mon-Sat; 11am-6pm Sun.
Admission *museum only* 30p; free under-16s, OAPs, students.

This is the oldest house in Bath, dating back to 1482, with fragments of Roman, Saxon and medieval buildings in the excavated cellar. Sally Lunn invented her Bath bun here in the 1680s, and they're still on sale today – along with an entire Lunn-related menu in the refreshment rooms.

Victoria Art Gallery

Bridge Street (01225 477233/www.victoriagal.org.uk).
Open 10am-5.30pm Tue-Fri; 10am-5pm Sat; 2-5pm Sun. **Admission** free.

Bath and North-East Somerset's excellent gallery houses a permanent collection of British and European art from the fifteenth century to the present day, plus temporary exhibitions.

William Herschel Museum

19 New King Street
(01225 311342/www.bath-preservation-trust.org.uk).
Open *Mar-Oct* 2-5pm daily; *Nov-Feb* 2-5pm Sat, Sun.
Admission £2.50; £1 4s-16s; £5 family.

Here's the very house where the great astronomer discovered Uranus in 1781. No giggling at the back, thank you.

Chippenham to Avebury

Prehistoric sites, historic houses and wonderful walking.

Opening the flood gates on one of the 29 locks on **Caen Hill**.

Bookended by its celebrity cousins – Bath (*see page 138*) and Marlborough – it is easy to speed through this corner of Wiltshire. But this is no poor relation, just a little shyer and quieter perhaps, with much more to recommend it than its famous pig rearing. Prick the surface for a hoard of ancient sites and historic houses. Dig deeper and duck down country lanes where delicious limestone hamlets and unspoilt country pubs are hiding out.

In the beginning...

To the east the landscape is marked by an openness and the gentle but often dramatic

skein of the Marlborough Downs. From Hackpen Hill the A361 slices through the village and famous stones of **Avebury** (*see page 149* **Stone me**). Other ancient world stars are **Silbury Hill** (Bronze Age 2700 BC), one of the largest man-made prehistoric mounds in Europe, and **West Kennet Long Barrow**, one of Britain's largest Neolithic burial tombs. Silbury Hill's purpose remains a mystery: some think it was once a stone circle used for black magic worship. This area is also a favourite spot for crop circles – phenomena that have been reported in over 40 countries, and often close to ancient sites. East of here, the town of **Marlborough** has an attractive high street lined with colonnaded Georgian and Tudor buildings.

Heading west on the A4, the 'ancient' gives way to the mere 'old' – historic houses like stunning **Bowood** near Derry Hill and settlements created by wool wealth in the

By train from London

Trains to **Chippenham** leave **Paddington** about every half an hour (journey time just over **1hr**).

seventeenth and eighteenth centuries. White Horses abound: **Cherhill**, on the site of **Oldbury Castle**, an Iron Age hillfort, is a good example – its four-foot-wide eye was once filled with upturned bottles giving it a winking sparkle until souvenir hunters robbed the horse of its twinkle. Highwaymen and women frequented this old coach route and the Cherhill Gang reputedly persuaded their victims to part with their riches by appearing naked. These days, it is safe to go the few miles down the road to **Calne**, which gained fame in the pig trade when the former Harris Bacon Factory became the first to use the principle of bacon curing in 1864. Take a jolly turn around the green to view the best houses.

Modern Devizes

Dipping south, the countryside irons itself out towards the Vale of Pewsey, the Kennet and Avon Canal and **Devizes**. Today, a tad faded with the elegant indoor market stuffed with cheap trainers and tea towels, the town retains a peeling charm, with 500 listed buildings and the chance to sample the excellent Wadworths beer in its many pubs. Some famous people made Devizes fashionable once upon a time – Judge Jeffreys lodged in the town and George Eliot had a steamy affair with the local Doctor Brabant. One senses that Devizes will have its day again. There are rumblings already – the groovy restored art deco Palace cinema and the revamped Wharfside; the town also boasts crafty shops, a good little theatre and is the starting point for the popular Devizes to Westminster canoe race on Good Friday. Just outside the town is the famous **Caen Hill** flight of 29 locks, the longest in the country. If utterly taken over by the romance of the canal, you can adopt a section of it; prices start from £2 to £100 for a whole lock, or you could take a trip or holiday on it (White Horse Boats, 8 Southgate Close, Pans Lane, Devizes; 01380 728504). Following the canal and the A365 west you come to **Melksham**, once a centre for the weaving trade, which also basks in past glory, with its smattering of seventeenth- and eighteenth-century merchants' houses.

Ways to go

There's good walking country all over the region, with many great pathways to latch on to, including the **Ridgeway**, the **Macmillan Way** and the **Cotswold Way**. For bikers, the **Wiltshire Cycleways** have some fantastic routes, notably Corsham to Great Bedwyn (about 41 miles in total). If you don't fancy the exercise, take a lazy leisure drive; there are plenty of lanes to explore, for instance, around **Bowden Hill** from A342 to **Lacock** (part of

The effortlessly romantic **Fosse Farmhouse**.

the old route taken by Pepys and others from London to Bath) and from the A4 at **Box**, taking in the divine village of **Colerne** and on up to **Ford**. Great hostelries pop up at every turn.

Chippenham and beyond

The largest town in this region is **Chippenham**. After negotiating Dantesque ring roads you arrive at its pedestrianised core to find a market town that holds more historical than contemporary interest – King Alfred sited his hunting lodge here – but if shopping is on the agenda, you will find all you need here. It's also worth a stroll round the lively market on Friday and Saturday mornings.

The western wedge of this area is the most attractive – all leafy, curvy, sexy, secret ups and downs. **Corsham**, founded on stone and cloth, is a historic treasure. Investigate the High Street, with houses dating back to 1540, the finest almshouses in the country on Pound Pill, built in 1668, and the only shaft stone mine in the world to be open to the public. The Hare & Hounds was once the residence of Moses Pickwick, Dickens' inspiration for *The Pickwick Papers*. The village at **Castle Combe** is for many people the prettiest in the country. It certainly has all the right elements – riverside setting, turreted church and gorgeous cottages, but can get very crowded with tourists. The village is also known for its motor-racing circuit (phone 01249 782417 if you fancy a whirl round it). Less-famous, and hence, less-crowded villages such as **Nettleton**, **West Kington** and **Biddestone** (home of Starfall pottery) are all well worth a gander.

At the Sign of the Angel

6 Church Street, Lacock, SN15 2LB (01249 730230/ fax 01249 730527/www.lacock.co.uk).
Rates (B&B) *single occupancy* £65; *double/twin* £90- £110; *deluxe double* £105-£125; *four-poster* £90- £125. Special breaks. **Rooms** (all en suite) 2 twin;

5 double; 1 deluxe double; 2 four-poster.
Cards AmEx, DC, Debit, MC, V.

George Hardy is the welcoming angel to this ship-like, creaks-and-squeaks fifteenth-century hotel, which has been run by his family for 40 years. Inside, it's Alice in Wonderland-goes-medieval, not least when you realise the cats (Henry, Sati and Felix) are kings of this castle, taking up the best seats; ghostly 'sightings' are not uncommon either. Four bedrooms are in the house, four in the cottage through the garden – comfy, cuddly, filled with lovingly collected antique furniture, as is the residents' panelled sitting room on the first floor. One of the doubles is dominated by a vast carved bed, which once belonged to Isambard Kingdom Brunel. Breakfast is stupendous. Children and dogs welcome. *See also p148.*
M4 J17 to Chippenham and Warminster; village is 3 miles S of Chippenham on A350; hotel is at far end of village.

Chilvester Hill House **Offer**

Calne, SN11 0LP (01249 813981/fax 01249 814217/ www.wolsey-lodges.co.uk).
Rates (B&B) *single occupancy* £45-£55; *twin/double* £75-£85. **Rooms** (all en suite) 3 double/twin.
Cards AmEx, DC, V.

Dr and Mrs John Dilley welcome guests into their Victorian family home (a member of the Wolsey Lodge group); it's full of curios, referred to as 'groupies' – check out the white ceramic jelly moulds on the landing. The three large bedrooms are blue, green and pink, and hugely flowery. The Dilleys do dinner from £18; everyone eats together. When it comes to food, Jill (army daugh-

ter and well travelled) likes to mix traditional English with the Middle East. Her wicked breakfasts were given 11 out of 10 by broadcaster Derek Cooper.
Take A4 from Calne towards Chippenham; after 1 mile turn right towards Bremhill and Ratford, then immediately right into hotel driveway.

Fosse Farmhouse

Nettleton Shrub, Nettleton, nr Chippenham, SN14 7NJ (01249 782286/fax 01249 783066/ caroncooper@compuserve.com).
Rates (B&B) *single* £58; *double* £88; *twin* £128; *four-poster* £128; *family* £135. **Rooms** (all en suite) 1 single; 2 double; 1 twin; 1 four-poster/family.
Cards AmEx, MC, V.

Vivacious Caron Cooper bought this derelict cottage by mistake. Not such a mistake, after all: now it's a fairy-tale retreat of French rustic charm and distressed chic; spot the crazy straw animals. Food, country antiques and decoration are Caron's forte. A stay can be tailored to your needs, culinary or otherwise: teas and cakes are served in the rambling gardens, and breakfast, lunch and supper in the dining room. Babies and children welcome. French and, more unusually, Japanese, are spoken.
M4 J17; follow signs to Castle Combe Race Circuit; pass Circuit on left of B4039; continue for 2 miles; arrive at Gib village; first left; 1 mile on right.

Lucknam Park

Colerne, SN14 8AZ (01225 742777/fax 01225 743536/ sales@lucknampark.co.uk/www.lucknampark.co.uk).

Lacock

Just south from Chippenham lies an enchanting antidote to modern living – the National Trust village of **Lacock**. A world within a world, Lacock is, however, a 'living' village that can best be appreciated when the tourists have gone home. Also, there is something charmingly disconcerting about feeling that the cottages could well be film sets. Lacock was indeed a location for *Pride and Prejudice* amongst other productions. The village, with its grid of four streets, remains today largely as it did in the eighteenth century. Stroll around and enjoy the buildings (and pubs): **Cruck House** is the oldest, dating from the fourteenth century and the massive tithe barn has an awesome virgin splendour – nothing converted or tampered with here. The bigger houses were built in the wool-rich days, as Lacock was placed on the 'cloth road' from Bristol to Bath. The **Lacock Bakery** provides gorgeous bread, buns and cakes and for a more lasting

take-away there is fabulous jewellery at the **Watling Goldsmith/Silversmith**.

Lacock Abbey has dominated the village since the thirteenth century. It was turned into a country house in 1539 when a brewery was added and, later, the Great Hall and Gothic archway, while still retaining Abbey elements with the cool cloisters running round its centre. William Fox Talbot made the Abbey his home in 1835 and invented photography here – his negative of the oriel windows is the oldest in existence. There is a museum next to the Abbey where you can see much of his work and wow at his ground-breaking achievements. The Abbey grounds, set within the tranquil meadow of Snaylesmeade where friendly cows loll about, are gorgeous.

Lacock Abbey & Grounds, & the Fox Talbot Museum (01249 730227). **Open** *Mar-Oct museum, grounds, & cloisters* 11am-5.30pm daily; *abbey* 1-5.30pm Mon, Wed-Sun; *Nov-Feb museum only* 11am-5.30pm Sat, Sun. **Admission** (NT) £5.70; £3.10 5s-18s; £15.50 family.

Rates (B&B) *single* £140; *double* £180; *deluxe* £230-£290; *suites* £390-£650; *lodge* £390. Special breaks. **Rooms** (all en suite) 1 single; 11 double; 18 deluxe; 11 suites; 1 lodge. **Cards** AmEx, DC, Debit, MC, V.

A Palladian country house hotel set in 500 acres of parkland, Lucknam Park is the ultimate in luxury escape. It's a magical initiation driving down the mile-long beech-and lime-lined drive, then a seamless check-in into your elegant, individually furnished room. Through the courtyard the gorgeous leisure spa beckons – pool, Jacuzzi, sauna, steam room – and just beyond, the beauty centre, tennis courts and equestrian centre. Unwind still further with afternoon tea by the croquet lawn or a cocktail in the drawing room. This is the stuff of dreams, with discreet staff attending to your every wish. Dinner, not surprisingly, is a lavish affair (*see p149*). Children welcome.

M4 J17; A350 towards Chippenham; take A420 towards Bristol; at Ford village follow signs to Colerne.

Manor House Hotel `Offer`

Castle Combe, SN14 7HR (01249 782206/ fax 01249 782159/enquiries@manor-house.co.uk/ www.manor-house.co.uk).
Rates (cottages) *double* £120-£350; (main house) *deluxe* £265; *four-poster* £285-£350. Breakfast £13 (Eng); £10 (Cont). **Rooms** (all en suite) 21 double/four-poster (main house); 26 double/four-poster (cottages). **Cards** AmEx, MC, V.

The perfect place to play Lord of the Manor or a round of golf. This impressive 'heraldic' traditional hotel, dating back to the fourteenth century, is approached by a sweeping drive over a weir and the trout-stuffed River Bybrook, and sits in 26 acres of grounds, including the romantic Italian gardens. The luxurious rooms, named after fields in the Castle Combe parish, were being upgraded as this guide went to press, with bathrooms being fitted with tellies, phones and rain bar showers. Many beds are four-posters. There's grand feasting in the barn-style restaurant (Sunday lunches are £20 per person and include a staggering cheese choice) and the chef is fond of themed mini-tasters like 'every which way to cook rhubarb and salmon'. Very accomplished and popular. Children welcome. No smoking throughout.

Castle Combe is off B4039.

Rudloe Hall Hotel `Offer`

Leafy Lane, Rudloe, SN13 0PA (01225 810555/ fax 01225 811412/www.rudloehall.co.uk).
Rates (B&B) *single occupancy* £65-£95; *double* £76-£153; *four-poster* £164-£186. **Rooms** (all en suite) 7 double; 4 four-poster. Special breaks.
Cards AmEx, DC, Debit, MC, V.

An exercise in Victorian kooky Gothic, Rudloe is run as a relaxed private house by its thoughtful owners John and May Lyndsey-Walker. The rooms are theatrically melodramatic – experience the grander variety with four posters, bathing alcoves with baths on legs and enjoy undressing behind a screen. Have your own fire lit in your room for £8.95 a day. Check out the relaxing gardens and spectacular vistas towards Bath (Rooms 6, 7 and 9 have the best views). Dinner is £21.95 for three courses and can be taken either in the candlelit dining room or your room. Dogs welcome.

At top of Box Hill on A4 between Box and Corsham (6 miles E of Bath).

Shurnhold House

Shurnhold, Melksham, SN12 8DG (01225 790555/fax 01225 793147).
Rates *double* £68-£78; *four-poster* £78; *family* £88-£98. Breakfast £5.75 (Eng); £3.50 (Cont).
Rooms (all en suite) 6 double; 1 four-poster; 1 family. **Cards** AmEx, Debit, MC, V.

Sue Tanir is the friendly owner of this delightful Jacobean house set within pretty gardens. There are flagstones on the ground floor, cavernous fireplaces, two cosy lounges, a licensed bar and all manner of comforts, including Sky Sports for those who need their fix. Immaculate, crisply decorated rooms. Children and dogs welcome. All bedrooms non-smoking.

1 mile W of Melksham on A365 towards Bath.

Where to eat & drink

There are some cracking boozers in this part of Wiltshire. Some gems are the **Rising Sun** near Lacock up Bowden Hill, the **Six Bells** in Colerne and the **White Horse** in Biddestone. Other musts include the **Quarryman's Arms** at Box (01225 743569) and the **Raven** at Poulshot (01380 828271), both with excellent restaurants, and the **Bear** in Devizes. There are two fantastic local breweries, **Moles** at Melksham and **Wadworths** at Devizes.

Ye Olde Pie Shoppe on Market Street, Devizes, around for donkey's years, is a good tip for a snack. For picnic goodies, try ham, bacon and Tracklements mustards and horseradish from **Michael Richards** on London Road in Calne or some smoked delights from **David Farquhar** at Foxham. Posh high teas are available at **Lucknam Park** and **Manor House Hotel** (for both, *see page 147 & 148*) or more down-to-earth but equally tasty ones at the **Stable Tea Rooms** at Lacock or the **Lock Cottage Tea Rooms** at the top of Caen Hill.

The best food is dominated by English and French cooking, with, perhaps the odd global influence, and a big emphasis on using local produce. There are plenty of wonderful restaurants to choose from, many attached to hotels and pubs.

At the Sign of the Angel

6 Church Street, Lacock, SN15 2LB (01249 730230).
Food served 7-9.30pm Mon; noon-2.30pm, 7-9.30pm, Tue-Sun.

Interconnecting dining rooms with roaring fires and wobbly beams contribute to the homey, oaky atmosphere here. Most veg and herbs are grown in the garden and contribute to the hearty, trad English fare. It's around £25 for a strapping good meal – starters such as crevettes with oriental sauces and pigeon terrine and damson, excellent roasts, beef and lamb, and good ol' English afters like blackberry and apple crumble. The house red is a winner. *See also p146.*

Stone me

Avebury was the greatest achievement in prehistoric Europe. More organic than Stonehenge (and you can get up close and personal too), the stones, village and landscape live together in a curious and spooky way. The stones attract all types of people, among them druids and credulous coach parties. How you interpret the stones is up to you – you may choose to throw yourself full-on into the whole spiritual thing, or simply enjoy playing 'what does that one look like? A monkey or a banana?'.

Avebury, originally built as a sun temple, was a real mecca for ritual worship and assembly. There were 200 stones here at one time; now only 27 remain – most smashed to pieces in the seventeenth and eighteenth centuries and used to build Avebury village and neighbouring farms. There was an outer and two inner circles, surrounded by a massive bank and ditch, connected by the West Kennet Avenue of standing stones to the Sanctuary on Overton Hill. The ditch may have been filled with water, not as a barricade but to symbolise the site as a holy island. As the centuries rolled by, pagan rites were taken over by Christian holy days. Today, though, the stones have been leased to freedom of expression: anything goes – pagan, secular or otherwise. The Henge Shop (open daily) wastes no opportunity to cash in on the popularity of the site – it's a veritable crystal-fest, with added temptations from dousing sticks (although a coat hanger seems to do the trick just as well) to chunks of semi-precious who-knows-what. Laugh at your peril.

George & Dragon
High Street, Rowde (01380 723053).
Food served noon-2pm, 7-10pm, Tue-Sat.
Cards Debit, MC, V.

Helen and Tim Withers run a top-quality restaurant renowned for its fish. It looks like a pub but don't be put off – the food is the thing; setting and decoration nowt special. Set lunches are fantastic value at £8.50 for two courses or £10 for three. The fresh market fish is delivered from Cornwall at least twice a week. Hannah and Katie, the chefs, have an instinct for creating delicious dishes that do not overpower – excellent crab and asparagus salad and lemon sole. A quiet atmosphere; everyone's too busy stuffing their faces to talk.

George Inn
4 West Street, Lacock (01249 730263).
Food served noon-2pm, 6-9pm, daily.
Cards Debit, MC, V.

A buzzing and jolly thirteenth-century pub. John Glass, a 'natural born landlord', loves to show you the old dog-wheel in the fireplace that once turned a spit. Portions are huge and prices reasonable (dishes around £4 at lunch; £12 in the evening). The menu offers no elaborate explanations – there's the like of swordfish steak with boozy mango sauce, Wiltshire Ham salad and treacle sponge. Mrs Natural Born Landlady runs Lower Home Farm, the B&B up the road, providing free transport to the pub for guests (01225 790045; single £25; double £40).

Lucknam Park
Colerne (01225 742777).
Food served 7.30-9.30pm Mon-Thur, Sun; 7-10pm Fri, Sat. **Set meal** £40 (3 courses). **Cards** AmEx, DC, Debit, MC, V.

The old ballroom of this swanky pad (*see p147*), now the dining room, is lavish with contemporary dashes, such as clay pots filled with herbs and flowers on tables. A battalion of waiters make service instinctive, and helps to foster an intimate mood. The food is exquisite; each course perfectly balanced down to final petit four – top marks to Head Chef and rising star Paul Collins (his appetisers include humorous touches like a mini bangers and mash). Wild mushroom consommé to start, followed by poached guinea fowl with noodles, and apple tart, rum and raisin ice-cream to finish – were all divine on a recent visit. There's an impressive special veggie menu with six starters and six mains. As you might expect, such top-notch nosh does not come cheap: be prepared to part with £20 for a main course.

Pear Tree
Top Lane, Whitley (01225 709131).
Food served noon-2pm, 6.30-9pm, Mon-Thur, Sun; noon-2pm, 6.30-9.30pm, Fri, Sat. **Set meals** *lunch* £8.95 (2 courses); £10.95 (3 courses). **Cards** DC, Debit, MC, V.

Despite fears from villagers of losing their darts and skittles local, Martin and Debbie Stills have triumphed in turning the Pear Tree into a class-act restaurant at the back serving Modern British fusion (Med and Far East) food, which won *The Publican*'s Catering Pub of the Year award 1999. Up front is the thriving pub. The interior is decorated with rustic curiosities and warm muted colours and the tables are well spaced and intimate; thankfully, too, it's a muzak-free zone. The menu might include such dishes as roasted duck breast with an apple and celeriac mash (£11.25) and Pimms cheesecake with a strawberry and mint compôte (£4.75). The set lunch is excellent value.

Stones
off High Street, Avebury (01672 539514).
Food served 10am-6pm daily. **Cards** Debit, MC, V.
The other famous Avebury Stones are of the vegetarian restaurant kind run by the charming Mike Pitts. The no-frills décor keeps the mind focused on the toothsome home-made, mostly organic and home-grown food from the garden, where you can sit and eat. Hot lunches are served every day; £7 buys a feast, such as egg hog with divine salad, home-made lemonade or Stonehenge Ale and a chocolate cherry Tiffin cake. Expect queues on Sundays and Summer Solstice. Children are welcome.

White Hart
Ford, nr Chippenham (01249 782213).
Food served noon-2pm, 7-9.30pm, daily.
Cards AmEx, Debit, MC, V.
This sixteenth-century Lionheart inn has bags of individual charm and a lovely setting with trout stream, ducks, pretty gardens and very comfortable reasonably priced (mostly four-poster) accommodation (single occupancy £59; double £79) separate from the pub. Sample ten real ales and two ciders including 'Black Rat', play pool on a revolving round table and eat superb food in the restaurant from chef Tony Farmer. Dinner is £20-£25 and might include ham hock, pork knuckle and black pudding to start and rack of lamb for a main, or at lunchtime cold roast beef for a fiver.

What to see & do

Tourist information centres
Avebury (01672 539425). **Open** 10am-5pm Wed-Sun.
The Citadel, Bath Road, **Chippenham**, SN15 2AA (01249 706333). **Open** *Apr-Oct* 9am-5.30pm Mon-Sat; *Nov-Mar* 9am-5pm Mon-Sat.
Cromwell House, The Market Place, **Devizes**, SN10 1JG (01380 729408). **Open** *Apr-Oct* 9.30am-5pm Mon-Sat; *Nov-Mar* 9.30am-4.30pm Mon-Sat.
An interactive exhibition takes you back to the twelfth century, when the town boasted what was said to be the finest castle in Europe, and was at the centre of a struggle between Empress Matilda and King Stephen for the English throne.
Church Street, **Melksham**, SN12 6LS (01225 707424).
Open *Apr-Oct* 9am-5pm Mon-Fri; 9.30am-4.30pm Sat; *Nov-Mar* 9.30am-4.30pm Mon-Fri; 10am-4pm Sat.

Bike hire
MJ Hiscock Cycles 59 Northgate Street, **Devizes** (01380 722236).

Alexander Kieller Museum
Avebury (01672 539250).
Open *Apr-Oct* 10am-6pm daily; *Nov-Mar* 10am-4pm daily. **Admission** (NT) £1.70; 80p 5s-16s.
Founded in the 1930s, this museum – the only one in the country devoted solely to the study of Stone Age excavation – displays many of the thrilling bits and bobs from the great archaeologist's excavations on Windmill Hill, north-west of Avebury. Note the curious curled remains of a child buried 5,000 years ago in a ditch below the hill.

Atwell Wilson Motor Museum Trust
Stockley Lane, Calne (01249 813119).
Open *Apr-Oct* 11am-5pm Mon-Thur, Sun; *Nov-Mar* 11am-4pm Mon-Thur, Sun.
Admission £2.50; £1 4s-14s; £2 OAPs, students.
Vintage classic cars and motorcycles from 1924 to 1983, lovingly restored and in perfect running order.

Avebury Manor
Avebury (01672 539250).
Open *gardens Apr-Oct* 11am-5.30pm Tue, Wed, Sat-Sun, bank hols; *house Apr-Oct* 2-5.30pm Tue, Wed, Sun, bank hols. **Admission** (NT) £3; £1.50 5s-16s.
Dating from 1550, Avebury Manor was extended in the seventeenth century, and is now set in grounds containing a formal Monk's Garden, topiary, fine borders, a wishing well and fountains. Charles II and Queen Anne stayed here.

Bowood House & Gardens
Off A4 at Derry Hill, between Calne and Chippenham (01249 812102/www.bowood-estate.co.uk).
Open *Apr-Oct* 11am-6pm daily.
Admission £5.50; £3.20 5s-15s; £4.50 OAPs.
Home of the Earl and Countess of Shelburne, Bowood was built in 1625. Two of the house's claims to fame are that Dr Joseph Priestly discovered oxygen here in 1774 and that Napoleon's death mask is on show. Capability Brown sculpted the gardens, with lawns running down to a long lake, grottoes, cascades and caves. The highlight in May and June are the astounding rhododendron walks. There's a fabulous treehouse adventure playground, and lovely teas and lunches.

Corsham Court
Off Church Street, Corsham (01249 701610).
Open *Jan-Mar, Oct, Nov* 2-4pm Sat, Sun; *Apr-Sept* 11am-5pm Tue-Sun.
This one-time royal manor in the days of the Saxon kings is currently home to the Methuen family. The core of the house is Elizabethan, dating back to 1582, and contains more than 140 paintings and statues. In the Capability Brown-designed grounds is a fine Gothic bathhouse. The house was the backdrop for the film *Remains of the Day*.

Devizes Museum
41 Long Street (01380 727369).
Open 10am-5pm Mon-Sat. **Admission** £2; 50p 5s-16s; £1.50 OAPs, students; £4.50 family.
Owned by the Wiltshire Archaeological and Natural History Society, the museum boasts one of the finest prehistoric collections in Europe.

Malmesbury & around

Walking, lazing, drinking, grazing.

Malmesbury Abbey – *the heart of the town. See page 155.*

ocals never tire of telling you that **Malmesbury** is the oldest borough in Britain, but few know what makes this fact so very significant. The best story about the town concerns the flying monk St Elmer, who leapt from the 620-foot west tower of the Abbey in 1010 in a home-made glider. To his credit, he travelled more than a furlong before becoming 'agitated by the violence of the wind and awareness of his rashness'. He broke both legs on landing. However, he reportedly lived happily ever after, so much so that he was barred from further vertiginous stunts and turned to astronomy instead.

With the exception of Elmer and certain other hedonistic monks in the Abbey's history, the people of Malmesbury have been a peaceable, undistinguished lot. The great and probably only exception is the philosopher Thomas Hobbes, who was born in Charlton, north-east of the town, in 1588. Anyone not believing there can be so little to this ancient borough should refer to Dr Bernulf Hodge's spirited pamphlet 'A History of Malmesbury', available from the tourist information centre in the Town Hall.

Malmesbury and the surrounding area is the perfect destination for a non-touristy, lazy weekend for those content with not doing a great deal. The characteristic honey-coloured stone buildings are pretty, but this is not an area of outstanding architectural interest. Happily, the **Cotswold Water Park** towards Cirencester keeps most activity maniacs occupied in one location and leaves the rest of us to mooch about doing little more than eat, sleep and, most importantly, drink. If that is what you fancy, this is the place for you.

Wiltshire & Bath

Go west

This area is divided east and west by the A429 and it is the west side, where Malmesbury and Tetbury are found, that is markedly more pastoral. In Malmesbury itself there is the largely ruined, partially used Abbey, an elaborately vaulted market cross of 1490 providing shelter from rain and the Abbey House gardens, with their 2,000 types of rose. And that's about it.

Likewise, the appeal of the pretty town of **Tetbury** is chiefly its comely appearance. The central feature is the Market House, built on stilts in 1655 as a sheltered market. The Georgian Gothic church of St Mary the Virgin, with the fourth-highest spire in England (built 1777-81) is worth a look. Certainly there is a profusion of antique shops and three good tearooms (notably the cosy Tetbury Gallery Tea Room, 18 Market Place; 01666 503412).

Where to stay

1 Cove House

Ashton Keynes, SN6 6NS (01285 861226).
Rates (B&B) £25-£32pp. **Rooms** (both en suite) 1 double; 1 twin.

Valerie Threlfall's colourful personality is stamped all over this beautifully appointed and femininely decorated manor house crouching behind a thick beard of green ivy. Val has a passion for interior design with a colourfully floral spin that reaches its apotheosis in the cosy red dining room lined with William Morris wallpaper. She is enormously warm and friendly, but you can seek out your own company in the sitting room in the bright attic or under the magnificent 250-year-old copper beech on the lawn, which rolls up to the unique ballroom, which is now occasionally used for concerts. Children welcome. No smoking throughout.
A419 towards Cirencester; follow signs for Cotswold Water Park and Ashton Keynes; turn left at White Hart pub, then left into driveway behind stone wall.

Calcot Manor

nr Tetbury, GL8 8YJ (01666 890391/fax 01666 890394/reception@calcotmanor.com).
Rates (B&B) *single occupancy* £105*; twin/double* £120-£140*; deluxe double/twin* £165*; family suites* £170. Special breaks. **Rooms** (all en suite) 6 double/twin; 12 deluxe double/twin; 10 family suites. **Cards** AmEx, DC, MC, V.

'A better class of people' stay at Calcot Manor, confided the proprietor of a local guesthouse. Sure enough: a nobbier sort of person (many proudly sporting a royal blue rinse) was found milling around in the manor's halls. Rooms are decently proportioned, smartly and prettily decorated (satisfying both corporate and private tastes) in soft colours, and some feature whirlpool baths for the more sybaritic. An excellent breakfast provides a good variation on the often all-too-full English breakfast. Facilities for those willing to struggle out of bed but who wish to stay in the verdant grounds include a croquet lawn, swimming pool and tennis courts. Children are competently catered for in the hotel's playroom.
A46 towards Stroud; after 12 miles turn right on to A4135 towards Tetbury; hotel is immediately on left.

Crudwell Court

Crudwell, nr Malmesbury, SN16 9EP (01666 577194/fax 01666 577853/crudwellcourt@compuserve.com).
Rates (B&B) *single* £50; *single occupancy* £60; *double/twin* £88; *double* £105-£114. Special breaks.
Rooms (all en suite) 2 single; 9 double/twin; 4 deluxe double/twin. **Cards** AmEx, DC, Debit, MC, V.

This crumbly seventeenth-century rectory is panelled and decorated in a soft Georgian style. Bedrooms are spacious if ordinarily furnished, but their best feature is the views of the floodlit lily pond gardens and neighbouring church. Nick Bristow, the owner, is fiercely proud of a hotel that is also his home (though the well-lived-in feel does tend to border on the slightly tired). The prettiness of the village and the gardens, which include a heated swimming pool, are ample compensation. *See also p153.*
J17 off M4; Crudwell Court is 3 miles N of Malmesbury on A429; next to church.

Manor Farmhouse

Crudwell, nr Malmesbury, SN16 9ER (01666 577375/fax 01666 823523).
Rates (B&B) £22.50-£25pp.
Rooms 1 double (en suite); 1 triple.

A good, clean, well-run, flagstone-floored B&B next to the manor house and church of the village. Owner Helen Carter runs a smart ship and avoids the flouncy touches that too often see 'homely' B&Bs garnished with chintz and teddy bears. Décor is therefore restrained; rooms have views of cows and the churchyard and gardens. Mrs Carter also bakes her own bread in the Aga and grows her own organic vegetables, which are often used in dishes as part of dinner (a very reasonable £15; BYOB). There is a tennis court in the garden with a rough tarmac surface. No smoking throughout.
3 miles N of Malmesbury on A429; turn right at Plough Inn in Crudwell; immediate left after church; house is behind church.

Manor Hill House

Purton, nr Swindon, SN5 9EG (01793 772311/fax 01793 772396).
Rates (B&B) *single* £35; *double/twin/four-poster* £44.
Rooms (all en suite) 2 single; 3 double; 1 twin; 1 four-poster.

*Malmesbury's venerable **Old Bell.***

An ivy-covered, Victorian house in the countryside near Purton. Filled with Victoriana and pictures, the house feels like a Victorian picture, with dark interiors pierced by strong light coming in through the windows. The brooding hallway with coloured tiles and an open fire leads to a reading room, dining room and TV room. The main feature, however, is the chunky farmhouse kitchen built round an Aga and a huge table, where breakfast is served. The rooms are smallish but bright and prettily decorated, each with varying en suite facilities and satellite TV. Children welcome. All bedrooms non-smoking.
M4 J16; towards Wootton Bassett; take Hook to Purton Road 2nd exit; follow road to main roundabout; take 3rd exit to Hook; through village; right at T junction to Lydiard Millicent; follow road to mini roundabout; take turning to Purton; house is 0.5 miles on right.

Old Bell
Abbey Row, Malmesbury, SN16 0AG (01666 822344/ fax 01666 825145/www.luxury-family-hotels.co.uk).
Rates (B&B) *single* £68-£75; *double* £95-£110; *deluxe* £130-£180. **Rooms** (all en suite) 3 single; 13 double; 15 deluxe double. **Cards** AmEx, DC, Debit, MC, V.

The most prestigious hotel in the district is set in a rambling old building plumb by the remains of the famous Abbey. In the main house, the hotel is filled with sturdy Victorian furnishings and illuminated by recessed mullioned windows. It features a comfortable lobby, a stately dining room and more cosy bistro bar furnished in dark wood. The Victorian solemnity of the main building contrasts with the coach house where the proprietors have created a similarly pared-down, faux-Japanese extension. Bedroom furnishings are consistent with these themes; in the main house the free-standing baths in spacious bathrooms hold much recumbent promise. Children are provided Z-beds at no extra charge and there is a well-appointed indoor playroom and playground to the rear of the main building. Dogs welcome.
A429 to Malmesbury; Old Bell is next to Abbey.

St Adhelm's
14 Gloucester Street, Malmesbury, SN16 0AA (01666 822145).
Rates (B&B) £22.50pp. **Rooms** 1 twin (en suite).

A thoroughly agreeable retreat in the centre of town, run by the friendly and urbane Batstones. The house is a pretty Georgian terrace, and the interior decoration is plain but light and attractive. The house is pleasantly infused with the smell of books thanks to a high-brow library. To the rear of the airy, white bathroom is a nicely kept garden and soothing views of the River Avon and rolling countryside. There is only one room so service is very personal – though the owners are very keen not to impose. Breakfast (with sausages and bacon from the impressive organic butcher over the road) is served in a delightful galleried dining room. No smoking throughout.
A429 to Malmesbury town centre; left at Market Cross at top of High Street; house is in angle by traffic mirror.

Whatley Manor
Easton Grey, Malmesbury, SN16 0RB (01666 822888/fax 01666 826120).
Rates (B&B) *Manor House: single occupancy* £96; *double/twin* £132; *Court House: single occupancy* £82; *double/twin* £96. Special breaks. **Rooms** (all en suite) 29 double/twin. **Cards** AmEx, DC, Debit, MC, V.

There's an Agatha Christie feel to this sprawling neo-Gothic, wood-panelled mansion-complex largely built in the 1920s by a wealthy polo enthusiast. But far from being murdered by Miss Scarlet in the library with the lead piping, you're more likely to enjoy a bath in the large en suite tubs in the bathrooms that adjoin the spacious bedrooms. There is a slight fustiness to some of the rooms and some of the 'period' furnishings could do with the attentions of an upholsterer, but this is all part of the hotel's eerie charm. The size and location (tucked away in a wooded dale) make the hotel an attractive corporate destination, but its anonymity also makes it an ideal hideaway. There is no shortage of facilities for the more outward bound – heated pool, tennis court, croquet lawn, billiard table and walks round the nearby infant Avon.
On B4040; 3 miles E of Malmesbury.

Where to eat & drink

In addition to the places below, **Whatley Manor** has an ambitious, if slightly pretentious restaurant; the **Pear Tree** at Church End, Purton (01793 772100), offers acclaimed Modern European cooking; the **Three Crowns** at Brinkworth (01666 510366) has a good line in snappy dishes like sautéed crocodile; and the **Horse & Groom** in Charlton (01666 823904) serves better-than-average pub grub.

Crudwell Court
Crudwell, nr Malmesbury (01666 577194).
Food served noon-2pm, 7.30-9pm, daily. **Set meals** *lunch* £8.50 (2 courses); *dinner* £19.50-£25.95. **Cards** AmEx, DC, Debit, MC, V.

Unusually, this esteemed no-smoking restaurant, set in an elegantly panelled room painted in creamy tones, has a unique pricing system. At first, you might baulk at the idea of paying £23.50 for grilled breast of duck with orange and thyme sauce, or £22 for pork medallions with wild mushroom sauce. Then you realise that this includes a choice of six starters, including fish terrine, pigeon breast and spinach in puff pastry, along with a good selection of English desserts (toffee pudding, pear and almond flan and so on). A good selection of wines, however, will soon loosen the purse strings. *See also p152.*

Gumstool Inn
Calcot Manor, nr Tetbury (01666 890391).
Food served noon-2pm, 7-9.30pm, Mon-Fri; noon-9.30pm Sat, Sun. **Cards** AmEx, DC, MC, V.

Whether you're dining in the smart, bright conservatory or in the crypto-rustic modern extension they call the Gumstool Inn, this is one of the more well-heeled eateries in the region. Both are fed by the same kitchen – the cooking is a little more rarefied in the conservatory, while the moderately priced Gumstool bistro provides a fine spread, which can be enjoyed out on the patio. Here, the cuisine ranges from devilled lamb's kidneys to Thai-spiced crab cakes for starters (£5-£6) and from char-grilled swordfish to a rich sausage and mash for mains (£9-£10). There is a good selection of classic wines in the Gumstool, and two tasty real ales on tap, all of which are also very reasonably priced for this kind of chichi establishment. *See also p152.*

Walk this way...

As the attentive reader will have discerned, Malmesbury is not the most exciting corner of the planet. So, hooray: you can stay in bed with a clear conscience. Alternatively, you can haul yourself out from under the sheets and go walking. Shoul you need any incentive for pulling on hiking boots, you'll be pleased to hear that the West Country has some of the best pubs and ales in the land. Here follow some ideas for rambling routes. The local tourist information centres have plenty of additional information.

Ways to go: the **Cotswold Way** – a 100-mile trek from Chipping Campden to Bath. The **Macmillan Way** – a 200-mile route from Rutland to Dorset. **Monarchs Way** – 610 miles from Worcester to Shoreham.

Cotswold Water Park (*see page 155*) – Apart from its 132 lakes, the park includes a nature reserve for those who would rather navigate terra firma.

Crop Circles – Folk can be more than a little kooky in these parts and Wiltshire is the undeclared capital of the crop circle world. Apparently, these phenomena 'appear' most frequently near ancient monuments and 'other sites with powerful natural energies'. Often located on private land, it is worth seeking permission from the owners if you don't want to be shot at by irate farmers whose subsidised crops you and the aliens may be destroying.

Lydiard Park (*see page 155*) – Pleasant Capability Brown-inspired grounds and woodlands around the Georgian mansion.

Town Trails – Malmesbury has a historic trail and a signposted two-mile riverside walk following the two branches of the surrounding River Avon. Both walks are set out in leaflets available at the tourist information centre in the Town Hall.

Westonbirt Arboretum (*see page 155*) In this arboreal paradise there are 17 miles of waymarked trails through the 600 acres of landscaped countryside.

Le Flambé

7-9 Gloucester Street, Malmesbury (01666 824545). **Food served** 7-10pm Mon, Sat; noon-2pm, 7-10pm, Tue-Fri. **Set meals** *lunch* £7.95 (2 courses), £10.50 (3 courses); *dinner* £18.75 (3 courses). **Cards** AmEx, Debit, MC, V.

Run by Canary Islands expat Manuel Pinero Paz, this a dark, intimate, trinket-full interior for a Mediterranean restaurant employing the venerable '70s tradition of flambé-ing as its core gimmick. However, it's not just tableside theatrics that pull the punters in – the overall choice of dishes is broad and attractive. The à la carte menu includes such delights as lemon sole poached in white wine with lobster sauce or rack of lamb in rosemary sauce (both £11.50). Trademark flambéed steaks diane and au poivre are about £12.

Old Bell

Abbey Row, Malmesbury (01666 822344). **Food served** 10am-10pm Mon-Sat. **Set meals** *lunch* £11.75 (2 courses), £15 (3 courses); *dinner* £19.75 (3 courses). **Cards** AmEx, DC, Debit, MC, V.

The Old Bell is considered by many locals to be *the* place to dine but, we were warned, service can be slow. The canny diner eats in the less-expensive bar-side bistro, which serves the same modern English cooking as the formal and imposing main dining room. It ain't cheap: a three-course roast Sunday lunch costs £16. The full dinner menu weighs in at £26 and has such mouth-watering prospects as raviolo of duck rillete and daube of beef with sweet potato mash and béarnaise sauce.

Rattlebone

Church Street, Sherston (01666 840871). **Food served** noon-2pm, 7-10pm, daily. **Set meals** *lunch* £9.95 (3 courses) Sun. **Cards** AmEx, Debit, MC, V.

A classic, unaffected, real McCoy, dark, olde-worlde inn. Not only does it offer an unusually fine selection of real ales and a promising battery of wines to be imbibed beside open fires, but locals also sing its praises as a restaurant. Starters at £3-£5 are good staples (pancakes, prawn fritters, pâté, etc), while, aside from daily specials, there is a plethora of mains for £6-£10 (from steak and kidney pie to a more nimble pasta with tomato sauce). Which is to say nothing of the home-made crumble, which heads the list of desserts (£3). Good food; great value.

Smoking Dog

62 High Street, Malmesbury (01666 825823). **Food served** noon-2pm, 7-9.30pm, daily. **Cards** AmEx, Debit, MC, V.

The people's choice in Malmesbury town, this is a good, simple, chatty pub with a chunky pine-furnished restaurant to the rear adorned with violently coloured pictures of shellfish. The menu enables you to mix light pastas and salads (both around £6-£7) or stuffed ciabattas (around £5) with main meals. Starters (including chargrilled calf's liver with rocket) are about £5 and mains (including blackened salmon creole or roast asparagus with couscous and lime) are £9-£13. The quality of cooking is reasonable even if service is more casual than you might like. Wines are basic but more competitively priced.

Vine Tree

Foxley Road, Norton, nr Malmesbury (01666 837654).
Food served noon-2pm, 7-9.30pm, daily.
Cards Debit, MC, V.

A good, unspoilt, flagstone-floored country boozer popular with locals and having a robust menu. Inside it's all
nooks and crannies, painted in strong, dark colours, and
round the back there's a paved beer garden. Starters for
under a fiver encompass wild boar sausages and moules
marinières, while mains for £8-£14 might feature puff
pastry vegetarian turnover, venison steak with cranberry sauce and fillet of beef with green peppercorn sauce.
Alternatively, get stuck into the real ales at the bar.

What to see & do

Tourist information centres

Town Hall, **Malmesbury**, SN16 9BZ (01666 823748).
Open *Easter-Sept* 9am-4.30pm Mon-Fri; 9am-4pm
Sat; *Oct-Easter* 9am-4.30pm Mon-Fri.

33 Church Street, **Tetbury**, GL8 8JG (01666 503552/
www.tetbury.org.uk). **Open** *Easter-Oct* 9.30am-
4.30pm Mon-Sat; *Nov-Easter* 11am-2pm Mon-Sat

Abbey House Gardens

Malmesbury (01666 822212).
Open *Easter-Oct* 11am-6pm daily.
Admission (NT) £3; £1 5s-15s.

A horticultural Eden, with five acres of gardens around
a late Tudor house next to the Abbey. Star attractions are
the 2,000 varieties of rose and similar number of herbs.

Cotswold Water Park

Spratsgate Lane, nr Somerford Keynes
(01285 861459/www.waterpark.org).
Open 9am-9pm daily. **Admission** free; phone for
details of activities.

No weekend, dirty or otherwise, would be complete without a spot of splashing about and so they invented
Britain's biggest water park. There is a ridiculous number of water-borne activities available on the 132 lakes
fashioned out of gravel quarries – sailing, canoeing,
windsurfing, water- and jet-skiing, sub-aqua diving,
power boating, coarse and fly fishing. Aquaphobes can
go walking, cycling, play golf or tennis, go horse riding,
settle down for wildlife- and bird-watching or visit the
shop or fossil exhibition. Children get to frolic in their
own beach and play area. The less energetic can sun-
bathe or simply spectate from the cafés and picnic sites.
Activities should be booked well in advance.

Lydiard House & Church

Lydiard Park, Lydiard Tregoze, nr Swindon
(01793 770401).
Open *Mar-June* 10am-1pm, 2-5pm, Mon-Sat; *July-
Sept* 10am-5pm Mon-Sat; 2-5pm Sun; *Nov-Feb* 10am-
1pm, 2-4pm, Mon-Sat. **Admission** £1.20; 60p 5s-16s.

Tucked away behind unlovely industrial estates and
new-town closes is this impressive Georgian residence
in elegant grounds. Beware: it is hard to find and there
are only six restored rooms for your admission fee. Also,
the key to the church must be booked and the St John
Triptych (a remarkable family portrait from 1615) can
only be viewed by prior appointment.

Malmesbury Abbey

Malmesbury (01666 826666/823126).
Open *Apr-Oct* 10am-6pm daily; *Nov-Mar* 10am-4pm
daily. **Admission** (EH) free; £2 suggested donation.

Time has not been kind to the Abbey, founded in the seventh century as a Benedictine monastery by St Aldhelm.
Three hundred years after its consecration in 1180 the
spire fell in and, following years of neglect by libertine
monks (one abbot was killed in a drunken brawl) and the
Dissolution of the monasteries in 1579, the site was sold.
It was then returned to the people of Malmesbury as a
parish church and now also functions more or less as a
retired people's social club. However, one or two features
make it worth a visit: the fabulously carved Norman arch
and the gloriously illuminated Bible of 1407.

Westonbirt Arboretum

Westonbirt, nr Tetbury
(01666 880220/www.forestry.gov.uk/westonbirt).
Open 10am-8pm daily. **Admission** £3.80;
£1 5s-16s; £3 OAPs.

This world-famous tree sanctuary (established in 1829)
features some 18,000 varieties of tree and shrub. It's
renowned for its huge banks of rhododendrons, azaleas
and magnolias as well as the Autumn Spectacular (which
lasts until mid-October), when seasonal changes produce
magnificent vistas of red, orange and gold. By night there
are musical events, fireworks and a walk along a mile-
long illuminated stretch called 'The Enchanted Wood'.

Trees are good at **Westonbirt Arboretum.**

The Cotswolds

STRATFORD & WARWICK
(page 174)

CHIPPING NORTON
TO BANBURY
(page 200)

WOODSTOCK
TO BURFORD
(page 194)

NORTH CHILTERNS
(page 214)

SOUTH
OXFORDSHIRE
(page 188)

OXFORD
(page 180)

NORTH
COTSWOLDS
(page 169)

CHELTENHAM
TO STOW
(page 163)

MALMESBURY
& AROUND
(page 151)

CIRENCESTER
TO GLOUCESTER
(page 157)

NORTHAMPTONSHIRE

BUCKINGHAM-SHIRE

OXFORDSHIRE

WARWICKSHIRE

WORCESTERSHIRE

GLOUCESTER-SHIRE

HEREFORD

MONMOUTH-SHIRE

© Copyright Time Out Group 1999

15 miles

25 km

Cirencester to Gloucester

The Cotswolds without tears.

The heart-stoppingly lovely **Painswick Valley** *above* **Cranham**.

For those who love the Cotswolds but hate the hordes of daytrippers who feel the same, this slice of glorious country balanced on the edge of the Gloucestershire Cotswold Hills is heaven. Between the Roman towns of Cirencester (Corinium) and Gloucester (Glevum) there's a fabulous spread of stonkingly beautiful countryside, historic houses, ancient sites and good eating and drinking.

By train from London

Trains from **Paddington** to **Gloucester** leave at least hourly (journey time is about **2hrs**) and every hour to **Stroud** (journey time is **1hr 30mins**). Trains from **Paddington** to **Kemble** leave hourly and take **1hr 30mins**; a linking bus service runs to **Cirencester**, four miles away.

The area is anything but isolated: the M4 and M5 aren't far away, there are major towns in abundance and a significant rural population. Yet there's a beguiling intimacy to this historically key corner of the country, perched on the doorstep of Wales and the South-West. The Cotswold Way bisects the region, meandering along woodland-clad ridges overlooking sheltered valleys, which are at their most seductive, perhaps, in the area around **Painswick**. This gem of a town ('Queen of the Cotswolds'), tumbling down the side of the valley, is hardly undiscovered yet has valiantly resisted the onslaught of the tearooms. The town centres on the Church of St Mary and its extraordinary churchyard, famed for its altar tombs and 99 yew trees (the oldest dating back to 1792); standing sentinel, they are trimmed into rather eerie shapes and, according to legend, are impossible to count (although that does beg a question...). Close by is Dennis French's wonderful shop Painswick Woodcrafts (New Street; 01452 814195), managed by his friendly, chatty wife. Dennis has been working in wood for more than 50 years, and his expertise shows in beautiful domestic pieces such as bowls and cheeseboards. Another must-see is the unique **Painswick Rococo Garden**.

A tour of the easy-going neighbouring villages of **Edge**, **Sheepscombe** and **Slad** is rewarding. If you've heard of the latter, chances are it is through the childhood recollections of Laurie Lee's *Cider with Rosie*. Lee grew up in Slad and was a long-time regular at the Woolpack. It's still a likeable, down-to-earth (and tiny) pub, even though the current owners are making more of its Lee connections than previously. Another (irregular) delight of Slad is Gill Wyatt Smith's **Yew Tree Gallery** (Steanbridge Lane; 01452 813601). A couple of times a year she turns her home into a display space for artists and craftsmen from all over the country; the range and quality of work, particularly ceramics, jewellery and painting/collage work, is superb. The gallery is open by appointment if an exhibition is not currently running. **Prinknash Abbey Park**, between here and Gloucester, offers the al fresco ecclesiastically inspired delights of birds, deer, fine walks and monk-made pottery.

Why did Dr Foster go to Gloucester?

Gloucester was described by Dickens as 'a wonderful and misleading city' and in some strange way, and despite what locals might say, it still is. It's actually a rather downmarket, working town but this is refreshing after the tweeness of nearby Cheltenham (*see page 163*) and most of the Cotswolds. Much of the centre is blighted by utterly characterless modern development, and strolling the streets is hardly a joy. Yet there are gems to be uncovered – the most rewarding of which is the wonderful Cathedral. The restored Victorian docks are also well worth a look. Within the buildings are the National Waterways Museum, the Museum of Advertising & Packaging and the Gloucester Antiques Centre, home to 90 dealers. The Gloucester City Museum & Art Gallery is also worth a visit.

Cirencester & around

Around 20 miles south-east of Gloucester lies the agreeable small town of **Cirencester**. A considerable leap of imagination is required to picture this gentle local centre as the one-time capital city of the Dobunni tribe and then the strategically vital Roman town of Corinium, commanding the juncture of the Fosse Way, Ermine Street and Akeman Street. It was once the second-largest Roman city in the country after London; the population today is little more than 15,000, but there is plenty of evidence of Cirencester's heyday. The Corinium Museum is the best source of Roman relics. To the west of the town are the remains of the second-century BC Roman amphitheatre. The other main sight in town is the wonderful 'wool' Church of St John the Baptist on Market Place, with its elaborate Perpendicular-style porch (around 1500).

Church lovers also shouldn't miss a tour of the **Dunt Valley**, just north-west of Cirencester off the A417, where there's a succession of superb small churches in villages such as **Elkstone**, **Winstone**, **Syde** and **Duntisbourne Rouse**.

Cirencester to the Severn

From Cirencester heading towards Stroud, it's through Royal country (Prince Charles's Highgrove and Princess Anne's Gatcombe Park are nearby) down into the **Golden Valley** (River Frome). The grand project for a canal joining the Severn and the Thames was completed in 1789 and immodestly but not inaccurately described by its own PR as 'an elaborate and stupendous work of art'. Its high point (literally) is the Sapperton Tunnel, running more than two miles through the Cotswold limestone. Stop at **Chalford**: pick up the old towpath and walk east up a delightful wooded valley to the tunnel portal (just under four miles there and back). Always short of water, the last boat went over the top in 1911, so don't expect much activity on what water remains, but there's plenty of wildlife and a pub at the halfway point.

Stroud is a working town, surprisingly into 'green alternative', but with little to appeal to visitors (although Moonflower and Moonflower Too on the High Street are worth a look, for appealing clothes, jewellery and gifts). The region to the south of the town is more densely populated than that to the north, but still well worth exploring. **Nailsworth** (almost a suburb of Stroud) is a sleepy little town, but does contain a number of surprises including two good restaurants, a cool shop called Krayfish (London House, Market Street; 01453 836656) selling some great 1950s knick-knacks and furniture, and progressive house and trance most Fridays and Saturdays at the Cross Inn (Market Street; 01453 836908).

There's bags of culture to be discovered in these parts, from the remnants of an Iron Age hill fort at **Uley** and the nearby long barrow (the magnificently named **Hetty Pegler's Tump**; both off the B4066), through Tudor **Owlpen Manor** to the spooky unfinished Victorian

*Lost in the **Dunt Valley**...*

masterpiece of **Woodchester Mansion** (*see page 161*). West of here the country flattens as it reaches the Severn – a perfect environment for a spot of twitching at the **Slimbridge Wildfowl & Wetlands Trust**.

Where to stay

Cardynham House

The Cross, Painswick, GL6 6XX (01452 814006/fax 01452 812321).
Rates (B&B) £27.50-£50pp. **Rooms** (all en suite) 9 double/twin/four-poster/family. **Cards** Debit, MC, V.
A stunner. Californian Carol Keyes has decorated every room in this outstanding B&B with a level of style and dash that most hotels can only envy. There are four-posters in every room bar one (and even that has a half-tester), and if you thought that theming was naff, just wait until you see 'Old Tuscany', 'Medieval Garden' or 'Palm Springs'. The huge room at the top of the house, 'Dovecote', is suitable for families, and, amazing as it seems, 'The Pool Room' actually contains a small swimming pool. Breakfasts are equally impressive. Book well in advance. Children welcome.
A46 N of Stroud; once in Painswick pass churchyard on right; take first right into Victoria Street; turn left at end of road; door to house is next to March Hare restaurant.

Frampton Court

Frampton-on-Severn, GL2 7EU (01452 740267).
Rates (B&B) £40-£45pp. **Rooms** 2 single (1 en

suite); 1 double/four-poster; 1 twin (en suite); 1 self-catering house.
The Clifford family have been living in Frampton since the eleventh century and their phenomenal Grade I-listed mansion gives up four bedrooms for B&B and also lets out the orangery for self-caterers (sleeps eight; £295-£595 per week). The B&B rooms are large – the double is hung with a Flemish tapestry and equipped with a double-tester bed; the twin enjoys wonderful views and some lovely wooden panelling. Frampton itself is an intriguing village, very close to the Severn estuary. Dogs welcome. Non-smoking throughout.
Take B4071 off A38; turn left and go through village green; house is on left (entrance between two large chestnut trees).

Grey Cottage

Bath Road, Leonard Stanley, GL10 3LU (tel/fax 01453 822515).
Rates (B&B) *single* £35; *double* £48-£50; *twin* £55.
Rooms 1 single (en suite); 1 double; 1 twin (en suite).
A warm welcome (and tea and scones) greets guests at Rosemary and Andrew Reeves' Grey Cottage. The décor is clean, fresh and free of extraneous frills and flounces. Of the two bedrooms, the twin (the beds can be shoved together) is the nicer and larger, with a size-able en suite shower room. Breakfast is outstanding – undyed haddock and poached eggs, full fry-up, smoked salmon with scrambled eggs, kedgeree, kippers – you name it. Leonard Stanley itself isn't a particularly appealing village, being mainly strung out along a main road, but it makes for a perfect base for exploring the area. All bedrooms non-smoking.
A419 W of Stroud towards M5 (Edley bypass); after 1 mile follow filter to Leonard Stanley; go through King's Stanley; 200m after Leonard Stanley Juniors pool, house is on left on bend.

Hampton Fields

Meysey Hampton, nr Cirencester, GL7 5JL (01285 850070/fax 01285 850993).
Rates (B&B) £30-£34pp. Single supplement by arrangement. **Rooms** 2 double (1 en suite); 1 twin.
Meysey Hampton's an appealing dozy little village, equipped with a good pub on the green and this welcoming B&B. Richard and Jill Barry make guests feel at home in their clean, fresh stone house, which enjoys considerable privacy, surrounded by a fine garden. Rooms are comfy and cossetting. The house is non-smoking throughout.
A417 E of Cirencester; at Meysey Hampton crossroads take left to Sun Hill; turn left after 1 mile at cottage.

Old Rectory

Meysey Hampton, GL7 5JX (01285 851200/fax 01285 850452).
Rates (B&B) £25-£40pp. **Rooms** (both en suite) 1 double; 1 twin.
This gorgeous seventeenth-century house, surrounded by six acres of gardens, is a treat. The interior is as immaculate as the outside, and the two bedrooms are unpretentiously yet classily decorated. Guests can use the outdoor heated swimming pool. The village pub is a short walk away and serves decent food. Children welcome. Non-smoking throughout.
A417 E of Cirencester; go through Meysey Hampton; turn right at Masons Arms; house is on left.

The Cotswolds

Painswick Hotel

Kemps Lane, Painswick, GL6 6YB
(01452 812160/fax 01452 814059).
Rates (B&B) *single* £75-£85; *double/twin* £110-
£155; *four-poster* £175; *family* £125-£140.
Rooms (all en suite) 2 single; 9 double; 4 twin;
2 four-poster; 2 family. **Cards** AmEx, Debit, MC, V.

Painswick's grandest accommodation option clings to
the hillside just down from the town's wonderful yew-
filled churchyard. It's a friendly place with some beautiful views from many of the well-proportioned rooms.
Relaxing gardens and a good restaurant serving upmarket dishes as well as light lunches are further attractions.
Children and dogs welcome.

*A46 N of Stroud; once in Painswick pass churchyard on
right, and turn right into Victoria Street; right at March
Hare; hotel is on right down hill.*

Southfield Mill

Southfield Road, Woodchester, nr Stroud
(01453 872896/fax 01452 872896).
Rates (B&B) £20-£25pp. Single supplement £3-£6.
Rooms (both en suite) 1 twin/double; 1 twin.

There's nothing stunning about the simply decorated
and furnished (yet very clean) bedrooms at Judy Sutch's
Southfield Mill, but the location next to a lake is lovely.
Guest rooms are located in a separate wing to the main
house and, thus, have their own entrance door, which
gives privacy not normally associated with B&Bs.
Children welcome. Bedrooms non-smoking, but there's
a shared guest living room where smoking is allowed.
*Take A46 S from Stroud; turn right after 2 miles to North
Woodchester; take 2nd left, down hill; house is on right.*

Where to eat & drink

There aren't a huge number of bona fide
restaurants in the area; the best eating options
are often the pubs. Alas, Painswick's **Country
Elephant** (01452 813564), long a gastronomic
beacon, was up for sale at the time this guide
went to press, but it's worth phoning to check
on its fate. The **Crown of Crucis** in Ampney
Crucis (east of Cirencester) is an ambitious
pub/restaurant/hotel (01285 851806). North-
west of here, the **Bathurst Arms** in North
Cerney (01285 831281) caters equally to diners
and drinkers. South of Cirencester, the comfy
Wild Duck in Ewen (01285 770310) does good
grub, and the **Eliot Arms** in South Cerney
(01285 860215) is another popular locals' haunt.
South of Stroud, there's more excellent food at
the **Old Lodge** in Minchinhampton (01453
834033), and bedrooms and working
waterwheels at the **Egypt Mill** in Nailsworth
(01453 833449). Try also the **Black Horse** in
Amberley for its great views. In Cranham,
north-east of Painswick, the tiny seventeenth-
century **Black Horse** (01452 812217) has
above-average food and beer. **Pizza Piazza** on
Gloucester Docks (1 Merchants Quay; 01452
311951) does excellent stone-ground pizzas.

Ban Thai at the March Hare

The Cross, Painswick, (01452 813452/814552).
Food served 7.30-9.15pm Wed-Sat. **Set meals**
dinner £19.50 (4 courses). **Cards** Debit, MC, V.

In the same building as Cardynham House B&B (*see
p159*), this separately run Thai restaurant offers unusually good food, freshly prepared by the proprietor's Thai
wife. There's no choice – but there are likely to be few
complaints about the set meal, which consists of a plate
of starters, followed by three well-balanced dishes – perhaps a curry, a noodle dish and veg, and then mango or
lemon sorbet. The short wine list is reasonably priced.

Butchers' Arms

Oakridge Lynch, nr Stroud (01285 760371).
Food served *bar* noon-2pm, 6.30-9.30pm, Mon, Tue;
restaurant noon-2pm, 6.30-9.30pm, Wed-Sat; noon-
2pm Sun. **Cards** Debit, MC, V.

A gem of a pub, with top-notch bar snacks as well as
the Stable Room restaurant. It's not far off the A419 but
feels utterly removed from urban civilisation. Potato
wedges with fillings are a speciality and very delicious,
too – the seafood version costs £6.50. Fine selection of
real ales including local brewery Berkleys' 'Old Friend'.

Kingshead House

Birdlip (01452 862299).
Food served 12.15-1.45pm, 7.30-9.45pm, Tue-Fri;
12.15-1.45pm Sun. **Set meals** *lunch* £16.50
(3 courses) Sun; *dinner* £27.50 (4 courses).
Cards AmEx, Debit, MC, V.

This cottagey restaurant with rooms does a good line in
English country cooking with the odd French or
Mediterranean influence thrown in. The set-price dinner
(determined by the price of the main course) might consist of warm onion and walnut tart, followed by rack of
lamb with red wine tomatoes, cucumber and mint, and
then crème brûlée with brandied cherries.

Owlpen Manor

Dursley, nr Uley (01453 860816).
Food served *Apr-Oct* noon-5pm Tue-Sun.
Set dinner £23.95 (3 courses) Sat.
Cards AmEx, Debit, MC, V.

The Cyder House restaurant at this romantic Tudor
manor house (*see also p162*) does a good line in home-
cooked lunches, trad cream teas and gourmet dinners.
Home-reared pheasant and beef are specialities (pheasant en cocotte and beef and Guinness pie are available
as part of the set menu or at lunch for £8.75 each).

Royal Oak

Church Road, North Woodchester (01453 872735).
Food served 12.15-2.15pm, 6.15-9.15pm, daily.
Cards Debit, MC, V.

This is a cracker of a dining pub – free of the affected-
ness that afflicts some country gastro-taverns, and with
an assured hand in the kitchen. It's a tiny place, with a
bar on one side of the entrance and a small, plainly decorated dining room on the other. Relaxed, casually
attired yet thoroughly professional staff dispense well-
crafted dishes such as goat's cheese pie (in filo pastry,
£4.50) and a lovely slab of pigeon with salad (£5.95), followed by beautifully cooked duck in a pungent, fruity
sauce (£13.50) and lamb niçoise (£11.95).

The Cotswolds

Woodchester Mansion

Hidden in a stunning, slender, wood-lined valley, a couple of miles south of Stroud, is one of the most unusual and enigmatic country houses in Britain. Much of the appeal of **Woodchester Mansion**, an extravagant exercise in Victorian Gothic, lies in the fact that it was never finished – and never will be. It's a unique example of a Victorian work-in-progress, and has been described as 'one of the great achievements of nineteenth-century domestic architecture in England'.

The house owes its existence to the (over-optimistic) vision of a tremendously wealthy and entirely humourless Catholic zealot, **Edward Leigh**. In 1845 the Ducie family sold the existing Georgian mansion, Spring Park, and the northern part of their estate in the valley to Leigh, a fervent convert whose family had made their money in trade in Liverpool and whose religious views had made him unpopular in his then-home in the Midlands.

Leigh decided that Spring Park was too classical for his tastes and, following the brief involvement of the celebrated (and expensive) Augustus Pugin, he appointed the cheaper Charles Hansom (brother of the inventor of the Hansom cab) to replace the old house. It was, though, a youthful local architect who was to most effectively stamp his mark on Woodchester. **Benjamin Bucknall**, a passionate fan of the French Gothic revivalist Viollet-le-Duc, was just 21 when he became involved in developing Hansom's ideas.

Work on the mansion started in 1858, but by the mid-1860s had sputtered to a halt. The fact that scaffolding and tools remained in the shell of the house suggests that Leigh did not intend to abandon the project, but by the end of the decade he was running short of funds. He died in 1873 and, although more work took place in the 1890s and the drawing room was used for many

functions over the years, the building had deteriorated signficantly when it was taken over by Stroud District Council in 1986. Both English Heritage (which has provided much money and support for the mansion) and the National Trust were too daunted by the scale of the restoration to take over the building and so a group of courageous (some say foolhardy) local enthusiasts formed the Woodchester Mansion Trust to stabilise the mansion, preserve it in its unfinished state, provide public access, and establish a centre for training in architecture, conservation and stonemasonry.

Although an £815,000 lottery grant has provided a large slice of the estimated £3 million repair bill, the job is still an immense one. Volunteer guides provide fascinating insights into the house and the progress of the restoration. Evidence of Leigh's fierce piety is everywhere, most noticeably in the astonishingly grand chapel (which has suffered severe water damage) with its fine rose window, and in the recently restored Grand Staircase. For all its grandeur (the gargoyles on the exterior are particularly impressive), it would never have been a comfortable house to live in, though – there was only one toilet, one bathroom, minimal plumbing and no central heating.

Woodchester Mansion
Woodchester, entrance outside of Nympsfield (Woodchester Mansion Trust 01453 750455/ training@wmtrust.free-online.co.uk/ www.wmtrust.free-online.co.uk).
Open *Easter-Oct* 11am-5pm (last tour 4pm) 1st Sat, Sun of month, plus every Sun in July, Aug, and bank hol weekends. Tours take place every half hour. **Admission** £4; £2 5s-16s, students.
There's no access to the house from Woodchester village. To reach it, drive to the mansion car park (a meadow), close to the Coaley Peak Picnic Site & Viewpoint on the B4066 Stroud to Dursley Road (about four miles SW of Stroud) and then walk down the one-mile woodland track to the house or take the regular free minibus.

What to see & do

Tourist information centres

Corn Hall, Market Place, **Cirencester**, GL7 2NW
(01285 654180). **Open** *Apr-Oct* 10am-5.30pm Mon;
9.30am-5.30pm Tue-Sat; *Nov-Mar* 10am-5pm Mon;
9.30am-5pm Tue-Sat.

28 Southgate Street, **Gloucester**, GL1 2DP
(01452 421188). **Open** *June-Sept* 10am-5pm Mon-Sat;
11am-3pm Sun.

Corinium Museum

Park Street, Cirencester (01285 655611).
Open *Nov-Mar* 10am-5pm Tue-Sat; 2-5pm Sun; *Apr-
Oct* 10am-5pm Mon-Sat; 2-5pm Sun. **Admission**
£2.50; 80p 5s-16s; £2 OAPs; £1 students.

This award-winning museum, as you can guess from its
name, concentrates on the Roman history of Cirencester.
There are reconstructions of a butcher's shop, dining
room and kitchen, but the museum is particularly strong
on mosaic floors. Children can have a go at mosaic building; the museum is as much aimed at kids as adults.

Gloucester Cathedral

Westgate Street, Gloucester (01452 528095).
Open 7.30am-6pm Mon-Fri; 7.30am-5pm Sat; 7.30am-
4pm Sun. **Admission** free; donations welcome.

While much of old Gloucester has gone, it's surprising
and refreshing to find its magnificent Cathedral in such
a fine state of preservation. A Saxon abbey stood on this
site, but the current building was started by Benedictine
monks in the eleventh century. When Gloucester agreed
to take the body of murdered King Edward II in 1327
(Bristol and Malmesbury had refused), the Cathedral
became a place of pilgrimage, financing the fourteenth-
and fifteenth-century development of the building into
the greatest example of the Perpendicular style in the
country. The huge expanse of the Great East Window
(1350) is magnificent, as is the fan vaulting in the cloisters (the first example of such vaulting in Britain).

Gloucester City Museum & Art Gallery

Brunswick Road, Gloucester (01452 524131).
Open *Oct-June* 10am-5pm Mon-Sat; *July-Sept* 10am-
5pm Mon-Sat; 10am-4pm Sun. **Admission** £2;
£1 OAPs, students; free under-18s.

The entertaining and informative city museum focuses
on Gloucestershire's early history, and includes dinosaur
bones and the re-creation of the appearance of the 2,000-
year-old 'Birdlip Lady'. There's also some fine eighteenth-century furniture and paintings by the likes of
Rembrandt, Gainsborough and Turner, plus enough
hands-on stuff to keep the kids amused.

Museum of Advertising & Packaging

Albert Warehouse, Gloucester Docks, Gloucester
(01452 302309/www.themuseum.co.uk).
Open *Mar-Oct* 10am-6pm daily; *Nov-Feb* 10am-5pm
Tue-Sun. **Admission** £3.50; £1.25 5s-16s; £2.30
OAPs, students; £8.50 family.

Plenty of 'do-you-remember-that?' moments in the world
of vintage packaging and ads. The new 'Time Tunnel
Experience' packs in toys, comics, sweeties, fags and
fashions from the 1940s to the 1970s.

National Waterways Museum

Llanthony Warehouse, Gloucester Docks, Gloucester
(01452 318054/www.nwm.org.uk).
Open 10am-5pm daily. **Admission** (EH) £4.75;
£3.75 5s-16s, OAPs, students; £11-£13 family.

The museum tells the 200-year story of Britain's canals,
using plenty of working models, engines, archive film,
hands-on and interactive exhibits to bring it all to life.

Owlpen Manor

Dursley, nr Uley (01453 860261/
www.1travel.com/owlpen).
Open *Apr-Oct* 2-5pm Tue-Sun.
Admission £4.50; £2 5s-14s; £12.50 family.

Formal terraced yew gardens and bluebell woods surround this lovely Tudor manor (1450-1616), home of the
Mander family. The interior contains some fine Arts and
Crafts furniture and seventeenth-century wall hangings.
Teas are served in the Tithe Barn. The house feels wonderfully remote – 'Owlpen – ah, what a dream is there!'
as Vita Sackville-West was moved to say. *See also p160.*

Painswick Rococo Garden

The Stables, Painswick House, Painswick
(01452 813204/www.beta.co.uk/painswick).
Open *mid-Jan-Sept* 11am-5pm Wed-Sun, bank hols;
July-Aug 11am-5pm daily. **Admission** £3.30; £1.75
5s-16s; £3 OAPs; £8 family.

Charles Hyett built Painswick House in the 1730s and, in
the following decade, his son Benjamin created a flamboyant rococo garden. Over the years, the six-acre garden became overgrown and it was only in the 1970s that
interest revived in what was the only surviving garden
from the rococo period of English garden design (1720-
60). Restoration work started in 1984. The result is wonderful – a combination of the formal (geometric patterns,
long vistas, architectural features) and the informal
(winding paths, off-centre designs, woodland walks).

Prinknash Abbey Park

Cranham (shop 01452 812066/bird park 01452 812727).
Open *park Apr-Sept* 10am-5pm daily; *Oct-Mar*
10am-4pm daily. **Admission** £3.40; £1.80 3s-16s;
£2.40 OAPs; £1.40 students.

The Benedictine Abbey of Prinknash (the 'k' is silent)
combines a working abbey with a pottery (where the
monks' creations can be bought), a bird park (packed
with peacocks and waterfowl) and a deer park (kids
love the tame fallow deer). There's also a Tudor Wendy
House, the 'Monks' Fish Pond', a lake, tearoom, gift shop
and the thirteenth-century 'Old Grange' building.

Slimbridge Wildfowl & Wetlands Trust

Slimbridge (01453 890333/www.wwt.org.uk).
Open *Apr-Oct* 9.30am-5pm daily; *Nov-Mar* 9.30am-
4pm daily. **Admission** £5.25; £3 5s-16s; £4.25
OAPs; £13.50 family.

The Wildfowl & Wetlands Trust was set up by artist
and naturalist Sir Peter Scott in 1946 to promote his central belief that the conservation message is best com-
municated by fostering the interaction of people and
wildlife. A wonderful range of birdlife can be seen,
including six types of flamingo and the world's largest
collection of ducks, geese and swans.

Cheltenham to Stow

Classic Cotswolds country and classical country town.

For a dose of Regency town and regal country, a visit to self-confident Cheltenham and the bucolic expanses stretching westward towards Stow is a winner. **Cheltenham** was an ordinary small Cotswold town until the spa was discovered in 1716 and its healing properties promoted by various nobles and literary figures, among them the Duke of Wellington and Charles Dickens. On the basis of this, the town developed into a genteel resort for the middle classes to take the water and enjoy a weekend reviving their spirits. In some ways, Cheltenham has changed little since. It still has an almost haughty complacency and a very conservative feel, which is tempered slightly when the music and literature festivals come to town, in July and October respectively (*see page 167* **Arts of the matter**). Nonetheless, Cheltenham boasts some beautiful architecture and graceful parks, making it a perfect place to stroll around in fine weather.

The Montpellier area, packed with upmarket shops, many selling antiques, is the most attractive part of Cheltenham. Heading north into the town centre you make your way along the Promenade – a handsome esplanade flanked with grand shops and parks and with the House of Fraser in grand residence in the shopping centre. Behind this are some very ordinary streets of shops and two shopping malls, one of which, the Regent Arcade, is made less anonymous and uniform by the addition of the Wishing Fish Clock, a fantastical clock designed by Kit Williams, who wrote and illustrated the book *Masquerade*. Children love to stand and gawp as the clock face regularly emits bubbles and small animals appear from hatches. While you're in town, it's worth

By train from London

There are five trains a day that run direct from **Paddington** to **Cheltenham**. The journey time is **2hrs 20mins**. Note that the station is about a mile from the town centre.

Cheltenham's stately Montpellier Walk.

popping into the Cheltenham Art Gallery & Museum. A real gem, it features an interesting mix of classic and contemporary work, with a significant collection of Arts and Crafts movement furniture.

Fans of horse racing will, of course, be familiar with the Cheltenham Races; the racecourse, at the foot of Cleeve Hill, a ten-minute walk north of Pittville Park, is the focus of the National Hunt Festival in March. Other meetings take place in April and from October to January (phone 01242 513014 for details).

Around Cheltenham

Tiny **Winchcombe**, to the north-east of Cheltenham, is a small, perfectly formed village best known for nearby **Sudeley Castle** and its nine stunning gardens. Winchcombe itself is pretty and pleasant to wander in, though you won't find much excitement here. Other cultural draws in the area include the once-mighty Cistercian **Hailes Abbey** (to the north) and the wonderfully situated **Belas Knap** Neolithic long barrow (to the south). It's a two-mile walk from Winchcombe to the latter – the most perfectly preserved burial chamber in England.

The distinctive pale yellow stone of the area gives the buildings and villages their warm, comfortable feel. Nowhere typifies this more than the disturbingly named but entirely unthreatening **Upper Slaughter** and **Lower Slaughter**, to the east of Cheltenham; Lower Slaughter, in particular, is stunning, with a small walled river winding through its heart and ducks and geese wandering lazily across the roads.

Stow-on-the-Wold

Stow-on-the-Wold, further east, means 'meeting place on the uplands' and, indeed, eight roads converge on the town. However, thankfully, none makes it into the centre, which is beautifully preserved. Stow is really its own main attraction, a pretty market town of honey-coloured stone houses and cottages with a fine central marketplace flanked on all sides by antique, bric-a-brac and teashops. If you're not offended by the gentility, it makes a good base.

The town is peaceful – if you discount the hordes of tourists who swarm through it every summer – but stay into the evening and the pace settles down. Have a look at the attractive King's Arms Old Posting House, which used to receive stage coaches through its huge broad arch as they stopped on their way to Cheltenham. Wander about and soak up the ambience, perhaps dropping in for a pint at the Queens Head; the more temperance-minded can enjoy a cup of tea at Edward's Café.

Northleach, south of Bourton-on-the-Water, is another village well worth a visit – pretty and peaceful with a beautiful fifteenth-century church boasting, if you're into that sort of thing, a collection of brasses. The village also offers the unexpected delights of Keith Harding's World of Mechanical Music (High Street; 01451 860181) – the pianolas, music boxes and other mechanical instruments on show make this a fun place to go with children. If you want to gain a fuller understanding of the area, then visit the Cotswold Heritage Centre (housed in a renovated eighteenth-century prison; 01451 860715; closed November to March), which traces the agricultural history of the region and includes a collection of antique farming equipment and tools.

Where to stay

Choose to stay in Regency splendour in the heart of Cheltenham or escape to a country house in one of the surrounding villages. Either way, you'll find a good selection of characterful and pleasant B&Bs and hotels, although be aware that this is not the area for bargain accommodation. Note, also, that many hotels get booked up weeks in advance before the National Hunt horse racing in March; the duration of the Festival of Music (July) and the Festival of Literature (October) are other busy times. In addition to the Lower Slaughter Manor, the village also boasts the equally luxurious **Lords of the Manor** (01451 820243; doubles from around £140). If you want to stay in Stow, the flower-festooned **Unicorn** (Sheep Street; 01451 830257; doubles from £105) and the lavish **Wyck Hill House** (01451 831936; doubles from £150) are both upmarket choices.

Cleeve Hill

Cleeve Hill, Cheltenham, GL52 3PR (01242 672052/fax 01242 679969).
Rates as the guide went to press the hotel was being taken over by new management. Phone for further details.
Cleeve Hill is set up high on the eponymous hill to the north-east of Cheltenham, affording tremendous views across the valley to the Malvern Hills. The bedrooms are of a respectable size and attractively decked out with dark repro furniture. There's an honour bar in the lounge and an amply proportioned breakfast is served in the conservatory.

Dial House Hotel

The Chestnuts, High Street, Bourton-on-the-Water, GL54 2AN (01451 822244/fax 01451 810126).
Rates (B&B) single/double/twin £49.50pp; four-poster £61.50pp; suite £49.50-£61.50pp.
Rooms (all en suite) 1 single; 8 double/twin; 3 four-poster; 1 suite. **Cards** AmEx, Debit, MC, V.
Situated in the heart of the tourist-heavy Bourton-on-the-Water, Dial House is a welcoming place with plenty of character. The house was built in 1698 and most of the 13 rooms reflect this, furnished with characterful antique pieces rather than in the anonymous chain-hotel style. There are four-posters for the romantically minded and a good restaurant downstairs, serving imaginative food (see p166). Make sure you request a room in the main house – those in the extension are more modern and less charming. No children under 12. Non-smoking rooms available.
4 miles SW of Stow-on-the-Wold off A429.

The Greenway

Shurdington, nr Cheltenham (01242 862352/fax 01242 862780/ real@greenway-hotel.demon.co.uk).
Rates (B&B) single £95; double £150-£205; four-poster suite £240. **Rooms** (all en suite) 2 single; 17 double; 1 four-poster suite. **Cards** AmEx, DC, Debit, MC, V.

The old stocks in **Stow-on-the-Wold**.

A classic country house hotel built of warm Cotswold stone and covered in creeper. The house is welcoming and luxurious without too formal a feel. Rooms are of a similarly high standard – clean, comfy and spacious and furnished with antiques and floral print fabrics. Though very much in the countryside, with beautiful scenery all around, the hotel is only a few minutes' drive from Cheltenham. The food in the restaurant is as elaborate and well executed as you'd expect. Children over seven welcome. Non-smoking rooms available.
On A46 2.5 miles SW of Cheltenham.

Hotel on the Park
Evesham Road, Cheltenham, GL52 2AH
(01242 518898/fax 01242 511526/
www.hotelonthepark.co.uk).
Rates *single occupancy £76.50-£139.50; double/twin £94.50-£114.50; four-poster £154.50; suite £124.50.* Breakfast £8.25 (Eng); £6 (cont). **Rooms** (all en suite) 10 double/twin; 1 four-poster; 1 suite.
Cards AmEx, DC, Debit, MC, V.

If you fancy playing out the fantasy of living the Regency life for the weekend, then this is a pretty good place to do it. The Hotel on the Park is a classy townhouse hotel with well-furnished rooms and plenty of home comforts. It's not in the centre of the town (the park in question is Pittville Park, across the road), but this isn't a bad thing as it's only a 10-15-minute walk into town. However, you do pay for your creature comforts, and breakfast is extra. No children under eight. All bedrooms non-smoking.

Lower Slaughter Manor
Lower Slaughter, GL54 2HP (01451 820456/
fax 01451 822150/lowsmanor@aol.com).
Rates (B&B) *single occupancy £135-£300; double*

£150; *deluxe double/twin £175-£300; four-poster £300; suite £300-£350.* **Rooms** (all en suite) 2 double; 9 deluxe double/twin; 2 four-posters; 3 suites.
Cards AmEx, DC, Debit, MC, V.

Set in the famously beautiful village of Lower Slaughter, this is a wonderful place to come for a luxurious weekend break. The current house was built in 1658 but a manor house has stood on this site for more than 1,000 years. The manor has its own private grounds with tennis courts and an indoor swimming pool. In winter the fireplaces roar and there is a reassuring sense that your every need will be met. You can also dine here (check out the impressive wine list), where smart casual dress is required. Children welcome.
A429 S of Stow-on-the-Wold; after 1.5 miles turn right after Esso garage towards the Slaughters; manor is on right.

Wesley House
High Street, Winchcombe, GL54 5LJ
(01242 602366/fax 01242 602405).
Rates (B&B) *single occupancy £48; double/twin £70-£75.* **Rooms** (all en suite) 5 double/twin.
Cards AmEx, Debit, MC, V.

The Wesley House is a restaurant and B&B in a superb beamed house in the middle of Winchcombe. The smallish bedrooms are right above the restaurant and are reached via a rickety little staircase. The place is clean, crisp and very pleasant, with good attention to detail – biscuits and fresh milk for tea and coffee await you in rooms, and breakfasts are big and delicious. Most bedrooms have showers rather than baths because the space is limited, but don't let that put you off – this is a lovely place to stay. Children welcome. All bedrooms non-smoking.
B4632 E of Cheltenham; Winchcombe is signposted to right; hotel is on right in High Street.

Where to eat & drink

Cheltenham is slowly but surely getting hipper in the food department. Previously, the town was guilty of an all-or-nothing approach to eating out, with cheap, unexceptional places at one end of the scale and lavish, ultra-expensive French restaurants at the other. Now, though, thanks to the likes of Raymond Blanc's understudies, the town provides a range of eating options that challenges those available in much larger cities.

On the other hand, Cheltenham isn't exactly overly endowed with characterful drinking dens. You could try the studenty **Whole Hog Ale House** or the All Bar One-ish **Circus Bar** on the Promenade. There are, however, plenty of good country boozers out of town. In Oddington, just east of Stow, the **Horse & Groom** has a good garden and play area for kids, while the **Fox** (01451 830584) is a top-notch dining pub. Close by is the **King's Head** in Birdlip (01452 862299), known for its excellent food and wines. Then there's the racing-memorabilia-packed **Hollow Bottom** in Guiting Power, between Bourton and Winchcombe; the tiny seventeenth-century **Plough** in Cold Aston; the cute **Halfway House** in Kineton, the racing-friendly **Plough** in Ford and the cheery **Black Horse** in Naunton are all nearby.

The Belgian Monk

47 Clarence Street, Cheltenham (01242 511717).
Food served 10am-10pm daily. **Set meals** *lunch* (noon-3pm); £5 (2 courses); *dinner* £10.50 (3 courses) Tue. **Cards** Debit, MC, V.

If Trappist beers or mussels take your fancy, then head down to the popular Belgian Monk. The bar offers good beer and reasonably priced meals along with a lively, relaxed atmosphere. Examples of dishes include wild boar sausages with Belgian mash (£5.75), platters of mussels with various sauces £8.25, and, of course, waffles for dessert.

Le Champignon Sauvage

24-26 Suffolk Road, Cheltenham (01242 573449).
Food served 12.30-1.30pm, 7.30-9.15pm, Tue-Sat.
Set meals *lunch* £14.50 (2 courses), £18.50 (3 courses); *dinner* £19.95/£36 (3 courses).
Cards AmEx, DC, Debit, MC, V.

One of Cheltenham's most celebrated (and inevitably pricey) restaurants has a careful eye for detail, not to mention well-constructed food and splendid home-made breads. Along with your meal expect pleasing little extras between courses and strong cooking skills applied to fish, fowl and flesh. If you want to control your spending urges, go for the set-price menus at lunch and dinner: examples of dishes include Cinderford lamb with sweetbreads and grain mustard, and, for pudding, coconut creamed rice. The wine list, surprisingly perhaps, is very reasonably priced, starting at £9.95.

Choirs

5-6 Well Walk, Cheltenham (01242 235578).
Food served noon-1.30pm, 7-9pm, Tue-Sat.
Set meals *dinner* £11.95 (2 courses), £14.95 (3 courses). **Cards** Debit, MC, V.

You're not going to find anything culinarily ground-breaking at Choirs, but that's no bad thing if all you fancy is a classic provincial French-style restaurant that's a treat without breaking the bank. The food is good and the prices reasonable, particularly at lunch-time, when baguettes, sandwiches and omelettes are on offer. Expect, from the set menu (there's no à la carte in the evening), starters such as herring roes fried in brown butter and vinegar, main courses such as steamed fillet of cod marinated in lemon and olive oil topped with provençal sauce and vegetables.

The Daffodil

18-20 Suffolk Parade, Cheltenham (01242 700055).
Food served noon-2.30pm, 6.30-10.30pm, Mon-Sat.
Cards AmEx, Debit, MC, V.

Another timely addition to Cheltenham's eating scene, this excellent lively restaurant (touted as 'Cheltenham's hottest restaurant' by Sophie Grigson) is housed in a remarkable art deco building (a former cinema). The cooking is modern (English with a dash of French and Mediterranean), interesting and fairly priced, and can be enjoyed in the relaxing ground-floor restaurant or the bar area upstairs, which is reached by a pair of sweeping staircases. Starters cost from £2.95 for soup up to £6.50 for home-cured salmon with dill bread and sour cream; the good range of main courses starts at £7.50 and peaks at £22.50.

Dial House Hotel

The Chestnuts, High Street, Bourton-on-the-Water (01451 822244).
Food served noon-2pm, 7-9pm, daily.
Cards AmEx, Debit, MC, V.

The Dial House Hotel offers a decent menu with well thought-out combinations and, unlike many restaurants, more than one (decent) vegetarian option. Prices are reasonable, with starters all less than a fiver and main courses rising to £16.50 for griddled fillet of beef on celeriac purée with red wine jus and baby onions. The pudding list (all £3.95) is good, if a little old school, with bread and butter pudding and crème brûlée with Bailey's Irish Cream; the selection of cheeses is imaginative and well worth investigating, too. *See also p164.*

The Imperial Gardens in **Cheltenham**.

Arts of the matter

Though the best-known event on the Cheltenham calendar is undoubtedly horse racing's Gold Cup, Cheltenham also has a thriving arts scene. The town boasts a brace of prestigious two-week annual events: the **International Festival of Music** in July and the **Festival of Literature** in October. The International Festival of Music, which began life in 1945, is an upmarket mixed bag of music. In past years it has attracted the likes of the BBC Philharmonic Orchestra, Julian Lloyd Webber and opera and ballet music from Covent Garden's Royal Opera House orchestra. The Festival of Literature, which was established a few years later (it celebrated 50 years in 1999), is thought to be the longest-running literary festival in the world. It comprises an impressive 250 literary events, including writing, poetry and drama. Running concurrently with the Festival of Literature is **Book It!**, a literary festival especially for children.

Phone 01242 237377 for a brochure on the festivals, or 01242 227979 for the box office, or check out the website at www.cheltenhamfestivals.co.uk.

Le Petit Blanc

The Queens Hotel, The Promenade, Cheltenham (01242 266800).
Food served noon-3pm, 6-10.30pm, Mon-Sat; noon-3pm, 6-10pm, Sun. **Set meals** lunch & dinner 6-7.30pm £12.50 (2 courses), £15 (3 courses).
Cards AmEx, DC, Debit, MC, V.

Part of Raymond Blanc's growing family of restaurants (whatever you do, don't call it a chain), Le Petit Blanc is an excellent addition to the culinary terrain of Cheltenham. It has a pleasant modern interior that manages to be both relaxed and smart, and caters to diners on a budget as well as those who want to go the whole hog. In addition to the excellent-value set menu, there is also a Blanc Vite menu from Monday to Friday (noon-3pm, 6-10pm), with baguettes from £3.25. Food, not surprisingly, is excellent: well-cooked and flavourful versions of both British and French classics. The wine list, too, is decent, with bottles starting at just £9.95. Children are not only welcome but even get their own, reasonably priced menu. The only downside is that service can be a bit patchy.

Lower Slaughter Manor

Lower Slaughter (01451 820456).
Food served noon-2pm, 7-9.30pm, daily. **Set meals** lunch £15.95 (2 courses), £19.95 (3 courses), Mon-Sat; £22.50 (4 courses) Sun. **Cards** AmEx, DC, Debit, MC, V.

If you're staying at the Manor (see p165) it probably makes a lot of sense to eat in the restaurant (after all, you're hardly likely to be watching the pennies); equally, if you're visiting the village and fancy pushing the boat out, then look no further. The food is classically rich and French with the odd nod to modernity. Expect dishes such as terrine of foie gras marinated in Saussignac wine with walnut and endive salad (£14.50) as a starter and pan-fried brill with creamed leeks, clams and mussels with a saffron emulsion (£21.50) as a main course; puddings carry on the indulgent theme. The wine list includes a few jaw-droppingly expensive bottles of legendary French vintages.

Wesley House

High Street, Winchcombe (01242 602366).
Food served noon-2pm, 6.45-9.30pm, Mon-Sat; noon-2pm Sun. **Set meals** dinner £23.50 (2 courses); £28.50 (3 courses). **Cards** AmEx, Debit, MC, V.

The Wesley House is the luxury restaurant of choice for many locals. Food could be described as French with a modern twist, with dishes such as monkfish and scampi tart with Thai spices on black linguini, and breast of Gressingham duck with pickled apples and calvados sauce (both from the set dinner menu). However, on a recent visit, food was awash with fussy additions that masked the true strengths of the main ingredients, and portions were almost overwhelmingly huge. The restaurant also favours South Africa in its wine list, though you will find a decent selection from other countries.

What to see & do

Tourist information centres

77 Promenade, **Cheltenham** (01242 226554/www.cheltenham.gov.uk). **Open** 9.30am-5.15pm Mon-Sat.
Cotswold Information Centre, Hollis House, The Square, **Stow-on-the-Wold**, GL54 1AF (01451 831082). **Open** Easter-Sept 9.30am-5.30pm Mon-Sat; 10.30am-4pm Sun; Oct-Easter 9.30am-4.30pm Mon-Sat.

Bike hire

Compass Holidays 48 Shurdington Road, Cheltenham (01242 250642).

Chedworth Roman Villa

Yanworth, nr Cheltenham (01242 890256).
Open late Feb-late Oct 10am-5pm Tue-Sun, bank hols; late Oct-late Nov 10am-4pm Tue-Sun. **Admission** (NT) £3.40; £1.70 5s-16s; £8.50 family.
Discovered in 1864, this sizeable second-century AD house is one of the best-exposed Romano-British villa sites in the country. The museum paints a vivid picture of domestic life in the villa, and there are plenty of mosaics, hypocausts and ancient latrines to gawp at.

Cheltenham Art Gallery & Museum

Clarence Street, Cheltenham
(01242 237431/www.cheltenham.gov.uk/agm).
Open 10am-5.20pm Mon-Sat. **Admission** free;
donations welcome.

A fine collection of furniture and silver made by craftsmen from the Arts and Crafts movement including
William Morris. The museum also includes material on
the social history of Cheltenham, plus oriental porcelain
and English ceramics.

Folly Farm

Bourton-on-the-Water (01451 820285).
Open *late Mar-Oct* 9am-5pm daily; *Nov-late Mar*
9am-4pm daily **Admission** £3.50; £1.50 5s-16s;
£2.50 OAPs.

A good place to bring children or the dedicated ornithol-
ogist in your life, Folly Farm is home to over 160 breeds
of wildfowl set in 50 acres of wildlife conservation area.

Hailes Abbey

nr Winchcombe (01242 602398).
Open phone for details.

This Cistercian Abbey was one of the pilgrimage centres in Britain during the twelfth century; its ruins are
still beautiful. The museum has some fine examples of
medieval sculpture and decorated floor tiles, and the
Abbey benefits from a very attractive setting on the
western fringe of the Cotswolds and is surrounded by
extensive woodlands.

Holst Birthplace Museum

4 Clarence Road, Cheltenham (01242 524846).
Open 10am-4.20pm Tue-Sat. **Admission** £2.25;
75p 4s-15s, OAPs, students.

This small museum in the Regency terrace house where
the composer of *The Planets* suite was born is now a
museum in his honour. Mug up on the story of Holst's
life, gaze at his original piano, and ponder on the classic 'upstairs-downstairs' life of Victorian and Edwardian
Britain while looking around the working kitchen.

Model Village

Bourton-on-the-Water (01451 820467).
Open *Apr-Oct* 9am-5.45pm daily; *Nov-Mar* 10am-
4pm daily. **Admission** £2; £1.50 5s-16s;
£1.80 students.

A perennial favourite with children, this isn't some fantasy village but a model of the actual village of Bourton
made of Cotswold stone in 1937, with rivers running
through it, and a model of the model as well.

Sudeley Castle & Gardens

Winchcombe, nr Cheltenham
(01242 602308/www.stratford.co.uk/sudeley).
Open *gardens, Mar-Oct* 10.30am-5.30pm daily;
castle Apr-Oct 11am-5pm daily. Last entry 4.30pm.
Admission *castle & gardens* £6.20; £3.20 5s-15s;
£5 OAPs, students; £17 family; *gardens* £4.70;
£2.50 5s-15s; £3.70 OAPs, students.

Throughout its turbulent 1,000-year history, the Castle
has been home to the likes of Katherine Parr (Henry
VIII's last wife), who lived here with Lady Jane Grey.
This ancient Castle has nine beautiful gardens plus an
impressive collection of furniture and paintings including works by Rubens, Turner and Van Dyck. The
Emma Dent Exhibition, named after the wife of John
Coucher Dent, who inherited the Castle in 1855, features
diaries, photographs and mementoes collected by her
when she lived here.

The tranquil ruins of **Sudeley Castle***'s tithe barn and the carp pond.*

The Cotswolds

North Cotswolds

A breath of fresh air for jaded urbanites.

The north Cotswolds signifies for many people the timeless essence of Englishness: a peaceful, naturally ordered Eden of drowsy hamlets and uncluttered market towns; golden-stoned cottages with immaculately manicured gardens; and handsome old moss-encrusted village churches – the very acme of dreamy bucolic splendour. The reality is that shepherds and silkmakers have long since been driven out by the wealthy Range Rover-driving, green welly-wearing, rentier classes. Much of the north Cotswolds quietly throbs with wealth: asked what local people did for a living, one well-spoken villager replied, only half tongue-in-cheek, 'We collect our dividends, darling!'

Nor are the area's pleasures a well-kept secret. Its accessibility and immense popularity mean that at peak times during the summer months you could, without careful planning, end up sharing your rural escape shoulder-to-shoulder with thousands of camcorder-wielding tourists. It's also worth pointing out that most of the discreet bourgeois charms of this area are adult-oriented: village-hopping, walking, visiting gardens, antiques browsing, eating and drinking. There are few attractions specifically aimed at energetic younger children, and it is always worth checking if smaller hotels and B&Bs are happy to cater for kids.

But having said all that, when the sun is shining and the road is clear, the north Cotswolds are gloriously seductive: slow-paced, sensuous and visually stunning. At its best, even the most hard-core urbanite will struggle to suppress subversive *Good Life* fantasies about giving it all up and moving here to while away summer evenings tending their cottage garden. Whether idling through the architecturally distinctive towns and villages, strolling along country footpaths, or grazing in the area's many top-class pubs and restaurants, it offers a tonic and a half for weary metropolitan senses.

By train from London

Trains from **Paddington** to **Moreton-in-Marsh** leave half hourly. Journey time is between **1hr 20mins** and **1hr 50mins**.

Moreton the point

The graceful market town of **Moreton-in-Marsh**, with its wide main street lined with seventeenth- and eighteenth-century coaching inns and pubs, has for centuries signified for Londoners their arrival in this part of the Cotswolds (it is on the old London-Worcester road, now the A44, and trains from Paddington stop here). It is worth a stroll down the main drag to admire the buildings, some of which claim diverting historical trivia of the 'King Charles I sheltered here during the Civil War' variety. You can restock your hamper and wallet here (cashpoints are thin on the ground elsewhere). Weekenders will miss the vast open-air market held in the town centre on Tuesdays.

In Broadway

To the west along the Worcester road lies **Broadway**, allegedly the Cotswolds' most-visited village, although one wonders if it is technically possible for a 'village' to have a mini-shopping mall. Again, its historical role as a coaching stop has bequeathed it an array of inns and hotels, pubs and tearooms. These are accompanied by numerous shops of varying degrees of frivolity and tweeness (laughably hyped in the brochures as the 'Bond Street of the Cotswolds'). Here you will find purveyors of taste-defying trinkets and souvenirs, as well as more upmarket wares, from jewellery to pastel pink trouser suits. A five-minute walk up the main street to the east takes you away from the madding crowds, however, and reminds you why the village was a magnet for William Morris and the Pre-Raphaelite artists. Serenely gorgeous limestone cottages abound, bedecked with wisteria, clematis and climbing roses. Morris used the eighteenth-century folly **Broadway Tower** (further up the hill to the east) as a retreat. This singular building boasts stunning views 'over 13 counties' on a clear day. Children can be safely let off the leash in the **Broadway Tower Country Park** next door.

Chipping with everything

Chipping Campden, just east of Broadway, rose to prominence on the back of the thriving wool trade of the Middle Ages; much of its lovingly preserved, eclectic architectural heritage dates back to then. Wealthy wool merchants bankrolled the towering church of

The Market Hall in **Chipping Campden**.

St James – brasses on the floor of the church pay tribute to their wisdom and munificence. The town's fortunes declined when the wool trade crashed, rising again when CR Ashbee made it the base for his bold Guild of Handicraft experiment in 1902 (*see page 173* **Crafty cockneys in the Cotswolds**). Although his Arts and Crafts project ultimately failed, the town has remained a centre for silversmiths, jewellers, wood carvers, cabinet makers and enamellers, as well as a mecca for Arts and Crafts movement devotees from all over the world. The town's rustic, unspoilt ambience is ironically the product of rigidly enforced modern planning strictures. The Campden Trust, formed by craftsmen and architects in 1929, restored many of the town's old buildings and set exacting conservation standards. Telegraph wires and power cables are buried underground or tucked away out of sight, while shops, pubs and restaurants are forced to maintain a discreet, understated presence.

Chipping Campden is a convenient base camp for ramblers: the 100-mile **Cotswold Way** starts here en route to Bath, and there are countless local walks. A strenuous one-mile hike up Dover's Hill to the north of the town repays with impressive views over the Vale of Evesham. A number of delightful villages lie within a five-mile radius of Chipping Campden, each conforming to the unwritten rule that all Cotswold villages must have at least one friendly, oak-beamed village pub serving real ales and grub.

Immediately south lies **Broad Campden**, where you can catch a glimpse of CR Ashbee's old house, a converted Norman chapel. **Blockley**, with its gently flowing brook, was the thriving centre of the silk industry in the eighteenth and nineteenth centuries. You can walk by the old silk mills, now converted into sumptuous houses. You may be lucky enough to catch a languorous afternoon's village cricket match at **Ebrington**, with its dinky pitch in the shadow of a fine old church.

Where to stay

Whether you fancy wallowing in five-star, four-poster luxury, a bog-standard B&B to crash for the night, or something in between, the north Cotswolds offers plenty of options. Here are some of the highlights – it is essential that you book these in advance. The tourist information offices (*see page 172*) can provide lists of more basic B&Bs at prices as low as £20 per room per night.

Collin House Hotel

Collin Lane, Broadway, WR12 7PB (01386 858354/collin.house@virgin.net/ www.broadway-cotswolds.co.uk/collin.html). **Rates** (B&B) *double* £92-£98; *four-poster* £102. **Rooms** (all en suite) 2 double; 2 deluxe double; 2 four-poster. **Cards** Debit, MC, V.

This serene and understated seventeenth-century house, situated a mile from Broadway village, has a cosy bar and lounge with oak beams, log fire and flag-stoned floors. The bedrooms are uncluttered and clean – ask for one overlooking the peaceful, elegant garden and orchard. The restaurant offers decent (if tradition-al) fare. Children are welcome. No smoking throughout the hotel.

A44 towards Evesham; follow signs to Broadway; turn right at 2nd roundabout after Fish Hill; follow signs to hotel.

Cotswold House Hotel

Chipping Campden, GL55 6AN (01386 840330/ fax 01386 840310/reception@cotswold-house.demon. co.uk/www.cotswold-house.demon.co.uk). **Rates** (B&B) *single* £55-£75; *double* £120-£150; *four-poster* £160. Special breaks. **Rooms** (all en suite) 3 single; 7 double; 4 twin; 1 four-poster. **Cards** AmEx, MC, V.

Overlooking Chipping Campden's main street, this handsome, solid and light hotel is a lot better value than some of its more gaudily furnished competitors. It boasts an impressive circular staircase that takes you up to the rooms, some of which overlook the gently stepped English walled garden to the rear. The restau-rant, which also overlooks the garden, is strictly non-smoking. Children are only allowed if they're staying in their own room.

A44 W of Moreton-in-Marsh; hotel is in square on main street in Chipping Campden, on B4081.

Holly House

Ebrington, nr Chipping Campden, GL55 6NL (01386 593213/fax 01386 593181). **Rates** (B&B) £20-£22pp. **Rooms** (all en suite) 1 double; 2 double/twin/family.

This clean, bright, unpretentious B&B in a modern fam-ily house is in the middle of the village of Ebrington, within staggering distance of the pub. It lacks the low-beamed rustic flavour of pricier rivals but is nonethe-less a reasonably priced launch pad for Hidcote, Chipping Campden and other neighbouring delights. Children welcome.

B4035 E from Chipping Campden; after 0.5 miles follow signs to Ebrington on left; house is in village centre after Ebrington Arms pub.

The Cotswolds

Lower Brook House

Lower Street, Blockley, GL56 9DS (tel/fax 01386
700286/lowerbrookhouse@compuserve.com).
Rates (B&B) *single occupancy* £65; *double* £80-£90;
four-poster £96; *apartment* £50pp. **Rooms** (all en
suite) 3 double; 4 four-poster; 1 apartment (sleeps 6).
Cards Debit, MC, V.

Winner of the *Sunday Times* 1999 Golden Pillow Award,
warm and relaxed Lower Brook House combines the
enthusiasm and personal touch of the best B&Bs with
the class and attention to detail of a good hotel. The
rooms are not especially large, and follow the flowery
décor conventions, but you will find chocolates and magazines in them on arrival. The breakfast is magnificent:
mounds of fresh fruit and a succulent fry-up. Children
welcome. Dogs allowed in the apartment only. All bedrooms are non-smoking.
*Off A44 between Moreton-in-Marsh and Broadway; at
Bourton-on-the-Hill take turning to Blockley; head down into
valley, which takes you straight into hotel drive.*

Lygon Arms

High Street, Broadway, WR12 7DU
(01386 852255/fax 01386 858611/
info@the-lygon-arms.co.uk/www.savoy-group.co.uk).
Rates (B&CB) *single occupancy* £143;
double £175-£215; *four-poster* £235-£395;
suite £370-£395. Breakfast £9.20 (Eng).
Rooms (all en suite) 52 double/twin; 11 four-
poster/suites. **Cards** AmEx, DC, Debit, MC, V.

Owned by the Savoy Group, and the place to come for
swish, the Lygon Arms offers Claridges-style splendour
with a flavour of Olde English coaching inn. The deceptively small sixteenth-century frontage extends back
through a warren of snug, wood-panelled sitting rooms
with log fires, to a health club with heated swimming
pool and fitness centre hidden at the rear. The cheaper
rooms are disappointingly bland; try the four-poster
rooms for the full, antique-stuffed, over-the-top period
effect. The restaurant's good too (*see p172*). Children
and dogs welcome. Non-smoking rooms available.
*Off A44 between Moreton-in-Marsh and Evesham; on High
Street in Broadway village centre.*

Malt House Hotel

Broad Campden, nr Chipping Campden, GL55 6UU
(01386 840295/fax 01386 841334/
nick@the-malt-house.freeserve.co.uk).
Rates (B&B) *single occupancy* £69.50-£89.50; *double*

*The tranquil **Malt House Hotel**.*

£96.50-£115; *suite/family* £120. **Rooms** (all en suite)
5 double/twin; 3 suites/family. **Cards** AmEx, DC,
Debit, MC, V.

There is a dreamy, secluded ambience to this sixteenth-
century building. All rooms look out over a couple of
acres of lush lawn bordered with flowers, an orchard
and a brook. The garden makes a picturesque setting
for evening drinks, and provides herbs, fruit and vegetables for the chef. Children and dogs welcome. All bedrooms non-smoking.
*A44 towards Evesham; take B4081 towards Chipping
Campden; follow signs to Broad Campden; hotel is in
centre of village.*

Where to eat & drink

For a lively pub crawl try Moreton-in-Marsh:
the **White Hart** (01608 650731), the
Redesdale Arms (01608 650308), and many
other pubs are all lined up, as they have been
for centuries, to provide refreshment for
travellers and market-goers. For more singular
drinking experiences largely free of jukeboxes
and slot machines, take your pick of several
traditional village pubs. In Chipping Campden,
the **Eight Bells** offers traditional ales in a
snug, low-beamed bar. Further down the main
street the **Malt House** bar (not to be confused
with the Malt House Hotel in Broad Campden)
is aesthetically undistinctive but allows
customers to take their drinks out into the
gorgeous back garden; get there early to grab
the tables beneath a big old yew tree.

The **Ebrington Arms** in Ebrington (01386
593223) serves Hook Norton real ales and basic
pub grub in its cheery bar. The **Baker's Arms**
in Broad Campden has also won plaudits for its
ales, and has a sizeable beer garden. The
National Trust-owned **Fleece Inn**, Bretforton,
dates back to 1339. Delightfully warped and
cramped, it serves idiosyncratic ales (Pigs Ear,
Piddle in the Wind) and eccentric-sounding
wines (parsnip, birch). It has an extensive, if
horticulturally undistinguished, beer garden.

Eating out can be a pleasure in these parts;
good-quality food is everywhere, in restaurants,
hotels, and typically, in the many restaurants-
masquerading-as-village-pubs. The following
is a small selection of the range on offer.

Churchill Arms

Paxford, Chipping Campden (01386 594000).
Food served noon-2pm, 7-9pm, daily.
Cards Debit, MC, V.

This massively popular village pub has an unfortunate
reputation as a magnet for metropolitan media types
down for the weekend. But on balance the superior food
– such as succulent braised lamb shank on saffron mash,
£11 – makes dodging the Volvos, fighting your way
through the scrum (no reservations taken) and perse-
vering with grumpy bar staff all seem worthwhile. The
beer garden is a further attraction.

The Cotswolds

St David's, **Moreton-in-Marsh**.

Crown Inn

High Street, Blockley (01386 700245).
Food served noon-2.30pm, 7-10pm, daily.
Cards AmEx, DC, MC, V.

The ambitious brasserie at this sixteenth-century coaching inn tries hard, but ultimately promises more than it can deliver. Despite its extensive ingredients, fricassée of monkfish fillet and langoustine tails with mushrooms, leeks and dried tomatoes in a light brandy and cream sauce with deep-fried basil managed to be strangely bland. Overpriced perhaps, at around £25 a head. On the other hand, the wine list is interesting, and at least you can crash out here without having to worry about finding somewhere else to stay for the night (double rooms £99).

Dormy House

Willersey Hill, Broadway (01386 852711).
Food served 7.30-10am, 12.30-2pm, 7-9.30pm, Mon-Fri; 7.30-10am, 7-9.30pm, Sat; 7-9pm Sun.
Set meals £30.50 (3 courses) Mon-Sat; £19.50 (3 courses) Sun. **Cards** AmEx, DC, MC, V.

This restaurant, hidden away at the top of the valley overlooking Broadway, is perhaps a little over-plush, while the hotel surroundings carry a disconcerting whiff of conference-venue blandness. But the detailed, inventive menu has a respected reputation locally. Again, dominated by meat – supreme of guinea fowl with potato and onion rösti served with a green lentil, tomato and thyme sauce may take your fancy. Choose wine from the lovingly prepared and impressively extensive list.

Lygon Arms

High Street, Broadway (01386 852255).
Food served 12.30-2.15pm, 7.30-9.15pm, Mon-Thur, Sun; 12.30-2.15pm, 7-9.30pm, Fri, Sat. **Set meals** *lunch* £25.50 (3 courses); *dinner* £39.50 (3 courses).
Cards AmEx, DC, Debit, MC, V.

The barrel-vaulted, wood-panelled dining room, its walls adorned with heraldry, suits of armour and stuffed stag heads, is a suitably imposing venue for this highly respected, meat-oriented restaurant. Roast loin of venison with a white sausage and plum millefeuille, baby fondant potatoes and cracked pepper sauce sets the tone. It's all very impressive, but once you've hit the wine list, don't expect any change out of £100. *See also p171.*

Marsh Goose

High Street, Moreton-in-Marsh (01608 653500).
Food served 12.30-2.15pm, 7.30-9.30pm, Tue-Sat; 12.30-2.30pm Sun. **Set meals** *dinner* £29.50 (3 courses). **Cards** AmEx, DC, Debit, MC, V.

On the main street, with its own delicatessen next door, this light, intimate restaurant matches efficient, friendly service with food of subtle excellence. Treats for meat eaters might include smoked Gloucester Old Spot bacon chop with black pudding and potato gâteau and Meaux mustard sauce; vegetarians may find options thin on the ground. Dinner costs around £30 per head.

What to see & do

Tourist information centres

1 Cotswold Court, **Broadway**, WR12 7AA (01386 852937). **Open** 10am-5pm daily.
High Street, **Chipping Campden**, GL55 6AL (01386 841206). **Open** 10am-5.30pm daily.
Cotswold District Council Offices, **Moreton-in-Marsh**, GL56 0AZ (01608 650881). **Open** 8.45am-5.15pm Mon-Wed; 8.45am-7.30pm Thur; 8.45am-4.45pm Fri.

Bike hire

Country Lanes Cycle Centre, Moreton-in-Marsh (01608 650065). Inside the train station. Only opens by prior arrangement when the weather's bad.

Broadway Tower Country Park

Just off A44 (01386 852390).
Open *tower Apr-Oct* 10am-6pm daily; *Nov-Mar* 10am-6pm Sat, Sun; *park Apr-Oct* 10am-4.30pm daily. **Admission** £3.20; £2.20 4s-16s; £2.50 OAPs; £9.50 family.

One-stop day out for all the family: spectacular views from the tower; a William Morris museum; adventure playground; picnic sites; walks; and a red deer enclosure offering the chance to ogle 'bambies' from mid-June.

Cotswold Falconry Centre & Batsford Arboretum

Batsford Park, off A44 (01386 701043).
Open *Mar-Nov* 10.30am-5.30pm daily.
Admission £3.50; £1.50 5s-16s.

Hour-long demonstrations of the art of falconry with eagles, falcons, hawks, kites and vultures, four times daily. The arboretum is next door.

Crafty cockneys in the Cotswolds

As you drink in the splendour of Chipping Campden, marvelling at how it appears to epitomise the timeless spirit of English country living, it is worth remembering that its character is due in no small part to the endeavours, earlier this century, of a group of cockney craftsmen – the **Guild of Handicraft** – who moved there from the backstreets of London's East End. The Guild was the brainchild of **CR Ashbee**, an idealistic Victorian toff with liberal leanings whose dream was to protect and promote traditional craft skills as a reaction against the mass production techniques of modern industry. He helped establish the Guild – comprising metal workers, silversmiths, cabinet makers and the like – in the Mile End Road in 1888, before moving it to Chipping Campden in 1902.

The grand 'back to the land' vision was initially successful: under Ashbee's guidance houses in the village were restored and converted; the old silk mill (empty at that stage for 60 years) was converted to house the Guild's workshops. A school of Arts and Crafts was set up (students came from all over the UK and the USA) and luminaries such as the writer John Masefield came to lecture. By 1908 the dream had gone sour. With what now

seems a familiar inevitability, the Guild was unable – or disinclined – to commercially exploit its original ideas and brilliant designs; mass production rivals imitated its goods, and sold them more cheaply. The Guild went bust.

Many of the guildsmen returned to London. Others stayed, including silversmith George Hart, whose grandson David Hart continues the family tradition in the silk mill workshop today. The **silk mill** (01386 841417) on Sheep Street, just off the main street (Apr-Oct 11am-5pm Tue-Sun; shorter opening times in winter; 50p entrance) is well worth a visit. It has a small exhibition of handicraft artefacts and a few fascinating photographs. But the real thrill is a look around the workshops upstairs, with many of the original workbenches and tools still in use. Look out for a century's worth of invoices impaled on nails, hanging from the ceiling like beehives. If all this inspires you to possess an Arts and Crafts design classic you could do worse than visit Robert Welch's studio shop in front of the silk mill (where he has a studio) on the High Street. There you will find his trademark cutlery and silverware, as well as a range of kitchen knick-knacks.

Hidcote Manor Garden

4 miles NE of Chipping Campden
(01684 8553700/www.nationaltrust.org.uk.)
Open *Apr, May* 11am-6pm Mon, Wed, Thur, Sat, Sun; *June, July* 11am-6pm Mon-Thur, Sat, Sun; *Aug-Oct* 11am-6pm Mon, Wed, Thur, Sat, Sun.
Admission (NT) £5.60; £2.80 5s-17s; £14 family.

Magnificent, highly influential formal gardens designed by the enigmatic artist-plantsman Lawrence Johnson in the first half of the twentieth century. The use of colour and texture is seminal, with hedges, water, walls and paving. Liable to serious overcrowding on Sundays.

Kiftsgate Court Garden

4 miles NE of Chipping Campden (01386 438777).
Open *Apr, May, Aug, Sept* 2-6pm Wed, Thur, Sun; *June, July* noon-6pm Wed, Thur, Sat, Sun.
Admission £3.50; £1 5s-16s.

A few minutes from Hidcote lies this flowing, sensuous and romantic garden designed by three generations of women. Set on the edge of the Cotswold escarpment with heart-stopping views over the Vale of Evesham, this is a space to treasure. Look out for the splendid swimming pool and the giant Kiftsgate Rose. Gardeners' heaven.

Sezincote House & Gardens

2 miles SW of Moreton-in-Marsh, off A44 (no phone).
Open *house May-July, Sept* 2.30-5.30pm Thur, Fri; *garden Jan-Nov* 2-6pm Thur, Fri, bank hols.
Admission £4.50; £1 5s-16s.

This elusive, exotic place is the third in a trio of spectacular gardens in the area, with bamboo and Japanese maples planted around a cascading stream. The house, inspired by Indian temples and fortresses, was the model for Brighton Pavilion. Sezincote is, infuriatingly, closed on Saturdays and Sundays; weekenders may catch it on Thursday and Friday or bank holiday Monday afternoons. Children under 16 are not allowed in the house.

Snowshill Manor

Snowshill, off A44 SW of Broadway (01684 855376).
Open *late Mar-Oct* 1-5pm Mon, Wed-Sun.
Admission (NT) £5; £2.50 5s-16s; £14 family.

An eclectic collection of objects is housed in this medieval manor house, from samurai armour to musical instruments and bicycles, linked by the theme 'craftsmanship'. Highly recommended gardens. Expect big crowds at weekends.

Stratford & Warwick

Battlements, boutiques and the Bard.

South Warwickshire is both literally and metaphorically the heart of England. The county's prominent place in English history is largely as a result of the River Avon and its tributaries, which traditionally provided both a means of transport and fertile land. Inevitably, though, the area's general past has been overshadowed by its association with William Shakespeare, with the unavoidable marketing of 'Shakespeare Country'.

Warwick

The county town of **Warwick**, a surprisingly small and low-key place, is chiefly (and justly) famed for its magnificent castle. The town grew from an eighth-century market – 'Werburgh's trading place'; stalls selling local produce can still be found trading in the Market Square on Saturdays. In 1694 a fire destroyed a large proportion of the original town, which accounts for today's Georgian town centre. Some of the medieval buildings on the outskirts survived the fire virtually intact. The Lord Leycester Hospital for war veterans (established 1571) is one of the best examples of a medieval building in the country.

Shakespeare-upon-Avon

Stratford and the surrounding area is the biggest tourist draw outside of London – and all because of one man. An otherwise unremarkable town, Stratford is inundated with visitors year round, most of whom come to pay homage to the world's most famous playwright. They follow the Shakespeare trail from the theatres to his birthplace on Henley Street, and then on to his grave at Holy Trinity

The waterside **Royal Shakespeare Theatre**.

Church in the Old Town. *See also page 177*

Where there's a Will...

Stratford's cutesy half-timbered architecture, cobbled mews and teashop culture isn't everyone's cup of char. Sheep Street, in particular, has fallen prey to pricey boutiques and restaurants, and ghastly souvenir shops. Yet it is all worth braving if you're a genuine Shakespeare junkie (and there is very pleasant walking along the canal); just make sure you have an escape route at the end of the day. For this reason, it may be better to stay in one of the farms or guesthouses in the surrounding villages rather than in Stratford itself.

So spa so good

Warwick has its castle; Stratford has its bard; **Royal Leamington Spa** (more commonly known as Leamington) has its shops. The attractive Parade and award-winning Royal Priors shopping centre have a good selection of high street and speciality shops. There's no fear of getting lost as the town is built on a grid, with wide tree-lined avenues, squares and a combination of grand Regency and Victorian architecture. A favourite with Queen Victoria (hence the royal prefix), the town was a playground for the rich and famous during its heyday as a fashionable spa resort. The supposed healing properties of the spa waters attracted thousands of credulous people over the years, including Charles Darwin and Florence Nightingale.

By train from London

Trains to **Warwick** and **Stratford-upon-Avon** leave **Paddington** four times a day. Journey time to **Warwick** is **1hr 45mins**; it is an additional **25mins** to **Stratford**. Trains to **Royal Leamington Spa** leave **Marylebone** hourly; the journey time is **1hr 40mins**.

Beyond the towns

If these tourist-heavy towns get too much, take heart in the fact there are many lesser-known (and hence generally less-crowded) places of interest worth seeing. Visit **Charlecote House**, with its gardens landscaped by Capability Brown, the old watermill at **Wellesbourne** (01789 470237; phone for opening times) or alternatively take a brisk walk up **Edgehill**, site of the first battle in the Civil War, in 1642, for fantastic views of Warwickshire with the Cotswolds on the horizon. There are dozens more – too many to include here, so contact the local tourist offices for brochures and leaflets before your trip.

Where to stay

Aylesford Hotel

1 High Street, Warwick, CV34 4AP (01926 492817/ fax 01926 493817/aylesford@freeuk.com).
Rates (B&B) *double* £75; *family room* £90-£100.
Rooms (all en suite) 4 double/twin; 4 family.
Cards DC, Debit, MC, V.

The hotel is one part of a local landmark, the 'Three Sisters', the tallest buildings in the area. Built after the fire in 1696, it has recently been refurbished to its full potential. The cellar has been converted into a restaurant, retaining its original features with bare brick walls and custom-made wrought iron furniture. The large bright bedrooms are clean, well equipped and thoughtfully decorated. Only a short walk from Warwick Castle and the town centre. Children and dogs welcome.

Caterham House

58-59 Rother Street, Stratford-upon-Avon, CV37 6LT (01789 267309/fax 01789 414836).
Rates (B&B) *double/twin* £76-£80.
Rooms (all en suite) 10 double/twin. **Cards** MC, V.

Five minutes from the Royal Shakespeare Theatre, this small private hotel is popular with both the actors and audience. Run for over 20 years by Anglo-French couple Dominique and Olive Maury, the atmosphere is friendly but unobtrusive. All the rooms are beautifully decorated, each with its own individual character; some have half-tester beds. The close proximity of Caterham House to the town centre makes it a good choice for those travelling by train or bicycle. Children and dogs are welcome.

Gravelside Barn

Binton, nr Stratford-upon-Avon, CV37 9TU (01789 750502/fax 01789 298056/ gravelside-barn@hotmail.com).
Rates (B&B) *double/twin* £60. **Rooms** (all en suite) 2 double; 1 twin. **Cards** Debit, MC, V.

Originally part of the Ragley Estate, owned by the Marquis of Hartford, this guesthouse is in a restored and renovated old barn. Set high on a hill, the views are spectacular, with the Malverns and Cotswolds on the horizon, farmland, woodland and small villages closer in. Binton itself is a pretty village, within easy reach of Stratford and the motorway. Non-smoking throughout.

A46 from Stratford towards Evesham; after 4 miles turn left towards Binton; turn left at Blue Boar pub; house 350m down hill on right; turn into drive; house is on left.

Leamington Hotel & Bistro

64 Upper Holly Walk, Royal Leamington Spa, CV32 4JL (01926 883777/fax 01926 330467).
Rates (B&ContB) *single* £37.50; *double/twin/four-posters* £55-£70. Breakfast £6.75 (Eng).
Rooms (all en suite) 1 single; 27 double/twin; 2 four-poster. **Cards** AmEx, DC, Debit, MC, V.

A five-minute walk up Lansdowne Crescent from the town centre, this small but grand hotel stands proudly on the corner. It is more reminiscent of a London hotel than the others in the area. The service is good but impersonal. Bedrooms are large, well maintained, and well equipped – Molton Brown goodies, hairdryers and tea and coffee-making facilities are examples. Downstairs the smart bar and restaurant serves reasonably priced British food. Children welcome. Non-smoking rooms available.

Loxley Farm

Loxley, CV35 9JN (01789 840265/fax 01789 840645).
Rates (B&B) *suite* £60. **Rooms** (both en suite) 2 suites.

The pretty, tranquil village of Loxley is a nice contrast to over-busy Warwick and Stratford. Guests stay in a converted seventeenth-century barn overlooking a well-kept English garden and late thirteenth-century thatched cottage. The bedrooms are equally charming; one boasts a private conservatory, while the other has

*This way to **Warwick**'s biggest draw.*

its own kitchen and lounge area. Combining the rooms would make it a good option for a family or two couples. An Aga-cooked English breakfast is served in the cottage where it is rumoured that King Charles I stayed after his defeat at Edgehill. Children and dogs welcome. Both bedrooms non-smoking.

A422 SE of Stratford; go through Loxley village to bottom of hill; turn left (towards Stratford); Loxley farm is 3rd house on right.

Mallory Court

Harbury Lane, Bishop's Tachbrook, Royal Leamington Spa, CV33 9QB (01926 330214/ 01926 451714/reception@mallory.co.uk).
Rates (B&CB) single occupancy £165-£225; double/twin £165-£295. Breakfast £11 (Eng). **Rooms** 18 double/twin (16 en suite). **Cards** Debit, MC, V.

This extensive country house, set in ten acres of beautiful grounds, is indisputably charming. There are gorgeous views from the spacious bedrooms, each decorated with attention to detail. Although the building looks Elizabethan from the outside, it was built during World War I, and many of the original art deco fittings can be found in the bathrooms. During winter, afternoon tea is served in front of log fires in one of the cosy lounges. On summer evenings guests dine by candlelight on the terrace overlooking the floodlit garden. Enjoy croquet on the lawn, a dip in the outdoor pool, a spot of tennis, or simply wander around the beautiful rose garden. Absolute luxury. Children welcome.

S of Leamington Spa off B4087.

Shrewley Pools Farm

Parish of Hasely, nr Warwick, CV35 7HB (01926 484315).
Rates (B&B) £45-£50 *double/twin/family*; £10 per child supplement. **Rooms** (both en suite) 1 twin; 1 double/family.

Built in 1630, the farmhouse has retained many of its original features – the exposed beams, uneven floors, leaded windows and mind-your-head doorways all breathe the building's history. The farm is still in action rearing turkeys, pigs and cows, and guests can commune with lambs, geese and the family dog. The house is surrounded by an acre of rambling garden, rhododendrons and herbaceous borders. With child-friendly facilities and prices, it makes a good destination for a break with the kids. Non-smoking throughout.

A4117 NW of Warwick towards Solihull; go through Hatton; at large roundabout take 1st exit into Five Ways Road signposted Shrewley and Claverdon; farm is 0.5 miles on left.

Victoria Spa Lodge

Bishopton Lane, Bishopton, Stratford-upon-Avon, CV37 9QY (01789 267985/204728/ ptozer@victoriaspalodge.demon.co.uk/ www.stratford-upon-avon.co.uk/victoriaspa.htm).
Rates (B&B) *double/twin* £60; *triple* £75.
Rooms (all en suite) 3 double; 1 twin; 3 family.
Cards MC, V.

Owners Paul and Dreen Trozer's guesthouse and home is a beautiful, well-restored Georgian country house. Paul's delicious breakfasts are served in a large room with velvet sofas, lacy tablecloths and an impressive collection of Wedgwood, which Dreen collected for years.

Each bedroom is spacious, comfortable, and meticulously clean. Some overlook the canal where a towpath leads to Stratford town centre in one direction and Mary Arden's cottage in the other. A favourite spot of Queen Victoria's, this was apparently the first place she officially gave her name to after she stayed here as a young princess. Children welcome. Non-smoking throughout.

A46 S; at A46 and A3400 intersection take 2nd exit (Bishopton Lane); Victoria Spa is 1st house on right after 500m just before bridge.

Most Stratford restaurants open early and close late, and offer good value pre- and post-theatre meals. If you're after a quick bite rather than a lengthy gastronomical experience, try the **Black Swan** (Stratford Way; 01789 297312), more commonly known as the 'Dirty Duck', where you may find yourself brushing shoulders with members of the RSC. For a snack in Stratford town centre check out the 'Light Bites' menu at **Vintner's** (Sheep Street; 01789 297259), the **Deli Café** (Meer Street; 01789 295705), or get into the spirit of the place with a dollop of clotted cream, jam and a scone to balance it on, washed down with a cuppa. **Hathaway's Tea Rooms** (High Street; 01789 292404) set in the eaves above its own bakery, serves a good cream tea. If you want a more elegant and luxurious setting, take high tea on the terraces of **Mallory Court** (*see above*).

There are plenty of good country boozers in the area. The **King's Head** at Aston Cantlow (01789 488242) is well worth a visit for its quality Italian and Mediterranean food. For good basic pub grub and a smooth pint of ale, try the **Fox** at Loxley (01789 840991), the **Bell** at Shottery (01789 269645), or watch the world go by at the **Tilted Wig** in Warwick's Market Place (01926 410466). For something posher, try the highly rated **Restaurant Bosquet** in Kenilworth (97A Warwick Road; 01926 852463) for the rich cooking of south-west France.

The Bell

Alderminster, nr Stratford-upon-Avon (01789 450414).
Food served noon-2pm, 7-9.30pm, daily.
Set meals *lunch* (Mon-Fri) £6.50 (2 courses).
Cards AmEx, DC, Debit, MC, V.

A cut above standard pub grub in quality and creativity, the menu at the Bell includes dishes like creamy fish pie with watercress mash (£8.95); Sunday lunch is very popular (roast beef and Yorkshire pudding, £7.95). The building was once a coaching inn, and there's plenty of evidence of times past – exposed beams, flagstone floors and horse paraphernalia. Most of the seating is reserved for diners, who can choose to eat in the restaurant, conservatory or garden – where they can enjoy views of the Stour Valley. Like all good trad country pubs, the Bell offers a wide range of quality cask ales.

Where there's a Will...

...there's a thriving tourist industry. Stratford and the surrounding area are packed with Shakespeare-related sights. Below we list the main ones.

Anne Hathaway's Cottage
Shottery, 2 miles W of Stratford (01789 204016). **Open** *mid-Mar-mid-Oct* 9am-5pm Mon-Sat; 9.30am-5pm Sun; *mid-Oct-mid-Mar* 9.30am-4pm Mon-Sat; 10am-4pm Sun. **Admission** £3.90; £1.60 5s-16s.

The thatched cottage belonging to Shakespeare's wife lies in beautiful gardens. There are many pleasant walks leading from the house.

Hall's Croft
Old Town, Stratford-upon-Avon (01789 292107). **Open** *mid-Mar-mid-Oct* 9.30am-5pm Mon-Sat; 10am-5pm Sun; *mid-Oct-mid-Mar* 10am-4pm Mon-Sat; 10.30am-4pm Sun. **Admission** £3.30; £1.60 5s-16s; £7.50 family.

This impressive sixteenth-century house contains an exhibition on medicine – appropriately, as it was the home of John Hall, the doctor husband of Shakespeare's eldest daughter Susanna.

Holy Trinity Church
Stratford-upon-Avon (01789 266316). **Open** 8.30am-6pm Mon-Sat; 2-5pm Sun. **Admission** 60p; 40p 5s-16s, OAPs, students.

On the banks of the Avon, one of England's most beautiful parish churches is famous for housing Shakespeare's grave. There's also a record of his baptism here.

Mary Arden's House & the Shakespeare Countryside Museum
Wilmcote, 4 miles NW of Stratford (01789 204016). **Open** *mid-Mar-mid-Oct* 9.30am-5pm Mon-Sat; 10am-5pm Sun; *mid-Oct-mid-Mar* 10am-4pm Mon-Sat; 10.30am-4.30pm Sun. **Admission** £4.40; £2.20 5s-16s.

This timbered farmhouse was the home of Shakespeare's mother before she married.

Nash's House & New Place
Chapel Street, Stratford-upon-Avon (01789 204016). **Open** *mid-Mar-mid-Oct* 9.30am-5pm Mon-Sat; 10am-5pm Sun; *mid-Oct-mid-Mar* 10am-4pm Mon-Sat; 10.30am-4.30pm Sun. **Admission** £3.30; £1.60 5s-16s.

Once owned by Thomas Nash, who married Shakespeare's granddaughter, the house still contains some of his original furniture. Outside is the site of Shakespeare's final home and his Elizabethan-style garden.

Royal Shakespeare Company
Waterside, Stratford-upon-Avon (box office 01789 403403/tours 01789 403405). **Tours** 1.30pm, 5.30pm, Mon-Sat; noon, 1pm, 2pm, 3pm, Sun (subject to performances). **Tickets** £4; £3 5s-18s, OAPs, students.

See a production of one of Shakespeare's plays or take a backstage tour. Booking is essential.

Shakespeare's Birthplace
Henley Street, Stratford-upon-Avon (01789 204016). **Open** *mid-Mar-mid-Oct* 9am-5pm Mon-Sat; 9.30am-5pm Sun; *mid-Oct-mid-Mar* 9.30am-4pm Mon-Sat; 10am-4pm Sun. **Admission** £4.90; £2.20 5s-16s.

This half-timbered house has an exhibition following Shakespeare's life and a traditional English garden. *See picture below.*

Desport's
13-14 Meer Street, Stratford-upon-Avon (01789 269304). **Food served** noon-2pm, 6-11pm, Tue-Sat. **Set meals** *lunch* £10.50 (2 courses), £14 (3 courses). **Cards** AmEx, DC, Debit, MC, V.

Despite being the new kid on the block in Stratford, Desport's has already established a good reputation. Former managers of Lamb's (Sheep Street), husband and wife team Paul and Julie Desport have applied imaginative modern interpretations to both the interior and the food. The restaurant is in the eaves above Desport's Deli, and the original features of the building are effectively combined with contemporary bright colours. The menu is divided equally between meat, fish and vegetarian, and is a hybrid of rich English, Mediterranean and Eastern food. Try, perhaps, the seared scallops with a sweet tomato risotto, crispy seaweed and vanilla oil (£13.95).

Findon's

7 Old Square, Warwick (01926 411755).
Food served noon-2pm, 7-9.30pm, Mon-Fri; 7-9.30pm Sat. **Set meals** *lunch* £4.95 (1 course), £8.95 (2 courses), £13.95 (3 courses); *dinner* £15.95 (2 courses). **Cards** AmEx, DC, Debit, MC, V.

Stylish and smart, everything at Findon's is well presented, from the efficient staff to the excellent food. The restaurant occupies an early Georgian townhouse, and décor is classic English. The rich, flavour-packed food, on the other hand, has a French slant. Breast of duck with cherries and cinnamon (£17.95) and paupiette of sea bass with shallot butter (£19.95) are just two of the temptations on offer. Vegetarians are not neglected, with imaginative options like wild mushroom tartlet with coriander and curry cream (£14.95). The high prices are matched by high quality – an all-round memorable dining experience.

The Opposition

13 Sheep Street, Stratford-upon-Avon (01789 269980).
Food served noon-2pm, 5.30-10.30pm, Mon-Sat; noon-2pm, 6-10pm, Sun. **Cards** Debit, MC, V.

Popular with locals and tourists, this small restaurant is highly rated by both. The bare brick walls, low beamed ceilings and candlelit tables are all in keeping with the sixteenth-century building. Staff are friendly and relaxed, and the food is consistently good (and slightly cheaper than sister restaurant **Lamb's** next door). The menu draws on a number of cuisines, with dishes such as breast of chicken with banana roasted in lime butter, served with basmati rice and mild curry paste (£9.25), and char-grilled Cumberland sausages with butter mash and caramelised onion gravy (£7.25). In summer there are tables outdoors in a courtyard. Book well in advance.

Russon's

8 Church Street, Stratford-upon-Avon (01789 268822).
Food served 11.30am-2pm, 5.30-10pm, Tue-Sat.
Cards AmEx, Debit, MC, V.

Russon's is probably the most highly rated restaurant in Stratford. The cooking employs arresting food combinations – for instance, fresh paw paw filled with prawns comes with a mango, ginger and mayonnaise dressing (£5.75). Although it has a reputation as the place to go for fish – daily specials, written on the blackboard, might include char-grilled marlin on roasted Mediterranean vegetables (£12.50) and halibut with fresh asparagus and sun-dried tomatoes in a creamy butter sauce (£13.95) – those inclined to meat dishes, and vegetarians, are equally satisfied. Prices are reasonable, especially the pre-theatre menu, which is à la carte but at lower prices.

Simpson's

101-103 Warwick Road, Kenilworth (01926 864567).
Food served 12.30-2pm, 7-10pm, Mon-Fri; 7-10pm Sat. **Set meals** *lunch* £12.50 (2 courses), £17.50 (3 courses); *lunch & dinner* £21.95 (2 courses), £27.95 (3 courses). **Cards** AmEx, Debit, MC, V.

Chef-patron Andreas Antona and his team serve modern English and Mediterranean dishes. Mr Antona's Greek origins mean that his kleftiko is unbeatable, and comes jazzed up with a Swiss chard and chickpea salsa. You might also be tempted by the roast squab pigeon with braised cabbage, or the mouthwatering desserts such as hot lemon soufflé and coconut ice-cream. Service is as first-rate as the food. Among the most highly rated restaurants in Warwickshire.

What to see & do

Tourist information centres

The Royal Pump Rooms, The Parade, **Royal Leamington Spa**, CV32 4AA (01926 311470/ www.shakespeare-country.co.uk). **Open** 9am-6pm Mon-Fri; 9.30am-6pm Sat; 10am-5pm Sun.

Bridgefoot, **Stratford-upon-Avon**, CV37 6TW (01789 293127/www.shakespeare-country.co.uk). **Open** *Easter-Oct* 9am-6pm Mon-Sat; 11am-5pm Sun; *Nov-Easter* 9am-5pm Mon-Sat.

The Court House, Jury Street, **Warwick**, CV34 4EW (01926 492212/www.warwick-uk.co.uk). **Open** 9.30am-4.30pm daily.

Bike hire

Off The Beaten Track Napton on the Hill (01926 817380). The company will deliver and collect bikes.

Charlecote Park

Charlecote, 5 miles E of Stratford-upon-Avon (01789 470277/www.nationaltrust.org.uk).
Open *Easter-Oct house* noon-5pm, *grounds* 11am-6pm, Mon, Tue, Fri-Sun. **Admission** (NT) £4.90; £2.45 5s-16s; £12.20 family.

Home of the Lucy family since 1247. The present house was built in the 1550s and visited by Queen Elizabeth I. Landscaped by Capability Brown, the park supports herds of red fallow deer and a flock of sheep.

Heritage Motor Centre

Banbury Road, Gaydon, 10 miles SE of Warwick (01926 641188).
Open 9am-5pm daily. **Admission** £6; £4 5s-16s; £5 OAPs, students.

The largest collection of historic British cars in the world – including one driven by Graham Hill at Le Mans – with a quad-bike track and children's roadway.

The **Lord Leycester Hospital** *in* **Warwick**.

Canal-life & waterways

The Stratford-upon-Avon Canal meets the River Avon at the Bancroft Basin and lock in front of the Royal Shakespeare Theatre. It eventually joins the Grand Union Canal, and the Avon flows down to meet the Severn at Evesham and Tewkesbury. This network of waterways was once crucial for local trade and communication. In the 1920s the length running through Stratford fell into disrepair. When the Board of Survey applied to abandon the section in 1955, there was massive public protest and local volunteers joined together to restore the canal, rebuilding locks and clearing the channel. As a result, in 1964 it was reopened as a fully navigable waterway.

Today, the canal is one of Stratford's greatest attractions, providing visitors with the chance to cruise, row, canoe, punt or just stroll or laze under willows on the grassy banks watching the activity. This is one of only five places in England where you can punt, and many consider it to be the finest, with a three-mile stretch of uninterrupted river. Below are some of the places where you can hire boats, punts and canoes, or book a table on a dinner cruise.

For information on activities, hire boat companies, leaflets, walks and education packs, phone or send an SAE to British Waterways, Brome Hall Lane, Lapworth, Solihull, B94 5RB (01564 784634).

Countess of Evesham Bancroft Gardens, Stratford-upon-Avon (01789 293477). Lunch and dinner cruises along the River Avon.

Prince Regent II Offchurch, 3 miles E of Royal Leamington Spa (01926 450317). Luxury cruising restaurant.

Roses Boathouse Swans Nest Lane, Stratford-upon-Avon (01789 267073). Edwardian craft available for short cruises or private charter. Rowing boats, punts and canoes can all be hired by the hour or day. Or ride in an authentic coal-powered steam boat or genuine Venetian gondola with a gondolier.

Stratford Marina Stratford Moat House Hotel (01789 269669). Regular hour-long cruises.

Kenilworth Castle

Kenilworth
(01926 852078/www.english-heritage.org.uk).
Open *Apr-Sept* 10am-6pm daily; *Oct* 10am-5pm daily; *Nov-Mar* 10am-4pm daily. **Admission** (EH) £3.50; £1.80 5s-16s; £2.60 OAPs, students.

The stunning red sandstone ruins are what is left of twelfth-century Kenilworth Castle. Visitors can see the Norman keep, Great Hall and the wonderful reconstructed Tudor gardens. Tape tours available (£1.50).

Lord Leycester Hospital

High Street, Warwick (01926 491422).
Open *Easter-Sept* 10am-5pm Tue-Sun, bank hols; *Oct-Easter* 10am-4pm Tue-Sun. **Admission** £2.75; £1.50 4s-16s; £2 OAPs, students.

Built in the fourteenth century, the Hospital was acquired by Robert Dudley Earl of Leicester in 1571. Visitors can see the chapel, great hall, guildhall, medieval galleried courtyard and geriatric restored garden (nearly 600 years old).

Royal Pump Rooms

Royal Leamington Spa (01926 311470).
Open 1.30-8pm Tue, Thur; 10.30am-5pm Wed-Sat; 11am-4pm Sun. **Admission** free.

Next to Jephson Gardens, the Pump Rooms are where people once came to take the healthful Leamington waters. Following a multi-million-pound restoration, the Pump Rooms now house an interesting art gallery, museum and library.

St John's House Museum

St John's, Warwick (01926 412132).
Open 10am-5.30pm Tue-Sat, bank hols; *May-Sept* 2.30-5pm Sun. **Admission** free; donations welcome.

An early Jacobean house with displays relating to the social history of Warwickshire, including costume and a nineteenth-century kitchen, parlour and schoolroom.

Warwick Castle

Warwick (01926 406600/www.warwick-castle.co.uk).
Open *Apr-Oct* 10am-6pm daily; *Nov-Mar* 10am-5pm daily. **Admission** £10.50; £6.25 4s-16s; £7.50 OAPs; £28 family.

Warwick Castle began life in 914, when the mound of earth upon which it sits was claimed by Ethelfleda. The motte and bailey were further fortified by William the Conqueror. Among the highlights of the present-day building are the Ghost Tower, which is said to be haunted by the ghost of Sir Fulke Greville, who owned the castle in the seventeenth century, the Great Hall, restored to its former glory after a devastating fire in 1871, the elegant State Rooms and the seventeenth-century chapel. Phone for details of special events.

Warwick County Museum

Market Place, Warwick (01926 412500).
Open 10am-5.30pm Mon-Sat; *May-Sept* 11am-5pm Sun. **Admission** free; donations welcome.

The seventeenth-century Market Hall houses displays of Warwickshire geology, biology and history, including giant fossils, live bees and the Sheldon tapestry map.

Oxford

Students and tourists – you just can't avoid 'em.

When a city has the irresistible twin draws of possibly the world's most famous university, and probably the best-loved and grumpiest detective on TV, Inspector Morse, it's no surprise that the locals sometimes feel under siege. Of Oxford's 118,000 inhabitants, some 15 per cent are reckoned to be the transient University population, and the streets fairly throb all year round with tourists and rucksacked European school parties. The city centre is dominated by the University, although there are other parts of town – notably Jericho and Summertown to the north, and Headington and Cowley to the west – with their own distinct identities and considerably fewer sightseers and students.

There is a certain perversity to place names in Oxford, ranging from downright mispronunciation (Magdalen is 'Maudlin', the River Cherwell is 'Charwell') to renaming in the case of the Isis (the Thames to anyone else) and strange predilection for dropping the 'street' part of road names (The High, The Turl, The Broad). In this latter category are a number of streets named solely after obscure saints (St Aldate's, St Ebbe's, St Giles').

Oxford arose as a Saxon burg built to defend Wessex from the dastardly Danes – the eleventh-century St Michael's Tower in Cornmarket Street is the only surviving building of this period. Its position at the confluence of the Cherwell and Isis was easy to defend, helped by the city wall built by the Normans (Charles I agreed, as he made the city his Royalist HQ during the Civil War).

Town v gown

By the twelfth century, Oxford saw its status as a market town becoming eclipsed by the nascent monastic colleges, which by the thirteenth century had developed into the

By train from London

Trains to **Oxford** leave **Paddington** about every half an hour; the journey time is about **1hr**.

*Ornithological and human water traffic on the **Cherwell**.*

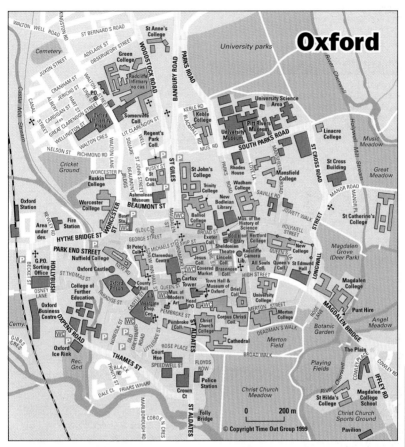

University, and this inevitably led to a degree of disharmony between town and gown.

This antipathy has often been fierce, and never more so than in the St Scholastica's Day Massacre of 10 February 1355. An affray in the Swindlestock Tavern (now the Abbey National at Carfax crossroads) erupted into a bloody riot, which left 60 students dead. The city's representatives were forced to attend a yearly penitential mass for nigh-on five centuries to rub their collective nose in their underdog status.

Car facts

The city finally got out from under the University's gown-tails thanks to the motor magnate William Morris, who graduated from a city-centre bicycle shop at the turn of the century to making 41 per cent of Britain's cars

in his Cowley plant by the mid-1920s. (His original garage can be seen on Longwall Street.) The Mini, Morris Minor and (no surprises here) Morris Oxford all came out of Cowley. The plant, now owned by Rover, has suffered an uncomfortable number of redundancies over the past decade, but remains one of the area's major employers.

Oddly, for a city with such close links to the motor industry, Oxford's council is vehemently anti-car. A medieval streetplan and one of the most tortuous one-way systems in the civilised world have recently been compounded by a programme of pedestrianisation that has entirely sealed off Cornmarket Street and half of Broad Street to traffic, and restricted access (buses only) to the High Street between 7.30am and 6.30pm. The clear message is that you should leave the car at home: fortunately, bus services are good and both the Oxford Tube and the CityLink run fast, frequent coaches to London.

This isn't a town packed with stylish places to stay, so pitch your expectations accordingly. Accommodation is split down the middle: hotels in the city centre tend to be expensive, whereas all the best B&Bs are a considerable distance out of town, near the ring road. It should be worth checking out the pricey but sleekly luxurious **Old Bank Hotel** (92-94 High Street; 01865 511115) when it opens in autumn 1999.

Bath Place Hotel

4 & 5 Bath Place, OX1 3SU (01865 791812/ fax 01865 791834/bathplace@compuserve.com/ www.bathplace.co.uk).
Rates (B&CB) *single occupancy £90-£125; double £95-£145; twin £100; four-poster £135-£145; cottage suite £125-£155.* **Rooms** (all en suite) 7 double; 2 twin; 2 four-posters; 2 suites.
Cards AmEx, MC, V.

Converted from Jacobean weavers' cottages built on the outer side of the city wall (sections of it are still visible in the restaurant and beside the neighbouring Turf Tavern), Bath Place has all the idiosyncrasies and hazardous staircases you would expect from buildings of this vintage. Heavy wooden beams and whitewashed walls predominate, and the uneven floors can induce seasickness – the alarm clock by one of the four-posters is in continual danger of sliding off its table. The hotel is family-run (by the Fawsitts), non-smoking (except in the bar), and is perhaps most notable for its restaurant, **Il Cortile** (*see p184*).

Chestnuts

45 Davenant Road (off Woodstock Road), OX2 8BU (tel/fax 01865 553375).
Rates (B&B) *single £40; double £62-£70; twin £62-£64.* **Rooms** (all en suite) 1 single; 3 double; 1 twin.
'Cead mile fáilte', reads the sign at the top of Tony and Ann O'Connor's pine staircase, and the weary traveller is certainly grateful for those hundred thousand welcomes after the lengthy trek into the extremities of north Oxford. The décor in this '50s suburban house could be described as 'Classic B&B' (chintz, knick-knacks, etc), with breakfast being served in an airy extension to the rear. Room sizes vary, but the best one is very spacious, boasting its own sofa and a commanding view of this sleepy wayfare of the Woodstock Road. No smoking throughout.

Cotswold House

363 Banbury Road, OX2 7PL (tel/fax 01865 310558/ d.r.walker@talk21.com).
Rates (B&B) *single £41-43; double £65-70; twin £65; family room £78.* **Rooms** (all en suite) 2 single; 2 double; 1 twin; 2 family. **Cards** Debit, MC, V.

Alan Clarke's successful north Oxford B&B takes its name from the warm Cotswold stone from which it is constructed. As far as the interior is concerned, it's distinctly suburban, with dark-wood furniture, fake beams on the ceiling, 'leaded' double-glazing and the obligatory Laura Ashley bedspreads. The atmosphere is friendly, and the large breakfasts (including vegetarian/vegan options, and additional fare such as kippers when the mood strikes) are very popular. Atheists may wish to steer clear of the devotional magazines that are strategically placed around the lounge. The house is entirely non-smoking, and only children over five are welcome.

Gables

6 Cumnor Hill, OX2 9HA (01865 862153/ fax 01865 864054/stay@gables-oxford.co.uk/ www.oxfordcity.co.uk/accom/gables).
Rates (B&B) *single £22-£28; double/twin £44-£48.*
Rooms (all en suite) 2 single; 4 double/twin.
Cards MC, V.

Sally and Tony Tompkins's friendly, competitively priced B&B is quite a long way down the Botley Road (where it turns into Cumnor Hill), but well worth the journey. Sally's motto would seem to be that you don't get anywhere in this business by standing still: she is continually redecorating the rooms to keep them fresh and creating impressive floral displays in the huge garden, as well as arranging a special deal with the local video shop so guests can hire films for the combined TV/video in every room. A scrapbook of her previous accolades ('Landlady of the Year', 'Britain in Bloom' et al) in the conservatory testifies to this. Children welcome. Non-smoking throughout.

Galaxie Hotel

180 Banbury Road, OX2 7BT (01865 515688/ fax 01865 556824/info@galaxie.co.uk/ www.oxlink.co.uk/oxford/hotels/galaxie.html).
Rates (B&B) *single £39-£50; double £72; twin £58-£72; four-poster £95; family room £81-£88.*
Rooms 6 single (4 en suite); 14 double (13 en suite); 7 twin (6 en suite); 1 four-poster (en suite); 4 family (all en suite). **Cards** Debit, MC, V.

A large, ivy-clad building in Summertown that caters mainly to a business crowd, the Galaxie strikes a mid-point in both price and location between the city-centre hotels and the peripheral B&Bs. The rooms are similarly yet individually decorated in restrained pastels (perhaps green, yellow or peach); despite the ashtrays, they are all non-smoking (though visitors can give in if they absolutely must). Check into the honeymoon room and you will find a four-poster bed, marble bathroom and a fabulously gimmicky pair of remote-controlled curtains. Breakfast is taken in a spacious conservatory (chandeliers, more ivy, floral curtains), and the garden even has a pool of placid koi carp. Children and dogs are welcome.

Old Parsonage Hotel

1 Banbury Road, OX2 6NN (01865 310210/ fax 01865 311262/info@oldparsonage-hotel.co.uk/ www.oxford-hotels-restaurants.co.uk).
Rates (B&B) *single occupancy £125; double £145-£195; twin £160-£195.* **Rooms** (all en suite) 30 double/twin. **Cards** AmEx, DC, Debit, MC, V.

*The historic **Old Parsonage Hotel**, one-time home to the young Oscar Wilde.*

Over the years, the Old Parsonage has been inhabited by nuns, a wigmaker, two mayors and the undergraduate Oscar Wilde. Since 1989, however, it has been easily one of the classiest hotels in Oxford; its rooms have a traditional, country-ish air, with authentically creaky floorboards but also luxurious marble bathrooms. The small Parsonage Bar is crammed with prints and paintings and offers a high-quality modern menu; food and drink are also available via 24-hour room service. They'll even arrange private guided tours of the colleges for you. The owner, Jeremy Mogford, is also responsible for **Gee's** restaurant (*see p184*) – meals there can be charged to your hotel account – and the new **Old Bank Hotel** (92-94 High Street; 01865 511115), which has a more contemporary, minimalist atmosphere. Children welcome.

The Randolph

Beaumont Street, OX1 2LN (01865 247481/ fax 01865 791678/GM1170@forte-hotels.com/ www.heritage-hotels.com).
Rates *single* £140; *double/twin* £170; *deluxe double/twin* £190; *four-poster* £210; *suite* £250-£400. Breakfast £13.75 (Eng); £10 (cont).
Rooms (all en suite) 32 single; 54 double; 16 twin; 7 deluxe double; 1 four-poster; 9 suites.
Cards AmEx, DC, Debit, MC, V.

Oxford's most famous hotel is inevitably pricey, but gives you a big dollop of grandeur for your money. The impressive main staircase won't let you forget which city you're in, with mirrored lancet arches and photographs from the Oxford Union. The rooms are individually decorated in the same self-consciously grand style, with William Morris (the designer, not the car magnate) wallpaper and heavy drapes; those converted from staff quarters on the top floor are more restrained. Suites are expensive but sumptuous, and named after individual colleges. The clientele tends towards the corporate/conference types – but Inspector Morse creator Colin Dexter can also be found propping up one of the hotel's bars on occasion. There's 24-hour room service. Children and dogs welcome. Non-smoking rooms available.

Where to eat & drink

While Oxford has a lot of good-quality restaurants, there are not that many in the city centre. Beyond the basic, deep-fried fare of the **Carfax Chip Shop**, there is the **Grand Café** (84 High Street; 01865 204463) on the site of the first coffee house in England (1641). Little Clarendon Street, at the Jericho end of St Giles', has a number of chain restaurants such as Café Rouge and Pierre Victoire, as well as the superior brasserie **Browns** (5-11 Woodstock Road; 01865 311415).

Down the vaguely bohemian Cowley Road are a large number of curry houses and Chinese takeaways, as well as **Mario & Mario** (109 Cowley Road; 01865 722955), an excellent pizzeria, and the **Hi-Lo Jamaican Eating House** (78 Cowley Road; 01865 725984), a Caribbean restaurant with dishes that change daily but normally include jerk chicken (£8) and curried goat (£8.50).

There are plenty of pubs to choose from in Oxford, with prices indiscernible from those in London and food indiscernible from one to the

The Cotswolds

Le Petit Blanc – *a little gem.*

next. Among the more student choices are the **King's Arms** at the corner of Holywell Street ('the KA' if you're trying too hard; overrated but strangely popular), the **Bear** on Blue Boar Street (low ceilings and a 'fascinating' collection of cut-off ties) and the **Turf Tavern** between Hertford and New Colleges (equally low-slung and Oxford's oldest inn). The **White House** behind the station is a gastro-pub with live, Chris Barber-ish jazz at Sunday lunchtime, while the part-thatched **Perch** on Binsey Lane has a big garden, a children's play area and is located close to the river.

Al-Shami
25 Walton Crescent (01865 310066).
Food served noon-midnight daily.
Set meals £15 (2 courses). **Cards** MC, V.
It is perhaps best to visit this Lebanese restaurant in a large group and concoct a meal from a selection of hors d'oeuvres – including Armenian spiced sausages (£3.20), fried sweetbread with lemon juice (£3.60) or even the Nkha'at Salatah (lamb's brain salad, £3.60). Main dishes – grilled lamb cubes with onions and tomatoes (£6.60), say – are less satisfying.

Cherwell Boathouse Restaurant
Bardwell Road (01865 552746).
Food served noon-2pm, 6.30-10pm, Tue-Sat; noon-2pm Sun. **Set meals** *lunch* £18.50 (3 courses); *dinner* £20.50 (3 courses). **Cards** AmEx, DC, Debit, MC, V.
Based at one of the city's major punting termini, the Boathouse Restaurant is hidden in an inauspicious pavilion down a north Oxford backstreet, where it is actually possible to see chaps sporting *Three Men in a Boat* candy-striped blazers. From the set menu you might choose straightforward but classy dishes such as an artichoke and tomato salad with peanut vinaigrette, or free-range loin of pork with a tomato, olive and herb salsa, and cap it off with tiramisu.

Gee's
61 Banbury Road (01865 553540).
Food served noon-2.30pm, 6-11pm, Mon-Sat; noon-11pm Sun. **Set meals** *lunch Mon-Sat* £9.75 (3 courses). **Cards** AmEx, Debit, MC, V.
For many years a florist's shop, Gee's Victorian conservatory dining room is still crammed with leafy green growth. The menu is broadly Modern European: linguine with wild mushrooms (£5.95) followed by pan-fried duck with smoked aubergine and polenta (£13.95); that sort of thing.

Il Cortile
4 & 5 Bath Place (01865 791812).
Food served 12.30-2.15pm, 7-9.30pm, Tue-Sat.
Set meals *lunch* £14.50 (2 courses).
Cards AmEx, MC, V.
The menu at the **Bath Place Hotel** (*see p182*) has moved south, from French to traditional Italian fare, and is refreshingly free of the standard pizza/pasta dishes. Instead, a typical meal might consist of an asparagus and Parmesan gazpacho (£6.50), followed by grilled sea bass on a bed of crispy risotto (£17.50) and home-made ice-cream (£6).

Lemon Tree
268 Woodstock Road (01865 311936).
Food served noon-11pm daily.
Cards AmEx, Debit, MC, V.
With its indoor palms, ceiling fans and curvy wicker chairs (which prove rather tricky to pull in to the table), Clinton Pugh's restaurant has a tropical, colonial atmosphere. The competently cooked, internationally-inspired food complements the setting: tomato consommé (£5.95), perhaps, followed by breast of chicken on a bed of tagliatelle (£13.95) or rump of Aberdeen Angus beef (£15.95).

Le Petit Blanc
71-72 Walton Street
(01865 510999/www.manoir.com).
Food served 11am-10.30pm Mon-Fri; 11am-10.45pm Sat, Sun. **Set meals** £12.50 (2 courses); £15 (3 courses). **Cards** AmEx, DC, Debit, MC, V.
Depending on which part of Raymond Blanc's Jericho brasserie you are sitting in, while you eat you can look at a bright mural of Oxford landmarks or an aluminium canteen hatch affair, beyond which food is prepared in view of the diners. Dishes such as a starter of mackerel escabeche (£4.95) and a confit of salmon, potato and dill cake with red wine jus (£12.50) betray the expected modern French influence. Children are actively welcomed and have their own menu.

Restaurant Elizabeth
82 St Aldate's (01865 242230).
Food served 12.30-2.30pm, 6.30-11pm, Tue-Sat; 12.30-2.30pm, 7-10.30pm, Sun. **Set meals** *lunch* £16 (3 courses). **Cards** AmEx, DC, Debit, MC, V.
With escargots à la bourguignonne (£6.50) among the starters, and main courses such as suprême de canard à l'orange (£16.50) and filet de boeuf maison (£17.75), Restaurant Elizabeth is the top spot in Oxford for no-nonsense, traditional French dishes that are not subject to the vagaries of gastronomic fashion.

The Cotswolds

What to see & do

Beware of the exploitative tourist honeypots, and the open-top tour buses claiming to offer unsurpassed views of the colleges, since large sections of the centre are inaccessible to them.

Tourist information centre

The Old School, Gloucester Green, OX1 2DA (01865 726871/www.oxford.gov.uk). **Open** *Easter-Oct* 9.30am-5pm Mon-Sat; 10am-3.30pm Sun; *Nov-Easter* 9.30am-5pm Mon-Sat.

Bike hire

Warlands 63 Botley Road (01865 241336). Not far from the station.

Ashmolean Museum

Beaumont Street (01865 278000/ www.ashmol.ox.ac.uk). **Open** 10am-5pm Tue-Sat; 2-5pm Sun. **Admission** free.

Home to the University's art collection (very big on Islamic and oriental stuff, ancient artefacts and the Pre-Raphaelites), the museum was founded by Elias Ashmole in 1683 – it was the first public museum in the country – although the current, neo-classical premises date from the 1840s. The museum is closed during St Giles' Fair in early September.

Bodleian Library

Broad Street (01865 277000/www.lib.ox.ac.uk/olis). **Open** *Apr-Dec* 10am-4pm Mon-Fri; 10am-12.30pm Sat; *Jan-Mar* Sat only (phone for details). Tours 10.30am, 11.30am, 2pm, 3pm, Mon-Fri; 10.30am, 11.30am, Sat. **Admission** *tour* £3.50.

The University's huge, reference-only library incorporates some of the most spectacular architecture in Oxford. Its earliest part is the fifteenth-century Divinity School, with a lierne vaulted ceiling; the Duke Humfrey's Library (1488), replete with wooden beams and resident deathwatch beetle, was home to the founder's collection of manuscripts. Post-printing press, the library was refounded by Thomas Bodley in 1602, which led to the construction of the Jacobean Old Schools Quadrangle, and later James Gibbs's reading rotunda, the Radcliffe Camera (1749). The library is entitled to a copy of every book published in Britain, and over six million of them are housed in its Stacks – miles of underground shelving. Note that children under 14 are not allowed. The guided tour lasts an hour.

Botanic Garden

High Street (01865 276920). **Open** *Apr-Sept* 9am-5pm daily; *Oct-Mar* 9am-4.30pm daily. **Admission** *Apr-Aug* £2; *Sept-Mar* donation; free under-12s.

Founded in 1621 to grow medicinal plants for University research, the Botanic Garden is the oldest in Britain. Look out for the century plant (Agave americana), which flowers only once in 10-30 years (originally thought to be once in a century).

Carfax Tower

Carfax (no phone). **Open** *Apr-Oct* 10am-5.30pm daily; *Nov-Mar* 10am-3.30pm daily. **Admission** £1.20; 60p 5s-16s.

The walk up the 99 steps of this thirteenth-century tower – the only surviving remnant of St Martin's Church, demolished to make room for traffic in 1896 – is hard on the calves, but rewarding on the eyes with a panoramic view of the city and the hills beyond.

The stately confines of Tom Quad in upper-crust **Christ Church College**. *See page 186.*

Secret Oxford

Not everything in Oxford is swamped by the tourist hordes. Here are a handful of the city's lesser-known treasures.

A fishy tale

The terraced house at 2 New High Street, Headington, is a work of conceptual art that predates Damien Hirst's shark by five years. It has a plaque saying 'Untitled 1986' where another house might read 'Dunroamin', and a bloody great fibreglass shark sticking out of the roof, much to the council's chagrin.

The king of rock

Among the stone heads decorating the tower at Magdalen is a bequiffed gargoyle bearing a curious resemblance to the King of Rock 'n' Roll. One of a number of replacements for those damaged in storms, it was put up in 1977 (the year of Elvis's death), and is best viewed from the quad behind the porter's lodge.

Magdalen is open noon-6pm daily (£2.50; £1.25 under-16s).

Let there be light

The fact that *The Light of the World* (1864), William Holman Hunt's Pre-Raphaelite painting of Christ, is in the chapel at Keble is actually quite well known, but is worth mentioning purely for the cheap irony that it can only be seen if a little lightbulb is switched on. Keble is open 2-5pm daily (admission free).

Zuleika's progress

As well as some amusingly poor copies of Pre-Raphaelite works, the Randolph hotel contains a set of 12 paintings by Osbert Lancaster depicting scenes from Beerbohm's comic novel *Zuleika Dobson*, including the 'Emperors' outside the Sheldonian sweating with lust, and the menfolk of Oxford drowning themselves in the river.

Colleges of Oxford University

The University, which has been in existence since at least the twelfth century, is undoubtedly the major touristic draw of the city. Over the years the colleges have seen to the education of vast numbers of the great and good, as well as every British Prime Minister of the twentieth century except James Callaghan and John Major. If, however, you are motivated by more than a rubberneck desire to see where Rupert Murdoch, say, went to college (Worcester, if you are that interested), the principal attraction has to be the architecture – the 'dreaming spires' of tourist-board cliché. The majority of the 41 colleges and halls are open to the public at differing times, usually in the afternoon (details are displayed at the porter's lodges; some colleges charge a fee for admission).

The largest of the colleges is **Christ Church** (founded 1525), whose Tom Tower – a Gothic spacerocket designed by Wren – dominates the St Aldate's skyline. The college also has its own gallery, full of Old Masters, and the chapel also serves as the city's cathedral. **Magdalen** (1458) has large gardens and a deer park, and choristers sing madrigals atop its tower at dawn on May Morning (1 May). The famous Bridge of Sighs can be found connecting the two parts of **Hertford** (1283), which also has an impressively quirky spiral staircase giving on to the main quad. The largely Hawksmoor-designed **All Souls** (1438) is reserved solely for Fellows; **Trinity** (1555) has extensive, beautiful gardens; **Merton** (1264) a stunning medieval chapel; and **Oriel** (1324) an impressive Jacobean quad. If you weary of seeing yet more Gothic buildings in that same yellowy stone, try the eighteenth-century classi-

cism of **Queen's** (founded 1341), the almost industrial Victorian brickwork of **Keble** (1868), or the clean Modernist lines at **St Catherine's** (1964) – entirely designed by Arne Jacobsen, even down to the cutlery.

Martyrs' Memorial

St Giles'.

George Gilbert Scott's 1841 Gothic spire commemorates the Protestant martyrs Cranmer, Latimer and Ridley, who Queen Mary burned around the corner in Broad Street (a cross marks the spot). Although gullible tourists are (apocryphally, at least) often told that the memorial is the steeple of an underground church, there is nothing beneath it but public toilets.

Museum of the History of Science

Broad Street (01865 277280/www.mhs.ox.ac.uk).
Open noon-4pm Tue-Sat. **Closed until September 2000. Admission** free.

The original premises of the Ashmolean, the seventeenth-century building is now crammed with a fascinating collection of timepieces, astrolabes, microscopes and other scientific ephemera, including Einstein's blackboard, on which the great man diligently shows all his working.

Museum of Modern Art

Pembroke Street (01865 722733).
Open 11am-6pm Tue-Sun. **Admission** £2.50; £1.50 OAPs, students; free under-16s.

A converted brewery with no permanent collection, the museum shows numerous temporary exhibitions of modern art, ranging from the pioneering to the pretentious.

The Cotswolds

Museum of Oxford

St Aldate's (01865 252761).
Open 10am-4pm Tue-Fri; 10am-5pm Sat;
noon-4pm Sun. **Admission** £2; 50p 5s-18s;
£1.50 OAPs, students.

A relatively informative trudge through Oxford's history since prehistoric times, but a number of the exhibits are showing their age.

The Oxford Story

Broad Street (01865 790055).
Open *Apr-June, Sept, Oct* 9.30am-5pm Mon-Sun;
July, Aug 9am-5.30pm daily; *Nov-Mar* 10am-4.30pm
Mon-Fri; 10am-5pm Sat, Sun. **Admission** £5.50;
£4.50 4s-16s, OAPs, students; £16.50 family.

As far as this tourist trap is concerned, the Oxford Story is pretty much restricted to that of the University. Visitors sit behind mobile desks and trundle through its history, re-enacted by a series of mannequins, with audio commentary by those academic luminaries Magnus Magnusson… and Timmy Mallett. There are better ways of spending an hour.

Pitt Rivers Museum

Parks Road (01865 270927/www.prm.ox.ac.uk).
Open 1-4.30pm Mon-Sat. **Closed until January
2000**. **Admission** free.

Reopening in 2000 with a spanking new roof, the Pitt Rivers is the anthropological annexe to the University Museum. Its dark corners house such arcane delights as voodoo dolls, shrunken heads, peace pipes and a totem pole, all marked with tiny, handwritten labels. Pull open the drawers to find more ethnological delights under glass. The museum may open on Sundays when it reopens in 2000; phone for details.

Punting

The quintessential Oxbridge pastime, punting has developed from a form of freight transportation to a lazy summer pursuit. The punter propels the boat with a long pole while standing in the hollow of the bow (there is no greater faux pas than punting from the other, 'Cambridge', end). There are two principal departure points for punting on the River Cherwell: **Magdalen Bridge** (01865 761586; punt hire £9-£10 per hour, plus £25 deposit) or the **Cherwell Boathouse** in Bardwell Road (01865 515978; £8-£10 per hour, plus £40-£50 deposit). The cushions are red at Magdalen and blue at Cherwell, so there is great kudos in manoeuvring a red-cushioned punt all the way up into blue waters.

Sheldonian Theatre

Broad Street (01865 277299).
Open *mid-Feb-mid-Nov* 10am-12.30pm, 2-4.30pm,
Mon-Sat; *mid-Nov-mid-Feb* 10am-3.30pm Mon-Sat.
Admission £1.50; £1 5s-16s.

This Restoration theatre was built – by Christopher Wren, then Professor of Astronomy at the University – for University degree ceremonies, although these days the grimacing cherubs painted on the ceiling also look down on concerts. The hirsute busts outside, sometimes referred to as emperors, sometimes as philosophers, are actually stylised versions of non-specific, off-the-shelf Romans.

University Museum

Parks Road (01865 272950).
Open noon-5pm daily. **Admission** free.

A taxidermist's dream, this natural history museum is stuffed with numerous beasties and dinosaurs. The museum is also worth visiting purely for its Victorian Gothic architecture and vaulted glass-and-iron roof.

The head of an anonymous Roman looks on from outside the **Sheldonian Theatre**.

South Oxfordshire

Mess about on the river, yomp along the Ridgeway, search out the haunts of literary lions.

The churchyard of the atmospheric Abbey at **Dorchester-on-Thames**.

The area south of Oxford is a gentle, unspectacular landscape, well cultivated (and populated) and packed with carefully groomed commuter villages and rich farmland. The River Thames cuts a swathe through its eastern flank, wending its way northwards through the university town and then west towards its source in Gloucestershire. To the south, the ancient Ridgeway path crosses the Berkshire Downs, lending a pagan dash of the primitive, the impressionistic slash of the chalk White Horse fuelling countless local legends and giving its name to the adjacent valley.

Around the towns

Abingdon, painted by Turner and admired by Ruskin, is the oldest continuously occupied town in England and the largest in the Vale of the White Horse. Sadly choked by traffic at the weekends, but with a good Thames-side setting and pleasant river walks, it contains an abbey that was founded in the late seventh century, a row of fifteenth-century almshouses still in use (the Long Alley Almshouses) and the magnificent English Baroque County Hall (now a museum), built by a protégé of Christopher Wren. It also boasts the area's only (and usually packed) branch of Pizza Express, along with plenty of tea and sandwich shops; there's an arts festival every April; and there are boats and bicycles for hire (for both, *see page 192-3*) to help you explore the surrounding countryside (enquire at the tourist information office on Bridge Street).

By train from London

Trains for **Dorchester** leave **Waterloo** hourly, and take **2hrs 30mins**. Unfortunately, there's no longer a train station in Abingdon: the nearest is at **Oxford** (*see page 180*). In addition, there are four trains an hour at weekends from **Paddington** to **Didcot Parkway**, taking between **40mins** and **1hr 20mins**.

The other main towns in the area are **Faringdon**, to the west off the A420, which was besieged by Cromwell's troops during the Civil War and is now famous for Lord Berners' 140-foot brick folly, built in the 1930s. Further south and east, the town of **Wantage** was the birthplace in 848 of Alfred the Great, warrior, statesman and educational pioneer. His statue is the centrepiece of the town square, also the site of a twice-weekly market (Wednesdays and Saturdays) and several small shops including a good baker and the India Shop, packed with Asian knick-knacks. At **Wallingford**, a town that strategically straddles the river to the east, there are the remains of Wallingford Castle, Saxon earthworks and a fine medieval bridge, as well as antique shops galore.

Village life

Among the many pretty villages that dominate the area is the thatched and half-timbered **Blewbury**, off the A417 south of Didcot, and **Buscot** (off the A417 beyond Faringdon to the west), whose church of St Mary contains a superb set of stained-glass windows designed by Edward Burne-Jones and manufactured by Morris and Company. The chancel dates from around 1200. The splendid Abbey at **Dorchester-on-Thames**, on the site of a Saxon cathedral, has been a centre of Christianity for nearly 14 centuries. The present building was begun during the twelfth century and still contains a Norman font, medieval floor tiles and the thirteenth-century effigy of an unknown knight in the act of drawing his sword, said to have influenced Henry Moore. It also contains the poignant memorial to one Sarah Fletcher, who died aged 29 on 7 June 1799, a 'martyr to excessive sensibility'. We know how she felt. The tranquil village, with a number of pubs, a couple of teashops and a distinctly classy antique dealer's, was spared the traffic-congested fate of Wallingford and Abingdon when the A4074 to Oxford was built round, not through, it.

Bookish bragging

South Oxfordshire boasts countless literary links. The churchyard at **Sutton Courtenay** contains the grave of one Eric Blair, better known as George Orwell (as well as a monument to the pre-World War I Prime Minister, Lord Asquith). The stretch of the River Thames occupied by the **Beetle & Wedge** hotel (*see below*) was immortalised in *The Wind in the Willows* (Kenneth Grahame lived in Blewbury between 1910 and 1924) and by Jerome K Jerome. It's one of several local hostelries that claim Jerome wrote *Three Men*

in a Boat while living there (as does the Two Brewers pub in Marlow; Jerome obviously got about a bit while researching his book). Like their creator, his hapless trio also stopped off at the Barley Mow in Clifton Hampden and the Anchor Inn at Abingdon Wharf, among others. **The Craven** in Uffington (*see page 190*) enjoys a walk-on part as 'a low-lying wayside inn' in *Tom Brown's Schooldays*, whose author Thomas Hughes lived nearby; the poet John Betjeman also lived in the village during the 1930s.

Where to stay

There is no shortage of unremarkable wayside inns, basic B&Bs or rooms-above-pubs in the area, though their proximity to London and Oxford tends to be reflected in their prices. Here are a few of the more noteworthy options. The **Lamb Inn** in Buckland (*see page 192*) also has rooms.

Beetle & Wedge

Ferry Lane, Moulsford-on-Thames, OX10 9JF (01491 651381/fax 01491 651376).
Rates (B&B) *single occupancy* £90-£110; *double/twin* £135-£150; *triple* £160. Special breaks.
Rooms (all en suite) 9 double/twin; 1 triple.
Cards AmEx, DC, Debit, MC, V.

George Orwell's grave in **Sutton Courtenay**.

*Crazy décor at the **Crazy Bear**, Stadhampton.*

If you don't want to lay down the £150 required for a room here, stop off and have a civilised pot of tea in front of the fire or in the garden instead. Given the enviable riverside setting, comfortable country house furnishings and impeccable service, it's not surprising that the Beetle is much-favoured by honeymooners. All rooms are luxurious doubles with spacious bathrooms, most have river views, and rates include a full English breakfast. You can eat in the formal (and expensive) dining room or the more laid-back, beamed-and-brick Boathouse restaurant, both overlooking the water. Splash out, book well in advance and pay the extra for that river view. Children welcome. All bedrooms non-smoking.

A329 NW of Reading; turn right at first crossroads in Moulsford into Ferry Lane; house is at end of lane by river.

The Craven

Fernham Road, Uffington, SN7 7RD (01367 820449).
Rates (B&B) *£28-£65pp.* **Rooms** 1 single; 3 double/twin; 2 four-poster (both en suite). **Cards** AmEx, MC, V.

An idyllic, 300-year-old thatched cottage on the northern edge of pretty Uffington village, near the White Horse and the Ridgeway. Carol Wadsworth treats her guests as part of the family (indeed, you half expect to be told to eat up your greens or asked to help with the washing up) and breakfast is shared by guests at a large table in the crimson-painted kitchen, complete with pine dresser and resident shaggy dog. One of the best rooms – the Elizabethan double, with chintz-hung four-poster and en suite bathroom – is on the ground floor; the others are up the crooked stairs and down winding passageways stocked with faded family photos and back copies of *Horse & Hound*. For a rather steep £17.50 you can have a three-course dinner cooked by Carol's daughter, who honed her skills at the stove working as a chalet girl. Children welcome. All bedrooms non-smoking.

B4000 to Lambourn; take B4001 N; turn left before Childrey on to B4057 to Kingston Lisle; turn right by White Horse Hill to Uffington; right after church on Fernham Road; house is 200m on left.

Crazy Bear

Bear Lane, Stadhampton, OX44 7UR
(01865 890714/fax 01865 400481).
Rates (B&CB) *single occupancy* £60-£80; *double* £80-£100; *four-poster* £100; *suite* £120; *cottage* £260-£280. Breakfast £8.50 (Eng). Special breaks. **Rooms** (all en suite) 3 double; 1 four-poster; 1 suite; 2 cottages (sleep 5 or 6). **Cards** AmEx, Debit, MC, V.

Crazy by name, crazy by nature. From the outside this sixteenth-century building looks like just another cute country pub, and the beamed, low-ceilinged bar (which serves draught champagne) could seem to confirm that impression, but eat in either of the two excellent restaurants (one contemporary, one Thai) or ascend to the extraordinary bedrooms and your expectations will be confounded. Some are very small, but all are remarkably decorated with zebra-print carpet, bold colours, spiralling sculptural metal bedsteads and beautifully chic bathrooms. One on its own. Children welcome. All bedrooms non-smoking.

A329 SE; in Stadhampton turn left after petrol station and left again into Bear Lane.

The George

High Street, Dorchester-on-Thames, OX10 7HH
(01865 340404/fax 01865 341620).
Rates (B&ContB) *single* £62.50; *single occupancy* £70; *double/twin* £80; *four-poster* £92.50; *family* £100. Breakfast £3.50 (Eng). Special breaks.
Rooms (all en suite) 2 single; 13 double/twin; 2 four-poster; 1 family. **Cards** AmEx, MC, V.

A fifteenth-century whitewashed coaching inn with oak beams much in evidence. Décor is unpretentious (the chintz factor is low, velour high) but some of the rooms are large, some have four-posters and the en suite bathrooms have toiletries and good-quality white bath towels. Avoid the motel-style rooms in the courtyard and make sure there's room at the inn. You can eat well and not too expensively at the pleasant bar, or opt for a more elaborate experience in the beamed Carriages restaurant, where a fillet steak will set you back a whopping £17.50. Children and dogs welcome. Non-smoking rooms available.

Le Manoir aux Quat' Saisons

Church Road, Great Milton, OX44 7PD
(01844 278881/fax 01844 278847/
lemanoir@blanc.co.uk/www.manoir.com).
Rates (B&ContB) *double/twin* £275-£340; *four-poster* £340-£475; *suite* £395-£475. Breakfast £6 (Eng). Special breaks. Min 2 nights if staying Sat, May-Sept. **Rooms** (all en suite) 8 double/twin; 5 four-poster; 13 suites. **Cards** AmEx, DC, Debit, MC, V.

Raymond Blanc's famous two Michelin-starred restaurant and rural retreat needs no introduction. The only hotel in Britain to hold Relais et Châteaux gongs for top-notch food *and* accommodation, the place is a positive paean to luxury living. If you've got a spare £500 or so to blow on a night of no-holds-barred indulgence, this is the place to come. Prices of the rooms (which were described by Terence Conran as 'a hymn to contemporary style') go up to a whopping £475 for a suite with his 'n' hers matching roll-top baths; all include fresh fruit and flowers, morning tea or coffee and a newspaper. M Blanc's much-lauded contemporary French *menu gourmand* in the restaurant costs £72 for seven courses, but there's also the option of a (relatively) bargain three-course set lunch for £32. Stop by for a plate of roast pheasant stuffed with wild mushrooms and a *parfait glacé aux marrons*, and take a stroll in the magnificent gardens – Japanese, vegetable, herb or formal – in which some of the ingredients will have been grown. Children are welcome and dogs allowed (kennels provided).

A329 S; signposted 'Great Milton Manor'.

The White Horse & the Ridgeway

The oldest and possibly most famous **White Horse** (of the 17 white horses in England) is a sketchy pagan beast - it isn't etched on the hillside like the others, but made from several 10-foot wide, chalk-filled trenches, which have to be weeded and refilled from time to time. This ritual has been carried out over the past 100 generations or so by locals who believed the horse was a Saxon memorial to the victory of King Alfred over the Danes in the ninth century, or that it was a Celtic tribute to the goddess Epona, protectoress of horses. The service is now carried out by the National Trust, which has dated the figure back nearly 3,000 years to the late Bronze or early Iron Age, and think it may have acted as a banner for the inhabitants of **Uffington Castle**, the hill fort whose remains lie nearby.

The distinctive, flat-topped hill below the horse is **Dragon Hill**, reputedly where St George slew the beast. And about a mile to the west along the ancient **Ridgeway Path** (which runs for 85 miles from near Avebury in Wiltshire to Ivinghoe Beacon in Hertfordshire) is the prehistoric chambered tomb known as **Wayland's Smithy**, where horses left overnight would be shod by Wayland the Anglo-Saxon smith god.

The White Horse and Ridgeway beyond are accessible up a narrow path leading off the B4507; although the approach is spectacular, the horse is best seen from a distance, near Fernham (south of Faringdon) or from the Highworth to Shrivenham road. The Ridgeway is popular with horse-riders and cyclists as well as walkers, and be warned that it can get extremely muddy.

Plough Inn
Clifton Hampden, OX14 3EG
(01865 407811/fax 01865 407136).
Rates (B&B) *single occupancy* £67.50; *double/twin/four-poster/family* £82.50.
Rooms (all en suite) 5 double/twin/family; 7 four-poster. **Cards** AmEx, Debit, MC, V.

Despite its position on the A415, the picturesque Plough is peaceful at night and ideally placed for local Thames-side walks and picnics. Eight bedrooms – all en suite – are located in the main thatched and half-timbered inn or in the adjoining (and less prepossessing) single-storey annexe. All contain four-posters or half-testers and giant colour TVs, the general décor a typical pub mix of genuine and naff. Bathrooms tend to be big and well appointed. Reasonably priced though unspectacular meals (stir-fried chicken with rice, tagliatelle with salmon and dill) can be eaten in the restaurant behind the snug flagstoned bar. Be warned, however: the Plough is popular with noisy wedding parties, so check this when you book. Children welcome. No-smoking throughout.
A329 S to Stadhampton; right on to B4015 to Clifton Hampden; Plough Inn is on right by traffic lights in village.

Where to eat & drink

The area is peppered with good pubs. Among those recommended for eating as well as drinking are the **Red Lion** (01865 890625) in Chalgrove, which has been owned by the local church for several hundred years, Pot Boy's bar in the **George** at Dorchester (*see page 190*), and the roadside **Chequers** (01865 407771) at Burcot, where salad and herbs for the kitchen

are grown in the garden at the back. The **Plough** (*see above*) and the **Barley Mow** are both in Clifton Hampden; the former has a thriving restaurant run by a Turkish family; the latter has a nice garden and is an ideal place to refuel after a Thames-side walk. Two excellent restaurants lurk within the zany **Crazy Bear** (*see page 190*) at Stadhampton, one serving cracking Modern European food, the other offering equally good Thai grub. The **Bear & Ragged Staff** at Cumnor has log fires in winter and sofas to slump in; further south, the **Boar's Head** at Ardington is part of the Ardington estate and in a pretty village. **The Harrow** at West Ilsley is popular with walkers taking a break from the nearby Ridgeway and overlooks its own well-kept cricket pitch. The **Beetle & Wedge** (*see page 189*) offers notable classic country cooking in two different restaurants, and **Le Manoir aux Quat' Saisons** (*see page 190*) offers an award-winning gourmet experience in a league of its own.

Crooked Billet
Newlands Lane, Stoke Row (01491 681048).
Food served noon-2.15pm, 7-10pm, daily.
Set meals £10 (2 courses); £14.95 (3 courses).
Cards AmEx, DC, MC, V

An endearing pub in a picturesque setting, offering reliable modern cooking at restaurant prices. This is the spot where Kate Winslet and Jim Threapleton tied the knot, favouring bangers and mash for their wedding breakfast. You don't have to follow suit: smoked goose breast with shredded celeriac and horseradish, caviar with smoked salmon and blinis, guinea fowl with pancetta, baby onions and roast garlic, or tuna with pak choi and yakisoba noodles have all featured recently on a menu that changes weekly. Most main courses are between £10 and £13 and the wine list is varied and well chosen, if rather pricey.

The Goose

Britwell Salome (01491 612304).
Food served 12.30-2.30pm, 7-9.30pm, Tue-Sat; 12.30-2.30pm Sun. **Set meals** *dinner* £20 (2 courses); £25 (3 courses). **Cards** Debit, MC, V.

A roadside pub-turned-restaurant, the Goose retains a front bar where you can have a drink and a snack, but it's the above-average cooking that's the point here. There's a short lunchtime menu listing about half a dozen main courses ranging in price from £10 to £16 (grilled tuna with flageolets, roast veg and garlic sauce, ultra-tender lamb with mushrooms and roast potatoes, lobster ravioli or chicken and asparagus terrine) and a set three-course menu that operates in the evenings. Décor is a somewhat uneasy mix of pub and something more serious, but the staff are thoroughly charming and the food is well worth the trip. There's a small garden at the back.

Lamb Inn

Lamb Lane, Buckland (01367 870484).
Food served noon-2pm Mon-Thur; noon-2pm, 7-9pm, Fri, Sat; noon-3pm, 7-9pm, Sun.
Set meals £19.50 (3 courses) Sun.
Cards AmEx, DC, MC, V.

Not one for pub-crawlers, the rather sedate Lamb Inn lies in the heart of a village filled with quaint thatched and clematis-covered cottages. Although you might find steak and kidney pie on the menu here, dishes like spiced salmon and prawn kedgeree (£8.95), goat's cheese salad with deep-fried celeriac and a walnut and herb dressing (£5.95) or confit of duck are more representative. Bread is good, crusty and home-made and the service attentive. You can eat in the bar, the restaurant or a small terrace at the back. The place also has four rooms, all with bath or shower and TV (£35-£55).

Leathern Bottel

Goring-on-Thames (01491 872667).
Food served noon-2pm, 7-9.30pm, Mon-Thur; noon-2pm, 7-9.30pm, Fri; noon-2.30pm, 7-9.30pm, Sat; noon-3.30pm Sun. **Set meals** *dinner* £19.50 (3 courses) Mon-Thur. **Cards** AmEx, Debit, MC, V.

The very essence of picture-postcard tranquillity, the Leathern Bottel has the advantage of a Thames-side terrace that seats 25. Inside, the two small dining rooms are stuffed to the gills with flowers and candlesticks, books and baskets and gilt-framed mirrors. A short, steeply priced menu runs from salads and soups to fusion dishes such as squid with tabouleh and crispy seaweed (£7.10), lamb with mint, spring onion, garlic and sweet potato (£18.75), or free range chicken flavoured with lime, pancetta and lemongrass (£15.60). The wine list is impressive but expensive.

White Hart

Fyefield (01865 390585).
Food served noon-2pm, 7-10pm, daily.
Cards AmEx, Debit, MC, V.

Don't be fooled by the unimpressive exterior: inside the medieval White Hart lie rambling rooms and a high-ceilinged, beamed main hall filled with refectory tables, benches and candles. There's an extensive blackboard bar menu aimed at filling the hungry punters (Stilton steaks, mushroom, steak and Guinness pie, treacle tart or sticky toffee pudding) and well-kept Theakstons Old Peculier, Boddingtons and Hook Norton Best among the ales on tap. The garden at the back is ideal for lazy summer lunches and there's even a better-than-average children's play area. A pub that should please everyone.

Tourist information centres

24 Bridge Street, **Abingdon**, OX14 3HN (01235 522711). **Open** *Apr-Oct* 10am-5pm Mon-Sat; 1.30-4.15pm Sun; *Nov-Mar* 10am-4pm Mon-Fri; 9.30am-2.30pm Sat.

7A Market Place, **Faringdon**, SN7 7HL (01367 242191). **Open** *Apr-Oct* 10am-1pm, 1.30-5pm Mon-Fri; 10am-1pm Sat; *Nov-Mar* 10am-1pm Mon-Sat.

Bike hire

H & N Bragg 2 High Street, **Abingdon** (01235 520034). If you're coming from Oxford, you'll need to catch a bus or taxi to Abingdon as there's no train station here.

Abingdon Museum

County Hall, Abingdon (01235 523703).
Open *Apr-Oct* 11am-5pm daily; *Nov-Mar* 11am-4pm daily. **Admission** free; donations welcome.

Housed in Abingdon's superb seventeenth-century town hall, the museum has exhibits relating to the town's history. Not everyone's cup of tea, admittedly.

Buscot Park

Faringdon (01367 240786).
Open *Apr-Sept* 2-6pm Wed-Fri.
Admission (NT) £4.40; £2.20 5s-16s.

Three miles west of Faringdon, towards Lechlade, Buscot is an eighteenth-century Adam-style house set in parkland with lakes, water gardens and a walled garden. The house contains the Faringdon Collection, including paintings by Rembrandt, Murillo, the Pre-Raphaelites Rossetti, Watts and Madox Brown, and Edward Burne-Jones's 'Briar Rose' paintings.

Didcot Rail Centre

Entrance through Didcot Parkway station, Didcot (01235 817200).
Open *Apr-Sept* 10am-5pm daily; *Oct-Mar* 10am-4pm Sat, Sun. **Admission** £4; £3 4s-16s; £3.50 OAPs.

If you're a steam fan, then this homage to Isambard Kingdom Brunel's Great Western Railway will be paradise. The centre contains a collection of steam locomotives, either lovingly restored or in the process of being renovated, and a variety of GWR passenger coaches and freight wagons. There's a country station complete with level crossing and signalbox, a travelling post office and mail exchange, and for the really besotted, special Railway Experience Days, when punters can drive a steam engine.

Rambling along the river

The 180-mile Thames Path runs from London to the river's source near Kemble in Gloucestershire and is well worth exploring. At Goring, the river meanders northwards towards Oxford, passing through Moulsford, Wallingford, Shillingford, Burcot and Abingdon, all of which are good starting points for relinquishing the car and striking out on foot. From the **Beetle & Wedge** in **Moulsford** (*see also page 189 & picture below*) you can follow the river path downriver to Streatley and then cut inland along a section of the Ridgeway path, returning to Moulsford by a footpath that leads through Unhill Wood, crosses the

A417 and ends up back at Moulsford, a total distance of about eight miles. At **Dorchester**, you can walk to the river (take the path opposite the Abbey at the end of Rotten Row), past allotments to Davy's Lock and on to Wittenham Clumps.

If you want to go with the flow, rather than walk beside it, boats can be hired in Abingdon and, four miles west of Faringdon, from Cotswold Boat Hire (01793 693933) based at the charming Trout Inn near Lechlade. Salter Brothers Ltd (01793 693933) runs trips by steamer from Nags Head Island in Abingdon to Oxford between May and September. For more on boating on the Thames, *see page 212.*

Kingston Bagpuize House & Garden

Kingston Bagpuize, nr Abingdon
(info 01235 522711).
Open *house & gardens Apr-Sept* (phone for details).
Admission *house & garden* £3.50; £2.50 5s-15s;
£3 OAPs; *garden only* £1.50; free under-5s.
This handsome red-brick baroque house is set in mature parkland containing an early Georgian gazebo and a notable collection of shrubs, trees and perennials. Inside, there's a riot of panelled rooms, a fine cantilevered staircase and some decent furniture and pictures. There's also a tearoom. No children under five are allowed in the house.

Little Wittenham Nature Reserve

(01865 407792).
This lovely reserve incorporates Little Wittenham Wood and Wittenham Clumps. Comfrey, teasel and tall meliot grow along the woodland paths and more than 30 different species of butterfly have been spotted in an area that combines woodland, grassland and riverside habitats and offers some splendid vistas (climb to the top of Round Hill for wonderful views over Oxfordshire, the Cotswolds, the Chilterns and the Ridgeway). On Castle Hill, you'll find the site of an Iron Age hill fort. Little Wittenham is located just off the A4074, near Dorchester.

Woodstock
to Burford

England at its most stereotypically glorious.

The word picturesque was invented for the Cotswolds. Clusters of fairytale stone cottages with thatched or lichened roofs and smoking chimneys give each village a beauty that's incredibly civilised and terribly, terribly English. Pheasants waddle through glowing fields of rape, rabbits leap in hedgerows, birds sing and blossom falls: the Cotswolds exemplify rural England. It's all fecundity, fresh air and four-wheel-drives.

Not surprisingly, the Cotswolds is now officially designated an Area of Outstanding Beauty. Visitors long to spend their twilight years surrounded by such all-out prettiness, and consequently the area functions as the ultimate free-range retirement home. It's a sedate beauty that attracts an older crowd, so anticipate fresh air and pub meals rather than a rave-up.

The Romans are ultimately responsible for the area's wealth; they introduced the long-woolled breed of sheep, the 'Cotswold Lion', to these parts. Cotswold wool quickly gained an international reputation, flourishing between 1300 and 1500, and the wealth it brought to the area paid for the churches and grand houses that still dominate the villages. In the Middle Ages, grazing sheep took priority over human residents, occupying great tracts of land; in some cases, villagers were even evacuated from villages to give them more room.

Nowadays, the Cotswolds' main industry is tourism, a fact that's reflected in some steep prices. Yet the main attractions are free. Planted deep in the rich countryside are ancient ruins and historical country piles. It's not surprising that some serious – and not-so-serious – creative types have been inspired to live here, from Chaucer, William Morris and Laurie Lee to Jilly Cooper. There are attractive walks between most of the small villages – and pubs en route to ease the effort. Aim to avoid the beaten track.

Eight miles north of Oxford, on the southern edge of the Cotswold hills, lies the historic market town of **Woodstock**, centred around one of the county's main attractions, **Blenheim Palace** (*see page 199*). For many centuries, Woodstock was known for two main crafts – glove-making and decorative steel work – and supplied royalty with both. Woodstock has certainly entertained its fair share of blue blood: legend has it that King Alfred stayed in the town in the year 890, while Henry II often frolicked here with his mistress during the twelfth century. One bizarre ritual continues from the eighteenth century: the Mock Mayor Elections, which harks back to the time when inhabitants, fed up with their pompous mayor, decided to hold their own elections. The people would elect a mayor and corporation for Old Woodstock with 'mock formality' and then throw him into the River Glyme, the boundary between Old and New Woodstock. Modern Woodstock is, in general, more sophisticated, with a good market and antique shops.

Heading west towards Burford, **Minster Lovell** is well worth a stop and a stroll. One of the quietest and most unspoilt villages in the area, it boasts not only a gorgeous fifteenth-century church but also the dramatic ruins of Minster Lovell Hall. Dating from the 1440s, the Hall and its well-restored medieval dovecote make an imposing sight on the banks of the River Windrush. The stunning thatched cottages are some of the prettiest around.

Burford, an elegant and historic coaching town by the Windrush, makes a good, if pricey, base from which to explore the surrounding area. The much-photographed main street comprises a welter of pretty cottages clinging to a steeply sloping hill, and is smattered with

By train from London

The nearest station to **Woodstock** is **Hanborough**, 2.5 miles away. The journey time from **Paddington** takes **1hr 13mins**. Buses from Hanborough to Woodstock are scarce, so you're better off getting a taxi (Woodstock Travel 01993 891365). For **Burford**, your best bet is to get a train to **Oxford** (*see page 180*), then a bus to Burford.

Climbing roses in **Woodstock**.

antique shops, tea rooms and an inordinate number of stripy shirt and jumper shops, plus a massive garden centre, to satisfy the visiting hordes. For much of the year, the entire village is chockful of traffic; aim to visit in early spring or winter.

Burford's Norman church, remodelled in the 1400s, is proud of its graffiti, inflicted during the seventeenth century by some of the 400 Leveller mutineers imprisoned here by Cromwell. There are plenty of good riverside walks; try the path to Taynton via the Barringtons or to nearby Swinbrook, where writer Nancy Mitford is buried. To the north, there are paintings and fragments of Roman mosaics in the tiny church at Widford. A few miles north of Burford, the petite village of **Shipton-under-Wychwood** boasts a pretty church, which has a stained-glass window designed by the William Morris company and some Pre-Raphaelite archangels. Taynton is a similarly picturesque, peaceful village with exquisite houses.

It's worth continuing about ten miles to the west of Burford to see the village described by William Morris as the most beautiful in England. It seems that the rest of England flocks to **Bibury** each year to check the truth of this statement – it oozes tourists. Based around

a wildfowl reserve, the Rack Isle, and the trout-filled River Windrush, Bibury has a certain tweeness but is undeniably pretty. Indeed, when Henry Ford visited in the 1920s he liked it so much he tried to take part of it back to the States with him. Fortunately he was stopped. The part in question, Arlington Row, is a crooked row of cottages that was originally a medieval agricultural building, converted into cottages in the seventeenth century as homes for the weavers who made cloth for the nearby mill (mentioned in the Domesday Book and now a museum). Try to hook your supper at the Bibury Trout Farm (open daily; 01285 740215), or buy a licence to fish for half a day from the Swan Hotel (£20). Off the main drag, the Saxon church of St Mary's, rebuilt by the Normans in 1156, is awesomely peaceful, with immaculate grounds. There's a lovely walk from Bibury along River Coln to Coln St Aldwyns.

Where to stay

In addition to the places below, the **Bay Tree** in Burford (Sheep Street; 01993 822791) is a classy option (doubles for £135).

Bibury Court Hotel

Bibury, GL7 5NT (01285 740337/fax 01285 740660). **Rates** (B&ContB) single £68; single occupancy £78; double/twin £87-£99; four-poster £99; suite £140. Breakfast £6 (Eng). Special breaks. **Rooms** 2 single (1 en suite); 9 double/twin (8 en suite); 7 four-poster (6 en suite); 1 suite. **Cards** AmEx, DC, Debit, MC, V.
Approach on the little road from Coln St Aldwyns for the most striking view of this grand building. Set in six acres of land by the River Coln, this 300-year-old Tudor mansion has an impressive setting. Despite its imposing appearance, however, its atmosphere is relaxed, informal and slightly quirky rather than luxurious. Rooms are spacious and filled with heavy antique furniture. The food is well rated, and in summer, lunch or afternoon tea can be taken in an attractive conservatory overlooking the orchard garden. Trout fishing is available for residents. Children and dogs are welcome.
A40 W of Oxford; take left on to B4425 to Bibury; hotel in village centre in front of church.

Burford House

99 High Street, Burford, OX18 4QA (01993 823151/ fax 01993 823240/burford@bestloved.com). **Rates** (B&B) single occupancy £75; double/twin/four-poster £80-£105; deluxe double/twin/four-poster £115-£115. **Rooms** (all en suite) 3 double; 2 twin; 2 four-poster. **Cards** AmEx, DC, Debit, MC, V.
The rooms of this pretty Tudor townhouse strike a winning combination of character and comfort; wonderful, sparkling bathrooms complement the homely, traditional furnishings. Taynton, for example, has a four-poster bed plus a giant free-standing bath and separate shower. Rooms are surprisingly quiet despite the hotel's position on Burford's sloping main street. Service is friendly; it's like staying at a friend's home. There are

sitting rooms with log fires and a courtyard for warmer days. There's no bar as such, but a selection of drinks is available. An exemplary English breakfast is served in the bright dining room overlooking the High Street. No wonder the visitor's book brims with enthusiasm. Children welcome. All bedrooms non-smoking.

Feathers Hotel

Market Street, Woodstock, OX20 1SX
(01993 812291/fax 01993 813158/
enquiries@feathers.co.uk/www.feathers.co.uk).
Rates (B&ContB) *single occupancy £99-£140; double/twin £105-£169; suite £220-£295.*
Breakfast £8.25 (Eng). Special breaks.
Rooms (all en suite) 17 double/twin; 5 suites.
Cards AmEx, DC, Debit, MC, V.

Woodstock's second-best-known institution (after Blenheim), the Feathers – made up of four townhouses seamlessly joined together – is elegant from the outside in. Stylish rather than swanky, it has smart yet homely rooms decorated with restrained floral prints, antiques and original paintings. Service is highly professional and entirely unsnooty. There's a cosy bar area, a large formal drawing room on the first floor and an attractive garden. The new wing has five rooms including a family suite with private patio and lounge. Book at least four weeks ahead in summer. Children and dogs welcome. *See also p198.*

Holmwood

6 High Street, Woodstock, OX20 1TF (01993 812266/
fax 01993 813233/christina@holm-wood.demon.
co.uk/www.oxlink.co.uk/woodstock/holmwood).
Rates (B&B) *single occupancy £60; suite £75.*
Rooms (both en suite) 2 suites.

This Queen Anne Cotswold stone house was built in 1710 – around the same time as Blenheim Palace itself. As a B&B, its main appeal lies in its friendly, personal atmosphere; Roberto and Christina Gramellini are charming and most welcoming. They have lovingly restored the house, which has oak beams, antique furniture and a striking red dining room, and, at the time this guide went to press, were working on the conservatory, which overlooks the garden. The spacious suites have king- or queen-sized beds, their own sitting room, colour TV and bathroom. A home from home. No smoking throughout.

Lamb Inn

Sheep Street, Burford, OX18 4LR
(01993 823155/fax 01993 822228).
Rates (B&B) *single occupancy £60-£75pp; double/twin/four-poster £47.50-£57.50pp.*
Special breaks. **Rooms** (all en suite) 14 double/twin;
1 four-poster. **Cards** Debit, MC, V.

This attractive inn, with its flagged floors and abundance of copper, brass and antiques, dates back to the fifteenth century. Bedrooms are individually decorated, with sloping ceilings, lead window frames and beams. The elegant sitting room and bar have roaring fires and great character, offering the comfort and charm of a country house without being over-quaint, and the food is renowned (*see p198*). There's also a pretty walled garden. There are golf facilities nearby (equipment can be hired). Not always the friendliest welcome, but you can't have it all. Children and dogs allowed.

Manor Farmhouse

9 Manor Road, Bladon, nr Woodstock
(tel/fax 01993 812168).
Rates (B&B) *double £55; twin £45.*
Rooms 1 twin, 1 double.

For a low-key, peaceful stay, this stylishly renovated Grade II-listed house is the business. The two bedrooms are pretty, both with tea-making facilities and colour TV; the larger double has a restrained Laura Ashley bedspread and furnishings and a white wrought iron bed. It's a quiet spot, the only sounds on a Sunday being church bells (Churchill is buried in the churchyard) and woodpigeons. The watercolours throughout the house are by owner Mrs Stevenson's mother. One word of warning: beware the pale carpets in muddy boots. Children welcome. Non-smoking throughout.

A44 NW of Oxford; take A4095 left after Begbroke; take last turn left in Bladon village into Manor Road; house has iron railings and is on second bend.

Mill & Old Swan Inn

Minster Lovell, OX8 5RN
(01993 774441/fax 01993 702002).
Rates (B&B) *Swan £50-£70pp; Mill £30-£50.*
Special breaks. **Rooms** (all en suite) *Swan* 2 single;
11 double/twin; 3 four-poster; *Mill* 2 single;
45 double/twin. **Cards** AmEx, DC, Debit, MC, V.

The older Swan and the more recent Mill are primarily run as conference centres, but don't let that put you off: they're set in 60 acres of land in a blissfully quiet spot. Previous visitors have included Richard III and Sir Winston Churchill. The Mill's rooms are modern Scandinavian style and spacious with good bathrooms, many with Jacuzzis; ask for a river room to have a private patio by the River Windrush. The Swan rooms, many with four-posters, are older and more characterful, hence the price difference. Facilities include a tennis court, fishing path, croquet lawn, putting, basketball, mountain bikes and a gym with a sauna. Service is first-class. Children and dogs welcome.

A40 W of Oxford; after 14 miles take sliproad on right signposted 'Carterton, Minster Lovell'; right at junction; through Minster Lovell; right at T junction; immediate left into vallley; left over stone bridge; hotel reception is on left.

New Inn

Coln St Aldwyns, nr Cirencester, GL7 5AN
(01285 750651/fax 01285 750657/
stay@new-inn.co.uk/www.new-inn.co.uk).
Rates (B&B) *single £68-£80; double/twin £96; deluxe double/twin £115.* Special breaks.
Rooms (all en suite) 1 single; 10 double/twin; 3 deluxe double/twin. **Cards** AmEx, DC, Debit, MC, V.

Old when Wren built St Paul's, this ivy-covered sixteenth-century coaching inn was born of a decree by Queen Elizabeth I that there should be a coaching inn within a day's travel of every major centre. It describes itself as a 'private castle of comfort' and, while this may be overstating the case, it's certainly cosy and quiet, with views over endless fields, and friendly, professional staff. Each room has been individually decorated by the manager's interior-designer wife, with tasteful floral prints and quirky bathrooms; many have beams and four-posters. The terracotta-floored bar has a homely smell of wood-burning stove and the food is excellent (*see p198*). If you

*The bow-fronted seventeenth-century **Angel** in Burford.*

see a man in a black coat, jangling keys, don't worry – it's just the resident ghost. Highly recommended.

A419 NE of Swindon to Preston; at Preston take A429 to B4425; follow signs between Arlington and Bibury to Coln St Aldwyns.

Shaven Crown Hotel

High Street, Shipton-under-Wychwood, OX7 6BA (01993 830330/fax 01993 832136).
Rates (B&B) *single occupancy* £45-£55; *double/twin* £85; *four-poster* £120. **Rooms** (all en suite) 8 double/twin; 1 four-poster. **Cards** AmEx, Debit, MC, V.

This fabulously historic hotel, overlooking the village's green and church, has a dramatic entrance through an ancient stone gateway into a courtyard with a 600-year-old garden. A monk's hospice in the fourteenth century, the building was confiscated by Henry VIII, who turned it into his hunting lodge. When Elizabeth I inherited it, she returned it to the village. Now, the Shaven Crown offers good value for a quirky stay. The medieval hall, now the lounge, has a vaulted ceiling and roaring fire, and a beamed dining room (it's worth staying for dinner). The hotel has the use of two tennis courts and a bowling green. Children and dogs welcome.

A40 W of Oxford past Witney; turn right at Burford on to A361 to Shipton-under-Wychwood; hotel faces church and village green.

Where to eat & drink

In general, the area cashes in on its appeal to tourists and prices are high. It will come as no surprise, then, that many recommended restaurants are within pricey hotels. Book well ahead for most restaurants, or you may be stuck for choice. On Burford High Street, the **Golden Pheasant** (01993 823223) and the **Old Bull** (01993 822220) both serve reasonable food

at reasonable prices. Away from the Burford hordes, the **Swan** (01844 281777) in Swinbrook is an unspoilt, down-to-earth old bar by the river serving food. In Bibury, **Jankowski's** offers reasonably priced snacks and lunches in a courtyard, while **Jenny Wren's** teashop (11 The Street; 01285 740555) does afternoon tea for just £3.50. For unexceptional but affordable food in a candlelit setting try **Vickers** (01993 811212), or there's the well-rated Chinese **Chef Imperial** (22 High Street; 01993 813593). The **Queen's Own** (59 Oxford Street; 01993 813582) is a hidden-away pub for a quiet pint. Two places worth travelling 20 minutes for are the **Hare & Hounds** at Fosscross near Chedworth (01285 720288) and the **Churchill Arms** at Paxford (01386 594000), both with good food.

Baker's

4 Lombard Street, Eynsham (01865 881888).
Food served noon-2.30pm, 7-10.30pm, Tue-Sat; 12.30-2.30pm Sun. **Set meals** *lunch* £12.50 (2 courses), £15.50 (3 courses); *dinner* £15.50 (2 courses), £19.50 (3 courses). **Cards** Debit, MC, V.

Light, airy Baker's has quickly earned a reputation, providing the area with an adventurous approach to dining for a younger clientele. The menus are quite a mouthful in themselves. A la carte there are starters such as cannelloni of crab with watercress and velouté of foie gras (£9.50), and mains like roast sea bass, aubergine and tomato caviar with langoustine, oyster and olive dressing vierge (£18.90). The set meals offer similarly wordy combinations. And as for desserts – get your mouth around caramelised pineapple filo rolls with vanilla butter sauce, coconut and rice pudding ice-cream. Accommodation is available (double rooms for £60).

Feathers Hotel

Market Street, Woodstock (01993 812291).
Food served 12.30-2.15pm, 7.30-9.15pm,
Mon-Thur, Sun; 12.30-2.15pm, 7.30-9.45pm, Fri, Sat.
Set meals *lunch* £17.50 (2 courses), £21 (3 courses).
Cards AmEx, DC, Debit, MC, V.

For a seriously swanky dining experience, splash out at
Feathers, where head chef Mark Treasure cooks up a
storm. Dinner in the formal oak-panelled dining room
(no smoking) includes starters (£7.25-£11.95), mains
such as salmon millefeuille, champagne and asparagus
(£17), or the six-course tasting menu (£44 per person), a
great idea whereby the whole table can sample a variety
of dishes. The lunch menu includes the likes of risotto of
foie gras with truffle oil, and nage of seafood, Jerusalem
artichokes and rocket. Non-residents can enjoy lunch,
tea or a drink in the pretty garden. *See also p196.*

King's Head Inn & Restaurant

Chapel Hill, Wootton, Woodstock (01993 811340).
Food served noon-2pm, 7-9pm, Mon-Sat;
noon-2pm Sun. **Cards** Debit, MC, V.

Local foodies head for Tony Fay's seventeenth-century
Cotswold stone house to relax in the cosy, salmon-pink
bar in large sofas by log fires and then pig out in the
candlelit restaurant. At a price. Few mains – for example, Cantonese braised leg and breast of duckling
(£15.95) and nori steamed fillet of salmon (£17.95), a
'Japanese concept with attitude' – lie much below the
£20 mark. Desserts at around £4.95 include caramelised
citrus tart and Tony's home-made ice-cream for £4.95.
There's an appealing 'wines of the month' selection
(£3.50 glass, £10.95 bottle).

Lamb Inn

Sheep Street, Burford (01993 823155).
Food served 7-9pm Mon-Sat; 12.30-2pm, 7-9pm,
Sun. **Set meals** *lunch* £19 (3 courses); *dinner* £20
(2 courses), £25 (3 courses). **Cards** Debit, MC, V.

Widely regarded as *the* place to eat in Burford, the
Lamb's gorgeously traditional bar and lounges, and light,
plant-filled dining room are constantly buzzing with diners tucking into lunch dishes such as sun-dried tomato
risotto with fricassée of wild mushroom, and ricotta
cheese or wild boar and apple sausages with mash and
onion gravy (£7.25), or a three-course evening meal (£25)
washed down by a great range of New and Old World
wine. The ambitious size of the menu can sometimes
compromise the quality at busy weekends, but food is
generally tasty and well presented. *See also p196.*

Lamb Inn

Shipton-under-Wychwood (01993 830465).
Food served noon-2pm, 7-9.30pm, daily.
Set meals *lunch* £16.95 (3 courses) Sun.
Cards AmEx, DC, Debit, MC, V.

This family-run bar/dining room/B&B has a mellow,
down-to-earth feel, with its beamed, stone-bricked dining room, hunting prints, fires and dark wooden furniture. Its traditional, award-winning food includes mains
such as rack of lamb or supreme of guinea fowl with
sherry, leeks and bacon (£7.95-£12.95), and the set three-
course Sunday lunch is a deal at £16.95. If you don't feel
like moving far afterwards, an overnight stay costs £65-
£75, or £95 for a four-poster. Refreshingly low-key.

New Inn

Coln St Aldwyns, nr Cirencester (01285 750651).
Food served noon-2pm, 7-9pm, Mon-Thur; noon-
2pm, 7-9.30pm, Fri, Sat; noon-2.30pm, 7-9pm, Sun.
Set meals *lunch* £15.50 (3 courses) Sun;
dinner £22.50 (2 courses), £26.50 (3 courses).
Cards AmEx, DC, Debit, MC, V.

Come early for lunch at the New Inn or be prepared to
wait. It's worth it. The bar menu ranges from £5.25 to
£9.50, and there are well-priced set meals. Renowned
head chef Stephen Morey's dinner, served in cosy dining rooms, includes starters such as medallion of monkfish with stir-fried vegetables and oriental dressing and
main courses like fillet of pork with prune and
Armagnac cream. Desserts include a killer apple tart
with honey ice-cream and a cider caramel, and there's
a solid wine list ranging from £10.50 to £23.50.
Constantly filled to overflowing, the New Inn represents
both quality and decent value. *See also p196.*

Swan at Southrop

nr Lechlade (01367 850205).
Food served noon-2pm, 7-9.30pm, Mon-Sat;
noon-2.30pm Sun. **Cards** AmEx, DC, Debit, MC, V.

Patrick and Sandra Keen's friendly, relaxed sixteenth-
century village pub serves consistently good food that's
always worth driving here for. Starters at around £3 to
£5 include tiger prawns with a spicy coconut, lemongrass and fresh coriander sauce and smoked haddock
and prawns in a creamy sauce. Mains include
Gressingham duck breast with a plum and sloe gin
sauce (£11.50) and rack of lamb with cranberry and
mint sauce (£11.50). Lunchtime dishes, at £6.95, might
include hearty sausage, bean and tomato hotpot with
garlic bread and courgettes plus never-fail staples like
sausages and mash and lasagne. Bizarrely, there's also
a skittle alley available for private hire. The best value
in the area.

What to see & do

Blenheim Palace (*see page 199*) is obviously
the big one, and is well worth a visit purely
on the grounds of, well, the grounds. A more
quirky place to go is **Glass Heritage** (113
High Street, Burford; 01993 822290), a
sixteenth-century building housing a stained-
glass studio, which runs regular weekend
courses for beginners and some one-day
workshops. Diehard shopaholics, on the other
hand, might be more interested in **Bicester
Village** (01869 323200; open daily), a big
shopping outlet a few miles east of Woodstock.

Tourist information centres

The Brewery, Sheep Street, **Burford**, OX18 4LP
(01993 823558/fax 01993 823590).
Open *Mar-Oct* 9.30am-5.30pm Mon-Sat; 10am-3pm
Sun; *Nov-Feb* 10am-4.30pm Mon-Sat.

The Oxfordshire Museum, Fletcher's House, Park
Street, **Woodstock**, OX20 1SN (01993 813276/
fax 01993 813632). **Open** *Apr-Oct* 9.30am-5.30pm
Mon-Sat; 1-5pm Sun; *Nov-Mar* 10am-5pm Mon-Sat;
1-5pm Sun.

Blenheim Palace

John Churchill, 1st Duke of Marlborough, must have been thrilled when he beat the French at the Battle of Blenheim in 1704; Queen Anne rewarded him not just with some paltry medal, but with the cash to build this rather smart place, designed by Sir John Vanbrugh and set in 2,100 acres of parkland landscaped by Capability Brown and built in the Cotswolds' distinctive pale stone. It wasn't all plain sailing, though, since his wife wanted Sir Christopher Wren as architect, and had furious rows with Vanbrugh. After all that, the duke didn't even live to see it finished.

Blenheim is Britain's only non-royal residence that's luxurious enough to earn the title 'palace'. Even if you decide not to tour the palace itself – with its extraordinary Long Library, gilded state rooms and Churchiliana exhibition (Sir Winston was born here, and buried in nearby Bladon; the graveyard has views over Blenheim) – there's plenty to do. The grounds are vast, and easy to get lost in; there's a butterfly house, a miniature railway and play areas (for children, that is), while, on the lake, you can hire a rowing boat, take a trip on a motor launch or go coarse fishing (call 01993 811432 for details). Otherwise, there's the Marlborough Maze – the world's largest symbolic hedge maze – and giant chess and draughts.

Woodstock (24hr recorded info 01993 811325).
Open *palace mid-Mar-Oct* 10.30am-5.30pm daily (last entry 4.45pm); *park* 9am-5pm daily.
Admission £8.50; £4.50 5s-15s; £6.50 OAPs; £22 family. Guided tours every 5-10 mins.

Bike hire
Burford Bike Hire Barns Lane, **Burford** (01993 823326/07971 363571). Phone ahead to book Monday to Friday. The shop is a one-minute walk from the bus stop.

Cogges Manor Farm Museum
Church Lane, Cogges, Witney (01993 772602).
Open *late Mar-Oct* 10.30am-5.30pm Tue-Fri; noon-5.30pm Sat, Sun. **Admission** £3.50; £1.75 3s-16s; £2.25 OAPs, students; £10 family.
At this working museum you can step back in time and discover rural Oxfordshire in Victorian times – the good old days before everything was a teashop. The 20-acre farm is stocked with traditional Victorian breeds of farm animals, plus displays of farm implements and machinery. In the historic manor house, which has recently been restored, displays include a Victorian bedroom and nursery, while the walled kitchen garden could inspire you to sort out those window boxes. Events, such as falconry displays, take place throughout the year.

Cotswold Wildlife Park
Burford (01993 823006/fax 01993 823807).
Open *Apr-Oct* 10am-5pm daily; *Nov-Mar* 10am-4pm daily. **Admission** £5.80; £3.80 3s-16s, OAPs, students.
Set in 160 acres of gardens and parkland around a listed Victorian manor house, this wildlife park is the place to see rhinos, zebras, ostriches, lions, leopards and red pandas in the very un-wild setting of an English country garden. Penguins, tropical birds, monkeys, meerkats and otters live in the Walled Gardens, while the reptile house, aquarium and insect house are home to more slimy and crawly inhabitants. There are also some 200 fruit bats. A mini-railway runs between April and October, and there's a children's farmyard and adventure playground for younger visitors.

Cotswold Woollen Weavers
Filkins, nr Lechlade (01367 860491).
Open 10am-6pm Mon-Sat; 2-6pm Sun.
Admission free.
Five hundred years ago, wealthy Cotswold wool merchants built the famous 'wool churches' like Burford and Northleach. At this working woollen mill you can watch fleece being woven into woollen fabric using age-old skills such as spinning and weaving. Then, in true Cotswold fashion, you can get out your cheque book and buy genuine Cotswold woollens. Coffee shop, free parking, picnic area.

Kelmscott Manor
Kelmscott, nr Lechlade (01367 252486).
Open *Apr, May, June, Sept* 11am-1pm, 2-5pm, Wed; 2-5pm 3rd Sat of month; *July, Aug* 11am-1pm, 2-5pm, Wed; 2-5pm 1st, 3rd Sat of month.
Admission £6; £3 5s-16s, OAPs, students.
Poet, artist, craftsman, printer and leader of the Arts and Crafts movement, William Morris lived at Kelmscott Manor from 1871 until his death in 1896. Time your weekend carefully to see this beautiful house and garden. The Morris Cottage nearby, built by Jane Morris as a memorial to her husband in 1902, and the village church, are also worth a look.

Chipping Norton to Banbury

An area lacking a distinct identity perhaps, but none the worse for it.

This area is an oddity in a way: you've passed throught the affluent commuter belt south of Oxford; to the east is the M1 and the dreary London overspill towns of Milton Keynes, Luton and Bedford. Out west are the ultra-twee honeypot villages of the Gloucestershire Cotswolds; and to the north the industrial Midlands. But sandwiched between them all are the Oxfordshire Cotswolds and the Ironstone villages of 'Banburyshire', a last bastion of untarnished, uneventful middle-England.

The landscape is a mix of cowparsley lanes, undulating cornfields, meadows, wooded hills and rivers, peppered with villages that haven't changed much in centuries. There's little modern building in the area and because stone has always been cheap round here, the houses are built in glorious red-brown ironstone, speckled with orange lichen, or rich, sun-soaking, tawny brown Cotswolds limestone.

Medieval wool money has made for many handsome, if not spectacular, churches, with local stone-cutting skills evident in fine tracery and other detailing. The medieval vocabulary of mullioned windows and gables is also much in evidence. You'll see strikingly beautiful Jacobean cottages, farmhouses and manor houses around every turn, and although the numerous perfect inglenook and beam pubs contain more than a fair smattering of American tourists and weekending Londoners in Range Rovers, there does remain at least some sense of reality – albeit a well-manicured one.

All the attractions of Oxford (*see page 180*), the baroque excess of Blenheim Palace (*see page 199*) and the mighty Warwick Castle (*see page 179*) are within easy reach, so you can combine big-time sightseeing further afield with the area's more provincial attractions. It's a place to hang out, chill out, walk, ride a bike or motor around, stopping at pubs and the odd landmark. Pretty much anywhere you head for within this area offers the same kind of pleasing vistas. It might be best to leave the kids at home, though – there's not much for them to do, and many of the best places to stay and visit are distinctly un-child friendly.

Chipping off the old block

Chipping Norton itself is a classic small market town. It's twee but not overwhelmingly touristy, with a mixture of normal shops and more artsy craftsy outlets on the elegant, fawn-stoned High Street and the lanes and alleyways running off it. There are lots of traditional teashops, inns and pubs, too, and the place has an affluent, relaxed feel. Terraced into the hillside, it's the highest town in Oxfordshire, and you can see glimpses of rolling countryside between the rooftops, as well as the bizarre and now-defunct Bliss Tweed Mill, designed to resemble a great stately home, except with a giant chimney plonked on the top. In addition to a small museum, there are lots of antiques shops to browse in in Chipping Norton, and you can buy bric a brac, plants and second-hand books in Albion Market, a narrow lane just off the main drag. Down on Church Lane are pretty seventeenth-century almshouses and the wool church of St Mary, which has one of the finest fifteenth-century interiors in the county.

Getting stoned

North and north-west of Chipping Norton are the pretty villages of **Little Rollright** – an unspoilt hamlet set among meadows – and **Great Rollright** – little grey stone cottages on a breezy hillside. Between them lie the **Rollright Stones** – no, not an ageing rock group, but a group of prehistoric stones said to be third in the stone-circle pecking order after

The church of St Mary in Chipping Norton.

Stonehenge and Avebury. There are beautiful walks to be had around this area, and it's not far to **Hook Norton**, a large ironstone village where the most wonderful beer of the same name – known locally as 'Hookey' – is brewed. Unsurprisingly, there are some good pubs in the village as well as an interesting rustic church. West of Chipping Norton, the A44 takes you further into the Cotswolds and to Chastleton House, one of the best-preserved Jacobean houses in the country, set in a cosy hillside nook. Continue on the A44 and you'll get to Moreton-in-Marsh (*see page 169*); taking the A436 will take you to Stow-on-the-Wold (*see page 163*).

The idyllic villages roll on; high on the hilltops above Hook are **Sibford Gower** and **Sibford Ferris**; **Shenington**; **Swalcliffe**; and across the border into Warwickshire, **Brailes** and a fantastically beautiful Tudor country house called **Compton Wynyates** – no longer open to the public but surrounded by lovely walks. From the nearby village of **Tysoe**, there's great hillwalking along **Edgehill**, and spectacular views across to Stratford-upon-Avon (*see page 174*). You can also visit the seventeenth-century **Upton House**, with its art collection and beautiful gardens descending in terraces to pools in the valley below.

Banbury and around

The north-east of this area is bounded by **Banbury**, a market town known for its cakes and its cloister, immortalised in the nursery rhyme *Ride a Cock-horse to Banbury Cross*. South-west of the town is the romantic **Broughton Castle** (*see page 205* **A manor of speaking**) and three pretty villages known for their imposing churches: '**Bloxham**, for length, **Adderbury** for strength, **Kings Sutton** for beauty' – so the local saying goes.

Further south, down the A4260, there's the historic and rather posh market town of **Deddington**, now a centre for antiques. Then, on the banks of the winding Cherwell river, the **Astons**: **North**, **Middle** and **Steeple**, with more fine walking and some excellent pubs, too. There's also **Rousham House**, a rather stern-looking Tudor Gothic pile with exquisite landscaped gardens designed by William Kent, 'the father of modern gardening'.

The Arcadian landscape of wooded hills and small villages continues from here back to Chipping Norton, by way of the Bartons, Kiddington, the Enstones, Glympton and the Tews. Taking the biscuit in the chocolate box stakes (so to speak) is the fabulously picturesque settlement of **Great Tew**, with

perfect thatched cottages nestling in a lushly wooded dell. It's no accident: in Victorian times, the village's owners planned this effect carefully, planting clumps of great trees and adding Gothic porches to all the cottages, so the village would complement the rest of their estate.

Where to stay

The Butts

Cherington, nr Shipston on Stour, CV36 5HZ (01608 686226/fax 01608 686524).
Rates (B&B) £30pp (£5 single supplement).
Rooms 3 double/twin.

Located outside the town, this elegantly symmetrical, large Victorian house has a big garden, which includes a (not over-heated) swimming poool, tennis court, monkey puzzle tree and lovely herb garden. Inside, the atmosphere is traditional but unstuffy, with decent furniture, lots of bookshelves, an open fire – you feel like you're staying at a smart friend's country house. There's a wonderful conservatory at the back, where breakfast is served with light streaming in and fine views across the open countryside. Of the two pretty first-floor bedrooms, the double with the sleigh bed is marginally preferable to the twin. There's also a pink family room on the top floor equipped with a rather rickety-looking but probably very comfortable brass bed. Dinner by arrangement. Children welcome. All bedrooms non-smoking.
B4035 W of Banbury; turn left towards Sutton-under-Brailes; keep village green on left in Sutton-under-Brailes (ignore signs for Cherington); right at T junction; right at next junction; house is on left (the one with the two-storey conservatory).

College Farmhouse

Kings Sutton, Banbury, OX17 3PS (01295 811473/fax 01295 812505/ sallday@compuserve.com).
Rates (B&B) *single occupancy* £34; *double/twin* £52.
Rooms (all en suite) 3 double/twin.

A creeper-covered eighteenth-century house on the outskirts of the village, whose beautiful, secluded garden has a tennis court and its own lake with tidy paths around it. There's a big inglenook fireplace and TV in the large, beamed sitting room overlooking the lawns; a smart, oval-tabled dining room in the middle of the house; and a long, airy kitchen/family room, where breakfast is served by the house's genial owners, Sara and Stephen. Sara is an interior decorator by trade and this is evident in the bright and elegant style of the farmhouse, which manages to be country-cosy without straying into twee territory. You're very much in a family house, but the atmosphere is relaxed and not at all overwhelming. If you really want to be alone, there's also the Barn Room in a separate outbuilding with its own little kitchen. Dinner costs £15 (3 courses) – by arrangement only. Children and dogs welcome. All bedrooms non-smoking.
M40 J11; follow signs from Banbury to Kings Sutton; take Astrop Road away from church towards Charlton; take last turning on right before leaving Kings Sutton; farmhouse is at end of lane.

*A deceptively uncompromising glimpse of the delightful **Falkland Arms**.*

Falkland Arms

Great Tew, Chipping Norton, OX7 4DB
(01608 683653/timnewman@btconnect.com).
Rates (B&B) *single* £40; *double* £65. **Rooms** (all en suite) 5 double; 1 single. **Cards** AmEx, Debit, MC, V.

The interior of the pub downstairs is every bit as idyllic as the honeystone and thatch village it's situated in, with inglenook fireplace, uneven flagstones, beams hung with old mugs and time-worn wooden furniture. The small, low-ceilinged and mullion-windowed bedrooms above it are also very much in style, furnished with antiques and reached by an old stone spiral staircase. They all have tellies and bathrooms, though, and two of the doubles have four-poster beds. The bluff northern manager here puts a priority on preserving his guests' tranquillity and no children under 14 are allowed. If you want a country cottage feel with an excellent pub at the bottom of the stairs, then this place is perfect. There's lunch and dinner available, too, although for the latter you'll need to book, even if you are a guest. All bedrooms non-smoking.

A361 SW from Banbury; follow signs to Great Tew on left.

La Madonette

North Newington, nr Banbury, OX15 6AA
(01295 730212/fax 01295 730363/
lamadonette@aol.com).
Rates (B&B) *single occupancy* £40, *double* £58; *four-poster* £85; *family room* £68. **Rooms** (all en suite) 2 double/twin; 1 four-poster; 2 family.
Cards DC, Debit, MC, V.

A honey-stoned, converted Jacobean millhouse very close to Banbury, La Madonette is stunningly beautiful from the outside, with climbing ivy, apple trees, well-tended lawns and a river running at the bottom of the garden, which also contains a discreetly hidden swimming pool. Inside the house, there's a small reception room with a licensed bar and an attractive, pink-walled dining room with crisp tablecloths, friendly staff and excellent breakfasts. Most of the beamed, low-ceilinged bedrooms are comfortable, with a fairly floral style – matching bedcovers and curtains, china wheelbarrows and baskets of dried flowers. They all have their own phones and views over the surrounding meadows. Room 2 is the biggest, best and most expensive, with a four-poster bed and huge bath. The two family rooms (3 and 6) are, at the time of writing, nothing special, but there are plans to redecorate them. Children welcome. All bedrooms non-smoking.

B4035 SW of Banbury; follow signs to North Newington, house is on right before village.

Sugarswell Farm

Shenington, Banbury, OX15 6HW
(01295 680512/fax 01295 688149).
Rates (B&B) *double* £50-£65.
Rooms (all en suite) 4 double.

Set in a remote location on high ground on the Oxfordshire-Warwickshire border, the accommodation at Sugarswell Farm comprises two large and two huge bedrooms in a comfortable modern country house. Although you do get the feeling you're in someone's home, the rooms have a rather bare, impersonal feel, with big '70s-style fitted cupboards, floral spreads and curtains, and damask carpets. Downstairs, there's a rather formal dining room with one big table, overlooked by seascapes in oils; there's also a large, spic and span sitting room. Sugarswell has many regular guests and one of the biggest draws is friendly owner Rosemary Nunneley's food. She used to run a restaurant in Stratford, but now only serves up her wholesome dishes using home-produced ingredients for her guests. Dinner is an extra £20. Non-smoking throughout.

A422 W of Banbury towards Stratford-upon-Avon; follow signs on left to Shenington; farmhouse is before village on left by airfield.

Tollgate Inn & Restaurant

Church Street, Kingham, OX7 6Y
(01608 658389/fax 01608 659467).
Rates (B&B) *single occupancy* £35; *double* £80; *twin* £60; *family room* £80-£105. **Rooms** (all en suite) 7 double; 2 twin; 1 family. **Cards** Debit, MC, V.

If you want a comfortable place to stay with the intimacy of a B&B but the professionalism of a top-notch hotel, then this is the place for you. Situated in the middle of Kingham in a converted Georgian farmhouse, the Tollgate's downstairs bar and reception rooms are all inglenook fireplaces, ticking clocks and country furniture. But the spotlighting, pastel walls, Habitat-style sofas and vases of fresh flowers give it a modern twist. The rooms are decorated individually and with some style; Room 4 has antique rustic French furniture and a hand-carved bed; Room 1 is the biggest and most traditional. Across the courtyard at the back there's the Hayloft, a barn-like family room with exposed beams. The Tollgate's emphasis on service and attention to detail is also evident in the restaurant, which serves classy but unpretentious modern food, using local and largely organic ingredients. Sunday breakfast includes home-made sausages and apple and onion cakes.

B4450 SW of Chipping Norton; follow signs on right to Kingham.

Where to eat & drink

North Oxfordshire is not exactly down-at-heel and neither is it too rural and isolated to have escaped '90s culinary trends. It will come as no surprise, then, that this area boasts a clutch of excellent restaurants. As for drinking, the area is littered with cosy hostelries serving good ales and, in some, classy food, too. These latter include the **Red Lion** in Steeple Aston and the **Fox & Hounds** in Great Wolford (*see below*); try also the **Blue Boar** in Chipping Norton (01608 643525); the **North Arms** in Wroxton (01295 730318); or, further afield, the **White Bear** in Shipston on Stour (01608 662612). The **Falkland Arms** (*see page 202*) has an extensive range of real ales, English country wines and real cider, it also serves decent lunches in the garden. For out and about drinking, try the popular **Pear Tree** in Hook Norton; the **Cherington Arms** in Cherington, where there's a lovely garden with a stream at its end. The **Tollgate Inn**, Kingham, is also well worth a dinner-time visit (*see above*).

Chavignol

7 Horsefair, Chipping Norton (01608 644490).
Food served 12.30-1.45pm, 7-9.30pm, Tue-Sat.
Set meals *lunch* £18.50-£25 (2 courses); *dinner* £25-£42.50 (2 courses). **Cards** AmEx, Debit, MC, V.

Probably the classiest restaurant in the area, and the only one with a Michelin star, Chavignol is a small place decorated with sunny yellow walls, rush matting, beams, royal blue tablecloths and biscuit-coloured upholstery. Staff are relaxed but super-attentive and the wine list is an oenophile's fantasy. Food verges on the over-elaborate but is extremely well cooked, covering the whole Modern European repertoire, but with an emphasis on local ingredients. Expect dishes like – wait for it – breasts of wood pigeon on a bed of braised cabbage with sautéed foie gras layered with crisp potato and caramelised apple in a pigeon and sherry vinegar sauce. Expect also to have to wait a long time between courses for these gourmet delights to be rustled up. A three-course evening meal clocks in at around £40 per head. Come here for a treat. Laudably, the restaurant offers a free pick-up and drop-off taxi service within a radius of ten miles.

Dexter's

Market Place, Deddington (01869 338813).
Food served noon-2.15, 7-9.15pm, Tue-Sat; noon-2.15pm Sun. **Set meals** £14.50 (2 courses); £18 (3 courses). **Cards** AmEx, Debit, MC, V.

A bit of a flashy-looking place this, with bare boards, modernist navy blue tables, twisted-metal wrought iron banisters and a metal swordfish displayed on the wall. On offer is standard modern eclectic fare – for example, marinated baked goat's cheese on rocket leaves with artichoke heads and balsamic vinegar as a starter, then veal and pork sausages with mash, red onion gravy and apple sauce to follow. Seasoning and flavouring are always capably handled and prices are reasonable – expect to pay around £30 a head for a three-course meal with wine.

Fox & Hounds

Great Wolford (01608 674220).

This sixteenth-century pub's low beams are hung with bunches of hops; stuffed animals line the walls; candles stand on the wooden tables and classical music plays softly in the gloom. There's a terrace in the courtyard and a fair smattering of Jags and Range Rovers parked there, too, but the place has a jolly enough atmosphere, and welcomes kids and those who just want to drink. It gets very full, so it's worth booking to eat. The food here is not cutting-edge but, despite the unnecessary big chunks of tomato and bushes of parsley garnish, it is more than competent. A standard pub grub menu is bolstered by a blackboard offering more snazzy dishes such as home-made salmon and tuna fish cakes with spinach, tomato coulis and potato wedges. There are also delicious roasts cooked up at Sunday lunchtime and an outstanding range of ales and whiskies as well. You should come away with change from £20 for three courses (just about). We would give you opening times but the rude person who answered the phone refused to tell us.

Morel's

2 Horsefair, Chipping Norton (01608 641075).
Food served noon-2pm, 7-9.30pm, Tue-Sat.
Set meals *lunch* £16.50 (3 courses); *dinner* £21 (2 courses), £25 (3 courses), £30 (4 courses).
Cards Debit, MC, V.

Situated over the road from Chavignol, Morel's offers a similarly upmarket menu. The restaurant is rag-rolled in orange, with damask tablecloths and country-style wooden chairs. A typical three-course meal, from the set menu, might be home-made shallot and parsley ravioli with pan-fried langoustines and seafood sauce, followed by spring rack of lamb with potato cake, garlic and lavender sauce, and for pud, red fruit crème brûlée with strawberry sorbet. Not bad value either.

Red Lion
Steeple Aston (01869 340225).
Food served 7.30-9pm Mon; noon-2pm, 7.30-9pm, Tue-Sat. **Cards** AmEx, Debit, MC, V.

Another perfect pub, with ticking clocks, beams, pewter mugs and fireplace, in a pretty village. You can sit out on the hanging basket-laden patio area for lunch in summer and eat sandwiches and straightforward dishes like whole fresh crab. On Friday and Saturday evenings, the tiny, old-fashioned, pub-style dining room is opened, serving wonderfully unpretentious dishes made from fresh, local ingredients: pea, lemon and mint soup; home-made pâté; saddle of spring lamb with onion purée; almond sponge with strawberries and cream. The proprietors are very friendly and three courses will set you back around £20-£25. Book well in advance.

What to see & do

This area is best for gentle meandering on foot, by bicycle or by car. The tourist information centre in Chipping Norton has useful leaflets outlining circular walks and bike rides. Generally, Oxfordshire's paths and bridleways all seem to be particularly well signposted.

Tourist information centre
The Guildhall, **Chipping Norton**, OX7 5NJ (tel/fax 01608 644379). **Open** *Mar-Oct* 9.30am-5.30pm Mon-Sat; *Nov-Feb* 10am-3pm Mon-Sat.

Chastleton House
Chastleton, off A44 NW of Chipping Norton (01608 674284).
Open *Apr-Oct* noon-4pm Wed-Sat.
Admission (NT) £5; £2.50 5s-15s; £12.50 family.

A superb, symmetrical gabled house built in 1603 by a rich wool merchant. Chastleton's interior is both elaborately decorated and perfectly preserved, but avoids a museumy atmosphere. The gardens display some fine imaginative topiary. It's now in the hands of the National Trust and, unfortunately, you have to pre-book to visit.

Hook Norton Brewery
Brewery Lane, Hook Norton (01608 737210).
Open *shop* 9am-4.30pm Mon-Fri.
Admission *tours* phone for details.

The pagoda-like brewery here, with its delicious brews, runs tours. They are hugely popular, too, and you'll need to book a long way in advance. Write to Mrs Paula Clarke, Hook Norton Brewery Co Ltd, Hook Norton, Oxon, OX15 5NY, requesting a date and time. A 'heritage centre' displaying brewery artefacts is due to open in October 1999.

Rollright Stones
S of A3400 NW of Chipping Norton (01295 277244/ www.rollright.demon.co.uk). **Open** sunrise-sunset daily. **Admission** 30p; 20p 5s-16s.

*A petrified army or a load of old rocks? See what you make of the **Rollright Stones**.*

A manor of speaking

You may recognise this absurdly romantic edifice as the moated location for *Shakespeare in Love*; **Broughton Castle** is also the most impressive medieval house in Oxfordshire. Built in about 1300 at the junction of three streams, it was bought 77 years later by William of Wykeham, founder of New College, Oxford, and has been kept in the same family ever since. Their surname changed to Fiennes in the fifteenth century, so actors Ralph and Joseph are cousins of the present owner, Nathaniel Fiennes, the 21st Lord Saye and Sele. So is explorer Ranulph Twisleton-Wykeham-Fiennes, for that matter.

Wykeham added a battlemented wall to the gatehouse. Even so, the word 'castle' is misleading – it is more an impressive manor house – though the building has seen its fair share of trouble, not least when it was besieged and captured by the Royalists after the battle of nearby Edgehill in 1642. Indeed, the house was a hotbed of anti-monarchical intrigue during the Civil War. Between 1629 and 1640 'The Providence Island Company' would meet regularly in the 'room without ears' at the top of the West stairs. The company was ostensibly formed to colonise certain

Caribbean islands. In fact, it was a front for assorted Parliamentarian bigwigs to assemble and plot against the King.

Elsewhere in the house there are some impressive plasterwork ceilings and atmospheric vaulted passages, as well as heirlooms connected with other colourful episodes in the family's history. You can also fight your way through the Japanese tourists to see snaps of thesps on location, but Broughton's greatest draw is the exterior's ravishing good looks.

Broughton Castle SW of Banbury (01295 262624). **Open** *mid-May-mid-Sept* 2-5pm Wed, Thur, Sun, bank hol Mon. **Admission** £4; £2 5s-15s; £3 OAPs.

A circle of 70-something pitted, prehistoric stones (you'll never count the same number of them twice, allegedly), about 30m in diameter and standing from a few centimetres to more than two metres high. Legend has it that the arrangement was formed when a king and his army were turned to stone by a witch. Some visitors may be filled with mystical awe by all this, others will just see a bunch of pockmarked old rocks.

Rousham Park House & Garden

nr Steeple Aston (01869 347110).
Open *house Apr-Sept* 2-4.30pm Wed, Sun, bank hol Mon; *garden* 10am-4.30pm daily.
Admission *house* £3; *garden* £3.

This imposing Jacobean mansion was remodelled in Tudor Gothic style by Wiliam Kent in the eighteenth century. He designed the extensive gardens, too, and these are quite outstanding, inspired by Italian landscape painting, with grouped trees, winding paths, glades and waterfalls interspersed with statues and temples. Rousham is totally uncommercialised, with no shop, tearoom or anything. This is a good thing: you're encouraged to bring a picnic and stay for the day wandering the grounds. 'NO CHILDREN (under 15) or DOGS' are allowed, as numerous rather fierce signs keep reminding you.

Upton House

off A422 S of Edgehill
(01295 670266/www.ntrustsevern.org.uk).
Open *Apr-Oct* 2-6pm Mon-Wed, Sat, Sun.
Admission (NT) £5.20; £2.60 5s-16s.

A late seventeenth-century house bequeathed to the National Trust in the 1920s by the son of the founder of Shell. He was a big art collector, as evident in the works of art displayed here, which include Stubbs, Brueghel, Hogarth, El Greco and more. The sloping gardens are spectacular, with ornamental pools and all kinds of colourful surprises.

Water Fowl Sanctuary & Children's Farm

Wiggington Heath, nr Hook Norton (01608 730252).
Open 10.30am-6pm/dusk daily. **Admission** £3; £2 1s-15s; £2.90 OAPs.

An eccentric place, with all the usual farmyard friends and an inordinate number of ducks in a series of ponds criss-crossed by pathways. Kids will find lots of things to play on scattered about the place – a broken-down tractor, a wooden tower – but the bit they'll like most is the petting room, where they can pick up baby rabbits, chicks and ducklings, under supervision.

The Chilterns to York

RUTLAND - (page 226)
LINCOLN - (page 231)
YORK - (page 239)

RUTLAND

Wymondham
Market Overton
Teigh
Clipsham
A6121
Langham
Burley-on-the-Hill
Barnsdale Gardens
Pickworth
Oakham
Braunston
Hambleton
Butterfly Farm & Aquatic Centre
Tallington
Brooke
Normanton Church Museum
Stamford
Rutland Water Nature Reserve
Burghley House
Wing
A6121
A47
A47
Uppingham
Seaton
King's Cliffe
Eyebrook Res
Stoke Dry

NORTHAMPTON

NORTHAMPTONSHIRE

Wellingborough

Olney
A509
Bedford
Kempston
A428
A421
A6

Newport Pagnell
MILTON KEYNES
Milton Keynes
M1

BEDFORDSHIRE

Woburn
A507
A507
Letchworth
Royston
A505
A10
A5120
Toddington
A6
Hitchin
A507

Leighton Buzzard
Dunstable
A418
A4146
LUTON
HERTFORDSHIRE (page 220)
Stevenage
A602

BUCKINGHAMSHIRE

Waddesdon Manor
NORTH CHILTERNS (page 214)
Brill
Hartwell House
Aylesbury
Aston Clinton
Tring
Whipsnade Wild Animal Park
Ashridge Estate
Knebworth House
Knebworth
Ayot St Lawrence
Shaw's Corner
Welwyn
Hertford
War
Dinton
Weston Turville
Wendover
Berkhamsted
Harpenden
St Albans
Welwyn Garden City
A41
Haddenham
Chiltern Brewery
Redbourn
Hatfield
A414
Hoddesdon
Thame
Hemel Hempstead
Gardens of the Rose
Bowman's Farm
Paradise Wildlife Park
Broxbour
A4129
Princes Risborough
Ridgeway Path
Chesham
Bovingdon
Kings Langley
A414
Cheshunt
Tetsworth
Prestwood
Great Missenden
A4010
Speen
Amersham
Chorleywood
Abbots Langley
Mosquito Aircraft Museum
Potters Bar
Cuffley
West Wycombe Caves
Hughenden Manor
Chalfont St Giles
Watford
Bushey
M25
West Wycombe
High Wycombe
Bekonscot Model Village
John Milton's Cottage
Rickmansworth
Turville
Beaconsfield
Gerrards Cross
Frieth
Odds Farm Park
Marlow
Bourne End
Cliveden
Fawley
Burnham
Henley-on-Thames
Fawley Court
Cookham
Shiplake Row
Maidenhead
Bray
A355
Wargrave
A404(M)
M4
Eton
Slough
LONDON
Twyford
WINDSOR & AROUND (page 207)
Windsor
Reading
Legoland
Old Windsor
Windsor Great Park
Runnymede
Wokingham
Savill Garden
Virginia Water

© Copyright Time Out Group 1999

0   15 miles
0   25 km

Windsor & around

Royal residences, historic hotels and food fit for a king.

Covering three counties (Oxfordshire, Buckinghamshire and Berkshire – sorry, 'Royal Berkshire', as it is better known), this region offers an easy-come, easy-go break from the city. While there is a clutch of impressive country houses and museums to satisfy the culture diehards, the main attraction is undoubtedly the many villages, walks and pubs that dot the area. Of all the towns here, **Windsor**, whose Castle is the most popular tourist attraction in the region, is the most agreeable place to spend a day or so.

Gone with the Windsor

It's hard to believe now, but in the mid-nineteenth century, Windsor was considered one of the dirtiest and unhealthiest towns in the country. Thankfully, things have improved: today it's a charming place that, despite its historical importance and resulting crowds, has managed to avoid becoming twee. **Windsor Castle** was strategically built at the top of the town by William the Conqueror a few years after his victory at Hastings; six centuries later

By train from London

Trains go from **Waterloo** to **Windsor & Eton Riverside** (direct). Trains to **Henley** go from **Paddington** (direct). Trains to **Marlow** leave from **Paddington** (change at Maidenhead). All these journeys take about **50mins**.

it was described, rather ineloquently, by Samuel Pepys as 'the most romantique castle that is in the world'. Occupied by the royal family since the Middle Ages, the Castle hit the headlines in 1992 when a worker's blowlamp sparked a fire, which devastated some of the State Rooms. Now completely restored, the Castle is the focal point of any trip to the town.

The cobbled precinct around the Castle is known as Guildhall Island, named for the Guildhall that stands within it, which was built by Windsor resident Sir Christopher Wren in the late seventeenth century. Today you can take tea in the curious, lop-sided timber

*Al fresco dining in **Windsor**.*

building, imaginatively called the Crooked House Tea Rooms (01753 857534): inside, you'll notice that the pillars don't quite reach the ceiling – this was Wren's way of cocking a snook at the town planners, who insisted that there be columns inside the building in the interest of safety.

Eton tidy

Joined with Windsor by a pedestrian bridge over the Thames at the foot of, er, Thames Street, **Eton** likes to consider itself separate from its royal neighbour. It boasts a unique identity, centred on its College (a clue to Eton's arrogance lies in the official title of the College: The King's College of Our Lady of Eton Beside Windsor). It sits at the end of the High Street, which is lined with antique shops, 'heritage' pubs and the Cockpit restaurant, which still has the original cock-fighting area from the seventeenth century. The College was founded in 1440 by Henry VI for just 70 pupils; the roll call probably takes slightly longer these days, with around 1,300 boys on the books. The best way to get to grips with the College's history is to arrange a guided tour.

Out in the country

If you're pining for some greenery after all those historic buildings, there are several parks and gardens within easy reach of Windsor, chief among them **Windsor Great Park**, south of the town, which covers a massive 4,800 acres (some of which is private) and incorporates the 35-acre **Savill Garden**. Running into the garden is **Virginia Water**, with its two-mile-long lake, said to be named after Queen Elizabeth I, the virgin Queen, and which incorporates a totem pole and an obelisk erected by George II. Monument spotters might also like to visit the nearby tiny island of **Runnymede**, reached via the A308, where King John sealed the Magna Carta in 1215; you can see the memorial erected by the American Bar Association to commemorate it in 1957, and, on the nearby hillside, a memorial to JFK.

Along the Thames

Just west of Eton and Windsor is **Bray**, the setting of John Donne's poem *The Vicar of Bray*, about turncoat vicar Simon Alwyn, who changed his politics repeatedly during the reign of four monarchs to keep his job. With its High Street of timbered cottages, the village is certainly picturesque, but the main reason for coming here is to sample the culinary delights of its rightly acclaimed restaurants (*see pages 211-212*).

Just north of Bray, off the A4094, is **Cookham**, a riverside, curate's egg of a village

Regattas, races & festivals

Windsor and the surrounding towns and villages host a wide range of events throughout the year. The following are our pick of the best. Windsor's Theatre Royal (01753 853888) also has a packed programme; phone for details.

Cliveden Festival
(box office 01494 755572).
Date late June-early July (5 days).
Two Shakespeare plays are performed every year outdoors in Cliveden's beautiful grounds.

Hambleden concerts (01491 574652).
Date May-Sept.
A series of classical music concerts, held once a month in summer at the church of St Mary the Virgin.

Henley Festival of Music & the Arts
(01491 843400; box office 834404).
Date July (5 days).
Music, theatre and visual arts, plus street theatre, cabaret and fireworks.

Henley Royal Regatta (01491 572153).
Date late June/early July (5 days).
World-renowned, and quintessentially upper-class English. If you don't know what it's about, you shouldn't be going.

Marlow Regatta (01491 575478).
Date mid-June (1 day).
Not as famous as Henley, perhaps, but at least you might get tickets for this one.

Royal Ascot (01344 622211).
Date mid-June (4 days).
Ladies' Day is on the Thursday, when the Queen makes an appearance.

Royal Windsor Horse Show (box office 0870 901 0600). **Date** mid-May (4 days).
International showjumping, dressage and other horsey events.

Windsor Festival (info 01753 743900).
Date late Sept-early Oct (15 days).
A varied programme of musical and other events in a variety of venues including St George's Hall in Windsor Castle.

thought to have been inhabited since Roman times. The village is best known as the birthplace of one of Britain's most famous – not to mention eccentric – artists, **Sir Stanley Spencer** (1891-1959; *see also page 97*). Spencer had the habit of painting allegorical scenes of Christ in biblical scenes set in and around his beloved Cookham, which he called, rather optimistically, 'a village in heaven'. The artist was born in the house called Fernlea on the High Street; the nearby village chapel has been converted into a museum showing his works. Cookham Dean, a short distance uphill, boasts several commendable pubs.

A trip to the area wouldn't be complete without seeing the splendour of **Cliveden**, set high on the hills. The stunning building – now a luxury hotel – began life as a hunting lodge in 1666, though the present central mansion dates from 1850, when it was rebuilt by Charles Barry, architect of the Houses of Parliament.

Marlow & around

While Cookham had its artist, **Marlow**, a few miles west on the A4155, has long been associated with its literary inhabitants, among them Jerome K Jerome, who is said to have penned *Three Men in a Boat* in the town's best pub, the Two Brewers, on St Peter's Street. Albion House on West Street was home to the Shelleys during the period when Mary wrote *Frankenstein*; TS Eliot lived at No.31 just down the road. Like its neighbour Henley, Marlow gets packed out in the summer with tourists eager to get close to the river, but is a less hectic place. The town's other claim to fame is its suspension bridge, built by William Tierney Clark, who was also responsible for the bridge over the Danube linking Buda with Pest. Nevertheless, Marlow has few proper sights, and even fewer pubs of any standing, and you'd be forgiven for not wanting to linger too long.

The country to the north-west of Marlow is an area of outstanding beauty, enough to bring out the walker in anyone. Villages of particular note include **Frieth**, with two fine country pubs and a recommended B&B, and **Turville**, where the *Vicar of Dibley* is filmed, and home to the excellent modern cooking of the Bull & Butcher (01491 638283).

Henley

A few miles west of Marlow, **Henley** is chiefly famed for its royal regatta (*see page 208* **Regattas, races & festivals**), which was established in 1839. The crowds and traffic in the town are bad at the best of times, but for five days in summer Henley is filled to bursting point with champagne-quaffing toffs. The town, which boasts some 300 listed buildings, was, at

the time of writing, the subject of an experimental pedestrianisation scheme.

Oenophiles might like to extend their interest to include, dare we say it, English wines: try one of the informative wine tastings at the Thames Valley Vineyards (just off the B3018 at Stanlake Park, Twyford; 01189 340176), or try before you buy at Old Luxters (off the A4155 going from Henley to Marlow past Hambleden; after 2.5 miles take the road to the left before Skirmett; 01491 638330).

If you're into walking, the area provides ample opportunities to get close to nature. Good places for starting walks include Remenham, Burnham Beeches and Boulter's Lock.

Where to stay

There are accommodation options aplenty in the area but, with a couple of notable exceptions listed below, there are few hotels of real character in the towns, and your best bet is to head for one of the B&Bs further out. In addition to the following places, the **Waterside Inn** (*see page 212*) and the **Walnut Tree** (*see page 211*) both offer accommodation. Lottery winners, meanwhile, might be interested in staying at **Cliveden** (*see page 213*).

Holmwood

Shiplake Row, Binfield Heath, RG9 4DP (01189 478747/fax 01189 478637).
Rates (B&B) *single* £35; *double/twin* £55.
Rooms (all en suite) 1 single; 2 double; 2 twin.
Cards Debit, MC, V.
This wonderful Georgian building, set back from the road behind a high wall, is about as far removed from a typical B&B as is possible. The grand, galleried entrance hall, complete with chandelier, sets the tone for the public rooms (lounge and dining room); the bedrooms are less awesome, though large and comfy and decorated with antiques (the bathrooms could only be called 'period' if you count the '70s). For once, the single traveller gets the best of the rooms – one with a single four-poster bed, where owner Brian slept as a child. Most overlook the immaculate four-acre gardens. Children over 12 only.
A4155 from Henley towards Reading; after 2.5 miles, turn right into Plough Lane just before Plowden Arms pub; Holmwood is up hill on left.

Inn on the Green

The Old Cricket Common, Cookham Dean, SL6 9NZ (01628 482638/fax 01628 487474/ www.theinnonthegreen.com).
Rates (B&B) *single/single occupancy* £55-£80; *double* £90-£100; *twin* £80-90; *four-poster* £100.
Rooms (all en suite) 1 single; 3 double; 3 twin; 1 four-poster. **Cards** AmEx, Debit, MC, V.
If nearby Cliveden is out of your budget, then the award-winning Inn on the Green is a cheaper alternative. The rooms have a real country feel: most have exposed beams, and the black slate in the stunning bathrooms

*No place like **Holmwood**. See page 209.*

contrasts starkly with the white fittings. The four-poster room, decked out in exotic oranges and dark greens, is saucily described by the management as the 'Karma Sutra' room. Best of all, though: there are no phones. Though quite pricey for what you get, the Inn is convenient for crashing out after sampling the delights of the restaurant in the attached pub. Children welcome.

A404 towards Marlow; follow signs from Marlow to Cookham Dean; turn left at war memorial after Jolly Farmer pub in Cookham Dean.

Little Parmoor

Frieth, RG9 6NL (01494 881447/fax 01494 883012).
Rates (B&B) £25pp. **Rooms** (all en suite) 1 single; 1 double; 1 twin.

Hosts Wynard and Julia Wallace go out of their way to make you feel at home in their wonderful Georgian house, set in farmland in the Chilterns. Rooms, decked out in floral bedspreads and wallpaper, are large and extremely comfortable, and guests are welcome to use the lovely panelled drawing room. Ask to be shown round the one-acre garden, complete with running water and vine-covered terrace, where visitors can breakfast in the summer. Guests are in good company at Little Parmoor: Wynard is a descendant of Inigo Jones, a portrait of whom hangs on the wall of the breakfast room. One-night bookings are sometimes refused at weekends. Children over five welcome; dinner by arrangement (£15). No smoking throughout.

Head through Frieth in direction of Henley and Hambleden and follow road round to left. House is 0.75 miles along on right.

Martens House

Willow Lane, Wargrave, RG10 8LH
(tel/fax 0118 940 3707).
Rates (B&B) *single occupancy* £30; *double/twin* £50.
Rooms 1 double; 2 twin (1 en suite).

A tranquil Thames-side base for river-centric pottering, Martens House is a sizeable, friendly late Victorian family home. Solidly and inoffensively decorated, the three bedrooms are comfy and relaxing; the best overlooks the lawns and the river. Children welcome.

A404 towards Reading; take A321 at Twyford roundabout towards Henley; straight over crossroads in Wargrave; left after George & Dragon pub into Willow Lane; over bridge; follow road to right; house is down a gravel drive on left.

Red Lion Hotel

Hart Street, Henley-on-Thames, RG9 2AR (01491 572161/fax 01491 410039).
Rates *single* £90; *single occupancy* £110; *double/twin* £120; *four-poster* £140; *family* £150.
Breakfast £11 (Eng); £8 (cont). **Rooms** (all en suite) 3 single; 11 double; 8 twin; 3 four-poster; 1 family.
Cards AmEx, Debit, MC, V.

This historic sixteenth-century wisteria-clad coaching inn wisely exploits its location right next to the Thames. The pricey but comfortable rooms feature all necessary modern trappings while largely retaining their original features: antiques and modern prints decorate the rooms, and the bright, marble-tiled bathrooms are of a high standard. Some overlook the river (thankfully, given the busy street below, their windows are double-glazed), though the four-poster room at the back of the hotel (hence without a riverside view) is undoubtedly the nicest. The food served in the restaurant is fine, if unexciting. The overall feel of the hotel is slightly stuffy, but this is probably the best accommodation in Henley. Children welcome.

A404 towards Maidenhead; follow signs to A4130 to Henley; hotel is on right after Henley Bridge.

Sir Christopher Wren's House Hotel

Thames Street, Windsor, SL4 1PX (01753 861354/fax 01753 860172/www.wrensgroup.com).
Rates (breakfast incl weekend only) *single* £99-£145; *double/twin* £135-£185; *deluxe double/twin/four-poster* £165-£225; *triple* £150-£200; *suite* £195-£250. Breakfast (Mon-Fri) £10.50 (Eng); £8.50 (cont). **Rooms** (all en suite) 11 single; 24 double; 8 twin; 16 deluxe double; 2 deluxe twin; 3 four-poster; 1 triple; 5 suites. **Cards** AmEx, DC, Debit, MC, V.

By far the nicest hotel in Windsor, the Sir Christopher Wren's House occupies several buildings on both sides of the street: the main building, and, opposite, a champagne and oyster bar and two apartments for longer stays. The rooms are of a high standard; many are decorated with antiques, with marble bathrooms and fireplaces. As the name suggests, the hotel was once the home of Sir Chris himself (the house has been significantly extended over the centuries); Room 2, with its beautiful wooden panelling, was the architect's bedroom, and is said to be haunted by his ghost (as is Room 1). The riverside restaurant, unlike many hotel restaurants, is bright and breezy, with Modern European dishes so well executed they would put many top London establishments to shame. Children welcome.

Where to eat & drink

Though this area is the domain of the country pub, banish all thoughts of the Ploughman's Lunch™. The fact that this is well-heeled Londoners-on-a-break territory means several things: high quality, inventive food… and hefty prices.

Surprisingly, while some villages, such as **Frieth** and **Shiplake Row**, have three or more decent pubs apiece (in the latter, the lovely **White Hart** – 01189 403673 – also serves good food), in towns such as Henley, you'll be hard-pushed to find one. **Bray**, on the other hand, seems to have the pick of the area rolled into one, with at least five notable pubs and restaurants; in addition to the places mentioned below, the **Fish** (Old Mill Lane; 01628 781111) and the **Crown** on the High Street (01628 621936) are also recommended. Beer lovers should note that **Henley** is the home of Brakspear bitter, so you're likely to come across it in most pubs in the area.

As well as the pubs and restaurants below, the restaurants in the **Sir Christopher Wren's House Hotel** and the **Inn on the Green** (for both, *see page 209*) are highly recommended, as is the Michelin-starred **Waldo's** at Cliveden (*see page 213*). If you fancy a decent Chinese or Indian, both can be found in Cookham. **The Peking Inn** (High Street; 01628 520900) serves high-quality Chinese food in swish surroundings. Alternatively, the **Cookham Tandoori** (High Street; 01628 522584) is in a refurbished pub, but food is a cut above that served in your average high-street Indian restaurant.

Al Fassia

27 St Leonard's Road, Windsor (01753 855370). **Food served** 11.30-2.30pm; 6.30-11pm Mon-Sat. **Set meals** £9.95 (2 courses); £12.95 (3 courses). **Cards** AmEx, DC, Debit, MC, V.

Admirably cheery staff and unusually good Moroccan food. If you know your briwats from your bastilla, you'll appreciate the authenticity of Al Fassia's very reasonably priced menu. Try dishes like salmon charmoula (with coriander, lemon juice, cumin, paprika, garlic, parsley and vinegar) and don't miss out on the fluffiest couscous in the Home Counties. A little gem.

Alfonso's

19-21 Station Hill Parade, Cookham (01628 525775). **Food served** 12.30-2pm, 7-10pm Mon-Thur; 12.30-2pm, 7-11pm Fri; 7-11pm Sat. **Set meals** *lunch* £7.50 (2 courses); *dinner* £18 (2 courses), £21.50 (3 courses). **Cards** AmEx, DC, Debit, MC, V.

Despite its less-than-glamorous setting (in a parade of shops near the train station), Alfonso's continues to attract plaudits for its down-to-earth atmosphere and inventive cooking influenced by the owners' native Spain. Starters could include creamed crab risotto deli-

cately infused with white truffle oil; a main dish might be fillets of sole baked with red onions and cider, flamed with brandy calvados; summer bottled cherry tart with a cool crème anglaise is a typical dessert.

Bottle & Glass

Binfield Heath (01491 575755). **Food served** noon-1.45, 7-9.30pm, Mon-Sat; noon-1.45, Sun. **Cards** AmEx, Debit, MC, V.

Parts of this cosy black-and-white-timbered pub date back to the fifteenth century. Upon entering, you get the impression that little has changed – there's a low, beamed bar, a huge open fireplace and, for a real sense of history, you can peruse the family records of earlier landlords etched into the windows. Food is traditional pub fare with a modern twist – a typical menu might feature beef Oxford (£8.25) – a local dish akin to steak casserole, with apricots and red wine; desserts, all £3.75, could include raspberry roulade or chocolate and orange cheesecake.

The Fat Duck

High Street, Bray (01628 580333). **Food served** noon-2pm, 7-9.30pm, Tue-Fri; noon-2pm, 7-10pm, Sat; noon-2.30pm Sun. **Set meals** *lunch* £23.50 (3 courses) Tue-Sat. **Cards** AmEx, Debit, MC, V.

If you like works of art on your plate as well as on your walls (and don't mind paying for them), you cannot fail to be impressed by Heston Blumenthal's Bray venture, which opened in 1995. On paper at least, many dishes seem to feature two or three ingredients too many, but once you've settled on a dish you're in for a treat. Examples include a starter of velouté of celeriac and tapioca, cabbage stuffed with pig's cheek and choucroute (£11.50); a main course of veal sweetbread roast in salt crust with hay, confit parsnips, cockles à la plancha, lettuce and truffle cream (yes, that's all one dish) (£27.50); and a dessert of millefeuille of pain d'épices ice-cream, pineapple and chilli jelly (£8.75).

The Walnut Tree

Fawley, nr Henley-on-Thames (tel/fax 01491 638360). **Food served** noon-2.30pm, 6-9.30pm daily. **Set meals** *lunch* £14.95 (3 courses) Sun; *dinner* £14.95 (3 courses) Mon-Fri. **Cards** Debit, MC, V.

You'd be forgiven for driving straight past the Walnut Tree and looking for something prettier. Don't: the food, not the setting (a nondescript '50s building with a

The Fat Duck *in Bray.*

The Chilterns to York

Splashing out

What better way to spend a sunny day than to pack up a picnic and cruise on the Thames? Several companies operate boat trips within the area covered in this chapter: among them are **Rivertime** (01628 530600), which offers a range of small boats, either skippered or self-manned, starting from various points between Windsor and Oxford. **French Brothers** (01753 851900), based in Windsor, covers the stretch of river from Runnymede to Hampton Court, and also runs trips from Windsor Promenade to Windsor racecourse on race days. **Kris Cruisers**, a family-run company based at Datchet, near Windsor (01753 543930), hires out a range of rowing boats and self-drive boats.

Most people take to the river for a leisurely mooch, eyeing up the riverside mansions of the rich and famous (a friendly local helps at this point). But, should you be tempted to step on to one of the islands in the Thames, be careful which one you pick: **Monkey Island** (near Bray), the site of the imaginatively named Monkey Island Hotel, and Eton College's very own **Queen's Eyot** (pronounced 'eight'; between Maidenhead and Windsor) and **Temple Island** (just downstream from Henley), named after the lovely Georgian folly located on it, are the jealously guarded preserve of corporate activities and tailor-made regattas.

modern conservatory) is the thing here. Perfectly executed dishes we've sampled include roasted best end of spring lamb with a potato and redcurrant rösti and jus (£11.95) and Moroccan spiced fish cakes with baker chips and aioli (£6.95). Desserts (£3.50) are displayed on the board, and are of the treacle tart and bakewell tart ilk. Owner Adam Dutton was previously the restaurant manager at Cliveden, and he obviously didn't lose any of his (considerable) skills when he moved here. Accommodation comes in the form of two double rooms (£50; £35 single occupancy).

The Waterside Inn
Ferry Road, Bray (01628 620691).
Food served noon-2pm, 7-9.30pm, Tue-Sun.
Set meals £30 (3 courses) Wed-Sat; £46 (3 courses) Sun. **Cards** AmEx, DC, Debit, MC, V.

OK, so the Waterside Inn may make its near-neighbour the Fat Duck look like a bargain, but what do you expect with Michel Roux at the helm and three Michelin stars under his belt? Food is distinctly Gallic, and worth breaking any diet (and budget) for: get your laughing gear around such delicacies as pan-fried lobster medallions with a white port and ginger sauce (£34.50), and roast Challandais duck served with stuffed cabbage and a spiced port jus (£63.50, for two people). The dining room, which overlooks the river, is best appreciated on a sunny day, when it's at its brightest and airiest. You could always go the whole hog and book a room for the night (from £135 for a double room). Closed for five weeks from Boxing Day.

The Yew Tree
Frieth (01494 882330).
Food served noon-3pm, 6-10.30pm, Mon-Sat; noon-3pm, 7-10pm, Sun. **Cards** AmEx, DC, Debit MC, V.

The Yew Tree is the sort of time-warp country pub once so common, but so rarely found nowadays – a warm, timbered room decorated with assorted trinkets, and complete with (friendly) old geezer drinking at the bar. The menu comprises classic '70s dishes at thoroughly '90s prices (mixed grill garni, £10.95; beef Wellington, £14.95; chocolate fudge cake, £3.50), and there's also a catch of the day special. It's obviously good enough for the local Aston Martin club, whose members meet here once a month.

What to see & do

Tourist information centres
Town Hall, Market Place, **Henley-on-Thames**, RG9 2AQ (01491 578034/fax 01491 411766/ www.henley-on-thames.org.uk).
Open *Apr-Sept* 10am-7pm daily; *Oct-Mar* 10am-4pm daily.
24 High Street, **Windsor**, SL4 1LH (01753 743900/ accommodation line 01753 743907/fax 01753 743904).
Open *Mar-Oct* 10am-5pm Mon-Sat; 10am-4.30pm Sun; *Nov-Feb* 10am-4pm daily.

Bike hire
Windsor Roller Rink & Cycle Hire Alexandra Gardens, Alma Road, **Windsor** (01753 830220). Just outside the train station, inside the coach park.

Cliveden
Off B476, Taplow, nr Maidenhead (01628 605069).
Open *estate & garden Mar-Dec* 11am-6pm
(till 4pm Nov-Dec); *mansion & Octagon Temple
(Chapel) Apr-Oct* 3-6pm Thur, Sun.
Admission (NT) *grounds* £5; £2.50 5s-18s;
£12.50 family; *mansion* £1 extra; 50p 5s-18s.

Set high on chalk cliffs overlooking the Thames and surrounded by 375 acres of gardens and parkland, this stunning nineteenth-century Italianate mansion is now a
National Trust property. Originally built by the 2nd
Duke of Buckingham in the seventeenth century, and
subsequently home to various earls, princes and the
Astors (William Waldorf gave the house to them as a
wedding present in 1905), it now seems fitting that such
a grand property is one of the country's most luxurious
hotels (and site of the notorious Profumo/Keeler swimming pool incident). Still, mere plebs can appreciate the
fabulous gardens, which feature roses, topiary, water
gardens, exquisite statuary, formal parterre and sweeping views over the cliffs. The mosaic interior of the
Octagon Temple (Chapel) and three mansion rooms are
also open during part of the year to non-residents.

Eton College
Eton High Street, Windsor
(01753 671177/www.etoncollege.com).
Open *term time* 2-4.30pm daily; *holidays* 10.30am-
4.30pm daily; *guided tours Apr-Sept* 2.15pm, 3.15pm,
daily. **Admission** £2.60; £2 7s-15s; *guided tour*
£3.80; £3 7s-15s.

Have a wander round or book a guided tour to get the
full low-down on the fifteenth-century College, which
has educated 18 British Prime Ministers.

Fawley Court
Off A4155 north of Henley (01491 574917).
Open *museum Mar-Oct* (except Easter and
Whitsun weekends) 2-5pm Wed, Thur, Sun.
Admission £4; £1.50 4s-16s; £3 OAPs.

Worth visiting for a gander at the elaborate ceiling by
Grinling Gibbons and the landscaped grounds by
Capability Brown that lead down to the river. Bed and
breakfast also available (phone for rates).

Legoland Windsor
Winkfield Road, Windsor (01753 626111/
www.legoland.co.uk).
Open *mid-Mar-Oct* 10am-6pm daily.
Admission £17; £14 3s-12s; £11 OAPs.

Whether or not the little plastic bricks are your idea of
fun, this award-winning theme park certainly does the
business with families (at a considerable price).
Favourite areas include Miniland, a tour of Europe made
from over 20 million Lego bricks, Duplo Gardens, and
the Lego Traffic area, where the little terrors can get
their own driving licence (2-12 years). Note that
Legoland is open till later during the school summer holidays; phone for details.

River & Rowing Museum
Mill Meadows, Henley-on-Thames
(01491 415600/www.rrm.co.uk).
Open *Easter-Oct* 10am-6.30pm Mon-Sat; 11am-
6.30pm Sun; *Nov-Easter* 10.30am-5pm daily.

The Round Tower of **Windsor Castle**.

Admission £4.95; £3.75 5s-16s, OAPs, students;
£13.95-£19.25 family.
A history of the regatta and life on the river.

Stanley Spencer Gallery
King's Hall, High Street, Cookham (01628 520890).
Open *Apr-Oct* 10.30am-5.30pm daily; *Nov-Mar*
11am-5pm Sat, Sun. **Admission** 50p; 10p 5s-16s;
25p OAPs, students.

Masterpieces on display include *The Last Supper* (1920)
and *Christ Preaching at Cookham Regatta* (1953-9),
which the artist was working on when he died. Phone
for details of specialist talks.

Windsor Castle
High Street, Windsor (01753 868286 ext 2347/24-hour
recorded info 01753 831118/www.royal.gov.uk.).
Open *Mar-Oct* 9.45am-5.15pm (last entry) daily;
Nov-Feb 10am-4.15pm (last entry) daily. Changing of
the Guard (weather permitting) *Apr-June* 11am daily;
July-Mar phone for details. **Admission** *Mon-Sat*
£10; £5 5s-16s; £7.50 OAPs; £22.50 family; *Sun*
£8.50; £4 5s-15s; £6.50 OAPs; £18.50 family.

Highlights include Queen Mary's Dolls' House, built on
a one-twelfth scale with such detail that even the toilets
flush. The State Rooms, destroyed by the 1992 fire, have
now been fully restored and are open to the public: they
include the opulent Waterloo Chamber, which was built
to celebrate the famous victory over the French in 1815.
The St George's Chapel is the burial place of Henry VIII
(note that the Chapel is closed to visitors on Sunday,
though worshippers are welcome). Try to coincide your
visit with the Changing of the Guard, which takes place
outside the Guardroom in the Lower Ward.

North Chilterns

See how the other half lives.

Anyone who has motored west down the M40 towards Oxford has driven through the Chilterns – literally, for the motorway passes through the massive chalk cutting that slices into the hilly tip of the Buckinghamshire Chilterns and continues out into Oxfordshire, lying flat and green as a billiard table below. Geographically blessed with the River Thames to the south, the Grand Union Canal to the north and the Chiltern Hundreds draped across the middle, it's little wonder that so many nobles and notables chose to live in the Chilterns. (Their modern equivalents – industrial fat cats, stinking-rich silks, etc – continue to do so today.) The undulating fields and bluebell woods are littered with their stately homes and parks.

Homes of the rich and famous

On this circle of waterways and roads surrounding the hills, at 12 o'clock is Bucks' agreeable but unremarkable county town **Aylesbury**, crouching in the fertile Vale of Aylesbury. Waddesdon Manor, a Renaissance-style château built in the 1870s for Baron Ferdinand de Rothschild with a stunning collection of eighteenth-century French decorative arts, is well worth a visit. Another of the area's fine houses is Hughenden Manor, the former home of Queen Victoria's favourite Prime Minister, Benjamin Disraeli.

These boots are made for walking

Possibly a greater attraction than the noble piles is the lure of quality rambling. Twice the national average of footpaths crosshatch the Chilterns area – that's four miles of path per square mile of countryside – all irresistibly studded with characterful pubs for refuelling.

Tring is within easy striking distance of three reservoirs and is a good starting point for

some splendid walks alongside the Grand Union Canal and the Ridgeway Path to Ivinghoe Beacon, the spectacular finale of the Chilterns. The prehistoric Ridgeway Path starts here and ambles 85 miles into Wiltshire, for much of the way following the Icknield Way, which, at 3,000 years old, is the oldest trackway in the country and runs from East Anglia to Dorset. Both paths have their merits, but prehistoric man's need for water means that both tend to follow the lower 'spring-lines', while the best views are to be had from the tops of the hills and more recent footpaths.

High Wycombe and around

High Wycombe is the largest town in Buckinghamshire and grew up around the furniture industry in the eighteenth and nineteenth centuries. Though undoubtedly a sprawling modern town, it's far from the industrial carbuncle you might expect, with buildings from as far back as 1237 sitting comfortably alongside modern shops, restaurants and the street market, held on Tuesday, Friday and Saturday. A few minutes' stroll east, the Rye is an area of open grassland with beech woods and an artificial lake. A mile or so north-west of here is Sir Francis Dashwood's estate and the dark secrets of West Wycombe Caves (*see page 219* **Sir Francis Dashwood and the Hellfire Club**).

From High Wycombe, take a scenic route to Bledlow Ridge for an unadvertised wonder: the mournful song and majestic sight of red kites soaring on air currents above the tumbling hills. Rarely seen in Britain, these raptors were introduced ten years ago to Bledlow Ridge so successfully that chances are you'll see at least half a dozen of them. Afterwards, lunch at the exemplary Sir Charles Napier (*see page 217*).

A few miles along the A40, the small drive-through village of **Tetsworth** – marked on the oldest-known map of England in 1382 – would quickly be left behind, but if antiques are your thing pull over at the Swan. A handsome coaching inn with foot-tripping floorboards and head-cracking lintels, it houses 10,000 square feet of old treasures. After a couple of hours' drooling, you might like to recover in the adjoining restaurant, or amble two miles down the road for impressive afternoon teas at Le Manoir aux Quat' Saisons (*see page 190*).

By train from London

Trains go direct from **Marylebone** to **Aylesbury** every half hour, and take approx **55mins** (stops include Wendover, Great Missenden and Amersham). There are four trains an hour from **Marylebone** to **High Wycombe**, which take between **30mins** and **40mins**; some stop at **Beaconsfield**.

Following in ancient footsteps – tramping the **Ridgeway Path.**

One of the numerous walks in the area can be started from Long Crendon. The Court House here was the first building to be purchased by the National Trust in 1900 and is still open to the public. Notley Abbey, founded in 1162 by the Augustinian monks, was reputedly one of the richest monasteries in the country and the church is at least twice the length of the present Oxford Cathedral. Buckinghamshire County Council has produced two booklets detailing historical and scenic walks, available from any of the area's tourist information centres.

Where to stay

There's a wealth of places to lay your head in the Chilterns. If those below are full, try the **Old Vicarage** in Mentmore (01296 661227; double £50), **Upper Green Farm** at Towersey near Thame (01844 212496; double £48-£60), the **Kings Arms** in Stokenchurch (01494 609090; doubles £89-£129) or **Holmdale**, Little Chalfont (01494 762527; double £50). If money's no option, head to the luxurious surroundings of **Champneys**, the posh health resort at Wigginton near Tring (01442 291000; double at £450 per night for the minimum two-night stay).

Bell Inn

Aston Clinton, HP22 5HP (01296 630252/ fax 01296 631250/info@thebellinn.com). **Rates** *double/twin* £65-£85; *four-poster* £85; *suite* £85-£130. Breakfast £9.50 (Eng), £6 (Cont).

Special breaks. **Rooms** (all en suite) 11 double/twin; 2 four-poster; 7 suites. **Cards** AmEx, DC, Debit, MC, V.

A cheery hello and the smell of wood fires and furniture wax welcome visitors to the Bell. Inside, the large, richly decorated rooms in this seventeenth-century coaching inn have been enjoyed by the likes of Pierce Brosnan and the inimitable Michael Winner. The deluxe suite 'Brewers House' is like having your own country cottage for the night. Cosseting service, attractive gardens, wonderfully leathery bars… all this plus great food in the curvaceous, mural-painted restaurant. Excellent-value breaks include breakfast, a six-course dinner, champagne and afternoon tea. Children welcome. Non-smoking rooms available.

off A41 SE of Aylesbury.

George & Dragon

High Street, West Wycombe, HP14 3AB (01494 464414/fax 01494 462432/enq@george-and-dragon.co.uk/www.george-and-dragon.co.uk). **Rates** (B&B) *single* £56; *double/twin* £66; *four-poster* £70. Special breaks. **Rooms** (all en suite) 1 single; 5 double; 1 twin; 2 four-poster. **Cards** AmEx, DC, Debit, MC, V.

More than a mere high street pub, this fourteenth-century inn with a large, quiet garden backing on to West Wycombe Park is squeezed into a fetching ancient village street. Back rooms are quaint and crooked with beamed ceilings; front rooms in the 'modern' extension (1720) are taller and brighter. The black-beamed, pumpkin-coloured bar looks comfortably well worn but is in fact spotlessly clean, and likewise a short menu seems pubby initially but deserves closer inspection. Homemade meat pies and grills plus pork and prawn creole stew and a soft and squishy stout cake with chocolate

Opulent **Hartwell House**.

sauce are all generously portioned and reasonably priced (between £5.85 and £12.95).

Off A40 SE of Stokenchurch.

Hartwell House

Oxford Road, nr Aylesbury, HP17 8NL (01296 747444/fax 01296 747500/info@hartwell-house.com). **Rates** *single* £130-£165; *double/twin* £205-305; *four-poster* £345; *suites* £305-£600. Breakfast £15.95 (Eng), £11.50 (cont). **Rooms** (all en suite) 7 single; 22 double/twin; 5 four-poster; 12 suites. **Cards** AmEx, Debit, MC, V.

Exquisitely restored by Historic House Hotels (who are also responsible for **Middlethorpe Hall** in York; *see p242)*, Hartwell House, one-time home of the exiled King Louis XVIII, is the place to come for unashamed luxury. Beautiful antiques, paintings and furnishings in all the rooms, distinguished service and unmissable bargain set lunches from £22 (Mon-Sat), which feature local produce such as Aylesbury duck. If you can bear to leave the house, 90 acres of parkland, soothing spa facilities and a 50-foot swimming pool are yours for the taking. Non-smoking rooms available.

A418 NE towards Aylesbury; hotel is signposted after Thame.

Old Trout

29-30 Lower High Street, Thame, OX9 2AA (01844 212146/212614/www.theoldtrouthotel.co.uk). **Rates** (B&B) *single* £55; *double/four-poster* £75. **Rooms** (all en suite) 2 single; 1 double; 4 four-poster. **Cards** Debit, MC, V.

Former owners of the acclaimed Angel Inn in nearby Long Crendon, Mark and Ruth Jones bring to Thame their sound policy of modern bistro-style food with comfortable rooms for those wanting a weekend moderate in price but extreme in relaxation, or for those who simply don't want to get back in the car after dinner. Both restaurant and bedrooms are warm, beamed and creaking with 500-year-old charm, and four rooms have prettily canopied, four-poster beds. A great breakfast is guaranteed. Children welcome.

Hotel is at lower end of Thame High Street, 200m before church and opposite courthouse.

Poletrees Farm

Luggershall Road, Brill, nr Aylesbury, HP18 9TZ (tel/fax 01844 238276). **Rates** (B&B) £22-£25pp. **Rooms** 3 double/twin (1 en suite); 1 suite.

A sixteenth-century former coaching inn on the old Oxford to Buckingham Roman road. This 150-acre mixed farm is set in the heart of the countryside but only eight miles from Oxford and six miles from Waddesdon Manor. Fulsome English breakfast with home produce and evening meals by arrangement. The village of Brill has a fascinating past, superb views and ruins dating from Neolithic times, which are easily accessible to the walker. Children welcome. No smoking throughout.

B4011 NW of Thame; follow signs to Brill on right; house is before railway bridge on sharp bend.

Wisteria Cottage

Bowood Lane, Wendover Dean, HP22 6PY (01296 625509/622141/wisteria.cottage@virgin.net). **Rates** (B&B) £22.50-£24. **Rooms** 2 double (1 en suite), 1 twin.

Tucked into lush, folded fields and threaded lanes, the aptly named Wisteria Cottage offers three spotless rooms with pitched, beamed ceilings and wonderful views. A large guest lounge provides extra space to get comfortable in. There's a TV and hot drinks facilities in each room, and a car service to restaurants on request. Children welcome. No smoking throughout.

A413 NW of Amersham; follow signs to Bowood Antiques on A413 between Great Missenden and Aylesbury; cottage is next to antiques shop.

Where to eat & drink

In addition to the hotels mentioned above, all of which serve reliable if not outstanding food, there's a wealth of good pubs in the area, many offering excellent grub. Among the best are the **Angel** in Long Crendon (01844 208268), the **Green Dragon** in Haddenham (01844 291403), the **Rising Sun** of Little Hampden (01494 488393) and the **Mole & Chicken** in Easington (01844 208387). Good drinking pubs include the **Seven Stars** in Dinton, the **Dinton Hermit** in Ford, the **Pheasant** in Brill, the **Crown** in Little Missenden, the **Polecat** in Prestwood, the **George & Dragon** in West Wycombe and the **Lions of Bledlow** in Bledlow.

La Chouette

Westlington Green, nr Dinton, Aylesbury (01296 747422). **Food served** noon-2pm, 7-9pm, Mon-Fri; 7-9pm Sat. **Set meals** £26.50 (4 courses). **Cards** AmEx, MC, V.

Allow an extra ten minutes to find La Chouette (signposted 'Westlington only' and down a dead end). Belgian Frédéric Desmette cooks and serves virtually single-handedly but has passion enough for a roomful of staff. Sample from a range of Belgian beers at the bar or move straight into the restaurant, which is olde worlde but not fussy, pandering instead to the desires of serious foodies. Belgian specialities are well advertised; asparagus with beurre noisette and hard-boiled egg is far more delicious than it sounds, and morels on toast and perfectly cooked pigeon with shallot sauce is lip-smackingly good. Starters cost £8-£12, mains £14, wines start at a very reasonable £10.50 and rise sharply through a mostly French list.

Steward of the Chiltern Hundreds

The part of Buckinghamshire south of the Chiltern Ridge enjoys a bizarre place in arcane Parliamentary tradition. Known as the Chiltern Hundreds, it is actually made up of three 'hundreds' (ancient divisions of a county) running roughly north-south: Stoke (around Gerrards Cross), Burnham (around Beaconsfield) and Desborough (around High Wycombe).

MPs are not allowed to resign during the life of a Parliament, so any member wishing to leave the Commons instead applies for the defunct office of Steward and Bailiff of the Chiltern Hundreds (or, alternatively, of the Manor of Northstead in Yorkshire), which, as (nominal) offices of profit under the Crown, disqualify the MP from the House. The two offices allow for the possibility of two MPs resigning at the same time. The ex-MPs hold these offices until the next member wishes to resign. Previous eminent stewards include John Stonehouse (1976), Roy Jenkins (1977), Matthew Parris (1986), Leon Brittan (1988) and Neil Kinnock (1995).

Green Dragon
Church End, Haddenham (01844 291403).
Food served noon-2pm, 7-9pm, Mon-Sat; noon-2pm Sun. **Cards** AmEx, Debit, MC, V.
Blue-and-yellow checks with aged pine tables give Mediterranean warmth to this pub-cum-restaurant by a duck pond in the picturesque village of Haddenham. Originally a twelfth-century coaching inn, it's still very much a combined food and comfort zone for locals. The menu has universal 'Mediterranean' appeal, with British and occasional Eastern influences popping up. Local wood pigeon and chicken pâté with spiced relish, marinated swordfish with tabouleh, bouillabaisse with rouille are typical. Starters £4-£5, mains £10-£13. Puddings are a nice mix of the expected and the surprising: bread and butter pudding perhaps, or mandarin and kumquat iced soufflé (£3-£5).

Old Plow Inn
Flowers Bottom Lane, Speen (01494 488300).
Food served noon-2pm, 7-9pm, Tue-Fri; 7-9pm Sat; noon-2pm Sun. **Set meals** *lunch* £17.95 (2 courses), £21.95 (3 courses); *dinner* £21.95 (2 courses), £26.95 (3 courses). **Cards** AmEx, Debit, MC, V.
Could any gnarled and ancient inn in a lane called Flowers Bottom fail to be enchanting? The Cowans have run this always-busy bistro and restaurant for ten years. A posher restaurant with starched linen is in one half and a lower-key bistro in the other, but both benefit from the same capable chef and polite front-of-house staff. Encouragingly, seafood only appears if maritime weather conditions are favourable and might be warm scallop salad with oriental dressing. Grilled loin of English lamb with soft apricot, mango and fresh mint preserve was deliciously rich, chargrilled veal with mushroom sauce equally so. Accompanying vegetables are treated as more than just add-ons and desserts of cappuccino ice-cream and toffee sauce and blackcurrant mousse cake are fresh and handmade. The bistro (à la carte only) is about £20 a head, the restaurant about £30.

La Petite Auberge
107 High Street, Great Missenden (01494 865370).
Food served 7.30-10.30pm daily. **Cards** DC, MC, V.
Deep in the woods, Great Missenden makes up for in Tudor-beamed character what it lacks in size, and it's worth wandering down a few side streets en route to La Petite Auberge. Ideal for a quiet dinner, accomplished, classic food is served with appropriately rural connotations. Typically, you'll find main courses such as medallions of roe deer with poivrade and cranberry sauce (£15.40), grey-leg partridge (that's the good one) with chestnuts and rack of lamb with coriander sauce. Innovative fish dishes include freshwater prawns wrapped in cabbage with caviar (£6.20) or tuna marinated in wholegrain mustard. The French-style desserts cost £4.

Sir Charles Napier
Spriggs Alley, nr Bledlow Ridge (01494 483011).
Food served noon-2pm, 7-9.30pm, Tue-Sat; noon-2pm Sun. **Set meals** £15.50 Tue-Fri (2 courses).
Cards AmEx, Debit, MC, V.
With 360° views and walks, the Sir Charles Napier restaurant is nationally acclaimed by food critics for its air of gentle debauchery – think roaring fires, red pigeon breasts and draught champagne. It isn't cheap and service can be patchy at weekends, but one visit and you'll be hooked for life. Champagne is served more often from the bottle than the barrel these days but memories hanker on undimmed for many, and the epic wine list is one to get deliciously lost in. Traditional roasts served with plenty of confidence and no surprises, together with comforting puddings, make leaving hard in more ways than one. About £30 a head plus wine.

What to see & do

Tourist information centres
8 Bourbon Street, **Aylesbury**, HP20 2RR (01296 330559). **Open** *Apr-July, Sept, Oct* 9.30am-5pm Mon-Sat; *Aug* 9.30am-5pm Mon-Sat; 10am-4.30pm Sun; *Nov-Apr* 10am-4.30pm Mon-Sat.
The Clock Tower, High Street, **Wendover**, HP22 6DU (01296 696759/www.chilternweb.co.uk/wendover). **Open** 9.30am-5pm Mon-Thur; 9.30am-4pm Fri, Sat.

The Chilterns to York

Bekonscot Model Village

Warwick Road, Beaconsfield
(01494 672919/www.bekonscot.org.uk).
Open *mid-Feb-Oct* 10am-5pm daily. **Admission**
£3.60; £2.20 3s-15s; £2.50 OAPs, students.

The oldest model village in the world (opened in 1929)
is a nostalgic portrayal of rural England from that era.
There are, in fact, six villages plus many moving models, including a Gauge 1 model railway. There are picnic areas here, and refreshments are available.

Blue Max Air Museum

Wycombe Air Park (01494 449810).
Open *Apr-Nov* 10am-4pm Mon-Fri; 11am-3pm Sun.
Admission £2.75; £1.65 5-16s, OAPs.

A historic collection of flying machines, many of which
have 'starred' in films.

Chiltern Brewery

on B4009 at Terrick, nr Aylesbury (01296 613647).
Open *museum* 9am-5pm Mon-Sat; *tours* phone for
details. **Admission** *museum* free; *tours* £3.50;
£2.50 5s-18s; £3 OAPs.

Buckinghamshire's oldest working brewery. Five
award-winning bespoke beers plus many others.

Chiltern Open Air Museum

Newlands Park, Gorelands Lane, Chalfont St Giles
(01494 871117).
Open *Apr-July, Sept, Oct* 10am-5pm Tue-Sun;
Aug 10am-5pm daily. **Admission** £4.50; £2.50 5-16s;
£3.50 OAPs, students; £13 family.

Historic buildings rescued from demolition and re-built
in 45 acres of countryside, with barns, granaries, stables, tollhouse, Iron Age house and even a 1940s prefab.

Hughenden Manor

High Wycombe
(01494 528051/www.nationaltrust.org.uk).
Open *house Apr-Oct* 1-5pm Wed-Sun;
Mar 1-5pm Sat, Sun; *garden* noon-5pm Wed-Sat.
Admission (NT) *house* £4.10; £2.05 5-16s; £10.20
family; *garden* £1.50; 75p 5s-16s.

Hughenden was home to Benjamin Disraeli from 1848
until his death in 1881. Many of the politician and
writer's pictures, furniture and books remain and genteel cricket games are played close to the chestnut trees
and stream in the surrounding park.

John Milton's Cottage

Chalfont St Giles (01494 872313).
Open *Mar-Oct* 10am-1pm, 2-6pm, Tue-Sun,
bank hols. **Admission** £2; 60p 4-15s.

This Grade I-listed sixteenth-century cottage was where
John Milton lived and wrote *Paradise Lost*. It is now a
museum of his first editions and poetry.

Odds Farm Park

Wooburn Common, nr Beaconsfield (01628
520188/www.btinternet.com/~oddsfarm.park).
Open *mid-Feb-Oct* 10am-5pm daily; *Nov-mid-Feb*
10am-4pm Thur-Sun. **Admission** £3.75; £2.75 2-16s;
£3 OAPs.

A wide range of animals moo, grunt, bray and cluck
away at this rare breeds farm, activities include bottle-
feeding lambs, cow- and goat-milking and tractor rides.

Steam trains

Scenic trips along the Icknield Way from Chinnor
to Princes Risborough. Call 01844 353535 for the
talking timetable.

*Lightly grilled bacon at **Odds Farm Park**.*

Sir Francis Dashwood and the Hellfire Club

Owner of West Wycombe Park, Sir Francis Dashwood (1708-81) notched up an enviable political CV as Chancellor of the Exchequer, Postmaster-General, MP, 1st Colonel of the Buckinghamshire Militia and 15th Baron Le Despenser. As well as being rich, influential and titled, he was a conscientious landowner and spent 30 years rebuilding and furnishing his Palladian mansion and providing locals with honest employment. The enigmatic golden ball spiking the church steeple at West Wycombe, visible for miles, was also built by Sir Frank and since the ball is big enough for three or four people to stand up in many a politician boasted of attending cocktail parties at 'The Globe Tavern'.

The wild side of Sir Francis found fulfilment in the Hellfire Club, which he founded in 1745. Membership was restricted to nobles such as Frederick, Prince of Wales, Benjamin Franklin, Lord Melcome and the Earl of Sandwich. They initially met at night in the grounds of Medmenham Abbey where, dressed in white monks' habits and assisted by mock nuns recruited from London Ladies of Pleasure, black masses were held in mockery of organised religion. Such behaviour, doubly shocking in men of society, fired the imagination of all those excluded so that rumours of 'unspeakable orgies' raged. West Wycombe Caves, excavated for Sir Francis after a few bad harvests to keep farm workers occupied, subsequently became a meeting place for the Hellfire Club. Nowadays, the damp, oversized rabbit burrows with crazy-eyed mannequins and piped psycho laughter rely heavily on wanton fiction rather than wanton action, so you might stick to the elegant rococo landscape of West Wycombe Park for entertainment and use your own imagination for the rest.

West Wycombe Caves West Wycombe Park Office, West Wycombe (01494 533739). **Open** *Mar-Oct* 11am-5.30pm daily; *Nov-Apr* 11am-5pm Sat, Sun. **Admission** £3; £1.50 5-16s, OAPs; £2 students.

Waddesdon Manor

nr Aylesbury (01296 651211/www.waddesdon.org.uk). **Open** *house Apr-June, Sept, Oct* 11am-4pm Thur-Sun; *July, Aug* 11am-4pm Wed-Sun; *grounds* 10am-5pm Wed-Sun. **Admission** (NT) *house & grounds* £10; £7.50 5-16s; *grounds only* £3; £1.50 5-16s.

Baron Ferdinand de Rothschild's French Renaissance-style château was built in the 1870s and now houses one of the world's foremost collections of eighteenth-century French decorative art and important English paintings, the garden is also famous for its specimen trees, seasonal bedding displays and rococo-style aviary of exotic birds.

Walter Rothschild Zoological Museum

Open 10am-5pm Mon-Sat; 2-5pm Sun. **Admission** £3; £1.50 OAPs; free under-17s.

Lord Rothschild's private collection, featuring over 4,000 species of animals, has been bequeathed to the nation (at a small charge), complete within its Victorian gentleman collector's setting. It's a delightfully quirky place, and represents the finest collection of stuffed mammals, birds, reptiles and insects in the country. Far from being full of dusty, flea-bitten relics, it's fascinating for anyone who hasn't seen a spotted wobbegong recently.

Wycombe Museum

Priory Avenue, High Wycombe (01494 421895/www.wycombe.gov.uk/museum). **Open** 10am-5pm Mon-Sat; 2-5pm Sun. **Admission** free.

High Wycombe was long dominated by the furniture industry, so it's no surprise that this entertaining local museum focuses (with the aid of interactive displays) on the 200-year history of the trade and its role in the town's development. There's a picnic area in the in the landscaped grounds, complete with pond. Also check out the Norman castle mound.

Hertfordshire

Far more than hideous new towns and golf courses...

Take a spin in George Bernard Shaw's revolving writing hut at **Shaw's Corner**. See page 225.

The Chilterns to York

If golf is your bag then a visit to Herts is a must. St Albans-born Samuel Ryder founded of the eponymous Cup and the county is home to both the English Open and British Masters. The rolling hills and green pastures of Hertfordshire are a perfect setting for the sport and, dotted between courses, there's many a fine house or park to enjoy. Admittedly, one glance at the map can be off-putting: Watford and the unalluring new towns of Stevenage and Welwyn Garden City glare back at you, but a trip to the area throws up plenty of pleasant surprises. From the market towns of Ware and St Albans, with its Cathedral and relics of Roman Verulamium, to the world-famous film studios at Elstree, Borehamwood and Leavesden (where scenes from the *Star Wars* prequel, *The Phantom Menace* were shot), Hertfordshire has much to offer. Served by several motorways (A1, M25 and M1) it is possible to be in the thick of meadows, glistening fairways and leafy lanes within 20 minutes of leaving London, while taking a more scenic route affords views of unspoilt villages and country inns.

St Albans

In AD 43 the first Roman fort was built to the north-east of the Belgic settlement of Verlamion. All that remains of this important stage in the history of **St Albans** are sections of the city walls and hypocaust in Verulamium Park and the famous thoroughfare of Watling Street. On Wednesdays and Saturdays St Albans market still bustles on St Peter's Street, offering a curious mix of wares, from bargain goods to local cheeses. Continue on past the Town Hall and the Clock Tower (pausing only briefly to ponder the notice on the small door at the side of the tower that reads 'commit no

By train from London

Probably the only Hertfordshire town with enough to do in itself to warrant a visit by train is **St Albans**. It is a mere **19mins** journey from **King's Cross Thameslink** by quarter-hourly fast trains.

nuisance'), before arriving at the junction of Chequer Street and High Street. Off to the right, past the upmarket designerwear shops on George Street, you'll see the Cathedral with its magnificent thirteenth-century wall paintings. Follow the road down to where it becomes Fishpool Street to enjoy a fine prospect of coaching houses, with Elizabethan, Georgian and medieval architectural styles all vying for attention.

Small town life
Directly west of St Albans is **Hemel Hempstead**. The town proper is about a mile or so from Hemel station, which is actually situated in Boxmoor on the Grand Union canal. Pass the shopping centre and you come to the Water Gardens, which link up with the vast municipal gardens alongside the unspoilt old town. The High Street is particularly noteworthy, with many a pleasant-looking pub and well-stocked antiques shop. Roughly half-way along High Street is the Old Town Hall, now the arts centre with theatre, gallery space and café, and behind this the charming flint-faced Norman church of St Mary.

Moving northwards, **Harpenden** is the next major town en route and, from the health shops, beauty salons, wine merchants and a superbly stocked delicatessen, it doesn't take a huge leap of the imagination to realise you've landed firmly in the well-to-do zone. Herts' golf courses have attracted many commuting businessmen, and the suburbs of Harpenden are where all their families have chosen to put down roots. There are plenty of bars, but not a lot on offer for the kids until they're old enough to cruise around with the stereo blaring and down a pint or two.

East of St Albans lies **Hatfield**, suffering somewhat from its concrete conurbation and the convergence of major roadways but encompassing one of England's most celebrated houses, **Hatfield House**, while further north-east is the attractive market town of **Ware**, characteristically huddled along its High Street, crowded with overhanging buildings and coaching houses. The side streets hark back to the industrial age when maltings were widespread in the area, though now high-class grocers and boutiques stand in their place.

A Shaw thing
Nearby are the **Ayots**. These are small villages whose names mean 'island', although not in a literal sense but rather meaning a clearing in the dense surrounding woodland. Nearby is the village of **Ayot St Lawrence**, where George Bernard Shaw set up his studio at the New Rectory, now named Shaw's Corner. The 'old'

church is undergoing restoration, but there's also a remarkable 'new' church set off in the fields close to Shaw's Corner, built in the classical style in 1778, looks more like a pagan temple than a Christian place of worship.

Hertfordshire's countryside has a tendency to swallow up its villages in swathes of verdure, so always persevere when venturing off the beaten track – you never know what you might find.

Where to stay
Hertfordshire has plenty of grand hotels, converted from illustrious but ill-fated country estates, plus some unique and remote guesthouses, and pub accommodation in most major towns. In addition to the places listed below, Harpenden's **Glen Eagle Hotel** (01582 760271) offers standard rooms at £55 for a single and £75 for a double at weekends.

Note that the restaurants in **Brocket Hall**, **Hanbury Manor**, **St Michael's Manor** and **Sopwell House** are all featured in detail on page 223.

Brocket Hall
Welwyn, AL8 7XG (01707 335241/ fax 01707 375166/www.brocket-hall.co.uk). **Rates** (B&B) *single* £138; *double* £150. **Rooms** *Melbourne Lodge* (all en suite) 4 single; 12 double. **Cards** AmEx, DC, Debit, MC, V.
Brocket Hall was home to the cuckolded 1st Lord Melbourne, whose spouse cavorted with George IV, while the second lord married Lady Caroline Lamb, whose love for Lord Byron was anything but discreet. The house proper is mainly used for conferences and parties. Although a golf's buggy journey away from the hall, Melbourne Lodge manages to maintain an air of opulence and, indeed, genuine romance with lashings of taffeta drapery and brocade, and wooded vistas. Since much of the parkland is given over to the golf course there are few places to take a stroll without fear of flying balls. Clay pigeon shooting, coarse and game fishing, croquet, tennis and archery are also available. Children welcome. Non-smoking rooms available.
A1 J4; follow signs to Wheathampstead and B653; once on Brocket Road, turn into entrance to golf club and restaurant for Melbourne Lodge.

Hanbury Manor
Ware, SG12 0SD (01920 487722/fax 01920 487692/ www.marriott.com/marriott/stngs). **Rates** (B&B) *single occupancy* £163-£240; *double/twin* £170-£230; *deluxe double* £188-£256; *four-posters/suites* £278-£430. **Rooms** (all en suite) 67 double/twin; 20 deluxe double; 9 four-posters/suites. **Cards** AmEx, DC, Debit, MC, V.
Last in the series of tragic manses, Hanbury was built in the Jacobean style by Edmund Hanbury as a tribute to his ambitious wife Amy. He ended up bankrupt and declining in health, while she succumbed slowly to madness. Primarily a golfing venue, the original Harry

Vardon golf course was developed by Jack Nicklaus II, and has since played host to the PGA European Tour and, more recently, the English Open. This is a beautifully preserved old house with a well-stocked library, medieval hall-style lounge, and bedrooms that feature all the extra touches you might expect, such as bathrobes. Suites are on several levels with separate sitting rooms built in, while rooms in the new section are more family-sized and are close to the fitness centre, pool and excellently secluded day crèche. Children and dogs welcome (£40 supplement for the latter). Non-smoking rooms available.

M25 J25; A10 towards Cambridge; hotel is on left after junction for Ware (where dual carriageway ends).

Homewood

Knebworth, SG3 6PP
(01438 812105/www.bestbandb.co.uk).
Rates (B&B) *single occupancy* £40; *double* £60 (£15 supplement per child). **Rooms** (all en suite) 1 double; 1 family/suite.

'A bit of friendly, gracious living,' says the brochure of this Edwardian English country house designed by Edwin Lutyens. Certainly, the informality of Homewood does its name justice. The grounds are spacious and include part of the nearby wood, and breakfast can be taken on the beautiful flowery terrace. Each room is different, one having been designed by the landlady's son along the lines of a gentleman's club, while others have more of a country cottage feel – all of them are light and airy, accessed off an intriguing landing decorated with old maps of central London and its environs. Children and dogs welcome. Non-smoking throughout. The owners request that potential visitors phone for a map, which gives detailed directions to Homewood.

Old Rectory

Ayot St Lawrence, Welwyn, AL6 9BT (01438 820429/fax 01438 821844/ayotbandb@aol.com).
Rates (B&B) *single* £35; *double/twin* £45-£70.
Rooms 1 single; 2 double/twin (both en suite).

Built around three sides of a courtyard, this is one part of a large group of buildings of former clergy accommodation. Sunlight dapples the cobbles and breezes waft the delicate scent of wisteria as you cross from the apartment bedrooms into the main house for breakfast. The farmhouse kitchen is dominated by a vast scrubbed table laden with cereals, jams and preserves, all in an easy come-as-you-please atmosphere. The rooms are newly decorated and have a bright, individual feel to them. The single room is quite small but that's reflected in the price, and the doubles are great value and less formal than you'd find in a larger place. There's even a squash court for those who can face it. All bedrooms non-smoking.

A1 J4; follow B653 towards Wheathampstead; after roundabout road bears right towards Luton; take first right after 1 mile; follow signs to Codicote and The Ayots; past golf course; left into Bride Hall Lane; Ayot St Lawrence is after 1 mile; entrance to Old Rectory on right 20m before phone box.

St Michael's Manor

Fishpool Street, St Albans, AL3 4RY (01727 864444/fax 01727 848909/manor@stalbans.co.uk).
Rates (B&B) *single* £105; *deluxe single* £115-£140;

double/twin £135; *deluxe double* £145-£185; *four-poster* £225; *suite* £275. Special breaks.
Rooms (all en suite) 3 single; 5 twin; 8 double; 6 deluxe double; 1 four-poster; 1 suite.
Cards AmEx, Debit, MC, V.

No two rooms are alike in this lovely independently owned hotel, which is only a minute's walk from the Cathedral and Verulamium Park, yet it's remarkably peaceful. Pampering is so complete visitors hardly need to bring any luggage – almost everything is provided. The higher up the creaky staircase you go the more quirky the rooms are, with sunken baths, and shower cubicles built in under the roof beams. All are en suite but opt for the suite with a balcony for a fine view of the garden. There are trays of strawberries and nuts in the lobby and lounges and the grounds are beautifully designed with fountains and wildfowl in abundance. Saturdays are popular for weddings. Children welcome. Non-smoking rooms available.

Follow High Street from St Albans town centre; left into George Street, which becomes Fishpool Street; hotel is on left.

Sopwell House

Cottonmill Lane, Sopwell, St Albans, AL1 2HQ
(01727 864477/fax 01727 844741).
Rates (B&B) *single* £79.75-£114.75; *double* £109.75-£144.75; *suites/apartments* £184.75. **Rooms** (all en suite) 12 single; 27 double; 2 suites; 16 apartments.
Cards AmEx, DC, Debit, MC, V.

Former country retreat of Lord Mountbatten, the original Georgian house has been substantially extended and further expansion has been in progress. There's lots of space to sit out on the terrace and take a walk over the bridge to view the fish, but note that the grounds are usually dominated by wedding parties at a weekend. The rooms offer a touch of nouveau splendour – cabinets with mock drawers to hide the tea things, stocky four-posters plus bed and chair settees in the suites, with peach décor throughout. Apartments offer the best family option, being self-catering and away from the bustle of the main building, with the option of hiring a babysitter should you wish to dine in the restaurant. The lounge has some truly ghastly design features but they seem to be a hit with the country club set. Perfect for a rejuvenating break (choose from spa, gym, golf, sauna, swimming pool and health treatments), but there's not much to do in the area save head for St Albans. The hotel's two restaurants offer a set dinner at £25.95 (*see p223*). Children welcome.

J21A M25; on A414 follow signs to Sopwell.

Where to eat & drink

Hemel old town's many pubs are backed up by a number of restaurants, a bistro, an Italian, plus a healthy and cheap selection at the theatre café. Then there's the creaking staircases and stifling atmosphere of the disappointing **Pie In The Sky** (01442 264309), which, despite its TV fame, offers tired vegetables at very lively prices. The **Rose & Crown** pub (01442 395054) comes highly recommended (and is very accommodating to children).

There are numerous real ale pubs in St Albans, including the oldest, the **Lower Red Lion** on Fishpool Street (01727 855669), which serves cask bitter, country wines and cheap eats including interesting toasties like brie and almond for £2. It also offers accommodation: doubles from £45. For entertainment, the **Horn** (01727 853143) on Victoria Street has jazz every Sunday lunchtime. The **George & Dragon**, Watton at Stone (01920 830285), offers good local food; the **White Lion** in Walkern (just east of Stevenage) is ideal for children, with an excellent play area, as is the **Brocket** at Ayot St Lawrence, which boasts a great garden and an amusingly taciturn landlord.

Shenley, on the road from Watford to Hatfield, has a couple of nice pubs with roomy beer gardens clustered around the duck pond and a curious dome-shaped outhouse (apparently once the local lock-up). The **Sow of Pigs** at Thundridge is also good for families, with a spacious garden and large rustic tables in the dining area. In Harpenden, the **Harpenden Arms** on the High Street (01582 712095) offers cheap Thai food, while the **Old Bell** (01582 712484) on Luton Road is recommended for more traditional family lunches. Alternatively, you can do it yourself at the **Silver Palate** deli on Vaughan Road (01582 713722), which has very fine wines, wonderful steeped olives, plus gourmet hampers for every occasion.

Auberge du Lac

Brocket Hall, Welwyn (01707 368888).
Food served noon-2.30pm, 7-10.30pm, Tue-Sat; noon-2.30pm Sun. **Set meals** *lunch* £18.50 (2 courses); £22.50 (3 courses).
Cards AmEx, DC, MC, V.

The place to be for highest-quality, value-for-money dining, adjacent to a lovely lake and overlooking Brocket Hall (*see p221*). Fine wines are available by the glass and Philippe Marques, the head sommelier, is happy to oblige to find wines to complement each course. The food is inspirational: layers of Cornish crab and avocado with crème fraîche in a spicy tomato coulis, and a crispy salad of green beans, globe artichokes and asparagus to start, followed by plump chicken breast with stuffing and onion gravy, and tagliatelle with sautéed shiitake mushrooms and basil cream. To finish, the fresh liquorice parfait with sweet pear chutney and Chantilly cream is an all-time great dessert. Three courses à la carte is around £38; table d'hôte lunch £22.50 (Sundays £25), excluding drinks. Expect new chef de cuisine Pascal Breant to stamp his signature blend of modern French with Asian influences on the menu.

The Conservatory

St Michael's Manor, Fishpool Street, St Albans (01727 864444). **Food served** 12.30-2pm, 7-9.30pm, Mon-Fri; 12.30-2pm, 7-10pm, Sat; 12.30-2pm, 7-9pm, Sun. **Set meals** *lunch* £15.75 (2 courses); £19.95 (3 courses); *dinner* £29.50 (3 courses).
Cards AmEx, Debit, MC, V.

A pleasant, airy conservatory overlooking the lawn and lake, with lots of tables making for a buzzing atmosphere of a Sunday lunch. Choose from dishes such as tartlet of deep-fried leeks with Lancashire cheese and quails' eggs, or more traditional options like Cumberland sausage in hot English mustard sauce to begin, followed by pan-fried Dover sole or venison sausage casserole. All of the numerous vegetarian starters can be had as main courses. Portions are ample, and are accompanied by – intriguingly – vegetables that have been boiled and then pan-fried. Desserts are irresistible – griddled honey apple fritters, bitter chocolate tart and the like.

. Magnolia Restaurant

Sopwell House Hotel, Sopwell, St Albans (01727 750513).
Food served 12.30-1.45pm, 7.30-9.45pm, Mon-Thur; 12.30-1.45pm, 7-9.45pm, Fri; 7-9.45pm Sat; 12.30-1.45pm Sun. **Set meals** *lunch* £15.95 (2 courses); £17.95 (3 courses); *dinner* £24.95 (3 courses); Sat £25.95 (3 courses). **Cards** AmEx, Debit, MC, V.

Dine under romantic magnolias only to find that although authentic tree trunks are in abundance the foliage is plastic. The meals are rich, not least the Châteaubriand for two, a generous beast the size of a horse (almost), served with, on our last visit, slightly-too-crisp vegetables but perfect roast potatoes; red snapper was much more pleasing. Starters varied from sublime wild mushroom tartlet to less-satisfactory cream-laden parsnip soup with sinewy strands. The Sopwell selection of desserts is always a must. Bejerano's Brasserie offers lighter meals and a less formal setting, though some might find the poolside aspect, with its faint hint of chlorine and backdrop of health-conscious swimmers, a little off-putting. Friday night 'Jazz in the Brazz' from 7.30pm. *See also p222.*

Royal Orchid Thai Cuisine

at back of Rose & Crown, High Street, Hemel Hempstead (01442 395054).
Food served 6-9.30pm Mon-Sat.
Set meals *dinner* £11.95-£19.95 (6 dishes).
Cards AmEx, Debit, MC, V.

Mountains of choice for carnivores and vegetarians, with all curry dishes available with or without meat. This is proper Thai (a popular trend in the region) with fragrant rice and crispy vegetables, a list of appetisers as long as your arm, seafood, meat dishes and spicy salads. It's all authentic, both in terms of ingredients and chilli-heat, with very reasonably priced set meals for two starting at £11.95 for six vegetarian dishes up to £19.95 for the Royal Platter with curried beef, savoury pork, seafood and stir-fried vegetables. The same grub is also available in the pub itself.

Zodiac & Vardon's Restaurants

Hanbury Manor, Ware (01920 487722/www.marriott.com/marriott/stngs).
Food served 12.30-2pm, 7.30-9.30pm, Mon-Thur; 12.30-2pm, 7-10pm, Fri; 7.30-9.30pm Sat; 12.30-2pm, 7.30-9pm, Sun. **Set meals** *lunch* £25 (3 courses); *dinner* £33 (3 courses). **Cards** AmEx, DC, Debit, MC, V.

The Chilterns to York

Gardens of the Rose

Hertfordshire certainly has a great deal to shout about when it comes to horticulture. Many privately owned houses throw open their green spaces from May to October in aid of charities like the National Gardens Scheme and the British Red Cross (leaflets available from tourist information centres; contact the Red Cross Herts branch on 01992 586609). **Knebworth**'s gardens are open periodically; Luton's **Stockwood Park**, with its variety of period gardens, is worth a visit, as are the **Physic Garden** at Hitchin and **Benington Lordship Gardens** near Stevenage, to name but a few.

Pride of place, however, must go to the queen of flowers, the noble rose, and here at the headquarters of the **Royal National Rose Society** there are over 30,000 of them in 1,700 varieties with which to overload your loved-one on a romantic break. There are also bulbs, herbaceous borders and over 100 types of clematis should other scents take your paramour's fancy. Walk through numerous arbours dripping with heady blooms or stroll through beds planted with old and modern plants, plus experimental future strains. You can also explore the water gardens, treasure trail, lawns and small-scale gardens. Plays, opera and classical concerts run throughout the summer.

Gardens of the Rose Chiswell Green, St Albans (01727 850461). **Open** *May-Sept* 9am-5pm Mon-Sat; 10am-6pm Sun. **Admission** £4.

Choose the **Zodiac** for more formal high dining (dressing up is essential but worth it just to smell the money around you). Head chef Robert Gleeson's award-winning delicacies include the likes of mushroom linguini with white truffle oil, and turbot with bok choi, water chestnuts and shiitake mushrooms in soy and ginger jus. The room is named after the elaborate plasterwork on the ceiling depicting all the astrological signs, a touch that is carried through in motifs on the china. **Vardon's** is more relaxed and family-friendly, with a special kids' Dragon Menu offering a Pizza Shield, Whopping Great Tiddlers from the Moat, and Maiden Macaroni Cheese, among other themed dishes. Adult meals are equally inventive from the crunchy pumpkin risotto to monkfish on sweet potato rösti or even an upmarket version of the humble sausage and mash. Starters in Vardon's begin at around £5; main courses £8.50-£19.50. *See also p221.*

What to see & do

Tourist information centres

Dacorum Information Centre, The Marlowes, **Hemel Hempstead**, HP1 1DT(01442 234222). **Open** 9.30am-5pm Mon-Fri; 10am-5pm Sat.

Town Hall, Market Place, **St Albans**, AL3 5DJ (01727 864511/www.bhl-tourism.org.uk). **Open** *Apr-June, mid-Sept, Oct* 9.30am-5.30pm Mon-Sat; *July-mid-Sept* 9.30am-5.30pm Mon-Sat; 10.30am-4pm Sun; *Nov-Mar* 10am-4pm Mon-Sat.

Ashridge Estate

Ringshall, Berkhamsted (01442 851227/recorded info 01494 755557). **Open** *monument* 2-5pm Mon-Thur, Sat, Sun; *estate* free access Mon-Thur, Sat, Sun. **Admission** (NT) £1; 50p 5-16s.

Situated on the Bucks/Herts border, the Ashridge Estate affords great opportunities to spot local flora and fauna along the ridge of the Chiltern Hills, through bluebell woods and verdant commons, taking in the monument erected to the Duke of Bridgewater in 1832. It's a touch ironic considering the Duke's contribution to Britain's industrial development.

Bowman's Farm

Coursers Road, London Colney (01727 822106). **Open** *mid-Feb-Oct* 10am-5.30pm, *Nov-mid-Feb* 10am-4.30pm, daily. **Admission** £3.75; £2.75 3-16s, OAPs. A good place for kids, with tractor rides and a mixed working farm with a milking gallery and pets corner.

Hatfield House

just off A1, Hatfield (01707 262823). **Open** *house late Mar-Sept* noon-4pm Tue-Thur; 1-4pm Sat, Sun; *gardens late Mar-Sept* 11am-6pm Tue-Sun. **Admission** *house & garden* £6; £3 5-15s; *garden only* £5.

Built by Robert Cecil, Earl of Salisbury, in 1611, this superb Jacobean mansion oozes history. In the grounds stands the remaining wing of the Royal Palace of Hatfield, the childhood home of Queen Elizabeth I, where in 1558 she held her first Council of State. The 42 acres of gardens include herb terraces, orchards and fountains restored to their former glory by the present marchioness. Both the house and grounds are open for pre-booked tours (no tours weekends or bank holidays).

Hertford Castle

Hertford (01992 584322). **Open** *May-Nov* (phone for details). **Admission** free. The ruins of the Norman motte and fifteenth-century gatehouse were converted into a stately home in the 1790s. Information boards in the grounds detail the castle's history. Note that the castle is only open about once a month (usually on a Sunday), so phone to check before you set off. There are free concerts in the castle grounds in summer.

Knebworth House & Gardens

Knebworth, near Stevenage
(01438 812661/www.knebworthhouse.com).
Open *May, June, Sept* noon-5pm Sat, Sun; *July-Aug* noon-5pm daily. **Admission** £6; £5.50 5-16s, OAPs; *garden only* £5.

Home to the Lyttons since 1490, this Gothically embellished Tudor mansion house is still the family residence. The 250-acre parkland also houses the formal gardens and woodland, the maze, 'Fort Knebworth' adventure playground and a miniature railway. Major rock concerts have added to the attractions since 1974 (with Led Zeppelin's legendary appearance in '79 and Oasis in '96). Car shows, craft fairs, flower festivals and classical concerts have since replaced the grinding guitars and metal posturing.

Mosquito Aircraft Museum

Salisbury Hall, London Colney, nr St Albans
(01727 822051).
Open *Apr-Oct* 2-5.30pm Tue, Thur, Sat; 10.30am-5.30pm Sun, bank hols. **Admission** £4; £2 5-15s, OAPs, students; £10 family.

Home of the de Havilland aircraft company since 1939, the museum displays over 20 types of aircraft and is open for visits, guided tours, model exhibitions, plus rallies, aerial displays and other events.

Museum of St Albans

Hatfield Road, St Albans (01727 819340).
Open 10am-5pm Mon-Sat, bank hols; 2-5pm Sun.
Admission free.

Impressive display of local history with plenty of medieval and Roman artefacts. Downstairs there's a fine collection of tools used in carpentry and agriculture, plus a gallery to the rear on two levels.

Paradise Wildlife Park

White Stubbs Lane, Broxbourne
(01992 468001/www.pwpark.com).
Open 10am-6pm daily. **Admission** £6.50; £4.50 2-15s, OAPs.

On the road to Ware, this is a good family stop-off point, with an adventure play area and indoor under-fives playroom, children's rides, walk-through farmyard, reptile encounter, plus monkeys, big cats, camels and birds of prey. Refreshments for visitors and feed for the animals are available.

Scott's Grotto

Scotts Road, Ware
(01920 464131/www.scotts-grotto.org).
Open *Apr-Sept* 2-4.30pm Sat, bank hols (other times by appointment). **Admission** by donation.

A series of quirky subterranean passages built by John Scott of Amwell House (now part of Ware College). Dating back to around 1760, and fronted by a flint-encrusted portico, the tunnels extend 67 feet into the hillside with seven chambers decorated with shells from around the world, plus local flints and minerals. Visitors are requested to bring a torch with them if possible.

Shaw's Corner

Ayot St Lawrence, nr Welwyn
(01438 820307/recorded info 01494 755567).
Open *Apr-Oct* 1-5pm Wed-Sun, bank hols.
Last admission 4.30pm. **Admission** (NT) £3.30; £1.65 5-16s; £8.25 family.

Home of George Bernard Shaw from 1906 to 1950. A sizeable brick dwelling with many rooms as the great man left them, including his restored revolving writing hut. Works undertaken by Shaw here include *Pygmalion* and *St Joan*. Plays are performed in the grounds in summer.

Verulamium Museum

St Michael's, St Albans (01727 751810).
Open 10am-5.30pm Mon-Sat; 2-5.30pm Sun.
Admission £3; £1.70 5-16s, OAPs, students; £7.50 family.

Featuring everything you ever wanted to know about the Romans and a little bit more, with reconstructions, mosaics, statuary and audio-visual presentations, conveniently close to the Roman ruins in Verulamium Park. The museum is much improved by extension work, which allows for some Iron Age scene-setting in the new gallery, as well as the splendid airy entrance, shops and display areas. The Legion XIIII are on guard roughly once a month.

Whipsnade Wild Animal Park

5 miles SW of Dunstable
(0990 200123/www.whipsnade.co.uk).
Open *Apr-Oct* 10am-6pm Mon-Sat; 10am-7pm Sun; *Nov-Mar* 10am-4pm Mon-Sat. **Admission** £9.50; £7.50 3-15s; £7 OAPs.

Although over the Bedfordshire border, London Zoo's out-of-town wild animal park, covering about 600 acres of prime countryside, is a sure-fire hit with the kids. There are plenty of roomy enclosures for the 2,500 or so creatures, plus a superb adventure playground and children's farm, allowing for close encounters with some less wild species.

*Magic mosaics at the **Verulamium Museum**.*

Rutland

The land that time forgot.

Rutland, the smallest and most laid-back county in England, offers a complete antidote to the noise and fumes of the hectic, breakneck city. A weekend break here shouldn't be planned around a manic itinerary of places to visit and sights to hoover up; best take it easy and enjoy the glorious absence of crowds and traffic and pressure.

Driving, cycling or walking through the Rutland countryside really is like stepping back 50 years in English history – an impression that is hardly shattered when civilisation is encountered. Quiet roads threading through still-life honey-stone villages recall the atmosphere of northern France; they could almost have been dreamt up by Enid Blyton or Agatha Christie. Thirty years ago there was only one set of traffic lights to be found in the whole county, this in the relatively seething metropolis of Oakham, the county town. In case you weaken and grow twitchy away from the capital's hurly-burly, the bustling medieval town of Stamford, lying on Rutland's doorstep, in Lincolnshire to the east, can up the excitement level a notch or two.

Otherwise, no matter where you travel in the county, you're never more than 15 minutes from its centrepiece, the calming, still waters of Empingham Reservoir – or 'Rutland Water', as proud locals renamed it during their long and savage war of independence (in the *Rutland Times*) against Leicestershire's faceless oppressors. Only the odd truncated B-road leading off into the shallows, and the recent disappearance of the prefix 'Upper' from the village of Hambleton, serve to remind that the area was only dammed and flooded in the early '70s and somewhere down there beneath the bobbing boats and ducks lies Lower Hambleton. You can take a trip round the reservoir with Rutland Belle Cruises (01572 787630), with commentary on the points of

Barn Hill in **Stamford**.

interest. The more energetic might like to hire a bike from the award-winning Rutland Water Cycling (01780 460705), located at Whitwell and Normanton car parks.

Town and country

Uppingham is a tiny toy market town (market day Friday) dominated by its sixteenth-century public school (tours June to September; 01572 822672), whose clock tower, cupolas and lawns are hidden away behind a towering stone façade better suited to a castle, or maybe a prison. The High Street, again, is quintessential film-set England, but agreeably unself-conscious of the fact – a beautiful place to wake up on Saturday morning. Look out for the three good bookshops, all open on Sundays: there's the 12-foot-square, three-storey Rutland Bookshop, the Tardis-like Forest Books, and Goldmark Books on Orange Street.

Oakham is larger and busier, its picture-book quality a little broken down by nominal progress, but still jumbled with some delightful Victorian streets, Georgian villas and older jewels. The public school is also sixteenth-century, nestling between the one-time castle's Great Hall and a superb little market square (market days Wednesday and Saturday), centred around the octagonal Butter Cross and its old public stocks.

Stamford's stock has risen sharply since it starred in the BBC's *Middlemarch* series. Barely a single building fails to conform to the symphony of weathered-yellow Lincolnshire stone, which still clings to a medieval street pattern on the Welland, ably assisted by the imposition of the country's first Conservation

By train from London

Trains for **Stamford** and **Oakham** leave **King's Cross** hourly. There is a change at **Peterborough**. Stamford is the stop before Oakham (journey time between **1hr** and **2hrs**).

The Chilterns to York

Area in 1967. Historically a wealthy textile town and staging point, Stamford was home to William Cecil, chief minister of Elizabeth I, who built his splendid **Burghley House** close by. Charles I spent his last days as a free man in Stamford, before riding to Southwell, where he was betrayed and handed over to Parliament. Sadly, the Stamford bull run and race meeting are now history, although the rumbustuous town-centre funfair is still held in the week following Mothering Sunday. North-east of Stamford is **Tallington Lakes** (01778 347000), a watersports centre featuring 160 acres of natural spring-fed water split between eight lakes, devoted to watersports of all kinds.

Away from the towns, the area is a noted centre for cycling, sailing, birdwatching and walking through the unspoiled pasturelands where deer were once hunted, and foxes still are. The **Viking Way** (marked with a Viking Helmet) passes through on its journey from the Humber to Oakham, while the **Jurassic Way** (look for the shell sign) runs between Stamford and Banbury. There are Forestry Commission woodlands at **Clipsham** (including the half-mile avenue of sculpted 150-year-old yew trees), **Southey Wood** (between the villages of Upton and Ufford), **Fineshade** (off the A43 east of King's Cliffe) and nearby **Wakerley Great Wood**.

Elsewhere in Rutland, the churchyard at **Braunston** features a stone carving of a pagan goddess; there's an 82-arch viaduct near Seaton; a medieval turf maze at **Wing**; John Betjeman's favourite church at **Brooke**; and the old smithy at **Burley-on-the-Hill**, which inspired the poem 'Underneath the Spreading Chestnut Tree'. Visit the picturesque hamlet of **Teigh**. Step into the church porch at **Stoke Dry**, where the Gunpowder Plot is said to have been hatched. Go fishing on the nearby **Eyebrook Reservoir**. See the stocks on the green at **Market Overton**, where Sir Isaac Newton played as a child. Explore the lime kiln at **Pickworth**, where pastoral poet John Clare laboured 200 years ago. And remember: take it easy in this green, relaxing, empty countryside.

Where to stay

There's an abundance of reinvented coaching inns and village pubs (all offering food, most with rooms) plus good farmhouse B&Bs scattered throughout the rich, rolling pasture-land of Rutland and south-west Lincolnshire.

Barnsdale Lodge Hotel

The Avenue, Rutland Water, nr Oakham, LE15 8AH (01572 724678/fax 01572 724961/barnsdale.lodge@ btconnect.com/home.btconnect.com/barnsdale lodge).

Rates (B&B) *single* £65; *double/twin* £89; *deluxe double/twin/four-poster/suite* £109.50; *family room* £129. **Rooms** (all en suite) 8 single; 23 double/twin; 5 deluxe double/twin; 2 four-poster; 5 suites; 2 family. **Cards** AmEx, DC, Debit, MC, V.

Just a couple of miles outside Oakham, this seventeenth-century farmhouse made a successful career switch when its land disappeared under the waves of Rutland Water. Now extended and expanded with the addition of bedrooms around a brightly planted courtyard, the stone walls and flagged floors of the old building retain great character amid a cornucopia of Edwardian-chic décor. The restaurant is recommended; there are also lighter meals and superb views from the conservatory. Children and dogs welcome. Non-smoking rooms available.
A1 N to A606 towards Oakham; through Empingham and Whitwell; hotel is on right.

The George

St Martins, Stamford, PE9 2LB (01780 750750/ fax 01780 750701/georgehotelofstamford@ btinternet.com/www.georgehotelofstamford.com).
Rates (B&B) *single* £78; *double/twin* £103-£125; *deluxe double* £150; *four-poster* £170; *suite* £140.
Rooms (all en suite) 11 single; 23 double/twin; 2 deluxe double; 4 four-poster; 7 suites.
Cards AmEx, DC, Debit, MC, V.

The George – 'perhaps England's greatest coaching inn' – boasts a cobbled, ivy-clad courtyard where Crusaders would once stop by for mead and a browse of the lunch-time bar menu, and rooms royally slumbered in by King Charles I and William III. The famous gallows sign spanning the road outside stands as a gesture of welcome to honest travellers, and a warning to highwaymen not to flout the ancient jacket-and-tie law (which still applies in the restaurant, by the way). Children and dogs welcome. Non-smoking bedrooms available.
A1 N; follow signs at roundabout to Stamford (right); hotel is on left down hill.

Hambleton Hall

Hambleton, Oakham, LE15 8TH (01572 756991/ fax 01572 724721/hotel@hambletonhall.com/ www.hambletonhall.com).
Rates (B&ContB) *single occupancy* £150-£295; *double/twin* £175-£195; *deluxe double/twin* £225-£295; *four-poster* £195. Breakfast £12 (Eng).
Rooms (all en suite) 10 double/twin; 4 deluxe double/twin; 1 four-poster. **Cards** AmEx, DC, Debit, MC, V.

*The perfect setting of **Hambleton Hall**.*

Imperiously overlooking Rutland Water from its own lush landscaped grounds on the central peninsula, Hambleton Hall is an English country hotel par excellence. 'Do as you please' is the order of the day emblazoned over the entrance, a throwback to wild Georgian party scenes – and, in keeping, Tim and Stefa Hart manage to uphold an atmosphere of relaxation amid the sumptuous chintz and Regency stripes. Bedrooms are individually themed, and stocked with elegant antique furniture. The dining room is agreeably intimate, seating 40 at most, with few of the luxurious dishes priced to intimidate: the six-course 'tasting menu' is a good place to start, at around £60. Children and dogs are welcome.

A1 N to A606 off A1; 10 miles towards Oakham; hotel is on peninsula of Rutland Water.

The Lake Isle

High Street East, Uppingham, LE15 9PZ
(tel/fax 01572 822951).
Rates (B&B) *single* £45-£52; *double/twin* £65-£69; *cottage suite* £65-£69. **Rooms** (all en suite) 1 single; 12 double/twin; 2 cottage suites. **Cards** AmEx, DC, MC, V.

An enjoyable, unpretentious restaurant with comfortable converted rooms to the rear, each named after a French wine region. The atmospheric decorative sprinkling of empty bottles of all sizes further reflects the pride in their bulging cellar, which is priced to enjoy. The details are all looked after, from the fresh biscuits, iced water and sherry waiting in every room, right down to the quality of the breakfast toast, mushrooms and bangers. Children and dogs welcome.

A1 to A47 towards Peterborough; follow signs W to Uppingham; hotel is in Uppingham town centre.

The Old Mill

Tallington, PE9 4RR
(01780 740815/fax 01780 740280).
Rates (B&B) *single occupancy* £35-£45; *double/twin* £50-£55; *family* £65.
Rooms (all en suite) 5 double/twin; 1 family.

This quaint eighteenth-century watermill on the River Welland east of Stamford makes for a fascinating breakfast (or night's sleep) amid the remaining cogs, shafts and winches of the old grinding gear – truly a triumph of conversion handiwork for your host, the former England rugger player John Olver. The best of the six bedrooms look out on to the river flowing beneath the mill, and one even has its own patio by the mill-pond. A relaxing haven of water-meadows, good food and plentiful ducks. Children and dogs welcome. Non-smoking throughout.

A1 to Stamford; A16 E from Stamford; house is on right in Tallington.

Where to eat & drink

In every published guide to decent pubs, pints and pub grub, the chunkiness of the Rutland chapter belies the diminutive size of the county. For foodie pubs, you could do a lot worse than aim for the friendly, flower-festooned **Old Plough** at Braunston, near Oakham (01572 722714); the beautifully located

Finches Arms in Hambleton (01572 756575), in the middle of Rutland Water; or the **Ram Jam Inn** at Stretton on the Great North Road (01780 410776). From the top of a lengthy list of more 'pubby' pubs are the **Hole in the Wall** (good for quality ales), up narrow, crooked Cheyne Lane in Stamford; the **Waggon & Horses**, High Street East, Uppingham; and the **Millstone Inn**, Millstone Lane, Barnack, Lincolnshire – good luck finding this last one!

Ask

St John's Street, Stamford (01780 765455).
Food served noon-10.30pm Mon-Thur, Sun; noon-11.30pm Fri, Sat. **Cards** AmEx, Debit, MC, V.

Everyday for London, perhaps, but in Rutland Ask is eye-catching for its sheer groovy trendiness in the midst of so much ancient yellow stone. Ask's clean white interior recalls a Hockney swimming pool, and is every bit as inviting on a hot summer's day. Stylish armchairs of red, purple and blue are set by the large open windows, making this an ideal spot to sit with a beer or a glass of wine and watch the traffic go by. The food is reliable pizza and pasta: starters are around £2; mains are £5.50-£6.50; desserts £2.25-£3.25.

King's Arms Inn

Top Street, Wing (01572 737634).
Food served noon-2pm, 7-9pm, Mon-Fri; noon-2pm, 6.30-9.30pm, Sat; noon-2pm, 7-8.30pm, Sun.
Cards AmEx, DC, Debit, MC, V.

Dating back to 1649, the King's Arms is yet another sprawling old local set in a two-horse Rutland village, offering real ales, superior pub nosh and reliable accommodation. The King's Bar is the oldest part of the inn, with flagstone floors, low beams, nooks and crannies and two open log fires for a totally cosy overkill outside the summer months. Local herb sausages, local trout and Rutland cheese feature on the perfect pub menu. Main courses will set you back anything from £6.95 to £12.75. Drop in at the **Cuckoo**, too, just along Top Street, on the way back from the medieval turf maze: it's another kind of pub, no less traditional, which offers a sunny garden, chat at the bar, a slightly warped pool table and the best pint of Pedigree you've ever tasted.

King's Cliffe House

31 West Street, King's Cliffe (01780 470172).
Food served 7-9.30pm Wed-Sat.

On the very fringes of our Rutland-and-around day-tripping region, King's Cliffe is within easy travelling distance of anywhere in this tiny county, and well worth a countryside spin south. King's Cliffe House is hidden away off the crooked village street, the semi-secret culinary laboratory of the kind and gentle Emma Jessop and Andrew Wilshaw. Restricting themselves to the politest possible opening hours on only four nights a week, the couple spend the rest of their time collecting fresh, semi-precious ingredients and preparing their immaculate country menu. Eels from the Nene. Home-made salt cod. Wild mushrooms. Quince. Prices are high-ish, with starters about £5.50, mains around £14, and desserts about £5.

Little & large

The county motto of Rutland is 'Multum in Parvo' – 'so much in so little' – and quite befitting an area that's not averse to blowing its own trumpet over its miniature stature, the area has its own little and large folk heroes. As you'll find on any trip to this area, size matters.

Three hundred years ago, Oakham was home to **Jeffrey Hudson**, a man notable chiefly for standing just 3 feet 6 inches tall. He worked at Burley-on-the-Hill for the Duke of Buckingham, where the Duchess used to dress him up as a pet poodle to show him off to visitors. When Jeffrey jumped out of a huge cold pie set before Charles I and his Queen Henrietta Maria, his future as her court toy seemed set. Fate, however, dictated that Jeff should be captured by pirates on a Channel crossing, sold into slavery on the Barbary Coast, and only returned to Oakham upon the payment of a ransom by the Duke. At this point, enter the town's other most famous son – **Titus Oates**, who made his name inventing popish plots against Charles II. Oates promptly shopped Hudson, who was thrown into prison.

Rutland's obsession with its size seeps over the border into Stamford, where the local museum has stuffed effigies of **Daniel Lambert** ('The Leicester Colossus') and **General Tom Thumb**, who once got together in Georgian Stamford to drum up a storm of publicity for the American's circus. Lambert, a modest, knowledgeable man, much sought after as a fashionable dinner guest, died in 1809 at the old Wagon & Horses Inn on St Martin's, while in town for the major social event of Stamford Races (not to mention the cock-fighting and bull-baiting). The window of his bedroom was famously removed to allow the removal of his corpse, after which he was lain to rest in the old churchyard of St Martin's, where his tombstone still pays tribute to this 'prodigy of nature, who was possessed of an exalted and convivial mind, and in personal greatness had no competitor'. Also duly recorded are Lambert's vital statistics: a substantial 52 stones 11 pounds, 9 feet 4 inches around the belly and 3 feet 1 inches around the leg.

Voujon Balti Hut

4 Burley Corner, High Street, Oakham (01572 723043). **Food served** 5.30pm-midnight daily. **Set meals** from £24.95 (4 courses; at least two people). **Cards** Debit, MC, V.

Although easy to miss at street level, the Voujon's lime-green faux flora act as a beacon to any traveller from Uppingham way, shining out as they do from the purple-trim windows above Thresher's off-licence. Duly installed on the more rewarding side of the double-glazing, looking down on the end of Oakham's High Street is a pleasure heightened via a shared sizzler serving of murgh sobzi bahar (chicken with onions, mushrooms and okra – 'a very tasteful dish', £7.95), gosht massala (diced lamb, minced lamb, egg, tomatoes), sag paneer and tandoori nan. The best Indian in Rutland.

The Whipper-Inn

Market Place, Oakham (01572 756971). **Food served** *restaurant* 7-9.30pm Mon-Sat; *bistro* 6-10pm Mon-Sat; 6-9pm Sun. **Cards** AmEx, DC, Debit, MC, V.

This stuccoed seventeenth-century coaching inn, looking out on to the market square, rates as one of Oakham's smartest places to stay or to dine. The Market Bar is popular with locals, too, which says a lot. A Modern British menu is prepared with love and precision: the triumvirate of flavours in the roast capsicum and cherry toma-

to soup (flavoured with a delicate smoked oil, £3.95) are expertly balanced – as is the fine fillet of beef with glazed shallots resting on champ with light leek essence (£13.95).

What to see & do

Tourist information centres

The Arts Centre, 27 St Mary's Street, **Stamford**, PE9 2EL (01780 755611/www.skdc.com). **Open** *Easter-Oct* 9.30am-5pm Mon-Sat; 10am-3pm Sun, bank hols; *Nov-Easter* 9.30am-5pm Mon-Sat; 10am-3pm bank hols.

Flore's House, 34 High Street, **Oakham**, LE15 6AL (01572 724329). **Open** *Apr-Sept* 9.30am-5pm Mon-Sat; 10am-3pm Sun; *Oct-Mar* 10am-4pm Mon, Wed, Fri, Sat; 10am-3pm Sun.

Bike hire

See p226 **Rutland Water Cycling**.

Barnsdale Gardens

The Avenue, Exton (01572 813200). **Open** *Mar-Oct* 10am-5pm daily. Last entry 3pm. **Admission** £5; free under-16s.

As a tribute to the work of Geoff Hamilton, his Barnsdale garden is now open to the public. It will be familiar to viewers of BBC2's *Gardener's World* as 'the garden that Geoff built'. Coffee shop and an excellent nursery.

Burghley House

1 mile E of Stamford on B1443 (01780 752451).
Open *Apr-Oct* 11am-4.30pm daily.
Admission £6.10; £3 5s-13s (one child goes
free with a paying adult); £5.85 OAPs.

One of the grandest Elizabethan houses in England, constructed from finely carved local limestone on the
remains of a twelfth-century monastery. Commissioned
by William Cecil, the 1st Lord Burghley, the house was
later used as a Royalist refuge in the Civil War, and laid
under siege by Cromwell, who luckily never carried out
his threat to raze it to the ground. Of the 18 magnificent
state rooms, those decorated with Antonio Verrio's lavish seventeenth-century frescoes are the most famous.
The art, sculpture and porcelain on display comprise
one of the most important private collections in the
world. There's also an extensive Deer Park, a 1932
Olympic silver medal courtesy of Lord 'Chariots of Fire'
Burghley, annual horse trials every September, and
Queen Victoria's hard, lumpy bed.

Lyddington Bede House

Lyddington (01572 8224380).
Open *Apr-Sept* 10am-6pm daily; *Oct* 10am-5pm
daily. **Admission** (EH) £2.50; £1.30 5s-16s;
£1.90 OAPs, students.

A medieval palace originally built for the sporting
Bishops of Lincoln, converted into almshouses for the
poor after the Reformation. Lovely, rambling honey-
stone house, sixteenth-century interiors, and events
throughout the summer.

Normanton Church Museum

nr Edith Weston, off A606 (01572 6530267).
Open *Apr-Aug* 11am-4pm Mon-Fri; 11am-5pm Sat,
Sun, bank hols; *Sept, Oct* 11am-4pm daily.
Admission 80p; 50p 5s-16s, OAPs; £2 family.

Rutland's best-known landmark, the Italianate Georgian
church from the submerged Normanton estate now
stands on a promontory on the edge of the reservoir, and
houses a display dedicated to the history of the Anglian
Water reservoir and surrounding area.

Oakham Castle

off Market Place, Oakham (01572 723654).
Open *Apr-Oct* 10am-1pm, 2-5.30pm, Tue-Sat;
2-5.30pm Sun; *Nov-Mar* 10am-1pm, 2-4pm, Tue-Sat;
2-4pm Sun. **Admission** free.

In its prime Oakham Castle was one of the finest examples of twelfth-century domestic architecture in
England. The marvellous arched Great Hall is all that's
left these days, complete with smashing collection of
horseshoes, presented by peers and royalty to Lords of
the Manor. Still in use as a court.

Rutland County Museum

Catmos Street, Oakham (01572 723654).
Open *Apr-Oct* 10am-5pm Mon-Sat; 2-5pm Sun;
Nov-Mar 10am-4pm Mon-Sat; 2-4pm Sun.
Admission free.

Housed in former Rutland Cavalry riding school, features 'The Volunteer Soldier in Leicestershire and
Rutland' gallery and loads on the rural life and agriculture of the historic county. Dig that vast rectangular
short-horn heifer.

Spying on nature at **Rutland Water**.

Rutland Open-Air Theatre

Tolethorpe Hall, Little Casterton (01780 756133).
Plays *June-Aug* (phone for details). **Tickets** £10;
£9 OAPs, under-18s.

The Stamford Shakespeare Company offers the Bard's
greatest hits in a 600-seater covered auditorium in an
idyllic woodland setting – so performances go ahead
whatever the weather. There's a bar, picnic areas in the
gardens and a pre-theatre restaurant seating 90. The
three-month season starts in June.

Rutland Water Butterfly Farm & Aquatic Centre

Sykes Lane car park, north shore, Rutland Water
(01780 460515).
Open *Apr-Oct* 10.30am-5pm daily. Last entry
4.30pm. **Admission** £3; £2 4s-15s; £2.50 OAPs,
students.

This is one of the best freshwater aquaria in the
country, packed with waterfalls, stream river and reservoir displays. Also, there's a heated exotic 'free flight'
butterfly house, complete with parrots, carp, terrapins
and iguanas in the undergrowth. 'The Twilight Zone',
domain of creepy-crawlies and reptiles, is not for
the faint-hearted.

Rutland Water Nature Reserve

Egleton Reserve, one mile south of Oakham; Lyndon
Reserve, one mile east of Manton on south shore
(01572 770651).
Open *Apr-Oct* 9am-5pm daily; *Nov-Mar* 9am-
4.30pm. **Admission** £3; £1 5s-16s.

Both of Rutland Water's informative and helpful visitor
centres contain well-stocked shops, and sell day permits.
They can also arrange wildlife and arts and crafts courses, bird walks with the wardens, 'Creatures of the Night'
walks, and more.

Stamford Museum

Broad Street, Stamford (01780 766317).
Open *Easter-Oct* 10am-5pm Mon-Sat; 2-5pm Sun;
Nov-Easter 10am-5pm Mon-Sat. **Admission** free.

Two full floors of information and displays on
Stamford's history – interesting if you're in the mood,
but many visitors cut straight to the chase and gawp at
the legendary bad-taste life-size models of General Tom
Thumb and the humongous Daniel Lambert (*see page
229* **Little & large**).

Lincoln

History off the beaten path.

When told of Lincoln, Americans tend to ask, 'Named after our great president?', but of course this beautiful city predates Abraham by almost 2,000 years. And from its Roman foundation in AD 48 right up to the seventeenth century, Lincoln was one of Europe's most important cities, a status that leaves it with a treasure trove of Roman and medieval architecture to equal York or Canterbury. However, after its glory years Lincoln drifted off into relative obscurity and third division football, and has only recently woken up to its tourism possibilities, making it a far more relaxing place to visit than any of its more popular competitors on the intensive British heritage trail.

Uptown top-ranking sights

The city is dominated by the magnificent **Cathedral**, a towering Gothic precipice perched on the only hill for miles around. At night it is spectacularly floodlit and if you arrive by train or car across the region's flat plains, it can look more fairytale than anything Walt Disney ever dreamt up. Its companion is the medieval **Castle**, built just after the Norman Conquest to keep the hairy local hordes in order. The surrounding uphill area, frequently the location for period films and costume dramas, crammed with cobbled streets and ancient houses, is largely car-free and has plenty of quirky traditional shops to mooch in and many a pub with above-average food in which to refuel. It's here you'll find most of the city's visitor attractions.

All downhill from here

The residential bulk of the city is downhill, including a busy pedestrianised High Street with extensive – if predictable – shopping possibilities and a vibrant covered market (local produce is sold on Fridays). Here you'll

Castle Square and the Cathedral.

also find the **Brayford Pool**, an expanse of water around which the original Celtic inhabitants settled. It became an important inland harbour for the Romans, and later, by the eighteenth century, when grain was brought in for the breweries that lined the Brayford's banks and local wool was taken away for export, this was the fourth busiest port in the whole of Britain. Nowadays it is a rather pleasant marina, with the new University of Lincoln taking up much of the land on its southern banks.

Lincoln started life as a Roman garrison, growing into a thriving community as legionnaires retired and settled here. There are plenty of remnants of the Roman era, including Newport Arch, the only surviving Roman arch in Britain that still has traffic driving through it. After the Romans left around AD 500 Lincoln became part of the Anglo-Saxon community of Lindsey, and later one of the principal 'burghs' of the Danelaw established by invading Vikings. The city received its charter in 1071 from William the Conquerer, who ordered the building of the Castle and Cathedral. By 1086 it was a walled metropolis of 5,000 people.

By train from London

There are, alas, no direct trains from London to Lincoln, but the service from **King's Cross** to **Newark Northgate** (one train an hour) takes **1hr 45mins**; from here, a connecting service to Lincoln takes **15mins**.

The Chilterns to York

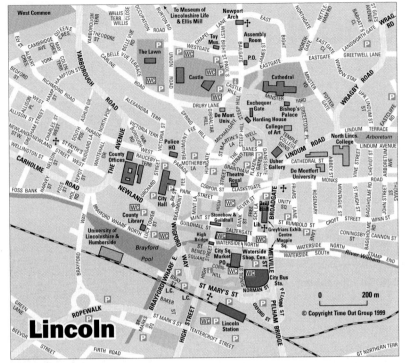

Medieval Lincoln can be seen best on the aptly named **Steep Hill**, the picturesque link between uphill and down, which is occupied by second-hand bookshops, vintage clothing stores, crafts and pottery shops, and an excellent florist. Here you'll see such ancient dwellings as the **Norman House** and the **Jews House**. The latter dates back to the 1170s and is Britain's oldest continuously occupied domestic building. Other later examples include the half-timbered houses on **High Bridge** – the nation's oldest bridge to have buildings over it – and the three surviving city gates, at Pottergate, Minster Yard and the Stonebow.

Lincoln's later prosperity was based on the fertile agricultural region surrounding the city, and this was what gave rise to its place as a centre of heavy industry. From the manufacture of steam tractors and threshing machines grew a series of foundries and engineering works, producing everything from earth-moving equipment to monumental gas turbines for power stations.

If you fancy a lazy trip along the local waterways (the River Witham and the Roman Foss Dyke canal), there are boat services from

the William IV pub by the Brayford and from the Waterside shopping centre. You get a nice view of Lincoln and a trip to the Pyewipe Inn, an above-average riverside pub just outside the city.

Young guns go for it

In 1996 Lincoln became a university town, and it plays its new academic role to the full. The rapidly growing campus now fills the wasteland left by the city's industrial past, bringing new life to the area around the Brayford Pool, and energising the city with an influx of young people. (Although it could probably do without the sudden rash of chain pubs and bars that now line the upper reaches of the High Street to cash in on unrestrained student drinking habits.) Lincoln is looking increasingly towards tourism for its income, and its annual one million visitors are well-catered for, with a wealth of places to stay and a growing number of good restaurants. However, there is, as yet, mercifully little of the intensive coach-party tourism and sightseeing-by-numbers you'll find in many similar British cities. Make the most of it while you can.

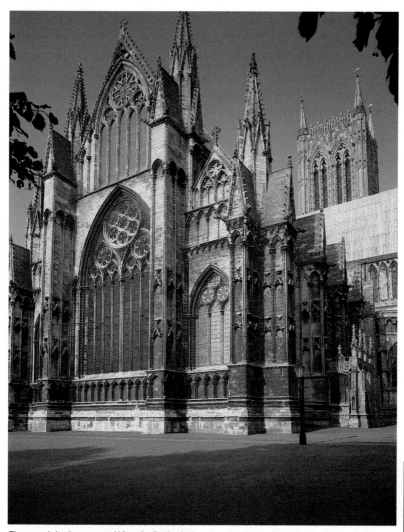

*The exquisite harmony of **Lincoln Cathedral**, a masterpiece of medieval craftsmanship.*

Where to stay

Lincoln lacks much truly characterful accommodation, but is teeming with B&Bs, especially in the 'West End' area of the city (try along Yarborough Road or West Parade). The city also has plenty of hotels: you'll find the older, more idiosyncratic places at the top of the hill, close to the Cathedral.

Castle Hotel

Westgate, LN1 3AS (01522 538801/
fax 01522 575457/www.castlehotel.net).
Rates (B&B) *single occupancy* £60; *double/twin* £74; *deluxe double/four-poster* £84; *family room* £84; *suite* £120. **Rooms** (all en suite) 16 double/twin; 2 deluxe double; 1 four-poster; 1 suite. **Cards** AmEx, DC, Debit, MC, V.

You can't see anything of it, but this hotel is built right over the centre of Roman Lincoln, in the area where the

The Chilterns to York

forum used to be, and behind it are the remains of the Roman mint. A stone's throw away is Bailgate, Castle Square and the Roman Newport Arch, and if you're heading for a conference at The Lawn, this is just round the corner. The hotel stands in the shadow of the Castle walls; all the bedrooms are named after a castle, and are clean and elegant with a country house ambience. The restaurant, Knights, is well above average and specialises in seafood. Non-smoking rooms available.

Courtyard by Marriott

Brayford Wharf North, LN1 1YW
(01522 544244/fax 01522 560805).
Rates (B&B) *single £51-£79; double/twin £64-£80.*
Rooms (all en suite) 49 single; 20 double; 20 twin.
Cards AmEx, DC, Debit, MC, V.

This hotel was a major part of the regeneration of Lincoln's Brayford pool area, built in a vaguely wharf-style design facing the very stylish University buildings across the water. The rooms are off-the-peg Marriott: clean, new, efficient, predictable, air-conditioned, and the location is handy for the central High Street shopping area. (It's a 15-minute walk uphill to the Cathedral.) Children welcome. Non-smoking rooms available.

D'Isney Place Hotel

Eastgate, LN2 4AA (01522 538881/fax 01522 511321).
Rates (B&B) *single occupancy £60; double/twin £76; family room £86; deluxe £96.* **Rooms** (all en suite) 13 double/twin; 3 deluxe/family. **Cards** AmEx, DC, Debit, MC, V.

The name could be misleading… There are no public rooms in this charming red-brick Georgian townhouse, but the guest rooms are all very pleasant and the atmosphere is very much home-from-home comfort. And as well as being close to the historic side of the city, there's a piece of it in the delightfully secluded garden: a 700-year-old tower, part of the old wall that once surrounded the Cathedral. Smoking and pets allowed by arrangement. Children welcome.

Edward King House

The Old Palace, Minster Yard, LN2 1PU
(01522 528778/fax 01522 527308).
Rates (B&ContB) *single £19; twin £37; family room £56.* Breakfast £2 (Eng). **Rooms** 5 single; 11 twin; 1 family. **Cards** MC, V.

If you don't mind sharing a bathroom, for a bargain price you can stay in the former official residence of the Bishop of Lincoln. Cosy and homely, and still run by the Church (your host is the Reverend Alex Adkins), this is close to the Cathedral (obviously) and has magnificent views over the city. It's a very quiet location overlooking the ruins of the medieval Bishop's Palace. No smoking throughout. Pets by arrangement. Children welcome.

Old Rectory Guest House

19 Newport, LN1 3DQ
(01522 514774/fax 01522 538893).
Rates (B&B) *single £20-£25; double/twin £38; family room £45.* **Rooms** 2 single (1 en suite); 4 double (all en suite); 1 twin (en suite).

Located just north of the Bailgate area, close to Newport Arch, this beautifully restored Edwardian townhouse is ideally situated for sightseeing and is a friendly place to stay. Children welcome. Non-smoking throughout.

Orchard House

119 Yarborough Road, LN1 1HR (01522 528795).
Rates (B&B) *single £18; double/twin £40.*
Rooms (all en suite) 1 single; 2 double/twin.

June and Graham Harrison run this small, family-style guesthouse. Despite being extremely central, it has ample off-street parking – unusual for Lincoln. Just a ten-minute walk puts you anywhere in the city, and with its hillside location there's the added benefit of panoramic views over towards the Trent Valley. Children and dogs welcome. All bedrooms non-smoking.

White Hart Hotel

Bailgate, LN1 3AR (01522 526222/fax 01522 531798).
Rates (B&B) *single £95; double/twin £105; deluxe double/twin £115; four-poster £135; suite £135.*
Special breaks. **Rooms** (all en suite) 6 single; 26 double/twin; 4 deluxe double/twin; 1 four-poster; 11 suites. **Cards** AmEx, DC, Debit, MC, V.

This is old Lincoln at its most luxurious; a historic coaching inn that dates back to the 1400s and is situated smack in between the Castle and the Cathedral, with about a 100-metre-walk to either. All the rooms have been recently renovated to a very high standard and the hotel is filled with antique porcelain, paintings and furnishings. In keeping with the White Hart's pre-eminence, the restaurant here is one of the best in the city. True Blue Tories might want to stay in the Thatcher Room. Children and dogs welcome. Non-smoking rooms available.

Where to eat & drink

Lincoln has several fine restaurants, and with its new student population to be fed, there are many new places serving good, reasonably priced meals. Hotel restaurants are dependable, especially the White Hart, the Eastgate and Knights at the Castle Hotel, as are many of the pubs, especially the **Duke William** (44 Bailgate; 01522 533351). If you fancy Indian food, the **Bombay Restaurant** (The Strait; 01522 523264) is very good, as is the **Raj Douth Tandoori** (Eastgate; 01522 548377). For dependable Italian there's **Gino's** (Gordon Road; 01522 513770) and for Spanish tapas head to **Miguel's** (High Street; 01522 532109), which is also a quiet spot for late drinking. **Pizza Express** (High Street; 01522 544701) and **Pierre Victoire** (Silver Street; 01522 544114) have just opened branches here, and by the Odeon multiplex on the way out of town you'll find the American diner menu of **Fatty Arbuckles** (Valentine Road; 01522 510515). Lincoln fish and chips are excellent as the city is well served by Grimsby's daily catch. Try the one on Newport next to Radio Lincolnshire – they still use dripping to fry their chips – mmm. While shopping on the High Street, **Stokes** coffee shop (High Street; 01522 513825), in the half-timbered house on High Bridge, is the ideal place for a cuppa, though the accompanying

Christmas twee

When the craze for twinning towns was running high, Lincoln found itself wedded to Neustadt an der Weinstrasse, a German wine-producing town. Subsequently, in the late '80s, when the city decided to inaugurate a faux-traditional Christmas market, it ended up with a feast as much Bavarian as Dickensian in its outlook. Sausages and mulled wine café off against roast chestnuts and Victorian carol singers for three and a half days of merriment.

A sea of fairground rides, festive lanterns and stalls selling all manner of

handicrafts and enticing winter belly fillers covers a vast area of uphill Lincoln, stretching from The Lawn to the Cathedral but centred on the Castle and Castle Square. The Christmas market is on the second weekend of December, starting on the Thursday night and lasting through till the Sunday (9-12 Dec 1999; 7-10 Dec 2000). Despite coach-loads of visitors descending on the city for the joint attraction of the market and some last-minute Christmas shopping, it is a surprisingly pleasant way to kick-start that Yuletide spirit.

snacks are the traditionally limp English fare. Up on Bailgate, try **Café Roxanna** (01522 546464) for either a light lunchtime bite or an evening meal. Another choice is the **Black Horse** (6 Eastgate; 01522 544404), a bistro carvery like the Wig & Mitre.

Brown's Pie Shop

33 Steep Hill (01522 527330).
Food served noon-3pm, 5.30-10pm, Mon-Sat.
Cards AmEx, Debit, MC, V.

Traditional British food comes in a pie. And it's followed by a sticky spongy pudding. That's the gospel according to Brown's, which, since 1987, has made a name for itself by serving up hearty meals at reasonable prices in this quaint Dickensian hillside restaurant. Steak and ale (£8.95; cheaper at lunchtime) is the favourite and there is always a wide selection of other fillings. You can also order steaks and grills, but you're best off plumping for a nice hot pie.

Jews House

15 The Strait (01522 524851).
Food served noon-2pm, 7-9pm, Tue-Sat.
Set meals *lunch* £7.95 (3 courses); *dinner* £23 (3 courses). **Cards** AmEx, DC, Debit, MC, V.

This is probably Lincoln's finest restaurant, set in what is possibly the oldest inhabited house in the country. The Jews House dates back to 1190 and chef Richard Gibbs has made it the setting for a quiet, smallish dining room. Service is informal, the setting is simple and cosy, and the food, Anglo-European, is excellent. Expect to pay around £4 for soups, up to £14.95 for mains, and around a fiver for desserts.

Victoria

6 Union Road (01522 536048).
Food served noon-4pm Mon-Fri; 11am-4pm Sat; noon-2pm Sun. **Cards** Debit, MC, V.

An excellent alehouse, filled to bubbling with amiable locals and visiting beer connoisseurs, the Victoria manages to squeeze in a lot to its smallish layout. In among

the open fire and the collection of pictures of the good Queen Vic herself, there's undoubtedly the best range of real ale in Lincoln, with better than serviceable pub grub including stews, and pies, as well as Sunday roasts, ploughman's and enormous chunky cob sandwiches. There's live music at least once a week, but no jukebox to distract from the atmosphere of seriously jovial pub-biness. Sadly, the staff can be a little brusque. Prices are low: soups are £1.60, mains are around £3.75 (about £5 on Sundays).

Wig & Mitre

30 Steep Hill (01522 535190).
Food served 8am-11pm daily.
Credit AmEx, DC, Debit, MC, V.

Named for the headwear of the judges in the Crown Court and the bishops in the Cathedral, both nearby, the Wig & Mitre (just 'the Wig' will do) has long been one of Lincoln's most civilised hostelries, with real ales, a lengthy wine list, a chatter-filled (music-free) atmosphere and excellent food. In 1999 it was forced to relocate a few doors down the hill and though it retains the same standards throughout, the ambience is a little less relaxed. Prices are high for Lincoln (about £9-£17 for main courses), but so is the quality, with a series of menus and blackboard specials ranging from trad pub fare to sophisticated French cuisine.

What to see & do

It helps to think of Lincoln in two parts – uphill and down – because you won't want to struggle up the hill too many times. It's a very walkable city, with the major attractions very close to each other, and with most of the centre completely pedestrianised. There are plenty of coffee shops and cafés close by for refuelling.

Tourist information centres

9 Castle Hill (Castle Square), LN1 3AA (01522 529828).
Open 9.30am-5.30pm Mon-Thur; 9.30am-5pm Fri; 10am-5pm Sat, Sun.

21 The Cornhill (High Street), LN5 7HB
(01522 579056). **Open** 9.30am-5.30pm Mon-Thur;
9.30am-5pm Fri; 10am-5pm Sat.
Ask about guided tours, too. Their website can be found
at www.lincoln-info.org.uk

Bishop's Palace

Minster Yard (01522 527468).
Open *Apr-Oct* 10am-6pm daily; *Nov-Mar* 10am-4pm
Sat, Sun. **Admission** (EH) £1.50; 80p 5s-15s; £1.10
OAPs, students.

Said to have once been Britain's most luxurious residence, the Bishop's Palace, with banqueting halls,
apartments and offices, was an important archaeological site, though not much of the original splendour sur-
vives except the restored Alnwick Tower. However,
displays here show just how well the medieval bishops
lived as they entertained monarchs and ran much of the
city. At one time a walled route had to be built to allow
them access to the Cathedral without being mobbed.
Access is through what remains of this VIP thoroughfare – Chesney Gate on the south side of Minster Yard.

Ellis Mill

Mill Road (01522 523870/528448).
Open *May-Sept* 2-6pm Sat, Sun; *Oct-Apr* 2pm-dusk
Sun. **Admission** 70p; 30p 5s-16s.

In days gone by the long ridge on which Lincoln is built
was peppered with windmills. Now there's just one, built
in 1798 and restored in 1981. If the wind's blowing and
they're grinding corn, it's a fascinating place to visit,
with Windy Miller on hand to tell you some history and
show off all the mechanics. After you've seen all the
whirling wooden cogs and gears you can take home
some fresh stoneground flour.

Greyfriars Exhibition Centre

Broadgate (01522 530401)
Open 10am-1pm, 2-4pm, Wed-Sat. **Admission** free.

Housed in a thirteenth-century building, this is a good
starting point for a tour of Lincoln's long history. It's a
changing display drawn from the collection of the old
City and County museum, and, as you'd expect, it covers aspects of Lincoln from its prehistory to around 1750,
including many objects retrieved from local archaeological excavations. An exhibition entitled 'Raiders and
Traders', detailing the Saxon and Viking legacy of the
area, runs until the end of April 2000. After this, there
will be an exhibition called 'Treasures', featuring a selection of artefacts from Lincoln's history.

Incredibly Fantastic Old Toy Show

26 Westgate (01522 520534).
Open *Easter-Sept* 11am-5pm Tue-Sat; noon-4pm
Sun, bank hol Mon; *Oct-Dec* 11am-5pm Sat;
noon-4pm Sun. **Admission** £1.90; £1 5s-16s;
£1.50 OAPs, students.

Whatever age you admit to, you can lose yourself here
in the toys of your youth, not to mention those of several generations before. Essentially a huge private collection of vintage toys displayed thematically, this is a
charming reminder that kiddie amusement didn't
always require a TV screen and a joystick. There are
also plenty of funfair mirrors and coin-operated mechanical attractions (for which you buy old pennies).

The Lawn

Union Road (01522 560306).
Open *Easter-Sept* 9am-5pm Mon-Fri; 10am-5pm Sat,
Sun; *Oct-Easter* 9am-4.30pm Mon-Fri; 10am-4pm Sat,
Sun. **Admission** free.

Remember in *The Madness of King George*, when the
nutty old monarch receives the very latest in eighteenth-
century psychiatric treatment from the Reverend Doctor
Francis Willis? Well, Willis was based in Lincoln and
thanks to his royal patronage was able to found a grand
and progressive mental institution here. He called it The
Lincoln Lunatic Asylum; later known as The Lawn,
it's now a multipurpose visitor centre. There's a tropical greenhouse, a delightful formal garden, a small aviation museum dedicated to local squadrons 50 and 61,
an archaeology centre, a café/bar/restaurant, and a host
of twee little gift shops, all set in very picnic-friendly
grounds. It's a diverting enough set of attractions,
though there's little of real substance here. There are
regular concerts, a series of international dance events
and outdoor music every Sunday afternoon from June
to September (for which you have to pay).

Lincoln Castle

Castle Hill (01522 511068).
Open *Apr-Oct* 9.30am-5.30pm Mon-Sat; 11am-
5.30pm Sun; *Nov-Mar* 9.30am-4pm Mon-Sat; 11am-
4pm Sun. **Admission** £2.50; £1 5s-15s; £1.50 OAPs,
students; £6.50 family.

Across a cobbled square, facing the Cathedral, is the
entrance to Lincoln Castle. Built immediately after the
Norman Conquest, this was a key defence for an important and wealthy town. It saw action in the 1140s during the Battle of Lincoln between King Stephen and the
invading Matilda, when it was besieged several times,
and then in 1644 when Cromwell's Parliamentary soldiers stormed it in less than an hour and booted the
King's soldiers out of the city. In more peaceful times
the Castle has been the site of a Victorian prison and a
Crown Court, which is still in operation. These days,
its grounds are the site of a busy programme of events
throughout the year, from fashion shows, Shakespeare
plays and classical concerts, to Civil War re-enactments, medieval jousting and demonstrations of
Roman soldiery. The Lincoln Castle Longbowmen are
here most weekends showing off their archery skills.
There's a coffee shop here, too.

Walk around the perimeter walls for some great
views of the city and surrounding countryside, or climb
the Observatory Tower, from which you can see as far
as Derbyshire to the west and Boston to the south. This
was actually built in the 1820s as an observation
tower for the prison, commissioned by a Governer
Merryweather, a keen astronomer who used it as a platform for his telescope. Round to the east, Cobb Tower
contains some grisly dungeons, complete with mana-
cles and prisoners' thirteenth-century carved graffiti.
This was the site of the city's public executions
throughout the nineteenth century. The prison is worth
a look, too, not least for its chapel, the only surviving
example of the 'Pentonville separate system', a maze of
interlocking doors, which kept prisoners completely isolated even while they were sitting next to each other.

Also housed in the prison building is the Magna
Carta, the foundation of the nation's civil liberties and
rule of law. This is one of the four surviving original

Roman around town

Whenever a large building is built in Lincoln, the developers have to allow time for the inevitable excavation of Roman remains. There's a lead mine under the police station, for example, and when City Hall was built the design had to be radically altered to allow a long chunk of Roman city wall to run underneath.

For nearly 500 years after its founding in AD 48, Lincoln was a vitally important outpost of the Roman Empire. The name is a contraction of 'Lindum Colonia' – the colony of Lindum, itself a Latinisation of the word 'Linden', meaning a hill settlement by a lake.

For a tour of the city's most prominent Roman remains, a good place to start is the section of wall under City Hall on Beaumont Fee. Here, as well as a long stretch of wall, you can see what's left of the lower west gate, including a fibreglass reconstruction of an ornately carved footstone. The original of this is in City Hall. This gate would have been where goods from the nearby Brayford Pool, then an inland harbour, were brought into the city.

From here, walk up the hill on a cobbled path to the left of the police station known as Motherby Hill. This traces the route of the Roman wall and you can see

that many of the buildings along the way have used stones from it, as did the builders of the Castle at the top of the hill. Head along Drury Lane, through Castle Square and you'll find yourself in Bailgate. This was the forum, or city centre of Roman Lincoln. The positions of the forum's pillars are marked in the road with red cobbles, and further up Bailgate is a small park where a well and a Roman church, the basilica of St Paul, have been excavated. Also near here was the mint, where coinage was made.

Head along Bailgate further still and you find Newport Arch, one of a pair of gates that marked the northern entrance to the city. This was built in the third century AD and boasts the distinction of being the only Roman arch in Britain that traffic still drives through. What you see is only the top of the original arch, as the ground level has risen a full eight feet since Roman times. A section of wall can be seen to the right of the arch, along with the base of a tower. At this point the wall was 12 feet thick with a ditch 30 feet deep and 100 yards across. Walk along East Bight and you will soon come to the remains of the eastern gate, now displayed in the car park of the Forte Posthouse Hotel.

documents that King John signed in 1215. It has been kept in Lincoln ever since. Guided tours of the Castle set off from the entrance at 11am and 2pm, and are included in the entrance fee.

Lincoln Cathedral

Minster Yard (01522 544544).
Open *June-Aug* 7.15am-8pm Mon-Sat; 7.15am-6pm Sun; *Sept-May* 7.15am-6pm Mon-Sat; 7.15am-5pm Sun. **Admission** (suggested donation) £4; £1.50 5s-15s, OAPs, students; £7 family.

For several centuries, when its three Gothic towers were capped by enormous spires, Lincoln Cathedral was (at 540 feet) the tallest building in the world. Today it remains among the most beautiful, described by John Ruskin as 'out and out the most precious piece of architecture in the British Isles'. It is visible from almost anywhere in the city and now that much of the exterior restoration is complete, its imposing west front is free of the scaffolding that obscured it for a decade.

The diocese of Lincoln once stretched from the Thames to the Humber, the largest in the country, so it was only appropriate that such a grand cathedral should be here. Most of what stands today was built by

St Hugh, a French monk who became Bishop of Lincoln in 1186. Hugh brought to the building an elegant continental style previously unknown in England, and this was followed throughout the four centuries of the building's construction, although the lower parts of the west front are the remnants of a much earlier cathedral, a 1072 Norman structure built by Remigius, the first Bishop of Lincoln. The rest of this was destroyed by an earthquake in 1141.

Lincoln Cathedral's most recent claim to fame was as the setting for some Trollope-esque ecclesiastical intrigue resulting from a long-running stand-off between the Dean and the Bishop over a 'tour' of Australia to show off the Cathedral's original of the Magna Carta (now kept in the Castle). Intervention by Mrs Thatcher and a 'randy vicar' sex scandal added fuel to the fire and the Church now refers to 'Lincoln' as one of its more embarrassing moments.

None of this affected the beautiful building, however, and a visit is a must, as the 900-year-old Cathedral boasts some of the finest medieval architecture and craftsmanship anywhere. See the beautiful Early English Angel Choir, where you'll find the Lincoln Imp, the city's devilish mascot; don't miss the fine wood carving (especially the hidden designs under the Bishops' perches), the fine stained glass throughout and the library, designed by Sir Christopher Wren. In the garden is a huge statue of Tennyson by George Frederick Watts (*see p93*).

Lincoln Cathedral is very much a working church, with a busy schedule of services and concerts. Visitors are made welcome, with regular guided tours at 11am, 1pm and 3pm in summer and at 11am and 2pm in the winter. These are free, as is entrance, although a donation is suggested. At certain times during the summer it is also possible to ascend the tower.

Museum of Lincolnshire Life

Burton Road (01522 528448).
Open *May-Sept* 10am-5.30pm daily;
Oct-Apr 10am-5.30pm Mon-Sat; 2-5.30pm Sun.
Admission £2; 60p 5s-16s, students.

This is a gem of a museum. It's the county's attic – a cluttered repository of junk representing all aspects of Lincolnshire's rich social and economic history. There's just enough of an educational angle to put things in context, but it's easy to ignore the labels and meander through this glorious time capsule full of period interiors (a printer's, a wheelwright's, a chemist shop, a school room…), weird agricultural implements, costumes, and scores of beautifully restored traction engines and horse-drawn carriages. Modern Lincoln was built on heavy engineering, so there are plenty of iron giants here, including the world's first tank (built in the city's foundries). Equally fascinating are the recordings of Lincolnshire dialect, an important inspiration for local poet Alfred Lord Tennyson, and the displays evoking rural life over the last two centuries or so. There are frequent talks and other events, and usually a few older visitors on hand to regale you with fond memories, giving the place a very human charm.

Stonebow & Guildhall

High Street (01522 881188).
Open 10.30am-noon, 1.30pm-4pm, Fri, 1st Sat of month. **Admission** free.

These days it's mostly a landmark for shopping rendezvous, with pram-pushing mums and mobile-toting teens arranging to meet each other under its clock. In the fifteenth and sixteenth centuries the Stonebow – a limestone archway that spans the pedestrianised High Street – was the southern gateway into the walled city, a replacement for one that the Romans erected centuries before (its companion gates exist in Pottergate and in Minster Yard between Castle and Cathedral). Inside is the council chamber and a room displaying a wealth of civic insignia: swords, seals and mayoral chains. Atop the Stonebow is a bell rung to call the council to meetings, with the curious inscription 'When any good man hears the bell let him open the bag…'

Usher Gallery

Lindum Road (01522 527980).
Open 10am-5.30pm Mon-Sat, bank hols; 2.30pm-5pm Sun. **Admission** £2; 50p 5-15s, students; free on Fri.

A fine provincial art gallery housing an acclaimed collection of coins, jewellery and timepieces, in keeping with the profession of its founder, James Ward Usher, a local jeweller. There are also watercolours by Turner, and a collection of work by Peter de Wint, as well as paintings by LS Lowry, John Piper, Walter Sickert and Ruskin Spear. Much of the work has a local theme or subject matter and there's a fine collection of memorabilia relating to Lincolnshire-born Poet Laureate Alfred Lord Tennyson. There is a programme of temporary exhibitions, workshops and talks. Coffee shop.

Lincoln Castle, *the city's number two visitor attraction.*

York

More than just history and teashops...

York Minster — *one of the finest Gothic churches in northern Europe. See page 246.*

Summer crowds aside, York makes for the perfect weekend urban break. The city that for much of the last 2,000 years was second in importance only to London is now less than two hours from the capital by rail. And the fact that it was largely bypassed by the Industrial Revolution (the coming of the iron horse excepted) means that its compact core has remained remarkably intact. It's the perfect walking city. Uniquely in the UK, a large portion of its heart is pedestrianised (a ring road and park and rides keep most traffic at a distance) and cycle lanes proliferate.

Large tracts of medieval wall ring an embarrassment of listed buildings – medieval, Tudor, Georgian – and some fine museums and other attractions, the list topped by the

magnificent Minster. The inevitable downside is that York is no secret. With a population of 100,000 and annual visitor numbers in the region of four million, the place can seem like a tourist-choked open-air heritage theme park in peak season. The city's at its best on a bright, crisp winter's day.

A bit of history

As with London, York is fundamentally a Roman creation. There may have been an Iron Age settlement in the area but it was the arrival of the legions in AD 71 and their setting up of a camp on the land between the Ouse and Foss rivers that marked the foundation of the city. Eboracum, as the fort was known (thought to mean 'place of the yew trees') soon grew into a permanent settlement and was subsequently taken over by the Saxons. The first church in York dates from the seventh century and the town, now the capital of the kingdom of Northumbria, soon became established as second only to Canterbury in the Church hierarchy, a position it retains today.

> **By train from London**
>
> Trains go direct to **York** from **King's Cross** every half an hour. The journey time is about **1hr 50mins**.

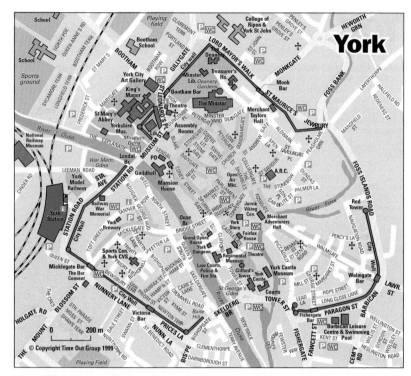

In the middle of the ninth century the
Vikings raided and then settled the entire north
of the country. Saxon Eoforwic became Norse
Jorvik. Although the Viking period lasted less
than a century, their street and place names
have proved more permanent. No little town in
Britain has more '-gate' (meaning 'street')
suffixed thoroughfares. Some of the street
names may refer to individuals (Goodramgate,
for instance), many refer to the trades carried
out there (Coppergate was home to the
carpenters, Skeldergate to the shield-makers).

The shape of the city changed little in
medieval times. Narrow ginnels (alleys) criss-
cross the centre, providing countless short cuts
(Coffee Yard, linking Stonegate with Grape
Lane, is only five foot ten inches high in places).
And Grape Lane itself was, of course, the haunt
of York's vintners. Not. Those down-to-earth
medieval folk were even more literal than that.
'Grap' meant 'grope', and when you know that
this was the city's red-light district you can
guess the rest.

The crazily teetering houses on York's best-
known street, The Shambles, were once home to

the city's butchers, and reputedly built so much
on top of one another to keep direct sunlight off
the meat. Now the overhanging eaves cool
overexcited tourists searching for ceramic
teddy bears and spurious coats of arms. There's
no little irony that what was once York's most
foul-smelling, pestilential street is now its twee-
most. At its southern end is the city's most
delightfully and bafflingly named street, Whip-
ma-Whop-ma-gate.

More useful high street stores are
concentrated along Coney Street, running
parallel to the Ouse, and in the purpose-built
Coppergate shopping centre not far from the
Castle Museum and Clifford's Tower.

That was then…

York is trying hard to shake off its fusty
teashop-and-tour-group image (although there's
still plenty of time-warp cake shops – and tour
groups). The University, just to the south-east
of the centre in Heslington, a big influx of
business and industry (particularly bioscience)
and the continuing presence of chocolate
companies (Terry's, Rowntree-Nestlé; one plant
nearby is devoted solely to the production of the

ever-popular Kit-Kat) means that this is no historical fossil. York now has its own Slug & Lettuce (well, you've got to start somewhere), its independent City Screen cinema has just got a permanent home on Coney Street and a massive new dual nightclub, Ikon and Diva, opened in 1999.

First Stop York by Train

If you visit York by train you can take advantage of the 'First Stop York by Train' scheme that entitles rail travellers to half-price admission to all the major sights (and ghost walks) plus discounts at a number of restaurants and York Theatre Royal. In addition, special rates are available at 30 of the city's hotels and guesthouses. Call the accommodation hotline on 01904 554499 as far in advance as possible to book (subject to a booking fee and a minimum two-night stay on Fridays and Saturdays). Ask for a 'First Stop York' voucher book when you book your rail tickets at any major station or at York station's Rail Travel Centre or the tourist information centre at 20 George Hudson Street.

Where to stay

There are surprisingly few hotels and B&Bs in the city centre. With the exception of Middlethorpe Hall, none of those mentioned below is more than a ten-minute walk from the city walls.

Bishops Hotel

135 Holgate Road, YO24 4DF (01904 628000). **Rates** (B&B) *single/double/twin* £30pp; *four-poster/canopy* £35pp. **Rooms** (all en suite) 2 single; 5 double/twin; 2 four-poster/canopy. **Cards** Debit, MC, V.

Since opening in 1998, Steve and Denise Magson's vibrant non-smoking hotel (run with great gusto by Denise and her sister Gill) has proved a huge success – and it's easy to see why. Nowhere else in York will you get such a winning combination of friendliness, competence, bright fresh décor and keen price. And few places are as well geared up for families, with family rooms, toys, kids' menus and, most importantly, a thoroughly relaxed and tolerant attitude. Ten minutes' walk from the walls and the rail station. Children welcome (the usual price for two adults and two children sharing is £80). Non-smoking throughout.

The Dairy

3 Scarcroft Road, YO24 1ND (01904 639367). **Rates** (B&B) *single occupancy* £28-£38; *double* £18-£22.50pp; *four-poster* £20pp; *family* £67.50. **Rooms** 4 double/family (2 en suite); 1 four-poster.

It's not going to have *Elle Deco* knocking on the door (lots of pine and flowery touches), but Keith Jackman's long-established (22 years and counting) guesthouse is as chilled, homey and competitively priced a B&B as you'll find in the city. Mini-hi-fis in the rooms betray Keith's musical passion (he's a part-time percussionist) and the creeper-clad courtyard of this former dairy is a haven in hot weather. The 'cottage' room on the courtyard offers the greatest privacy. Children and dogs welcome. Non-smoking throughout.

On the site of the original Norman castle stands **Clifford's Tower**. *See page 245.*

The Chilterns to York

Easton's

90 Bishopthorpe Road, YO23 1JS (01904 626646).
Rates (B&B) *single occupancy £36-£62;
double/twin £41-£69; family £65-£78*. Special breaks.
Rooms (all en suite) 10 double/twin/family.

A good few notches better than your average B&B, not
only does Easton's offer swathes of rich William Morris
wallpapers and fabrics, a lovely sitting room and good-
sized bedrooms, but a breakfast menu that includes such
scandalously forgotten Victorian gems as kedgeree and
devilled kidneys. Children over five welcome. Non-
smoking throughout.

The Grange

1 Clifton, Y30 6AA (01904 644744/fax 01904 612453/
info@grangehotel.co.uk/www.grangehotel.co.uk).
Rates (B&B) *single occupancy £99-£160;
double £120; deluxe double/twin £135-£165;
four-poste*r £180; *suite £210*. **Rooms** (all en suite)
11 double/twin; 16 deluxe double/twin; 2 four-poster;
1 suite. **Cards** AmEx, DC, Debit, MC, V.

It's not cheap, but the Grange is certainly a classy operation. The pink-columned entrance hall and impressive
spiral staircase lead on to a wide range of bedrooms, all
individually decorated in classical, no-nonsense wallpapers and fabrics. Shirley Bassey has stayed in the
sizeable suite (having a running machine moved in to
satisfy her exercise requirements). Further attractions
include three restaurants – an informal brasserie and
bar in the basement (mains £8-£9), the more formal Ivy
restaurant (mains around £16) and its offshoot, the
Dom Ruinart seafood bar, which sits within its own
handsome stripy-muralled pavilion. Front rooms suf-
fer a little from traffic noise. The Grange is about ten
minutes' walk from the Minster to the north-west of the
city. Children and dogs welcome.

Grasmead House Hotel

1 Scarcroft Hill, YO24 1DF (tel/fax 01904 629996/
www.uktourism.com/yk-grasmead).
Rates (B&B) *four-poster £65-£70; family four-poster
£87-£92*. **Rooms** (all en suite) 4 four-posters; 2
family four-posters. **Cards** AmEx, DC, Debit, MC, V.

If you've got a thing for four-posters, Grasmead House
is the place for you – all six rooms have one (and they're
all antique, one dating from 1730). You don't get much
room to go with the beds, but you can relax in the cosy
lounge with its own small bar, wind-up gramophone and
cock-eared china dog. Micklegate is ten minutes' walk
away. Children welcome. All bedrooms non-smoking.

Holmwood House

114 Holgate Road, YO24 4BB (01904 626183/fax
01904 670899/holmwood.house@dial.pipex.com/
www.holmwoodhousehotel.co.uk).
Rates (B&B) *single occupancy £45-£65; double £55-
£85; twin £65-£80; four-poster £70; triple £75; family
suite £130-£140*. **Rooms** (all en suite) 11
double/twin/family suites; 2 four-posters; 1 triple.
Cards AmEx, Debit, MC, V.

Bill Pitts and Rosie Blanksby's highly successful establishment lies not much more than five minutes' walk
from the rail station and city walls. Décorwise it's pretty, and pretty conservative, with plenty of Laura Ashley-
esque floral motifs in evidence. The top-floor rooms (11

York's finest lodgings: **Middlethorpe Hall**.

and 12) are in a more cottage style and enjoy the best
views of the Minster, while the plushest room has a massive bed and spa bath. Breakfasts in the basement
restaurant include excellent kippers and croissants
imported from France. Gourmet breaks are organised in
association with Melton's (*see p244*); phone for details.
Children over eight welcome. Non-smoking throughout.

Middlethorpe Hall

Bishopthorpe Road, YO23 2GB (01904 641241/fax
01904 620176/info@middlethorpe.u-net.com).
Rates *single £99; single occupancy £125; double/twin
£145; deluxe double/twin £160; four-poster £225;
suite £185-£250*. Special breaks. Breakfast £12.50
(Eng); £9.50 (cont). **Rooms** (all en suite) 4 single;
12 double/twin; 6 deluxe double/twin; 2 four-posters;
7 suites. **Cards** Debit, MC, V.

The place to splurge in York, Middlethorpe Hall lies a
couple of miles south of the centre opposite York racecourse. This fabulous house, one-time home of diarist
Lady Mary Wortley Montagu, was rescued from neglect
(and Superman wallpaper in one room) by Historic
House Hotels (who also run Hartwell House near
Aylesbury). Set in 26 acres of grounds, the William III
building is now back to its full country house splendour,
the formality of its period fittings balanced by the easy
cheeriness and efficiency of the staff. Rooms vary greatly in size and décor, but all are in keeping with the overall classically restrained mood of the house. Some are in
the courtyard block to the side of the main building. The
formal wood-panelled restaurant offers highly competent classical French-based cuisine (*see p244*). A health
spa with indoor swimming pool opened in early 1999.

The tranquillity of the beautiful, extensive park and gardens is, alas, marred by the streaming traffic on the adjacent A-road. Children over eight welcome.

M1 J45; A1 to A64 to York; follow signs to Bishopthorpe and Middlethorpe; hotel is 0.5 miles after St Andrew's church on right.

Mount Royale

The Mount, YO24 1GU (01904 628856/fax 01904 611171/reservations@mountroyale.co.uk/ www.mountroyale.co.uk).
Rates (B&B) *single occupancy* £85-£105; *double/twin* £95; *deluxe double/twin* £105; *four-poster* £105; *suite* £140. Special breaks. **Rooms** (all en suite) 9 double/twin; 5 deluxe double/twin; 3 four-posters; 6 suites. **Cards** AmEx, DC, Debit, MC, V.
This grand old stager of the York hotel scene, occupying two William IV houses, has been run by the Oxtoby family for more than 30 years. It's not going to win any prizes for its rough-at-the-edges décor and fittings, but an air of faded grandeur is part of its charm; the other part is exemplary service. Exhibitionists can flounce on the extraordinarily gaudy Italian carved bed in room 15, or you might prefer the private patio of the garden room, which looks out on to the lovely award-winning garden. Guests can sup in the compact, wood-heavy bar surrounded by pics of Brucie and other celeb guests, eat in the pricey but first-rate trad restaurant or plunge in the heated outdoor pool (in summer). One on its own. Children and dogs welcome.

York Backpackers

Micklegate House, 88-90 Micklegate, YO1 6JX (01904 627720/fax 01904 339350/yorkbackpackers @cwcom.net/www.yorkbackpackers.mcmail.com).
Rates £9-£15pp. Breakfast £3 (Eng); £2 (cont).
Rooms (140 beds) 1 double; 7 dorms (sleep 8-20); 3 family rooms (sleep 7). **Cards** Debit, MC, V.
There can't be a hostel in the country in a grander setting than this Grade-I listed Georgian mansion within the city walls. Exuberantly run, it offers a vaulted cellar (with pool table), a beamed bar, and extraordinary value. It's particularly popular with good-time weekender groups and stag and hen parties.

Where to eat & drink

York has plenty of places to eat, but surprisingly few of real quality. **The Grange** (*see page 242*) and **Mount Royale** hotels (*see above*) both have excellent restaurants that are worth patronising even if you're staying elsewhere. For something less formal, there's a **Pizza Express** at 17 Museum Street (01904 672904) and, even more casual, **Petergate Fisheries** (97 Low Petergate; 01904 624788) for the best takeaway fish and chips in town. For a lunchtime snack or a coffee and cake, try the airy **Spurriergate Centre** in the former church of St Michael on Spurriergate (01904 629393), or the admirable **Blake Head Bookshop & Café** at 104 Micklegate (01904 623767) for warming veggie fare and bargain-priced books. An all-day place, very popular

with the locals, is **Café Concerto** at 21 High Petergate (01904 610478). The tourist-trap **Betty's** teashop in St Helen's Square (01904 659142) caters for those who like tourist-trap teashops. More rewarding, perhaps, are the plethora of old-style bakeries that churn out the sort of retro pastries most of us thought were extinct – cream horn, vicar?

The opening of the gargantuan **Ikon/Diva** nightclub has injected some much-needed metropolitan urgency into York's sleepy nightlife, but, for most locals and students, a night out still revolves around the pub. Happily, the city is well provided with characterful taverns and good beer at (by southern standards) low prices (though pub food is generally poor). Among the best boozers are the **Blue Bell** (53 Fossgate; a tiny, chummy drinkers' pub), the **Olde Starre** (Stonegate; the oldest licensed pub in the city – 1644 – though parts of the building are much older), the **Black Swan** (Peaseholme Green; famed for its ghosts), the **King's Arms** (by the Ouse Bridge; regularly floods) and the **Spread Eagle** (98 Walmgate; good beer and a lively atmosphere).

19 Grape Lane

19 Grape Lane (01904 636366).
Food served noon-2pm, 6-9pm, Tue-Fri; noon-2pm, 6-10pm, Sat. **Set meals** *lunch* £5 (1 course), £9 (2 courses), £12 (3 courses); *dinner* £19 (3 courses) before 7pm. **Cards** Debit, MC, V.
Goat's cheese with black olive and basil vinaigrette (£3.35) and wild rabbit with garlic and a balsamic cream on bacon and honey-roasted parsnips (£13.50) are typical of the simple, well-executed English and French dishes at this cosy restaurant in the centre of the city. A low, beamed ceiling, inoffensive cottagey décor and an intriguing New World-biased wine list are further attractions.

The Blue Bicycle

34 Fossgate (01904 673990).
Food served noon-2.30pm, 7-10pm, daily.
Cards AmEx, DC, Debit, MC, V.
One of the newer names on the York restaurant scene, and one of the most popular, the BB is broadly French and fishy, knocking out good versions of such classics as moules marinières (£5.25) and calf's liver with caramelised onions and a rich gravy (£14.95) in an informal, thoroughly agreeable atmosphere.

Kites

13 Grape Lane (01904 641750).
Food served noon-2.30pm, 6.30-10.30pm, Mon-Sat. **Set meals** *lunch* £10.95 (2 courses); £12.95 (3 courses). **Cards** AmEx, DC, Debit, MC, V.
Just a few doors down from 19 Grape Lane (*see above*), Kites presents a more modern face of York dining, with deep red walls, wooden floors and internationally influenced dishes such as bang bang chicken (£5.25) and seared tuna with spiced lentil salsa (£12.95).

Melton's

7 Scarcroft Road (01904 634341).
Food served 5.30-10pm Mon; noon-2pm, 5.30-
10pm, Tue-Sat; noon-2pm Sun. **Set meals** *lunch*
£15 (3 course); *dinner* £19.50 (3 courses).
Cards Debit, MC, V.

Located in a residential area, just south of the city walls,
Michael and Lucy Hjort's unassuming little restaurant
is without doubt the York dining destination for foodies. A simply decorated room (salmon-pinky-red walls
hung with miscellaneous pictures and a specially commissioned Melton's mural) provides a warm setting for
the inventive, sometimes idiosyncratic, dishes that are
chef Michael's forte. A typical meal might consist of dar-
iole of langoustine and salmon tartare (£6.50), roast confit of duck with bitter leaves and a warm potato salad
(£12.30), with Melton's boozy trifle (£4.40) to finish.

Middlethorpe Hall

Bishopthorpe Road (01904 641241).
Food served 12.30-1.45pm, 7-9.45pm, daily. **Set
meals** *lunch* £14.50 (2 courses), £17.50 (3 courses);
dinner £32 (3 courses). **Cards** Debit, MC, V.

You've got to be in the mood for it... but if you fancy a
bit of starched linen, creaking floors, classically rich cuisine and wood-panelled formality, then Middlethorpe
supplies it in spades. For £32 you get three courses (plus
canapés) along the lines of rillette of pork and prunes
with garlic purée and a bean salad, followed by turbot
Mouginoise with roasted salsify, confit of garlic and fondant potatoes, then banana and gingerbread parfait with
a butterscotch sauce – and the chance to relax afterwards in the stunning drawing room. The wine list is,
inevitably, heavy on major French regions. Good value,
considering the quality of food and peerless setting.

What to see & do

York is packed with museums and other visitor
attractions – too many, in fact. Many are rather
insubstantial and unashamedly aimed at the
tourist market. The best are listed below. The
main sights tend to be clustered either to the
north of the centre around the Minster or to the
south around the Castle area.

Tourist information centre

De Grey Rooms, Exhibition Square, YO10 7HB
(01904 621756/www.york.gov.uk). **Open** 9am-6pm
daily. There's also a branch within York railway
station and at 20 George Hudson Street.

Bike hire

Bob Trotter's, 13 Lord Mayor's Walk (01904
622868). A ten-minute walk from the train station.

ARC

St Saviourgate (01904 654324).
Open 10am-5pm Mon-Fri; 1-5pm Sat.
Last entry 3.30pm. **Admission** (EH) £3.60.
The Archaeological Resource Centre, located within the
old church of St Saviour, is an admirable attempt to
make archaeology accessible. Its hands-on exhibits,
mainly aimed at children, illuminate York's history.

Barley Hall

2 Coffee Yard, off Stonegate (01904 610275).
Open *Mar-Oct* 10am-4pm Mon-Fri; noon-4pm Sat,
Sun; *Nov-Feb* 11am-3.30pm Wed-Sun.
Admission £3.50; £2.50 10s-18s, OAPs, students.
A splendid fifteenth-century house that has now been
fully restored by the Archaeological Trust.

Castle Museum

Tower Street (01904 613161).
Open *Apr-Oct* 9.30am-5pm daily; *Nov-Mar* 9.30am-
4.30pm daily. **Admission** £4.95; £3.50 5s-16s,
OAPs, students; £14.80 family.
Undoubtedly York's best museum, this inspired collection of everyday objects from the past 300 years was
started by Dr John Kirk, who wanted to preserve evidence of a vanishing way of life. One room still presents
exhibits in glass cases as Kirk intended in 1935 when
he donated his collection to the City of York. Happily,
far more modern presentation techniques prevail elsewhere. There are carefully reconstructed period rooms,
a plethora of vintage domestic appliances, tons of old
toys and extensive recreated Victorian and Edwardian
streets and shops. Kids love it, particularly the informative and entertaining section on chocolate. Amid the
everyday there are also some unique gems, chief among
which is the most complete Anglo-Saxon helmet yet
found in Britain. The museum is housed in old prison
buildings on the site of York Castle, next to Clifford's
Tower (*see p245*).

The teetering rooftops of **The Shambles**.

Annual events in York

York is a big horse-racing town. The Knavesmire course, a couple of miles south of the centre, hosts major **flat race meetings** every month from May to October, the biggest being the August Ebor Meeting. Unless you're a turf fan, it's wise to avoid the city at these times as it can be all but impossible to find accommodation or a seat in any pub or restaurant.

February witnesses the popular (particularly with kids) **Viking Festival**, which encompasses a variety of vigorous Nordic events and culminates in the burning of a replica Viking boat at Knavesmire race course (no longer, alas, on the Ouse).

From May to September the **Summer in the City** programme features a wide range of music, dance, art and street theatre including a busking festival and an outdoor chess competition.

The **York Early Music Festival** in July is the finest of its type in the country, attracting top international artists. The festival includes the famous **York Mystery Plays**, which in 2000 (22 June-22 July) will be performed in the Minster for the first time. For details and advance booking call 01904 635444.

Started in 1997, the nine-day **Festival of Food & Drink** (end Sept) has been a huge success and has grown in size in each subsequent year. Also over one weekend in September are the **Heritage Open Days** when buildings not normally open to the public allow the great unwashed through their doors. The **York National Book Fair** also takes place over one September weekend. Held in the Barbican Centre, it's Britain's biggest antiquarian book fair.

For all of the above, phone the tourist office (*see page 244*) for precise dates.

City Walls

Strolling the extensive surviving sections of York's medieval (thirteenth- and fourteenth-century) walls is one of the greatest pleasures of a visit to the city. Stretching for three miles, they are punctuated by four bars (gates) – Micklegate Bar (on the original road to London), Bootham Bar, Monk Bar and Walmgate Bar (unique in the UK in still retaining its barbican, a projecting extension that provided an extra line of defence). There's a small museum in Micklegate Bar and an exhibition on Richard III in Monk Bar.

Clifford's Tower

Tower Street (01904 646940).
Open *Apr-June* 10am-6pm daily; *July, Aug* 9.30am-7pm daily; *Oct-Mar* 10am-4pm daily. **Admission** (EH) £1.80; 90p 5s-16s; £1.40 OAPs, students.

One of York's most immediately recognisable landmarks, the bluff white-stone tower sits on a mound raised by William the Conqueror to allow him to keep an eye on the troublesome citizens. The original Norman keep was destroyed by the same locals in 1109 in a shameful episode when the city's Jews sheltered from a mob inside and committed suicide rather than face the rabble. The current structure dates from 1245. There's nothing much more than a shell here, but it's an evocative shell, and there are good views from the walls.

Fairfax House

Castlegate (01904 655543).
Open *late Feb-early Jan* 11am-4.30pm Mon-Thur, Sat; 1.30-4.30pm Sun; *guided tours* 11am, 2pm, Fri. **Admission** £4; £1.50 5s-16s; £3.50 OAPs, students.

This fine Georgian house was designed by John Carr for the 9th Viscount Fairfax of Emley in 1750. It was meticulously restored during the 1980s and is now home to the splendid Noel Terry (of chocolate fame) collection of Georgian furniture.

Guildhall

St Helen's Square (01904 613161).
Open *May-Oct* 9am-5pm Mon-Fri; 10am-5pm Sat; 2-5pm Sun; *Nov-Apr* 9am-5pm Mon-Fri. **Admission** free.

The one-time administrative centre of the city is best viewed from the south side of Lendal bridge. The medieval riverside building, standing on the site of the first Roman bridge across the Ouse, was all but obliterated by bombs during World War II but has been beautifully restored and the interior can be toured.

Jorvik Viking Centre

Coppergate (01904 643211/advance booking 01904 543403/www.jorvik-viking-centre.co.uk).
Open *Apr-Oct* 9am-5.30pm daily; *Nov-Mar* 9am-3.40pm daily. **Admission** £5.35; £3.99 5s-15s; £4.60 OAPs, students; £17 family.

York's number one tourist draw has them queuing round the block. When it opened in the 1980s, it was a pioneer of the then-new time-car-ride-through-history type of visitor attraction. The idea is that time has stopped one October day in 948 and you pass through the sights, sounds and smells of recreated Viking York, before disembarking and examining some of the actual finds that were excavated from Coppergate between 1976 and 1981. Frankly, it's all looking rather tired now, and is certainly not worth an hour's queuing.

Merchant Adventurers' Hall

Piccadilly (01904 654818).
Open *Easter-Sept* 9.30am-5pm Mon-Sat; noon-4pm
Sun; *Oct-Easter* 9.30am-3.30pm Mon-Sat. **Admission**
(EH) £1.90; 60p 5s-16s; £1.60 OAPs, students.

One-time home to the city's most powerful guild, this
massive medieval building (completed in 1362) is in a
wonderful state of preservation.

National Railway Museum

Leeman Road (01904 621261/www.nmsi.ac.uk/nrm).
Open 10am-6pm daily. **Admission** £5.90; £4.90
OAPs; £3.90 students, free under-17s.

The two huge halls that make up the NRM are heavily
geared towards children (rides on 'Thomas the Tank
Engine', stories from the Fat Controller) and railway
junkies. The whole history of the railway is here, including such locomotive icons as Stephenson's stumpy 1829
Rocket and the undeniably beautiful Mallard. There are
engines galore, plus pots of memorabilia, but not a lot
to convert the unconvinced into a rail fanatic.

St William's College

College Street, opposite Minster (01904 557233).
Open 9am-5pm daily. **Admission** 60p; 30p 5s-16s.

Built around 1475, this fine half-timbered building was
once home to 23 priests and a provost. The modest
restaurant within the building spills into the lovely interior courtyard in summer. Some of the medieval rooms
can be viewed.

Treasurer's House

Chapter House Street (01904 624247).
Open *Apr-Oct* 10.30am-5pm daily.
Admission (NT) £3.50; £1.75 5s-16s; £8.50 family.

Built on the site of the original eleventh-century house
of the Treasurer of York Minster, the current late six-
teenth-/early seventeenth-century building contains
some fine furniture and features an exhibition on the history of the house and its predecessors.

York Brewery

12 Toft Green (01904 621162).
Open *tours* 11.30am, 12.30pm, 2.30pm, 4pm,
6pm, 7pm, Mon-Sat; 4pm, 5pm, 6pm, 7pm, Sun.
Admission £3.75; £2.75 14s-17s, £3 OAPs;
£3.40 students.

The **Merchant Adventurers' Hall**.

This tiny independent brewery has only been operational since 1996, bringing brewing back within the city
walls for the first time in 40 years. Sample a half of its
Stonewall bitter before an entertaining and informative
half-hour tour that's capped with a half of the admirably
sharp Yorkshire Terrier.

York City Art Gallery

Exhibition Square (01904 551861).
Open 10am-5.30pm Mon-Sat. Last entry 4.30pm.
Admission free.

This easily digestible municipal collection spans 600
years (though large swathes of that are only covered
very sketchily) and is a little too heavy on workaday
British nineteenth-century paintings. It is notable, however, for a large number of works by York-born William
Etty, and for its good-quality and imaginative temporary exhibitions.

York Minster

(01904 557216/www.yorkminster.org).
Open *Mar-Oct* 7am-8.30pm daily; *Nov-Feb* 7am-6pm
daily. **Admission** *foundations* £2; £1 5s-15s;
£1.50 OAPs, students; *chapter house* 70p;
30p 5s-15s; *central tower* £2.50; £1 5s-15s;
crypt 70p; 30p 5s-15s.

York's chief glory is its Minster. The sheer scale of the
honey-stoned building – at 500 feet long, 100 feet wide
and with a central tower almost 200 feet high, it's the
largest Gothic church north of the Alps – is testament
to the city's prominent role in medieval England. Begun
in the 1220s by Archbishop Walter de Grey, the building took 250 years to complete, employing a variety of
architectural styles. Broadly speaking, the transepts are
in Early English style (1220-70), the nave is Decorated
Gothic (1280-1350) and the chancel is Perpendicular
style (1361-1472). The nave is the widest of its type in
Europe, but it is, perhaps, the proliferation of wonderful medieval stained glass that impresses most. The
Great West Window (1338), with its flamboyant tracery,
is affectionately known as the 'Heart of Yorkshire', the
Great East Window (1405-8) at the far end of the chancel contains the world's largest surviving piece of
medieval stained glass, while the Five Sisters' Window
in the north transept is the oldest complete window in
the Minster (1260).

Entrance to the Minster is free, but there are individual charges to climb the tower, see the chapter
house, crypt and foundations. The harmonious chapter house is a gem. Built in the 1270s and 1280s, it is
unusual in having no central supporting pillar. Less
compelling is the crypt, which contains a variety of
architectural fragments. The (decidedly tough) climb
to the top of the tower is rewarded by fine views
(although, strangely, York looks more impressive from
ground level than above). If you're short of time (or
money), though, make the foundations your priority.
In the late 1960s, excavation work to secure the foundations of the central tower (which was threatening to
collapse) uncovered not just parts of the Norman cathedral but also an Anglo-Saxon and Anglo-Scandinavian
cemetery and evidence of the original Roman basilica.
It was within this building that, in all probability,
Constantine the Great was proclaimed Roman Emperor
by his troops on the death of his father in AD 306. It's
a tremendously evocative display.

The Chilterns to York

Grabbed by the ghoulies

York's seen a lot of history, so perhaps it's not surprising that it boasts of being one of the most haunted cities in the land. Here's a run-down of the major spooks and where they hang out.

Treasurer's House

In 1953 a plumber's apprentice working in the cellar heard a blast of a trumpet and looked up to see a Roman legion march through the wall across the floor of the cellar and disappear through the wall on the opposite side... and they only appeared from their knees up. The house stands on a Roman road and it has been suggested that its level was probably lower than the cellar floor, hence the cut-off legs.

Cock & Bottle, Skeldergate

The naughtiest ghost in town is that of infamous rake George Villiers, 2nd Duke of Buckingham. This is the Georgie Porgie who kissed the girls and made them cry; his spectre appears only to women, sometimes going as far as having a sly grope.

King's Manor

Probably the city's most haunted building, there have been reports of a ghostly monk (the Manor was built in the thirteenth century as part of the neighbouring St Mary's Abbey), a women in a green dress holding a bunch of roses and ghostly groans of pain (the building was used as a makeshift hospital after the Battle of Marston Moor in 1644). The **Old Starre** pub on Stonegate was also used to treat wounded soldiers and ghastly cries have also been reported there.

Church of Holy Trinity, Goodramgate

This church is said to be haunted by the headless ghost of Thomas Percy, Earl of Northumberland, who was beheaded in 1572 for rebelling against Elizabeth I.

Holy Trinity Church, Micklegate

In the Middle Ages a man died in an accident, leaving his wife and child destitute. The child then died of the plague, and the heartbroken mother soon followed them both to the grave. Her ghost has been reported wandering amid the gravestones, searching for her lost child.

Black Swan, Peaseholme Green

The ancient Black Swan is probably the most haunted pub in the city. A beautiful young woman clad in a long white dress, and a Victorian gent in a bowler hat have both been spotted here.

York Cells Tearooms, Parliament Street

The basement here once housed police cells and is said to be haunted by one Benjamin Wallis who was arrested and suffocated here in 1865.

Ghost walks are big business in York, and most are thoroughly entertaining. The three best-known are…

The Original Ghost Walk of York (01759 373090) goes from the King's Arms pub by the Ouse Bridge at 8pm daily (£3; £2 4s-14s).

The Ghost Trail of York (01904 633276) starts at 7.30pm every night at the front door of the Minster (£3; £2 4s-16s).

The Ghost Hunt of York (01904 608700) from The Shambles at 7.30pm every day (£3; £2 4s-16s).

York Model Railway

York station (01904 630169).
Open *Apr-Oct* 9.30am-6pm daily; *Nov-Mar* 10am-5.30pm daily. **Admission** £2.95; £1.95 4s-15s; £2.65 OAPs, students; £7.95 family.

One for little boys of all ages. The scale of the display (incorporating 600 buildings, 1,000 vehicles and 2,500 tiny people) certainly impresses.

Yorkshire Museum

Museum Gardens (01904 629745).
Open 10am-5pm daily. **Admission** £4.25; £2.70 5s-16s, OAPs, students; £12.95 family.

Well worth a visit for its enlightening displays on the history of the city and region from Roman times. There's a welter of facts, but they're imaginatively presented, with displays on the daily life of monks and some of the oddities of Roman cuisine ensuring that kids don't get bored. The reconstructed vestibule of the chapter house of the Abbey of St Mary (the ruins of which can be seen outside the museum in Museum Gardens), complete with monkish chanting, is particularly well done and very atmospheric. Another of the museum's prize exhibits is the tiny but exquisite fifteenth-century pendant known as the Middleham Jewel. A good place to escape the city crowds.

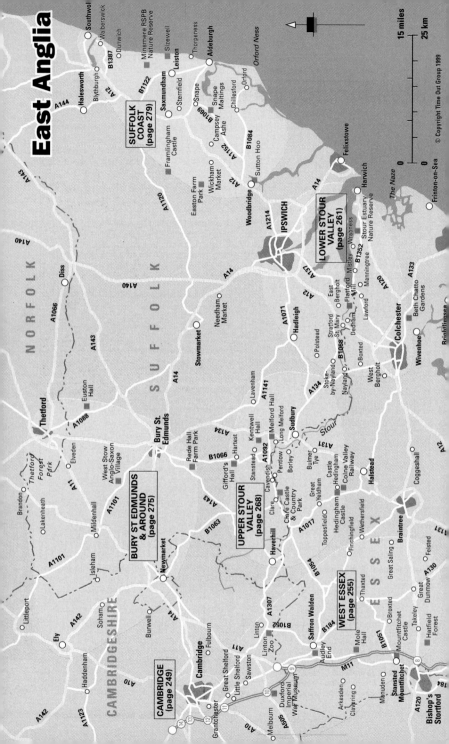

Cambridge

As cities go, they don't come much more laid-back...

*A rural idyll in the centre of a city – cows grazing on **The Backs**.*

There is a casual air to Cambridge that lingers in the stonework of the old town centre, that drifts in the breeze above the rippling waters of the River Cam and permeates the grassy glades that edge the town to the south and west and encroach upon parts of the centre that should, by rights, be built up with houses and roads and multi-storey car parks. This is a green and pleasant town, with a character that intermingles the lofty and distracted mind of academia (the kind that sits around waiting for an apple to drop) and the mildly more industrious life of a market town.

Cambridge stretches out across its grass commons and pastures, but the historic centre

of town (where the majority of the sights are situated) is compact and easily walkable. Indeed, much of the central area is semi-pedestrianised, the red-brick roads encouraging the unwary to wander with carefree abandon. This, however, is just what the cyclists are waiting for, and with a stealthy silence they will mow you down with an equally free abandon, chiming their little bells in celebration.

Many of these bell-ringing free-wheelers are students of the University, and it is the college buildings that draw in the majority of visitors who throng here. Cambridge became a centre of learning in the thirteenth century, when some sort of fracas at Oxford – apparently involving a dead woman, an arrow and a scholar holding a bow – led to some of the learned minds bidding a hasty farewell to Oxford and a hearty hello to Cambridge. Cambridge was chosen because of its ecclesiastical connections – there were several orders of monks in the town and they were looked to for the provision of teachers. The first college, Peterhouse, was established in 1284 and the most recent,

By train from London

Trains run direct from **King's Cross** to **Cambridge** twice an hour and take about **50mins**. Note that the railway station is a good mile's walk from the city centre.

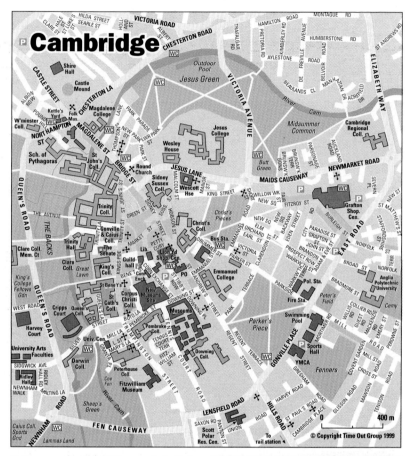

Robinson, was built in 1977 – a reminder that Cambridge isn't all history and is very much a thriving centre of academic (and particularly scientific) research.

Cambridge is certainly a town for those who love their architecture, and the legacy in stone includes the Saxon St Bene't Church, the late Gothic magnificence of King's College Chapel and the classicism of Christopher Wren (the Wren Library and Emmanuel College) and James Gibbs (King's College). Such culturally high-brow material probably won't hold the same attraction for kids, but then, so long as the weather is fine, strolling The Backs (the cattle-grazed grasslands behind the colleges bordering the Cam), splashing about in boats and picnicking in Grantchester Meadows offer simpler and timeless pleasures.

Where to stay

Cambridge is notoriously lacking in classy accommodation in all price brackets. The top of the range – the **Garden House Hotel** (01223 259988) – is frighteningly expensive, while many of the B&Bs are functional, fusty and rather dull. We've attempted to sift out the best in all categories, but be warned that it doesn't pay to have too high expectations in this town.

46 Panton Street

46 Panton Street, CB2 1HS
(01223 365285/fax 01223 461142).
Rates (B&B) *double/twin* £65. **Rooms** 1 double (en suite); 1 twin. **Cards** MC, V.

This small nineteenth-century terrace house is on a quiet street just around the corner from the Botanic Gardens. There's a pleasant-looking pub across the road and the town centre is no more than a ten-minute walk. Just two rooms are available and this obviously makes for an intimate atmosphere. The proprietor, Alice Percival, is clearly proud of her elegant and well-maintained rooms, and this is very much a place for a quiet and sedate stay. As there are no communal areas, guests are asked to vacate the property during the day. Non-smoking throughout.

Arundel House Hotel

Chesterton Road, CB4 3AN
(01223 367701/fax 01223 367721).
Rates (B&ContB) *single* £49-£69; *double/twin* £65-£92.50; *family* £89.50-£98. Breakfast £3.95 (Eng).
Rooms (all en suite) 40 single; 65 double/twin/family. **Cards** AmEx, DC, Debit, MC, V.

Arundel House receives a lot of recommendations, but this must be more for its proximity to the centre of town (five minutes' walk) and views over Jesus Green than for the bedrooms, which feature uninspiring expanses of magnolia porridge paper. Though hardly the most luxurious of places, the décor in the rooms is constantly being updated. An old coaching inn at the back of the building has been converted into bedrooms and conference facilities; the rooms are a little fresher than those in the main building. Children welcome. Non-smoking rooms available.

Garden House Hotel

Granta Place, Mill Lane, CB2 1RT
(01223 259988/fax 01223 316605).
Rates *single occupancy* £135-£160; *double* £165-£190; *deluxe double/twin* £245; *suite* £360. Breakfast £13.50 (Eng); £11.50 (cont). **Rooms** (all en suite) 63 double; 32 twin; 21 deluxe double/twin/suites. **Cards** AmEx, DC, Debit, MC, V.

A modern hotel in a prime location with a private garden on the banks of the River Cam. About half of the rooms overlook the river and the meadows beyond, and although this concrete and brick affair isn't what you might call pretty, it does offer more elegant and spacious rooms than most, as well as an indoor (unheated) swimming pool and riverside restaurant. Children welcome. Non-smoking rooms available.

Holiday Inn

Downing Street, CB2 3DT (01223 464466/fax 01223 464440/www.holiday-inn.co.uk/camb).
Rates *single occupancy* £122-£157; *double/twin* £149; *deluxe double/twin* £156-£164; *suite* £174-£187. Breakfast £11.95 (cont/Eng). **Rooms** (all en suite) 141 double/twin; 18 deluxe double/twin; 6 suites. **Cards** AmEx, DC, Debit, MC, V.

The façade of this large hotel, plumb in the centre of town, is a mild-mannered piece of 1980s neo-classicism, which more or less sets the tone for what you find inside – an atmosphere that, like Switzerland, is keen to maintain its neutrality. The Holiday Inn's principal attractions are location and the guarantee of a certain standard, with pristine air-conditioned rooms. There is, of course, a restaurant and also a well-patronised bar. The best deals on rates can be picked up either from Teletext or the Internet, bringing the cost down to around the price of one of the more expensive B&Bs. Children and dogs welcome. Non-smoking rooms available. Some rooms fully equipped for disabled visitors.

Sleeperz Hotel: *good, cheap, very popular.*

Sleeperz Hotel

Station Road, CB1 2TZ (01223 304050/fax 01223 357286/info@sleeperz.com/www.sleeperz.com).
Rates (B&ContB) *single* £25-£32; *twin* £38; *double* £47; *family* £55. **Rooms** (all en suite) 4 double; 20 twin; 1 family. **Cards** Debit, MC, V.

This relatively new hotel, next to the station, was hewn from a former granary. The conversion has made exceptional use of space, creating simple modern cells influenced in equal measure by Scandinavia and Japan. Each room, in which the swing of a cat would result in a swift call from the RSPCA, has an en suite shower and a small portable TV. Twin rooms make use of space-saving bunks, while doubles use low-slung futon bases but with more substantial mattresses. Sleeperz is ideal for youngish or just youthful visitors who will be out and about for most of the day and evening. Excellent value for money. Children welcome. Non-smoking throughout.

Suffolk House

69 Milton Road, CB4 1XA
(01223 352016/fax 01223 566816).
Rates (B&B) *double/twin* £65-£75; *family* £75-£90.
Rooms (all en suite) 4 double; 2 twin; 2 family.
Cards AmEx, Debit, MC, V.

Suffolk House is one of many undistinguished B&Bs on roads towards the edge of the town centre. Milton Road is to the north and the guesthouse is equidistant from the Grafton Shopping Centre and the heart of Cambridge (about a 15-minute walk to each). The rooms are clean and tidy with floral print wallpaper and a few prints of the Cambridge colleges dotted around. The breakfast room looks out over a surprisingly large and attractive garden. All rooms have TVs. Non-smoking throughout.

Where to eat & drink

Surprisingly for a town with so much wealth splashing around, there are few really good restaurants in Cambridge. In fact, if the weather is fine, a picnic assembled from the various delis, bakeries and wine merchants in the centre of town and taken to The Backs or Grantchester Meadows would be the ideal way to partake of a leisurely lunch or early evening repast. That said, there are of course exceptions to the rule; **Midsummer House Restaurant** being the most notable. If you want your spending to be rather more modest, it's worth knowing that there's a **Café Rouge** on Bridge Street opposite St John's College (01223 364961), and a **Dôme** on St Andrew's Street (01223 313818), right next to the Varsity. Alternatively, if you just want something basic to eat, perhaps washed down with some of the rather good Suffolk ales that are served hereabouts, then it is as well to stick to a pub. You can usually get a meal for about a fiver in some kind of creaky old inn with twisted floorboards and scalp-taking beams. The **Eagle** on Bene't Street (01223 505020) is the one that usually receives all the plaudits, but in truth there are many of equal merit, including the **Pickeral Inn** on Magdalene Street just to the north of the bridge (01223 355068), **Fort St George** by the river on Midsummer Common (01223 354327), the **Mill** (01223 357026) and the **Anchor** (01223 353554), which are practically next door to each other on the river between Granta Place and Silver Street, and **Bath Ale House**, back on Bene't Street (01223 350969).

22 Chesterton Road

22 Chesterton Road (01223 351880).
Food served 7-9.45pm Tue-Sat. **Set meals** £23.50 (4 courses). **Cards** AmEx, DC, Debit, MC, V.

This tiny, candlelit restaurant close to the Cam offers a globally influenced menu. Not everything comes off, but there are more hits than misses, and a very good wine list. Examples of mains include roast skate wings with pancetta, capers and herbs, and grilled herb polenta with roast vegetables, black olives and pesto dressing; desserts include pear and walnut upside down pudding.

Copper Kettle

King's Parade (01223 365068).
Food served 8.30am-5.30pm Mon-Sat; 9am-5.30pm Sun.

Not actually a restaurant, but a good place for tea and cakes just beyond the shadow of King's College Chapel. The view from the glass-fronted room takes in the fanciful gateway to the courtyard of King's College and the James Gibbs neo-classical building beyond.

Dojo

Miller's Yard, Mill Lane (01223 363471).
Food served noon-2.30pm, 5.30-11pm, Mon-Thur; noon-11pm Fri-Sun. **Cards** Debit, MC, V.

Essentially a Japanese restaurant with the emphasis on noodles, the menu at Dojo extends around the Pacific Rim to take in a smattering of Chinese fry-ups and one or two Thai-style dishes: expect to find such delights as mussels with onion and chillis in a spicy black bean sauce, and ramen with char-grilled chicken in teriyaki sauce. The small interior is simple and geometric, with plain wooden furniture. A meal with a Kirin shouldn't set you back more than a tenner.

Loch Fyne Oyster Restaurant

37 Trumpington Street (01223 362433).
Food served 11.30am-10pm Mon-Sat; 11.30am-8pm Sun. **Cards** AmEx, Debit, MC, V.

This is one of a handful of offshoots from the Loch Fyne Oyster Bar in Western Scotland, where the restaurants' smokehouse and oyster beds are situated. It's an informal place and you are welcome to pick and mix your dishes from across the menu. The shellfish platters served on ice (£16.95) are utterly sumptuous, if a trifle daunting, while a more rustic soup will cost £3-£6.

Michel's

21-24 Northampton Street (01223 353110).
Food served noon-2.30pm, 6-10.30pm, daily.
Set meals *lunch* £6.95 (2 courses); £8.45 (3 courses).
Cards AmEx, DC, Debit, MC, V.

This is a bright and breezy restaurant, just to the north of Magdalene Bridge and, therefore, outside the throng of the town centre. It has two pleasant rooms of white-clothed tables and a Modern European menu that has a hankering for Italy. Healthy foods such as fish, pasta and chicken predominate and there are great lunchtime deals to be had: two courses for £6.95; three for £8.45.

Midsummer House Restaurant

Midsummer Common (01223 369299).
Food served noon-2pm, 7-10pm, Tue-Fri; 7-10pm Sat; noon-2pm Sun. **Set meals** *lunch* £19.50 (3 courses) Mon-Fri; £25 (3 courses) Sun; *dinner* £39.50 (3 courses). **Cards** AmEx, Debit, MC, V.

This is a great restaurant by any standards, and in Cambridge it stands out a mile, enticingly sited on the northern edge of Midsummer Common by the banks of the Cam. The menu is inventive and modern, offering a short selection of mainly French-influenced dishes; the wine list is extensive, and the choice of house wines (six red, six white) starts at £12. Vegetarian meals are cooked on request, but it's a good idea to call ahead of time to ensure a decent choice. Service is friendly, and a passion for food is evident from waiters, who are keen to explain the nuances of the dishes.

Varsity

St Andrew's Street (01223 356060).
Food served noon-2.30pm, 5.30-10.45pm, Mon-Sat; noon-10pm Sun. **Set meals** £9.95 (4 courses).
Cards AmEx, DC, Debit, MC, V.

The Varsity, heading south from the town centre on the road to the station, offers a Cypriot menu. The vegetable mezedes (£8.50) give vegetarians a fair number of options, while the grills (from £5.90) cater for the more carnivorous. The décor is simple, with plenty of exposed wood, plain white walls and a scattering of mirrors and glass to add to the illusion of space.

What to see & do

Cambridge is essentially a small, semi-rural town in a beautiful setting. The main attraction is more the town itself than specific things within it, and people come to imbibe the centuries of history and that deep-scented ambience of academia. When the weather's fine, a walk along The Backs will give a sense of the pastoral side of Cambridge, and a stroll across Coe Fen from Mill Lane will take you in the direction of the Fitzwilliam Museum.

Punting to Grantchester

Grantchester is a tiny village, lying just two miles upriver from Cambridge. It is famed for its association with Rupert Brooke, who grew up there and penned a paean to the village (*The Old Vicarage, Grantchester*) in which he famously asked 'And is there honey still for tea?' Indeed there is, at the **Orchard Tea Rooms**, which also functions as a homage to the poet. There's also beer and grub at the three pubs that service this rural idyll - the **Red Lion**, **Green Man** and **Rupert Brooke**.

The meadows between Grantchester and Cambridge were more recently made famous by Pink Floyd, in one of their quieter moments from the 1960s *Ummagumma* album. When the weather is balmy and the lush grasslands sway in the East Anglian summer breeze, Grantchester makes for a splendid little escape from the bustle of the town, and the traditional means of getting there is by punt.

Now, in the modern world, with its sextants and oars and suchlike, using a long stick to push a boat may seem an outmoded means of aquatic propulsion, but then Cambridge is a town that thrives on its well-worn traditions. If you do take to one of these flat-bottomed boats, the thing to remember is that punting is a meditative experience and should be undertaken in the manner of a gliding swan. If you ever reach walking pace, you are clearly over-exerting yourself. A booklet published by Scudamore's Boatyards in Granta Place advises you on the correct technique.

Punting to Grantchester can take between an hour and an hour and a half. Given that you'll probably want to stay in the village for an hour or two, the whole trip could take about four or five hours and at £10 per hour this may prove quite expensive, depending on how many there are of you. A shorter but still delightful trip would be to punt into the meadows for a picnic. And if you are put off by the technicalities of punting, chauffeured boats, cycling or walking along the towpath are all agreeable alternatives (and almost certainly quicker).

East Anglia

Tourist information centre

The Old Library, Wheeler Street, CB2 3QB (01223 322640/www.cambridge.gov.uk/leisure/index.htm). **Open** *Apr-Oct* 10am-6.30pm Mon-Fri; 10am-5pm Sat; 11am-4pm Sun; *Nov-Mar* 10am-5.30pm Mon-Fri; 10am-5pm Sat.

Bike hire

Geoff's Bike Hire, 65 Devonshire Road (01223 365629). Conveniently located near the train station.

Botanic Gardens

Corey Lodge, Bateman Street (01223 336265). **Open** *Apr-Sept* 10am-6pm daily; *Nov-Mar* 10am-4pm daily. **Admission** £2; £1.50 5s-17s, OAPs.

The Botanic Gardens belong to the University and was established in the early nineteenth century. The layout is quite formal for an English garden, with a broad central avenue leading up to a fountain and terrace garden. Though pleasant, the low rumble of traffic is never far away, and so, if you simply want to escape the rigours of city life, a walk along the towpath to the meadows is a better option. If you're into your botany, however, the alkaline soil here supports plants of a contrasting nature to the national collections at Kew and Edinburgh.

The Colleges

Trinity College Trinity Street (01223 338400); *Emmanuel College* St Andrew's Street (01223 334200); *Clare College* Trinity Lane (01223 333200).

Each of the colleges is independently run and the cost and times for being allowed to wander through the hallowed halls and around the green courtyards vary from college to college. What you can expect for your money also varies greatly, from the splendour of **Trinity** (one of the largest) and the elegance of Wren's **Emmanuel College** to the dreary **Clare College**, its dark hall hung with some dreadful old portraits of its alumni. There are many restrictions imposed upon visitors (which parts of the colleges are accessible, etc) and during exam time (May and early June) most colleges are closed to the public while students get their heads down. So don't go expecting to see more than the surface veneer of university life. However, with a vivid imagination, it is fun to conjure up the great names of the past who would have passed this way – a young Lord Byron bathing in the fountain at Trinity with his pet bear (regulations forbade the keeping of a dog); Wittgenstein reclining in his deckchair; and Newton, sitting on the grass outside the gate of Trinity, still waiting for that apple to drop. Check out the college's website at www.cam.ac.uk.

Fitzwilliam Museum

Trumpington Street (01223 332900/www.fitzmuseum.cam.ac.uk). **Open** 10am-5pm Tue-Sat; 2.15-5pm Sun. **Admission** free.

This is a wonderfully diverse and much under-visited museum. Some of the highlights include the Egyptian collection, which, besides some great funerary gear, includes surprising smaller finds, such as a broken section of frieze depicting a jackal attacking a duck's nest and the blue-glazed snout of a hippopotamus. Among the great paintings in the collection are a portable altarpiece by Fra Filippo Lippi, some Rubens oil sketches and Joos van Cleve's *Virgin and Child*.

Kettle's Yard

Castle Street (01223 352124/www.kettlesyard.co.uk). **Open** *house* 1.30-4.30pm Tue-Sat; 2-4.30pm Sun, bank hols; *gallery* 12.30-5.30pm Tue-Sat; 2-5.30pm Sun, bank hols. **Admission** free.

Located to the north of the town centre, just a short stroll over Magdalene Bridge, Kettle's Yard comprises a house with a collection of twentieth-century artworks, among them works by Brancusi, Miró and Hepworth, and an art gallery with a changing programme of contemporary and modern art. Phone for details of chamber music concerts held in the house.

King's College Chapel

Kings Parade (01223 331155/www.kings.cam.ac.uk). **Open** *term time* 9.30am-3.30pm daily; *holidays* 9.30am-4.30pm daily. **Admission** £3; £2 12s-16s, students.

The narrowness of this lengthy chapel emphasises its height to great effect, as do the slender, linear columns that stretch up to an explosion of fan vaulting – a Perpendicular Gothic extravagance that has no equal in Britain. The altarpiece below the east window comes from Rubens' workshop (a much earlier version of Andy Warhol's Factory). Concerts and services take place throughout the year, which visitors may attend.

Round Church (Church of the Holy Sepulchre)

Bridge Street (01223 518219). **Open** 9.30am-5pm daily; *Oct-Mar* 11.30am-4.30pm daily. **Admission** free.

A twelfth-century medieval church, although the Norman appearance is a style lent to it much later (in the nineteenth century) by some overzealous restorers. Its circular format is very rare in Britain and was based upon the Church of the Holy Sepulchre in Jerusalem.

St Bene't Church

Bene't Street (01223 353903). **Open** 8.30am-6pm daily. **Admission** free.

With its Saxon tower, St Bene't (a contraction of St Benedict) is the oldest surviving building in Cambridge. It was the original chapel of Corpus Christi College and is handily located just opposite the Eagle pub and the Bath Ale House.

Punting under the bridges

This slow-paced means of transport is ideal for casting a leisurely eye over the colleges, their manicured gardens and the bridges that link the town to the country. And if you are feeling too lazy even for this minor jaunt, you can hire someone else to do the work in a chauffeured punt. This is quite a good idea, in fact, as chauffeurs double as guides to the colleges and bridges, such as Bridge of Sighs (a copy of the Venetian original) and the Mathematical Bridge (now in its third incarnation since first built in the mid-eighteenth century). Punts are available at various points along the river, though most are hired from Granta Place at the end of Mill Lane (*see page 253* **Punting to Grantchester**).

West Essex

Its heyday may be over, but this pocket of the country still boasts plenty of lost-in-time charm.

The bookish charms of **Saffron Walden**.

While most attempts to recreate Olde England appear contrived or unconvincing, this pocket of Essex ('Uttlesford', as the area is sometimes referred to) on the western edge of East Anglia is suspiciously close to the picture-book past we always imagined. It's a working landscape, not a living museum, but at the same time it's one of those places where the classic elements of our assumed past – thatched wooden cottages; rolling countryside; windmills; winding lanes; ancient forests; obscure traditions – are all present and correct.

Saffron Walden was something of a boom town in the Middle Ages, benefitting from its proximity to Roman trade routes and its agricultural resources, but with additional wealth from ephemeral moneyspinners such as saffron and cutlery, there was extra cash to throw around. Evidence of those medieval good times is still plentiful today, in the form of orderly market towns, sprawling manor houses and extravagantly well-appointed churches, but the Uttlesford miracle was never destined to last. The Industrial Revolution passed the area by almost completely, and by the eighteenth century fortunes were ultimately tied to agriculture, until the lucre of London began to draw away the population.

Less is more

The silver lining to this steady decline, and one of the most persuasive reasons for coming here, is, of course, a rustic tranquillity that most of the country lost hundreds of years ago. Apart from the M11, which runs through the middle of the area, between Stansted Airport to the south and Cambridge to the north, there is very little to

By train from London

The nearest station to Saffron Walden is **Audley End**: about four trains an hour go there direct from **Liverpool Street**. The journey takes about **1hr**.

interfere with the peace and quiet. Despite being easily accessible and close to tourist-friendly Cambridge, it's off the viewfinder for most foreign coach parties – again an advantage for those in search of the urban antidote.

There's not necessarily a great deal to *do*, in the modern theme-park, passive-entertainment sense. But with innumerable public footpaths, quiet roads and large tracts of common land, it's ideal country for walking, cycling or even horse riding. What sights there are are typically historical remnants free of tourist-grabbing gimmickry and commercial repackaging, although city kids might find these subtleties just downright boring. Attempts to re-brand the area along the lines of neighbouring 'Constable Country' should be discouraged; there's already a Dick Turpin heritage route (he was born in Hempstead), and a few disturbing references to the area as 'Lovejoy Country' (*see also page 260*).

Running north-south alongside the M11 and the River Cam, the B184 connects three principal historic towns, Saffron Walden, Thaxted and Great Dunmow, although virtually any road out of these towns will pass through a picturesque little village.

Mellow yellow

Saffron Walden dates back to pre-Roman times, and received its name and much of its wealth from the obscure source of the saffron crocus (it was originally called Chipping Walden), which was prized for its colouring, flavouring and medicinal applications. Uttlesford was the national saffron centre between the fifteenth and eighteenth centuries, until explorers discovered it could be obtained abroad for a fraction of the price. Now a Conservation Area, the town's compact centre hasn't changed much since those times, consisting of a central Market Square (there's still a market on Tuesday and Saturday) surrounded by narrow lanes (now dominated by antiques shops, as much of the region seems to be) and thinning out to generous townhouses towards the outskirts. Some 400 wobbly, oak-framed and wattle-and-daubed buildings survive, displaying characteristics you'll find throughout the region such as overhanging upper storeys and pastel-coloured plasterwork with ornate patterns known as pargetting – for the most extreme example visit the Sun Inn on Church Street. Later Georgian and Victorian architecture also abounds, particularly the Italianate Corn Exchange (now the library) in the Square. East of the Square, on the ancient common, is an even older relic – the turf maze, said to be the largest in the country and to date back more than 800 years. It's more than a mile long in total, and not as easy to master as it

looks. There's also a Victorian hedge maze, modelled on Hampton Court's, in the attractive Bridge End Gardens, though an appointment is required.

Thaxted life

Ten minutes down the B184, **Thaxted** has a similar history and make-up to Saffron Walden, but fewer twentieth-century interventions like high street stores and banks (although there's an intriguing armour shop). It has been consistently praised over the years as one of the most charming villages in the country; John Betjeman admired its 'beauty, compactness and juxtaposition of medieval and Georgian architecture', composer Gustav Holst completed *The Planets* here (the music festival he originated still takes place here during June-July; 01371 831421), and many London émigrés have decamped to Thaxted, adding a cosmopolitan edge to its friendly, everyone-knows-everyone atmosphere. A precarious three-storey Guildhall is the town's centrepiece, and one of the best surviving examples in the country, although its widely touted connection with the Cutlers' Guild is disputed by some historians. On the hill behind it, next to the windmill, the magnificent fourteenth-century church is another source of local pride (the

Saffron Walden's *Sun Inn*.

East Anglia

finest in England, they'll tell you), with a white-painted perpendicular-arched interior and intricately carved ceiling. Even the graveyard is pretty. The vicar, Father Richard, is a genial source of local knowledge, although his predecessor in the 1920s, Conrad Noel, is remembered less fondly for running up the communist and Sinn Fein flags and slashing the tyres of incensed protesters. Noel's wife was, however, instrumental in turning the village into a Morris-dancing mecca (*see page 259* **Stick it**).

Bringing home the bacon

Carry on south down the same road and you'll reach **Great Dunmow**, another ancient market town, similar to Saffron Walden and Thaxted. Great Dunmow's claim to fame is the Flitch Trials, in which a flitch of bacon is awarded to couples who manage not to 'quarrel, differ or dispute' for a year and a day after their marriage. They are then paraded through town on the 'bacon chair', which sits in Little Dunmow parish church. The none-too-serious custom dates back to the twelfth century and was revived this century, taking place every leap year.

There are innumerable stereotypically lovely villages in the surrounding area, most notably **Clavering**, **Manuden** and **Hazel End**, along the Stort Valley to the west of the M11, and **Linton** and **Melbourn Bury**, just south of Cambridge. East of Thaxted, complete with duck pond, river, windmill and village green, **Finchingfield** is commonly labelled 'the most photogenic village in Essex', if not necessarily the most peaceful. The area is popular with motorcyclists, who like to congregate in the village after speeding through these otherwise serene country roads of a weekend, much to the retired villagers' consternation.

Where to stay

In this area, large hotels are uncommon, and even B&Bs are relatively thin on the ground and consequently fill up rapidly during the summer. Many family-run places prefer to cater for weekly business clients and have the weekend to themselves. Below are some of the most amenable to weekend guests.

Crossways Guest House

32 Town Street, Thaxted, CM6 2LA (01371 830348). **Rates** (B&B) *single occupancy* £30; *double/twin* £48. **Rooms** (all en suite) 2 double; 1 double/twin.

Right in the centre of town, just opposite the Guildhall, this sixteenth-century townhouse is perfectly situated and immaculately presented. Proprietors Michael and Pepe have been in the business for 20 years, and have their presentation and unpretentious cooking down to a tee. There are two double rooms upstairs overlooking the High Street, and an adjoining lodge in the back garden with a twin/double, all with en suite bathrooms and décor that stops just short of kitsch. There's also a pleasant tearoom at the front. Children welcome. All bedrooms non-smoking.

Homelye Farm

Braintree Road, Great Dunmow, CM6 3AW (01371 872127/876528). **Rates** (B&B) *single* £25-£30; *double/twin* £45; *family* £65. **Rooms** (all en suite) 3 single; 3 double; 2 twin; 1 family. **Cards** Debit, MC, V.

A secluded working farmstead just off the A120 (though only ten minutes from Stansted Airport) with a converted fourteenth-century stable block next to the house containing three cosy little doubles, each with en suite shower. Wholesome English breakfasts as you'd expect, and in the summer, there's a small meadow where guests can eat al fresco, looking over the rolling fields. The Pickford family will happily provide a tour of the farm. Children welcome. Non-smoking throughout.

1 mile E of Great Dunmow off A120; turn into lane opposite water tower; farm is at bottom of lane.

Purlins

12 High Street, Little Shelford, CB2 5ES (tel/fax 01223 842643). **Rates** (B&B) *single occupancy* £35-£40; *double* £43-£55. **Rooms** (all en suite) 3 double.

This unconventional house was built in 1978 to the design of proprietors Olga and David Hindley, and features plenty of light, a conservatory, full-height central space and period 1970s furnishings throughout. Rooms (two at the back upstairs, one downstairs facing the road but well sound-insulated) are fairly small but homely. A major plus, though you'd never guess from the street, is the two-acre back garden, gloriously untended and populated by wild flowers, pheasants and the occasional deer. Another is the owners: David is a former music lecturer at Cambridge University, and was once the subject of a QED documentary! No smoking throughout. Children aged eight or over welcome.

A1301 S from Cambridge; follow signs on right to Little Shelford.

Recorders House

Town Street, Thaxted, CM6 2LD (01371 830438/fax 01371 831645). **Rates** (B&B) *single occupancy* £40/£50; *double* £60/£75. **Rooms** (both en suite) 2 double. **Cards** MC, V.

Something of a well-kept secret, the two double rooms above the restaurant (*see p258*) are just about the best in the area if you're looking for something historic and out of the ordinary. The house dates back to the seventeenth century and much of the original linenfold wood panelling is still present, not to mention strange angles and, of course, exposed beams. There are also open fireplaces for those winter nights, though there's nothing primitive about the rest of the facilities. The top room is larger and more expensive but also has a Jacuzzi. No smoking in bedrooms.

Springfield

16 Horn Lane, Linton, CB1 6HT (01223 891383/fax 01223 890335/

East Anglia

www.smoothhound.co.uk/hotels/springf2.html).
Rates (B&B) £20-£22pp. Special breaks.
Rooms 2 double (1 en suite).

An elegant converted Victorian schoolhouse in a quiet corner of another historic village. Two airy double bedrooms (another twin is available at a push) look out on to a pretty river at the bottom of extensive gardens. Guests also have their own dining room and lounge downstairs, and there's a grass tennis court in the garden. The house retains original Regency décor and fittings, plus a fragrant plant-filled conservatory, which is pleasant to dine in. Serene proprietor Judith Rossiter lives here with dog and children, and can arrange horse riding on the nearby Ickfield Way. Meals other than breakfast are not provided but there is decent food available at the Crown Inn around the corner. Children welcome. Non-smoking throughout.

Approaching Linton along A1307 SW of Cambridge; left into High Street then first right after the Crown pub into Horn Lane; house on right next to chapel.

The Starr

Market Place, Great Dunmow, CM6 1AX
(01371 874321/www.zynet.co.uk/menu/starr).
Rates (B&B) *single occupancy* £60; *double/twin* £90-£105; *four-poster* £105. **Rooms** (all en suite) 1 twin; 6 double; 1 four-poster. **Cards** AmEx, DC, Debit, MC, V.

A sixteenth-century former coaching inn, now a popular restaurant (*see p259*) with eight rooms in a converted stable block behind. Jovial proprietor Brian Jones designed the interiors himself, each with an individual theme and colour scheme (Lemon, Peach, Poppy, etc). The facilities are reassuringly modern but there are well-selected antique furnishings, too. On the downside, none of the rooms is extravagantly spacious, though all are well lit; also, being situated on the main road, views are limited, though noise is not a problem. Two of the rooms are slightly more expensive – the flagship Oak Room includes a Victorian iron bathtub at the foot of the four-poster bed. The breakfasts are also a point in favour. Children and dogs welcome. All bedrooms non-smoking.

Great Dunmow is where the A120 meets A130.

Whitehall

Church End, Broxted, CM6 2BZ (01279 850603).
Rates *single* £90; *double/twin* £115; *deluxe double* £145; *suite* £220. Breakfast £10 (cont.), £6 (cont.).
Rooms (all en suite) 5 twin; 14 double; 6 deluxe double; 1 suite. **Cards** AmEx, DC, Debit, MC, V.

Close to Stansted Airport, this sprawling Elizabethan manor house has been sensitively refurbished, and provides some of the most luxurious accommodation in the area. Rooms are individually named; those in the original house are more pleasant than those in the new extension (exposed beams, wonky angles, original furnishings, including oak panelling and a stone fireplace in the Garden Room), though all are spacious with good views over the well-maintained gardens. The restaurant/bar/lounge areas are similarly well appointed, especially the double-height medieval banquet hall with its exposed studwork. Special weekend food-and-board packages are a good option if you've just come to put your feet up and relax. One drawback is that the hotel regularly hosts wedding parties, during which times peace and quiet may become rare commodities.

Take A120 E of Stansted Airport; follow signs for Broxted.

You won't need to drive far in this area to find a decent country pub, though you might have trouble finding a specific destination in this maze of country lanes. Fine dining, as you'd expect, is thinner on the ground, but not altogether absent.

In addition to the places below, there's good grub at the sixteenth-century **Cricketers** in Clavering (01799 550442) and good drinking at the **Flitch of Bacon** in Little Dunmow, the **Eight Bells** in Saffron Walden and a big garden and good animal-petting at the **Bell** in Wendens Ambo. TV chef Steven Saunders's **Pink Geranium** (23 Station Road, Melbourn; 01763 260215) and recently acquired **Sheene Mill** (also in Melbourn; 01763 261393), 12 or so miles south-west of Cambridge, are also local destination dining spots.

Axe & Compasses

Arkesden (01799 550272).
Food served noon-2pm, 6.45-9.30pm, daily.
Set meals *lunch* £12 (3 courses) Sun.
Cards Debit, MC, V.

One of the most renowned pubs in the region, for both its relaxed atmosphere and exceptional food. It's a thatched seventeenth-century building situated in an attractive corner of the middle of nowhere, and is divided into several spaces, with dark beams, polished brasses, horse paraphernalia and open fireplaces. Food is extensive in range and slightly more than provincial in scope, from snacks like focaccia topped with Stilton and onions up to monkfish or roast pepper sauce or grilled polenta with stir-fried vegetables. The steak and kidney pie is a winner. Mains range from about £6.95 to £15.

Dicken's Restaurant

The Green, Wethersfield (01371 850723).
Food served 12.30-2pm, 7.30-9.30pm, Wed-Sat; 12.30-2pm Sun. **Set meals** £9.75 (2 courses).
Cards Debit, MC, V.

Owner of this relaxed and popular place (it's often fully booked on a Saturday night), John Dicken adds his personal touch to the olde-worlde charm provided by the interior. Food is traditional-based with Mediterranean accents: wholesome soups (fish is a favourite); game dishes that manage to be sumptuous without requiring a health warning; simple desserts and a respectable wine list. Good value for money. Mains start at £10.75.

Recorders House Restaurant

Town Street, Thaxted (01371 830438).
Food served noon-2pm, 7-10pm, Tue-Sat; noon-2pm Sun. **Set meals** *lunch* £8.75 (one course), £10.75 (two courses), £12.75 (three courses) Tue-Sat; £14.75 (two courses), £17.95 (three courses) Sun.
Cards MC, V.

Lee Newsome used to be head chef at the Savoy, and he has given a new lease of life to this long-running institution with imaginative, refreshingly cosmopolitan dishes of fresh fish, meat and game, such as braised pig's trotter stuffed with goose liver and wild mushrooms

Stick it

Visit Thaxted on the first weekend after Spring Bank Holiday and you'll find the entire town taken over by white-shirted men with bells on their stockings, waving scarves, banging sticks together and exclaiming things like 'Wassail!'. It may be laughable to outsiders, but Morris dancing is very much a cherished rural tradition, not just in this area but across the country; it's intensively studied, analysed and practised, and dances are often unfathomably complex (is that the Upton-upon-Severn Stick Dance or Ladies of Pleasure in the Bledington Tradition?). At the heart of this living folklore, Thaxted is host to the Morris community's annual get-together, and on the day, a carnival-like atmosphere pervades the town. More than 200 dancers from across the country converge on the town, touring the local pubs and villages over the afternoon before filling the High Street in the evening for mass dances and drinking (in roughly equal proportions), culminating in the 'Abbots Bromley' Horn Dance, performed by the Thaxted Morris in splendid antler-headed costume.

Morris dancing didn't originate in Essex, but Thaxted was instrumental in its modern revival. Nobody really knows where it started. It's one of those traditions that's been shaped by our imagined folk heritage as much as actual events, and it's such a quintessential part of Englishness that it's almost disappointing to discover it hasn't been around forever. Like maypoles, hobby horses and cheese rolling, it's often held as a relic of our pagan past, though it's just as likely to have come from France or Spain as recently as the fourteenth century. Wherever it started, it had just about died out altogether at the beginning of the 1900s, until various middle-class academics, particularly Cecil Sharp, inspired by a general revival in all things folkloric, decided to 'take the Morris back to the villages'. The Morris Ring was founded in 1934 and Thaxted was designated as its meeting place.

Throughout the summer, especially on bank holidays, Morris dancers are a common sight in the country pubs of the area, whether the academic, men-only Ring Side or the unisex 'let's just have a laugh' Open Side (fiercely opposing poles in the Morris world, apparently). Traditionally, the landlord buys them the first round, after which they usually call upon the charity of drinkers. Mock them at your peril: they carry big sticks.

with minted pea purée and Madeira jus, or seared panache of fish, julienne of leek and beetroot in a chive beurre blanc sauce, and that's just the starters (£6-£8; mains are £16-£20). Perplexingly elaborate but knowledgeably handled. The refurbished sixteenth-century interior features an open fireplace, and extends into a large conservatory out the back. *See also p257.*

The Restaurant
Church Street, Saffron Walden (01799 526444).
Food served noon-2pm, 7.30-10pm, Tue-Sat.
Cards Debit, MC, V.
If you've seen enough exposed beams to last a lifetime and crave a breath of modernity, this newish venture is a sound option. It's a basement space, divided into smoking and non-smoking rooms, with bare brick walls and clean colours. The simple décor is matched by a refreshingly concise menu, which includes dishes such as monkfish with a Thai-style green curry sauce, and pan-fried spring lamb stuffed with fresh herbs served with a port wine sauce. Produce is organic wherever possible, the wine cellar is well stocked and reasonably priced, and service is polite but casual. Main courses start from £8.95 and go up to £15.95.

The Starr
Market Place, Great Dunmow (01371 874321).
Food served noon-1.30pm, 7-9.30pm, Mon-Sat; noon-1.30pm Sun. **Set meals** *lunch* £11-£19.50 (2 courses), £24.50 (3 courses); *dinner* £21.80-£35 (3 courses). **Cards** AmEx, DC, Debit, MC, V.
The interior of this local institution matches the cuisine: built on traditional foundations, but with a modern touch to satisfy late turn-of-the-millennium demands. Thus, the 500-year-old interior has been kept up to date, with shiny brass fittings and light furnishings and modern lighting, and a spacious conservatory at the back adds to the openness. On the food front, it's a combination of country standards and international gloss: from the set menu, choose from the likes of fillet of English beef with Roquefort ravioli and horseradish jus; or escalope of veal on fresh leaf spinach with warm pea salsa and mustard cream. Not cutting edge but not, thankfully, over-ambitious either. A good place for Sunday lunch.

White Hart
The Street, Great Saling (01731 850341).
Food served noon-2.30pm, 7-9.30pm, daily.
Cards Debit, MC, V.

*Frolics outside **Audley End House**.*

Another local landmark, partly due to its connection with the *Lovejoy* television series. It's the home of the 'huffer', a traditional, triangular sandwich of soft white bread that forms a decent lunchtime snack. The restaurant proper, in a separate wing, extends to exotica such as red snapper and wild mushroom crumble with herb and hazelnut topping, but at a price (mains from about £8-£11, or £6-£10 in the bar).

What to see & do

Tourist information centres

District Council Offices, 46 High Street, **Great Dunmow**, CM6 1AN (01799 510490). **Open** 8.30am-5pm Mon-Thur; 8.30am-4.30pm Fri.

1 Market Place, **Saffron Walden**, CB10 1HR (01799 510444). **Open** *Apr-Oct* 9.30am-5.30pm Mon-Sat; *Nov-Mar* 10am-5pm Mon-Sat.

Audley End House & Gardens

Saffron Walden (01799 522399).
Open *Apr-Sept* 11am-5pm Wed-Sun; *Oct guided tours only* 10am-3pm Wed-Sun. **Admission** (EH) £6; £3 5s-16s; £4.50 OAPs, students; £15 family.

An unmissable Jacobean house on the grandest of scales, dating back to 1605. Jam-packed with the accumulated wealth of successive aristocratic owners: opulent furnishings; priceless books and artworks; a monumental collection of stuffed birds and animals; an elegant suite of rooms designed by Robert Adam; and beautiful grounds on the River Cam, landscaped by Capability Brown. There are no dry information labels; a guide in each room tells you all you need to know. Phone to book a guided tour (October only).

Duxford Imperial War Museum

Duxford (01223 835000/www.iwm.org.uk/duxford.htm).
Open *Apr-Oct* 10am-6pm daily; *Nov-Mar* 10am-4pm daily. **Admission** £7.20; £5 OAPs; £3.50 students; free under-16s.

Aviation heaven, with over 150 historic aircraft from biplanes to Concorde. Norman Foster designed an award-winning building here (as well as Stansted Airport down the road). Air shows throughout the summer.

Flitch Way

Good route for walking, cycling or riding, along 15 miles of disused railway line from Hatfield Forest through Great

Dunmow to Braintree. Wild flowers and animals as well as Victorian railway architecture. Get the tourist office at Great Dunmow (01799 510490) to send you a leaflet.

Fry Art Gallery

Castle Street, Saffron Walden (01799 513779).
Open *Easter-Oct* 2.30-5.30pm Sat, Sun, bank hols. **Admission** free.

Work by local artists including Eric Ravilious, Edward Bawden and Michael Rothstein.

Hatfield Forest

Takeley, off A120 (01279 870678/
www.nationaltrust.org.uk).
Open *car park Easter-Oct* 10am-5pm daily; *shell house Easter-Oct* 10am-4pm Sat, Sun. **Admission** (NT) *car park* £3 per car; *shell house* donation.

Former medieval royal hunting forest, now pleasant woodland and nature reserve. Plenty of 400-year-old pollarded trees, plus ornamental lakes and an eighteenth-century Shell House, named for its interior, which is decorated with, yes, you guessed it, shells. Pedestrians are allowed into the forest all year round, but the car park inside the forest is open Easter to October only.

Linton Zoo

Hadstock Road, Linton (01223 891308).
Open *Apr-Oct* 10am-6pm daily; *Nov-Mar* 10am-4pm daily. **Admission** £4.50; £3.50 2s-13s; £4.25 OAPs.

Conservation-oriented zoo with emphasis on breeding. Big cats, including white tigers and snow leopards, and other exotic creatures.

Mole Hall

Widdington, nr Newport, Saffron Walden (01799 540400).
Open *Apr-Oct* 10.30am-6pm daily; *Nov-Mar* 10am-4pm daily. **Admission** £4.50; £3.20 3s-15s; £3.80 OAPs; £14 family.

Kid-friendly, family-run wildlife park in 20 acres of grounds, with small monkeys, deer, otters, reptiles and a butterfly hall (closed in winter).

Mountfitchet Castle & House on the Hill Toy Museum

Stansted Mountfitchet
(01279 813237/www.gold.enta.net).
Open *castle mid-Nov-mid-Mar* 10am-5pm daily; *museum* 10am-5pm daily. **Admission** *castle* £4.50; £3.50 2s-14s; £3.80 OAPs; *museum* £3.50; £2.50 2s-14s; £3.20 OAPs.

Award-winning reconstructed Norman motte and bailey castle and village built on an original site, complete with siege weapons and retro farm animals. The adjacent toy museum has over 50,000 exhibits, including a museum of slot machines.

Saffron Walden Museum

Museum Street, Saffron Walden (01799 510333).
Open *Mar-Oct* 10am-5pm Mon-Sat; 2-5pm Sun; *Nov-Feb* 10am-4.30pm Mon-Sat; 2-4.30pm Sun, bank hols. **Admission** £1; OAPs, students; free under-18s.

Good local history from the year dot onwards, plus anthropological, geological and costume exhibitions. Adjacent to the remains of the Norman castle keep.

East Anglia

Lower Stour Valley

On the Constable trail...

The elegant **Wakes Colne Chappel Viaduct**.

John Constable is sometimes credited with having invented the English countryside as we now know it. His images of lush wheatfields and placid rivers have passed into everyone's subconsciousness, and when organisations are set up to protect 'rural England', it's a fair bet to say that most people assume it's a Constable landscape they're most concerned to preserve.

The pieces that make up the Constable picture – locks and mill-ponds, spreading oaks and willows, tumbledown cottages and giant brick waterside mills – are all inseparable from the painter's own home patch of Dedham Vale,

running roughly west and north along the lower Stour (which roughly rhymes with 'brewer', not 'flower') from Dedham up to Nayland and Hadleigh. Ironically, some of the elements that add most to its rural charm – especially the massive mills, built for cleaning wool as well as grinding corn – are due to the area's earlier prominence as one of the economic hubs of England, as a major centre of the medieval wool trade. Similarly, nearly all the villages have especially grand, near cathedral-scale fifteenth-century churches with emphatic towers and spires, paid for in their day by local wool merchants.

Even if you're not interested in painting-spotting, the Vale is still unquestionably beautiful. It's a soft, gentle landscape with an ideal mixture of greenery and water, of dipping valleys and hills to provide variety and expansive views. Roads roll up, down and around between the villages in no apparent order, and even what look like main routes on the map can be quite insignificant (so it's easy to get lost). Within the villages – often

By train from London

Trains for **Colchester** and **Ipswich** leave **Liverpool Street** about every 10mins. Journey time to **Colchester** is **55mins**, **Ipswich** is a further **20mins**. For **Harwich** change at **Colchester** or **Manningtree**. Journey time an extra **20-25mins**.

East Anglia

unusually rambling and spread-out – there are mixtures of Georgian brick and bulging-walled half-timbered cottages, prettified all the more by the odd local custom of using pink- and yellow-washes on walls instead of just white. This is above all an ideal area for relaxing, unstressed walking. There are as many footpaths as there are roads, most of which are easy to find, and you're never too far from a village and a pub.

With all its fame, Dedham Vale predictably attracts its share of weekend visitors and second-home owners, but even so there's nothing like a 'Constable Experience' anywhere nearby, and pleasantly few alterations have been made to any of the villages to maximise their tourist-twee potential. Consequently, they're still friendly, easygoing places, and away from holiday weekends it's surprisingly easy to avoid any crowds.

Dedham good

Dedham itself is the main centre and visitor-hub of the Vale, with the old grammar school attended by Constable next to the town cross and the enormous St Mary's Church. The charm of its main street is Dedham's greatest attraction, but it also has an Art & Craft Centre (and toy museum) housed in an old mill and showcasing the work of local artists, plus pubs, shops, cafés, small art galleries and Dedham Vale Family Farm, with animals for kids to pet. Boats can be hired on the Stour. On the south side of the village is the Sir Alfred Munnings Museum, where the once-fashionable painter of horses and rural scenes lived until his death in 1959. From Dedham it's a 1½-mile walk along the river or a more roundabout drive to the sites most closely associated with Constable at Flatford.

Constable's birthplace is in the beautifully peaceful village of **East Bergholt**, a couple of miles north of Dedham. The house where he lived has long been demolished, but still there are his first tiny studio, and the house (now a hairdressers') of John Dunthorne, the village handyman who first helped him to draw. Bergholt has another grand church, with the distinction of a tower that has been standing half in ruins for nearly 500 years. The church was due to be given an all-new spire in the 1520s, to be paid for by Henry VIII's minister Cardinal Wolsey; however, the fall of the Cardinal and the Reformation meant that money was cut off, the tower was never finished, and ever since the church's bells have been housed in the unique Bell Cage at ground level, a remarkable timber structure in the churchyard. Next to it is the grave of Constable's parents.

The Bell Cage at **East Bergholt** *church.*

West of Dedham, **Stratford St Mary** is another attractive village with good pubs and pleasant riverside walks. North of the Stour the land climbs steadily up to **Stoke-by-Nayland**, on the highest point in Dedham Vale, with spectacular views back to the east and a magnificent church with a soaring 120ft tower (the village is also a great place to eat). Just west again, **Nayland** itself is a large village with an especially pretty main street of up-and-down roofs and in-and-out pink and timber frontages, relics of its sixteenth-century wealth, and another fine big church with an altarpiece by Constable (not one of his best, to be frank).

This side of the Vale is much more hilly than the area further east. North of Stoke-by-Nayland, **Polstead** is yet another attractive village, spread over hills; it was once famous as the site of one of the most celebrated of Victorian-era murders, that of Maria Marten, apparently by her lover, in the once-legendary 'Red Barn'. North of here, several roads wind up to the largest settlement in Dedham Vale, **Hadleigh**, a likeable old wool town with a very long high street, down which sheep were once driven, that's lined with a whole variety of architecture from the sixteenth to the nineteenth centuries. At its centre is the Guildhall, much of it dating from 1438, one of the most impressive buildings in the area.

Different views

To the east of Dedham and Flatford, the scenery of the Stour Estuary is quite different from that of Dedham Vale, a flat, open landscape of marshes, reeds, water and flocks of wading birds that can be atmospherically bleak when the weather turns grey. Villages are further apart, and there are good longer walks that are great for seeing birds and taking in the misty riverscapes.

Manningtree, at the head of the estuary, is a neat Georgian harbour town that grew wealthy by sending grain (and especially malt) downriver to the London breweries. The overflow from the town's maltings are believed to be what has attracted one of England's largest swan populations to the Stour. Manningtree and neighbouring **Mistley** are both still working ports. On Mistley's main street above the river there is the ancient Thorn Inn, which during the Civil War was used as headquarters by the 'Witchfinder-General' Matthew Hopkins in his purges of the neighbourhood in search of practitioners of witchcraft. The oddest buildings nearby, though, are the Mistley Towers on the Manningtree road. These two large neo-classical towers are all that remain of a neo-Roman temple built by Robert Adam in 1776 for Richard Rigby MP, who had a plan to turn Mistley into a fashionable resort. The temple was finished, but after Rigby died in 1788 there was little interest in the scheme. The church was later knocked down but the towers, oddly, were allowed to stay.

A few miles east of Mistley is the turn off for **Wrabness**, a widely dispersed village in glorious, windblown isolation on a slope above the Stour – it's the best jumping-off point for estuary walks. Birdwatchers are drawn especially to the **Stour Estuary Nature Reserve**, alongside it.

Beyond here, the main roads soon run into **Harwich**, known to most people only as a ferry port. It's worth continuing on, though, past the ferry terminal to the very eastern end of Harwich and its Old Town, a tiny but engaging knot of narrow streets and sixteenth-to-twentieth century buildings. Many have maritime associations, such as the Harwich Redoubt fort (01255 503429; closed Mon-Sat from September to April), the 1818 Lighthouses or the home of Christopher Jones, captain of the *Mayflower*, which took the first Pilgrims to America.

Jumping-off points

If you can't take too much village life and want somewhere bigger, the two cities north and south of the Stour Valley each have their attractions. **Colchester**, 'the oldest town in Britain' and capital of Roman Britain before Queen Boudicca took it apart and forced a move to London in 60AD, has one of the best town museums in its Norman Castle, particularly good on local Roman relics. It's also a student town, and central Colchester is one of the best examples in Britain of redevelopment and Shopping-Centre-isation without (entirely) sucking all vitality out of the historic centre, which has a noticeably lively street life amid its often-quirky old buildings.

Ipswich is further from Dedham Vale but also has its points, with a compact historic centre and a centuries-old dock area, a string of

medieval churches and many fine buildings such as the magnificent Ancient House, with a lavishly carved façade from the 1670s. The Christchurch Mansion houses a fine art collection, and a point of pilgrimage for contemporary architecture followers is the 1975 Willis Corroon building, a monolithic black glass drum by Norman Foster.

Where to stay

There are plenty of bed & breakfasts scattered around the Stour Valley villages. If those listed here are full others worth looking for are **May's Barn Farm** (01206 323191; doubles from £43) in Dedham, **Gladwins Farm** (01206 262261; doubles around £56) in Nayland and **Ryegate House** (01206 263679; doubles £46) in Stoke-by-Nayland.

Aldhams

Bromley Road, Lawford, Manningtree, CO11 2NE (tel/fax 01206 393210).
Rates (B&B) *single occupancy* £30-£35; *double/twin* £40-£50. **Rooms** 1 double (en suite), 2 twin (1 en suite).

A gem of a B&B on the edge of the main Dedham Vale just south of Manningtree. The house is a massive Queen Anne farmhouse, beautifully restored in the 1930s with superb wood panelling; the gardens and tranquil location are delightful, and the big, airy rooms and bathrooms have every comfort, but what really makes the difference is the warmth of the hospitality. Owners Coral and Christopher McEwen could not be more welcoming, providing a full-scale afternoon tea with delicious home-made cakes – although should you just wish to retire to your room and rest they don't overwhelm you either. As you settle in you discover all kinds of extras in the rooms as well, and the large double, with windowseat, is particularly pretty. Evening meals are not provided, but the McEwens advise on local restaurants and make bookings as part of the service. Christopher is also a keen walker and can point you towards walks nearby. Children welcome. Non-smoking throughout.
A12 3rd Colchester exit for A120 to Harwich; after a few miles turn left to Little Bromley; house on right after 3 miles.

Angel Inn

Stoke-by-Nayland, CO6 4SA (01206 263245/fax 01206 263245).
Rates (B&B) *single occupancy* £47.50; *double/twin* £61. **Rooms** (all en suite) 5 double, 1 twin.
Cards AmEx, DC, Debit, MC, V.

Behind a rambling, up-and-down whitewashed façade – testimony to many earlier alterations and rebuildings – the Angel has been functioning as an inn in the middle of one of the most attractive Dedham Vale villages since the sixteenth century. In the last few years it has been refurbished to combine high-standard modern facilities with its oak beams and giant brick fireplaces. All rooms (one of which is in an annex next to the main inn) have been individually and sensitively decorated, and are extremely comfortable; staff are also very helpful and obliging. Book well ahead, as it's popular; guests also have first call on bookings in the restaurant, one of the best in the area (see p266). Children welcome.

A134 from Colchester towards Sudbury; after 8 miles turn right at Nayland onto B1087; through Nayland village into Stoke-by-Nayland; house is on left at crossroads.

Dedham Hall

Brook Street, Dedham, CO7 6AD (01206 323027/fax 01206 323293/jimsarton@dedhamhall.demon.co.uk).
Rates (B&B) *single occupancy* £50; *double/twin* £75; *family* £85-£95. **Rooms** (all en suite) 1 single; 4 double/twin; 1 family. **Cards** Debit, MC, V.

Dedham Hall consists of a fifteenth-century farmhouse and its attached cottages, joined together to make one big, meandering house set amid gardens, fields and duckponds between Dedham village and the Stour, right beside the footpath to Constable's mill at Flatford. Inside, there seem to be any number of staircases and low-ceilinged lounges with wood panelling and giant comfy sofas, as well as a tiny bar and pretty dining rooms, but despite its size it has a strong feel of a private home, given many personal touches by owners Wendy and Jim Sarton. Half-board rates, with dinner in the **Fountain House** restaurant (see p266), offer exceptional value; enquire about rates and, if you're interested, the painting courses held here. Children welcome.

A12 E towards Colchester; 2 miles after last exit to Colchester follow signs to Dedham into High Street; hall is at the end on left.

Dimbols Farm

Station Road, Wrabness, CO11 2TH (tel/fax 01255 880328).
Rates (B&B) *single occupancy* £22; *double* £32; *family* £50-£56. **Rooms** 1 double, 1 family room.

This Georgian farmhouse, part of a working farm, stands in a great location with a wonderful view down over the Stour estuary from just west of Wrabness village. The house and rooms are very warm, cosy and comfortable, and Mrs Macaulay provides all the traditional B&B amenities (plus TV and tea and coffee-making facilities in each room). Note that neither room is en suite. She doesn't offer lunch or dinner, but the Wheatsheaf pub is an easy walk away. Dimbols is very well placed for beginning estuary walks, or for anyone wishing to get straight into the countryside on the way to or from Harwich. Children welcome (special rates).

A120 E towards Harwich; turn left towards Wrabness; straight over crossroads; through village of Wrabness; Dimbols is 500 yards after village on left.

Edgehill Hotel

2 High Street, Hadleigh, IP7 5AP (01473 822458/fax 01473 827751).
Rates (B&B) *single* £30-£45; *double/twin* £50-£75; *four-poster* £70-£75; *family room* £65-£85 **Rooms** (all en suite) 2 single; 5 double/twin; 1 four-poster; 2 family.

Despite its Georgian façade, the Edgehill is one of the most venerable buildings in the old wool town of Hadleigh, with parts dating from the 1590s; further back, around the large garden (where afternoon tea can be served) there are modern additions as well. Nowadays it's a likeably relaxed family-run country hotel, with a flagstoned hall, chandeliers in the main lounge, and bedrooms – though all equally well-equipped and comfort-

able – of differing sizes and styles: the large four-poster room is romantically aged, others (particularly in the Lodge at the rear) are smaller and more modern. Mrs Rolfe's morning cook-ups are a treat; more home-cooking can be provided for evening meals (with advance notice). Dogs welcome. Non-smoking rooms available.

A12 E from Ipswich; follow signs to Hadleigh & B1070; follow road to T-junction; house on right opposite war memorial.

Maison Talbooth

Stratford Road, Dedham, CO7 6HN (01206 322367/ fax 01206 322752/mtreception@talbooth.co.uk/ www.talbooth.com).
Rates (B&CB) *single occupancy* £95-£130; *suite* £115-£175. Breakfast £7.50 (Eng). Special breaks. **Rooms** (all en suite) 10 suites. **Cards** AmEx, DC, Debit, MC, V.

The only choice for those going for an all-out splurge in Dedham Vale. Gerald Milsom's Maison Talbooth is a big pink-washed Victorian house in its own grounds with a commanding view over the Vale, transformed into an all-suites opulent hideaway suitable for Joan Collins in her prime. The huge ground floor suites like the 'Shakespeare' and the 'Keats' – with a giant two-seater peach-coloured Jacuzzi with gold taps and surrounded by Grecian columns – are the pinnacle of Essex-meets-Beverly Hills style; those above are a tad more restrained, but still distinctly ritzy. Weddings and honeymoons are a speciality; special short break deals also help soften the prices. There's no restaurant at the hotel (breakfast is served in the rooms), but a courtesy car service is provided to the Milsom-owned **Le Talbooth** (see p266) just down the road. Children welcome.

A12 NE of Colchester; take Dedham & Stratford St. Mary exit; house is 2 miles on right.

The Pier at Harwich

The Quay, Harwich, CO12 3HH (01255 241212/ fax 01255 551922/chris@thepieratharwich.co.uk/ www.talbooth.com).
Rates (B&CB) *single occupancy* £52.50-67.50; *double/twin* £75-£85. Breakfast £4 (Eng). **Rooms** (all en suite) 6 double/twin. **Cards** AmEx, DC, Debit, MC, V.

Although the Pier is owned by Gerald Milsom of the Maison Talbooth, its rooms – while still possessing every modern comfort – are far more conventional than those in Dedham. Bathrooms are big but non-decadent, and the décor is in straightforward pastel shades. They occupy the top floor of the building, an engaging old Victorian hotel built to cater for passengers off some of the very first Holland-Harwich ferries, and comprehensively renovated in the 1980s. A great attraction of the rooms is their airiness: 1-3 have a great outlook northwards across the Stour estuary and all its activity; 4-6 are at the side of the hotel, have less of a view and so are a little cheaper. With room 3, a big room on a corner, you get the benefit of views in both directions.

Round Hill House

Parsonage Hill, Boxted, nr Colchester, CO4 5ST (tel/fax 01206 272392).
Rates (B&B) *single occupancy* £30; *double/twin* £45-£48; *family room* from £50. **Rooms** 1 double; 1 twin (en suite); 1 family (en suite).

Postcards of home

No British artist is so closely associated
with a particular place as **John Constable**.
All his major paintings depict scenes
within a ten-mile radius of **East Bergholt**,
where he was born in 1776, and the most
important are all of places a short walk
from **Flatford Mill**, which was owned by
his father. The label 'Constable Country'
was already being applied to **Dedham
Vale** before his death, in 1837.

If these paintings appeal so widely to a
sense of longing for a rural retreat today
it's probably in good part because
Constable felt similarly himself. He moved
to London to become a professional
painter when he was 23, but the only part
of the big city he ever painted was
Hampstead Heath. He went back home to
Dedham Vale whenever he could,
sketching and re-sketching the same
scenes over again in oil roughs that were
then painted up into huge finished
canvases in his London studio, in
Charlotte Street.

Constable was a slow worker, putting
years of studies into a final painting. He
was in his late forties when he painted
his most famous pictures, after having

been unsuccessful and short of money
for most of his career. Another feature of
this creator of English icons is that he
was first recognised by... the French. His
first great success came at the Paris
Salon of 1824, where he was awarded
the Gold Medal and acclaimed by
Delacroix and Géricault; his innovative
free-flowing brush techniques were also
picked up by the Impressionists. In
England, meanwhile, after a brief period
in fashion in the 1830s, Constable was
dismissed for most of the Victorian era
as just a sloppy draftsman, until the
twentieth century rediscovered him as a
national institution.

A B&B in a large, modern hilltop house surrounded by
lush scenery on the edge of Dedham Vale. The house may
not be historic but the rooms are very comfortable. Mrs
Carter's hefty breakfasts are served in an attractive dining room with log fire or, if weather allows, outside in the
fine garden. The house also has its own tennis court, paddock, coarse fishing stream, expansive living room with
baby grand piano and memorabilia from Colonel Carter's
earlier military career, which adds a touch of eccentrici-
ty to the place. The Carters take great care of their guests,
offering plenty of room for children (they ask to be told
of their arrival in advance), and have many repeat customers. Evening meals are available by prior arrangement; otherwise the Carters can tell you about local
restaurants. Dogs welcome. All bedrooms non-smoking.
*A12 signposted Colchester central; A134 towards Sudbury
passed Colchester station; through Great Horkesley (ignore
signs to Boxted); turn right at crossroads into Church Road
towards Boxted; after 2 miles turn left into Church Street
signposted Higham; Round Hill is last house on left before
sharp Z bend.*

Where to eat & drink

The Stour Valley has a variety of decent eating
places, which might surprise anyone who
thinks of this region as lost in the country.

Some pubs, like the **Angel** and the **Cock**
below, contain high-standard restaurants;
another is the Roux-brothers-owned **White
Hart** in Nayland (01206 263382), which
reopened in August 1999 with an all-new menu.
Others offer more conventional pub fare. Of the
two in Dedham, the **Marlborough Head** and
the **Sun**, the latter has a more genuine
atmosphere. Also check out **Josephine's**
(01206 322677), a likeable vegetarian
restaurant-tea room in the village's Art & Craft
Centre. In East Bergholt, the **Red Lion** right in
the centre of the village, is a likeable, unfussy
old pub with a decent garden; in Stratford St
Mary the **Swan** benefits from a sizeable
garden alongside the river. Another lovely
riverside **Swan** (this time the river is the Colne,
just south of the Stour) is in Chappel, just off
the A1124; in Stoke-by-Nayland, there's the
Black Horse (01206 262504) a popular,
buzzing place with a bargain-priced menu of
Indian food. Hadleigh has almost a pub row
along its High Street: the **Ram**, on the Market
Square, is a peaceful old tavern with good beer;

East Anglia

the **King's Head** is an un-prettified, lively locals' boozer.

Pubs are thinner on the ground along the Stour estuary, but the **Thorn** on the quay at Mistley (01206 392821) and the **Wheatsheaf** in Wrabness (01255 870200) are both popular locally for their food. In Harwich, the **Angel** (01255 507241) is a relaxed alternative that also offers well-priced grub, and a harbour view.

Angel Inn

Stoke-by-Nayland (01206 263245).
Food served noon-2.30pm, 6-9.30pm, daily.
Cards AmEx, DC, Debit, MC, V.
The Angel offers a choice of a sophisticated traditional/modern British menu, served in the beautifully restored, high-timbered Well Room (booking essential), or superior pub food, served in bars that have as much dark wood as you could ask of a country pub (no reservations taken). Both lists feature high-quality, imaginative dishes, making good use of local produce – deliciously fresh fish dishes, such as grilled skate wings or a salad of trout fillets, are a speciality, but meats and game are also excellent. Diners from across the region converge on the pub, but even so prices are reasonable, with a full meal with wine around £20-£25 a head.

The Cock Inn

The Green, Polstead (01206 263150).
Food served noon-2pm, 7-9pm, Tue-Sat;
noon-2pm Sun. **Cards** Debit, MC, V.
Another venerable old village pub, unmissable on Polstead Green, with brick floors and oak beams, and now occupied by a restaurant with an innovative contemporary menu. Proprietor Michael Leviseur does his own smoking, so smoked salmon, trout or even prawns are specialities; other dishes might be aubergine tempura with a soy ginger dip, honey glazed duck with gnocchi and a fruit sauce, or wild mushroom stroganoff with fresh pasta, plus very moreish fruity puddings. The wine list is just as interesting, and prices are accessible (about £25 per person, with wine).

The Fountain House

Dedham Hall, Brook Street, Dedham (01206 323027).
Food served 7-9.30pm Tue-Sat. **Set meals** £21.50
(3 courses). **Cards** Debit, MC, V.
Snugly comfortable, the restaurant at Dedham Hall (*see p264*) offers fine food with a distinctly personal feel – owner Wendy Sarton handles the cooking herself, and all the activity in the farmhouse-style kitchen is easy to view. Her fixed-price dinner menu is exceptionally generous, with an ample choice of skilfully prepared dishes with great fresh ingredients such as a rocket salad with Stilton and pine nuts, a brochette of mixed fish or fillet of beef with a delicious red onion sauce. The enterprising wine list is excellent too, which, with the relaxed atmosphere, all helps toward a very enjoyable meal.

The Pier at Harwich

The Quay, Harwich (01255 241212).
Food served noon-2pm, 6-9.30pm, daily.
Set meals *lunch* £14.50 (2 courses), £17.50
(3 courses) Mon-Sat; *dinner* £19.50 (3 courses).
Cards AmEx, DC, Debit, MC, V.

Le Talbooth – *plush, flash but not too pricey.*

One of the East Coast's most prestigious seafood restaurants, the Pier is another place that offers a choice of styles and prices. The first floor (with the best view) houses the reservation-only, traditionally comfortable Harbourside Restaurant, with fixed-price menus and an extensive, pretty traditional à la carte list; on the ground floor is the much more casual, no-reservation Ha'penny Pier, with simpler dishes (such as a very superior fish and chips) and meals for under £10, including plenty of things aimed at kids. Both feature excellent quality, wonderfully fresh fish and seafood, and both are extremely popular.

Stour Bay Café

39-43 High Street, Manningtree (01206 396687).
Food served noon-2pm, 7-9.30pm, Tue-Fri;
7-9.30pm Sat. **Set meals** *lunch* £8.50 (2 courses),
£10 (3 courses). **Cards** AmEx, DC, Debit, MC, V.
A friendly, comfortable restaurant on Manningtree's main street with a light, modern and eclectically international menu that seeks to make the most of local produce, especially fish. A la carte dinner costs about £20 per person. Menu regulars include goat's cheese and red pepper cheesecake, a warm salad of grilled tiger prawns with chilli, grilled skate on 'Stour Bay cassoulet' and roast lamb marinated in harissa with couscous. Desserts, wines and trimmings show the same degree of care and imagination.

Le Talbooth

Gun Hill, Dedham (01206 323150).
Food served noon-2pm, 7-9pm, daily.
Set meals *lunch* £19 (3 courses); *dinner* £24
(3 courses). **Cards** AmEx, DC, Debit, MC, V.
The 'tollbooth' is a giant half-timbered Elizabethan building where duties were once charged on traffic crossing the Stour (pictures of which often turn up in brochures as archetypal images of Englishness). Over the last 40 years it has been painstakingly restored by owner Gerald Milsom and built up as the region's favourite luxury restaurant. The style is unreserved old-English plush, with crisp pink linen, masses of silverware, flowers and brocade-covered furniture, a white piano, smoothly oiled service and a ravishingly pretty riverside terrace where meals are served when weather allows. The menu is a mainly traditional Anglo-French haute-cuisine selection, and, despite all the opulence, not as expensive as you might think. The wine list is also impressive.

What to see & do

The best way to appreciate the Stour Valley is, naturally, to walk it. For non-strenuous strolling, one easy but enjoyable route is the circular path from Flatford to Dedham and back (around 1½ hours) or, with a bit more exertion, as far west as Stratford St Mary; another is the path between Dedham and East Bergholt, taken by Constable every day on his way to school, and which features in *The Cornfield*. As well as at tourist offices, walking maps and guides are available from the National Trust shop in Flatford and bookshops in Dedham and East Bergholt. For less widely known walks along the marshes near Mistley and Wrabness, a useful guide is the Tendring Trails booklet, available from Harwich TIC and other Essex offices.

Tourist information centres

One peculiarity of this area is that, although 'Constable Country' covers both sides of the Stour, as far as the counties of Suffolk and Essex are concerned this little river seems to be a very important boundary indeed: leaflets given you on the Essex side tend to ignore anywhere north of the river, and vice versa. The Visitor Centre and National Trust shop in Flatford have more material that deals with the area in one go.

1 Queen Street, **Colchester**, CO1 2PG (01206 282920/ www.colchester.gov.uk/leisure/leisure.htm). **Open** *Apr-Oct* 9.30am-6pm Mon, Tue, Thur-Sat; 10am-6pm Wed; 10am-5pm Sun; *Nov-Mar* 10am-5pm Mon-Sat.
Iconfield Park, **Harwich**, CO12 4EN (01255 506139). **Open** *Apr-Sept* 8.30am-7pm daily; *Oct-Mar* 8.30am-5.30pm Mon-Fri; 9am-4pm Sat.
St Stephen's Church, St Stephen's Lane, **Ipswich**, IP1 1DP (01473 258070/www.ipswich.gov.uk). **Open** 9am-5pm Mon-Sat.

Bike hire

Action Bikes 24 Crouch Street, **Colchester** (01206 541744). One mile from the train station.

Beth Chatto Gardens

Elmstead Market, nr Colchester (01206 822007). **Open** *Mar-Oct* 9am-5pm Mon-Sat; *Nov-Feb* 9am-4pm Mon-Fri. **Admission** £3; free under-14s.

Created from scratch – before 1960 this was farm wasteland – Beth Chatto's garden is a showpiece for what can be achieved by adapting to, rather than fighting, existing conditions. So, for example, drought-loving Mediterranean plants dominate in the gravel garden, while lush foliage surrounds the ponds (created by damming a ditch). Many of the unusual plants seen in the garden are for sale. Note that there's no café, but there is space for picnics alongside the (grassy) car-park.

Christchurch Mansion & Wolsey Art Gallery

Christchurch Park, Ipswich (01473 253246). **Open** *Mar-Oct* 10am-5pm Tue-Sat, bank hols; 2.30-4.30pm Sun; *Nov-Feb* 10am-4pm/dusk Tue-Sat 2.30-4pm/dusk Sun. **Admission** free.

This Elizabethan mansion, set in its own grounds just north of Ipswich town centre and recently restored, contains the most important collection of Constable's works outside London, together with paintings by Gainsborough, Wilson Steer and other local artists, relics from the long history of the house, and a whole variety of other objects with Suffolk connections such as seventeenth-century furniture and Lowestoft porcelain.

Colchester Castle Museum

Castle Park, Colchester (01206 282931). **Open** *Apr-Oct* 10am-5pm Mon-Sat; 1-5pm Sun; *Mar-Nov* 10am-5pm Mon-Sat. **Admission** £3.70; £2.40 5-15s, OAPs, students; £9.90 family.

The largest Norman keep in England, built over a Roman temple and begun in 1076, Colchester Castle now houses one of the best collections in the country from Roman Britain, an inventive display with priceless relics of the time when Colchester was a capital city, together with exhibits on later events such as Civil War sieges and Puritan witch-trials.

Flatford

Bridge Cottage, Flatford (01206 298260/www.nationaltrust.org.uk). **Open** *Bridge Cottage Mar, Apr, Oct* 11am-5.30pm Wed-Sun; *May-Sept* 10am-5.30pm daily; *Nov, Dec* 11am-3.30pm Wed-Sun; *Jan, Feb* 11am-3pm Sat, Sun; *tours Apr-Oct* 11am, 1pm, 2.30pm daily. **Admission** *Bridge Cottage* (NT) free; *tours* £1.80.

Most of the tiny clutch of buildings at Flatford, the subject of Constable's most famous paintings, are now in the care of the National Trust. As an arch-famous beauty spot it naturally gets crowded on some sunny weekends, but at other times the place is surprisingly low-key, with very little to disrupt the beauty of the location, the river or the mill buildings. One, Bridge Cottage, now houses a café, a very good small exhibition on Constable and a shop, from where guided tours and other talks and trips run daily (Apr-Sept). They are well-planned and worth taking, and often include a visit inside Flatford Mill, otherwise closed to the public. The Mill itself and Willy Lott's Cottage (the house shown in *The Haywain*) are occupied by a study centre of the Field Studies Council, which hosts a wide range of residential courses and weekends through the year (info 01206 298283). On many summer weekends you can also hire boats on the Stour, from next to Flatford bridge. If you're planning a visit in early 2000, phone first to check that the sights are open, as there are plans for renovation work.

Stour Estuary Nature Reserve

Ramsey, nr Harwich (01255 886043). **Open** free access. **Admission** free; donations welcome.

Run by the RSPB, this reserve covers a large area of woodland and marshes along the Stour shoreline just east of Wrabness. From the main entry gate and car park, on the road from Wrabness to Ramsey, there's about a 40-minute walk through woods before you cross the railway line and descend onto the marshes, where there is a choice of paths and hides with information on the wildlife to be seen. Giant flocks of migratory wading birds pass through the estuary in August and September, but at many times of year you can see a wide variety of ducks, plovers, redshanks and others. The paths are often very muddy.

East Anglia

Upper Stour Valley

The subtle charms of the Suffolk/Essex borders.

Sleepy Suffolk – less somnolent since the tribes of commuters in search of their own personal *lebensraum* burst across the banks of the river Stour (which roughly rhymes with 'brewer') – has often been unfairly disparaged as a place where nothing happens, where there's nothing to look at. True, its clay and flint-crop soils (Robert Louis Stevenson, on visiting Cockfield in 1872, reported himself 'afraid of the clay soil') and gentle undulations lack the high drama of, say the North Yorkshire Moors, but there's plenty in East Anglia to make the visitor wuther, not least the biting easterly winds that can arrive, at any time, from Siberia and the North Sea. Indeed, their sting has been credited – erroneously or not: the Oxford English is silent on this matter – with the development of East Anglian dialect, in which locals speak from the corner of a barely opened mouth.

The Stour Valley is a 60-mile stretch that flows from south of Newmarket, past Haverhill and then west-east, forming the Essex/Suffolk border, through the lovely Suffolk-pinked villages of Clare, Cavendish and Long Melford, past Dedham and Flatford Mill to its estuary in the east at the Cattawade Marshes. This break concentrates on the river's upper reaches, from Haverhill to Sudbury. (For the **Lower Stour Valley**, *see page 261*.)

Historic associations

A fire swept through **Haverhill** (pronounced 'Ave-rill) in 1665, and there has been little of interest in this unlovely former wool town since. But to the east, the cluster of villages within a ten-mile radius around Sudbury represents some of the best that Suffolk has to offer. There is the grand medieval architecture of unmissable **Lavenham**, a village which grew rich on the wool trade; the thriving market town of **Sudbury**; the myriad farms and cottages. Much of Suffolk's beauty is in the detail: look for cottages covered with decorated

Lavenham – *half-timbered heaven.*

plasterwork known as pargetting (a house by Clare churchyard offers a fine example) and painted in the distinctive colour of Suffolk Pink. Many of the villages – such as **Cavendish**, with its village green and thatched cottages – have entered a kind of folk memory as the image of what an English village should look like. It is also an area that wears its history in its place names: Latin, Saxon, Scandinavian and, finally, Norman French tongues inform whole clusters of village names. Similarly so in the architecture: the Romans, who made their capital 30 miles to the south-east at Colchester, have left their mark in roads and numerous archaeological sites along the routes; the Saxons and, especially the Normans, can be seen more clearly in their ruined castles and churches. The splendour of Elizabethan England is evident in such great manor houses as **Melford Hall** (Elizabeth I stayed there) and

By train from London

Trains to go from **Liverpool Street** about once every hour (changing at **Marks Tey**) to **Sudbury**. The journey takes about **1hr 15mins**.

Kentwell Hall, both in Long Melford. That the area was once rich and powerful is not in any doubt: the Domesday Book recounts numerous manors and holdings in Suffolk and – in the days when position and money were inextricably linked – Simon Theobald – also known as Simon of Sudbury – became Archbishop of Canterbury and Chancellor to the court of Richard II (*see page 273* **Off with their heads**). Centuries later, during Henry VIII's Reformation, the lucrative Abbey of Bury St Edmunds was sacked and the images of grave, great churches like that of Long Melford and Lavenham, destroyed: one can still see the vacant plinths on the outside walls of the latter edifice.

You will find, too, that history has left a living trace on the landscape. At **Great Yeldham**, a 1000-year-old oak still stands, even if it is girt with iron bands, and at **Clare**, a huge man-made mound topped with a few ruins is all that remains of the Norman castle. (Incidentally, during the Hundred Years War, the Lord of Clare was presented with lands in France and the local wine – claret – still bears his name). At **Pentlow**, just south of Cavendish, the Norman round tower church stands at the foot of the hill that leads up to the Essex border village. Why? Because the Black Death was in Cavendish and the Pentlow community sought to evade it by moving itself. Three miles away, **Long Melford** – so called because it is a 'ribbon' village of about two miles in length – shows its continuing growth in its development. The village, now closing onto the town boundaries of Sudbury itself, contains a wonderful church, two noble halls, and, in general, is over-supplied with antique shops: 39 at the last count and more than any village needs. It is no coincidence that the BBC filmed its popular series *Lovejoy* around this area. Long Melford's old village school (situated by the bridge and more or less opposite a house once owned by World War I poet Edmund Blunden) hosts very popular antiques fairs every bank holiday.

A few miles from Melford, lies the village of **Borley**, famous in the earlier part of this century for its extravagant ghosts. Once known as the 'most haunted house in Britain', the Rectory – built on the site of an old convent – apparently had the lot: ghostly nuns, carriages drawn by coal-black horses, wailings and all kinds of nasty noises until a careless poltergeist burnt the place down in 1939. Or at least, that's the story. Even now, spookologists stake out Borley church trying to capture a glimpse of something that goes bump in the night. The site of the former rectory is now private land and thus unvisitable.

Situated in a loop in the River Stour, the ancient town of **Sudbury** is still, more than 1,000 years after its foundation, a thriving market town. Every Thursday and Saturday, a lively market takes place in the town square, just at the foot of painter Thomas Gainsborough's statue. Author Dodie Smith uses this statue as a meeting place for the dogs in her sequel to *101 Dalmatians, The Starlight Barking*. Dickens modelled the rotten borough of Eatanswill in *The Pickwick Papers* on Sudbury: a fiction that is commemorated on Boxing Day, when a stage coach travels from Haverhill to Sudbury, via Cavendish and Long Melford. It's a fine town in which to spend a few hours: you can go rowing (the boathouse is at Ballingdon Hill); take in an exhibition at Gainsborough's House; eat lunch and then lose it over the head of poor Simon of Sudbury.

Where to stay

Note that many pubs/restaurants in the area double up as B&Bs. *See page 271.*

The Bull

High Street, Long Melford, CO10 9JG (01787 378494/fax 01787 880307).
Rates (B&B) *single* £65; *double/twin* £100; *suite* £130; *family room* £110. **Rooms** (all en suite) 3 single; 17 double/twin; 3 family; 2 suites.
Cards AmEx, DC, Debit, MC, V.

Lavenham Priory. *See page 270.*

A well-established hotel and pub situated on the Lavenham corner in the centre of this historic village and instantly recognisable by it beamed exterior. Rooms have a period charm, while the two suites have separate lounge areas and king-size beds with canopies. The hotel menu tends towards the roast beef of olde England variety. Children and dogs welcome. Non-smoking rooms available.

Bulmer Tye House

Bulmer Tye, nr Sudbury, CO10 7ED
(tel/fax 01787 269315).
Rates (B&B) *single* £20; *double* £40.
Rooms 2 single (1 en suite); 2 double.

Two miles south of Sudbury is this welcoming B&B set in a handsome Victorian house. Offering two double rooms (neither en suite) and two single rooms (with a bathroom between them), Peter and Noël Owen have created a homely and imaginative atmosphere – the house is filled with books and wooden cabinets – and the grounds are nice too. In the village, there is a famous brickworks, which uses old methods to replicate Tudor bricks needed for restoring the old homes of England and other countries. Children and dogs welcome. Non-smoking throughout. Note that breakfast, while not a fry-up, includes a delicious spread of cereals, fruit, home-baked bread, boiled eggs and so on.
Take A131 from Halstead N towards Sudbury; house is 0.25 miles before Fox Pub.

Lavenham Priory

Water Street, Lavenham, CO10 9RW (01787 247404/248472/www.btinternet.com/~lavpriory).
Rates (B&B) *single occupancy* £50-£60; *double/four-poster* £90; *twin* £70. **Rooms** (all en suite) 1 double; 1 twin; 2 four-poster. **Cards** Debit, MC, V.

Without doubt one of Lavenham's most unusual and beautiful spots. This thirteenth-century house was once home to a Benedictine order; now its owners have restored the building to its Elizabethan grandeur, and it's a picture to behold. Oak floors set the mood for the timelessly quiet house and the bedrooms – divided between the great, painted and gallery chambers. Guests can use the great hall (complete with real fire in winter). The three-acre gardens (with a separate walled herb garden) are as pretty as one could imagine. Non-smoking throughout.

Oliver's Farm

Toppesfield, CO9 4LS (01787 237642/fax 01787 237602).
Rates (B&B) *double/twin* £50.
Rooms 2 double/twin (1 en suite).

Adjacent to a working farm, and set in two acres of landscaped gardens, Oliver's Farm is a 1650 house (think: big arched fireplace and carved beams) set in the total quiet of the Essex countryside. The two bedrooms are comfortable and, downstairs, a dining and sitting room and terrace are on offer. Mrs Blackie's full English breakfasts – including home-made bread and jams and bacon smoked locally in Sudbury – are fortifying in their excellence. Heritage hunters may be thrilled to know that the house was built by the Symonds family (their crest adorns the building), whose son emigrated to the fledgling US and became big pals with Groton-born John Winthrop, Puritan leader and first governor of Massachusetts. Non-smoking throughout.

A1017 N of Braintree towards Haverhill, turn left to Toppesfield off A1017 before Great Yeldham; 1.5 miles to Toppesfield Hall on right, then next turn on left into farmhouse drive.

Red House

29 Bolton Street, Lavenham, CO10 9RG
(01787 248074/www.lavenham.demon.co.uk/accommodation/redhouse).
Rates (B&B) *double* £45.
Rooms (all en suite) 3 double.

A homely and personable B&B is offered in this elegantly proportioned Victorian country house by Diana Schofield. The three double rooms all feature subtly colour-cordinated furnishings and the gardens are pretty to sit in. Dinners can be ordered (£15 for 3 courses; BYOB) by prior arrangement. Children and dogs welcome. Non-smoking throughout.

The Swan

High Street, Lavenham, CO10 9QA
(01787 247477/fax 01787 248286).
Rates *single* £75; *single occupancy* £105; *double/twin* £120; *deluxe double/twin/four-poster* £130; *suite* £145. Special breaks. Breakfast £10.95 (Eng/cont).
Rooms (all en suite) 7 single; 14 double; 12 twin; 7 deluxe double; 1 deluxe twin; 3 four-poster; 2 suites.
Cards AmEx, DC, Debit, MC, V.

This impressive fourteenth-century hotel is located in the centre of Lavenham and within minutes of all the central sites. A hotel since at least 1667, the Swan was originally three houses converted into one 100 years ago. More recent restoration has been sensitive and the rooms are comfortable and tastefully decorated. Two bars and a restaurant add to the appeal of the place. Children and dogs welcome. Non-smoking rooms available.

Western House

High Street, Cavendish, CO10 8AR (01787 280550).
Rates (B&B) *double/twin* £32.
Rooms 1 double; 1 twin.

Situated in a large house – its foundations are eleventh-century, although the interior is mostly Elizabethan, Western House is built on the Roman Way – the legions' route from their capital at Colchester to Bristol. During the eighteenth century it was a stop for westward carriages: an old coachhouse, with a chimney large enough to hold several small sweeps, is the old inn. Owners Peter and Jean Marshall have made the book-lined house highly popular among those wanting an oasis of calm and a mature one-acre organic garden in which to reflect. All bedrooms are beamed and cosy. Full breakfasts (home-made bread is a feature) are vegetarian and the house's popularity is reflected in the guests who return regularly. Children welcome.
W of Long Melford on A1092.

Where to eat & drink

Note that many of the places listed below also provided bed and breakfast. Additionally, good drinking (and often eating) can also be found at the cheery **Bell** in Castle Hedingham (01787 460350) and the hilltop **Plough** in Hundon (01440 786789).

The Angel

Market Place, Lavenham (01787 247388).
Food served noon-2.15pm, 6.45-9.15pm, daily.
Cards AmEx, Debit, MC, V.

Licensed premises since 1420, the Angel offers solid, rural food – fresh pork pies, steaks and some unexpected fish items: red snapper, for instance – that aims itself squarely at the upper end of the pub grub spectrum. Eat snacks in the beamed pub, all atmosphere and charm, or repair to a quieter dining room. A meal without drinks comes to around £15 per person. The eight bedrooms (all ensuite) make the best of this crooked, winding building. Doubles from £69.

The Bull

High Street, Cavendish (01787 280245).
Food served noon-2pm, 6.30-9pm, Tue-Sun.
Cards Debit, MC, V.

You can certainly sample weighty ploughman's lunches at the Bull, but this busy country pub has made a name for itself with all its food: colossal plates of fresh fish and home-made chips, home-made steak and kidney pies or, should you prefer, vegetarian options such as pastas and ratatouille. It's all served in a period inn, with exposed beams stripped of their lathe and plasterwork, enabling one to peep through from the bar area into a dining section set slightly to one side. Children are welcome; booking essential on Sundays and bank holidays. There are also bedrooms at the Bull (doubles £45).

The Countrymen

Church Walk, Long Melford (01787 312356).
Food served *wine bar* noon-2pm, 7-9.30pm, Tue-Sun; *restaurant* 7-9.30pm Tue-Sun. **Set meals** £9.95 (3 courses). **Cards** AmEx, Debit, MC, V.

Refurbished a few years ago from its incarnation as the Black Lion, a large and above-standard country hostelry just by the church, the Countrymen is indicative of the rebranding of Suffolk as a place fit for townies to set foot. Accordingly, modern British cuisine dominates the restaurant (open evenings only; a main course with all the trimmings is around £15-£20); bistro food is served in the wine bar. The B&B side of things is also comfortable: period knick-knacks adorn the building, but manage to add charm rather than annoy. Double rooms from £65.

Food for Thought

8 Market Place, Lavenham (Lavenham Books 01787 247941). **Open** phone for details.

A minuscule tea rooms offering Aga-toasted teacakes, warm scones and home-baked cakes. With only seven tables, this is very much a local business, owned by the bookshop next door, with a delightful old-fashioned feel to it, right down to home-style baking and the wispy young waiter who looked faint at the idea of the hordes from London descending.

The Great House

Market Place, Lavenham (01787 247431).
Food served noon-2pm, 7-9.30pm, Tue-Sat.
Set meals *lunch* £9.95 (2 courses), £14.95 (3 courses); *dinner* £18.95 (3 courses).
Cards AmEx, Debit, MC, V.

This was once Stephen Spender's house; now it's an elegantly formal yet relaxed French restaurant and bed and breakfast run with Gallic verve and precision by Régis and Martine Crépy. A Georgian façade conceals a medieval interior; the dining room is dominated by a large fireplace and the menu, reputedly one of the best in Suffolk, is strong on subtle flavours. An excellent à la carte dinner menu (three courses, £18.95) offers such delights as pan-fried calf's liver with Dijon mustard sauce and paupiette of sole and brill with smoked salmon and fish mousse. Meat and fish dishes are favoured and, while vegetarians are catered for, the chef asks for some advance warning to enable him to prepare some suitably lovely suggestions. A more than competent wine list enhances the meats and cheeses which follow dessert (from £4.75), and coffee and home-made chocolates add the final flourish to a perfect meal. Children are welcome, particularly for Sunday lunch (£18.95, three courses, £9.95 child's portion). Double rooms from £70.

Red Onion

57 Ballingdon Street, Sudbury (01787 376777).
Food served noon-2pm, 6.30-9.30pm, Mon-Sat.
Set meals *lunch* £6.25 (2 courses), £8.25 (3 courses); *dinner* £8.25 (2 courses), £10.25 (3 courses). **Cards** Debit, MC, V.

The Red Onion's conversion from an old motor factors' shop into a bistro is so successful, diners would have never believe that ten years ago the kitchen may have been knee-deep in sump oil. With about 12 tables, the Red Onion is a bright, cheerful place offering a short but first class menu, with many vegetarian and fish options, at prices that are hard to beat. Filling soups and some wonderfully stodgy puddings top and tail meals here. A three-course meal without drinks is around £12.

Scutcher's

Westgate Street, Long Melford (01787 310200).
Food served noon-2.30pm, 7-9.30pm, Tue-Sat.
Cards AmEx, Debit, MC, V.

Scutcher's has had to live down a reputation as a lacklustre pub in its former existence. Bought by its current owners in 1991, the Grade-II Georgian building has been completely refurbished and offers a menu and an atmosphere totally at odds with its past. The menu steers a tasty course through grills (whole Dover sole, £16.90), sirloin steak £12.90), roasts and vegetarian options, such as wild mushroom, asparagus and noodles (£8.50), with daily specials shown on a blackboard. A large wine list with over 200 choices features nine marques of champagne and four dessert wines. And, if you're interested, scutching is the action of trimming a hedge or striking the grain from a head of corn.

White Hart

Poole Street, Great Yeldham (01787 237250).
Food served noon-2pm, 6.30-9.30pm, Mon-Fri; noon-2pm, 6.30-10pm, Sat, Sun. **Set meals** *lunch* £8.50 (2 courses). **Cards** AmEx, DC, Debit, MC, V.

This large, relaxed and deservedly busy restaurant is set off of a pub within a higgledy-piggeldy Tudor farmhouse. The kitchen can turn its hand to first-grade bar snacks such as pastas and a range of ploughmans, as well as a more formal menu which combines trad British heartiness (roasts, etc) with Mediterranean flavours in dishes such as spinach and Parmesan tar with tomato and chilli confit and tossed rocket salad. A three-course meal without drinks comes to around £25 a head.

See also the Essex and Suffolk County Council websites (www.essexcc.gov.uk and www.suffolkcc.gov.uk respectively) for information and full local transport timetables.

Tourist infomation centres

Lady Street, **Lavenham**, CO10 9RA (01787 248207/www.babergh-south-suffolk.gov.uk). **Open** *Easter-June, Sept, Oct* 10am-4.45pm daily; *July, Aug* 10am-4.45pm Mon-Thur, Sun; 10am-5.45pm Fri, Sat; *Nov-Dec, Mar* 10am-3pm Sat, Sun.

Town Hall, Market Hill, **Sudbury**, CO10 1TL(01787 881320/www.babergh-south-suffolk.gov.uk). **Open** *Easter-Oct* 10am-4.45pm Mon-Sat; *Nov-Easter* 10am-2.45pm Mon-Sat.

Bike hire

Street Life bus station, Hamilton Road, **Sudbury** (01787 310940). Close to the train station.

Cavendish Manor Vineyards

Nether Hall, Cavendish (01787 280221). **Open** by appointment only. **Admission** £2.50; free under-16s.

Up the road between Cavendish Green on the one side and the pink almshouses and St Mary's church on the other is Nether Hall, a timbered manor dating from the fourteenth century. Vines were planted in 1972, and within three years had produced a national prize-winner. It's debatable as to whether Romans first introduced wines to the area: Nether Hall is close to where a Roman villa has been located. The house and its grounds are open to the public, as is the small crafts museum.

Clare Castle & Country Park

Maltings Lane, Clare (rangers 01787 277491). **Open** free access to castle and grounds; *visitors centre May-Sept* 10am-5pm daily; *Apr, Oct* 10am-5pm Sat, Sun; *Nov-Easter* by appointment only. **Admission** free.

All that is left of Richard de Bienfait's eleventh-century castle now is a motte, encircled by a spiralling path, and the ruins of the old walls that once protected the inner bailey. The view from the motte's top is pleasant enough and the untamed open space – there are picnic and conservation parking areas – is inviting. The remnants of the old Clare railway station are also contained in the

park in the form of the two old platforms; a sometimes-muddy walkway along the river completes the picture. In Clare itself, the splendid parish church of St Peter and St Paul (built 1450) is worth a visit too.

Colne Valley Railway

Yeldham Road, Castle Hedingham (01787 461174/www.cvr.uk.com). **Open** *museum Mar-Dec* 10am-5pm daily; *trains Mar-Oct* Sun only (phone for details). **Admission** £3; £1.50 3s-16s, OAPs; £7.50 family. **Tickets** *steam trains* £5; £2.50 3s-16s; £4 OAPs; £12.50 family; *heritage diesel trains* £4; £2 3s-16s; £3 OAPs; £10 family.

Run by the Colne Valley Railway Preservation Society, the restored Pullman carriages of this working steam and diesel railway will shunt you into the past. Now in its 25th year, the museum has been built up lovingly by enthusiasts, and it offers various diversifications: train-driving courses, Sunday lunches aboard the Pullman as it travels its private line (departing 12.45pm; booking essential) and various Agatha Christie-inspired murder mystery evenings. Entrance to the museum also gives admittance to the 30 acres of the **Colne Valley Farm Park** where sheep, cattle and goats graze in traditional water meadows.

Gainsborough's House

46 Gainsborough Street, Sudbury (01787 372958). **Open** *Apr-Oct* 10am-5pm Tue-Sat; 2-5pm Sun; *Nov-Mar* 10am-5pm Tue-Fri; 10am-4pm Sat; 2-4pm Sun. **Admission** £3; £1.50 5s-16s, students; £2.50 OAPs.

Part museum, part gallery, the birthplace of painter Thomas Gainsborough (1727-88) is unusual in that it manages to combine both roles well. The house, older than its Georgian façade suggests, is a roomy, winding affair and each room highlights a different aspect of the artist's work: there are etchings, a bronze of a horse (the only known sculpture by him) and paintings from throughout his career, including *A Wooded Landscape With Cattle by a Pool* (1782). Regular visiting exhibitions of contemporary art and craft are also held and a working print workshop in the old coach house offers courses to the public. A lovely mature garden, including a lavender tree and a mulberry tree, make an atmospheric accompaniment.

Gifford's Hall

Hartest (01284 830464). **Open** *Apr-Oct* 11am-6pm daily. **Admission** £3.25; £2.75 OAPs; free under-16s.

The good life made flesh? This 33-acre small holding, centred around a Georgian homestead, is a self-sufficient farm with gardens, vineyards, meadows filled with wild flowers and animals ranging from a flock of St Kilda sheep to posse of Rhode Island Red hens. Bees from the Hall's ten hives buzz about the sweet peas and the fruits of their labours can be bought, just a waggle-dance away, at the farm shop. Gifford's Hall also has tea rooms and offers bed and breakfast (double room from £40).

Hedingham Castle

Castle Hedingham (01787 460261). **Open** *Easter-Oct* 10am-5pm daily. **Admission** (EH) £3.50; £2.50 5s-16s; £3 OAPs, students; £10.50 family.

The garden of **Gainsborough's House**.

East Anglia

Off with their heads

Considering that Suffolk has had, to put it mildly, a rigorous history, it's quite surprising that the county does not have a larger trove of bloody stories to relate. True, there is the stirring tale of **Edmund**, King of East Anglia (841-869), who, following his death at the hands of the invading Danes, didn't give up the ghost. Far from it: his head, concealed beneath a bush, alerted his kinsman to its whereabouts, allowing them to re-assemble the dead Edmund back home in the renamed Bury St Edmunds.

Thereafter, local sporadic unrest broke out from time to time, but it was not until the **Peasants' Revolt** (1381), led by Wat Tyler, that another notable spate of beheading began. This time, it was the turn of **Simon Theobald** from Sudbury (1317-81), an adherent of John of Gaunt and Archbishop of Canterbury and Lord Chancellor of England: in 1377, he had crowned Richard II. When the mob reached London they caught Theobald, beheaded him at Tower Hill and stuck his head on a spike: friends spirited the head back to Sudbury, where the revolt had been suppressed bloodily: rebels were executed in the marketplace following their defeat in Essex. Simon's body ended up in Canterbury Cathedral – it's still there, next to the Black Prince. His head, now lodged in the theological college he had founded at St Gregory's (Gregory Street, Sudbury; *see picture*), meanwhile acquired a miraculous reputation. Pilgrims visited it regularly, and took its teeth away

as relics. Once Simon was down to his last molars, St Gregory's decided on a little decorum: Simon was locked away in a little wall cupboard in the church's vestry. He's still there (the vestry is locked and you will need the permission of a church official to see him; 01787 372611): small, and yellowish and very much without his two front teeth.

This solid Norman castle, rising 110ft, was built by the Earl of Oxford, Aubrey de Vere, in 1140. A Tudor bridge over the dry moat is a more recent addition to the castle, which retains its original four floors, great arched banqueting hall and minstrels' gallery. Somehow Hederingham managed to avoid the fate of Clare Castle which, bit by bit, was dismantled to provide stone for building. On bank holidays and other festive occasions, jousting tournaments are organised with mounted knights in full fig.

Kentwell Hall

Kentwell Hall, Long Melford (01787 310207/ www.kentwell.co.uk).
Open *Apr-mid-July, Sept, Oct* noon-5pm Sun; *mid-July, Aug* noon-5pm daily; *public days* 11am-6pm.
Admission £5.25; £3.20 5s-15s; £4.50 OAPs; *public days* £7.75; £5.20 5s-15s; £6.70 OAPs.

Twenty-five years ago, this magnificent brick Tudor mansion, once seat to the Clopton family, was a ramble of neglect and decrepitude. Slowly, Kentwell's new owners – barrister Patrick Phillips and his family – have brought about the hall's resurrection. It is not a stately home in the mould of Melford Hall, a mile away: this is a working house where Elizabethan kitchens, gardens and animals are still maintained. The Hall regularly holds historical recreations ('public days'), which are immensely popular with visitors and out-of-work actors who nonny-nonny-no from morning 'til night. If you can overlook the artifice of all this (and the tacky thatched hovel, occupied by pretend yokels during recreations), the rose garden maze, open-air Shakespearean theatre (July only) and various outhouses – brewery, dairy and stables, with heavy Suffolk Punch horses – are sites to let your imagination wander.

One of the finest sixteenth-century buildings in the country – Lavenham's **Guildhall**.

Lavenham

The village of Lavenham is the jewel in Suffolk's crown. Growing rich on the medieval wool trade, many of its timbered buildings and halls date from the fourteenth century. Start off at the church, an imposing and martial-looking structure, that rises up black and grey against the fields behind. Moving on down Church Street, past the pedestrian Old Tea Shop, the pink, timbered cottages, all exposed beams and crooked angles come into view. They are typical of Lavenham and indicative of its charm. Most of these houses are private and, while their owners have learnt to live with enthusiastic tourists, try not to press your noses against their windows. Instead, save your curiosity for two of the town's centre-pieces: the **Guildhall of Corpus Christi** (01787 247646; *Apr-Oct* 11am-5pm daily; (NT) £2.80; free under-17s) and **Little Hall** (01787 247179; *Apr-Oct* 2-5.30pm Wed, Thur, Sat, Sun, bank hols; £1.50). Dating from the 1520s, the Guildhall is justly celebrated as one of the most outstanding medieval buildings in England: architectural historians will swoon over it, as should everyone. Close by is the slightly more recent Little Hall, another delightfully timbered building with gardens attached.

Melford Hall

Long Melford (01787 880286).
Open *Apr, Oct* 2-5.30pm Sat, Sun;
May-Sept 2-5.30pm Wed-Sun, bank hols.
Admission (NT) £4.30; £2.15 5s-15s.

This turreted Tudor mansion is a well-maintained and mannered example of Suffolk's stately homes. Home to the Hyde Parker family since 1786, Melford Hall offers many set pieces: its original panelled banqueting hall; an eighteenth-century drawing room and a Regency library. Furniture and Chinese porcelain, captured from a Spanish galleon (the Hyde Parkers produced a number of admirals) are on display, while outside the gardens have a wonderful air of tranquillity; the walled garden is especially beautiful. A country fare is held in the grounds each June; in November, it is also the venue for a vast conflagration in honour of Guy Fawkes' night. Less hands-on and frenetic than Kentwell Hall, Melford Hall proceeds at its own pace – one which probably hasn't varied since Elizabeth I stayed here in 1578. While you're in Melford, visit Holy Trinity church, just up the lane by the sixteenth-century almshouse, founded in 1573 for 12 poor men and two women. The battlemented church, with flint panelling known as flushwork, has a fine Lady Chapel.

Sue Ryder Museum

Cavendish (01787 280653).
Open 10am-5.30pm daily.
Admission 80p; 40p 5s-15s, OAPs.

Situated behind the duck pond and to the side of the Ryder Foundation's lovely Tudor house is a tiny amateur museum that makes up for in heart what it lacks in a rigorous taxonomy. At the end of World War II, its eponymous founder was a FANY (no sniggering at the back: the Female Auxiliary Nursing Yeomanry were a top-notch outfit) who saw at first hand the horror of the concentration camps, particularly in Poland. Sue Ryder converted her Cavendish premises into a refugee home and built a lasting link with Poland as a consequence. The museum has various uniforms, some rather ropey tableaux showing improvised hospitals, plus artifacts from the concentration camps, including – in somewhat dubious taste – a tin of Zyklon B. Other exhibits focus on more jolly things such as the Foundations's global work.

Bury St Edmunds & around

Conservatism still rules.

Dickens was a regular visitor to **Bury St Edmunds**, describing it in *The Pickwick Papers* as 'a handsome little town of thriving and cleanly appearance'. Back then, in the early nineteenth century, Bury made its money from textiles. Now sugar and beer are the dominant industries, but there's still a sense in which it resembles a prosperous Victorian burgher – solid, upright, intolerant of decadence and disorder. The streets positively gleam, and the presence of 'save our pound' demonstrations and the like seem to confirm Bury as a High Tory haven of snobbish insularity. Yet in all other respects, Bury is remarkably welcoming, with a helpful tourist information office and a sedate, intelligent take on its past, which extends to the obvious efforts made to keep monuments just-so and stop modernity from encroaching on the town in too brash and inappropriate a manner.

Bury grew up around the Benedictine Abbey of St Edmund in medieval times and was for centuries a place of pilgrimage (Edmund was England's patron saint until George unseated him) until 1539, when the monastery was dissolved by Henry VIII and fell into ruin. Bury's motto is 'Shrine of a king, cradle of the law', a reference to the legend that in 1214, the barons of England met in the Abbey church and swore an oath to force King John to accept demands that became enshrined in the Magna Carta.

Bury has long been a busy market town. Until 1871, when it was disbanded after complaints of 'rowdyism', the market stretched all the way across Angel Hill, the gentle slope – now an enormous car park – which runs parallel to the Abbey gardens, overlooked on one side by the ivy-festooned Angel Hotel and at the far end by the Athenaeum assembly rooms. The market (the largest of its kind in East Anglia) now takes place on Wednesdays and Saturdays in the area around Cornhill and the Butter Market, best reached via Abbeygate Street, the main shopping thoroughfare.

Beyond Bury

Though there's more than enough in Bury to keep you busy for a weekend, it's worth remembering its proximity to **Newmarket** racecourse (20 minutes' drive away), **Ely** (*see page 277* **Ely does it**) and **Cambridge** (*see page 249*). Another worthwhile excursion is 12 miles north to **Thetford**, just over the Norfolk border. This handsome town, with plenty of gardens and riverside walks, was once seat of the kings and bishops of East Anglia and more recently spawned eighteenth-century radical Thomas Paine. Born in White Hart Street, he is represented in the Ancient House Museum in the same street. The tourist office is here too.

A few miles south-west of Thetford in the local churchyard of the tiny village of **Elveden** is the unlikely last resting place of Prince Duleep Singh (died 1893), the last Sikh Maharajah, who was given the huge Elveden estate in return for his Punjab kingdom and the Koh-i-Noor diamond. Elveden Hall is, alas, not open to the public. Those wanting a country house experience could, instead, view **Euston Hall**, not far away, just off the A1088.

The dominating feature of this sparsely populated area is the massive **Thetford Forest**, planted in drearily regular rows by the Forestry Commission in the 1920s. The High Lodge Forest Centre (off the B1107 east of Brandon) has details of forest walks.

By train from London

Trains to **Bury St Edmunds** leave **King's Cross** approximately every 20 mins and **Liverpool Street** about every half hour; the fastest takes around **1hr 45mins**.

Where to stay

Abbey Hotel

35 Southgate Street, Bury St Edmunds, IP33 2AZ (01284 762020/fax 01284 724770).
Rates (B&B) *single occupancy* £55; *double/twin* £60-£68; *family room* £75-£85; *suite* £75; *St Botolph's Cottage* (sleeps 4) £75 as double, then £7.50pp.
Rooms (all en suite) 12 double/twin; 2 family; 1 suite. **Cards** AmEx, MC, V.

East Anglia

Ten minutes' walk from the town centre, the Abbey comprises a former Tudor hostelry (connected to the adjacent maltings at Oast Court) along with more recent extensions. It's comfortable rather than luxurious, and a number of the rooms feel slightly makeshift. Baut it does have a low-ceilinged charm, and some of the bedrooms are on the original site of the medieval Chapel of St Botolph. The former landlord's stable and hayloft in the rear yard has been converted into snug cottage accommodation.

Angel Hotel

3 Angel Hill, Bury St Edmunds, IP33 1LT (01284 753926/fax 01284 750092/sales@theangel.co.uk/www.theangel.co.uk).
Rates *single* £68; *double* £86 *four-poster* £130. Special breaks. **Rooms** (all en suite) 9 single; 38 double; 4 four-poster. **Cards** AmEx, DC, Debit, MC, V.
Managerial musical chairs and the sheer expense of upkeep are taking their toll on this, Dickens' hostel of choice on his sundry visits to the town. (You can still stay in his favoured room.) The posher suites impress, but they're expensive and the standard rooms are shockingly basic. The Abbeygate restaurant serves creditable fare, though its recent, rather outré refurbishment in mismatched blues and golds has provoked much local consternation. Children welcome.

Chantry Hotel

8 Sparhawk Street, Bury St Edmunds, IP33 1RY (01284 767427/fax 01284 760946).
Rates (B&B) *single* £44.50-£54.50; *standard double/twin* £59.50; *superior double/suite* £67.50.
Rooms (all en suite) 3 single; 3 twin; 9 double; 1 suite. **Cards** AmEx, DC, Debit, MC, V.
Standing on the site of a twelfth-century chantry chapel, the main building is actually Georgian. One of the adjacent Tudor buildings has been incorporated into the hotel. Not quite as plush as some of its rivals (though there's a smattering of mahogany and wrought iron in the dearer rooms), but it is a bit cheaper, and headily close to the brewery. Children are welcome; pets by arrangement only. No smoking in dining room.

Old Egremont House

31 Egremont Street, Ely, CB6 1AE (tel/fax 01353 663118).
Rates (B&B) *single*; £29; *double/twin* £44.
Rooms 1 single (en suite); 2 double/twin.

The richly decorated **Twelve Angel Hill**.

A B&B is your best bet if you do decide you want to stay in Ely. Sadly, the atmospheric Black Hostelry next to the cathedral has now closed, but this upscale establishment, run by Sheila Friend-Smith, is just as good and has a great view of the cathedral from the garden. Breakfasts use fresh local produce. Children welcome. No smoking throughout.

Ounce House

Northgate Street, Bury St Edmunds, IP33 1HP (01284 761779/fax 01284 768315/pott@globalnet.co.uk).
Rates *single occupancy* £50-£60; *double/twin* £80-£90; *family room* £100. **Rooms** (all en suite) 1 twin; 2 double. **Cards** AmEx, MC, V.
A former Victorian merchant's house with a large garden at the back and ample car-parking space. Rooms are spacious; antiques and paintings contribute to an air of solid bourgeois gentility. Guests breakfast together around a single long table, which can be awkward if you're not in the mood for conversation. The friendly owners, Simon and Jenny Pott, are key figures in the local community, and an excellent source of tips and gossip. Children by arrangement. No smoking throughout.

Twelve Angel Hill

12 Angel Hill, Bury St Edmunds, IP33 1UZ (01284 704088/fax 01284 725549).
Rates (B&B) *single* £50-£55; *single occupancy* £60-£65; *double/twin* £80-£85; *suite/four-poster* £85.
Rooms (all en suite) 2 single; 1 twin; 2 double; 1 four-poster; 1 suite. **Cards** AmEx, DC, MC, V.
John and Bernie Clarke's B&B is top class, and the deserving recipient of numerous awards, including one for its (incredible) breakfasts. It's smartly decorated, too, with daubed yellow walls in the hall and a rich red, oak-panelled bar/lounge, which dates back to the sixteenth century. Rooms are large (the single is the size of doubles in most other places), well equipped and named after classic wine-growing regions. No smoking throughout. No children under 16.

There isn't a huge amount of choice in Bury, but the better restaurants deserve their local reputations. If you're in a hurry or not fussy, a number of chains have opened in the past year. In terms of boozers, there's the quirky **Nutshell Pub** on Skinner Street, a Greene King pub which, at 16ft by 7.5ft, is said to be the smallest pub in Britain. Another of its 'attractions' is the dead cat hanging from its ceiling.

Leaping Hare

Wyken Hall, Stanton, Bury St Edmunds (01359 250287).
Food served 10am-6pm Wed, Thur, Sun; 10am-6pm, 7-9.30pm, Fri, Sat. **Cards** Debit, MC, V.
Housed in a 400-year-old barn next to the Elizabethan manor house Wyken Hall, the Leaping Hare is ten minutes' drive from Bury. The food manages to be Olde English and Modern Mediterranean at the same time. The brief menu changes every day and might include such inventive dishes as black pudding and snail salad

Ely does it

Half an hour's drive away along the A14 and A142, **Ely** is perhaps most familiar to nostalgic thirtysomethings as the place Tom and Hatty skate to along the frozen Great Ouse in Philippa Pearce's children's classic, *Tom's Midnight Garden*: 'They walked through the town, making for the cathedral, and went in through the great west door. Inside, the failing of winter daylight was beginning to fill the vastness with gloom. Through this they walked down the nave towards the octagon; and it seemed to Tom as if the roof of the cathedral were like a lesser sky, for, although they walked steadily, when they looked upwards, it moved very little in relation to its spaces. Hatty walked with dazzled eyes: "Oh, I never thought there was anything so big – so beautiful!" she said.'

John Major might have had Ely in mind when he waffled cheerily about warm beer, old maids on bicycles, cricket on the village green, etc. In truth, it's stranger than that: a place where, you sense, countless evacuee childhoods were unspent. Ely Cathedral knocks spots of Bury's and so dominates the town that the shopping and riverside areas feel a bit dour and depleted in comparison. The Cathedral was founded as a monastery in 673 by Saxon princess St Etheldreda, a shrine to whom you can find in front of the High Altar. The octagon which so impressed Tom and Hatty is breathtaking: 200 tons of timber, glass and lead, it was built after the original Norman central tower collapsed in 1322, and appears to just hang there unsupported.

Also worth checking out on a day trip are **Oliver Cromwell's House** (also the tourist information centre; 01353 662062), which the Lord Protector inherited in 1636 and now features a Portrait Room, a Civil War exhibition, Cromwell's Study, a Haunted Bedroom and a room devoted to the history of the drainage of The Fens; **Ely Museum** at the Old Gaol (01353 666655); and the **Stained Glass Museum** in the South Triforium of the cathedral (01353 660347). For food, try the Old Fire Engine House at 25 St Mary's Street (01353 662582), which serves generous helpings of no-nonsense English fare like noisette of lamb and plum crumble with custard.

or tomato tart with Suffolk sheep's brie and olives, followed by yummy comfort-food desserts like buttermilk pudding with rhubarb. You can sample their own wine, too. Three courses with wine should work out at just over £20 per head.

Maison Bleue at Mortimer's

30-31 Churchgate Street, Bury St Edmunds (01284 760623).
Food served noon-2.30pm, 7-9.30pm, Mon-Sat.
Set meals *lunch* £14.95 (3 courses); *dinner* £17.95 (3 courses) Mon-Fri. **Cards** AmEx, DC, Debit, MC, V.
This fish restaurant is generally held to be the best in Bury. All the fish is locally caught. The platter of fruits de mer – a tottering tower of steaming crustacea you have to order a few days in advance – is especially fine, as is the poached brill with grilled aubergine and pepper, though there's plenty for the piscatorially sceptical (shank of lamb in red wine, for instance). Expect to pay about £30 per head.

Pizza Express

40 Abbeygate Street, Bury St Edmunds (01284 704802).
Food served 11.30am-midnight daily.
Cards AmEx, Debit, MC, V.
No, we're not being funny. This recently opened branch is light, airy and (by Bury standards) daringly minimalist in its décor. The pizzas are as good, but definitely seem more generously topped, than their London brethren. No bookings taken.

Somewhere Else

1 Langton Place, Bury St Edmunds (01284 760750).
Food served 10.30am-10.30pm Tue-Sat.
Cards MC, V.
Low-key but impressive, Somewhere Else is the perfect lunch stop, with a menu which takes in all manner of toasted and open sandwiches, from brie, avocado and garlic mushroom to cottage cheese, chive salad and walnut, all from £2.75-3.80.

What to see & do

Tourist information centres

6 Angel Hill, **Bury St Edmunds**, IP33 1UZ (01284 764667). **Open** *Easter-Oct* 9.30am-5.30pm Mon-Sat;

East Anglia

10am-3pm Sun; *Nov-Easter* 10am-4pm Mon-Fri; 10am-1pm Sat.

Ancient House Museum, White Hart Street, **Thetford**, IP24 1AA (01842 752599). **Open** *June-Aug* 10am-12,30pm, 1-5pm, Mon-Sat; 2-5pm Sun; *Sept-May* 10am-12.30pm, 1-5pm, Mon-Sat.

Bike hire

Mick's Cycles 68 St John's Street, **Bury St Edmunds** (01284 753946). About 10-15 minutes' walk from the station.

Abbey ruins & gardens

Bury St Edmunds (01284 763110/www.stedmundsbury.gov.uk). **Open** *gardens* 7.30am-dusk Mon-Sat; 9am-dusk Sun. **Admission** *audio tour* £1.50; £1 5s-16s, OAPs, students.

The abbey gardens, with their roses, yew hedges and carefully tended beds of forget-me-nots, are great for a peaceful stroll, but the ruins themselves are lumpily underwhelming. For some context, make for the Abbey Visitors Centre in Samson's Tower, part of the Abbey's West Front, where you can pick up the necessary gear for an audio tour, or call the tourist information centre (01284 764667) to arrange a guided tour. On Saturdays between June and September (10.30am and noon) you can be shown around by one Brother Jocelin de Brakelond, who lived in Bury in the twelfth century. He'll tell you all about the travails of Benedictine life under Abbot Samson. Or, for the hardy of stomach, there's Victorian graveyard warden William Hunter (Saturdays 1.30pm and 3pm), who spins pleasurably grisly yarns about resurrection men and the charnel house. These guided tours cost £2.50 for adults and £1 for children.

Greene King Brewery

Westgate Brewery Westgate Street, Bury St Edmunds (01284 714382). **Open** *tours* 10am, 2pm, Mon-Thur. **Admission** £5 (no under-18s).

Follow your nose. Greene King has been brewing beer here on Westgate Street since 1799. The brewery still uses the same traditional methods, and the pungent results – Abbot Ale and St Edmund Ale – are enough to make you grow a beard and start wearing roll-necks. Tours of the brewhouse and fermenting room are available most weekdays, starting at 10am and 2pm. Pre-booking is essential.

Manor House Museum

5 Honey Hill, Bury St Edmunds (01284 757072). **Open** *Apr-Oct* 10am-5pm Tue-Sun, bank hols; *Nov-Mar* 10am-4pm Tue-Sun. **Admission** £2.85; £1.85 5s-16s, OAPs, students.

Built by John Hervey, the first Earl of Bristol, this Georgian mansion has been converted into an offbeat museum full of paintings, furniture, costume, objets d'art and lots and lots of clocks. One can, you'll rapidly discover, have too many clocks, though the touch-sensitive computer screens in each room make fact-gleaning easy. If you're planning a visit in early 2000, phone to check first as the museum may be closed during this period.

Moyse's Hall Museum

Cornhill, Bury St Edmunds (01284 757488). **Open** 10am-5pm Mon-Sat; 2-5pm Sun. **Admission** £1.60; £1 5s-16s, OAPs, students.

Moyse's Hall has been many things in its 800-year history, including a tavern, a synagogue and a prison. Now it's a museum of local history and archaeology which numbers among its more ghoulish exhibits a lock of Mary Tudor's hair and a book covered in the skin of William Corder, the man convicted of the notorious 'Red Barn' murder in 1827, as well as his flayed scalp. One for the kids.

Rede Hall Park Farm

Rede, Bury St Edmunds (01284 850695). **Open** *Apr-Sept* 10am-5pm daily. **Admission** £3, £2 2s-15s, OAPs.

A working farm, utilising machinery and methods from an era where genetically modified vegetables were not even dreamt of. The wagons and 1930s tractors introduce an altogether slower pace to life. Cart rides, pets' corners, a farming museum and the like are among the attractions.

St Edmundsbury Cathedral

Angel Hill, Bury St Edmunds (01284 754933). **Open** *June-Aug* 8am-8pm daily; *Sept-May* 8am-6pm daily. **Admission** donation.

Over 1,100 years old and still not finished. St Edmundsbury was only granted cathedral status in 1914, and even then it was a toss-up between it and nearby St Mary's as to who would get it. The cathedral's entrance porch, quire, crossings and lady chapel were built as late as the 1960s. A £5-million Millennium Commission grant has made it possible to complete the St Edmund Chapel, transept, cloisters and tower. Architecturally it's hit and miss, but stumbling upon a choir practice can be an unexpected, transporting joy. For guided tours, call the Cathedral Visitor Officer on the above number. The Cathedral Refectory is popular for morning coffee and light snacks.

Theatre Royal

Westgate Street, Bury St Edmunds (01284 769505/www.theatreroyal.org).

Owned by Greene King, who once used it to store hops (it's opposite the brewery on Westgate Street), the Theatre Royal is leased to the National Trust and is one of the smallest and oldest working theatres in the country. Ironically, its size works in its favour, attracting interesting Almeida-scale productions. It's well worth phoning for a brochure (01284 769505).

West Stow Anglo-Saxon Village

Icklingham Road, West Stow (01284 728718). **Open** 10am-5pm daily. Last entry 4pm. **Admission** £4.50; £3.50 5s-16s, OAPs, students.

This replica village is built on the site of a genuine Anglo-Saxon dwelling excavated between 1965 and 1972. Hire an audio guide and wander from the Weaving House to the Living House to the Sunken House, learning all about life in fifth-century East Anglia. Pigs and hens and crops add to the 'realism'. There's also a 125-acre country park, with nature and wildfowl reserves and two Visitors' Centres. West Stow is a short drive from Bury along the A1101.

East Anglia

Suffolk Coast

A singular seaside experience.

*Two of the hundreds of brightly painted beach huts which line the seafront at **Southwold**.*

Very odd, Suffolk. And it's not easy to say why. Perhaps it's because the county is not really on the way to anywhere (apart from very flat Norfolk, and the sea) that it's managed to maintain its own distinct identity and a subtle otherness. Nowhere in the county is this more true than along the coast. The more sensitive visitor will revel in the marginally uneasy juxtaposition of the cosy and the bleak, the cultivated and the wild. It's perfect Barbara Vine territory, and it's no wonder that Ruth Rendell's darker alter ego has set several of her claustrophobic novels in the county (including *No Night is Too Long*, which makes use of Orford and Aldeburgh). This frisson is probably at its least noticeable during the height of the summer when crowds of demob-happy Essex folk frolic on Southwold's shingle, and cravat-enhanced music-lovers attend the Proms season at Snape Maltings. But if you ever happen to be in, say, Orford, on a biting winter's day, walking in the shadow of the grim castle keep, past the fulminating fug of the blackened smokehouse, and down to the quayside as the mist rolls slowly and silently in from the River Alde, you'll know you're somewhere pretty special.

Woodbridge to Aldeburgh

There's not a lot specifically to *do* along the coast (and beaches are predominantly pebbly, the sea icy) – in fact, locals rather look down their noses at 'attractions'. You come here to *be* rather than to *do*. **Woodbridge**, a few miles north-east of Ipswich, may be inland but this lively one-time Elizabethan ship-building port makes an agreeable introduction to the area. Stretching back up a hill from the River Deben, you'll find a scattering of minor sights (Woodbridge Tide Mill, the Suffolk Horse

By train from London

One or two trains an hour go from **Liverpool Street** to **Woodbridge**, with a change at **Ipswich**. The entire journey takes **1hr 45mins** to **2hrs**.

A trio of Suffolk's distinctive town signs.

Museum, Woodbridge Museum), antiques shops, the odd good pub and restaurant, and plenty of stress-free strolling. Not far out of town is the site of probably the most celebrated archaeological find ever made in Britain, **Sutton Hoo** – the fabulous treasure-stuffed ship of a seventh-century East Anglian king.

Between Woodbridge and the coast, the wind-whipped Rendlesham and Tunstall Forests provide a barrier which only adds to the invigorating feeling of isolation in little **Orford**. Overlooked by its twelfth-century keep, there's little to do here but walk, eat and drink and contemplate the immense expanse of **Orford Ness**. In the twelfth century the then-nascent shingle spit provided a sheltered harbour for Orford. Unfortunately, it wouldn't stop growing and, expanding by around 16 metres a year, it now all but cuts the village off from the sea. Boat trips run from the quay. While you're in Orford, pick up picnic goodies from Richardsons Smokehouse, and take a quick look at the Norman church of St Bartholomew – there's a fine font inside and a huge rosemary bush in the churchyard.

The next major settlement on the coast heading north is **Aldeburgh**. It's a classy place and knows it (so pronounce it 'orl-brer' if you want to create the right impression). There are deliberately few concessions to the tourist industry along the long, wide High Street that runs parallel to the sea, but it's a relaxed spot to hang out nonetheless. Constant erosion of the coastline means that the current seafront is something of a jumble – it was never meant to face the ocean. The oldest building in town is here – the sixteenth-century moot hall – as is a shiny modern lifeboat station. If you don't fancy eating out at one of the town's surprising

number of excellent restaurants, then join the often considerable High Street queues at the Aldeburgh Fish & Chip Shop and the Golden Galleon and then take your booty on to the pebbly beach.

No-one is more associated with his native region that **Benjamin Britten** is with the Suffolk Coast. He was born in Lowestoft in 1913 and lived the majority of his life in the area. In 1947 Britten moved with the celebrated tenor (and his lifelong partner) Peter Pears to Crag House on Crabbe Street in Aldeburgh. Together with the producer and librettist Eric Crozier they came up with the idea of starting a modest musical festival. Today, the **Aldeburgh Festival** (now held a few miles inland at Snape Maltings) is one of the world's premier classical music and opera festivals. Many of Britten's works are set in Suffolk, most notably the tragic story of the Aldeburgh fisherman Peter Grimes (inspired by local poet George Crabbe's *The Borough*). Fans should get hold of the 'Britten Trail' leaflet available at the tourist office.

Snape Maltings, a large collection of Victorian malthouses and granaries on the banks of the Alde, has been developed as far more than just a concert venue. It now encompasses a music school and a 'unique shopping experience', consisting of a music shop, gallery, kitchen shop, crafts shop, 'period home centre', clothes store, a pub and tea shop. Frankly, it's all rather unreal and over-priced. More appealing are the range of painting, craft and decorative arts courses run from here (01728 688305) and the regular river trips.

North to Southwold

Thorpeness, a couple of miles north of Aldeburgh, is a surreal little place. With its rows of black-boarded and faux half-timbered houses, it has the air of a Tudor theme village. It's hardly a surprise when you learn that the entire settlement was dreamed up as a fashionable resort by GS Ogilvie when he bought the Sizewell estate in 1910. Go for a row on the Meare, dug by hand by navvies, and sprinkled with 20 islands named after characters in *Peter Pan* in honour of Ogilvie's friend JM Barrie. He also created a well and used a windmill to pump the water to a tank on top of a 26-m tower, which he disguised as a overgrown house, known as the 'House in the Clouds'. The windmill can be visited, and the Dolphin Inn is good for a spot of refreshment.

A little further up the coast is the area's most controversial presence: **Sizewell**. Apart from the legion of pylons striding purposefully across the coastal flats, the twin nuclear power stations are a surprisingly low-key presence. The huge dome of Sizewell B, the UK's only pressurised water reactor, is the most distinctive feature. There's even a moderately popular beach by the power station for the truly blithe.

Unlikely as it seems, **Dunwich** (the 'w' is silent), a diminutive village with a good pub (the Ship), a few remaining beach-launched fishing boats and a seaside café serving up possibly the freshest fish and chips in the country, was once a major port (*see page 283* **The city that fell into the sea**). Little evidence now remains beyond the sparse ruins of Greyfriars Abbey and the salvaged remains of All Saints church and leper chapel in the churchyard of St James's. Don't miss the superb **Dunwich Museum**, which tells the remarkable story of this unique place.

The northern extent of this break is marked by **Southwold**. It's the biggest 'resort' on this stretch of coast, yet in Suffolk all this means is that (in season) you get a lot of lobster-hued holidaymakers picnicking outside the brightly painted beach huts that stretch along the entire promenade (plus one tiny amusement arcade on the soon-to-be-rebuilt rump of the pier), while the town up on the cliffs gets on with its own life. When you consider that one of Southwold's premier attractions is 'the only purpose-built museum dedicated to the story and history of amber' you get an idea of the sort of place it is. Low key to a fault.

The most dominant force in Southwold life is the estimable Adnams Brewery, which owns the town's best two hotels (the Crown and the Swan, which it is situated behind). The Sole Bay Brewery, founded in the early seventeenth century, was based on the same site; it was bought by the Adnams family in 1872. There are few Southwold pleasures like supping an

Adnams brew on one of the many greens that speckle the town.

Another must is the 20-minute walk along the seafront or cross-country to the rowing-boat ferry over the River Blyth to **Walberswick**. This somnolent little village was once home to painter Philip Wilson Steer and, apart from the excellent Bell Inn, boasts a curious church-within-a-church. In the Middle Ages, Walberswick was a sizeable port and the original fifteenth-century St Andrew's was to be a mighty church to reflect the status of the town. But Walberswick's fortunes declined before the church was finished and much of it was dismantled to build the much smaller current church which now stands within the older building's ruins. Another notable church close by is in **Blythburgh**. The huge Holy Trinity, known as the 'Cathedral of the Marshes' has a wonderfully ornate exterior and is filled with light inside.

Where to stay

The Suffolk Coast can be a bugger of a place to find a free room. Book as far in advance as possible, and if the places reviewed below are full, try the **Uplands Hotel** in Aldeburgh (01728 452420; £69), **Ferry House** in Walberswick (01502 723384; £42), **Theberton Grange** in Theberton (01728 830625; £80) or the **Crown Inn** in Snape (01728 688324; £50). If you want to stay in Orford, there are rooms at the **King's Head** (01394 450271; £45), the **Crown & Castle** (01394 450205; £70) and, near the quay, the **Jolly Sailor** (01394 450243; £35). All prices quoted are for the cheapest double rooms.

Acton Lodge
18 South Green, Southwold, IP18 6HB (01502 723217). **Rates** *single occupancy* £25-£35; *double/twin* £44-£70. **Rooms** 3 double/twin (2 en suite).
Enjoying a fantastic location close to the sea on one of Southwold's characteristic and immensely characterful greens, this weighty Victorian guesthouse is packed with original features and has been furnished in an appropriately antiquey style. Bedrooms are smart and have the usual tea and coffee making facilities. Breakfasts are above average. A good value choice. Children welcome. Non-smoking throughout.

Bell Inn
Ferry Road, Walberswick, IP18 6TN (01502 723109/fax 01502 722728). **Rates** (B&B) *single occupancy* £30; *double/twin* £60; *family* £80-£100. **Rooms** (all en suite) 4 double; 1 twin; 1 family. **Cards** Debit, MC, V.
On the light-suffused apex of Walberswick's estuary and rivermouth, with views of both, this pleasingly plain 600-year-old pub has old stone floors eroded to a polish, wooden settles, fires and good fish dinners and ceilings

East Anglia

*The beach-side **Ocean House** in Aldeburgh.*

to suit the height of a fourteenth-century population. The six rooms above have twentieth-century flourishes – en suite bathrooms, tea and coffee-making facilities – but nothing (fortunately) can be done about their basically medieval character. Great garden. Children and dogs welcome. All bedrooms non-smoking.

A12 N; take B1387 E to Walberswick; inn is signposted in village; follow signs up track; hotel is on right.

The Crown

90 High Street, Southwold, IP18 6DP
(01502 722275/fax 01502 727263).
Rates (B&ContB) *single* £47; *double/twin* £72; *family* £98. Breakfast £4 (Eng). **Rooms** 2 single (both en suite); 5 double (4 en suite); 4 twin (3 en suite).

The number two Adnams-owned hotel in Southwold (there's also the **Cricketers**, just outside town in Reydon; 01502 723603; doubles from £59), is considerably smaller and cheaper than the nearby Swan. Bedrooms tend towards the diminutive and are simply decorated, but the hotel's great plus is its snug marine-inspired Back Bar and a buzzing front bar-brasserie – the best place to eat and drink in Southwold (*see p284*). Behind the Crown is the HQ, cellar and kitchen shop of the much-respected Adnams Wine Merchants. Children and dogs welcome.

Ocean House

25 Crag Path, Aldeburgh, IP15 5BS
(01728 452094/jbreroh@aol.com).
Rates (B&B) *single occupancy* £60; *double/twin* £65. Special breaks. **Rooms** (both en suite) 2 double/twin.

Wonderfully situated overlooking Aldeburgh's pebbly beach, Ocean House is a mid-Victorian monolith that's been sensitively restored to its original condition by Phil and Juliet Brereton. The bedrooms have views out over the icy North Sea, and there's a games room in the basement. The hearty breakfasts are excellent. No children or dogs. No smoking throughout the house.

A12 N; take A1094 E to Aldeburgh; hotel is on seafront between two look-out towers.

Old Rectory

Campsea Ashe, IP13 0PU (tel/fax 01728 746524).
Rates (B&B) *single* £38; *double/twin* £58; *four-poster* £58-£69; *family* £69. **Rooms** (all en suite) 2 single; 5 double/twin; 2 four-poster; 1 family.

It's not on the coast, but the Old Rectory, in a small, tranquil village near Woodbridge, is a quirky and fun place to stay. Owner Stewart Bassett encourages an informal atmosphere in the sizeable Georgian house. There's a good range of bedrooms, from the big four-poster room overlooking the garden to the cosy attic room. A no-choice dinner can be prepared on request (Monday to Saturday, three courses for £18). Children and dogs welcome. Non-smoking throughout.

A12 N; take B1078 E to Campsea Ashe; go through village; over bridge; house is on right next to church.

Sternfield House

Sternfield, nr Saxmundham, IP17 1RS (01728 602252).
Rates (B&B) *single* £30; *double* £90; *twin* £30.
Rooms 1 single; 5 double (all en suite); 3 twin.

This must be Suffolk's grandest family home B&B – the building (constructed around 1700) is one of the finest Queen Anne houses in East Anglia. During the last war it was commandeered by the military and much of the planning for the Normandy landings took place here. A sweeping drive cuts through the extensive grounds, which are dotted with pergolas, summer houses, lovely vistas and a tennis court and swimming pool (both of which guests can use). Bedrooms are large, decorated in a somewhat heavy style, but very comfortable. Breakfast, served on a table of gargantuan proportions, is excellent. Pricey for a B&B, but worth it for the setting. Children welcome. Non-smoking throughout.

A12 N; take B1121 E to Sternfield; first right over humped back bridge; first driveway on left.

The Swan

Market Place, Southwold, IP18 6EG (01502 722186/ fax 01502 724800/hotels@adnams.co.uk).
Rates (B&B) *single* £59-£65; *double/twin* £95-£108; *deluxe double/twin* £115-£130; *four-poster* £165; *suites* £155. **Rooms** (all en suite) 4 single; 28 double/twin; 8 deluxe double/twin; 1 four-poster; 2 suites. **Cards** AmEx, DC, Debit, MC, V.

The jewel in the Adnams hotel crown, the Swan has always been the most prestigious inn in Southwold and remains so today. The most characterful parts of the building (such as the stone-flagged lobby), date from the seventeenth century. The airy portrait-hung lounge and leathery bar are great places to chill out and the stately restaurant is well worth trying. There are 25 bedrooms in the main hotel and a further 18 around an old bowling green in the garden (stay in the former if possible); décor is unobtrusive – pale wallpapers, framed pics of local scenes – and bathrooms are spick and shiny.

Breakfast is outstandiing. But, all this aside, what impresses most about the Swan is the breezy friendliness and efficiency of the staff. A hotel very much at ease with itself. Children and dogs welcome.

Wateringfield

Golf Lane, Aldeburgh, IP15 5PY (01728 453163).
Rates (B&B) *single £20; double/twin £38-£45.*
Rooms 1 single; 2 double (1 en suite); 3 twin.
This 1930s house, sitting in a fine garden, is a good value option. Much care has been taken over the décor and the bedrooms are kitted out with well-chosen wallpapers and furniture. Helpful owner Linda Connah is happy to advise on local amenities. Non-smoking throughout.
A12 N; take A1094 E to Aldeburgh, then B1122 N; turn right into Golf Lane; house is 500m on right.

Where to eat & drink

There aren't any stunning pubs in Southwold – the best are those which allow al fresco spillover in fine weather. Try the **Lord Nelson**, between Market Hill and the sea (and take your pint of Adnams to the seafront) or the **Red Lion**, where drinkers chill out on the lovely South Green. In Woodbridge, the best pub is the **King's Head** on Market Hill (01502 724517), which offers a wide range of good food. For a snack in Aldeburgh, the excellent café and sandwich shop **Scandelicious** (163 High Street; 01728 452880), specialises in Nordic goodies.

Other pubs worth a visit are the **Crown Inn** (good for nosh; 01728 688324), and the **Golden Key** (01728 688510), both in Snape. In Aldeburgh, try the **White Lion**, the **Mill** or the flower-festooned **Cross Keys**.

Butley Orford Oysterage

Market Hill, Orford (01394 450277).
Food served *Apr-Oct* noon-2.15pm, 7-9pm, Mon-Fri; noon-2.15pm, 6-9pm, Sat; noon-2.15pm, 6.30-9pm, Sun; *Nov-Mar* noon-2.15pm Mon-Thur, Sun; noon-2.15pm, 7-9pm Fri, noon-2.15pm, 6-9pm, Sat.
Cards Debit, MC, V.
The best spot in Orford for some quality local seafood. It's fairly spartan inside, so there's little to detract from the keenly priced and feisty-fresh fish – perhaps simple baked mullet (£7.95) or cod in parsley sauce (£6.90), or

The city that fell into the sea

'I defy anyone, at desolate, exquisite Dunwich, to be disappointed in anything.'
(Henry James)

Dunwich is an unremarkable hamlet with an extraordinary history. For, in early medieval times, this tiny settlement was the region's most populous city, and one of the largest ports in the country.

At its peak, the walled city supported a population of between 4,000 and 5,000 people, ministering to their needs with more than a dozen churches, monasteries, hospitals, palaces, and even a mint. It was a cosmopolitan place, importing furs, fish and timber from the Baltic and Iceland, wine from France and fine cloth from the Low Countries, and exporting grain and raw wool. Wealthy merchants built tall, timber-framed houses for themselves on the roads down to the docks which were famed for their ships and ship-building. In 1241 Dunwich was able to send 80 ships to help the king (the same number as supplied by London).

Yet less than 50 years later a huge storm marked the beginning of the end. Erosion of the sandy cliffs had always been a problem, but the townfolk had previously managed to take effective preventative measures. In 1286, though, a three-day battering, combined with an unusually high spring tide, washed away part of the city. In the fourteenth century, the harbour started seriously silting up and the coast continued to be eroded. Decline was rapid. The harbour had effectively gone by the sixteenth century and Dunwich's fine churches and houses gradually toppled over the receding cliffs into the sea. The last medieval church, All Saints, disappeared in the early twentieth century. The erosion continues today. The story of Dunwich is told in the excellent **Dunwich Museum**.

St James Street, Dunwich (01728 648796).
Open *Apr-Sept* 11.30am-4.30pm daily; *Oct* noon-4pm daily. **Admission** free.

One of the last fishermen in Dunwich.

more unusual dishes such as pork and cockle stew‑ (£6.40). Start, perhaps, with oyster soup (£3.60) or smoked cod roe on toast (£5.80), and don't miss the local samphire (£3.80) when it's in season.

Café 152

152 High Street, Aldeburgh (01728 454152).
Food served *Apr-Sept* noon-2.30pm, 6-9pm, Mon, Wed-Sun; *Oct-Mar* noon-2.30pm, 6-9pm, Wed-Sun.
Cards DC, Debit, MC, V.

Café 152 offers perhaps the most intimate dining experience in Aldeburgh. Warm terracotta paint and candlelight provided a soothing backdrop for equally warming Med-influenced dishes like Moroccan tomato, saffron and roast garlic soup (£3.25), risotto nero topped with griddled squid (£7.25) and marinaded lamb steak with roasted vegetables, olives and aioli (£8.75).

Captain's Table

3 Quay Street, Woodbridge (01394 383145).
Food served noon-2pm, 6.30-9.30pm, Tue-Thur; noon-2pm, 6.30-10pm, Fri, Sat; noon-2pm Sun.
Cards Debit, MC, V.

The name isn't particularly promising, but while there's plenty of fish on the regular and specials menus, the lack of nautical decorative theming in the three interconnecting dining rooms gives a clue that this pub/restaurant is of a superior breed. Modernity makes its presence felt in dishes such as spiced salmon with lime and coriander, but there's more simply cooked piscean treats like grilled Dover sole too. A refreshing lack of pretention in presenation and service are further plus points. Around £25 a head excluding wine for three courses.

The Crown

90 High Street, Southwold (01502 722275).
Food served 12.30-1.30pm, 7.30-9.30pm, daily.
Set meals *lunch* £14.50 (2 courses), £17.50 (3 courses); *dinner* £19.50 (2 courses), £24.50 (3 courses). **Cards** AmEx, DC, Debit, MC, V.

Probably the premier dining spot in town, such is the Crown's popularity that tables can spill across the entrance hall from the lively bar-brasserie to the more sedate 'Parlour'. The set-price dinner menu offers carefully presented starters such as antipasti of bresaola, aubergine, mozzarella, courgette and anchovy dressing, and a selection of smoked and marinated seafood with guacamole and herb salad. There's ambition aplenty in mains like lasagne of grilled monkfish tail with minty crushed potatoes, cherry tomatoes and tapenade cream, and pleasing simplicity in the likes of roast fillet of sea bass with spring onion mash, crispy bacon and sweet tomato dressing. As Adnams Wine Merchants is based behind the Crown, you'd expect a varied and interesting wine list – and that is exactly what you get.

Froize Inn

Chillesford (01394 450282).
Food served noon-2pm, 7-9pm, Tue-Sun.

For many years Alistair Shaw was the man behind the pans at Orford's King's Head. Now he and his wife Joy run this top-notch pub just a few miles away. Part of the building dates from the fifteenth century and was once a friary – the friars used to serve up a type of savoury pancake called a 'froize' to weary travellers, hence the name. Today's weary travellers will find far more vari-

ety on Alistair's ambitious and assured menu. Start perhaps with boudin blanc on red onion marmalade with smokey bacon and potato cake (£6.95) and go on to one of the excellent fish dishes such as Orford plaice with grilled chicory and herb butter (£12.95). Very friendly service, and as welcoming if you just want a drink as a full meal. Bedrooms available (£55 for a double).

Lighthouse

77 High Street, Aldeburgh (01728 453377).
Food served noon-2.30pm, 7-11pm, daily.
Set meal *lunch & dinner* £13.50 (2 courses), £15.75 (3 courses). **Cards** Debit, MC, V.

Café and deli by day, the versatile Lighthouse shines brightest in the evening when its excellent value fixed-priced menu delivers such goodies as fresh spaghetti with crab (in an unannounced Thai curry-like sauce) and toothsome potted shrimps on toast, followed by grilled fresh tuna on a Mexican bean and chilli salad, and roast chicken breast on Puy lentils with a rich Parmesan butter. Boozy banana pancake is a classy way to finish. The wine list is notable – both for range and quality of bottles and the very reasonable prices.

Regatta

171 High Street, Aldeburgh (01728 452011).
Food served noon-2pm, 6-10pm, days vary seasonally. **Cards** AmEx, DC, Debit, MC, V.

There is, as might be expected, some maritime theming to this popular restaurant, but it's understated and the cool-flagged floor and clean lines make for a relaxed eating environment. There's a certain global jiggery-pokery to the menu, which offers most dishes as either starters and mains. You might find steamed couscous with roasted tomatoes and baked goat's cheese (£5/£8), Peking duck salad with hoisin dressing (£5/£8) or fish specials like sea trout (£11) or skate (£8.50). Regatta also puts on regular events and can provide excellent beach picnics complete with plates and cutlery.

Spice

17 The Thoroughfare, Woodbridge (01394 382557).
Food served noon-2pm, 7-10pm, Mon-Sat.
Cards AmEx, Debit, MC, V.

Spice offers an unusual mix of oriental and occidental – perhaps Asian-flavoured aubergine crostini (£3.75), fresh tuna with olive oil, roasted plum tomatoes and basil (£8.50), nasi goreng (£6.25) or spinach and chick-pea curry with baked eggs (£5.95). At lunch-times, there's an 'Express' menu with two courses for £8.25.

The Swan

Market Place, Southwold (01502 722186).
Food served noon-1.30pm 7-9.30pm daily.
Set meals *lunch* £16 (2 courses), £18 (3 courses); *dinner* £24-£28.50 (3 courses), £34 (5 courses).
Cards AmEx, DC, Debit, MC, V.

The salmon-pink restaurant at the estimable Swan can't quite shake off the feeling that it's a hotel dining room, but don't let that put you off. The napery may be starched but the service isn't, and the set dinner menu promises such ambitious delights as tempura battered oysters with soy and ginger, seared fillet of beef with a blue cheese tartlet, beetroot crisps and a Madeira jus, and hot passionfruit soufflé. All are cooked with flair. The bar is open for lunch from Easter to December.

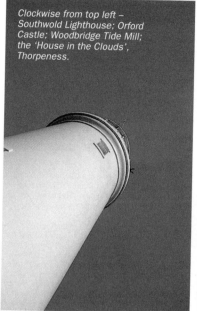

Clockwise from top left –
Southwold Lighthouse; Orford
Castle; Woodbridge Tide Mill;
the 'House in the Clouds',
Thorpeness.

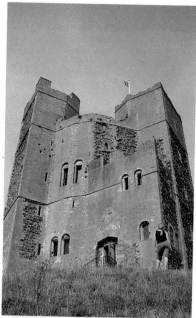

East Anglia

Tourist information centres

The Cinema, High Street, **Aldeburgh**, IP15 5AU (01728 453637/www.suffolkcoastal.gov.uk). **Open** *Easter-Oct* 9am-5.15pm Mon-Fri; 10am-5.15pm Sat, Sun.

Town Hall, Market Place, **Southwold**, IP18 6EF (01502 724729). **Open** *Easter-Oct* 11am-1pm, 1.45-5pm, Mon-Fri; 10am-5.30pm Sat; 11am-4pm Sun.

Station Buildings, **Woodbridge**, IP12 4AJ (01394 382240). **Open** *Easter-Sept* 9am-5.30pm Mon-Fri; 9.30am-5pm Sat, Sun; *Oct-Easter* 9am-5.30pm Mon-Fri; 10am-4pm Sat; 10am-1pm Sun.

Aldeburgh Festival

Snape Maltings (box office 01728 453543/ enquiries@aldeburghfestivals.org).

With the appointment in 1999 of 28-year-old composer Thomas Adès as artistic director, Jonathan Reekie of the Almeida Theatre as chief executive and the dynamic Dennis Stevenson as chairman, this famed but fusty music festival is set to radically reinvent itself for the next millennium. The Britten-Pears School, based at the Maltings, puts on events throughout the year, but the big ones are the main festival in June and the August Proms season. In addition, there's the annual Early Music Festival at Easter (featuring mainly Baroque music), and in October there's a festival of music by Benjamin Britten (which returns in 2000 following a break in 1999). For all these events, you should check the dates with the local tourist information office and book as far in advance as possible (particularly accommodation). There's also a major poetry festival here in November.

Easton Farm Park

Easton, nr Wickham Market (01728 746475/ www.easton-farm-park@freeserve.com).
Open *late Mar-June, Sept* 10.30am-6pm Tue-Sun, bank hols; *July, Aug* 10.30am-6pm daily.
Admission £4.25; £2.75 3s-16s; £3.75 OAPs.

There's petting aplenty in the beautifully situated 35 acres of Easton Farm Park. Highlights for the wee ones include the Victorian dairy in full milking action, pony rides, feeding the fauna and the adventure playground.

Framlingham Castle

Framlingham (01728 724189).
Open *Apr-Sept* 10am-6pm daily; *Oct-Mar* 10am-4.30pm/dusk. **Admission** (EH) £3.10; £1.60 5s-16s; £2.30 OAPs, students.

While **Orford Castle** has its keep but no curtain walls, Framlingham has its walls but no keep. The current castle – stronghold of the Bigod family – dates from the late twelfth century. Edward VI gave it to his sister Mary, who was proclaimed queen here in 1553. Accompanied by the free audio tour, visitors can follow in her footsteps along the battlements, punctuated by 13 towers.

Minsmere RSPB Nature Reserve

nr Westleton (01728 648281).
Open 9am-9pm/dusk Mon, Wed-Sun. **Admission** £4; £1 5s-16s; £2.50 OAPs, students; £8 family.

Follow the signs from the A12 or Westleton to reach Minsmere, one of Eastern England's most important reserves for wading birds. Upwards of 100 species of bird have been recorded here, including avocets, marsh harriers and bitterns. There's a shop, tearoom, nature trails, hides and frequent guided walks and events.

Orford Castle

Orford (01394 450472).
Open *Apr-Oct* 10am-6pm daily; *Nov-Mar* 10am-4pm Wed-Sun. **Admission** (EH) £2.50; £1.30 5s-16s; £1.90 OAPs, students.

Henry II built Orford Castle in 1165-73 in order to counter the considerably local power of uppity Hugh Bigod, who was based at nearby **Framlingham Castle**. The castle's original curtain walls are long gone, but the impressive keep – one of the best preserved in Britain – remains. There's not much to see inside, but the views from the top over Orford Ness are lovely.

Orford Ness

(access info & ferry crossings 01394 450057).
Ferries *Apr-Oct* 10am-2pm Thur-Sat (last return ferry leaves Orford Ness at 5pm). **Tickets** *return* £5.20; £2.60 5s-15s; NT members £3.20; £1.60 5s-15s; *guided tours* £12.50.

Probably the most desolate spot in East Anglia, this ten-mile long expanse is the 'largest vegetated shingle spit in Europe' and a unique habitat for plants and birds. Here you'll find such botanical treats as the yellow horned poppy and the purple flowering sea pea and, on neighbouring Havergate Island, a major nesting site for avocets. Access is from Orford Quay but is deliberately limited to preserve the fragile ecostructure. There are monthly guided walks (Apr-Oct, book in advance) on the Ness with the National Trust Warden (call 01394 450900 for details). The Ness was the site of 'secret' military experiments since World War I (until taken over by the National Trust in the early 1990s), and strange MOD buildings still pepper the landscape.

Sizewell

Nr Leiston (01728 653890).
Open *Easter-Oct* 10am-4pm daily. **Admission** free.

British Energy is desperately keen to persuade us of the safety of nuclear energy and of Britain's only pressurised water reactor, Sizewell B. And it does it quite well. The visitors' centre explains how nuclear power works and compares the environmental impact of different ways of making electricity. The highlight, though, is the tour of the power station itself – now that you trust them....

Sutton Hoo

nr Woodbridge (tourist info 01394 382240).
Guided tours *Easter-Oct* 2pm, 3pm, Sat, Sun.
Tickets £2; £1 10s-18s.

Anyone with any archaeological interest will be familiar with the name Sutton Hoo. From the 20 grave mounds set high on a hillside by the River Deben the richest archaeological treasure ever found in Britain was excavated (in 1938). The centrepiece was a 27-m long ship, the likely last resting place of Anglo-Saxon king of East Anglia, Raedwald. The magnificent cache of treasure found here can now be seen in the British Museum. Visitor facilities are planned to open in 2001, but until then there are 45-minute guided tours of the site, which is only accessible by foot from the B1083. Opposite the turning to Hollesley, take the footpath signposted to Sutton Hoo; it's a 20-minute walk.

East Anglia

The best for...

In a book of this nature a conventional index would be of only very limited use. Therefore, we have instead compiled the following list of attractions by type, so that, say, the Roman-obsessed motoring enthusiast with kids to placate and a partner who's into beer and East Asian art can find the break with the maximum number of attractions to suit them.

Index

In a nutshell, these are the strengths of the 44 breaks in this book...

Kent

North Kent Coast
kids, seaside (class to tack)
Canterbury
architecture, churches, history, kids
Sandwich to Sandgate
castles, kids
North Kent Downs
walking
Rye, Dungeness & Romney Marsh
on-beat and off-beat charm, seaside
The Heart of Kent
country houses, gardens, vineyards
The Kent Weald
country houses, gardens, oasthouses

Sussex & Surrey

Battle & Hastings
history
The Ashdown Forest
gardens, walking
Lewes & around
a bit of everything
Brighton
fun, kids, seaside
South-west Sussex
country houses, gardens, Romans, sculpture
North Surrey Downs
country houses, walking
The Three Counties
pubs, walking

Hampshire & Isle of Wight

Around Newbury
country houses, horses & rabbits
Winchester & around
churches, walking
The New Forest
walking
Isle of Wight
kids, nostalgia, seaside, walking
Bournemouth & Poole
kids, seaside

Wiltshire & Bath

Salisbury & Stonehenge
ancient sites, churches
Bradford-on-Avon & around
architecture, canals
Bath
architecture, history, museums, restaurants
Chippenham to Avebury
ancient sites
Malmesbury & around
pubs, walking

The Cotswolds

Cirencester to Gloucester
a bit of everything
Cheltenham to Stow
town & country, walking
North Cotswolds
gardens, walking
Stratford & Warwick
castles, Shakespeare
Oxford
architecture, history, museums

South Oxfordshire
ancient sites, the Thames
Woodstock to Burford
walking
Chipping Norton to Banbury
a bit of everything

The Chilterns to York

Windsor & around
kids, the Thames, town & country
Northern Chilterns
walking
Hertfordshire
kids, Romans
Rutland
emptiness
Lincoln
architecture, churches, history
York
architecture, churches, history, museums

East Anglia

Cambridge
architecture, history
West Essex
morris dancers
Lower Stour Valley
Constable, villages
Upper Stour Valley
villages, walking
Bury St Edmunds & around
churches
The Suffolk Coast
otherworldliness, seaside

Weekend Breaks
Advertisers' Directory

The advertisements in this section are colour-coded for each area of the guide. Simply refer to the coloured number as shown in the chart below.

1 Kent

2 Sussex & Surrey

3 Hampshire & Isle of Wight

4 Wiltshire & Bath

5 The Cotswolds

6 The Chilterns to York

7 East Anglia